Bitmapped Graphics Programming in C++

MARV LUSE

 Addison-Wesley Publishing Company

Reading, Massachusetts   Menlo Park, California   New York
Don Mills, Ontario   Wokingham, England   Amsterdam   Bonn
Sydney   Singapore   Tokyo   Madrid   San Juan   Paris   Seoul
Milan   Mexico City   Taipei

Library of Congress Cataloging-in-Publication Data

Luse, Marv.
    Bitmapped graphics programming in C++ / Marv Luse.
      p. cm.
    Includes index.
    1. Bit-mapped graphics. 2. C++ (Computer program language)
    I. Title.
    T385.L87   1993
    006.6'762—dc20
                                                    92-38363
                                                  CIP

Cover design by Abrams Design Group
Set in 10-pt. Palatino by ST Associates, Inc., Wakefield, MA

ISBN 0–201–63209–8
1 2 3 4 5 6 7 8 9-MA-9796959493
First printing, June 1993

Contents

Acknowledgments

I would like to thank the many people who contributed to the production of this book. Their efforts are greatly appreciated.

My associate K. Wade Turner spent many hours scouring the Internet for sources of information and sample graphics files. My wife and business partner Judy Spose provided much encouragement. She also kept the wolves at bay while I scratched my head over the vagaries of graphics formats. A special note of thanks to Claire Horne of Addison-Wesley. Her good humor and meticulous work were an immeasurable asset.

There were many people who influenced the outcome of the book, whether directly or indirectly, and I would like to acknowledge them here: Joe Huffman of Flash Tek, my good friend Andrew Binstock, and Dr. Attilio Catanzano. I would also like to thank MicroGrafx for contributing a copy of Picture Publisher to this undertaking. Their fine product proved to be invaluable on many occasions. Finally, a fond salute to Kirsten Simmonds.

Preface

One of my goals in writing this book was to create a reasonably complete, single-source reference on the subject of bitmapped graphics file formats. I also wanted to cover enough theoretical background in sufficient detail that the interested reader would not have to seek out other references to obtain adequate explanations of concepts and techniques.

As is often the case, the territory I set out to explore was far greater in scope than I had anticipated. Indeed, the material proved to be an expansive and eclectic jungle! However, I feel that enough of the objective was achieved to warrant the effort, and I hope you find that the results bear this out.

Those who scour source code for principle should know that I am fond of the practical and the empirical. For instance, C++ aficionados may be alarmed at my extensive use of the functions in `stdio.h` (for example, `printf()`) instead of the more stylistically correct `iostreams` classes. The approach I take, however, results in code that is more palatable to the C-only programmer at no cost in functionality—a good practical objective.

I should also warn you that some of the coding techniques in this book are potentially sensitive to compiler options and environmental dependencies. Many programmers try to avoid such techniques, but in certain situations taking a slight *risk* yields simpler, smaller, and faster code, an unarguable advantage. Consider the example of reading complex binary structures as a single operation:

```
struct some_struct s;
fread( &s, sizeof(some_struct), 1, fileptr );
```

This practice, while sensitive to the compiler's packing assumptions, is completely reliable if no member alignment is performed. The alternative—reading each element of the structure separately—defeats the goal of using a structure definition, namely, treating a complex, multi-element data instance as a single object.

For those new to the C++ language, note that the preceding technique will not work on structures or classes possessing virtual functions. For one thing, the `sizeof()` operator is currently sensitive to certain implementation details of the language, and returns, in effect, an erroneous result for structures and classes containing virtual functions. C++ contains many such conceptual anomalies, but it is nonetheless an excellent language for software development.

One final note concerns the formats themselves. The overall selection of formats is representative but not a complete survey of the topic. Several important examples were omitted, and if your own favorite format is missing, my apologies. Time and space dictate that at some point a book be called done, whether or not the author is ready to stop writing. In this regard books are not unlike programs, which are never finished but merely abandoned.

Marv Luse
Boulder, Colorado

Introduction

During the years following the release of the original IBM PC, computing grew and evolved with all of the vigor of a living organism. It is a phenomenon seen in few areas of human endeavor. Perhaps the only comparable examples in this century are the developments that have occurred in the fields of aviation and spaceflight.

Some of the most interesting advances in computing have occurred in the interface between human and computer. At one time, the only way to communicate with the beast was with paper tape and punch cards. In the years since, the computer has developed many senses and abilities that rival those of humans themselves—sight, sound, tactile perception, the ability to read and write and draw—and before long it will no doubt acquire speech and verbal communication skills. Who knows? Perhaps someday, like the vast machine in Robert Heinlein's *The Moon Is a Harsh Mistress*, the computer will develop self-awareness. In the meantime, however, its lowbrow but stunning graphics capabilities constitute one of its most important traits.

Visual communication has always been important to humans. A picture can often convey in a second or two what would require minutes or even hours of speech. Imagine a map or an architect's plan implemented using text only! Clearly, the computer's abilities of visual display are important, and the rich and robust nature of the field of computer graphics bears this out.

It may seem surprising, but graphics computing developed and matured primarily on smaller, single-user computers like the IBM PC and the Macintosh, and on so-called workstation machines typified by Sun SPARCs. As late as 1986, computer graphics was a poorly implemented novelty on large IBM mainframes; the same was true for many other large machines. At the same point in time, however, literally millions of PC users were acquainted with ZSoft's PC Paintbrush, primarily because Microsoft bundled the program with just about everything it sold. If for no other reason than sheer numbers, PC Paintbrush was one of the first important graphics applications for computers.

In the same time frame, the industry produced the first commercially successful graphical operating system interface, used on the Apple Macintosh, and the first important desktop publishing program, Ventura Publisher. Graphics computing has procreated with wild abandon ever since, and now there are literally dozens of graphically oriented niches for computer applications software. System software and desktop publishing remain important. There are also illustration applications like Corel Draw, image-editing software like Micrografx's Picture Publisher, graphical spreadsheets like Microsoft's Excel, and so on. Animation and photo-realistic rendering are now important fields that contribute to such diverse endeavors as motion-picture making, aircraft flight simulation, and even situation and evidence recreation for use in court trials.

We now possess an incredible store of graphical computer data, especially data in the form of imagery. All of it resides in computer files, and all of it is encoded in a bewildering variety of file formats. These graphics file formats constitute the subject of this book.

The Formats

There are two broad categories of graphics file formats, termed bitmapped formats and vector formats. They are fundamentally very different: a **bitmapped format** stores a complete, digitally encoded image; a **vector format** stores the individual graphical elements that make up an image. This book covers bitmapped formats only. Vector formats will be dealt with another time in another book.

There are literally dozens of bitmapped file formats, and new ones are being invented on a regular basis. Indeed, it is probably only a slight exaggeration to state that there are as many bitmapped formats as there are breeds of dogs and cats. Many started life as proprietary formats of important applications. As the number of an application's users grew, so grew the importance of its format, to the point that the format became a standard of sorts. The PCX format, which originated as the native format of ZSoft's PC Paintbrush, is a good example of a format that developed in this way.

Other formats were designed with specific uses or application niches in mind. CompuServe's GIF format, for example, was developed to transmit and display graphical imagery by means of a modem. To this end, the format utilizes data compression to reduce transmission times and also supports interlaced imagery. **Interlacing** allows a rough view of the complete image to become apparent quickly, and the image appears to fill in gradually as all scan lines are drawn.

Most of the various TIFF standard classes were developed for specific applications. For example, TIFF Class F is designed to meet the requirements of bilevel fax imagery. This particular subformat of the TIFF standard allows specification of fax-related data such as image quality or number of bad scan lines (that is, scan lines corrupted in transmission).

Formats can be categorized by complexity as well as by origin. The MacPaint format, for example, is perhaps the simplest of all formats dealt with in this book. It consists of a brief file header followed by a single monochrome bitmap of fixed dimensions. In contrast, the TIFF format is large, complex, and open-ended. It supports all types of bitmaps and bitmap-related measures and allows vendor-specific extensions to the baseline format. Writing code to deal with all possible aspects of the TIFF format is a substantial undertaking.

One last observation about graphics file formats concerns, regrettably, the realm of lawyers and the law. At least one format, GIF, is copyrighted, and although it can be freely used, any software that reads or writes the format must acknowledge the copyright. The GIF format also employs LZW compression, which is covered by a patent owned by UniSys Corporation. The developer of a commercial software product that uses any format would be wise to investigate potential legal restrictions on its use. Any restrictions I know about are mentioned, but these things can, and do, change with time.

The following table lists the formats that are covered in this book and briefly describes each. Note that they are listed alphabetically in the table, but will be covered within the book in an ordering based, more or less, on the complexity of each format, its importance, and related considerations. Bear in mind that these are my own predilections and are not intended to be taken as an authoritative judgment.

Bitmapped Graphics File Formats

BMP	Microsoft Windows Bitmap Format. A general-purpose format for storing bitmapped imagery.
EPS	Encapsulated PostScript Format. Used for graphics import and export with PostScript-based applications.
GIF	CompuServe Graphics Interchange Format. A general-purpose format designed to facilitate image transmission by means of modem.
IMG	GEM Image Format. A bitmap format developed for use under Digital Research's GEM environment.
MSP	Microsoft Paint Bitmap Format. Functionally similar to IMG and PCX, but less important than those two formats.
PCX	ZSoft PC Paintbrush Format. A widely supported format, intended primarily for storing screen imagery.
PNTG	Apple MacPaint Format. The native format of the Macintosh MacPaint program.
RAS	Sun Microsystems Raster Format. The native bitmap format used on Sun SPARCs.
TGA	AT&T Targa Format. Format for 16-bit and 24-bit full-color imagery created with the Truevision system.
TIFF	Aldus Tagged Image File Format. A complex, multipurpose format developed jointly by Aldus and Microsoft.
WPG	WordPerfect Graphics Format. A vector-based format (like EPS) that also supports bitmapped imagery.
XBM	X Windows X-11 Bitmap Format. A general-purpose format for storing bitmapped imagery.

Software Issues

It is not practical to deal with the use of all these formats under all potentially important hardware platforms, operating systems, programming languages, and compilers in a single book. It is therefore necessary to define a specific environment that will be used to present each format. This environment will consist primarily of MS-DOS on an Intel 80x86 processor, with occasional references to other operating systems and processors. All source code in the book is written in either C++ or assembly language and was developed and tested using Borland C++ 3.1 and Borland's Turbo Assembler.

The use of C++ in a book of this sort may seem a bit unusual. However, it is rapidly becoming the language of choice for large-scale application development, and it can generally be read by the typical C-only programmer. Also, the more arcane features of the language have been avoided, which is always a good practice where portability is a concern.

MS-DOS is perhaps the only operating system environment in which assembly language is routinely used by the C or C++ developer. Given the constraints of DOS and of Intel processors operating in real mode, it is almost unavoidable. While many low-level OS and BIOS services can be invoked from C using the `int86()` library function, such code is very inefficient, especially in performance-critical situations (and what other kinds are there?). For this reason functions of this type are always presented in assembly language.

The most practical approach to dealing with a bitmapped image is to treat it as a collection of scan lines. In a software sense, this means writing functions that read and write scan lines, display scan lines, and so forth. Unfortunately, few, if any, commercial graphics packages provide scan-line-oriented operations, so some discussion will be devoted to dealing with scan lines on representative display hardware.

What's Ahead

Before we test the murky waters of graphics file formats, we should consider some general theoretical and practical information as background. To this end, the chapters in Part I cover such topics as color models, dithering, compression, memory management, and display hardware. Along the way, source code implementations of the various functions and concepts are presented. Taken together they form a reasonably complete and self-contained (though modest) image manipulation and display system.

Following this extended introduction, the formats themselves are presented, one per chapter, Part II comprising simple formats and Part III comprising complex formats. The discussion of each format includes, where appropriate, source code to both read and write the format. The code deals with the format as a collection of encoded scan lines, which is the actual arrangement in many formats. Other formats ignore the breakdown of the image data into lines and deal instead with the complete image. For these formats, the scan-line paradigm is less natural, but is still employed when possible, it being important from a design standpoint to maintain a consistent software interface regardless of the format.

Part One

Concepts and Techniques

1
Color ──────────────────

If you think about it, a graphical image is nothing more than a collection of organized colors intended to communicate some information. In the case of a scene or abstract image, the intent may primarily be to influence one's aesthetic sense. On the other hand, a quarterly revenues graph might be intended to influence a stockholder's blood pressure. Ultimately, however, both boil down to the same thing, a collection of colors.

Many people are surprised to learn that color has no physical reality. It is nothing more than the psycho-physiological response of the human eye and brain to light energy of varying wavelengths and intensities. Light energy is sensed by the eye and interpreted by the brain as color. Indeed, much of the science of color is based on the sensory characteristics of the eye.

Despite this mundane assessment, color is a very important component of graphical imagery. Many of the tasks associated with the manipulation and display of graphics files involve color-related operations.

Of Pixels and Palettes

Despite their variety, all bitmapped graphics file formats have one thing in common—a bitmap. In this usage, bitmap is synonymous with image, which may be taken to mean a two-dimensional array of values. Each element of the array corresponds to a single dot in a picture, and is referred to as a **pixel** or a pel. Both words represent contractions of the term **picture element**.

In most cases a pixel's value is an index into a table of colors, indicating that the pixel is to be displayed using the color pointed to by the index. The colors in the table are collectively referred to as a **palette**.

The use of an index for the pixel value rather than what the index points to serves two purposes. First, if the palette is sufficiently small, the index is generally smaller than the corresponding color definition, reducing memory requirements for an image. Second, the indexing scheme serves to virtualize the image definition. The value of the latter can be demonstrated by considering the task of changing one color in the image—instead of modifying all pixels of that color in the image, only the palette entry for that color need be modified.

Three commonly used palette sizes include 2, 16, or 256 colors. Note that the corresponding index sizes are 1, 4, and 8 bits and that these are referenced as the number of **bits per pixel**. As you might expect, the size of a bitmap's pixels influences its physical organization. In a bitmap of 1 bit per pixel, each byte holds 8 separate pixel values. In a bitmap of 8 bits per pixel, each byte represents a single pixel. A 16-color bitmap is an odd duck of sorts, in that there is no single implied bitmap organization. In one representation, two 4-bit pixels are packed into each byte. Another common representation, that used by the EGA and VGA display adapters, uses four separate bit planes, and a pixel value is synthesized using a bit from each plane.

Bitmaps that represent very large numbers of colors simultaneously generally do not employ the palette scheme because it becomes too costly in terms of memory. In these cases a pixel's value is no longer an index, but directly defines a color. This type of bitmap is employed on 16-bit and 24-bit display hardware. A little math illustrates the problem of using a palette for large numbers of colors. In 16-bit hardware, 15 bits are actually used, allowing 32,768 possible colors; 24-bit hardware allows 16,277,216 possible colors. A 24-bit palette requires space for over 16 million 3-byte values, for a total of 48 megabytes!

There are numerous ways to define a color, but virtually all computer display hardware uses the RGB color representation. In this scheme, a color is defined by the relative amounts (intensities) of three primary colors (red, green, and blue) that are required to produce the given color. Intensity can range from 0 to 100 percent, and the number of bits used to represent intensity determines the intensity resolution and therefore the number of possible colors. Note that zero intensity for all primaries represents the color black and 100-percent intensity for all primaries represents the color white.

In the case of 24-bit display hardware, each 24-bit pixel value defines a color consisting of 8-bit intensities of each of red, green, and blue. A value of 00000000 represents zero intensity; a value of 11111111 represents 100-percent intensity. The same scheme holds for 16-bit hardware, except that intensities are represented using 5-bit quantities.

If you've ever been impressed with the realistic quality typical of 256-color video imagery, you might be inclined to wonder if 24-bit color is really necessary. As it turns out, it is in some cases, because 24-bit color represents the limit of the human eye's ability to differentiate colors. Thus, to the human eye, there is no perceptible difference between a 24-bit color image of an object and the object viewed directly. For this reason 24-bit color is referred to as **true color**.

Color Models

The RGB system is an example of a **color model**, which is a formal system for defining and representing colors. A somewhat synonymous term is **photometric interpretation**. We would say that computer video displays are based on an RGB photometric interpretation of color.

Numerous color models have been developed, but three in particular are important in dealing with graphic imagery. They are RGB, which we have already mentioned, CMY (or CMYK), and YCbCr (or YIQ). Table 1.1 lists these and other important color models.

Table 1.1   Important Color Models

Model	Description
RGB	Red, green, and blue primaries. An additive primary system.
CMY(K)	Cyan, magenta, yellow, (and black). A subtractive primary system.
YCbCr	Luminance (Y) and two chrominance components (Cb and Cr). Used in television broadcasting. Same as the YIQ model.
HSB	Hue, saturation, and brightness. A model based on human perception of color.
HLS	Hue, lightness, and saturation. Similar to HSB.

As noted in Table 1.1, RGB is an **additive** primary system, meaning that color is generated by combining the light energy of the three primaries in various proportions. By contrast, CMY is a **subtractive** system, wherein colors are generated by absorbing (removing) various components of white light.

CMY is the color model generally employed by color printers. The pigments in the inks deposited on the printing medium absorb specific colors, removing them from the reflected light received by the eye. Where no ink is deposited, close to 100 percent of the light spectrum is reflected and we perceive white. Where all three primaries are deposited, close to zero percent of the visible light spectrum is reflected, and we perceive black.

The inclusion of black ink along with the CMY inks is referred to as the CMYK model. This model represents a concession to the real world: because of physical impurities in printing inks it is difficult to achieve 100-percent absorption of light. The result to the eye is that blacks printed with CMY alone appear muddy and not perfectly black. The addition of the fourth primary improves the quality of blacks in printed imagery.

The addition of black to CMY to obtain CMYK means that the relative intensities of CMY must be reduced to compensate for the increased absorption. The general rule for conversion of CMY to CMYK is that K is set to the minimum of the three CMY intensities, and then K is subtracted from each of the CMY intensities. In other words, to convert a CMY triple to a CMYK quadruple, do the following:

```
K = min( C, M, Y )
C -= K, M -= K, and Y -= K
```

The astute reader may have suspected that CMY and RGB are related in some way, which is indeed the case. Cyan ink, for instance, filters out (absorbs) red light. What is left is green and blue light, which mix to form cyan. Similarly, magenta ink absorbs green light, leaving red and blue, and yellow ink removes blue light, leaving red and green. These facts allow colors expressed in one model to be converted to colors expressed in the other model. Assuming an intensity range of 0 to 1, the following hold:

$$\begin{bmatrix} C \\ M \\ Y \end{bmatrix} = \begin{bmatrix} 1 \\ 1 \\ 1 \end{bmatrix} - \begin{bmatrix} R \\ G \\ B \end{bmatrix}$$

In other words, C = 1 - R, and so forth. The equations can be rearranged to obtain the inverse mapping: R = 1 - C and so on. In an actual situation, the two sets of values would be scaled to the same maximum, and 1 in the equations would be replaced by that maximum. Throughout this book, 255 is the maximum that is used.

The YCbCr color model is rarely encountered in graphics files, but is important for other reasons. As noted in the table, this is the color model that is encoded in a color television broadcast signal. When received by a black and white set, only the Y component, luminance, is utilized; in other words, luminance represents color brightness. This suggests how a color expressed as an RGB triple can be converted to a gray-scale value.

There are several standards for conversion between YCbCr and RGB models; perhaps the most common is that defined by CCIR Recommendation 601-1. The suggested luminance calculation is:

```
Y = 0.299xR + 0.587xG + 0.114xB
```

Note that the coefficients sum to 1, implying that an RGB of (1,1,1) has a luminance of 1 and therefore is expressed by the same range of values. This is important, because it implies that luminance values need not be scaled to match an existing primary intensity range.

Color-Model Classes

Because manipulation of color models and palettes is involved in the display and printing of graphic imagery, the development of a set of C++ color-model classes is warranted. A suitable implementation containing class definitions for the RGB, CMY, and CMYK models is presented in Listings 1.1 and 1.2.

Of particular interest are the operator functions, which implement commonly used arithmetic computations on primary intensity values. Primary intensities are most often expressed as values in the range 0 to 255 using an `unsigned character` representation. Since the VGA adapter uses 6-bit primary intensity values, these are right-shifted 2 bits before use. Given a `structure` such as the following:

```
struct rgb
{
    unsigned char red;
    unsigned char grn;
    unsigned char blu;
};
```

the C programmer would code it as follows, assuming that `pal` is a pointer to an instance of `rgb`:

```
pal->red >>= 2;
pal->grn >>= 2;
pal->blu >>= 2;
```

Here, a **shift-right-equals** operator function for the `rgb` structure has been implemented. In place of the C version, the code is:

```
*pal >>= 2;
```

The code-saving benefits of the C++ version should be obvious.

Also worth noting is the use of type conversion constructors to obtain translations from one color model to another. These are used as in the following example:

```
rgb R( 100, 100, 100 );
    :
cmy C( R );
```

The cmy class contains a constructor overload that, given an rgb triple, initializes an instance of cmy with cyan, magenta, and yellow intensities computed from the rgb's red, green, and blue intensity values. Similar constructors are provided in the other classes.

Listing 1.1   COLOR.HPP

```
//----------------------------------------------------------//
//                                                          //
//    File:      COLOR.HPP                                  //
//                                                          //
//    Desc:      Classes for implementation of various     //
//               color models and their conversion.        //
//                                                          //
//----------------------------------------------------------//

#ifndef _COLOR_HPP_
#define _COLOR_HPP_

struct rgb;
struct cmy;
struct cmyk;

//.............an RGB class

struct rgb
{
   unsigned char red;
   unsigned char grn;
   unsigned char blu;

   rgb( )
   {
      red = grn = blu = 0;
   }
   rgb( int r, int g, int b )
   {
      red = r;
      grn = g;
      blu = b;
   }
   rgb( rgb& x )
   {
      red = x.red;
      grn = x.grn;
      blu = x.blu;
   }
```

Listing 1.1 COLOR.HPP (continued)

```
    rgb( cmy& x );
    rgb( cmyk& x );
    unsigned char graylevel( void );

    rgb& operator = ( rgb& x )
    {
        red = x.red;
        grn = x.grn;
        blu = x.blu;
        return *this;
    }
    rgb operator << ( int i )
    {
        rgb x( red<<i, grn<<i, blu<<i );
        return x;
    }
    rgb& operator <<= ( int i )
    {
        red <<= i;
        grn <<= i;
        blu <<= i;
        return *this;
    }
    rgb operator >> ( int i )
    {
        rgb x( red>>i, grn>>i, blu>>i );
        return x;
    }
    rgb& operator >>= ( int i )
    {
        red >>= i;
        grn >>= i;
        blu >>= i;
        return *this;
    }
};

//..............a CMY class

struct cmy
{
    unsigned char cyn;
    unsigned char mag;
    unsigned char yel;
```

Listing 1.1   COLOR.HPP (continued)

```
cmy( )
{
    cyn = mag = yel = 0;
cmy( int c, int m, int y )
{
    cyn = c;
    mag = m;
    yel = y;
}
cmy( cmy& x )
{
    cyn = x.cyn;
    mag = x.mag;
    yel = x.yel;
}

cmy( rgb& x );
cmy( cmyk& x );
unsigned char graylevel( void );

cmy& operator = ( cmy& x )
{
    cyn = x.cyn;
    mag = x.mag;
    yel = x.yel;
    return *this;
}
cmy operator << ( int i )
{
    cmy x( cyn<<i, mag<<i, yel<<i );
    return x;
}
cmy& operator <<= ( int i )
{
    cyn <<= i;
    mag <<= i;
    yel <<= i;
    return *this;
}
cmy operator >> ( int i )
{
    cmy x( cyn>>i, mag>>i, yel>>i );
    return x;
}
cmy& operator >>= ( int i )
{
    cyn >>= i;
    mag >>= i;
```

Listing 1.1   COLOR.HPP (continued)

```
            yel >>= i;
            return *this;
    }
};

//..............a CMYK class

struct cmyk
{
    unsigned char cyn;
    unsigned char mag;
    unsigned char yel;
    unsigned char blk;

    cmyk( )
    {
        cyn = mag = yel = blk = 0;
    }
    cmyk( int c, int y, int m, int k )
    {
        cyn = c;
        mag = m;
        yel = y;
        blk = k;
    }
    cmyk( cmyk& x )
    {
        cyn = x.cyn;
        mag = x.mag;
        yel = x.yel;
        blk = x.blk;
    }

    cmyk( rgb& x );
    cmyk( cmy& x );
    unsigned char graylevel( void );

    cmyk& operator = ( cmyk& x )
    {
        cyn = x.cyn;
        mag = x.mag;
        yel = x.yel;
        blk = x.blk;
        return *this;
    }
    cmyk operator << ( int i )
    {
        cmyk x( cyn<<i, mag<<i, yel<<i, blk<<i );
```

Listing 1.1   COLOR.HPP (continued)

```
            return x;
    }
    cmyk& operator <<= ( int i )
    {
        cyn <<= i;
        mag <<= i;
        yel <<= i;
        blk <<= i;
        return *this;
    }
    cmyk operator >> ( int i )
    {
        cmyk x( cyn>>i, mag>>i, yel>>i, blk>>i );
        return x;
    }
    cmyk& operator >>= ( int i )
    {
        cyn >>= i;
        mag >>= i;
        yel >>= i;
        blk >>= i;
        return *this;
    }
};

//..............an RGB palette class

struct RgbPalette
{
    rgb *colors;
    int  ncolors;

    RgbPalette( )
    {
        colors = 0;
        ncolors = 0;
    }
    RgbPalette( rgb *clrs, int nclrs )
    {
        colors = clrs;
        ncolors = nclrs;
    }
    ~RgbPalette( )
    {
    }
};

#endif
```

Listing 1.2   COLOR.CPP

```cpp
//--------------------------------------------------------//
//                                                        //
//    File:      COLOR.CPP                                //
//                                                        //
//    Desc:      Classes for implementation of various    //
//               color models and their conversion.       //
//                                                        //
//--------------------------------------------------------//

extern "C"
{
    // see iscale.asm
    int iscale( int i, int m, int d );
}

#include "color.hpp"

//............the RGB class

rgb::rgb( cmy& x )
{
    red = 255 - x.cyn;
    grn = 255 - x.mag;
    blu = 255 - x.yel;
}

rgb::rgb( cmyk& x )
{
    int i = x.cyn + x.blk;
    red = (i > 255) ? 0 : 255 - i;
    i = x.mag + x.blk;
    grn = (i > 255) ? 0 : 255 - i;
    i = x.yel + x.blk;
    blu = (i > 255) ? 0 : 255 - i;
}

unsigned char rgb::graylevel( void )
{
    int gry = iscale( red, 299, 1000 );
    gry += iscale( grn, 587, 1000 );
    gry += iscale( blu, 114, 1000 );
    return (unsigned char) gry;
}

//............the CMY class

cmy::cmy( rgb& x )
```

Listing 1.2   COLOR.CPP (continued)

```
{
   cyn = 255 - x.red;
   mag = 255 - x.grn;
   yel = 255 - x.blu;
}

cmy::cmy( cmyk& x )
{
   int i = x.cyn + x.blk;
   cyn = (i > 255) ? 255 : i;
   i = x.mag + x.blk;
   mag = (i > 255) ? 255 : i;
   i = x.yel + x.blk;
   yel = (i > 255) ? 255 : i;
}

unsigned char cmy::graylevel( void )
{
   int gry = iscale( 255-cyn, 299, 1000 );
   gry += iscale( 255-mag, 587, 1000 );
   gry += iscale( 255-yel, 114, 1000 );
   return (unsigned char) gry;
}

//............the CMYK class

cmyk::cmyk( rgb& x )
{
   cmy C( x );
   int k = C.cyn;
   if( C.mag < k ) k = C.mag;
   if( C.yel < k ) k = C.yel;
   cyn = C.cyn - k;
   mag = C.mag - k;
   yel = C.yel - k;
   blk = k;
}

cmyk::cmyk( cmy& x )
{
   int k = x.cyn;
   if( x.mag < k ) k = x.mag;
   if( x.yel < k ) k = x.yel;
   cyn = x.cyn - k;
   mag = x.mag - k;
   yel = x.yel - k;
   blk = k;
}
```

Listing 1.2   COLOR.CPP (continued)

```
unsigned char cmyk::graylevel( void )
{
    cmy C( *this );
    return C.graylevel();
}
```

Integer Scaling

Note in Listing 1.2 that the various `graylevel()` methods are implemented using calls to the function `iscale()`. The purpose of the `iscale()` function is to perform integer scaling as in the following expression

```
(grn * 587) / 1000
```

This kind of computation can potentially cause an overflow if 16-bit integers are used for intermediate results. In order to prevent this, 32-bit integers, or longs, must be used, which of course requires long arithmetic. Virtually all 16-bit compilers use calls to their run-time libraries to perform long arithmetic. On 80x86 processors, however, 16-bit multiplies generate a 32-bit result, and 16-bit divides use a 32-bit dividend, so there is no need to use longs if these operations are performed directly in assembly language. A suitable implementation of the function is presented in Listing 1.3, and you will find frequent calls to it throughout the source code in this book.

If you are wondering why 32-bit arithmetic is being avoided, the answer is speed. Some very dramatic time savings can be obtained in situations such as scaling a large bitmap. One bitmap-oriented operation I tested took 44 seconds to process an image using long arithmetic. The same process using calls to `iscale()` in place of expressions containing longs took only 25 seconds to complete.

Listing 1.3   ISCALE.ASM

```
;-------------------------------------------------------
;
;  File:    ISCALE.ASM
;
;  Desc:    Function to perform 16-bit integer scaling
;           using a scale define as the fraction n/d
;
;-------------------------------------------------------

.model large

; argument addressing - 16-bit far calls
```

Listing 1.3   ISCALE.ASM (continued)

```
arg1    equ    [bp+6]
arg2    equ    [bp+8]
arg3    equ    [bp+10]

public _iscale

.code

;------------------------------------------------------------
;  Desc:   Perform 16-bit integer scaling
;  Use:    int iscale( int i, int n, int d );
;  Ret:    The quantity  (i * n) / d
;------------------------------------------------------------

_iscale proc far
        push   bp
        mov    bp, sp
        push   bx

        mov    ax, arg1
        imul   word ptr arg2
        mov    bx, arg3
        idiv   bx
        shl    dx, 1
        inc    dx
        sub    bx, dx
        adc    ax, 0

        pop    bx
        pop    bp
        ret
_iscale endp

end
```

Color Measurement and Comparison

We have already discussed one color-related measure, luminance, which is a measure of a color's intrinsic brightness. Luminance, however, tells us little about the *color* of a color. For instance, suppose we want to approximate the color gold and our only choices are a light blue and a dark yellow. It doesn't take much thought to select yellow as the best available substitute—the determination is intuitive. If we try to use luminance as an objective measure to verify our choice, we find it isn't at all helpful, because the luminance measures of colors can be similar even when their *colors* are not. Whatever the mechanism, we recognize yellow and gold as being more similar than blue and gold.

The process of approximating one color with another is one that continually arises in the display of graphical imagery. Consider, for example, the task of displaying a 256-color image on a system with only 16 available colors. Assuming that the 16-color palette is settable, we can properly show 16 of the image's colors, but that still leaves 240 colors unaccounted for.

Although it sounds like an unpleasant chore, it is necessary to find some way of approximating the 256-color image using only 16 colors. To state the problem in a general sense, given an n-color image and an m-color display, $n > m$, find the closest approximation of the image using m colors.

Obviously, any solution to this problem will rely on a means of measuring the closeness of two colors. As it turns out, this part of the problem is relatively straightforward; the measure we are after is nothing more than one of distance. Assume, in the RGB color model, that each RGB triple is treated as a point in three-dimensional space, where the traditional x, y, and z axes of solid geometry are replaced by red intensity, green intensity, and blue intensity. The distance(d) between two colors (r_1, g_1, b_1) and (r_1, g_1, b_1) is then

$$d_{12} = \sqrt{(r_1 - r_2)^2 + (g_1 - g_2)^2 + (b_1 - b_2)^2}$$

This defines a relative measure of how closely the two colors resemble each other. The concept is illustrated graphically in Figure 1.1, which shows RGB color space using the range 0 to 1 for mapping intensity.

With the measure of color distance, we can now measure the closeness of pairs of colors. However, this still does not tell us how to pick 16 colors to approximate a 256-color palette. The solution to this problem depends on how the image is to be rendered; that is, how the 16-color image is to be derived from the 256-color image. There are numerous techniques for this, but most involve some form of dithering or error diffusion—subjects that will be discussed in the next chapter. For now, let us suppose we will use a simple mapping function that maps each color in the 256-color palette to the closest color in the 16-color palette.

The color mapping function is conceptually quite simple. For each color in the 256-color palette, we substitute the color from the 16-color palette whose RGB distance to the given color is smallest. In actual practice, we replace each image pixel value in the range 0 to 255 with a device pixel value in the range 0 to 15. Now for the tough part—picking the best 16 colors to use.

It makes sense to start by selecting the 16 display colors from the set of 256 image colors. This ensures that the display palette will at least be related to the image palette. Suppose, for example, that the image to be rendered is an autumn scene containing mostly reds, yellows, oranges, and browns. In such an image, colors like blue and cyan occur very infrequently and can be reasonably omitted.

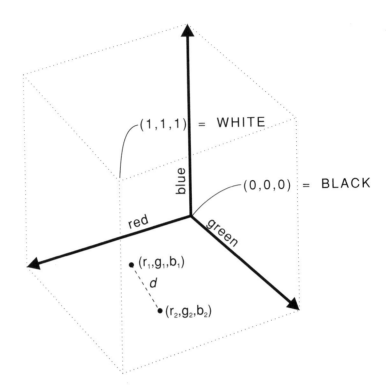

Figure 1.1 The RGB Color Cube

One way to select the 16 display colors is to construct a frequency histogram by counting the number of times each of the image's colors appears. The 16 most frequently used colors are then selected. However, there is no guarantee that this approach would work on all images, and more importantly, the process of computing the histogram would be costly in terms of time. A better approach is definitely called for.

Beyond requiring that the display colors be selected from the image palette, we can specify that the 16 colors be maximally far apart. They should be spread out in RGB color space so that the volume they occupy comes closest to the volume containing the original 256 colors, and the distances between individual colors are as close to being the same as possible. These qualifications ensure that the range of color in the reduced palette is close in extent to the range of the original palette, and that no two colors in the reduced palette are any closer to each other than necessary.

Determining a palette in which the 16 colors are maximally far apart involves computing a measure that is a function of color distance. For a given color c_i, where i ranges from 0 to 255, we compute the quantity

$$f(i) = \sum_{c_j \neq c_i} \frac{1}{d^2}$$

This produces a measure of how far away a given color is, on average, from its neighbors. We want to select those colors for which this metric is smallest. While it might seem that we should sum distance and pick the maximum, this does not work in practice. Consider the case of three colinear points in RGB space. We can position the middle point anywhere between the other two and the sum of distance remains constant—the distance metric tells us nothing in this case. However, summing the inverse of distance from the middle point to the end points varies with the midpoint's position and achieves a minimum value when the middle point is exactly halfway between the other two.

In practice, the optimum reduced palette is elegantly determined by sorting the image palette using the inverse-distance measure as the comparison function. The initial color picked from the palette is the color closest in distance to the origin of RGB space (which, of course, represents pure black). This palette entry is swapped with entry 0 to form the initial color of the reduced palette. Then, each succeeding entry, from 1 to the number of required colors, is filled by picking the color from those remaining whose measure is smallest, computed over all colors already selected for the reduced palette. This is perhaps more easily understood by looking at the source code itself, which is presented in Listings 1.4 and 1.5. Note that, in order to avoid floating-point arithmetic, the code computes *large-integer/distance-squared* rather than *1/distance-squared*.

The technique just described does a reasonably good job of determining a subset of a given palette with which to approximate the full palette. However, an even better approximation can be obtained in most cases by performing an additional step, which is to apply to the reduced palette an averaging filter derived from the full palette.

Remember, once the reduced palette has been determined, the full palette must be mapped to this new palette. In the example cited earlier, a 256-color palette is reduced to a 16-color palette, and pixel values in the range 0 to 255 are mapped to pixel values in the range 0 to 15 by finding the 16-color palette entry closest in distance to each 256-color palette entry.

Note that this process effectively partitions the 256-color palette into 16 groups of similar colors, and that each group contains one entry from the reduced 16-color palette. All that is required to implement the averaging filter is to replace each 16-color palette entry with the average of the RGBs found in the corresponding color group determined from the full palette. We can further weight each average toward the corresponding reduced palette entry by averaging in more than one occurrence of that entry.

The averaging technique is included in Listings 1.4 and 1.5, along with the palette reduction logic. This source code module implements palette modification and color mapping capabilities.

Listing 1.4   COLORMAP.HPP

```
//------------------------------------------------------//
//                                                      //
//   File:     COLORMAP.HPP                             //
//                                                      //
//   Desc:     Palette modification and color mapping   //
//             functions.                               //
//                                                      //
//------------------------------------------------------//

#ifndef _COLORMAP_HPP_
#define _COLORMAP_HPP_

#include "color.hpp"

void xchg_rgb( rgb *pal, int m, int n );

int  closest_rgb( rgb x, rgb *pal, int npal );

int  maximal_rgb( rgb *pal, int mid, int max );

void reduce_palette( rgb *pal, int npal, int nsub );

void color_map( rgb *img, int nimg, rgb *dev, int ndev,
                int *cmap, int smooth_wt );

#endif
```

Listing 1.5 COLORMAP.CPP

```
//------------------------------------------------------//
//                                                      //
//   File:     COLORMAP.CPP                             //
//                                                      //
//   Desc:     Palette modification and color mapping   //
//             functions.                               //
//                                                      //
//------------------------------------------------------//

#include "colormap.hpp"

extern "C"
```

Listing 1.5   COLORMAP.CPP (continued)

```cpp
    {
        // see iscale.asm
        int iscale( int i, int m, int d );
        // see dist3.asm
        long dist3( int r1, int r2, int g1, int g2,
                    int b1, int b2 );
    }

    //.................swap two palette entries

    void xchg_rgb( rgb *pal, int m, int n )
    {
        rgb tmp = pal[m];
        pal[m] = pal[n];
        pal[n] = tmp;
    }

    //.................determine closest rgb in a list

    int closest_rgb( rgb x, rgb *pal, int npal )
    {
        long dmin = dist3( x.red, pal[0].red,
                           x.grn, pal[0].grn,
                           x.blu, pal[0].blu );
        int closest = 0;

        for( int i=1; i<npal; i++ )
        {
            long d = dist3( x.red, pal[i].red,
                            x.grn, pal[i].grn,
                            x.blu, pal[i].blu );
            if( d < dmin )
            {
                dmin = d;
                closest = i;
            }
        }

        return closest;
    }

    //.................find rgb in mid..max maximal to 0..mid-1

    int maximal_rgb( rgb *pal, int mid, int max )
    {
        long n = 1L << 30;  // a large number
        long dmin = n;
```

Listing 1.5   COLORMAP.CPP (continued)

```
    int  maximal = mid;
    for( int i=mid; i<max; i++ )
    {
        long dsum = 0;
        for( int j=0; j<mid; j++ )
        {
            long d = dist3( pal[i].red, pal[j].red,
                            pal[i].grn, pal[j].grn,
                            pal[i].blu, pal[j].blu );
            if( d == 0 )
            {
                dsum = n;
                break;
            }
            dsum += n / d;
        }
        if( dsum < dmin )
        {
            dmin = dsum;
            maximal = i;
        }
    }
    return maximal;
}

//...............compute maximally apart reduced palette

void reduce_palette( rgb *pal, int npal, int nsub )
{
    // find "blackest" entry as a starting point
    int  i = closest_rgb( rgb(0,0,0), pal, npal );

    // reorder palette so that first nsub entries
    // are maximally far apart
    int imin = 0;
    while( imin < nsub )
    {
        xchg_rgb( pal, i, imin++ );
        i = maximal_rgb( pal, imin, npal );
    }
}

//...............compute color map, optionally smooth

void color_map( rgb *img, int nimg, rgb *dev, int ndev,
                int *cmap, int smooth_wt )
```

Listing 1.5   COLORMAP.CPP (continued)

```
{
    int  *ccnt = 0;
    long *rsum = 0,
         *gsum = 0,
         *bsum = 0;

    // smooth_wt > 0 enables averaging filter
    {
        ccnt = new int [ndev];
        rsum = new long [ndev*3];
        if( (ccnt == 0) || (rsum == 0) )
        {
            smooth_wt = 0;
            if( ccnt ) delete ccnt;
            if( rsum ) delete rsum;
        }
        else
        {
            gsum = rsum + ndev;
            bsum = gsum + ndev;
            // initialize weighted sums
            int n = smooth_wt - 1;
            for( int i=0; i<ndev; i++ )
            {
                rsum[i] = dev[i].red;  rsum[i] *= n;
                gsum[i] = dev[i].grn;  gsum[i] *= n;
                bsum[i] = dev[i].blu;  bsum[i] *= n;
                ccnt[i] = n;
            }
        }
    }

    // compute the color map
    for( int i=0; i<nimg; i++ )
    {
        int j = closest_rgb( img[i], dev, ndev );
        cmap[i] = j;
        if( smooth_wt > 0 )
        {
            ccnt[j] += 1;
            rsum[j] += img[i].red;
            gsum[j] += img[i].grn;
            bsum[j] += img[i].blu;
        }
    }

    // smooth the device palette
    if( smooth_wt > 0 )
```

Listing 1.5   COLORMAP.CPP (continued)

```
{
    for( i=0; i<ndev; i++ )
    {
        rsum[i] /= ccnt[i];
        dev[i].red = rsum[i];
        gsum[i] /= ccnt[i];
        dev[i].grn = gsum[i];
        bsum[i] /= ccnt[i];
        dev[i].blu = bsum[i];
    }
}

if( ccnt ) delete ccnt;
if( rsum ) delete rsum;
}
```

Computing Distance

Despite the fact that we are using 8-bit RGB intensity values, the computation of the distance between two colors can generate intermediate results that exceed the range expressible with a 16-bit integer, so once again, 32-bit integer arithmetic is required. As was the case with integer scaling, the distance computation can be significantly speeded up on 16-bit systems by coding the distance function in assembly language.

An additional concession to speed is to omit the final step of taking the square root of the sum of squares, thereby computing the square of distance rather than true distance. This shortcut is feasible because we use distance only in a comparative sense and do not require its precise magnitude.

A suitable assembly language implementation of the squared-distance function is presented in Listing 1.6.

Listing 1.6   DIST3.ASM

```
;------------------------------------------------------------
;
;   File:   DIST3.ASM
;
;   Desc:   Function to compute distance-squared between two
;           integer triples, such as two RGB's.
;
;------------------------------------------------------------

.model large
```

Listing 1.6   DIST3.ASM (continued)

```asm
; argument addressing - 16-bit far calls

arg1    equ    [bp+6]
arg2    equ    [bp+8]
arg3    equ    [bp+10]
arg4    equ    [bp+12]
arg5    equ    [bp+14]
arg6    equ    [bp+16]


; local temporaries

tmp1    equ    [bp-2]
tmp2    equ    [bp-4]
tmp3    equ    [bp-6]
tmp4    equ    [bp-8]


ntmp    equ    8


public  _dist3


.code


;-----------------------------------------------------------
;   Desc: Compute sum of deltas squared
;   Use:  long dist3( int r1, int r2, int g1, int g2,
;                     int b1, int b2 );
;   Ret:    (r1-r2)^2 + (g1-g2)^2 + (b1-b2)^2
;-----------------------------------------------------------


_dist3 proc far

        push   bp
        mov    bp, sp
        push   bx
        push   cx

        ; accumulate result in cx:bx
        xor    bx, bx
        xor    cx, cx

        mov    ax, arg1
        sub    ax, arg2
        imul   ax
        add    bx, ax
        adc    cx, dx
```

Listing 1.6   DIST3.ASM (continued)

```
        mov     ax, arg3
        sub     ax, arg4
        imul    ax
        add     bx, ax
        adc     cx, dx

        mov     ax, arg5
        sub     ax, arg6
        imul    ax
        add     bx, ax
        adc     cx, dx

        ; set dx:ax = cx:bx
        xchg    ax, bx
        xchg    dx, cx

        pop     cx
        pop     bx
        pop     bp
        ret

_dist3 endp

end
```

This concludes our look at color by itself, but the subject will reappear several times in future chapters, generally in conjunction with an additional topic. The next chapter in particular, which deals with dithering, is related to color and its manipulation, and will add to the base of information presented in this chapter. The two subjects, as we shall see, are strongly connected.

2

Dithering _____

In Chapter 1, we took a first look at the subject of color. We discussed the problem of rendering an image on a display device having fewer color or intensity resources than the original image. The range and effectiveness of solutions to this problem are significantly enhanced when dithering techniques are included. In this chapter we investigate the subject of dithering in general and discuss it's application to the problem of rendering an image.

While the subject of dithering is well grounded in scientific principles, there is an element of aesthetics to it as well. Indeed, its fundamental purpose is perhaps best stated as "fooling the human eye." In this regard, it is no different from the fascinating tricks performed by a good magician. But where the magician pulls rabbits from a hat, a dithered image fools you into thinking it contains more colors or gray levels than it actually has.

Photometric Properties of the Eye

As we have noted, the eye is a light sensor and has a known set of response characteristics. These characteristics help to explain many of the principles of dithering and also determine the operational characteristics of a given dithering algorithm.

The eye itself has a resolution limit of about 1 minute of arc. At a distance of 10 to 12 inches, a typical viewing distance for a printed page, this corresponds to a width of about 0.003 inches (and as it turns out, 0.003 inches is about the size of the dots printed by a 300-dpi laser printer). Note that this does not mean that the eye cannot see objects smaller than 0.003 inches at a distance of a foot. Rather, it means that two objects (such as the dots produced by a laser printer) that are closer together than 0.003 inches cannot be distinguished at that distance.

We do not always "see" to this resolution limit, however. On complex imagery the human brain performs spatial integration, averaging intensities in small areas to reduce the image's apparent complexity. A simple example shows how this works.

Consider a sheet of paper that contains a single dot printed by a laser printer. We can definitely see such a dot (although we would most likely interpret it as an imperfection in the paper). Now consider a sheet of paper with 4 or 5 such dots printed closely together but not touching. In most cases this would be seen as a single, slightly larger gray dot. In other words, the brain averages the white and black intensities in the neighborhood of the dots and interprets them as an area of uniform average intensity. This behavior of the eye–brain apparatus explains how dithering works.

Another important property of the eye is its intensity response characteristic, which can be thought of as a graph of actual versus perceived intensity. This is not linear, as you might expect, but logarithmic. Thus, the perceived relative brightness of two light sources is based on the ratio of their intensities, not the difference of their intensities. The smallest intensity change the eye can detect, its intensity resolution limit, is an intensity ratio of about 1.01. This value has important implications for image rendering.

The intensity characteristic must be considered in **continuous-tone** imagery. A continuous-tone image is one in which intensity changes between adjacent image areas are fine enough that the eye cannot perceive discrete differences. In the case of a black and white gray-scale image, for example, this occurs when the intensity ratio of consecutive gray levels is 1.01 or less—that is, below the eye's intensity resolution threshold.

To understand how this works, consider again the sheet of paper from the 300-dpi laser printer and assume it is being viewed under normal lighting conditions. A region of bare paper reflects close to 100 percent of incoming light and produces the brightest perceived intensity. We'll call it I_1. A region of solid black absorbs close to 100 percent of incoming light and produces the least bright intensity, I_0. The ratio of these two numbers, I_1/I_0, is referred to as the medium's **dynamic range**.

There must be enough reproducible intensities, or gray levels, between the two intensity extremes such that successive intensities vary by a ratio of 1.01 or less in order to produce continuous-tone imagery. In other words, the minimum number of required gray levels, n, is:

$$n = \log_{1.01}(I_1/I_0)$$

These relationships are generally presented in a normalized form, where the maximum intensity is given the value 1. We then have the following:

$$r = 1/I_0$$
$$n = \log_{1.01}(r)$$

Physical measurement has established the dynamic ranges of various media. Newsprint, for example, has a dynamic range of about 10, and the paper typically used in a laser printer or copier has a dynamic range of perhaps 20. The corresponding minimum number of intensities are 230 and 300, respectively. This implies that 256-level gray-scale imagery should appear continuous or close to continuous on these media.

Bilevel Dithering

There are literally dozens of ways to implement dithering. These depend on the algorithm employed, the type of image to be rendered, and the characteristics of the display medium. Bilevel dithering refers to those techniques used to dither an image for a two-tone medium, such as that of a black and white printer or a monochrome video mode. This class of dithering techniques is especially important, because most video displays use color and most printers do not. Without these techniques, it would be impossible to reproduce a color screen image on a monochrome printer.

The two types of dithering algorithms most commonly encountered are **dot-ordered** dithers and **error-diffusion** dithers. Another useful technique, **thresholding**, is perhaps the simplest of all dithering methods. In this section we explore all three of these methods within the context of producing bilevel dithered renditions of both gray-scale and color imagery.

Dot-Ordered Dithering

A monochrome printer can produce only two intensity levels, black and white. So how can 256 gray levels can be produced? The answer is with dithering. Recall that the brain performs intensity averaging on small areas of an image seen with the eye. If we partition a 300-dpi bitmap into cells of 2x2 or 4x4 dots, and then print it with varying numbers of dots in each cell set to black, the intensity averaging performed by the brain will cause us to perceive individual cells as larger dots of varying intensities of black; that is, as gray-scale values.

The size of the cell controls the number of apparent gray levels. A 2x2 cell provides five different possibilities; a 4x4 cell provides seventeen different possibilities. It is important that the size of a cell not be too large, otherwise we begin to perceive detail within a cell itself and its function as a single gray dot is lost. Obviously, the cell size limit is related to the resolution of the printing device; this in turn limits the number of reproducible gray levels.

As it turns out, 4x4 is about the limit for a 300-dpi laser printer, implying that it cannot come anywhere close to producing continuous-tone imagery. Sixteen distinct gray levels is about the best it can muster, which may come as a surprise. In contrast, a 2400-dpi linotronic device has 8 times the spatial resolution and therefore 64 times the intensity resolution of the 300-dpi laser printer. It thus can produce continuous-tone imagery quite comfortably.

The individual cells used in dithering are referred to as **dither patterns**. The scheme used to generate them has important visual implications. The most commonly used scheme generates cell $n+1$ from cell n by turning on (or off) dots adjacent to those already turned on (or off) in the previous cell. The effect of this is a series of increasingly larger (or smaller) dots. Such a scheme is referred to as a **clustered-dot-ordered** dither. An example of a 3x3 clustered-dot-ordered dither is illustrated in Figure 2.1.

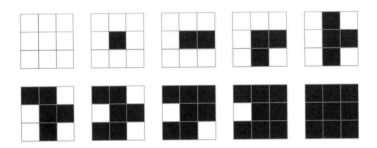

Figure 2.1 Example of a 3x3 Clustered-Dot-Ordered Dither

The cell order must be selected to accommodate the type of display device being used. On an RGB-based monitor, the order moves from all zeroes to all ones, yielding a luminance scale running from black to white. On a typical printer, the order is reversed if the dither is to model luminance. This is normally the case, because the source image is most frequently a screen display. The reverse order can be thought of as modeling gray level, where 100 percent gray, corresponding to a cell of all ones, represents black.

Other algorithms for generating dither patterns are, of course, possible. If the algorithm avoids turning on consecutive adjacent dots then the resulting dither is referred to as a **dispersed-dot-ordered** dither. Other possibilities include the use of geometric patterns. For example, if the setting pattern is constrained to dots in the same row, then a pattern of horizontal lines results.

Ordered dithers are easily notated using a **dither matrix.** This is an $m \times n$ matrix; the dimensions of the dither cell are $m \times n$. The matrix elements are integer numbers in the range 1 to $m*n$, which indicate the order in which dots are turned on (or off) to generate the cell sequence. For example, the dither illustrated in Figure 2.1 can be notated as follows:

$$\begin{bmatrix} 5 & 4 & 7 \\ 9 & 1 & 2 \\ 6 & 3 & 8 \end{bmatrix}$$

One noteworthy aspect of a dithering algorithm is the apparent intensity of individual cells as a function of their position in the cell sequence. For instance, a dither in which the nth cell has n white dots produces a linear intensity progression. In order to cater to the eye's logarithmic response characteristic it is necessary to discard many of the possible cells, retaining only those in which the ratio of white dots in consecutive cells is more or less constant. This, of course, reduces the number of possible gray levels. If only ten or so are available to begin with, then the construction of a logarithmic progression is a self-defeating proposition.

Implementation of a Dot–Ordered Dither

The vast majority of printers have resolutions in the 100- to 300-dpi range. At these resolutions a 4x4 ordered dither is a good choice for printing graphical imagery. As we noted, a 4x4 size generates seventeen possible cells, with 0 to 16 dots per cell set on or off. We discard one of these cell choices to produce a 16-level dither set.

Because most printers interpret a 1-bit as black (the most notable exception being PostScript printers), we will order the dither set from 16 bits on to 0 bits on, and discard the cell having 15 bits on. With this setup, the cells are ordered by increasing intensity (luminance) from black to white. Each cell will be stored in a byte array, with each cell row beginning on a byte boundary. The entire dither set is then referenced by an array of pointers to `unsigned char.`

To illustrate the use of our dither set, suppose we are printing a 16-color VGA screen image. An initial step is to read the video card's palette and obtain a set of 16 RGB triples. These are scaled to 8-bit quantities (0 to 255) and converted to luminance using the RGB class's `graylevel()` member function.

The next step is to scan the image a pixel at a time and read each pixel's value. Note that the position and value of each pixel effectively represents a triple, (x,y,i), where x is the pixel's column coordinate, y is the pixel's row coordinate, and i is the pixel's palette index. This triple is used to determine the value of the bit in the corresponding position on the printed bitmap as follows: the pixel's palette index is converted to a gray-scale value by reference to a table of the luminance values. The value is scaled from the luminance range (0 to 255) to the cell range (0 to 15) to determine which dither cell to use. Then, the pixel's position is used to select a bit from the 4x4 dither cell by using y modulo 4 for the row index and x modulo 4 for the column index. The printer bitmap bit takes the value of the selected bit.

The scheme just described prints the source image at a scale of one to one, demonstrating that the dithered image does not necessarily have to be four times the size of the source image. This technique depends on a certain amount of spatial coherence in the source image, which is almost always the case. If the source image is a completely random pattern, the chances are that the dithered representation would bear little resemblance to it.

See Listings 2.1 and 2.2 for source code implementations of various ordered dithers.

Thresholding and Error Diffusion

The clustered-dot-ordered dither technique just described is widely used. It is attractive because of its ease of implementation and computational simplicity. The latter is, of course, important if execution speed is a critical requirement. The clustered-dot-ordered dither, however, is not necessarily the best algorithm when judged by its resulting image quality. Other, more sophisticated techniques generally produce better image quality with a sacrifice of execution speed. One of the more important of such classes of algorithms involves thresholding and error diffusion.

Thresholding can be thought of as a 1x1 patterned dither, in that both techniques produce a bilevel image. A bilevel image can be derived from an n-level gray-scale image by replacing each gray-scale pixel value with either a 1 or a 0. The method for determining the bilevel value is simple: if the gray-scale luminance value exceeds some predetermined value, the threshold, assign a value of 1 to the corresponding bilevel pixel; otherwise assign a value of 0.

Thresholding alone can produce surprisingly good results; in general, however, images rendered in this manner lack much of the detail of the original. This is, of course, to be expected if 16 or 256 intensity values are mapped to just two. However, thresholding is important as the first step of a gray-scale dither technique based on error diffusion.

Consider a 256-level gray-scale image, with intensities ranging from 0 to 255. Suppose we want to convert it to a bilevel image using a threshold value of 127. A pixel with a value of 150, for instance, is mapped to 1. Since 1 is equivalent to 255 (both represent maximum intensity), the approximation of the pixel's value using 1 has an error of 255 – 150 or 155. In other words, the approximated value is 155 intensity levels too high. Similarly, a pixel with a value of 90 is approximated by a value of 0, which is 90 intensity levels too low.

We can compensate for the intensity error by adjusting the intensity values of nearby pixels by some percentage of the error such that the total intensity adjustment over all affected pixels sums to the total error. This is error diffusion. There are many schemes for its implementation, which generally differ in two regards: how the nearby pixels are selected and how the total error is divided among them.

Perhaps the most commonly employed error-diffusion algorithm is the Floyd–Steinberg algorithm, which was first described by R. W. Floyd and L. Steinberg in 1975. This algorithm distributes the error at each pixel among four neighboring pixels, using 7/16ths, 5/16ths, 3/16ths, and 1/16th of the total error (ε). The algorithm is diagrammed in Figure 2.2.

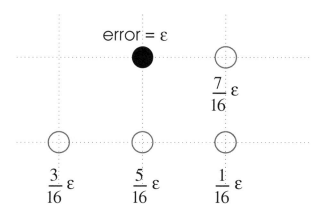

Figure 2.2   Diagram of Floyd–Steinberg Error Diffusion

One important difference between error-diffusion algorithms such as the Floyd–Steinberg algorithm and traditional dot-ordered algorithms is that the latter are pointwise processes whereas the former are not. That is, a pixel in a dot-ordered dithered image derives its value from a single pixel in the source image. In contrast, the Floyd–Steinberg algorithm requires manipulation of five pixels at a time taken from two consecutive rows of the source image. These traits influence the complexity of software implementations of the algorithms, and also, as we have noted, impact execution speed.

Implementation of a Floyd–Steinberg Dither

Because error diffusion is not a pointwise process, some form of temporary storage is required for its implementation. The Floyd–Steinberg algorithm operates on pixels in the current and next scan lines, so normally two work arrays are required, one for each of the affected scan lines. Also, keep in mind that accumulated error can exceed the range of possible pixel values, and is a signed value as well. Thus, while a scan line in our implementation is an array of `unsigned char`, the two error arrays must store signed 16-bit quantities.

Some implementations of error-diffusion filters, of which the Floyd–Steinberg algorithm is an example, utilize what is known as a **serpentine scan** of the source image. A normal scan processes each scan line in consecutive order, always proceeding from left to right. A serpentine scan processes even scan lines from left to right and odd scan lines from right to left (or vice versa). The path traced through an image by this example is a line that meanders back and forth, hence the name.

Employing a serpentine scan helps to reduce the occurrence of visual artifacts in a dithered image. These artifacts, which are manifested as spatial noise patterns in the dither, are a natural side effect of any filtering process. One of the goals in designing a diffusion filter is to minimize their impact. In most situations, the use of a serpentine scan is an unnecessary refinement and will not produce dramatic image enhancement. For this reason, we'll omit it from our implementation.

A final note regarding execution speed: compared with a simple ordered dither, the Floyd–Steinberg algorithm requires a great deal more computation and is therefore slower. It makes sense to optimize such code for speed wherever possible. One obvious enhancement that can be made is based on the fact that error terms are expressed as sixteenths of the total error. This allows us to replace integer divides by 16 with right shifts by 4.

The Floyd–Steinberg algorithm, along with simple thresholding, is implemented in Listings 2.1 and 2.2. Listings 2.1 and 2.2 also contain color dithering classes, which we will be discussing shortly.

Listing 2.1   DITHER.HPP

```
//----------------------------------------------------------//
//                                                          //
//    File:     DITHER.HPP                                  //
//                                                          //
//    Desc:     Bilevel and Color Dithering Classes         //
//                                                          //
//----------------------------------------------------------//

#ifndef _DITHER_HPP_
#define _DITHER_HPP_
```

Listing 2.1   DITHER.HPP (continued)

```
#include "color.hpp"
#include "colormap.hpp"

//................dither matrix

struct DitherMatrix
{
    unsigned char width;
    unsigned char height;
    unsigned char *order;

    DitherMatrix( );
    DitherMatrix( int w, int h, unsigned char *ord );
   ~DitherMatrix( );
};

//................basic dither types

enum DitherTypes
{
    ditNone,
    ditOrdered,
    ditThresholded,
    ditErrDiffused,
    ditClrThresholded,
    ditClrErrDiffused
};

//................dither base class

class Dither
{
    public:
        int type;

    public:
        Dither( ) { type = ditNone; }
       ~Dither( ) { }
        virtual void dither( unsigned char *px, int npx ) = 0;
};

//................ordered dither (bilevel)

class OrderedDither : public Dither
{
    protected :
        int cellw;
        int cellh;
```

Listing 2.1   DITHER.HPP (continued)

```
        int ncells;
        int rowbytes;
        int on_value;
        int off_value;
        int rowcnt;
        unsigned char **cells;

    public:
        OrderedDither( );
        OrderedDither( DitherMatrix& dm,
                        int von=1, int voff=0 );
       ~OrderedDither( );
        int dotval( int p, int x, int y );
        virtual void dither( unsigned char *pxls, int npxls );
};

//.................thresholded dither (bilevel)

class ThresholdDither : public Dither
{
    protected:
        int threshold;
        int on_value;
        int off_value;

    public:
        ThresholdDither( );
        ThresholdDither( int t, int von=1, int voff=0 );
       ~ThresholdDither( );
        virtual void dither( unsigned char *pxls, int npxls );
};

//.................error diffusion dither (bilevel)

class DiffusionDither : public Dither
{
    protected:
        int threshold;
        int ewidth;
        int on_value;
        int off_value;
        int *err1;
        int *err2;

    public:
        DiffusionDither( );
        DiffusionDither( int t, int maxwidth,
                        int von=1, int voff=0 );
```

Listing 2.1 DITHER.HPP (continued)

```
      ~DiffusionDither( );
      virtual void dither( unsigned char *pxls, int npxls );
      void reset( void );
};

//.................thresholded dither (color)

rgb * ColorThresholdPalette( void );
int   ColorThresholdSize( void );

class ColorThresholdDither : public Dither
{
   protected:
      int  threshold;        // normally 127
      int  nimgcolors;       // number of image colors
      rgb *imgcolors;        // image colors

   public:
      ColorThresholdDither( );
      ColorThresholdDither( int t, rgb *img, int nimg );
     ~ColorThresholdDither( );
      virtual void dither( unsigned char *pxls, int npxls );
};

//.................error diffusion dither (color)

rgb * ColorDiffusionPalette( void );
int   ColorDiffusionSize( void );

class ColorDiffusionDither : public Dither
{
   protected:
      int  ndevcolors;       // number of device colors
      rgb *devcolors;        // device colors
      int  nimgcolors;       // number of image colors
      rgb *imgcolors;        // image colors
      int *rerr1, *rerr2;    // red error accumulators
      int *gerr1, *gerr2;    // green error accumulators
      int *berr1, *berr2;    // blue error accumulators
      int  ewidth;           // error array sizes

   private:
      int  bestdevclr( int r, int g, int b );

   public:
      ColorDiffusionDither( );
      ColorDiffusionDither( int maxw, rgb *img, int nimg,
                            rgb *dev, int ndev );
```

Listing 2.1   DITHER.HPP (continued)

```
        ~ColorDiffusionDither( );
         virtual void dither( unsigned char *pxls, int npxls );
         void rgbdither( unsigned char *pxls, rgb *clrs,
                                        int npxls );
         void reset( void );
    };

    #endif
```

Listing 2.2   DITHER.CPP

```
//-----------------------------------------------------//
//                                                     //
//    File:    DITHER.CPP                              //
//                                                     //
//    Desc:    Bilevel and Color Dithering Classes     //
//                                                     //
//-----------------------------------------------------//

#include "string.h"

#include "dither.hpp"

extern "C"
{
    int iscale( int, int, int );
    long dist3( int, int, int, int, int, int );
}

//.................dither matrix

DitherMatrix::DitherMatrix( )
{
    width = height = 0;
    order = 0;
}

DitherMatrix::DitherMatrix( int w, int h, unsigned char *ord )
{
    width = height = 0;
    order = new unsigned char [w*h];
    if( order == 0 ) return;
    width = w;
    height = h;
    for( int i=0; i<w*h; i++ )
       order[i] = ord[i];
```

Listing 2.2   DITHER.CPP (continued)

```cpp
DitherMatrix::~DitherMatrix( )
{
   if( order ) delete order;
}

//.................ordered dither (bilevel)

OrderedDither::OrderedDither( ) : Dither( )
{
   type = ditOrdered;
   cellw = cellh = ncells = 0;
   on_value = off_value = 0;
   rowcnt = rowbytes = 0;
   cells = 0;
}

OrderedDither::OrderedDither( DitherMatrix& dm,
                             int von, int voff ) : Dither( )
{
   type = ditOrdered;
   cellw = dm.width;
   cellh = dm.height;
   ncells = cellw * cellh;
   rowbytes = (cellw + 7) / 8;
   on_value = von;
   off_value = voff;
   rowcnt = 0;
   cells = new unsigned char * [ncells];
   if( cells == 0 ) return;
   int nbytes = rowbytes * cellh;
   for( int i=0; i<ncells; i++ )
   {
      cells[i] = new unsigned char [nbytes];
      if( cells[i] == 0 ) return;
      memset( cells[i], 0, nbytes );
      // fill in cell pattern
      unsigned char *ord = dm.order;
      for( int m=0; m<cellh; m++ )
      {
         unsigned char *row = cells[i] + rowbytes * m;
         unsigned char mask = 0x80;
         for( int n=0; n<cellw; n++ )
         {
            if( *ord++ <= i ) *row |= mask;
            if( (mask >>= 1 ) == 0 )
            {
               mask = 0x80;
               row++;
```

Listing 2.2   DITHER.CPP (continued)

```cpp
                   }
                }
             }
          }
       }
    }

    OrderedDither::~OrderedDither( )
    {
       if( cells )
       {
          for( int i=0; i<ncells; i++ )
             if( cells[i] ) delete cells[i];
          delete cells;
       }
    }

    int OrderedDither::dotval( int p, int x, int y )
    {
       int ix = x % cellw;
       int iy = y % cellh;
       unsigned char *byte = cells[p] +
                             (iy * rowbytes) +
                             (ix >> 3);
       unsigned char mask = 0x80 >> (ix & 7);
       return (*byte & mask) ? on_value : off_value;
    }

    void OrderedDither::dither( unsigned char *pxls, int npxls )
    {
       for( int i=0; i<npxls; i++ )
       {
          int p = iscale( pxls[i], ncells-1, 255 );
          pxls[i] = dotval( p, i, rowcnt );
       }
       rowcnt++;
    }

    //................thresholded dither (bilevel)

    ThresholdDither::ThresholdDither( ) : Dither( )
    {
       type = ditThresholded;
       threshold = 127;
       on_value  = 1;
       off_value = 0;
    }
```

Listing 2.2   DITHER.CPP (continued)

```cpp
ThresholdDither::ThresholdDither( int t,
            int von, int voff ) : Dither( )
{
   type = ditThresholded;
   threshold = t;
   on_value  = von;
   off_value = voff;
}

ThresholdDither::~ThresholdDither( )
{
}

void ThresholdDither::dither( unsigned char *pxls, int npxls )
{
   for( int i=0; i<npxls; i++ )
      pxls[i] = pxls[i] > threshold ? on_value : off_value;
}

//................diffusion dither (bilevel)

DiffusionDither::DiffusionDither( ) : Dither( )
{
   type = ditErrDiffused;
   threshold = 127;
   on_value  = 1;
   off_value = 0;
   err1 = err2 = 0;
   ewidth = 0;
}

DiffusionDither::DiffusionDither( int t, int maxwidth,
            int von, int voff ) : Dither( )
{
   type = ditErrDiffused;
   threshold = t;
   on_value  = von;
   off_value = voff;
   ewidth = maxwidth;
   err1 = new int [ewidth*2];
   if( err1 )
   {
      err2 = err1 + ewidth;
      memset( err1, 0, ewidth*2*sizeof(int) );
   }
   else
   {
      err2 = 0;
```

Listing 2.2   DITHER.CPP (continued)

```cpp
        ewidth = 0;
    }
}

DiffusionDither::~DiffusionDither( )
{
    if( err1 ) delete [] err1;
}

void DiffusionDither::dither( unsigned char *pxls, int npxls )
{
    int n = (ewidth < npxls) ? ewidth : npxls;

    // add error from previous call to current scan line
    for( int i=0; i<n; i++ )
    {
        err1[i] = err2[i] + pxls[i];
        err2[i] = 0;
    }

    // threshold each error-corrected pixel value
    pxls[0] = (err1[0] > threshold) ? on_value :
                                      off_value;
    for( i=1; i<n-1; i++ )
    {
        int err = (err1[i] > threshold ) ? err1[i]-255 :
                                           err1[i];
        pxls[i] = (err1[i] > threshold ) ? on_value :
                                           off_value;
        // diffuse error
        err1[i+1] += (err * 7) >> 4;
        err2[i-1] += (err * 3) >> 4;
        err2[i]   += (err * 5) >> 4;
        err2[i+1] += (err * 1) >> 4;
    }
    pxls[n-1] = (err1[n-1] > threshold) ? on_value :
                                          off_value;
}

void DiffusionDither::reset( void )
{
    if( err1 )
        memset( err1, 0, ewidth*2*sizeof(int) );
}

//.................palette for color threshold dither

static rgb threshold_pal[] =
```

Listing 2.2   DITHER.CPP (continued)

```
{
   rgb(    0,    0,    0 ),
   rgb(    0,    0,  255 ),
   rgb(    0,  255,    0 ),
   rgb(    0,  255,  255 ),
   rgb(  255,    0,    0 ),
   rgb(  255,    0,  255 ),
   rgb(  255,  255,    0 ),
   rgb(  255,  255,  255 )
};

rgb * ColorThresholdPalette( void )
{
   return threshold_pal;
}

int ColorThresholdSize( void )
{
   return sizeof(threshold_pal) / sizeof(rgb);
}

//................thresholded dither (color)

ColorThresholdDither::ColorThresholdDither( ) : Dither( )
{
   type = ditClrThresholded;
   threshold = nimgcolors = 0;
   imgcolors = 0;
}

ColorThresholdDither::ColorThresholdDither( int t, rgb *img,
                      int nimg ) : Dither( )
{
   type = ditClrThresholded;
   threshold  = t;
   nimgcolors = nimg;
   imgcolors  = img;
}

ColorThresholdDither::~ColorThresholdDither( )
{
}

void ColorThresholdDither::dither( unsigned char *pxls,
                                   int npxls )
{
   for( int i=0; i<npxls; i++ )
   {
```

Listing 2.2   DITHER.CPP (continued)

```cpp
        int j = pxls[i];
        int k = 0;
        k += (imgcolors[j].red > threshold) ? 4 : 0;
        k += (imgcolors[j].grn > threshold) ? 2 : 0;
        k += (imgcolors[j].blu > threshold) ? 1 : 0;
        pxls[i] = k;
    }
}

//.................palette for color diffusion dither

static rgb diffusion_pal[] =
{
    rgb(   0,   0,   0 ),
    rgb(   0,   0, 255 ),
    rgb(   0, 255,   0 ),
    rgb(   0, 255, 255 ),
    rgb( 255,   0,   0 ),
    rgb( 255,   0, 255 ),
    rgb( 255, 255,   0 ),
    rgb( 255, 255, 255 ),
    rgb(  85,  85,  85 ),
    rgb(   0,   0, 127 ),
    rgb(   0, 127,   0 ),
    rgb(   0, 127, 127 ),
    rgb( 127,   0,   0 ),
    rgb( 127,   0, 127 ),
    rgb( 127, 127,   0 ),
    rgb( 170, 170, 170 )
};

rgb * ColorDiffusionPalette( void )
{
    return diffusion_pal;
}

int ColorDiffusionSize( void )
{
    return sizeof(diffusion_pal) / sizeof(rgb);
}

//.................error diffusion dither (color)

ColorDiffusionDither::ColorDiffusionDither( ) : Dither( )
{
    type = ditClrErrDiffused;
    ndevcolors = nimgcolors = 0;
    devcolors  = imgcolors  = 0;
```

Listing 2.2 DITHER.CPP (continued)

```
        rerr1 = rerr2 = 0;
        gerr1 = gerr2 = 0;
        berr1 = berr2 = 0;
        ewidth = 0;
    }

    ColorDiffusionDither::ColorDiffusionDither( int maxw,
                         rgb *img, int nimg,
                     rgb *dev, int ndev ) : Dither( )
    {
        type = ditClrErrDiffused;
        ndevcolors = ndev;
        nimgcolors = nimg;
        devcolors  = dev;
        imgcolors  = img;
        ewidth = maxw;
        rerr1 = new int [ewidth*2];
        gerr1 = new int [ewidth*2];
        berr1 = new int [ewidth*2];
        if( (rerr1==0) || (gerr1==0) || (berr1==0) )
        {
            ewidth = 0;
            rerr2 = gerr2 = berr2 = 0;
        }
        else
        {
            memset( rerr1, 0, sizeof(int)*2*ewidth );
            rerr2 = rerr1 + ewidth;
            memset( gerr1, 0, sizeof(int)*2*ewidth );
            gerr2 = gerr1 + ewidth;
            memset( berr1, 0, sizeof(int)*2*ewidth );
            berr2 = berr1 + ewidth;
        }
    }

    ColorDiffusionDither::~ColorDiffusionDither( )
    {
        if( rerr1 ) delete [] rerr1;
        if( gerr1 ) delete [] gerr1;
        if( berr1 ) delete [] berr1;
    }

    int ColorDiffusionDither::bestdevclr( int r, int g, int b )
    {
        long dmin = dist3( r, devcolors[0].red,
                           g, devcolors[0].grn,
                           b, devcolors[0].blu );
        int best = 0;
```

Listing 2.2   DITHER.CPP (continued)

```cpp
    for( int i=1; i<ndevcolors; i++ )
    {
       long d = dist3( r, devcolors[i].red,
                       g, devcolors[i].grn,
                       b, devcolors[i].blu );
       if( d < dmin )
       {
          dmin = d;
          best = i;
       }
    }
    return best;
}

void ColorDiffusionDither::reset( void )
{
    if( ewidth > 0 )
    {
       memset( rerr1, 0, sizeof(int)*2*ewidth );
       memset( gerr1, 0, sizeof(int)*2*ewidth );
       memset( berr1, 0, sizeof(int)*2*ewidth );
    }
}

void ColorDiffusionDither::dither( unsigned char *pxls,
                                   int npxls )
{
    int npx = (ewidth < npxls) ? ewidth : npxls;

    // ?err1 contains current primary intensities plus
    // error accumulated from previous line...
    for( int i=0; i<npx; i++ )
    {
       int n = pxls[i];
       rerr1[i] = rerr2[i] + imgcolors[n].red;
       rerr2[i] = 0;
       gerr1[i] = gerr2[i] + imgcolors[n].grn;
       gerr2[i] = 0;
       berr1[i] = berr2[i] + imgcolors[n].blu;
       berr2[i] = 0;
    }

    // traverse current image line and set pixel values
    // for this line from available device palette
    pxls[0] = bestdevclr( rerr1[0], gerr1[0], berr1[0] );
    for( i=1; i<npx-1; i++ )
    {
       int j = bestdevclr( rerr1[i], gerr1[i], berr1[i] );
```

Listing 2.2   DITHER.CPP (continued)

```
        pxls[i] = j;

        // compute error in each primary
        int rerr = rerr1[i];   rerr -= devcolors[j].red;
        int gerr = gerr1[i];   gerr -= devcolors[j].grn;
        int berr = berr1[i];   berr -= devcolors[j].blu;

        // diffuse red error
        rerr1[i+1] += (rerr * 7) >> 4;
        rerr2[i-1] += (rerr * 3) >> 4;
        rerr2[i]   += (rerr * 5) >> 4;
        rerr2[i+1] += (rerr * 1) >> 4;

        // diffuse green error
        gerr1[i+1] += (gerr * 7) >> 4;
        gerr2[i-1] += (gerr * 3) >> 4;
        gerr2[i]   += (gerr * 5) >> 4;
        gerr2[i+1] += (gerr * 1) >> 4;

        // diffuse blue error
        berr1[i+1] += (berr * 7) >> 4;
        berr2[i-1] += (berr * 3) >> 4;
        berr2[i]   += (berr * 5) >> 4;
        berr2[i+1] += (berr * 1) >> 4;
    }
    pxls[npx-1] = bestdevclr( rerr1[npx-1],
                              gerr1[npx-1],
                              berr1[npx-1] );
}

void ColorDiffusionDither::rgbdither( unsigned char *pxls,
                                      rgb *clrs, int npxls )
{
    int npx = (ewidth < npxls) ? ewidth : npxls;

    // ?err1 contains current primary intensities plus
    // error accumulated from previous line...
    for( int i=0; i<npx; i++ )
    {
        rerr1[i] = rerr2[i] + clrs[i].red;
        rerr2[i] = 0;
        gerr1[i] = gerr2[i] + clrs[i].grn;
        gerr2[i] = 0;
        berr1[i] = berr2[i] + clrs[i].blu;
        berr2[i] = 0;
    }

    // traverse current image line and set pixel values
    // for this line from available device palette
```

Listing 2.2   DITHER.CPP (continued)

```
pxls[0] = bestdevclr( rerr1[0], gerr1[0], berr1[0] );
for( i=1; i<npx-1; i++ )
{
    int j = bestdevclr( rerr1[i], gerr1[i], berr1[i] );
    pxls[i] = j;

    // compute error in each primary
    int rerr = rerr1[i];   rerr -= devcolors[j].red;
    int gerr = gerr1[i];   gerr -= devcolors[j].grn;
    int berr = berr1[i];   berr -= devcolors[j].blu;

    // diffuse red error
    rerr1[i+1] += (rerr * 7) >> 4;
    rerr2[i-1] += (rerr * 3) >> 4;
    rerr2[i]   += (rerr * 5) >> 4;
    rerr2[i+1] += (rerr * 1) >> 4;

    // diffuse green error
    gerr1[i+1] += (gerr * 7) >> 4;
    gerr2[i-1] += (gerr * 3) >> 4;
    gerr2[i]   += (gerr * 5) >> 4;
    gerr2[i+1] += (gerr * 1) >> 4;

    // diffuse blue error
    berr1[i+1] += (berr * 7) >> 4;
    berr2[i-1] += (berr * 3) >> 4;
    berr2[i]   += (berr * 5) >> 4;
    berr2[i+1] += (berr * 1) >> 4;
}
pxls[npx-1] = bestdevclr( rerr1[npx-1],
                          gerr1[npx-1],
                          berr1[npx-1] );

}
```

Intensity Mapping

The simple threshold dither described previously is also an example of a contrast- enhancement function. As a matter of fact, it represents the maximum limit of contrast enhancement that can be imposed on an image: low intensities are forced to zero and high intensities are forced to one.

Contrast enhancement is an example of intensity mapping, and can be defined as a process that amplifies, or enhances, the intensity differences between the lighter and darker elements of an image. Note that this process does not scale or alter the intensity *range* of an image. If the possible intensity range is

0 to 255 before alteration, it will also be 0 to 255 after alteration. That is, the range of an intensity mapping must be the same as its domain.

   This process is perhaps best understood visually. Figure 2.3 shows several possible contrast mapping functions. If an intensity value maps to itself; that is if *f(x) = x*, no intensity change occurs, and the function graphs as a straight line of slope 1. The thresholding process graphs as a step function with only two possible function values, 0 or 1. These two functions represent the extremes of possible contrast enhancement; generally, a function that maps between the two extremes is used. The third function graphed in Figure 2.3 shows a typical choice. Note that a contrast enhancement function that is inflected to the opposite side of the one-to-one mapping (also shown in Figure 2.3) yields a **contrast reduction** function.

   In actual practice, the exact contrast mapping function used is not important as long as it generally conforms to the behavior shown in Figure 2.3. For example, the sine function exhibits this behavior over the domain $-/\pi/2$ to $\pi/2$, and can be used to perform contrast mapping with suitable scaling and translation of intensity values to the function's domain and from the function's range. Assuming that *i* represents an intensity value with a possible intensity range of 0 to *m*, the following expression can be used to compute an intensity delta:

$$\theta = \pi \left(\frac{i}{m} - \frac{1}{2} \right) m$$

$$(f\theta) = \frac{m}{2} \ (\sin(\theta) + 1) - i$$

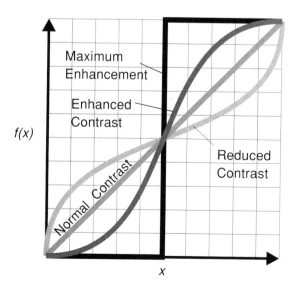

Figure 2.3   Contrast Mapping Functions

This delta can be added to intensity values to perform contrast enhancement or subtracted from intensity values to perform contrast reduction.

To see the results of contrast enhancement, try running one of the two dither demonstration programs presented later in this chapter. You will find that the appearance of most dithered images is improved if the palette of the source image is contrast enhanced prior to dithering.

Brightness mapping is another type of intensity mapping. Its process is similar to that of contrast mapping. Where contrast alteration maps low and high intensity values differently, however, brightness mapping maps them in the same way. Both highs and lows are increased when an intensity range is mapped for increased brightness. This is shown in Figure 2.4.

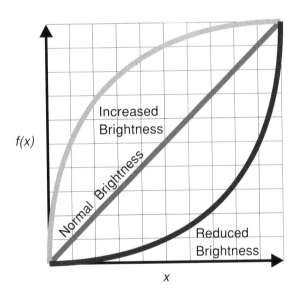

Figure 2.4   Brightness Mapping Functions

Listings 2.3 and 2.4 present the source code for an intensity mapping module, which provides both contrast and brightness mapping functions. The actual mapping is performed by the two functions `contrast_delta()` and `brightness_delta()`. The contrast map uses the sine-based function described earlier. The brightness map uses the following function:

$$f(i) = \left(\sqrt{\frac{i}{m}} - \frac{i}{m} \right) m$$

These functions represent empirical implementations; feel free to experiment with them to obtain possibly better results. There are only two restrictions on a function used to map intensity: it must be single valued and its range must be the same as its domain.

Listing 2.3   INTENMAP.HPP

```
//--------------------------------------------------------------//
//                                                              //
//    File:    INTENMAP.HPP                                     //
//                                                              //
//    Desc:    Intensity mapping functions.                    //
//                                                              //
//--------------------------------------------------------------//

#ifndef _INTENMAP_HPP_
#define _INTENMAP_HPP_

#include "color.hpp"

#define  iMORE    1
#define  iLESS   -1

int  contrast_delta( int ival, int imax );
void contrast_alter( unsigned char *ivals,
                     int icnt, int isign );
void contrast_alter( int *ivals, int icnt, int isign );
void contrast_alter( rgb *iclrs, int icnt, int isign );

int  brightness_delta( int ival, int imax );
void brightness_alter( unsigned char *ivals,
                       int icnt, int isign );
void brightness_alter( int *ivals, int icnt, int isign );
void brightness_alter( rgb *iclrs, int icnt, int isign );

#endif
```

Listing 2.4   INTENMAP.CPP

```
//--------------------------------------------------------------//
//                                                              //
//    File:    INTENMAP.CPP                                     //
//                                                              //
//    Desc:    Intensity mapping functions.                    //
//                                                              //
//--------------------------------------------------------------//
```

Listing 2.4   INTENMAP.CPP (continued)

```cpp
#include "math.h"

#include "intenmap.hpp"

//.................compute contrast intensity delta

int contrast_delta( int ival, int imax )
{
   // map 0..imax to -pi/2..+pi/2
   double m = double( imax );
   double x = double( ival ) - m/2.0;
   double theta = (x * 3.14159265) / m;

   // convert back to 0..imax
   x = (sin(theta) + 1.0) * m/2.0;
   int inew = int( x );

   return inew - ival;
}

//.................contrast-alter a byte intensity array

void contrast_alter( unsigned char *ivals,
                    int icnt, int isign )
{
   for( int i=0; i<icnt; i++ )
      ivals[i] += contrast_delta( ivals[i], 255 ) * isign;
}

//.................contrast-alter an int intensity array

void contrast_alter( int *ivals, int icnt, int isign )
{
   for( int i=0; i<icnt; i++ )
      ivals[i] += contrast_delta( ivals[i], 255 ) * isign;
}

//.................contrast-alter an rgb color array

void contrast_alter( rgb *iclrs, int icnt, int isign )
{
   for( int i=0; i<icnt; i++ )
   {
      iclrs[i].red += contrast_delta( iclrs[i].red, 255 )
                      * isign;
      iclrs[i].grn += contrast_delta( iclrs[i].grn, 255 )
                      * isign;
      iclrs[i].blu += contrast_delta( iclrs[i].blu, 255 )
```

Listing 2.4   INTENMAP.CPP (continued)

```cpp
                             * isign;
    }
}

//................compute brightness intensity delta

int brightness_delta( int ival, int imax )
{
// // map 0..imax to 0..pi/2
// double m = double( imax );
// double x = double( ival );
// double theta = (x * 1.57079633) / m;
//
// // convert back to 0..imax
// x = sin(theta) * m;
// int inew = int( x );
  // map 0..imax to 0..1.0
  double m = double( imax );
  double x = double( ival ) / m;

  // compute function value
  double y = pow( x, 0.5 );

  // map 0..1.0 to 0..imax
  y*= m;
  int inew = int( y );

  return inew - ival;
}

//................brightness-alter a byte intensity array

void brightness_alter( unsigned char *ivals,
                       int icnt, int isign )
{
   for( int i=0; i<icnt; i++ )
      ivals[i] += brightness_delta( ivals[i], 255 ) * isign;
}

//................brightness-alter an int intensity array

void brightness_alter( int *ivals, int icnt, int isign )
{
   for( int i=0; i<icnt; i++ )
      ivals[i] += brightness_delta( ivals[i], 255 ) * isign;
}

//................brightness-alter an rgb color array
```

Listing 2.4   INTENMAP.CPP (continued)

```
void brightness_alter( rgb *iclrs, int icnt, int isign )
{
   for( int i=0; i<icnt; i++ )
   {
      iclrs[i].red += brightness_delta( iclrs[i].red, 255 )
                         * isign;
      iclrs[i].grn += brightness_delta( iclrs[i].grn, 255 )
                         * isign;
      iclrs[i].blu += brightness_delta( iclrs[i].blu, 255 )
                         * isign;
   }
}
```

A Dither Demonstration Program

Dithering as a technique is highly empirical despite its firm grounding in scientific principles. The results of a particular dither can vary widely with the type and particular nuances of the source image. Because the whole point to dithering is to deceive the human eye, it is also sensitive to the "eye of the beholder" in a quite literal sense.

Although dithering is most commonly employed to render printed (that is, black and white) imagery, it can also be used to render color imagery in monochrome video display modes (or color display modes, for that matter—see the section on color dithering later in this chapter). A program to do this is presented in Listing 2.5, which uses VGA mode 12h with a gray-scale palette to provide four views of a color input image: a clustered-dot-ordered dither, a dispersed-dot-ordered dither, a bilevel threshold, and a bilevel threshold with Floyd–Steinberg error diffusion.

The program uses VGA-based graphics functions that will be described in detail in Chapter 5. They are used here without comment. Also, because we have yet to cover a graphical file format, no format is assumed. The image is read as a simple array of bytes from a disk file with no compression or other formatting. The image's palette is read from a simple ASCII file containing 256 RGB triples with intensity values in the range 0 to 255. A suitable test image was created for the program from a 256-color GIF file. Figures 2.5 through 2.8 illustrate the four bilevel versions of the test image as they were printed by an HP LaserJet II printer. The image, by the way, is from a painting by the renowned Spanish painter, El Greco.

Figure 2.5 An Image Rendered with Simple Thresholding

Figure 2.6 An Image Rendered with a Clustered-Dot Ordered Dither

Figure 2.7 An Image Rendered with a Dispersed-Dot Ordered Dither

Figure 2.8 An Image Rendered with Floyd–Steinberg Error Diffusion

Listing 2.5   MDITDEMO.CPP

```cpp
//-----------------------------------------------------------//
//                                                           //
//   File:     MDITDEMO.CPP                                  //
//                                                           //
//   Desc:     Monochrome dithering demonstration            //
//                                                           //
//-----------------------------------------------------------//

#include "stdlib.h"
#include "stdio.h"
#include "string.h"
#include "conio.h"

#include "color.hpp"
#include "colormap.hpp"
#include "intenmap.hpp"
#include "display.hpp"
#include "dither.hpp"
#include "dithers.hpp"

//.................test image metrics

char * palname     = "EL-GRECO.PAL";
char * imgname     = "EL-GRECO.IMG";
int    imgwidth    = 354;
int    imgheight   = 446;
int    imgcolors   = 256;
rgb  * imgpalette  = 0;
int  * imggrays    = 0;

//.................read test image palette

rgb * read_palette( char *fn, int ncolors )
{
   rgb *pal = new rgb [ncolors];
   if( pal == 0 )
   {
      printf( "No memory for palette\n" );
      exit( 0 );
   }
   FILE *f = fopen( fn, "rt" );
   if( f == 0 )
   {
      printf( "Palette file not found\n" );
      exit( 0 );
   }
   for( int i=0; i<ncolors; i++ )
```

Listing 2.5   MDITDEMO.CPP (continued)

```
      {
         int r, g, b;
         fscanf( f, "%d %d %d", &r, &g, &b );
         if( ferror(f) || feof(f) )
         {
            printf( "Error reading palette\n" );
            exit( 0 );
         }
         pal[i] = rgb( r, g, b );
      }
      fclose( f );
      return pal;
   }

   //.................get grayscale values from palette

   int * compute_grays( rgb *pal, int ncolors )
   {
      int *glvl = new int [ncolors];
      if( glvl == 0 )
      {
         printf( "No memory for grayscale\n" );
         exit( 0 );
      }
      for( int i=0; i<ncolors; i++ )
         glvl[i] = pal[i].graylevel();
      return glvl;
   }

   //.................dither and display the image

   unsigned char scanline[640];

   void dither_image( FILE *img, VgaDisplay& vga, Dither& dit )
   {
      fseek( img, 0L, SEEK_SET );
      for( int i=0; i<imgheight; i++ )
      {
         fread( scanline, imgwidth, 1, img );
         for( int j=0; j<imgwidth; j++ )
            scanline[j] = imggrays[ scanline[j] ];
         dit.dither( scanline, imgwidth );
         vga.putscanline( scanline, imgwidth, 0, i );
      }
      getch();
   }
```

Listing 2.5   MDITDEMO.CPP (continued)

```cpp
//.................main

int main( void )
{
   // get image palette and grayscale
   imgpalette = read_palette( palname, imgcolors );
   imggrays  = compute_grays( imgpalette, imgcolors );

   // open image file for reading
   FILE *f = fopen( imgname, "rb" );
   if( f == 0 )
   {
      printf( "Image file not found\n" );
      exit( 0 );
   }

   // create a mode 12h VGA display
   VgaDisplay vga( 0x12 );

   // perform the demonstrations...
   // notes:  (1) in a mono display mode use 1, 0
   //             in place of 15, 0.
   //         (2) in a color mode try using 7, 8
   //             in place of 15, 0.

   OrderedDither cdit( ClustMat, 15, 0 );
   dither_image( f, vga, cdit );

   OrderedDither ddit( DispMat, 15, 0 );
   dither_image( f, vga, ddit );

   ThresholdDither tdit( 127, 15, 0 );
   dither_image( f, vga, tdit );

   DiffusionDither edit( 127, imgwidth, 15, 0 );
   dither_image( f, vga, edit );

   contrast_alter( imggrays, imgcolors, iMORE );
   edit.reset( );
   dither_image( f, vga, edit );

   // cleanup and exit
   fclose( f );
   delete [] imgpalette;
   delete [] imggrays;
   return 0;
}
```

Color Dithering

All the dithering techniques that have been discussed here were illustrated within the context of bilevel imagery, either for a black and white printer or a monochrome video mode. However, they can be used with equal facility to create imagery for gray-scale or color output devices. Potential applications of dithering include the display of 24-bit color images in a 256-color VGA display mode or printing a 256-color image on a color printer.

To explore how this works, let us consider printing a 256-color image on a color-ribbon dot-matrix printer. Such printers are based on the CMYK color model and are generally equipped with a four-color ribbon containing blue, red, yellow, and black. Blue and red can be treated as cyan and magenta for printing purposes.

In the dither demonstration program in the preceding section, the image's RGB palette was converted to gray-scale levels for dithering. If we are printing to a color-ribbon printer, the palette is converted instead to CMY (or CMYK) values, and three (or four) separate dithers are computed and printed, one for each primary in the color model.

Choosing between CMY and CMYK is somewhat arbitrary with a color-ribbon printer. If CMY is used, then black in the printed image will look more like a muddy brown. On the other hand, the nonblack colors in a CMYK rendering often look "dirty." On most other color printers the CMYK model generally gives a better result.

The same techniques apply whether we are rendering 256-color images in 16-color video display modes, or 16-bit and 24-bit color images in 256-color video display modes. Here, of course, no color translation is required; we can work directly with the image's RGB palette.

The implementation of video-based color dithering differs from its printer-based cousin in one important respect—the number of available primary intensities. The color printer is still essentially a bilevel device, in the sense that ink is either placed on the page or is not placed on the page. It's just that it has more than one ink color to work with. By contrast, the standard VGA adapter has 64 possible intensities of each primary. This capability can be exploited to improve upon the binary nature of classic dithering.

As a starting point, let's first consider dithering with bilevel primaries. Three primaries, each having two possible intensities, generate a palette of eight colors. If we use 0 and 1 to represent intensities, this is equivalent to the following set of numbers:

```
0   0   0
0   0   1
0   1   0
0   1   1
1   0   0
1   0   1
1   1   0
1   1   1
```

This is nothing more than the binary representation of the numbers 0 through 7. We can therefore take an arbitrary RGB value from an image and convert it to an index in the range 0 to 7 by thresholding each primary intensity separately and then concatenating the three binary values. A VGA adapter's palette can then be modified to allow use of indexes computed in this way as actual pixel values. Here is the corresponding VGA device palette:

```
 0    0    0
 0    0   63
 0   63    0
 0   63   63
63    0    0
63    0   63
63   63    0
63   63   63
```

Note that only 8 of 16 possible colors are actually used (assuming VGA mode 12h); this technique is suitable for rendering images of 256 colors or more.

While bilevel dithering with 8 colors is fast, it is not particularly effective, and obviously does not exploit the full capabilities of the video hardware. A better approach is to use a 16-color palette with some form of error diffusion, such as Floyd–Steinberg. The results obtainable with this approach are quite impressive, although the process is much slower.

One disadvantage of any dithering technique used at typical screen resolutions is that the texture of the resulting images is quite grainy. However, subtle color details are preserved much better than they are with the faster and less grainy techniques of palette mapping discussed in the previous chapter.

The techniques we have just described are implemented as a set of dithering classes in Listings 2.1 and 2.2. Both an 8-color thresholded and an n-color error-diffusion dither are presented. The error diffusion dither can employ any device palette, but the best results are obtained with a palette that is optimally maximal with respect to the color capabilities of the display device. An example of such a palette with 16 colors is shown.

A Demonstration Program for a Colored Dither

Recall that the test image used in the monochrome dither demonstration is a 256-color image. It is interesting to compare the results from that demonstration with the results obtainable using a colored dither on the same image. A program to do this is presented in Listing 2.6. All dithers performed by the program use the special 8-color palette, described previously, in VGA display mode 12h. This setup produces results that are typical of a color printer, but still do not fully exploit the capabilities of the VGA adapter. An optimum VGA implementation will be postponed until Chapter 7, when we will combine palette reduction with dithering.

Listing 2.6   CDITDEMO.CPP

```
//------------------------------------------------------------//
//                                                            //
//    File:      CDITDEMO.CPP                                 //
//                                                            //
//    Desc:      Color dithering demonstration                //
//                                                            //
//------------------------------------------------------------//

#include "stdlib.h"
#include "stdio.h"
#include "string.h"
#include "conio.h"

#include "color.hpp"
#include "colormap.hpp"
#include "intenmap.hpp"
#include "display.hpp"
#include "dither.hpp"

//.................test image metrics

char * palname     = "EL-GRECO.PAL";
char * imgname     = "EL-GRECO.IMG";
int    imgwidth    = 354;
int    imgheight   = 446;
int    imgcolors   = 256;
rgb  * imgpalette = 0;

//.................read test image palette

rgb * read_palette( char *fn, int ncolors )
{
   rgb *pal = new rgb [ncolors];
   if( pal == 0 )
```

Listing 2.6   CDITDEMO.CPP (continued)

```cpp
      {
         printf( "No memory for palette\n" );
         exit( 0 );
      }
      FILE *f = fopen( fn, "rt" );
      if( f == 0 )
      {
         printf( "Palette file not found\n" );
         exit( 0 );
      }
      for( int i=0; i<ncolors; i++ )
      {
         int r, g, b;
         fscanf( f, "%d %d %d", &r, &g, &b );
         if( ferror(f) || feof(f) )
         {
            printf( "Error reading palette\n" );
            exit( 0 );
         }
         pal[i] = rgb( r, g, b );
      }
      fclose( f );
      return pal;
   }

   //.................dither and display the image

   unsigned char scanline[640];

   void dither_image( FILE *img, VgaDisplay& vga, Dither& dit )
   {
      fseek( img, 0L, SEEK_SET );
      for( int i=0; i<imgheight; i++ )
      {
         fread( scanline, imgwidth, 1, img );
         dit.dither( scanline, imgwidth );
         vga.putscanline( scanline, imgwidth, 0, i );
      }
      getch();
   }

   //.................main

   int main( void )
   {
      // get image palette
      imgpalette = read_palette( palname, imgcolors );
```

Listing 2.6   CDITDEMO.CPP (continued)

```cpp
    // open image file for reading
    FILE *f = fopen( imgname, "rb" );
    if( f == 0 )
    {
        printf( "Image file not found\n" );
        exit( 0 );
    }

    // create mode 12h display, set special palette
    VgaDisplay vga( 0x12 );

    // thresholded dither...
    vga.putpalette( ColorThresholdPalette(),
                    ColorThresholdSize() );
    ColorThresholdDither tdit( 127, imgpalette, imgcolors );
    dither_image( f, vga, tdit );

    // error diffusion dither....
    vga.putpalette( ColorDiffusionPalette(),
                    ColorDiffusionSize() );
    ColorDiffusionDither ddit( imgwidth, imgpalette, imgcolors,
                               ColorDiffusionPalette(),
                               ColorDiffusionSize() );
    dither_image( f, vga, ddit );

    // error diffusion dither with enhanced contrast...
    contrast_alter( imgpalette, imgcolors, iMORE );
    ddit.reset( );
    dither_image( f, vga, ddit );

    // cleanup and exit
    fclose( f );
    delete [] imgpalette;
    return 0;
}
```

This completes our look at dithering. It is a capability that should be included in any program that displays or prints images. Without it, the results obtainable when an image's color resolution exceeds the capabilities of the display device are less than satisfactory. We will explore practical implementations of image display and printing that include dithering capabilities in Chapter 7. We turn next to the subject of data compression.

3

Compression Techniques

At the heart of every bitmapped file format there is a compression scheme. It is the compression scheme, more than anything else, that determines the "personality" of a format. This is evident in the way we refer to specific formats. For example, the PCX Format is a "run-length-encoded" format, and the GIF format is an "LZW-compressed" format.

The importance of compression reflects the most salient aspect of bitmaps—their size. They tend to be quite large and, therefore, quite unwieldy. The memory requirements of various VGA graphic modes provide some typical numbers: 640x480x256 colors require 307,200 bytes of memory and 1024x768x256 colors require 786,432 bytes of memory. Bitmaps for 16-bit and 24-bit display hardware are two and three times the size of those for a corresponding 256-color mode.

This chapter looks at the subject of compression and provides implementations of three commonly used compression schemes. These schemes will come in handy later when the specific formats that make use of them are presented. We begin with an overview of compression terms and concepts.

Compression Overview

Compression is a special case of a general technique known as **encoding**. Encoding can be described as a process that takes as input a string of symbols (called a message or a data set) and outputs a code for each input symbol or datum. The output of the process is thus an **encoded representation** of its input.

There are many reasons for using encoding algorithms. Because encoded data typically look like jumbled mush and bear little apparent relation to their unencoded representation, an encoding algorithm serves to **encrypt** its input, making it unintelligible. This use of encoding is obviously of interest to spies and others in similar occupations. It is not, however, the reason it is of interest to the programmer trying to decipher a compressed bitmap.

If the encoded output of an encoding algorithm is smaller in size than its unencoded input, we have a compression algorithm. In this case, we are interested not in the fact that the encoded output looks like mush (although it does) but in the fact that it is smaller in size than its corresponding unencoded input.

For every encoding algorithm there is an inverse process, called a **decoding** algorithm. The decoding algorithm, when applied to the output of the encoding algorithm, reproduces the original input that was processed by the encoding algorithm. Obviously, without the decoding algorithm there would be little point in using an encoding algorithm.

If the output of a decoding algorithm reproduces exactly the input to the corresponding encoding algorithm then the algorithm is said to be **lossless**. Algorithms that are not lossless are said to be **lossy**. Although an algorithm that is not lossless might seem to have little practical use, this is not the case. A compression algorithm and its corresponding decompression algorithm are collectively referred to as a **codec**. This term is a contraction of "compressor-decompressor."

One of the most interesting aspects of the subject of compression is the fact that no compression algorithm is guaranteed to work. For every compression algorithm that is either lossless or minimally lossy, it is relatively easy to concoct a data sample on which it fails. Indeed, most algorithms, when applied to pathological data cases, typically produce a compressed representation that is larger than the uncompressed input. The reason for this behavior is that compression depends on, and takes advantage of, the redundancy present in most information. If a piece of information possesses sufficiently low redundancy, it is not compressible by standard means.

This idea can be illustrated with a hypothetical algorithm intended to compress English text. The algorithm itself is quite simple: replace each sentence with a noun, a verb, and an object. Let's try the algorithm on a few sample sentences. The sentence

The girl with blonde hair rides her bicycle.

compresses to

Girl rides bicycle.

The algorithm did a pretty fair job here; eight words compressed down to three. Note, however, that the algorithm is lossy. We have lost the information about the girl's hair color and the implied fact that she owns the bicycle. Now consider this sentence:

He eats.

This compresses to

He eats something.

Remember, our algorithm requires a noun, a verb, and an object. Because the original sentence in this example does not contain an object, a generic object is supplied, making the "compressed" form of the sentence larger than the original. The original is a pathological case for this algorithm.

Our text-compression algorithm is not particularly robust, and I seriously doubt that the patent office would grant us a patent for it, but it does illustrate the concepts involved.

In the case of graphic imagery, redundancy is manifest as repeating colors and repeating patterns of colors. Most images exhibit a high degree of both. A line of pixels all of the same value (that is, color) is referred to as a **run**. The simplest practical compression scheme replaces all runs in an image with a two-value code, representing the pixel's value and the number of times to repeat it. Algorithms based on this technique are referred to as **run-length-encoding** algorithms (RLE for short). They do a reasonably good job on images that are either simple or contain only a few colors. One example of this class of algorithm is the so-called PackBits algorithm used in MacPaint files, which we will be looking at shortly.

An obvious shortcoming of run-length encoding is that it is effectively limited to 1-byte patterns. That is, a sequence of bytes such as 1A1A1A1A can be viewed as repetitions of the 1-byte pattern 1A. This sequence can be compressed by an RLE algorithm. However, an RLE algorithm has no effect on the sequence 1A2B1A2B1A2B, which consists of three repetitions of the 2-byte pattern 1A2B. Other classes of compression algorithms do encode multibyte patterns. Perhaps the most notable example is LZW compression, which we will also look at in some detail in connection with the GIF format.

One class of imagery that does not compress well using traditional methods is continuous-tone photographic-style imagery. Such images contain a large number of colors, which reduces the kind of simple redundancy that is the forte of traditional compression methods. Since photographic imagery has become increasingly important over the past few years, new compression methods have been devised to cope with its typically complex images. Most of these techniques involve the use of complex mathematical transforms and filters. These are typically used to preprocess images to enhance their redundancy and thus make them more amenable to standard compression techniques.

Having briefly surveyed the subject, we now turn to the particulars and actual software implementations of three important compression schemes: PackBits, the MacPaint RLE algorithm; Huffman encoding, which is commonly used on fax imagery; and LZW compression, which is used in the GIF format. Additional algorithms will be described as they occur during the presentation of the actual file formats. These three, however, are important in that they are all supported by more than one format. We begin with a discussion of a suitable C++ class design for handling compression and decompression and then consider the specific algorithms.

A C++ Codec Class Design

Collectively, the various compression schemes mentioned represent a class of objects that are "similar yet different." This situation, commonly encountered in software design, is generally best handled if the objects can be made to appear exactly the same. That is, we want to treat the various compression schemes as black boxes that all look the same on the outside but may differ substantially on the inside.

The programming paradigm that we have just described is standard fare for the C++ language, and is one of the many reasons C++ is preferable to C. Note that, while there is no reason why the same approach cannot be implemented in C, it is much less natural in C and would probably require more effort on the part of the programmer.

A good approach to handling compression and decompression with a class hierarchy is to devise a virtual base class from which specific codec classes are derived. Each algorithm is then implemented in such a fashion that they all appear identical from the outside and they all make access to each class's functional capabilities through the same set of virtual functions. This approach has the advantage that any piece of code designed for one codec works without modification with another codec. This reusability simplifies the programmer's task tremendously.

To illustrate the use of this paradigm, suppose we create a `Compressor` base class with a virtual `encode()` function that encodes and outputs a single scan line:

```
class Compressor
{
        :
    public:
```

```
        void encode( unsigned char *scanline,
                int npixels ) = 0;
            :
};
```

If we then derive, say, some RLE-based compressor class, as in

```
class RleXCompressor : public Compressor
```

and write a function that outputs a compressed bitmap, such as

```
void write_bm( Compressor& cmp, unsigned char **img,
            int width, int height )
{
    for( int i=0; i<height; i++ )
        cmp.encode( img[i], width );
}
```

we can then write code such as

```
RleXCompressor rleX;
    :
write_bm( rleX, rows, w, h );
```

Later on, if we create, say, an LZW–based compressor derived from the same base class, then the write-bitmap function works with this new class without modification, as in

```
LzwCompressor lzw;
    :
write_bm( lzw, rows, w, h );
```

This design makes for a compression package that's wonderfully easy to use. Keep in mind, however, that the coding inside the boxes is probably more complicated in such a design than it is in a more traditional approach. This is especially true for a compression scheme designed to operate on a complete image without regard to its structure as a collection of scan lines. In our example, the virtual encode function is designed to be scan-line based.

Even though the box internals are more complex, the net result is well worth the effort—we will implement such a design in this chapter. As a starting point, the implementations of the base classes to be used are presented in Listing 3.1. Note the use of separate encoder (compressor) and decoder (decompressor) classes—a complete codec requires implementation of both.

Listing 3.1 CODEC.HPP

```cpp
//----------------------------------------------------------//
//                                                          //
//    File:      CODEC.HPP                                   //
//                                                          //
//    Desc:      Base class definitions for data            //
//               compressors and decompressors.             //
//                                                          //
//----------------------------------------------------------//

#ifndef _CODEC_HPP_
#define _CODEC_HPP_

//.................codec types

enum tCodecTypes
{
    tNONE,
    tRLE,
    tPACKBITS,
    tHUFFMAN,
    tGROUP3,
    tLZW,
    tGIFLZW
};

//.................status codes

enum xStatusCodes
{
    xOKAY        = 0x00,
    xENDOFIMAGE  = 0x01,
    xENDOFFILE   = 0x02,
    xIOERROR     = 0x04,
    xNOMEMORY    = 0x08,
    xOUTOFSYNC   = 0x10,
    xOVERFLOW    = 0x20,
    xBADPARAM    = 0x40,
    xUNSUPPORTED = 0x80
};

//.................the encoder (compressor) base class

class Encoder
{
    public:
        int type;        // encoder identifier
```

Listing 3.1 CODEC.HPP (continued)

```
        Encoder( int encoder_type = tNONE )
        { type = encoder_type; }
        ~Encoder( )
        { }
        virtual int encode( unsigned char *buf,
                            int nbytes ) = 0;
        virtual int init( void ) = 0;
        virtual int term( void ) = 0;
        virtual int status( void ) = 0;
};

//................the decoder (decompressor) base class

class Decoder
{
    public:
        int    type;        // decoder type

        Decoder( int decoder_type = tNONE )
        { type = decoder_type; }
        ~Decoder( )
        { }
        virtual int decode( unsigned char *buf,
                            int nbytes ) = 0;
        virtual int init( void ) = 0;
        virtual int term( void ) = 0;
        virtual int status( void ) = 0;
};


#endif
```

Both the encoder and decoder classes include virtual initialization and termination functions. Depending on the algorithm being implemented, these may or may not be required. When they are not required, they will be implemented as stubs that simply return a status code. Usually the code for these functions properly belongs in the class constructor and destructor, respectively. Their implementation here as separate functions is designed to free the programmer from having to consider an object's scope in controlling the encode or decode process, and to allow a single object instance to encode or decode multiple images.

To illustrate how this is intended to work, let us return to the hypothetical LzwCompressor class mentioned previously. A typical calling sequence would go something like this:

```
LzwCompressor lzw;
    :
lzw.init( );
write_bm( lzw, img1_rows, w1, h1 );
lzw.term( );
    :
lzw.init( );
write_bm( lzw, img2_rows, w2, h2 );
lzw.term( );
```

PackBits Compression

PackBits is a simple byte-oriented run-length compression scheme that was originally developed for use in the MacPaint image file format and is one of several schemes supported by the TIFF format. The PackBits algorithm encodes a stream of bytes into a series of packets consisting of an index byte followed by some number of data bytes. The easiest way to explain the algorithm is to describe the decoding process. Here it is in pseudocode:

```
Loop until desired number of bytes have been decoded.
    N = next byte from input.
    If N < 0
        Read next byte from input and
        repeat it 1-N times.
    Else
        Read next N+1 bytes from input.
Endloop.
```

Here are some notes and rules concerning the algorithm:

1. Each scan line of an image must be encoded separately. Thus, packets in the compressed data stream cannot span scan lines.

2. Note that index values are always incremented by 1 before use in the decoding process. Thus, an index of 0 implies a count of 1, an index of 1 implies a count of 2, an index of –5 implies a count of 6, and so on.

3. Valid index values range from –127 to 127. This yields counts in the range 1 to 128. Note that the index value –128 is never used.

In most RLE-based compression schemes, the logic required to perform encoding is more complex than the logic for decoding. PackBits is typical in this regard. This results principally from the fact that a given data stream seldom produces a unique encoded representation, regardless of the algorithm, so some decision making invariably accompanies the encoding process. For example, consider the byte sequence AAB. This could be encoded by the PackBits algorithm in several different ways. One way would be as two repeating runs, two As followed by one B. Another would be as a single nonrepeating sequence of three bytes, AAB. As it turns out, both forms generate four encoded bytes, so neither one is desirable.

It is possible with sufficient effort to determine the optimum encoding for a given data string, but the results seldom justify the effort. For this reason, in this book we will always implement encoding in the simplest, most straight-forward fashion.

Listings 3.2 and 3.3 present C++ source code for the PackBits compressor and decompressor classes. Keep in mind that there are numerous variations on the RLE concept, of which PackBits is just one. We will encounter others when we discuss the formats that use them.

Listing 3.2 PACKBITS.HPP

```
//------------------------------------------------------------//
//                                                            //
//    File:      PACKBITS.HPP                                 //
//                                                            //
//    Desc:      Class definitions for PackBits               //
//               compressor and decompressor.                //
//                                                            //
//------------------------------------------------------------//

#ifndef _PACKBITS_HPP_
#define _PACKBITS_HPP_

#include "stdio.h"

#include "codec.hpp"

//.................PackBits encoder

class PackBitsEncoder : public Encoder
{
   protected:
      FILE *outfile;

   public:
      PackBitsEncoder( FILE *f_out ) : Encoder( tPACKBITS )
      {
         outfile = f_out;
      }
      ~PackBitsEncoder( )
      {
      }
      virtual int init( void );
```

Listing 3.2 PACKBITS.HPP (continued)

```
        virtual int term( void );
        virtual int encode( unsigned char *line, int size );
        virtual int status( void );
};

//................PackBits decoder

class PackBitsDecoder : public Decoder
{
    protected:
        FILE *infile;

    public:
        PackBitsDecoder( FILE *f_in ) : Decoder( tPACKBITS )
        {
            infile = f_in;
        }
        ~PackBitsDecoder( )
        {
        }
        virtual int init( void );
        virtual int term( void );
        virtual int decode( unsigned char *line, int size );
        virtual int status( void );
};

#endif
```

Listing 3.3 PACKBITS.CPP

```
//----------------------------------------------------------//
//                                                          //
//   File:    PACKBITS.CPP                                  //
//                                                          //
//   Desc:    Encode and Decode functions for the          //
//            PackBits compression algorithm                //
//                                                          //
//----------------------------------------------------------//

#include "packbits.hpp"

//................class PackBitsEncoder

int PackBitsEncoder::init( void )
{
    return status( );
}
```

Listing 3.3 PACKBITS.CPP (continued)

```cpp
int PackBitsEncoder::term( void )
{
   return status( );
}

int PackBitsEncoder::status( void )
{
   if( ferror(outfile) ) return xIOERROR;
   return xOKAY;
}

int PackBitsEncoder::encode( unsigned char *line, int size )
{
   int cnt = 0;   // bytes encoded

   while( cnt < size )
   {
      int i = cnt;
      int j = i + 1;
      int jmax = i + 126;
      if( jmax >= size ) jmax = size-1;

      if( i == size-1 )   //................last byte alone
      {
         fputc( 0, outfile );
         fputc( line[i], outfile );
         cnt++;
      }
      else if( line[i] == line[j] )   //....run
      {
         while( (j<jmax) && (line[j]==line[j+1]) )
             j++;
         fputc( i-j, outfile );
         fputc( line[i], outfile );
         cnt += j-i+1;
      }
      else   //...........................sequence
      {
         while( (j<jmax) && (line[j]!=line[j+1]) )
            j++;
         fputc( j-i, outfile );
         fwrite( line+i, j-i+1, 1, outfile );
         cnt += j-i+1;
      }
   }

   return status( );
}
```

Listing 3.3 PACKBITS.CPP (continued)

```cpp
//.................class PackBitsDecoder

int PackBitsDecoder::init( void )
{
   return status( );
}

int PackBitsDecoder::term( void )
{
   return status( );
}

int PackBitsDecoder::status( void )
{
   if( feof(infile) )    return xENDOFFILE;
   if( ferror(infile) ) return xIOERROR;
   return xOKAY;
}

int PackBitsDecoder::decode( unsigned char *line, int size )
{
   int n = 0;                 // number of bytes decoded

   while( n < size )
   {
      int ix = fgetc( infile );    // get index byte
      if( feof( infile ) ) break;

      char cx = ix;
      if( cx == -128 ) continue;

      if( cx < 0 )  //............run
      {
         int i = 1 - cx;
         char ch = fgetc( infile );
         while( i-- )
         {
            // test for buffer overflow
            if( n == size ) return -1;
            line[n++] = ch;
         }
      }
      else  //....................seq
      {
         int i = cx + 1;
         while( i-- )
         {
            // test for buffer overflow
```

Listing 3.3 PACKBITS.CPP (continued)

```
                if( n == size ) return -1;
                line[n++] = fgetc( infile );
            }
        }
    }

    return feof( infile );
}
```

Huffman Compression

By computing standards, Huffman compression is a venerable technique, having been first described by D. A. Huffman in 1952. It nonetheless remains an important and useful compression technique and is specified by the CCITT Group 3 Facsimile Standard, which is supported by the TIFF format. The Group 3 standard actually specifies a variant of the classic Huffman algorithm, but is still generally referred to as Huffman compression.

Huffman compression encodes a byte stream into a sequence of variable-length bit codes. The principle behind the algorithm is to determine the statistical frequency of the various symbols in the input stream and to encode the message using short bit codes for the most frequent symbols and longer bit codes for less frequent symbols.

As an illustration, consider an ASCII file encoded as a sequence of fixed-length 8-bit codes. The letter A is encoded as 01000001 (41h) and the letter Z is encoded as 01011010 (5Ah). However, on average, the letter A occurs more frequently than the letter Z. So if we encode A with a short code, say 011, and Z with a longer code, say 0111111, then we will have reduced the number of bits needed to represent a file.

This technique, referred to as **variable-length encoding**, is not what Huffman actually described. Huffman's contribution was an algorithm for determining the optimal code set for a given data set to be encoded. This is done by ordering the input symbols by frequency and then constructing a binary tree from them. The bit code for a given symbol is then determined by the path to that symbol in the tree. At each level a left branch contributes a 1 bit to the symbol encoding and a right branch contributes a 0 bit. When a terminal node is reached, the input symbol found there is encoded with the bit pattern constructed from the path to that symbol. During decoding, bits are read from the input stream and are used to traverse the tree. When a terminal node is reached, the symbol associated with that node is output to the decoded stream.

The actual tree, referred to as a **Huffman tree**, is constructed from the bottom up, starting with all the terminal nodes ordered by increasing frequency. The two nodes with the lowest frequency are combined to form a parent node whose frequency is defined to be the sum of the frequencies of its two children nodes. This process is repeated until a single node, the root of the tree, is reached. Note that the tree used to encode a data stream is required to decode the compressed representation of the data stream.

Two problems with Huffman compression are (1) that it requires two passes over a file, one to determine symbol frequency and one for the actual encoding, and (2) that the bitwise manipulation required of the encoded representation is computationally more expensive than byte-oriented manipulation. The first problem can be solved by assuming a standard symbol frequency distribution and bit code set, which is the case with the Group 3 Facsimile Standard.

CCITT Group 3 Compression

The CCITT Group 3 compression algorithm was developed specifically for compression of bilevel (monochrome) facsimile images. Each scan line in an image is encoded separately, and what is encoded is the length, in bits, of alternating runs of white and black pixels. For example, consider a scan line such as the following:

```
00001110000000001110000
```

Assuming that a 1 bit represents black, this scan line can be described as a sequence of 4 white pixels, 3 black pixels, 8 white pixels, 3 black pixels, and 4 white pixels. It would be encoded as the sequence of bit codes representing 4w–3b–8w–3b–4w.

Because the Group 3 standard specifies the set of bit codes to use, files can be compressed in a single pass. The Group 3 bit code set is listed in Appendix A. Note that two types of codes are defined, terminating codes and make-up codes. **Terminating codes** have bit counts in the range 0 to 63, and **make-up** codes have bit counts that are multiples of 64. A given bit count is encoded as zero or more make-up codes followed by exactly one terminating code. When counts greater than 63 are encoded, the make-up code that is closest to but not greater than the count is used, followed by the terminating code representing the difference between the two. For example, the count 64 is encoded as 64m–0t, the count 120 as 64m–56t, and so on. When counts that are greater than the range accommodated by the table are encoded, as many make-up codes as necessary are used to represent the count, followed by the required terminating code.

The code table contains separate codes for black and white pixel counts. Note, however, that make-up codes for counts of 1792 and greater can represent either black or white pixels. In actual practice, it is a good rule to determine pixel color from the terminating codes only. TIFF format scan lines must always begin with a white run (even if of length zero). Because pixel colors alternate, this ensures that the decoder is always synchronized with the encoder as far as pixel color is concerned.

Here are some notes and rules regarding the Group 3 algorithm:

1. Scan lines are encoded separately, and encoding always begins on a byte boundary.

2. Encoded scan lines always begin with a white run. If the actual scan line begins with a black pixel then the initial white run specifies a count of zero.

3. Run lengths for an encoded scan line should sum to the image width. It is considered an error if they do not.

4. Don't forget, this compression scheme is for monochrome imagery only. Scan lines should thus contain only pixel values 0 and 1.

Listings 3.4 and 3.5 present the source code to a CCITT Group 3 codec.

Listing 3.4 GROUP3.HPP

```
//----------------------------------------------------------//
//                                                          //
//   File:     GROUP3.HPP                                   //
//                                                          //
//   Desc:     Class definitions for CCITT Group 3          //
//             compressor and decompressor.                 //
//                                                          //
//----------------------------------------------------------//

#ifndef _GROUP3_HPP_
#define _GROUP3_HPP_

#include "stdio.h"

#include "codec.hpp"

//.................Group 3 encoder

class Group3Encoder : public Encoder
```

Listing 3.4 GROUP3.HPP (continued)

```
{
  protected:
     FILE            *outfile;
     unsigned char   codebyte;
     unsigned char   codemask;

  private:
     int  runlength( int pxval, int maxcnt,
                     unsigned char *pxls );
     int  wrtbitcode( int code, int len );
     int  wrtrun( int pxval, int cnt );

  public:
     Group3Encoder( FILE *f_out ) : Encoder( tGROUP3 )
     {
        outfile = f_out;
     }
     ~Group3Encoder( )
     {
     }
     virtual int init( void );
     virtual int term( void );
     virtual int encode( unsigned char *line, int size );
     virtual int status( void );
};

//................Group 3 decoder

class Group3Decoder : public Decoder
{
  protected:
     FILE            *infile;
     int             cond;
     unsigned char   codebyte;
     unsigned char   codemask;

  private:
     int  rdbit( void );
     int  rdcode( int pxval );

  public:
     Group3Decoder( FILE *f_in ) : Decoder( tGROUP3 )
     {
        infile = f_in;
        cond = xOKAY;
     }
     ~Group3Decoder( )
```

Listing 3.4 GROUP3.HPP (continued)

```
            {
            }
            virtual int init( void );
            virtual int term( void );
            virtual int decode( unsigned char *line, int size );
            virtual int status( void );
    };

    #endif
```

Listing 3.5   GROUP3.CPP

```
    //----------------------------------------------------------//
    //                                                          //
    //    File:     GROUP3.CPP                                  //
    //                                                          //
    //    Desc:     Class implementations for CCITT Group 3     //
    //              compressor and decompressor.                //
    //                                                          //
    //----------------------------------------------------------//

    #include "group3.hpp"

    //.................structure to hold code definitions

    struct codedef
    {
       short bitcode;    // encoded representation
       short codelen;    // length of bitcode in bits
       short runlen;     // run length in pixels
    };

    // table entry count — note that EOL codes are omitted

    #define TBLSIZE 104

    // code table for black runs, ordered by code length

    static codedef black_bits[] =
    {
       { 0x8000,  2,     3 },   { 0xC000,  2,     2 },
       { 0x4000,  3,     1 },   { 0x6000,  3,     4 },
       { 0x2000,  4,     6 },   { 0x3000,  4,     5 },
       { 0x1800,  5,     7 },   { 0x1000,  6,     9 },
       { 0x1400,  6,     8 },   { 0x0800,  7,    10 },
       { 0x0A00,  7,    11 },   { 0x0E00,  7,    12 },
       { 0x0400,  8,    13 },   { 0x0700,  8,    14 },
```

Listing 3.5 GROUP3.CPP (continued)

```
    { 0x0C00,  9,    15 },      { 0x0DC0, 10,     0 },
    { 0x05C0, 10,    16 },      { 0x0600, 10,    17 },
    { 0x0200, 10,    18 },      { 0x03C0, 10,    64 },
    { 0x0CE0, 11,    19 },      { 0x0D00, 11,    20 },
    { 0x0D80, 11,    21 },      { 0x06E0, 11,    22 },
    { 0x0500, 11,    23 },      { 0x02E0, 11,    24 },
    { 0x0300, 11,    25 },      { 0x0100, 11, 1792 },
    { 0x0180, 11, 1856 },       { 0x01A0, 11, 1920 },
    { 0x0CA0, 12,    26 },      { 0x0CB0, 12,    27 },
    { 0x0CC0, 12,    28 },      { 0x0CD0, 12,    29 },
    { 0x0680, 12,    30 },      { 0x0690, 12,    31 },
    { 0x06A0, 12,    32 },      { 0x06B0, 12,    33 },
    { 0x0D20, 12,    34 },      { 0x0D30, 12,    35 },
    { 0x0D40, 12,    36 },      { 0x0D50, 12,    37 },
    { 0x0D60, 12,    38 },      { 0x0D70, 12,    39 },
    { 0x06C0, 12,    40 },      { 0x06D0, 12,    41 },
    { 0x0DA0, 12,    42 },      { 0x0DB0, 12,    43 },
    { 0x0540, 12,    44 },      { 0x0550, 12,    45 },
    { 0x0560, 12,    46 },      { 0x0570, 12,    47 },
    { 0x0640, 12,    48 },      { 0x0650, 12,    49 },
    { 0x0520, 12,    50 },      { 0x0530, 12,    51 },
    { 0x0240, 12,    52 },      { 0x0370, 12,    53 },
    { 0x0380, 12,    54 },      { 0x0270, 12,    55 },
    { 0x0280, 12,    56 },      { 0x0580, 12,    57 },
    { 0x0590, 12,    58 },      { 0x02B0, 12,    59 },
    { 0x02C0, 12,    60 },      { 0x05A0, 12,    61 },
    { 0x0660, 12,    62 },      { 0x0670, 12,    63 },
    { 0x0C80, 12,   128 },      { 0x0C90, 12,   192 },
    { 0x05B0, 12,   256 },      { 0x0330, 12,   320 },
    { 0x0340, 12,   384 },      { 0x0350, 12,   448 },
    { 0x0120, 12, 1984 },       { 0x0130, 12, 2048 },
    { 0x0140, 12, 2112 },       { 0x0150, 12, 2176 },
    { 0x0160, 12, 2240 },       { 0x0170, 12, 2304 },
    { 0x01C0, 12, 2368 },       { 0x01D0, 12, 2432 },
    { 0x01E0, 12, 2496 },       { 0x01F0, 12, 2560 },
    { 0x0360, 13,   512 },      { 0x0368, 13,   576 },
    { 0x0250, 13,   640 },      { 0x0258, 13,   704 },
    { 0x0260, 13,   768 },      { 0x0268, 13,   832 },
    { 0x0390, 13,   896 },      { 0x0398, 13,   960 },
    { 0x03A0, 13, 1024 },       { 0x03A8, 13, 1088 },
    { 0x03B0, 13, 1152 },       { 0x03B8, 13, 1216 },
    { 0x0290, 13, 1280 },       { 0x0298, 13, 1344 },
    { 0x02A0, 13, 1408 },       { 0x02A8, 13, 1472 },
    { 0x02D0, 13, 1536 },       { 0x02D8, 13, 1600 },
    { 0x0320, 13, 1664 },       { 0x0328, 13, 1728 },
};
```

Listing 3.5 GROUP3.CPP (continued)

```
// code table for black runs, ordered by run length

static codedef black_runs[] =
{
    { 0x0DC0, 10,    0 },    { 0x4000,  3,    1 },
    { 0xC000,  2,    2 },    { 0x8000,  2,    3 },
    { 0x6000,  3,    4 },    { 0x3000,  4,    5 },
    { 0x2000,  4,    6 },    { 0x1800,  5,    7 },
    { 0x1400,  6,    8 },    { 0x1000,  6,    9 },
    { 0x0800,  7,   10 },    { 0x0A00,  7,   11 },
    { 0x0E00,  7,   12 },    { 0x0400,  8,   13 },
    { 0x0700,  8,   14 },    { 0x0C00,  9,   15 },
    { 0x05C0, 10,   16 },    { 0x0600, 10,   17 },
    { 0x0200, 10,   18 },    { 0x0CE0, 11,   19 },
    { 0x0D00, 11,   20 },    { 0x0D80, 11,   21 },
    { 0x06E0, 11,   22 },    { 0x0500, 11,   23 },
    { 0x02E0, 11,   24 },    { 0x0300, 11,   25 },
    { 0x0CA0, 12,   26 },    { 0x0CB0, 12,   27 },
    { 0x0CC0, 12,   28 },    { 0x0CD0, 12,   29 },
    { 0x0680, 12,   30 },    { 0x0690, 12,   31 },
    { 0x06A0, 12,   32 },    { 0x06B0, 12,   33 },
    { 0x0D20, 12,   34 },    { 0x0D30, 12,   35 },
    { 0x0D40, 12,   36 },    { 0x0D50, 12,   37 },
    { 0x0D60, 12,   38 },    { 0x0D70, 12,   39 },
    { 0x06C0, 12,   40 },    { 0x06D0, 12,   41 },
    { 0x0DA0, 12,   42 },    { 0x0DB0, 12,   43 },
    { 0x0540, 12,   44 },    { 0x0550, 12,   45 },
    { 0x0560, 12,   46 },    { 0x0570, 12,   47 },
    { 0x0640, 12,   48 },    { 0x0650, 12,   49 },
    { 0x0520, 12,   50 },    { 0x0530, 12,   51 },
    { 0x0240, 12,   52 },    { 0x0370, 12,   53 },
    { 0x0380, 12,   54 },    { 0x0270, 12,   55 },
    { 0x0280, 12,   56 },    { 0x0580, 12,   57 },
    { 0x0590, 12,   58 },    { 0x02B0, 12,   59 },
    { 0x02C0, 12,   60 },    { 0x05A0, 12,   61 },
    { 0x0660, 12,   62 },    { 0x0670, 12,   63 },
    { 0x03C0, 10,   64 },    { 0x0C80, 12,  128 },
    { 0x0C90, 12,  192 },    { 0x05B0, 12,  256 },
    { 0x0330, 12,  320 },    { 0x0340, 12,  384 },
    { 0x0350, 12,  448 },    { 0x0360, 13,  512 },
    { 0x0368, 13,  576 },    { 0x0250, 13,  640 },
    { 0x0258, 13,  704 },    { 0x0260, 13,  768 },
    { 0x0268, 13,  832 },    { 0x0390, 13,  896 },
    { 0x0398, 13,  960 },    { 0x03A0, 13, 1024 },
    { 0x03A8, 13, 1088 },    { 0x03B0, 13, 1152 },
    { 0x03B8, 13, 1216 },    { 0x0290, 13, 1280 },
    { 0x0298, 13, 1344 },    { 0x02A0, 13, 1408 },
    { 0x02A8, 13, 1472 },    { 0x02D0, 13, 1536 },
```

Listing 3.5 GROUP3.CPP (continued)

```
        { 0x02D8, 13, 1600 },   { 0x0320, 13, 1664 },
        { 0x0328, 13, 1728 },   { 0x0100, 11, 1792 },
        { 0x0180, 11, 1856 },   { 0x01A0, 11, 1920 },
        { 0x0120, 12, 1984 },   { 0x0130, 12, 2048 },
        { 0x0140, 12, 2112 },   { 0x0150, 12, 2176 },
        { 0x0160, 12, 2240 },   { 0x0170, 12, 2304 },
        { 0x01C0, 12, 2368 },   { 0x01D0, 12, 2432 },
        { 0x01E0, 12, 2496 },   { 0x01F0, 12, 2560 },
    };

    // code table for white runs, ordered by code length

    static codedef white_bits[] =
    {
        { 0x7000, 4,    2 },   { 0x8000, 4,    3 },
        { 0xB000, 4,    4 },   { 0xC000, 4,    5 },
        { 0xE000, 4,    6 },   { 0xF000, 4,    7 },
        { 0x3800, 5,   10 },   { 0x4000, 5,   11 },
        { 0xA000, 5,    9 },   { 0x9800, 5,    8 },
        { 0xD800, 5,   64 },   { 0x9000, 5,  128 },
        { 0x0C00, 6,   13 },   { 0x1C00, 6,    1 },
        { 0x2000, 6,   12 },   { 0xA800, 6,   16 },
        { 0xAC00, 6,   17 },   { 0xD000, 6,   14 },
        { 0xD400, 6,   15 },   { 0x5C00, 6,  192 },
        { 0x6000, 6, 1664 },   { 0x4E00, 7,   18 },
        { 0x1800, 7,   19 },   { 0x1000, 7,   20 },
        { 0x2E00, 7,   21 },   { 0x0600, 7,   22 },
        { 0x0800, 7,   23 },   { 0x5000, 7,   24 },
        { 0x5600, 7,   25 },   { 0x2600, 7,   26 },
        { 0x4800, 7,   27 },   { 0x3000, 7,   28 },
        { 0x6E00, 7,  256 },   { 0x3500, 8,    0 },
        { 0x0200, 8,   29 },   { 0x0300, 8,   30 },
        { 0x1A00, 8,   31 },   { 0x1B00, 8,   32 },
        { 0x1200, 8,   33 },   { 0x1300, 8,   34 },
        { 0x1400, 8,   35 },   { 0x1500, 8,   36 },
        { 0x1600, 8,   37 },   { 0x1700, 8,   38 },
        { 0x2800, 8,   39 },   { 0x2900, 8,   40 },
        { 0x2A00, 8,   41 },   { 0x2B00, 8,   42 },
        { 0x2C00, 8,   43 },   { 0x2D00, 8,   44 },
        { 0x0400, 8,   45 },   { 0x0500, 8,   46 },
        { 0x0A00, 8,   47 },   { 0x0B00, 8,   48 },
        { 0x5200, 8,   49 },   { 0x5300, 8,   50 },
        { 0x5400, 8,   51 },   { 0x5500, 8,   52 },
        { 0x2400, 8,   53 },   { 0x2500, 8,   54 },
        { 0x5800, 8,   55 },   { 0x5900, 8,   56 },
        { 0x5A00, 8,   57 },   { 0x5B00, 8,   58 },
        { 0x4A00, 8,   59 },   { 0x4B00, 8,   60 },
        { 0x3200, 8,   61 },   { 0x3300, 8,   62 },
```

Listing 3.5 GROUP3.CPP (continued)

```
    { 0x3400,  8,   63 },    { 0x3600,  8,   320 },
    { 0x3700,  8,  384 },    { 0x6400,  8,   448 },
    { 0x6500,  8,  512 },    { 0x6800,  8,   576 },
    { 0x6700,  8,  640 },    { 0x6600,  9,   704 },
    { 0x6680,  9,  768 },    { 0x6900,  9,   832 },
    { 0x6980,  9,  896 },    { 0x6A00,  9,   960 },
    { 0x6A80,  9, 1024 },    { 0x6B00,  9,  1088 },
    { 0x6B80,  9, 1152 },    { 0x6C00,  9,  1216 },
    { 0x6C80,  9, 1280 },    { 0x6D00,  9,  1344 },
    { 0x6D80,  9, 1408 },    { 0x4C00,  9,  1472 },
    { 0x4C80,  9, 1536 },    { 0x4D00,  9,  1600 },
    { 0x4D80,  9, 1728 },    { 0x0100, 11,  1792 },
    { 0x0180, 11, 1856 },    { 0x01A0, 11,  1920 },
    { 0x0120, 12, 1984 },    { 0x0130, 12,  2048 },
    { 0x0140, 12, 2112 },    { 0x0150, 12,  2176 },
    { 0x0160, 12, 2240 },    { 0x0170, 12,  2304 },
    { 0x01C0, 12, 2368 },    { 0x01D0, 12,  2432 },
    { 0x01E0, 12, 2496 },    { 0x01F0, 12,  2560 },
};

// code table for white runs, ordered by run length

static codedef white_runs[] =
{
    { 0x3500,  8,    0 },    { 0x1C00,  6,    1 },
    { 0x7000,  4,    2 },    { 0x8000,  4,    3 },
    { 0xB000,  4,    4 },    { 0xC000,  4,    5 },
    { 0xE000,  4,    6 },    { 0xF000,  4,    7 },
    { 0x9800,  5,    8 },    { 0xA000,  5,    9 },
    { 0x3800,  5,   10 },    { 0x4000,  5,   11 },
    { 0x2000,  6,   12 },    { 0x0C00,  6,   13 },
    { 0xD000,  6,   14 },    { 0xD400,  6,   15 },
    { 0xA800,  6,   16 },    { 0xAC00,  6,   17 },
    { 0x4E00,  7,   18 },    { 0x1800,  7,   19 },
    { 0x1000,  7,   20 },    { 0x2E00,  7,   21 },
    { 0x0600,  7,   22 },    { 0x0800,  7,   23 },
    { 0x5000,  7,   24 },    { 0x5600,  7,   25 },
    { 0x2600,  7,   26 },    { 0x4800,  7,   27 },
    { 0x3000,  7,   28 },    { 0x0200,  8,   29 },
    { 0x0300,  8,   30 },    { 0x1A00,  8,   31 },
    { 0x1B00,  8,   32 },    { 0x1200,  8,   33 },
    { 0x1300,  8,   34 },    { 0x1400,  8,   35 },
    { 0x1500,  8,   36 },    { 0x1600,  8,   37 },
    { 0x1700,  8,   38 },    { 0x2800,  8,   39 },
    { 0x2900,  8,   40 },    { 0x2A00,  8,   41 },
    { 0x2B00,  8,   42 },    { 0x2C00,  8,   43 },
    { 0x2D00,  8,   44 },    { 0x0400,  8,   45 },
    { 0x0500,  8,   46 },    { 0x0A00,  8,   47 },
```

Listing 3.5 GROUP3.CPP (continued)

```
        { 0x0B00,  8,    48 },   { 0x5200,  8,    49 },
        { 0x5300,  8,    50 },   { 0x5400,  8,    51 },
        { 0x5500,  8,    52 },   { 0x2400,  8,    53 },
        { 0x2500,  8,    54 },   { 0x5800,  8,    55 },
        { 0x5900,  8,    56 },   { 0x5A00,  8,    57 },
        { 0x5B00,  8,    58 },   { 0x4A00,  8,    59 },
        { 0x4B00,  8,    60 },   { 0x3200,  8,    61 },
        { 0x3300,  8,    62 },   { 0x3400,  8,    63 },
        { 0xD800,  5,    64 },   { 0x9000,  5,   128 },
        { 0x5C00,  6,   192 },   { 0x6E00,  7,   256 },
        { 0x3600,  8,   320 },   { 0x3700,  8,   384 },
        { 0x6400,  8,   448 },   { 0x6500,  8,   512 },
        { 0x6800,  8,   576 },   { 0x6700,  8,   640 },
        { 0x6600,  9,   704 },   { 0x6680,  9,   768 },
        { 0x6900,  9,   832 },   { 0x6980,  9,   896 },
        { 0x6A00,  9,   960 },   { 0x6A80,  9,  1024 },
        { 0x6B00,  9,  1088 },   { 0x6B80,  9,  1152 },
        { 0x6C00,  9,  1216 },   { 0x6C80,  9,  1280 },
        { 0x6D00,  9,  1344 },   { 0x6D80,  9,  1408 },
        { 0x4C00,  9,  1472 },   { 0x4C80,  9,  1536 },
        { 0x4D00,  9,  1600 },   { 0x6000,  6,  1664 },
        { 0x4D80,  9,  1728 },   { 0x0100, 11,  1792 },
        { 0x0180, 11,  1856 },   { 0x01A0, 11,  1920 },
        { 0x0120, 12,  1984 },   { 0x0130, 12,  2048 },
        { 0x0140, 12,  2112 },   { 0x0150, 12,  2176 },
        { 0x0160, 12,  2240 },   { 0x0170, 12,  2304 },
        { 0x01C0, 12,  2368 },   { 0x01D0, 12,  2432 },
        { 0x01E0, 12,  2496 },   { 0x01F0, 12,  2560 },
};

//.................class Group3Encoder

int Group3Encoder::init( void )
{
    return status( );
}

int Group3Encoder::term( void )
{
    return status( );
}

int Group3Encoder::status( void )
{
    if( ferror( outfile ) ) return xIOERROR;
    return xOKAY;
}
```

Listing 3.5 GROUP3.CPP (continued)

```cpp
int Group3Encoder::runlength( int pxval, int maxcnt,
                              unsigned char *pxls )
{
   int cnt = 0;
   while( (pxls[cnt]==pxval) && (cnt < maxcnt) )
      cnt++;
   return cnt;
}

int Group3Encoder::wrtbitcode( int code, int len )
{
   unsigned short mask = 0x8000;
   while( len-- )
   {
      if( code & mask )
         codebyte |= codemask;
      mask >>= 1;
      if( (codemask >>= 1) == 0 )
      {
         if( fputc( codebyte, outfile ) < 0 )
            break;
         codebyte = 0;
         codemask = 0x80;
      }
   }
   return status( );
}

int Group3Encoder::wrtrun( int pxval, int cnt )
{
   codedef *tbl = pxval ? black_runs : white_runs;
   while( cnt >= 2624 )
   {
      if( wrtbitcode( tbl[TBLSIZE-1].bitcode,
                      tbl[TBLSIZE-1].codelen ) != xOKAY )
         return status( );
      cnt -= 2560;
   }
   if( cnt > 63 )
   {
      int n = cnt >> 6;    // n=pxcnt/64
      int i = n + 63;
      if( wrtbitcode( tbl[i].bitcode,
                      tbl[i].codelen ) != xOKAY )
         return status( );
      n <<= 6;                // n=n*64
      cnt -= n;
   }
```

Listing 3.5 GROUP3.CPP (continued)

```cpp
      return wrtbitcode( tbl[cnt].bitcode,
                         tbl[cnt].codelen );
   }

   int Group3Encoder::encode( unsigned char *line, int size )
   {
      // scan line initialization
      codebyte = 0;
      codemask = 0x80;

      // start with 0 run
      int pxval = 0;

      // encode the scan line
      while( (size > 0) && (status( ) == xOKAY) )
      {
         int cnt = runlength( pxval, size, line );
         wrtrun( pxval, cnt );
         line += cnt;
         size -= cnt;
         pxval = 1 - pxval;
      }

      // flush a partial code byte
      if( (codebyte != 0x80) && (status( ) == xOKAY) )
         fputc( codebyte, outfile );

      return status( );
   }

   //.................class Group3Decoder

   int Group3Decoder::init( void )
   {
      cond = xOKAY;
      return status( );
   }

   int Group3Decoder::term( void )
   {
      return status( );
   }

   int Group3Decoder::status( void )
```

Listing 3.5 GROUP3.CPP (continued)

```cpp
{
   if( feof( infile ) )    return xENDOFFILE;
   if( ferror( infile ) ) return xIOERROR;
   return cond;
}

int Group3Decoder::rdbit( void )
{
   if( (codemask>>=1) == 0 )
   {
      codebyte = fgetc( infile );
      codemask = 0x80;
   }
   return (codebyte & codemask) ? 1 : 0;
}

int Group3Decoder::rdcode( int pxval )
{
   codedef *tbl = pxval ? black_bits : white_bits;
   short code = 0;
   unsigned short mask = 0x8000;
   int len = 0;
   int n = 0;

   while( n < TBLSIZE )
   {
      while( len < tbl[n].codelen )
      {
         if( rdbit() ) code |= mask;
         len++;
         mask >>= 1;
      }
      while( tbl[n].codelen == len )
      {
         if( tbl[n].bitcode == code )
            return tbl[n].runlen;
         n++;
      }
   }

   // getting here is an error - no match found!
   cond = xOUTOFSYNC;
   return -1;
}

int Group3Decoder::decode( unsigned char *line, int size )
{
```

Listing 3.5 GROUP3.CPP (continued)

```
// scan line initialization
codebyte = 0;
codemask = 0;
int cnt = 0;
int pxval = 0;

while( (size > 0) && (status( ) == xOKAY) )
{
   // get next code
   if( (cnt = rdcode( pxval )) < 0 )
      break;

   // fill in scan line
   int n = cnt;
   while( (n-) && (size > 0) )
   {
      *line++ = pxval;
      size--;
   }

   // switch pixel values if terminating code
   if( cnt < 64 )
      pxval = 1 - pxval;

}

return status( );
}
```

LZW Compression

In 1977 J. Ziv and A. Limpel published an algorithm for data compression that was subsequently refined by T. Welsh. The modified algorithm has come to be known as LZW compression. The algorithm is widely used; a variant of it is specified by CompuServe's GIF bitmap format. It is, unfortunately, covered by a patent owned by UniSys Corporation, so use of the algorithm in commercial software requires a license from UniSys.

The essence of the algorithm is to replace repeating strings of one or more characters in an input stream with n-bit codes in an output stream. Since the codes are generally shorter than the strings they represent, compression takes place. What is unique to the LZW algorithm is the technique by which the codes are generated by the compressor and interpreted by the decompressor.

The workings of the algorithm depend on three objects: a charstream, a codestream, and a string table. During compression, the charstream is input and the codestream is output; during decompression, the codestream is input and the charstream is output. The string table is used to store character strings and their corresponding codes, and is used by both the compressor and the decompressor to convert either strings to codes or codes to strings.

The unusual feature of LZW compression is that the string table is constructed on the fly, by both the compressor and decompressor, as the input stream is scanned. Unlike Huffman compression, therefore, only a single pass over the input data is required, and the table does not need to accompany the compressed representation of the data.

Assuming n-bit character codes, the string table uses N-bit compression codes, where $N > n$. For example, if a charstream consists of 8-bit bytes, an LZW compressor might use 12-bit compression codes. This allows a string table with 4096 entries, indexed by compression codes with values in the range 0 to 4095.

Here is a thumbnail sketch of the compressor: The table is initialized with all one-character strings, which are assigned the first 2^n codes, $0..2^n-1$. In our example this corresponds to all 8-bit ASCII characters with code values of 0 to 255. (One-character strings are referred to as **roots**.) A current prefix (a string) is initialized to null.

The compressor reads characters one at a time. As each character is read, a current string is constructed. It consists of the current character appended to the current prefix. A search of the string table is made to see if the current string is in the table. If the current string is found in the table, the current prefix is set to the current string. If it is not found, the current string is added to the table, the code for the current prefix is output to the codestream, and the current prefix is set to the current character. This process is repeated for each input character until no characters remain. As a final step, the code for the current prefix is output.

Notice that the codestream in our example consists of a sequence of 12-bit codes. These are packed so that there are no unused padding bits in the codestream. Furthermore, low-order code bits are placed in the low-order bits of the next available codestream byte. If a code is represented as BA9876543210 then the codestream is laid out as follows:

`76543210` `3210`**`BA98`** `BA987654`

This example shows two 12-bit codes, one of which is printed in bold.

GIF LZW Compression

The implementation of LZW compression with the GIF format adds two refinements to the basic algorithm: command codes and variable-length compression codes. The string table is initialized as described previously, where the first 2^n-1 codes represent string roots. The next two available codes, with values of 2^n and 2^n+1, are reserved as a clear code and an end-of-input code, respectively. The end-of-input code is more of a convenience than anything else. It allows the decompressor to terminate with no further processing when an end-of-input code is read. This slightly simplifies the decompressor logic.

The clear code is used to instruct the decompressor to reinitialize its string table. This is done because in actual use the string table can become full, after which compression must be aborted. In the classic algorithm there is no recovery from this state. It is therefore necessary to pick a code size large enough to accommodate largest-case data files, or else design a compressor that restarts the compression with a larger code size when the table becomes full. The GIF variant is an elegant solution to this problem.

GIF specifies a maximum code size of 12 bits and an initial code size of $n+1$ bits, where n is the number of bits used to represent a pixel value in an image. For example, a 256-color image uses 8 bits per pixel and is encoded using an initial code size of 9 bits. The only exception to this rule is for bilevel (1-bit-per-pixel) images, where n is assumed to be 2 and the initial code size is 3 bits.

The format of the image data in a GIF file has some effect on the design of the GIF LZW codec. Specifically, image data are blocked into packets that are 0 to 255 bytes in length. Each image block is preceded by a 1-byte size field that specifies the number of data bytes to follow. Thus, both the compressor and decompressor should perform blocked I/O.

Note that in the GIF format, images are compressed without regard to scan line boundaries. This makes it difficult to structure encode and decode functions that operate on individual scan lines, as was done with the PackBits and Group 3 functions. We want to maintain the scan-line-oriented paradigm, however, to preserve the virtual design of the codec base classes.

The GIF LZW codec is presented in Listings 3.6 and 3.7. Here are some implementation notes:

1. Because of the complexity of the GIF LZW algorithm, the implementation is partitioned into several different functional classes.

2. The encoder string table is accessed by a hashing function, which requires that the table size be a prime number. This can be any prime larger than the required capacity of 4096 entries. We have used 4099 in this

implementation. Note that, without the use of hashing, the table would have to be searched sequentially, and the algorithm run time would be unacceptably slow.

3. The I/O requirements of both encoder and decoder are handled by the `CodeFile` class. Refer to the listings for specific details.

4. Because strings are decoded from last byte to first byte, they are pushed onto a stack and then popped off in the proper order during decoding. This mechanism is implemented as the `ByteStack` class.

5. The GIF format is the copyrighted property of CompuServe Incorporated, and the term GIF is a service mark of CompuServe. Be sure to acknowledge these in any code that uses the format.

Listing 3.6 GIFLZW.HPP

```
//----------------------------------------------------------//
//                                                          //
//    File:      GIFLZW.HPP                                 //
//                                                          //
//    Desc:      Encoder and Decoder classes for GIF/LZW    //
//                                                          //
//----------------------------------------------------------//

#ifndef _GIFLZW_HPP_
#define _GIFLZW_HPP_

#include "stdio.h"
#include "string.h"

#include "codec.hpp"

//.................A Code File I/O Class

// This class encapsulates the I/O requirements of GIF/LZW
// compression.  These are (1) blocked reads and writes of
// up to 255 bytes at a time, and (2) reading and writing
// values with a variable number of bits.

class CodeFile
{
    public:
        int    cond;        // condition code;

    protected:
        FILE *filep;        // open stream pointer
        int    capacity;    // size of I/O buffer
        char *buffer;       // I/O buffer
```

Listing 3.6 GIFLZW.HPP (continued)

```
        int    codesize;   // bits per code
        int    bytecnt;    // number of bytes in buffer
        int    curbyte;    // current byte in buffer
        int    curbit;     // current bit of current byte

   public:
      CodeFile( FILE* f, int nbits );
     ~CodeFile( );
      void clearbuf( void );
      int flushbuf( void );
      int loadbuf( void );
      void putcode( int code );
      int getcode( void );
      void dumpcode( int code );
      void setsize( int nbits )
         { codesize = nbits; }
      int getsize( void )
         { return codesize; }
};

//.................An Encoder String Table Class

// This implementation of the string table is for the
// encoder and uses a hashing function for searching
// and addition.  Performance is generally unacceptable
// if some form of hashing is not used.

class  LzwEncoderTable
{
   public:
      int  cond;          // condition code

   protected:
      int  capacity;      // table size
      int  next_code;     // next code value
      int  root_size;     // root size in bits
      int *code_value;    // code value array
      int *prefix_code;   // prefix code array
      int *append_char;   // char for this code

   public:
      LzwEncoderTable( int rootsize );
     ~LzwEncoderTable( );
      void cleartbl( void );
      int findstr( int pfx, int chr );
      int addstr( int pfx, int chr, int index );
};
```

Listing 3.6 GIFLZW.HPP (continued)

```cpp
//.................A GIF/LZW Encoder Class

class GifEncoder : public Encoder,
                   public CodeFile,
                   public LzwEncoderTable
{
   public:
      int cond;        // condition code;

   protected:
      int minbits;     // min # bits per code
      int curbits;     // current # bits per code
      int maxcode;     // max code value for cur # bits
      int clearcode;   // nroots
      int endcode;     // nroots+1;
      int string;      // current prefix
      int character;   // current character

   public:
      GifEncoder( FILE* outfile, int pixelsize );
      ~GifEncoder( );
      virtual int init( void );
      virtual int term( void );
      virtual int encode( unsigned char *line, int size );
      virtual int status( void );
};

//.................A Byte Stack Class

// This class is used by the GIF/LZW decoder to output
// decoded strings.  Because of the design of the algorithm
// strings are decoded last char to first char, so a stack
// is used to reverse the character order for output.

class ByteStack
{
   public:
      int cond;        // condition code

   protected:
      int    capacity; // size in bytes
      char *top;       // top of stack
      char *bot;       // bottom of stack
      char *sp;        // current stack pointer

   public:
      ByteStack( int size );
      ~ByteStack( );
```

Listing 3.6 GIFLZW.HPP (continued)

```
        void push( int x );
        int pop( void );
        void purge( void );
        int empty( void )
            { return (sp == top) ? 1 : 0; }
};

//.................A Decoder String Table Class

// This implementation of the string table is for the
// decoder.  Entries are directly addressed with a
// code value, so searching requires no implementation.

class  LzwDecoderTable
{
   public:
       int cond;            // condition code;

   protected:
       int  capacity;       // table size
       int  next_code;      // next code value
       int  root_size;      // root size in bits
       int *prefix_code;    // prefix code array
       int *append_char;    // char for this code

   public:
       LzwDecoderTable( int rootsize );
      ~LzwDecoderTable( );
       void cleartbl( void );
       int addstr( int pfx, int chr );
       int findstr( int code )
       {
          return ((code >= 0) && (code < next_code)) ?
                 1 : 0;
       }
};

//.................A GIF/LZW Decoder Class

class GifDecoder : public Decoder,
                   public CodeFile,
                   public ByteStack,
                   public LzwDecoderTable
{
   public:
       int cond;            // condition code;
```

Listing 3.6 GIFLZW.HPP (continued)

```
    protected:
        int minbits;       // min # bits per code
        int curbits;       // current # bits per code
        int maxcode;       // max code value for cur # bits
        int clearcode;     // nroots
        int endcode;       // nroots+1;
        int oldcode;       // prev input code
        int newcode;       // cur input code
        int firstch;       // first char of decoded string

    public:
        GifDecoder( FILE* infile, int pixelsize );
        ~GifDecoder( );
        virtual int init( void );
        virtual int term( void );
        virtual int decode( unsigned char *line, int size );
        virtual int status( void );
        int pushstr( int code );
    };

    #endif
```

Listing 3.7 GIFLZW.CPP

```
    //-----------------------------------------------------------//
    //                                                           //
    //   File:     GIFLZW.CPP                                    //
    //                                                           //
    //   Desc:     Encoder and Decoder classes for GIF/LZW       //
    //                                                           //
    //-----------------------------------------------------------//

    #include "giflzw.hpp"

    //.................defines

    #define   MAXBITS      12
    #define   TBLSIZE      (1 << MAXBITS)
    #define   HASHSIZE     4099
    #define   HASHBITS     4
    #define   NULLCHAR     -1
    #define   NULLCODE     -1
    #define   SIGNAL       -99
    #define   BUFSIZE      255
    #define   ROOTSIZ( x ) ( x > 1 ? x+1 : 3 )
    #define   NROOTS( x )  ( x > 1 ? (1 << x) : 4 )
```

Listing 3.7 GIFLZW.CPP (continued)

```cpp
//................class CodeFile

CodeFile::CodeFile( FILE* f, int nbits )
{
   cond = xOKAY;
   capacity = BUFSIZE;
   buffer = new char [capacity];
   if( buffer == 0 )
   {
      cond = xNOMEMORY;
      capacity = 0;
      return;
   }
   filep = f;
   codesize = nbits+1;
}

CodeFile::~CodeFile( )
{
   if( buffer ) delete buffer;
}

void CodeFile::clearbuf( void )
{
   memset( buffer, 0, capacity );
   bytecnt = 0;
   curbyte = 0;
   curbit = 1;
}

int CodeFile::flushbuf( void )
{
   if( bytecnt > 0 )
   {
      fputc( bytecnt, filep );
      fwrite( buffer, bytecnt, 1, filep );
      if( ferror(filep) ) cond = xIOERROR;
      clearbuf();
   }
   return cond;
}

int CodeFile::loadbuf( void )
{
   curbyte = 0;
   curbit = 1;
   bytecnt = fgetc( filep );
```

Listing 3.7 GIFLZW.CPP (continued)

```cpp
        if( bytecnt > 0 )
            fread( buffer, bytecnt, 1, filep );
        if( feof(filep) )
            cond = xENDOFFILE;
        else if( ferror(filep) )
            cond = xIOERROR;
        return cond;
    }

    int CodeFile::getcode( void )
    {
        if( bytecnt == 0 )
            loadbuf();
        int code = 0;
        int mask = 1;
        for( int i=0; i<codesize; i++ )
        {
            if( buffer[curbyte] & curbit )
                code |= mask;
            mask <<= 1;
            curbit <<= 1;
            if( curbit > 128 )
            {
                curbit = 1;
                curbyte++;
                bytecnt--;
                if( bytecnt == 0 )
                    loadbuf();
            }
        }
        return code;
    }

    void CodeFile::putcode( int code )
    {
        int mask = 1;
        for( int i=0; i<codesize; i++ )
        {
            if( code & mask )
                buffer[curbyte] |= curbit;
            mask <<= 1;
            curbit <<= 1;
            if( curbit > 128 )
            {
                curbit = 1;
                curbyte++;
```

Listing 3.7 GIFLZW.CPP (continued)

```cpp
            if( curbyte == capacity )
               flushbuf();
        }
        else if( curbit == 2 )
           bytecnt++;
    }
}

// this function is not required, but is handy
// for debugging and other purposes.

void CodeFile::dumpcode( int code )
{
    int mask = 1 << codesize;
    for( int i=0; i<codesize; i++ )
    {
       mask >>= 1;
       if( code & mask ) printf( "1" );
       else              printf( "0" );
    }
}

//.................class LzwEncoderTable

LzwEncoderTable::LzwEncoderTable( int rootsize )
{
    cond = xOKAY;
    capacity = HASHSIZE;
    root_size = rootsize;
    code_value = new int [capacity];
    prefix_code = new int [capacity];
    append_char = new int [capacity];
    if( (code_value == 0) ||
        (prefix_code == 0) ||
        (append_char == 0) )
    {
       cond = xNOMEMORY;
       capacity = 0;
    }
    else
       cleartbl();
}

LzwEncoderTable::~LzwEncoderTable( )
{
    if( code_value ) delete code_value;
    if( prefix_code ) delete prefix_code;
```

Listing 3.7 GIFLZW.CPP (continued)

```cpp
      if( append_char ) delete append_char;
   }

   void LzwEncoderTable::cleartbl( void )
   {
      next_code = (1 << root_size) + 2;
      for( int i=0; i<capacity; i++ )
         code_value[i] = NULLCODE;
   }

   int LzwEncoderTable::findstr( int pfx, int chr )
   {
      int i = (chr << HASHBITS) ^ pfx;
      int di = (i==0) ? 1 : capacity - i;
      while( 1 )
      {
         if( code_value[i] == NULLCODE )
            break;
         if( (prefix_code[i] == pfx) &&
             (append_char[i] == chr) )
            break;
         i -= di;
         if( i < 0 ) i += capacity;
      }
      return i;
   }

   int LzwEncoderTable::addstr( int pfx, int chr, int index )
   {
      code_value[index]  = next_code++;
      prefix_code[index] = pfx;
      append_char[index] = chr;
      if( next_code > TBLSIZE ) cond = xOVERFLOW;
      return code_value[index];
   }

   //.................class GifEncoder

   GifEncoder::GifEncoder( FILE* outfile, int pixelsize ) :
               Encoder( tGIFLZW ),
               CodeFile( outfile, pixelsize ),
               LzwEncoderTable( pixelsize )
   {
      minbits = pixelsize > 1 ? pixelsize+1 : pixelsize+2;
      clearcode = 1 << pixelsize;
      endcode = clearcode + 1;
   }
```

Listing 3.7 GIFLZW.CPP (continued)

```
GifEncoder::~GifEncoder( )
{
}

int GifEncoder::init( void )
{
    cond = xOKAY;
    curbits = minbits;
    maxcode = (1 << curbits) - 1;
    clearbuf();
    putcode( clearcode );
    string = SIGNAL;
    return status();
}

int GifEncoder::term( void )
{
    putcode( string );
    putcode( endcode );
    flushbuf();
    return status();
}

int GifEncoder::encode( unsigned char *line, int size )
{
    if( string == SIGNAL )
    {
        string = *line++;
        size--;
    }
    while( (size > 0) && (status() == xOKAY) )
    {
        character = *line++;
        size--;
        int index = findstr( string, character );
        if( code_value[index] != -1 )  // string found
        {
            string = code_value[index];
        }
        else // string not found
        {
            int code = addstr( string, character, index );
            putcode( string );
            string = character;
            if( code > maxcode )
            {
                curbits++;
                if( curbits > MAXBITS )
```

Listing 3.7 GIFLZW.CPP (continued)

```cpp
                {
                    putcode( clearcode );
                    curbits = minbits;
                    cleartbl();
                }
                maxcode = (1 << curbits) - 1;
                if( curbits == MAXBITS ) maxcode--;
                setsize( curbits );
            }
        }
    }
    return status();
}

int GifEncoder::status( void )
{
    return cond | CodeFile::cond | LzwEncoderTable::cond;
}

//.................class ByteStack

ByteStack::ByteStack( int size )
{
    cond = xOKAY;
    capacity = size;
    top = bot = sp = 0;
    bot = new char [size];
    if( bot == 0 )
    {
        cond = xNOMEMORY;
        capacity = 0;
        return;
    }
    top = bot + size;
    sp = top;
}

ByteStack::~ByteStack(  )
{
    if( bot ) delete bot;
}

void ByteStack::push( int x )
{
    if( sp > bot ) *--sp = x;
    else cond = xOVERFLOW;
}
```

Listing 3.7 GIFLZW.CPP (continued)

```cpp
int ByteStack::pop( void )
{
   if( sp < top ) return *sp++;
   return NULLCHAR;
}

void ByteStack::purge( void )
{
   sp = top;
}

//................. class LzwDecoderTable

LzwDecoderTable::LzwDecoderTable( int rootsize )
{
   cond = xOKAY;
   capacity = TBLSIZE;
   root_size = rootsize;
   prefix_code = new int [capacity];
   append_char = new int [capacity];
   if( (prefix_code == 0) ||
       (append_char == 0) )
   {
      cond = xNOMEMORY;
      capacity = 0;
   }
   else
      cleartbl();
}

LzwDecoderTable::~LzwDecoderTable( )
{
   if( prefix_code ) delete prefix_code;
   if( append_char ) delete append_char;
}

void LzwDecoderTable::cleartbl( void )
{
   next_code = (1 << root_size) + 2;
   for( int i=0; i<next_code; i++ )
   {
      append_char[i] = i;
      prefix_code[i] = NULLCODE;
   }
}

int LzwDecoderTable::addstr( int pfx, int chr )
```

Listing 3.7 GIFLZW.CPP (continued)

```cpp
{
   if( next_code < capacity )
   {
      prefix_code[next_code] = pfx;
      append_char[next_code] = chr;
      next_code++;
      return next_code;
   }
   cond = xOVERFLOW;
   return NULLCODE;
}

//.................class GifDecoder

GifDecoder::GifDecoder( FILE* infile, int pixelsize ) :
            Decoder( tGIFLZW ),
            CodeFile( infile, pixelsize ),
            ByteStack( TBLSIZE ),
            LzwDecoderTable( pixelsize )
{
   minbits = pixelsize > 1 ? pixelsize+1 : pixelsize+2;
   clearcode = 1 << pixelsize;
   endcode = clearcode + 1;
}

GifDecoder::~GifDecoder( )
{
}

int GifDecoder::pushstr( int code )
{
   while( code != NULLCODE )
   {
      push( append_char[code] );
      code = prefix_code[code];
      if( code == prefix_code[code] ) break;
   }
   return *sp;
}

int GifDecoder::init( void )
{
   cond = xOKAY;
   curbits = minbits;
   maxcode = (1 << curbits) - 1;
   cleartbl();
   purge();
   clearbuf();
```

Listing 3.7 GIFLZW.CPP (continued)

```cpp
    while( (oldcode = getcode()) == clearcode ) { }
    push( oldcode );
    return status();
}

int GifDecoder::term( void )
{
    return status();
}

int GifDecoder::status( void )
{
    return cond | CodeFile::cond |
           LzwDecoderTable::cond | ByteStack::cond;
}

int GifDecoder::decode(  unsigned char *line, int size )
{
    // output any previously decoded bytes
    while( (! empty()) && (size > 0) )
    {
        *line++ = pop();
         size--;
    }

    // decode remainder of the row
    while( (size > 0) && (status() == xOKAY) )
    {
        // get a new code
        newcode = getcode();

        // decode it
        if( (newcode == endcode) || (newcode == NULLCODE) )
           break;
        else if( newcode == clearcode )
        {
           cleartbl();
           setsize( minbits );
           curbits = minbits;
           maxcode = (1 << codesize) - 1;
           oldcode = getcode();
           push( oldcode );
        }
        else
        {
           if( findstr( newcode ) )
```

Listing 3.7 GIFLZW.CPP (continued)

```
            {
                firstch = pushstr( newcode );
            }
            else
         0  {
                push( firstch );
                firstch = pushstr( oldcode );
            }
            if( addstr( oldcode, firstch ) > maxcode )
            {
                curbits++;
                if( curbits > MAXBITS )
                {
                    // we should have gotten a clearcode
                    // before this - we try to continue
                    cond = xOUTOFSYNC;
                    curbits = minbits;
                    cleartbl();
                }
                setsize( curbits );
                maxcode = (1 << curbits) - 1;
            }
            oldcode = newcode;
        }

        // output the just-decoded string
        while( (! empty()) && (size > 0) )
        {
            *line++ = pop();
            size--;
        }
    }

    return status();
}
```

This concludes our overview of compression, but we are far from being done with the subject. In later chapters, when the individual file formats are discussed, we will encounter additional compression schemes. In particular, numerous RLE schemes will be covered, in conjunction with formats such as BMP and PCX. Keep in mind that, while some of these compression schemes are unique to a specific format, we will nonetheless continue to implement them as derived classes of the virtual codec base classes. This not only preserves the operational methodology we have devised for handling compression, it also ensures the future extendibility of each of the individual algorithms to new formats and uses.

4

Memory Management _

Most of us have seen or used programs that work nicely with small data files but that head for the weeds when asked to digest a sufficiently large data case. There are few things in computing more frustrating.

Applications that deal with bitmapped imagery are especially vulnerable to this type of problem because of the large memory requirements of most bitmaps. As time passes, these requirements only get larger. The original PC was designed around a 64K video buffer; nowadays the average new system comes equipped with a one-megabyte video card. At the present time, we appear headed toward an eventual standard video capability of 1024 by 768 resolution with 24-bit color, which will require more than 2Mb of video memory.

Given these numbers, the venerable MS-DOS 640K limit, which once was only incredibly irritating, is now incredibly ridiculous. We can probably expect someday to see a viable alternative to DOS that lacks this crippling limitation, but even then DOS is likely to persist for some time as a lucrative marketplace. The bottom line is that developers of applications for the desktop will probably continue bumping their heads on 640K for years to come.

Fortunately, there are ways to cope with large images under DOS—they are the subject of this chapter. The most common way to deal with large images involves the use of either EMS or XMS memory on an AT-compatible system. I doubt that anyone is attempting to do serious work on a PC or XT anymore, but if you must support these antiques, then some form of virtual disk storage is required.

Nonconventional Memory

From the 16-bit real-mode viewpoint of DOS, EMS and XMS memory are examples of **nonconventional memory**. As its name implies, this is memory that cannot be used in a conventional fashion. You cannot allocate EMS or XMS memory with `malloc()`, and with some minor exceptions, you cannot execute program code in EMS or XMS. What you can do is store data in nonconventional memory. Because most systems contain a minimum of 1Mb of such memory, some very large images can be accommodated.

The acronyms EMS and XMS stand for expanded memory specification and extended memory specification, respectively. Expanded and extended are easily confused and are an unfortunate choice of terms. At one time there were true physical differences between EMS and XMS memory. Nowadays, however, EMS is generally simulated using extended memory, so they are effectively two different ways to access the same memory.

EMS memory was originally designed to be accessed by means of a system's expansion bus and was situated on a card plugged into an expansion slot. In this regard it was very much like a high-end video card. A segment of the total available memory was mapped into the processor's address space below the 1Mb boundary, where it could be accessed conventionally.

By contrast, XMS, or extended memory, is physical memory that can be accessed directly by the processor. It is accessed by means of the processor's so-called local bus, just as it is in conventional memory. The only problem with it is that when the processor is operating in real mode, as when DOS is running, 20-bit physical addressing is used, which can map a maximum of 1Mb. All the extended memory above 1Mb is thus out of reach, like a ripe apple tantalizingly hanging eight feet off of the ground. What is needed is some way of getting up into the tree.

All Intel processors starting with the 286 were designed to operate in protected mode, but also supported real mode operation for backward compatibility with previous processors. This also allowed the newer processors to run DOS, whose evolution effectively ended with release 2.0, and which remains, even today, the same real-mode fossil. Protected mode operation inaugurated many new capabilities—perhaps the most important from the application developer's point of view was the potential of accessing more than 1Mb of memory.

Under DOS this access is normally accomplished by some kind of extended-memory manager, such as Microsoft's HIMEM.SYS. The memory manager temporarily switches the processor to protected mode operation to gain access to memory above 1Mb. In this state the memory manager can, for instance, copy data between extended and conventional memory. Following such a move, the manager switches the processor back to real mode and returns to the caller.

This same capability is available through a so-called DOS extender, but an extender goes far beyond the services of a simple memory manager, and actually implements what are rightfully termed operating-system services. In effect, the DOS extender switches the processor to protected mode and leaves it there. It also provides some form of interface layer to DOS and to the system's BIOS, which both execute only in real mode, allowing an application access to those services. The net result is a kind of hybrid protected-mode operating-system environment. DOS extenders represent an excellent solution to the limitations of DOS alone. Keep in mind, however, that programs that use them cannot execute on pre-286 hardware and that 32-bit extender environments will not work on the 80286.

It is unlikely that memory availability will ever be a problem on EMS- or XMS-equipped systems. Should it happen, however, an application can always resort to disk for storage of large data objects. Given the impressive performance of most of today's hard disks, the resulting performance penalty is frequently quite acceptable. Manipulating bitmapped imagery on a scan-line basis is itself compatible with blocked disk I/O, and represents a good fit with that strategy. It is a good rule to support virtual memory on disk only as a last resort.

Now that you have an overview of alternative types of memory, we turn to a further look at the different types and a discussion of actual implementation details.

EMS Memory

For a full treatment of the EMS specification, the interested reader is directed to the *MS-DOS Encyclopedia*, edited by Ray Duncan. Here I will cover only the basics and implement the minimal functionality needed to utilize EMS memory.

An application using EMS memory communicates with an EMS device driver using interrupt 67h. A function code is placed in the AH register, any additional parameters are placed in specified registers, and interrupt 67h is invoked. The EMS driver returns a status code in the AH register. A value of zero indicates a successful call. Any other value represents an error code. All EMS error codes have the high-order bit set, so all EMS error codes will have numeric values of 80h or higher. Memory is referenced by a handle, which is returned by the EMS driver when EMS memory is allocated.

EMS memory is organized into 16K pages. The specification (version 4.0 and later) supports up to 32Mb of total memory. This memory is accessed by an application by means of a **page-frame buffer**, typically a 64K segment located in the area between 640K and 1Mb. One to four physical 16K pages are mapped into the page-frame buffer and are then accessed the way conventional memory is. Note that an application can "see" only four 16K pages at a time. If an application allocates 512K of EMS memory, it has a total of 32 pages to use (16K × 32 = 512K), but could only access them four at a time. This technique, called **bank switching**, requires that you map a specified physical page to a specified logical page within the page-frame buffer before the physical memory can be accessed. (This is essentially the same technique used to implement extended VGA video modes requiring more than 64K of video memory—a 64K page is mapped into the video segment, usually at A000h, before being accessed.)

An EMS interface must perform at least the following five functions: (1) test for EMS driver, (2) get page-frame address, (3) allocate pages, (4) free pages, and (5) map page. The only unusual operation is determining if an EMS driver is installed. Unfortunately, interrupt 67h does not provide this service. The standard method of determining the presence of an EMS driver is to inspect the device-driver header, assuming interrupt 67h points to a valid device driver, for the guaranteed device name EMMXXXX0. See Listing 4.1 for details.

There is one important caveat regarding EMS usage: Be sure that your program always frees any allocated EMS memory before it terminates. DOS knows nothing about the presence of EMS memory, so it remains allocated until explicitly freed or until the system is rebooted.

Four quantities are required for storing or retrieving data in EMS: (1) the EMS handle, (2) the logical page number, (3) the physical page number, and (4) an offset into the physical page (which will be the same as the offset into the logical page). The procedure to access a given location in EMS consists of the following steps:

1. Map a desired logical page to one of the four physical pages. This operation requires the EMS handle returned by `EMS_alloc()`.

2. Get a far pointer to the specified physical page using `EMS_pgframeaddr()`.

3. Add any required offset to the pointer. Note that we are dealing with 16K pages here, so the offset will be less than 16K. Also note that it is possible to create an address outside the desired physical page.

4. Perform the memory access as with conventional memory, using the far pointer in a normal fashion.

Listing 4.1 presents an assembler implementation for a minimal EMS access module. We will make use of this module later in the chapter when we discuss the implementation of a C++ class hierarchy for storing bitmapped images.

Listing 4.1   EMS.ASM

```
;----------------------------------------------------------
;
;  File:    EMS.ASM
;
;  Desc:    Minimal function set required to utilize
```

Listing 4.1   EMS.ASM (continued)

```
;              EMS memory from DOS real mode application
;
;-----------------------------------------------------------

.model large

; argument addressing - 16-bit far calls

arg1   equ   [bp+6]
arg2   equ   [bp+8]
arg3   equ   [bp+10]
arg4   equ   [bp+12]
arg5   equ   [bp+14]

public _EMS_installed, _EMS_pgframeaddr
public _EMS_alloc, _EMS_free, _EMS_mappage

.data

dd_name db 'EMMXXXX0'

.code

;-----------------------------------------------------------
; Desc:  Test for presence of EMS driver. Returns 1 if
;        found or 0 if not found.
; Use:   int EMS_installed( void );
;-----------------------------------------------------------

_EMS_installed proc far

     ; save registers
     push ds
     push es
     push di
     push si

     ; es:di -> name in device drvr hdr
     mov  al, 67h
     mov  ah, 35h
     int  21h
     mov  di, 10

     ; ds:si -> expected name
     mov  si, seg dd_name
     mov  ds, si
     mov  si, offset dd_name
```

Listing 4.1   EMS.ASM (continued)

```
        ; compare names
        mov  cx, 8
        cld
        repz cmpsb
        jnz  EMS_installed_1

        ; EMS driver found
        mov  ax, 1
        jmp  short EMS_installed_2

    EMS_installed_1:
        ; EMS driver not found
        xor  ax, ax

    EMS_installed_2:
        pop  si
        pop  di
        pop  es
        pop  ds
        ret

_EMS_installed endp


;------------------------------------------------------------
;  Desc:  Get address of specified physical page in
;         EMS page frame buffer.
;  Use:   char * EMS_pgframeaddr( int physical_pg );
;  In:    logical page number (0 - 3)
;  Out:   far pointer to specified page
;------------------------------------------------------------

_EMS_pgframeaddr proc far

    push bp
    mov  bp, sp
    push bx

    ; page frame seg in bx
    mov  ah, 41h
    int  67h

    ; test for error
    or   ah, ah
    jz   EMS_pgframeaddr_1

    ; error - return null pointer
    xor  dx, dx
```

Listing 4.1   EMS.ASM (continued)

```
        xor   ax, ax
        jmp short EMS_pgframeaddr_2

    EMS_pgframeaddr_1:
      ; set dx:ax to requested address
      push bx
      mov  ax, 4000h    ; page size
      mov  bx, arg1     ; page number
      mul  bx
      pop  dx

    EMS_pgframeaddr_2:
      pop  bx
      pop  bp
      ret

_EMS_pgframeaddr endp

;-------------------------------------------------------
;  Desc:   Allocate EMS memory
;  Use:    int EMS_alloc( int npages );
;  In :    Number of 16K pages to allocate
;  Out:    EMS handle or -1 on error
;-------------------------------------------------------

_EMS_alloc proc far

      push bp
      mov  bp, sp

      ; request allocation
      mov  bx, arg1     ; bx = page count
      mov  ah, 43h      ; func 43h = alloc pages
      int  67h

      ; test for error
      or   ah, ah
      jz   EMS_alloc_1

      ; allocation failed
      mov  ax, 0FFFFh
      jmp  short EMS_alloc_2

    EMS_alloc_1:
      ;allocation successful
      mov  ax, dx    ; ax = handle
```

Listing 4.1   EMS.ASM (continued)

```
    EMS_alloc_2:
      pop  bp
      ret

_EMS_alloc endp


;----------------------------------------------------------
;  Desc:  Free EMS memory
;  Use:   void EMS_free( int EMShandle );
;  In :   Handle returned by EMS_alloc()
;----------------------------------------------------------


_EMS_free proc far

        push bp
        mov  bp, sp

        mov  dx, arg1     ; DX = EMS handle
        mov  ah, 45h      ; func 45h = free pages
        int  67h

        pop  bp
        ret

_EMS_free endp


;----------------------------------------------------------
;  Desc:  Map EMS logical page to physical page
;  Use:   int EMS_mappage( int hand, int lpage, int ppage );
;  In :   hand - EMS handle from EMS_alloc
;         lpage - logical page number
;         ppage - physical page in frame buffer
;  Out :  EMS return code (0 = success)
;----------------------------------------------------------


_EMS_mappage proc far

        push bp
        mov  bp, sp
        push bx

        ; map page
        mov  dx, arg1
        mov  bx, arg2
        mov  al, arg3
        mov  ah, 44h
        int  67h
```

Listing 4.1   EMS.ASM (continued)

```
        ; reformat return code
        xchg ah, al
        xor  ah, ah

        pop  bx
        pop  bp
        ret
_EMS_mappage endp

end
```

XMS Memory

The XMS specification is similar in many respects to the EMS specification in its treatment of memory above 1Mb. The primary exception is that a page-ordered layout of memory is not used. The XMS specification is much more involved, however, because it deals not only with normal extended memory but also with upper-memory blocks and the high-memory area. Interested readers can obtain a copy of the XMS specification from Microsoft Corporation. It can also be downloaded from the Microsoft area on CompuServe.

Upper-memory blocks (UMBs) are small blocks of free memory that are scattered throughout the BIOS area between 640K and 1Mb. The **high-memory area** (HMA) is the first 64K above 1Mb, and it is treated separately for two reasons: (1) it is addressable as conventional real memory using a segment address of 0FFFFh (which requires that the A20 address line be enabled), and (2) code can be executed in the HMA. Unfortunately, there are also many pitfalls in using the HMA. Because our interest is solely in storing image data, there is no compelling reason to deal with either UMBs or the HMA, and we will not. The XMS implementation described here will utilize conventional extended memory only.

An application communicates with an XMS memory manager by means of a control function, the address of which can be obtained using interrupt 2Fh. Why the XMS API was not implemented completely by interrupt 2Fh or another interrupt is an unanswered question. The interrupt itself is used only to determine the presence of an XMS manager and to get the control-function address.

API functions are provided to allocate and free blocks of XMS memory. XMS memory blocks are referenced by a 16-bit handle in much the same way EMS memory is. In place of the EMS paging mechanism, the XMS API provides a function to move (that is, copy) memory from one location to another. Either location can reference either conventional memory or a previously allocated XMS memory block.

Given this scheme, using XMS is a matter of creating data in conventional memory and copying it into an allocated XMS block using the API move function. Retrieving data stored in this fashion entails copying it from XMS into a conventional memory buffer. This scheme is necessary because it is not possible to address XMS memory directly when an application is running in DOS real mode.

One restriction on XMS usage should be kept in mind. It is not possible to use XMS memory if a VDISK or compatible virtual-disk device driver is installed. In this situation XMS allocations will fail, although it appears that the system has plenty of spare XMS memory.

Listing 4.2 contains the assembly source code of a minimal XMS interface, one that ignores UMBs and the HMA. It is intended to be used exclusively for data storage, in our case for storage of bitmapped images. We will make use of it later in this chapter when we discuss the implementation of an image-storage subsystem.

Listing 4.2   XMS.ASM

```
;----------------------------------------------------------
;
;   File:    XMS.ASM
;
;   Desc:    Minimal function set required to utilize
;            XMS memory from DOS real mode application
;
;----------------------------------------------------------

.model large

; argument addressing - 16-bit far calls

arg1   equ   [bp+6]
arg2   equ   [bp+8]
arg3   equ   [bp+10]
arg4   equ   [bp+12]
arg5   equ   [bp+14]

public _XMS_installed, _XMS_alloc, _XMS_free, _XMS_move

.data

XMSctl label dword
             dw  ?
             dw  ?
```

Listing 4.2   XMS.ASM (continued)

```
.code

;------------------------------------------------------------
;  Desc:   Test for presence of XMS driver.
;  Use:    int XMS_installed( void );
;  In:     Nothing
;  Out:    Returns 1 if found, 0 otherwise
;------------------------------------------------------------

_XMS_installed proc far

        mov  ax, 4300h
        int  2Fh
        cmp  al, 80h
        jne  XMS_installed_1
        mov  ax, 1
        jmp short XMS_installed_2
    XMS_installed_1:
        xor  ax, ax
    XMS_installed_2:
        ret

_XMS_installed endp

;------------------------------------------------------------
;  Desc:   Allocate XMS memory.
;  Use:    unsigned XMS_alloc( int nKBytes );
;  In:     Number of KB to allocate
;  Out:    XMS handle (0 implies failure)
;------------------------------------------------------------

_XMS_alloc proc far

        push bp
        mov  bp, sp
        push es
        push bx

        ; get control function address
        mov  ax, 4310h
        int  2Fh
        mov  word ptr [XMSctl], bx
        mov  word ptr [XMSctl+2], es

        ; make alloc request
        mov  dx, arg1
        mov  ah, 09h
        call [XMSctl]
```

Listing 4.2 XMS.ASM (continued)

```asm
            ; check for failure
            or   ax, ax
            jz   XMS_alloc_1

            ; all is well
            mov  ax, dx

    XMS_alloc_1:
        pop  bx
        pop  es
        pop  bp
        ret

_XMS_alloc endp


;-------------------------------------------------------
; Desc:   Free XMS memory.
; Use:    void XMS_free( unsigned XMShand );
; In:     Handle returned by XMS_alloc()
; Out:    Nothing
;-------------------------------------------------------


_XMS_free proc far

        push bp
        mov  bp, sp
        push bx
        push es

        ; get control function address
        mov  ax, 4310h
        int  2Fh
        mov  word ptr [XMSctl], bx
        mov  word ptr [XMSctl+2], es

        ; make free request
        mov  dx, arg1
        mov  ah, 0Ah
        call [XMSctl]

        pop  bx
        pop  es
        pop  bp
        ret

_XMS_free endp
```

Listing 4.2   XMS.ASM (continued)

```
;------------------------------------------------------
;  Desc:   Move XMS memory block
;  Use:    int XMS_move( XMSmovestruct *ms );
;  In:     Pointer to an XMS move structure
;  Out:    0 -> success
;------------------------------------------------------

_XMS_move proc far

      push bp
      mov  bp, sp
      push bx
      push es
      push ds
      push si

      ; get control function address
      mov  ax, 4310h
      int  2Fh
      mov  word ptr [XMSctl], bx
      mov  word ptr [XMSctl+2], es

      ; make move request
      xor  bx, bx
      mov  si, ds
      mov  es, si
      mov  si, arg2
      mov  ds, si
      mov  si, arg1
      mov  ah, 0Bh
      call es:[XMSctl]

      ; set return code
      xor  ax, ax
      mov  al, bl

   XMS_move_1:
      pop  si
      pop  ds
      pop  es
      pop  bx
      pop  bp
      ret

_XMS_move endp

end
```

Virtual Disk Storage

Disk storage is the third type of nonconventional memory; it should normally be considered the choice of last resort. Although disk access can be surprisingly fast, it nonetheless will normally be the slowest of the three alternatives. The use of disk storage remains an important option, however, because for most purposes it effectively represents a limitless memory pool.

Implementation of blocked or paged memory storage using disk is less intricate than for either EMS or XMS, and can be done completely within the confines of a compiler's run-time library. Because it is likely that an application will use these run-time file access services anyway, it makes good sense to use these and avoid adding yet another layer to the program's complexity.

Implementation of the disk-based storage medium will be presented in Listings 4.3 and 4.4, which contain the full image-storage class hierarchy.

Memory Management Strategies

Because we are dealing with very specific entities, bitmapped images, it is useful to discuss strategies for storing them in memory for subsequent manipulation. Recall that our overall approach is to treat a bitmapped image as a collection of scan lines. This suggests allocating separate buffers for each scan line and maintaining an array of pointers to individual scan lines.

A collection of many small buffers rather than one large buffer is the better architecture for conventional memory, because heap fragmentation and use can potentially foil the allocation of a single large buffer. However, the small-buffer approach is less desirable with EMS or XMS memory, because each allocation requires a unique handle, and handle resources are generally quite sparse. EMS, for example, supports a maximum of 255 handles, although the actual number is frequently smaller. The suggested approach for an EMS or XMS bitmap is therefore to allocate a single memory block large enough for the full image and to maintain separate row pointers, or offsets, that point into the block. The same approach is suggested for disk usage.

The main problem in supporting EMS, XMS, and disk memory in addition to conventional memory is that separate pointer formats are involved. This is illustrated graphically in Figure 4.1. This type of problem is addressed quite elegantly in C++ using inheritance and virtual functions. A generic image-storage class can be created and used as a base class for the derivation of memory-specific implementations. Because classes are accessed by the base class, a uniform interface is presented. The type of memory actually used is determined from the derived class constructor that is called.

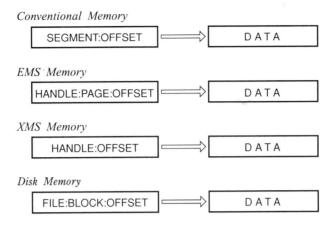

Conventional Memory

| SEGMENT:OFFSET | ⟹ | D A T A |

EMS Memory

| HANDLE:PAGE:OFFSET | ⟹ | D A T A |

XMS Memory

| HANDLE:OFFSET | ⟹ | D A T A |

Disk Memory

| FILE:BLOCK:OFFSET | ⟹ | D A T A |

Figure 4.1   Pointer Requirements for Various Memory Types

An Image-Storage Class Hierarchy

Listings 4.3 and 4.4 present a suitable implementation of the image-storage class hierarchy. Memory allocation and deallocation are handled by the class constructors and destructors respectively. Only a few additional member functions are required to provide access to the allocated image structure.

In the conventional-memory version, a separate buffer is allocated for each scan line and the pointers are stored in an array, one for each row. Getting a pointer to a row is therefore only a matter of an array access.

In the EMS version, a sufficient number of 16K pages are allocated to hold the image. Each 16K page holds some integral number of scan lines, and the start of each scan line is aligned on a double word boundary. Scan lines are guaranteed not to cross a page boundary. Because of the regular layout, the page and offset of each scan line are easily calculated, so these are not maintained in arrays.

The XMS version is similar to the EMS version, except that only an offset is required. Note that the EMS version requires 16-bit offsets and the XMS version requires 32-bit offsets. The XMS version also maintains its own conventional-memory buffer. When a scan line is accessed, it is moved from XMS into this buffer, and a pointer to the buffer is returned to the application.

The disk version is treated much like EMS, except that a file pointer replaces the EMS handle, and the block size, which corresponds to the EMS page size, can be set to an arbitrary size. For large images, the size of a scan line represents a good choice, although slightly better performance may be realized if a block holds two or more scan lines.

Listing 4.3   IMGSTORE.HPP

```cpp
//----------------------------------------------------------//
//                                                          //
//    File:      IMGSTORE.HPP                               //
//                                                          //
//    Desc:      Memory management classes for storing and  //
//               manipulating bitmapped images.             //
//                                                          //
//----------------------------------------------------------//

#ifndef _IMGSTORE_HPP_
#define _IMGSTORE_HPP_

#include "stdio.h"
#include "string.h"
#include "ems.h"
#include "xms.h"


//.............status codes

enum ImgStoreStatus
{
   imgstoreOKAY,
   imgstoreNOMEM,
   imgstoreNODRVR,
   imgstoreNODISK
};

//.............the base class

class ImgStore
{
   public:
      int status;      // okay or failed
      int flags;       // for the app's use

   protected:
      int rowcnt;      // row count
      int colcnt;      // pixels per row
      int pxlbits;     // bits per pixel
      int rowbytes;    // bytes per row

   public:
      ImgStore( int nrows, int ncols, int nbits )
      {
         status = imgstoreOKAY;
         flags = 0;
         rowcnt = nrows;
         colcnt = ncols;
```

Listing 4.3   IMGSTORE.HPP (continued)

```
            pxlbits = nbits;
            rowbytes = ((nbits * ncols) + 7) / 8;
        }
        virtual ~ImgStore( )
        {
        }
        virtual void put( unsigned char *data, int row ) = 0;
        virtual unsigned char *get( int row ) = 0;
        virtual void cpy( unsigned char *dest, int row ) = 0;
        virtual void cpy( unsigned char *dest, int row,
                          int col, int cnt ) = 0;
        int width( void )     { return colcnt; }
        int height( void )    { return rowcnt; }
        int depth( void )     { return pxlbits; }
        int scanbytes( void ) { return rowbytes; }
};

//..............conventional memory

class CnvImgStore : public ImgStore
{
    protected:
        unsigned char **rowptrs;

    public:
        CnvImgStore( int nrows, int ncols, int nbits );
        virtual ~CnvImgStore( );
        virtual void put( unsigned char *data, int row );
        virtual unsigned char *get( int row );
        virtual void cpy( unsigned char *dest, int row );
        virtual void cpy( unsigned char *dest, int row,
                          int col, int cnt );
};

//..............EMS memory

class EmsImgStore : public ImgStore
{
    protected:
        int handle;      // EMS handle
        int npages;      // number of alloc'd pages
        int phypage;     // physical page used
        int blkcnt;      // rows per 16K page
        int blklen;      // padded row length
        char *pgframe;   // pointer to physical page
```

Listing 4.3   IMGSTORE.HPP (continued)

```
    public:
        EmsImgStore( int nrows, int ncols, int nbits );
        virtual ~EmsImgStore( );
        virtual void put( unsigned char *data, int row );
        virtual unsigned char *get( int row );
        virtual void cpy( unsigned char *dest, int row );
        virtual void cpy( unsigned char *dest, int row,
                          int col, int cnt );
};

//..............XMS memory

class XmsImgStore : public ImgStore
{
    protected:
        unsigned handle;      // xms handle
        int blklen;           // padded row length
        char *buffer;         // cnv mem buffer
        XMSmovestruct c2x;    // for move to xms
        XMSmovestruct x2c;    // for move to cnv

    public:
        XmsImgStore( int nrows, int ncols, int nbits );
        virtual ~XmsImgStore( );
        virtual void put( unsigned char *data, int row );
        virtual unsigned char *get( int row );
        virtual void cpy( unsigned char *dest, int row );
        virtual void cpy( unsigned char *dest, int row,
                          int col, int cnt );
};

//..............Disk memory

class DskImgStore : public ImgStore
{
    protected:
        FILE *fstor;       // file pointer
        int blklen;        // padded row length
        char *buffer;      // cnv mem buffer

    public:
        DskImgStore( int nrows, int ncols, int nbits );
        virtual ~DskImgStore( );
        virtual void put( unsigned char *data, int row );
        virtual unsigned char *get( int row );
        virtual void cpy( unsigned char *dest, int row );
```

Listing 4.3   IMGSTORE.HPP (continued)

```
        virtual void cpy( unsigned char *dest, int row,
                          int col, int cnt );
};


#endif
```

Listing 4.4   IMGSTORE.CPP

```
//----------------------------------------------------------//
//                                                          //
//    File:      IMAGSTORE.CPP                              //
//                                                          //
//    Desc:      Memory management classes for storing and  //
//               manipulating bitmapped images.             //
//                                                          //
//----------------------------------------------------------//


#include "imgstore.hpp"


//...............Conventional Memory

CnvImgStore::CnvImgStore( int nrows, int ncols, int nbits ) :
            ImgStore( nrows, ncols, nbits )
{
    int nerrors = 1;
    rowptrs = new unsigned char * [rowcnt];
    if( rowptrs )
    {
        nerrors—;
        for( int i=0; i<rowcnt; i++ )
        {
            rowptrs[i] = new unsigned char [rowbytes];
            if( rowptrs[i] )
                memset( rowptrs[i], 0, rowbytes );
            else
                nerrors++;
        }
    }
    if( nerrors > 0 ) status = imgstoreNOMEM;
}


CnvImgStore::~CnvImgStore( )
{
    if( rowptrs )
    {
        for( int i=0; i<rowcnt; i++ )
        {
            if( rowptrs[i] ) delete rowptrs[i];
```

Listing 4.4   IMGSTORE.CPP (continued)

```cpp
        }
        delete rowptrs;
    }
}

void CnvImgStore::put( unsigned char *data, int row )
{
    if( status == imgstoreOKAY )
        if( (row >= 0) && (row < rowcnt) )
            memcpy( rowptrs[row], data, rowbytes );
}

unsigned char * CnvImgStore::get( int row )
{
    if( status == imgstoreOKAY )
        if( (row >= 0) && (row < rowcnt) )
            return rowptrs[row];
    return 0;
}

void CnvImgStore::cpy( unsigned char *dest, int row )
{
    if( status == imgstoreOKAY )
        if( (row >= 0) && (row < rowcnt) )
            memcpy( dest, rowptrs[row], rowbytes );
}

void CnvImgStore::cpy( unsigned char *dest, int row,
                        int col, int cnt )
{
    if( status == imgstoreOKAY )
        if( (row >= 0) && (row < rowcnt) )
            memcpy( dest, rowptrs[row]+col, cnt );
}

//..............EMS Memory

EmsImgStore::EmsImgStore( int nrows, int ncols, int nbits ) :
            ImgStore( nrows, ncols, nbits )
{
    if( EMS_installed() )
    {
        // we use only 1 of the 4 physical pages
        // in the page frame buffer.  phypage
        // is set to desired page (0-3).
        phypage = 0;
        pgframe = EMS_pgframeaddr( phypage );
```

Listing 4.4   IMGSTORE.CPP (continued)

```cpp
            // blklen is rowlen padded to multiple of 4.
            // blkcnt is number of padded rows that
            // fit in a 16K page.
            int n  = (rowbytes + 3) / 4;
            blklen = n * 4;
            blkcnt = 16384 / blklen;

            npages = (rowcnt + blkcnt - 1) / blkcnt;
            handle = EMS_alloc( npages );
            if( handle != -1 )
            {
                for( int i=0; i<npages; i++ )
                {
                    EMS_mappage( handle, i, phypage );
                    memset( pgframe, 0, 16384 );
                }
            }
            else
                status = imgstoreNOMEM;
        }
        else
            status = imgstoreNODRVR;
    }

EmsImgStore::~EmsImgStore( )
{
    if( status == imgstoreOKAY )
        EMS_free( handle );
}

void EmsImgStore::put( unsigned char *data, int row )
{
    if( status == imgstoreOKAY )
        if( (row >= 0) && (row < rowcnt) )
        {
            int page = row / blkcnt;
            EMS_mappage( handle, page, phypage );
            int ofs  = (row % blkcnt) * blklen;
            memcpy( pgframe+ofs, data, rowbytes );
        }
}

unsigned char * EmsImgStore::get( int row )
{
    if( status == imgstoreOKAY )
        if( (row >= 0) && (row < rowcnt) )
        {
            int page = row / blkcnt;
```

Listing 4.4   IMGSTORE.CPP (continued)

```cpp
            EMS_mappage( handle, page, phypage );
            int ofs  = (row % blkcnt) * blklen;
            return (unsigned char *) pgframe+ofs;
        }
    return 0;
}

void EmsImgStore::cpy( unsigned char *dest, int row )
{
   if( status == imgstoreOKAY )
      if( (row >= 0) && (row < rowcnt) )
         memcpy( dest, get(row), rowbytes );
}

void EmsImgStore::cpy( unsigned char *dest, int row,
                       int col, int cnt )
{
   if( status == imgstoreOKAY )
      if( (row >= 0) && (row < rowcnt) )
         memcpy( dest, get(row)+col, cnt );
}

//...............XMS Memory

XmsImgStore::XmsImgStore( int nrows, int ncols, int nbits ) :
           ImgStore( nrows, ncols, nbits )
{
   if( XMS_installed() )
   {
      // blklen is rowlen padded to multiple of 4.
      int n  = (rowbytes + 3) / 4;
      blklen = n * 4;

      // allocate a cnv mem row buffer
      buffer = new char [blklen];
      if( buffer )
      {
         memset( buffer, 0, blklen );

         // total xms bytes required
         long nbytes = blklen; nbytes *= rowcnt;

         // convert to KB
         nbytes += 1023;
         nbytes /= 1024;
         n = (int) nbytes;
```

Listing 4.4   IMGSTORE.CPP (continued)

```cpp
                // and attempt to allocate
                handle = XMS_alloc( n );
                if( handle != 0 )
                {
                    // set up move structs
                    c2x.nbytes = blklen;
                    c2x.srchandle = 0;
                    c2x.srcoffset = (long) buffer;
                    c2x.dsthandle = handle;
                    c2x.dstoffset = 0;

                    x2c.nbytes = blklen;
                    x2c.srchandle = handle;
                    x2c.srcoffset = 0;
                    x2c.dsthandle = 0;
                    x2c.dstoffset = (long) buffer;

                    // zero the image
                    for( int i=0; i<rowcnt; i++ )
                    {
                        XMS_move( &c2x );
                        c2x.dstoffset += blklen;
                    }
                }
                else
                {
                    status = imgstoreNOMEM;
                    delete buffer;
                }
            }
            else
                status = imgstoreNOMEM;
        }
        else
            status = imgstoreNODRVR;
    }

XmsImgStore::~XmsImgStore( )
{
    if( status == imgstoreOKAY )
    {
        delete buffer;
        XMS_free( handle );
    }
}

void XmsImgStore::put( unsigned char *data, int row )
{
```

Listing 4.4   IMGSTORE.CPP (continued)

```cpp
   if( status == imgstoreOKAY )
      if( (row >= 0) && (row < rowcnt) )
      {
         c2x.srcoffset = (long) data;
         c2x.dstoffset = long( blklen ) * row;
         XMS_move( &c2x );
      }
}

unsigned char * XmsImgStore::get( int row )
{
   if( status == imgstoreOKAY )
      if( (row >= 0) && (row < rowcnt) )
      {
         x2c.srcoffset = long( blklen ) * row;
         XMS_move( &x2c );
         return (unsigned char *) buffer;
      }
   return 0;
}

void XmsImgStore::cpy( unsigned char *dest, int row )
{
   if( status == imgstoreOKAY )
      if( (row >= 0) && (row < rowcnt) )
         memcpy( dest, get(row), rowbytes );
}

void XmsImgStore::cpy( unsigned char *dest, int row,
                       int col, int cnt )
{
   if( status == imgstoreOKAY )
      if( (row >= 0) && (row < rowcnt) )
         memcpy( dest, get(row)+col, cnt );
}

//..............Disk Memory

DskImgStore::DskImgStore( int nrows, int ncols, int nbits ) :
            ImgStore( nrows, ncols, nbits )
{
   // blklen is rowlen padded to multiple of 4.
   int n  = (rowbytes + 3) / 4;
   blklen = n * 4;

   // allocate a cnv mem row buffer
   buffer = new char [blklen];
   if( buffer )
```

Listing 4.4   IMGSTORE.CPP (continued)

```cpp
   {
      memset( buffer, 0, blklen );

      // initialize the disk file
      fstor = fopen( "IMGSTORE.MEM", "w+b" );
      if( fstor )
      {
         for( int i=0; i<nrows; i++ )
         {
            fwrite( buffer, blklen, 1, fstor );
            if( ferror(fstor) )
            {
               fclose( fstor );
               delete buffer;
               status = imgstoreNODISK;
               break;
            }
         }
      }
      else
      {
         delete buffer;
         status = imgstoreNODISK;
      }
   }
   else
      status = imgstoreNOMEM;
}

DskImgStore::~DskImgStore( )
{
   if( status == imgstoreOKAY )
   {
      delete buffer;
      fclose( fstor );
   }
}

void DskImgStore::put( unsigned char *data, int row )
{
   if( status == imgstoreOKAY )
      if( (row >= 0) && (row < rowcnt) )
      {
         long offset = blklen;
         offset *= row;
         fseek( fstor, offset, SEEK_SET );
         fwrite( (char *) data, blklen, 1, fstor );
```

Listing 4.4 IMGSTORE.CPP (continued)

```
        }
}

unsigned char * DskImgStore::get( int row )
{
    if( status == imgstoreOKAY )
        if( (row >= 0) && (row < rowcnt) )
        {
            long offset = blklen;
            offset *= row;
            fseek( fstor, offset, SEEK_SET );
            fread( buffer, blklen, 1, fstor );
            return (unsigned char *) buffer;
        }
    return 0;
}

void DskImgStore::cpy( unsigned char *dest, int row )
{
    if( status == imgstoreOKAY )
        if( (row >= 0) && (row < rowcnt) )
            memcpy( dest, get(row), rowbytes );
}

void DskImgStore::cpy( unsigned char *dest, int row,
                       int col, int cnt )
{
    if( status == imgstoreOKAY )
        if( (row >= 0) && (row < rowcnt) )
            memcpy( dest, get(row)+col, cnt );
}
```

This concludes our look at memory management. We will return to the topic briefly in Chapter 7, when we consider the overall process of image display and printing. Before we do that, however, we need to discuss the hardware used to display and print bitmapped images.

5
Video Display Hardware

The access to video display hardware that was provided in the original IBM PC design was both minimal and, for the most part, character oriented. It was also relegated to the BIOS, specifically to interrupt 10h. Interestingly, DOS itself provides no graphical display functionality.

Interrupt 10h does a good job with control issues—such as palette setting and mode switching—that arise in connection with video hardware, but its actual drawing capabilities are acutely meager. Beyond the output of text, the only graphic operations it supports are read pixel and write pixel. Because of this, the use of a third-party graphics primitive library is the standard procedure for all graphics-based DOS applications.

Bitmapped images present their own special set of display problems, and these are not always well addressed by commercial graphics primitive libraries. In particular, most such libraries do not provide scan-line-oriented operations. Because of this, we will take the time in this chapter to discuss various aspects of video-display hardware. Design techniques and implementations for scan-line-oriented primitives will be illustrated. The intent is to describe a self-contained graphics environment suitable for dealing with bitmapped imagery.

The VGA Display

On Intel-based systems, the VGA adapter is perhaps the closest thing there is to a display-hardware standard. Developed originally by IBM for its PS/2 line and for use under MS-DOS, it is now widely supported by Unix variants, OS/2, Windows, and other operating-system environments. I deal with the VGA standard in some depth here, because it is both widely used and one of the more difficult hardware designs to deal with in software. Many of the VGA's quirks are hereditary in nature. It was developed from the earlier EGA adapter and was intended to be backward compatible with it. The quirkiness of the VGA is especially evident in the VGA's palette registers, as you will see.

As time goes by, earlier display standards are becoming less important. This is particularly true in view of the industry's move toward the graphical interface. It is now doubtful whether it is worth the trouble to support display standards such as CGA, EGA, PGA, or Hercules in a graphics application. Of these, the CGA continues to be resurrected from time to time for use in specialized embedded systems, and the Hercules adapter is still found on inexpensive, low-end MS-DOS systems. However, both are inadequate for handling mainstream graphic imagery, which is typically of high resolution and in color.

It should be noted that the VGA's repertoire of display modes includes all modes of the earlier CGA and EGA adapters. These are useful for preserving the aspect ratio of images created on the older adapters, but except for this specialized use there is no compelling reason to support them.

In the following sections, several aspects of the VGA adapter will be discussed, including mode switching, adapter detection, palette setting, and scan-line drawing primitives. Discussion will be confined to video modes 12h (640x480x16-colors) and 13h (320x200x256-colors) of the standard VGA, but will also include mode 62h (640x480x256-colors) of the ATI series of adapters and mode 2Eh (640x480x256-colors) of the Tseng 4000 chip set to illustrate extended VGA modes. The Tseng chip set is widely used on VGA-compatible adapters, one example being the Orchid ProDesigner series of video cards.

The "official" method of interfacing to a VGA adapter in software is by the BIOS video services interrupt, 10h. Where possible, it is best to use interrupt 10h instead of programming the video hardware directly. However, in the real world it is seldom possible to get by with using interrupt 10h alone, either because of performance limitations or because a required function is not implemented. Keep in mind that the video BIOS is a component of the adapter itself, and so it varies from card to card and manufacturer to manufacturer.

Mode Switching

Before graphical imagery can be drawn on a VGA display, it is necessary to put it into an appropriate graphics mode. All modes are selected in the same fashion, using function 00h of interrupt 10h. You will normally want to reset the adapter to its previous mode (presumably a text mode) at the end of a graphics application. Using function 0Fh of interrupt 10h before switching to graphics mode allows you to determine the current mode.

Listing 5.1 presents a suitable assembly-language implementation of functions to perform these two tasks. They are typically used as in the following code fragment:

```
        // graphics setup
        int tmode = getvideomode( );
        setvideomode( desired_graphics_mode );

            :

        // restore display when done
        setvideomode( tmode );
```

Listing 5.1   VMODE.ASM

```
;--------------------------------------------------------
;
;  File:    VMODE.ASM
;
;  Desc:    Functions to query and set the video mode
;           on a VGA or compatible display adapter
;
;--------------------------------------------------------

.model large

; argument addressing - 16-bit far calls

arg1   equ   [bp+6]
arg2   equ   [bp+8]

public _getvideomode, _setvideomode

.code

;--------------------------------------------------------
;  Desc:   Return current video mode
;  Use:    int getvideomode( void )
;  In:     Nothing
;  Out:    Current mode number
;--------------------------------------------------------

_getvideomode proc far

    push bx
    mov  ah, 0Fh
    int  10h
    xor  ah, ah
    pop  bx
    ret

_getvideomode endp
```

Listing 5.1   VMODE.ASM (continued)

```
;------------------------------------------------------------
;  Desc:   Set current video mode
;  Use:    void setvideomode( int mode )
;  In:     Desired mode number
;  Out:    Nothing
;------------------------------------------------------------

_setvideomode proc far

        push bp
        mov  bp, sp
        mov  ax, arg1
        xor  ah, ah
        int  10h
        pop  bp
        ret

_setvideomode endp

end
```

VGA Detection

In general, video-adapter detection is a tricky and unreliable process. The original video BIOS design of the IBM PC never anticipated the need for such a service, and the mix of commercially available adapters plus their varied modes and configurations makes for a complex domain of possibilities. Nonetheless, it is customary for graphics software to make the attempt, so we will look at the process here.

The code needed to detect a standard VGA adapter is fairly minimal. Function 1Ah of interrupt 10h supports reading or setting the video-display combination code maintained by the BIOS in the video-display-data area. After the video-display combination code is read, two byte values are returned, one indicating the active display and one indicating the inactive display. A value of 07h for the active display indicates a monochrome VGA, and you can then assume the availability of display mode 11h. A value of 08h indicates a color VGA and you can assume the availability of VGA modes 12h and 13h.

The fun begins when you attempt to identify the presence of an extended VGA adapter and to determine what specific display modes are available. The latter is a function of the amount of video RAM that is present, so the problem boils down to (1) determining the chip set, and (2) determining the amount of video memory present on the board. In some cases it may not be possible to determine one or the other of these two values, so in a general sense the problem is not completely solvable.

There is, however, another way to go. Video-adapter manufacturers assign mode numbers to the various display modes supported by their cards. These are used to select specific display modes with interrupt 10h. Because these are unique on a given adapter, and because there is little overlap among manufacturers, an adapter can often be identified by the simple expedient of setting a display mode unique to the card in question and then querying the display mode to see if the mode-select operation succeeded. The only potential snag with this process is that there is no guarantee that a given mode number is truly unique.

There is now an industry standard for this. Developed by the Video Electronics Standards Association, it allows a program to obtain video information in a straightforward and well-defined manner. Unfortunately, most video adapters currently on the market predate the standard, so it is still of little practical use. Someday, when the last non–VESA display adapter bites the dust, video detection will become a moot subject. Until then, however, we'll continue to rely on the tricks described here.

Listing 5.2 presents the assembler source code for several functions that are useful in identifying video hardware. Some of the functions are specific to the ATI and Tseng chip sets, and others are generally applicable. Refer to the listing for details.

Listing 5.2   VGAQUERY.ASM

```
;---------------------------------------------------------
;
;   File:     VGAQUERY.ASM
;
;   Desc:     Functions for detecting various VGA compatible
;             displays and display modes
;
;---------------------------------------------------------

.model large

; argument addressing - 16-bit far calls

arg1   equ   [bp+6]
arg2   equ   [bp+8]

public _is_vga, _is_ati, _test_mode

.data
```

Listing 5.2   VGAQUERY.ASM (continued)

```
; ROM signature of all ATI cards
ati_size  dw  9
ati_sign  db  '761295520'

.code

;------------------------------------------------------------
; Desc:  Test if a specified video mode is supported
; Use:   int test_mode( int mode );
; Ret:   0 - Not supported
;        mode - Mode is supported
;------------------------------------------------------------

_test_mode proc far

     push bp
     mov  bp, sp

     ; get current video mode and save
     mov  ah, 0Fh
     int  10h
     push ax

     ; set passed mode
     mov  ax, arg1
     xor  ah, ah
     mov  dx, ax     ; dx = passed mode
     int  10h

     ; get current mode again
     mov  ah, 0Fh
     int  10h
     xor  ah, ah
     xor  dx, ax     ; dx=0 -> mode supported

     ; restore previous mode
     pop  ax
     xor  ah, ah
     int  10h

     ; set return code
     xor  ax, ax
     or   dx, dx
     jnz  test_mode_1
     mov  ax, arg1
```

Listing 5.2   VGAQUERY.ASM (continued)

```
      test_mode_1:
        pop  bp
        ret

  _test_mode endp

  ;----------------------------------------------------------
  ; Desc:  Test for standard VGA adapter and display
  ; Use:   int is_vga( void );
  ; Ret:   0 - Not a VGA
  ;        1 - Monochrome VGA
  ;        2 - Color VGA
  ;----------------------------------------------------------

  _is_vga proc far

        push bx

        ; get active display
        mov  ax, 1A00h
        mov  bl, 99h
        int  10h

        ; bl = active display
        cmp  bl, 07h
        je   is_vga_1
        cmp  bl, 08h
        je   is_vga_2
        xor  ax, ax
        jmp short is_vga_3

     is_vga_1:
        mov  ax, 1
        jmp short is_vga_3

     is_vga_2:
        mov  ax, 2
        jmp short is_vga_3

     is_vga_3:
        pop  bx
        ret

  _is_vga endp

  ;----------------------------------------------------------
  ; Desc:  Test for presence of an ATI adapter
  ; Use:   int is_ati( void );
```

Listing 5.2   VGAQUERY.ASM (continued)

```
;   Ret:    0 - Not an ATI
;           1 - Is an ATI
;-------------------------------------------------------


_is_ati proc far

        push es
        push di
        push si
        push cx

        xor  ax, ax
        mov  si, offset DGROUP:ati_sign
        mov  di, 0C000h
        mov  es, di
        mov  di, 0031h
        mov  cx, ati_size
        cld
        repz cmpsb
        or   cx, cx
        jnz  is_ati_1
        inc  ax
     is_ati_1:
        pop  cx
        pop  si
        pop  di
        pop  es
        ret

_is_ati endp


;-------------------------------------------------------
;   Desc:   Test for presence of a Tseng chip set
;   Use:    int is_tseng( void );
;   Ret:    0 - Not a Tseng
;           1 - Is a Tseng
;-------------------------------------------------------


_is_tseng proc far

        ; check for Tseng by testing support
        ; for a known Tseng super vga mode
        mov ax, 29h
        call _test_mode
        or   ax, ax
        jz   is_tseng_1
```

Listing 5.2   VGAQUERY.ASM (continued)

```
        mov    ax, 1
    is_tseng_1:
      ret

_is_tseng endp

end
```

VGA Palette Manipulation

A critical requirement for displaying graphics files is the ability to manipulate the video display's palette. Virtually all important formats provide for the specification of a palette, and most of the commercial applications that produce them allow the program user to modify an image's palette.

Setting a 16-color palette for VGA mode 12h is a confusing process unless you know how palettes were implemented for the EGA adapter and how the VGA designers implemented backward compatibility with the EGA adapter. On the EGA there are sixteen 8-bit palette registers. The contents of each palette register control the intensities of the three primaries for that color. Only six of a register's eight bits are used, two bits each for red, green, and blue. This design provides for four possible intensities of each of the three primaries, for a total of 64 possible colors. A pixel's value is actually an index in the range 0 to 15 that selects one of the palette registers. The pixel is displayed with the color defined by that register.

Here are typical default palette register values for an EGA adapter:

```
    unsigned char ega_default_pal[16] =
    {
        0x00, 0x01, 0x02, 0x03,
        0x04, 0x05, 0x14, 0x07,
        0x38, 0x39, 0x3A, 0x3B,
        0x3C, 0x3D, 0x3E, 0x3F
    };
```

Each 8-bit value is interpreted as xxRGBrgb, where Rr is the 2-bit red intensity, Gg is the 2-bit green intensity, and Bb is the 2-bit blue intensity. The two high-order bits are unused and should be set to zero.

For backward compatibility with the EGA, the VGA contains the same set of sixteen palette registers, and these are used in mode 12h. However, their value no longer defines a color. Instead, a palette register is used as an index to select one of the card's 256 DAC registers (DAC stands for Digital to Analog Convertor). Each DAC register contains an 18-bit quantity that defines a color as three 6-bit intensity values for each of the color's primaries. An 18-bit value allows for 262,144 possible colors, compared to the EGA's 64. In either case, only 16 of the possible colors are displayable at any one time in the 16-color video modes.

Mode 13h (320x200x256-colors) is handled differently. A pixel in this mode is an 8-bit quantity that directly selects one of the 256 DAC registers. The pixel is displayed with the color defined by the DAC register.

One other difference between the EGA and VGA adapters is worth mentioning. While the VGA's palette and DAC registers can be both read and written, the EGA's palette registers are write only. This means that on an EGA you must initialize the palette to a known state if you are to be sure about the current palette's colors. The EGA's meager capabilities and many limitations are two good reasons to avoid it if possible.

Given this background, the procedure for setting the palette color for a given pixel value on the VGA in mode 12h is as follows:

1. Get a palette register value using the pixel value as an index to select the palette register.
2. Set the contents of a DAC register using the palette register value as an index to select the DAC register.

Mode 13h is much more straightforward:

1. Set the contents of a DAC register using the pixel value as an index to select the DAC register.

These same methods work with all extended VGA adapters and display modes. A 16-color palette is set as described for mode 12h, and a 256-color palette is set as described for mode 13h. Listing 5.3 presents assembler code to read and write the VGA palette and DAC registers.

Listing 5.3 VGAPAL.ASM

```
;---------------------------------------------------------
;
;   File:    VGAPAL.ASM
;
;   Desc:    Functions for reading and writing the VGA'a
;            adapter's palette and DAC registers
;
;---------------------------------------------------------

.model large

; argument addressing - 16-bit far calls
```

Listing 5.3   VGAPAL.ASM (continued)

```
arg1    equ    [bp+6]
arg2    equ    [bp+8]
arg3    equ    [bp+10]
arg4    equ    [bp+12]


public _get_vga_pal_reg, _set_vga_pal_reg
public _get_vga_dac_reg, _set_vga_dac_reg

.code

;-------------------------------------------------------
;  Desc:  Get the value of a VGA palette register
;  Use:   int get_vga_pal_reg( int reg_no );
;-------------------------------------------------------

_get_vga_pal_reg proc far
    push bp
    mov  bp, sp
    push bx
    mov  bl, arg1        ; register number
    mov  ax, 1007h       ; func 10h, subfunc 07h
    int  10h
    xor  ax, ax
    mov  al, bh          ; ax = register value
    pop  bx
    pop  bp
    ret
_get_vga_pal_reg endp

;-------------------------------------------------------
;  Desc:  Set the value of a VGA palette register
;  Use:   void set_vga_pal_reg( int reg_no, int reg_val );
;-------------------------------------------------------

_set_vga_pal_reg proc far
    push bp
    mov  bp, sp
    push bx
    mov  ax, 1000h       ; func 10h subfunc 00h
    mov  bl, arg1        ; bl = register number
    mov  bh, arg2        ; bh = register value
    int  10h
    pop  bx
    pop  bp
    ret
_set_vga_pal_reg endp
```

Listing 5.3   VGAPAL.ASM (continued)

```
;----------------------------------------------------------
;  Desc:  Get the value of a VGA DAC register
;  Use:   long get_vga_dac_reg( int reg_no );
;----------------------------------------------------------

_get_vga_dac_reg proc far
    push bp
    mov  bp, sp
    push bx
    push cx
    mov  ax, 1015h      ; func 10h subfunc 15h
    mov  bx, arg1       ; bl = register number
    int  10h
    xor  dl, dl
    xchg dl, dh
    mov  ax, cx         ; DX:AX = xRGB
    pop  cx
    pop  bx
    pop  bp
    ret
_get_vga_dac_reg endp


;----------------------------------------------------------
;  Desc:  Set the value of a VGA DAC register
;  Use:   void set_vga_dac_reg( int reg_no,
;                               int r, int g, int b );
;----------------------------------------------------------

_set_vga_dac_reg proc far
    push bp
    mov  bp, sp
    push bx
    push cx
    mov  ax, 1010h      ; func 10h subfunc 10h
    mov  bx, arg1       ; register number
    mov  dh, arg2       ; red component
    mov  ch, arg3       ; green component
    mov  cl, arg4       ; blue component
    int  10h
    pop  cx
    pop  bx
    pop  bp
    ret
_set_vga_dac_reg endp

    end
```

Note that in Listing 5.3 all register numbers should be in the range 0 to 255, and all primary intensities should have values in the range 0 to 63. The `long` value returned by `get_vga_dac_reg` is formatted as `00000000 00RRRRRR 00GGGGGG 00BBBBBB`. The individual primary values can be extracted with appropriate shifts and masks, as in this example:

```
int red = (get_vga_dac_reg( n ) >> 16) & 0x3F;

int green = (get_vga_dac_reg( n ) >> 8) & 0x3F;

int blue = get_vga_dac_reg( n ) & 0x3F;
```

VGA Scan–Line Operations

As we have noted, few commercial graphics packages provide specific scan-line-oriented primitives, yet this is perhaps the best way to deal with bitmapped graphic formats. Without these primitives, two approaches are generally taken. One is to read and write images a pixel at a time; the other is to construct in-memory bitmap structures that can then be read or written using virtual bitmap functions. The first approach is unacceptably slow, and the second approach generally requires substantial amounts of memory, conventional or other.

In many cases there is no practical alternative to the second approach, and a virtual bitmap must be used. This is particularly true for an application that must implement image-editing or fast pan and zoom operations, because an entire copy of the image must be maintained off screen. Even in this case, however, scan-line operations are useful, because both bitmapped formats and virtual bitmap structures tend to be scan-line oriented.

In this section, techniques for reading and writing scan lines in VGA mode 12h and 13h are illustrated. These same processes will also be illustrated for mode 62h of ATI's series of extended VGA cards (640x480x256-colors) and mode 2Eh of the Tseng 4000 chip set. The same principles are generally applicable to other display types.

The most important difference among the four modes is how video memory is organized. This organization is illustrated in Figure 5.1. Of the four modes, only mode 13h can be handled in a completely straightforward fashion, because it is the only mode requiring 64K or less of video memory. The other modes require more than 64K, but note that mode 12h uses the complex hardware design of the VGA adapter to appear to the processor as only 38K. This is not possible with modes 62h and 2Eh. In these modes, individual 64K pages must be bank switched by the software into the processor's address space at segment 0A000h.

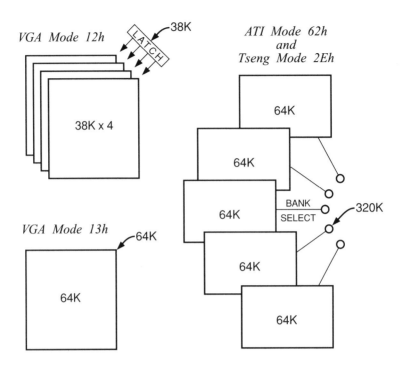

Figure 5.1   Video Memory Organization in Various Modes

Turning to the software design, we first need to define what we mean by a scan line. This is simply one full row of pixels in an image. What is not readily apparent from this definition, however, is how the row of pixels is physically or conceptually implemented. As we have seen, it could consist of single rows from each of the bit planes in a multiplane image, it could consist of one or more pixel values packed into each byte, or it could consist of single- or double-word values for each pixel.

Obviously, if an application is going to display any format from any source on any possible display, then there are a lot of possibilities to be accounted for. This points to the need for a single, intermediate scan-line representation. With this approach, the format-interface layer translates to and from this representation, while the display-interface layer reads and writes the representation from and to the display device.

Probably the best general-purpose definition of a scan line is an array of 32-bit pixel values. This can handle 15-bit and 24-bit display hardware in addition to normal VGA modes. If we ignore the 15-bit and 24-bit hardware, we can treat a scan line as an array of unsigned characters consisting of 8-bit pixel values. Because it is simpler, we will use the latter definition here. Modifying this scanline definition to handle larger pixel values, if necessary, is easily accomplished. Keep in mind that limiting pixels to 8 bits does not prevent the display and manipulation of 24-bit imagery, only that such images must be approximated in the display sense. This involves the use of techniques presented in Chapters 1 and 2, and will be discussed further in Chapter 7.

Regardless of the pixel size, we require functions that take as input an (x,y) screen location in pixel coordinates, a pixel count, and a pixel array that will write the array to the display as a horizontal line starting at the specified location. In the following discussion, keep in mind that screen locations are measured from the upper left corner of the display, and that the very first pixel at that location has the coordinate position (0,0).

Listing 5.4 presents functions to read and write scan lines in VGA mode 12h, which is 640x480x16-colors. Of the four modes, this is actually the most complex to handle, because video memory is organized as four separate bit planes. Writing a pixel value is performed as a single operation that updates all four bit planes at once and uses read mode 1 and write mode 2 of the VGA adapter. Reading a pixel value, on the other hand, involves reading each bit plane in turn and accumulating the four separate bits into a single value. This uses read mode 0 and write mode 0 of the adapter.

For the purpose of determining the video address of a given pixel location in this mode, we treat the pixel size as 1 bit. Thus, each scan line is treated as 80 bytes in length (that is, 640/8), although a scan line's worth of pixel values requires 320 bytes of memory (that is, [640 pixels x 4 bits per pixel]/8). This is a result of the VGA adapter's parallel addressing of the four bit planes used in this mode.

One note on the performance of the code presented in Listing 5.4: although it is a tight assembler implementation it is nonetheless only moderately fast. This results from our design decision to treat scan lines as arrays of 8-bit pixels. The only way to get really fast performance out of mode 12h is to perform large updates of individual bit planes, which requires that pixel data in program memory be organized as bit planes as well.

Listing 5.4   VGA12.ASM

```
;------------------------------------------------------------
;
;   File:    VGA12.ASM
;
;   Desc:    Functions to read and write scan lines in
;            VGA mode 12h (640 x 480 x 16-colors)
;
;------------------------------------------------------------
```

Listing 5.4   VGA12.ASM (continued)

```
.model large

; argument addressing - 16-bit far calls

arg1    equ   [bp+6]
arg2    equ   [bp+8]
arg3    equ   [bp+10]
arg4    equ   [bp+12]
arg5    equ   [bp+14]

public _put_pixels_12, _get_pixels_12

.code

;----------------------------------------------------------
; Desc:   Compute video memory address and a pixel
;         bitmask from an (x,y) pixel coordinate
; In:     CX = X, BX = Y
; Out:    ES:DI = video address, BH = bitmask
;----------------------------------------------------------

pixel_addr proc near

        mov   ax, 0A000h
        mov   es, ax        ; es = video seg addr
        mov   ax, 80        ; bytes-per-row
        mul   bx            ; ax = Y * bytes-per-row
        mov   di, cx
        shr   di, 1
        shr   di, 1
        shr   di, 1         ; di = row byte offset
        add   di, ax        ; di = video offset
        and   cx, 07h       ; cx = X % 8
        mov   bh, 80h
        shr   bh, cl        ; bh = pixel bitmask
        ret

pixel_addr endp

;----------------------------------------------------------
; Desc:   Write scan line in VGA mode 12h
; Use:    void put_pixels_12( unsigned char *pixels,
;                             int npixels, int x, int y );
;----------------------------------------------------------

_put_pixels_12 proc far
        ; stack frame, save regs
        push bp
```

Listing 5.4   VGA12.ASM (continued)

```asm
        mov  bp, sp
        push ds
        push es
        push di
        push si

        ; setup memory addressing
        mov  si, arg2
        mov  ds, si
        mov  si, arg1      ; ds:si -> pixel array
        mov  bx, arg5      ; bx = Y
        mov  cx, arg4      ; cx = X
        call pixel_addr    ; es:di -> video buffer

        ; initialize VGA controller
        mov  dx, 03CEh     ; dx = addr reg port
        mov  ax, 0A05h     ; RM=1, WM=2
        out  dx, ax
        mov  ax, 0003h     ; rot/func select
        out  dx, ax
        mov  ax, 0007h     ; color select
        out  dx, ax

        ; other setup
        mov  cx, arg3      ; cx = pixel count
        mov  al, 8         ; al = bmask reg no
        mov  ah, bh        ; ah = bitmask

        ; loop
put_pixels_12_1:
        out  dx, ax        ; set bitmask reg
        mov  bh, ds:[si]   ; get pixel value
        and  es:[di], bh   ; set pixel
        inc  si            ; next pixel addr
        ror  ah, 1         ; next bitmask
        jnc  put_pixels_12_2
        inc  di            ; next video byte
put_pixels_12_2:
        loop put_pixels_12_1

        ; restore VGA controller
        mov  ax, 0FF08h
        out  dx, ax
        mov  ax, 0F07h
        out  dx, ax
        mov  ax, 0005h
        out  dx, ax
```

Listing 5.4   VGA12.ASM (continued)

```
        ; restore regs
        pop  si
        pop  di
        pop  es
        pop  ds
        pop  bp
        ret
_put_pixels_12 endp

;-------------------------------------------------------
; Desc:  Read scan line in VGA mode 12h
; Use:   void get_pixels_12( unsigned char *pixels,
;                            int npixels, int x, int y );
;-------------------------------------------------------

_get_pixels_12 proc far
        ; stack frame, save regs
        push bp
        mov  bp, sp
        push ds
        push es
        push di
        push si

        ; zero the pixel buffer
        mov  di, arg2
        mov  es, di
        mov  di, arg1     ; es:di -> pixel array
        mov  cx, arg3     ; cx = pixel count
        xor  al, al
        cld
        rep  stosb

        ; initialize VGA controller
        mov  dx, 03CEh    ; dx = addr reg port
        mov  ax, 0005h    ; RM=0, WM=0
        out  dx, ax

        ; bitplane number and mask
        mov  bh, 3
        mov  bl, 08h

        ; loop for each bitplane
    get_pixels_12_1:
      push bx
      push bx

        ; select bitplane
```

Listing 5.4   VGA12.ASM (continued)

```
        mov   dx, 03CEh      ; dx = addr reg port
        mov   al, 04h        ; al = map select reg
        mov   ah, bh
        out   dx, ax

        ; setup memory addressing
        mov   si, arg2
        mov   ds, si
        mov   si, arg1       ; ds:si -> pixel array
        mov   bx, arg5       ; bx = Y
        mov   cx, arg4       ; cx = X
        call  pixel_addr     ; es:di -> video buffer

        ; other setup
        mov   ah, bh         ; ah = cur pixel mask
        pop   bx             ; bl = plane mask
        mov   cx, arg3       ; cx = pixel count

        ; loop for each pixel
get_pixels_12_2:
        mov   bh, es:[di]    ; bh = plane latch
        and   bh, ah         ; isolate pixel bit
        jz    get_pixels_12_3
        or    ds:[si], bl
get_pixels_12_3:
        inc   si             ; next pixel addr
        ror   ah, 1          ; next bitmask
        jnc   get_pixels_12_4
        inc   di             ; next video byte
get_pixels_12_4:
        loop  get_pixels_12_2

        ; next bitplane
        pop   bx
        dec   bh
        ror   bl, 1
        jnc   get_pixels_12_1

        ; restore regs
        pop   si
        pop   di
        pop   es
        pop   ds
        pop   bp
        ret
_get_pixels_12 endp

    end
```

Listing 5.5 shows the scan-line functions for VGA mode 13h. This mode is 320x200 pixels in size and uses 8-bit pixels (256 colors). The rationale for its poor spatial resolution is that the entire video bitmap fits within a single 64K segment. From a programming perspective this is the easiest of the four modes to deal with. Once the mode has been set, no further interaction with the video hardware is necessary. Pixel reads and writes are accomplished by getting a byte from video memory or putting a byte into video memory. For addressing purposes, each scan line in this mode is 320 bytes in length.

Listing 5.5   VGA13.ASM

```
;--------------------------------------------------------
;
;  File:    VGA13.ASM
;
;  Desc:    Functions to read and write scan lines in
;           VGA mode 13h (320 x 200 x 256-colors)
;
;--------------------------------------------------------

.model large

; argument addressing - 16-bit far calls

arg1    equ    [bp+6]
arg2    equ    [bp+8]
arg3    equ    [bp+10]
arg4    equ    [bp+12]
arg5    equ    [bp+14]

public _put_pixels_13, _get_pixels_13

.code

;--------------------------------------------------------
;  Desc:  Write scan line in VGA mode 13h
;  Use:   void put_pixels_13( unsigned char *pixels
;                             int npixels, int x, int y );
;--------------------------------------------------------

_put_pixels_13 proc far
    ; stack frame, save regs
    push bp
    mov  bp, sp
    push ds
    push es
    push di
    push si
```

Listing 5.5 VGA13.ASM (continued)

```
        ; source address
        mov  si, arg2
        mov  ds, si
        mov  si, arg1      ; ds:si -> pixel array

        ; destination address
        mov  di, 0A000h
        mov  es, di
        mov  ax, 320
        mov  bx, arg5
        mul  bx
        mov  di, arg4
        add  di, ax        ; es:di ->video buffer

        ; do block pixel move
        mov  cx, arg3      ; cx = pixel count
        rep  movsb

        ; restore regs
        pop  si
        pop  di
        pop  es
        pop  ds
        pop  bp
        ret
_put_pixels_13 endp

;-----------------------------------------------------
; Desc:  Read scan line in VGA mode 13h
; Use:   void get_pixels_13( unsigned char *pixels
;                            int npixels, int x, int y );
;-----------------------------------------------------

_get_pixels_13 proc far
        ; stack frame, save regs
        push bp
        mov  bp, sp
        push ds
        push es
        push di
        push si

        ; source address
        mov  si, 0A000h
        mov  ds, si
        mov  ax, 320
        mov  bx, arg5
        mul  bx
```

Listing 5.5   VGA13.ASM (continued)

```
        mov   si, arg4
        add   si, ax        ; es:di ->video buffer

        ; destination address
        mov   di, arg2
        mov   es, di
        mov   di, arg1      ; ds:si -> pixel array

        ; do block pixel move
        mov   cx, arg3      ; cx = pixel count
        rep   movsb

        ; restore regs
        pop   si
        pop   di
        pop   es
        pop   ds
        pop   bp
        ret
_get_pixels_13 endp

end
```

Listing 5.6 shows the scan-line functions for mode 62h of ATI's series of extended VGA cards. This mode is 640x480 pixels in size with 8-bit pixels (256 colors). Note that it requires video-memory bank switching, because the video buffer is larger than 64K (307,200 bytes to be exact). Bank switching is relatively straightforward to implement, but does require a program to access the video hardware. The exact procedure varies from adapter to adapter, but the versions implemented here for ATI and later for Tseng-based hardware (Listing 5.7) are typical.

From the point of view of the processor, there is only 64K of video memory, which is accessed at physical addresses A000:000 to A000:FFFF. The 300K of memory required by mode 62h and actually present on the video card, is divided into five 64K pages. At any given time, one of these five pages, numbered 0 through 4, is accessible to the processor at segment address A000. Which page is currently accessible is determined by programming the video adapter.

The 480 scan lines of mode 62h, each 640 bytes in length, are ordered linearly, one after another, in the video card's on-board RAM. To access a pixel at a given location (x,y) it is necessary to determine in which page the pixel resides and what its offset is from the start of the page. These are computed as follows:

```
unsigned long nbytes;
unsigned short page_no, offset;
      :
nbytes = (((long) y) * 640) + x;
page_no = (unsigned short) (nbytes >> 16);
offset = (unsigned short) nbytes;
```

Note that these expressions, written for C, require long arithmetic to avoid overflows. The same computations implemented in assembly language are extraordinarily simple:

```
mov   dx, 0
mov   ax, 640
mov   bx, y
mul   bx
add   ax, y
adc   dx, 0
```

At the completion of these six instructions, the content of dx is the desired page number and the content of ax is the desired offset into the page.

Listing 5.6   ATI62.ASM

```
;------------------------------------------------------------
;
;  File:    ATI62.ASM
;
;  Desc:    Functions to read and write scan lines in
;           ATI mode 62h (640 x 480 x 256-colors)
;
;------------------------------------------------------------

.model large

; argument addressing - 16-bit far calls

arg1   equ   [bp+6]
arg2   equ   [bp+8]
arg3   equ   [bp+10]
arg4   equ   [bp+12]
arg5   equ   [bp+14]


; local variables

tmp1   equ   [bp-2]
ntmp   equ   2


public _put_pixels_62, _get_pixels_62
```

Listing 5.6   ATI62.ASM (continued)

```
        .code

;-----------------------------------------------------------
;  Desc:   Map extended video memory page
;  In:     CH = page number (0-4 for mode 62h)
;  Out:    nothing (all registers preserved)
;-----------------------------------------------------------

map_page proc near
        ; save regs
        push es
        push ax
        push bx
        push cx
        push dx

        ; disable interrupts
        cli

        ; get ATI extended reg port address
        mov   bx, 0C000h
        mov   es, bx
        mov   bx, 0010h
        mov   dx, es:[bx]

        ; map the page
        mov   al, 0B2h    ; page select
        out   dx, al
        inc   dl
        in    al, dx
        mov   ah, al
        and   ah, 0E1h    ; page mask
        shl   ch, 1
        or    ah, ch
        mov   al, 0B2h    ; page select
        dec   dl
        out   dx, ax

        ; enable interrupts
        sti

        ; restore regs
        pop   dx
        pop   cx
        pop   bx
        pop   ax
        pop   es
```

Listing 5.6 ATI62.ASM (continued)

```
        ret
map_page endp


;-----------------------------------------------------
;  Desc:   Compute page and offset of X,Y pixel coordinate
;  In:     BX = Y
;          CX = X
;  Out:    AX = Offset
;          CH = Page
;-----------------------------------------------------

pxl_addr proc near
        mov  ax, 640    ; bytes per row
        mul  bx
        add  ax, cx     ; ax = offset
        adc  dx, 0      ; dl = page
        xor  cx, cx
        xchg ch, dl     ; ch = page
        ret
pxl_addr endp


;-----------------------------------------------------
;  Desc:   Write scan line in ATI mode 62h
;  Use:    void put_pixels_62( unsigned char *pixels
;                              int npixels, int x, int y );
;-----------------------------------------------------

_put_pixels_62 proc
        ; stack frame, save regs
        push bp
        mov  bp, sp
        sub  sp, ntmp
        push ds
        push es
        push di
        push si

        ; get page/offset, map page
        mov  bx, arg5
        mov  cx, arg4
        call pxl_addr
        mov  tmp1, cx    ; save page
        call map_page

        ; memory addressing
        mov  si, arg2
        mov  ds, si
        mov  si, arg1    ; ds:si -> pixel array
```

Listing 5.6   ATI62.ASM (continued)

```
        mov   di, 0A000h
        mov   es, di
        mov   di, ax          ; es:di -> video buffer
        mov   cx, arg3        ; cx = pixel count

        ; does scan line cross page boundary?
        or    di, di          ; zero offset ?
        jz    put_pixels_62_1
        mov   ax, 0FFFFh
        sub   ax, di
        inc   ax              ; ax = space in page
        cmp   ax, cx          ; room for cx pixels?
        jae   put_pixels_62_1

        ; fill what's left of current page
        xchg  ax, cx          ; cx = cnt in cur page
        sub   ax, cx          ; ax = cnt in next page
        cld
        rep   movsb
        mov   cx, tmp1        ; ch = cur page
        inc   ch              ; ch = next page
        call  map_page
        xchg  cx, ax          ; cx = pixel count

    put_pixels_62_1:
        cld
        rep   movsb

        ; restore regs
        pop   si
        pop   di
        pop   es
        pop   ds
        add   sp, ntmp
        pop   bp
        ret
_put_pixels_62 endp


;------------------------------------------------------
; Desc:  Read scan line in ATI mode 62h
; Use:   void get_pixels_62( unsigned char *pixels
;                            int npixels, int x, int y );
;------------------------------------------------------

_get_pixels_62 proc
        ; stack frame, save regs
        push bp
        mov  bp, sp
```

Listing 5.6   ATI62.ASM (continued)

```
        sub  sp, ntmp
        push ds
        push es
        push di
        push si

        ; get page/offset, map page
        mov  bx, arg5
        mov  cx, arg4
        call pxl_addr
        mov  tmp1, cx      ; save page
        call map_page

        ; memory addressing
        mov  di, arg2
        mov  es, di
        mov  di, arg1      ; es:di -> pixel array
        mov  si, 0A000h
        mov  ds, si
        mov  si, ax        ; ds:si -> video buffer
        mov  cx, arg3      ; cx = pixel count

        ; does scan line cross page boundary?
        or   di, di        ; zero offset ?
        jz   get_pixels_62_1
        mov  ax, 0FFFFh
        sub  ax, di
        inc  ax            ; ax = space in page
        cmp  ax, cx        ; room for cx pixels?
        jae  get_pixels_62_1

        ; fill what's left of current page
        xchg ax, cx        ; cx = cnt in cur page
        sub  ax, cx        ; ax = cnt in next page
        cld
        rep  movsb
        mov  cx, tmp1      ; ch = cur page
        inc  ch            ; ch = next page
        call map_page
        xchg cx, ax        ; cx = pixel count

get_pixels_62_1:
  cld
  rep  movsb

        ; restore regs
        pop  si
        pop  di
```

Listing 5.6   ATI62.ASM (continued)

```
        pop   es
        pop   ds
        add   sp, ntmp
        pop   bp
        ret
_get_pixels_62 endp

end
```

Listing 5.7 shows the scan-line primitives implemented for mode 2Eh of the Tseng 4000 chip set, which is also 640x480 pixels in size with 8-bit pixels (256 colors). Note that these implementations are almost identical to those for ATI mode 62h. The only difference is in the code to map a video page.

Listing 5.7 TSE2E.ASM

```
;------------------------------------------------------
;
;
;   File:    TSE2E.ASM
;
;   Desc:    Functions to read and write scan lines in
;            mode 2Eh (640 x 480 x 256-colors) of the
;            Tseng ET4000 chip set
;
;
;------------------------------------------------------


.model large

; argument addressing - 16-bit far calls

arg1   equ   [bp+6]
arg2   equ   [bp+8]
arg3   equ   [bp+10]
arg4   equ   [bp+12]
arg5   equ   [bp+14]


; local variables

tmp1   equ   [bp-2]
ntmp   equ   2

public _put_pixels_2e, _get_pixels_2e

.code

;------------------------------------------------------
; Desc:  Map extended video memory page
```

Listing 5.7 TSE2E.ASM (continued)

```
;  In:    CH = page number (0-4 for mode 2Eh)
;  Out:   nothing (all registers preserved)
;-------------------------------------------------

map_page proc near
     push ax
     push dx
     ; set "key" for seg-select register access
     mov  dx, 03BFh
     mov  al, 3
     out  dx, al
     mov  dx, 03D8h
     mov  al, 0A0h
     out  dx, al
     ; select segment - bits 0..3 of AL specifies
     ; write seg, bits 4..7 specifies read seg.
     mov  al, ch
     shl  al, 1
     shl  al, 1
     shl  al, 1
     shl  al, 1
     or   al, ch
     mov  dx, 03CDh
     out  dx, al
     pop  dx
     pop  ax
     ret
map_page endp


;-------------------------------------------------
;  Desc:  Compute page and offset of X,Y pixel coordinate
;  In:    BX = Y
;         CX = X
;  Out:   AX = Offset
;         CH = Page
;-------------------------------------------------

pxl_addr proc near
     mov  ax, 640    ; bytes per row
     mul  bx
     add  ax, cx     ; ax = offset
     adc  dx, 0      ; dl = page
     xor  cx, cx
     xchg ch, dl     ; ch = page
     ret
pxl_addr endp
```

Listing 5.7 TSE2E.ASM (continued)

```
;------------------------------------------------------
;  Desc:   Write scan line in Tseng 4000 mode 2Eh
;  Use:    void put_pixels_2e( unsigned char *pixels
;                             int npixels, int x, int y );
;------------------------------------------------------

_put_pixels_2e proc
     ; stack frame, save regs
     push bp
     mov  bp, sp
     sub  sp, ntmp
     push ds
     push es
     push di
     push si

     ; get page/offset, map page
     mov  bx, arg5
     mov  cx, arg4
     call pxl_addr
     mov  tmp1, cx       ; save page
     call map_page

     ; memory addressing
     mov  si, arg2
     mov  ds, si
     mov  si, arg1       ; ds:si -> pixel array
     mov  di, 0A000h
     mov  es, di
     mov  di, ax         ; es:di -> video buffer
     mov  cx, arg3       ; cx = pixel count

     ; does scan line cross page boundary?
     or   di, di         ; zero offset ?
     jz   put_pixels_2e_1
     mov  ax, 0FFFFh
     sub  ax, di
     inc  ax             ; ax = space in page
     cmp  ax, cx         ; room for cx pixels?
     jae  put_pixels_2e_1

     ; fill what's left of current page
     xchg ax, cx         ; cx = cnt in cur page
     sub  ax, cx         ; ax = cnt in next page
     cld
     rep  movsb
     mov  cx, tmp1       ; ch = cur page
     inc  ch             ; ch = next page
```

Listing 5.7 TSE2E.ASM (continued)

```
        call map_page
        xchg cx, ax          ; cx = pixel count

    put_pixels_2e_1:
        cld
        rep   movsb

        ; restore regs
        pop  si
        pop  di
        pop  es
        pop  ds
        add  sp, ntmp
        pop  bp
        ret
_put_pixels_2e endp

;----------------------------------------------------------
;  Desc:  Read scan line in Tseng 4000 mode 2Eh
;  Use:   void get_pixels_2e( unsigned char *pixels
;                             int npixels, int x, int y );
;----------------------------------------------------------


_get_pixels_2e proc
        ; stack frame, save regs
        push bp
        mov  bp, sp
        sub  sp, ntmp
        push ds
        push es
        push di
        push si

        ; get page/offset, map page
        mov  bx, arg5
        mov  cx, arg4
        call pxl_addr
        mov  tmp1, cx        ; save page
        call map_page

        ; memory addressing
        mov  di, arg2
        mov  es, di
        mov  di, arg1        ; es:di -> pixel array
        mov  si, 0A000h
        mov  ds, si
        mov  si, ax          ; ds:si -> video buffer
        mov  cx, arg3        ; cx = pixel count
```

Listing 5.7 TSE2E.ASM (continued)

```
        ; does scan line cross page boundary?
        or   di, di        ; zero offset ?
        jz   get_pixels_2e_1
        mov  ax, 0FFFFh
        sub  ax, di
        inc  ax            ; ax = space in page
        cmp  ax, cx        ; room for cx pixels?
        jae  get_pixels_2e_1

        ; fill what's left of current page
        xchg ax, cx        ; cx = cnt in cur page
        sub  ax, cx        ; ax = cnt in next page
        cld
        rep  movsb
        mov  cx, tmp1      ; ch = cur page
        inc  ch            ; ch = next page
        call map_page
        xchg cx, ax        ; cx = pixel count

get_pixels_2e_1:
    cld
    rep    movsb

        ; restore regs
        pop  si
        pop  di
        pop  es
        pop  ds
        add  sp, ntmp
        pop  bp
        ret
_get_pixels_2e endp

end
```

The code for the four video modes we have just discussed was purposely written to be highly adapter and mode dependent, which makes the code easier to follow and understand. In a real application setting, you would probably want to modify these functions to make them as generic as possible, and also eliminate the high degree of redundancy that they exhibit. Changes you would want to make would be to make scan-line lengths a variable parameter and to invoke the video-page-mapping function by a function pointer.

With these changes, only three versions of each primitive would be required to cover almost all VGA-adapter/mode combinations. The only exceptions would be in handling the 1024x768x16-color modes of various adapters. This mode is problematic in that even a single bit plane requires more than 64K of memory. If video memory in this mode is organized the way it is in mode 12h, it would still require bank switching. Some adapters take this approach anyway; others abandon it in favor of packing two 4-bit pixel values into each video byte.

A C++ Video-Display Class Hierarchy

We have covered all the individual aspects of dealing with VGA displays. We now turn to the task of organizing and encapsulating all the individual pieces into a single class-hierarchy structure. What we are after is a single display class that supports video-mode detection and setting, palette reading and setting, and scan-line reading and writing on a variety of hardware designs. We further want to hide all environmental discrepancies within the class itself so that a user of the class does not need to be concerned with specific hardware or video-mode differences.

This is a reasonably tall order, so in order to keep the task manageable we will continue to confine the discussion to the four previously discussed VGA video-mode and hardware combinations. The design principles remain pretty much the same regardless of the size of our display domain.

There are two areas in particular that must be addressed: the various measures that define the adapter/mode environment and the set of methods used to make things actually happen. Each area can be handled separately, with its own class definition. Our display class can either be derived from these or contain an instance of each. To this end, we define two classes, `ModeMetric` and `ModeDriver`. Refer to Listing 5.8 for the definition of these two classes as well as the definition of the `VgaDisplay` class.

Listing 5.8   DISPLAY.HPP

```
//---------------------------------------------------------//
//                                                         //
//   File:      DISPLAY.HPP                                //
//                                                         //
//   Desc:      A video display class for handling the     //
//              display of bitmapped images on VGA         //
//              compatible hardware                        //
//                                                         //
//---------------------------------------------------------//

#ifndef _DISPLAY_HPP_
#define _DISPLAY_HPP_

#include "color.hpp"
#include "gffasm.h"
```

Listing 5.8   DISPLAY.HPP (continued)

```
//..............function pointer types

typedef void (*ScanLinePrim) ( unsigned char *,
                                int, int, int );

typedef void (*PalettePrim) ( rgb *, int );

//..............a display mode metric structure

struct ModeMetric
{
   int mode;        // mode for this metric set
   int nrows;       // display height in pixels
   int ncolumns;    // display width in pixels
   int nbits;       // pixel size in bits
   int nplanes;     // number of bit planes
   int ncolors;     // max simultaneous colors
   ModeMetric( )
   {
      mode = nrows = ncolumns = 0;
      nbits = nplanes = ncolors = 0;
   }
   ModeMetric( int m, int nr, int nc,
               int nb, int np, int ns )
   {
      mode = m;  nrows = nr;  ncolumns = nc;
      nbits = nb;  nplanes = np;  ncolors = ns;
   }
   ~ModeMetric( )
   {
   }
};

//..............a display mode driver structure

struct ModeDriver
{
   int mode;               // mode for this driver
   ScanLinePrim putln;     // write a scan line
   ScanLinePrim getln;     // read a scan line
   PalettePrim  putpl;     // set a palette
   PalettePrim  getpl;     // read the palette
   ModeDriver( )
   {
      mode = 0;
      putln = getln = 0;
      putpl = getpl = 0;
   }
```

Listing 5.8   DISPLAY.HPP (continued)

```cpp
    ModeDriver( int m,
                ScanLinePrim pl, ScanLinePrim gl,
                PalettePrim pp, PalettePrim gp )
    {
       mode = m;
       putln = pl;  getln = gl;
       putpl = pp;  getpl = gp;
    }
   ~ModeDriver( )
    {
    }
};

//.............the display class

class VgaDisplay
{
   public:
       int gmode;          // current graphics mode
       int pmode;          // previous mode
       ModeMetric metric;  // current mode's metrics
       ModeDriver driver;  // current mode's driver

       VgaDisplay( int mode=0x12 );
      ~VgaDisplay( );
       void putscanline( unsigned char *pxls, int npxls,
                     int x, int y )
       {
          (*driver.putln)( pxls, npxls, x, y );
       }
       void getscanline( unsigned char *pxls, int npxls,
                     int x, int y )
       {
          (*driver.getln)( pxls, npxls, x, y );
       }
       void putpalette( rgb * pal, int nc = 0 )
       {
          (*driver.putpl)( pal, nc );
       }
       void getpalette( rgb * pal, int nc = 0 )
       {
          (*driver.getpl)( pal, nc );
       }
};

#endif
```

Note that the driver class consists of a set of functions pointers. These are set based on the adapter and video mode being used, and are actually called by various methods of the VgaDisplay class. This design technique is commonly used in commercial graphics libraries, and is a good way to help mask environmental differences.

The class implementations are presented in Listing 5.9. Note that two static tables are employed, one consisting of an array of ModeMetric structures and the other an array of ModeDriver structures. Additional adapter support can be added simply by creating a new entry for each table. Indeed, this architecture can be extended to support non–VGA hardware without modification to the VgaDisplay class.

Listing 5.9 DISPLAY.CPP

```
//----------------------------------------------------------//
//                                                          //
//    File:      DISPLAY.CPP                                //
//                                                          //
//    Desc:      A video display class for handling the     //
//               display of bitmapped images on VGA         //
//               compatible hardware                        //
//                                                          //
//----------------------------------------------------------//

#include "display.hpp"

#define NMODES ( sizeof(supported_modes) / \
                 sizeof(ModeMetric) )

//..............a mode metrics table

static ModeMetric supported_modes[] =
{
    ModeMetric( 0x12, 480, 640, 1, 4, 16 ),
    ModeMetric( 0x13, 200, 320, 8, 1, 256 ),
    ModeMetric( 0x2e, 480, 640, 8, 1, 256 ),
    ModeMetric( 0x62, 480, 640, 8, 1, 256 )
};

static ModeMetric null_metric;

//..............select a metric from a mode

static ModeMetric& get_metric( int mode )
{
    for( int i=0; i<NMODES; i++ )
        if( mode == supported_modes[i].mode )
```

Listing 5.9   DISPLAY.CPP (continued)

```cpp
            return supported_modes[i];
    return null_metric;
}

//..............palette setting, 16 and 256 colors

static void set16( rgb * pal, int nclrs )
{
    int nc = (nclrs==0) ? 16 : nclrs;
    for( int i=0; i<nc; i++ )
    {
        rgb c = pal[i] >> 2;
        int r = get_vga_pal_reg( i );
        set_vga_dac_reg( r, c.red, c.grn, c.blu );
    }
}

static void set256( rgb * pal, int nclrs )
{
    int nc = (nclrs==0) ? 256 : nclrs;
    for( int i=0; i<nc; i++ )
    {
        rgb c = pal[i] >> 2;
        set_vga_dac_reg( i, c.red, c.grn, c.blu );
    }
}

//..............palette reading, 16 and 256 colors

static void get16( rgb * pal, int nclrs )
{
    int nc = (nclrs==0) ? 16 : nclrs;
    for( int i=0; i<nc; i++ )
    {
        int  r = get_vga_pal_reg( i );
        long c = get_vga_dac_reg( r );
        int blu = int( c & 0x3F );
        c >>= 8;
        int grn = int( c & 0x3F );
        c >>= 8;
        int red = int( c & 0x3F );
        pal[i] = rgb( red, grn, blu ) << 2;
    }
}

static void get256( rgb * pal, int nclrs )
{
```

Listing 5.9   DISPLAY.CPP (continued)

```cpp
    int nc = (nclrs==0) ? 256 : nclrs;
    for( int i=0; i<nc; i++ )
    {
        long c = get_vga_dac_reg( i );
        int blu = int( c & 0x3F );
        c >>= 8;
        int grn = int( c & 0x3F );
        c >>= 8;
        int red = int( c & 0x3F );
        pal[i] = rgb( red, grn, blu ) << 2;
    }
}

//..............a mode driver table

static ModeDriver drivers[] =
{
    ModeDriver( 0x12, put_pixels_12, get_pixels_12,
                set16, get16 ),
    ModeDriver( 0x13, put_pixels_13, get_pixels_13,
                set256, get256 ),
    ModeDriver( 0x2e, put_pixels_2e, get_pixels_2e,
                set256, get256 ),
    ModeDriver( 0x62, put_pixels_62, get_pixels_62,
                set256, get256 )
};

static ModeDriver null_driver;

//..............select a driver from a mode

static ModeDriver& get_driver( int mode )
{
    for( int i=0; i<NMODES; i++ )
        if( mode == drivers[i].mode )
            return drivers[i];
    return null_driver;
}

//..............the display class

VgaDisplay::VgaDisplay( int mode ) :
            metric( ), driver( )
{
    pmode = getvideomode();
    metric = get_metric( mode );
    driver = get_driver( mode );
    gmode = metric.mode;
```

Listing 5.9   DISPLAY.CPP (continued)

```
    if( gmode )
        setvideomode( gmode );
}

VgaDisplay::~VgaDisplay( )
{
    if( getvideomode() != pmode )
        setvideomode( pmode );
}
```

To illustrate the use of our display class we return to the El Greco sample image that was used earlier. Recall that we had two files, one containing the image's palette and the other containing the image's bitmap. Listing 5.10 presents a brief program that uses the `VgaDisplay` class to display the image using mode 2Eh of the Tseng 4000 chip set.

Listing 5.10   DISPTEST.CPP

```
//----------------------------------------------------------//
//                                                          //
//   File:      DISPTEST.CPP                                //
//                                                          //
//   Desc:      Program to illustrate the use of the        //
//              VgaDisplay class hierarchy                  //
//                                                          //
//----------------------------------------------------------//

#include "stdio.h"
#include "conio.h"

#include "display.hpp"

// test image metrics

#define  PALNAME     "EL-GRECO.PAL"
#define  IMGNAME     "EL-GRECO.IMG"
#define  IMGWIDTH    354
#define  IMGHEIGHT   446
#define  IMGCOLORS   256

rgb imgpalette[IMGCOLORS];

void read_palette( void )
{
    FILE *f = fopen( PALNAME, "rt" );
    for( int i=0; i<IMGCOLORS; i++ )
```

Listing 5.10   DISPTEST.CPP (continued)

```cpp
    {
        int r, g, b;
        fscanf( f, "%d %d %d", &r, &g, &b );
        imgpalette[i] = rgb( r, g, b );
    }
    fclose( f );
}

int main( void )
{
    // read the image's palette
    read_palette();

    // create display and set palette
    VgaDisplay Vga( 0x2E );
    Vga.putpalette( imgpalette, IMGCOLORS );

    // read and display the image
    unsigned char line[IMGWIDTH];
    FILE *fimg = fopen( IMGNAME, "rb" );
    for( int i=0; i<IMGHEIGHT; i++ )
    {
        fread( line, IMGWIDTH, 1, fimg );
        Vga.putscanline( line, IMGWIDTH, 150, 10+i );
    }
    fclose( fimg );

    // wait for a key and exit
    getch();
    return 0;
}
```

The techniques and functional designs that have been presented in this chapter will cover a surprisingly large array of video hardware. Keep in mind, however, that several important classes of non–VGA hardware were omitted from the discussion. These include IBM's XGA adapter, Texas Instrument's TIGA design, Display PostScript, and others. Handling all potentially important video hardware is a large, complex subject that exceeds the bounds of a single chapter.

We now move on, in the next chapter, to hardcopy devices, specifically printers, yet another voluminous subject.

6

Hardcopy Devices _____

The term **hardcopy devices** encompasses many types of hardware. In the realm of computers it generally means *printers*. In this chapter we take a look at printers and explore the problems associated with the printing of graphical imagery.

In many ways, the printer is the black sheep of the computer peripherals. It is by nature slow and mechanical, it does not attach to the PC's expansion bus the way other devices do, and its support by the operating system and the BIOS is minimal.

MS-DOS itself provides only two commands that are printer specific. The PRINT command performs background printing of text files, and in most cases it will not print a binary print file properly. The GRAPHICS command loads a TSR for printing the screen, and it does support graphics modes. However, it provides few options and supports only a very few, albeit important, printers.

The BIOS contains no actual support for printers. What it does provide is functionality for communication over serial and parallel ports, which is how a printer is normally connected to a system. However, the BIOS knows nothing of the actual device at the other side of the port, except what an 8-bit status register tells it.

This paucity of software support for printers extends into the third-party library market as well. There are few commercial offerings available to the developer that can be used to add printer support to an application.

Although printer software resources are generally meager, the same is not true of the hardware itself. The industry has produced more models of printers than just about any other kind of device. These printers encompass a bewildering variety of hardware technologies and software interfaces. If ever an industry niche needed a standards organization it was the printer industry of ten to fifteen years ago. What we have today can only be described as a "robust jungle."

Printer Characteristics

From a software standpoint it is important to categorize printers by their interface requirements. In most cases, the interface requirement is influenced to a great degree by a printer's actual hardware design, so one generally jibes with the other. Our concern here, however, is the software interface, and from this point of view, there are three important printer characteristics. These concern whether the printer is (1) a page or a line printer, (2) a multiline swath or a single-line swath printer, and (3) a color or a monochrome printer.

The HP LaserJet is a good example of a **page printer**, so categorized because the printer constructs an entire representation of the printed page in memory before it actually begins to process a physical sheet of paper. By contrast, all dot-matrix printers are **line printers**. They print each line of text or swath of image as they receive it progressing down the page a line at a time.

One important feature of line printers is that they do not support arbitrary page positioning of text and graphic elements. In other words, if you've just printed a line of text in the bottom half of a page you cannot back up and print a title at the top of the same page. Within the same line, however, you can back up and, for instance, print at the left margin after printing something near the right margin.

This line-oriented positioning capability is implemented using special control characters, including the carriage return (0Dh), the backspace character (08h), and the tab character (09h). Some dot-matrix printers implement a negative line-feed character, but its use is frequently constrained and does not support moving backward more than a line or two. In general, arbitrary vertical positioning is not possible with a dot-matrix printer.

The second printer characteristic, swath height, often correlates with page versus line categorization, but not always. A good place to begin understanding swath height is to look at the print-head mechanism of dot-matrix printers.

There are two common types of print heads on dot-matrix printers, a 9-pin head and a 24-pin head. The ninth pin of a 9-pin head is almost never used for graphics printing, so for all practical purposes it can be considered an 8-pin head. The pins are arranged vertically on the print head, and as the print head tracks horizontally across the page the pins trace a pattern of horizontal lines.

The print head does not have continuous horizontal movement, having instead a discrete number of horizontal positions. The pin spacing and horizontal position spacing are typically the same as, or close to, the pin diameter, so a traverse of the print head from left to right traces out a pattern of adjacent dot positions. This is illustrated graphically in Figure 6.1. The dot

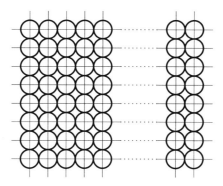

Figure 6.1   Dot Positions in an 8-pin Print-Head Swath

pattern produced by a print head traverse is referred to as a **swath**, and its height, in dots, is the **swath height**. Note that if all pins on the print head are used then the swath height is obviously the same as the print head height.

The importance of a printer's swath height becomes apparent when we see how graphical data are printed. In an 8-pin swath, each byte of data sent to the printer controls the activation of the 8 pins on the print head at one horizontal head position. Where a bit in a byte is set, the corresponding pin "fires," striking the printer's ribbon against the paper and producing a dot. A zero bit causes no action.

This arrangement results in a big software headache. Because of the way graphical images are stored in memory, each byte of a single-plane bilevel bitmap in memory represents eight horizontal pixel positions. However, the 8-pin dot-matrix printer interprets, and prints, each graphical byte as eight vertical dot positions. Thus, in order to print an image on a dot-matrix printer, each printer byte must be synthesized from a given bit position in eight different image bytes. This requirement not only complicates the printer driver's logic, it also slows it down. In actual practice, however, the speed penalty is not important; the mechanical nature of the print process is the usual limiting factor in terms of performance.

It may have occurred to you that a 1-pin print head would not require this data reformatting, which is indeed true. Conceptually, page printers like the LaserJet possess the equivalent of a 1-pin head, so each byte sent to these printers controls eight horizontal dot positions, just as a byte in memory does. For this reason page printers are normally easier to program.

The third printer characteristic, color versus monochrome, has obvious software implications. If a color image is to be printed on a monochrome printer, then color values must first be converted to luminance values, and some form of dithering, as discussed in Chapter 2, will likely be needed. The problem of printing a color image on a color printer is, paradoxically, potentially more complex. Because a color printer can potentially utilize any one of several different color models, there are more possibilities to be dealt with.

The typical color dot-matrix printer utilizes a four-color ribbon, which implements a CMYK model of sorts. It is not a true CMYK device, however, because the ribbon contains blue instead of cyan and red instead of magenta. By overprinting multiple ribbon colors at the same dot position the color dot-matrix printer can effectively produce any of nine different colors. These are listed in Table 6.1.

Table 6.1   Colors Producible with a Four-color Printer Ribbon

Color	Ribbon Color			
	Yellow	Red	Blue	Black
Yellow	X			
Red		X		
Blue			X	
Black				X
Orange	X	X		
Green	X		X	
Purple		X	X	
Brown	X	X	X	
White				

Note that combining black with any other ribbon color produces black, so the black portion of the ribbon is always used alone. Also note that the quality and consistency of the color brown produced in this fashion is seldom very good. One final important note concerns the order in which the ribbon colors are used. If possible, when more than one ribbon color is printed at the same position, the colors should be printed in the order yellow, red, blue, and then black. This ordering helps minimize the unavoidable effect of ribbon contamination that occurs with overprinting.

The easiest way to print an RGB-based image on a color dot-matrix printer is to treat the printer as a true CMYK device by converting each RGB color to its equivalent CMYK value. This color mapping produces reasonable, if not chromatically correct, results. Each CMYK primary is computed and printed on separate print-head passes over each swath. Each primary plane can be separately dithered using one of the techniques presented in Chapter 2. Keep in mind that some form of dithering is useful because the printer can produce only two primary intensities, zero and full.

A more involved technique, which generally produces more faithful color reproduction, uses a printer palette containing accurate RGB values for the actual colors producible by the printer's ribbon. Each pixel in an image to be printed is approximated by the closest printer RGB and its color error is diffused to surrounding pixels. This approach is computationally more expensive than the simpler method of treating the ribbon colors as a true CMYK palette. This factor is often not evident in practice, however, because, as we have noted, the mechanical action of the printer is the main performance limitation.

Other color-printer technologies involve the use of ink jets or wax transfer devices to deposit color on the printing medium. These printers typically use true CMY or CMYK primary colors. If the software interface to such a printer allows for control of the individual primaries then that printer can be treated much like a color dot-matrix printer as far as color production is concerned. On the other hand, many color printers possess firmware that performs intelligent translation of RGB or other color model values, so it is not always necessary to convert image RGBs to printer CMYKs. Another scheme used on some printers is to print an image from an array of pixel values, in much the same manner as the typical palette-based video display. With this type of printer, a palette is first specified by sending appropriate commands to the printer, and then an array of pixel values is sent to the printer. The printer's firmware uses the palette to translate pixel values into colors. This palette-based approach is used on the HP PaintJet. The printer's palette is specified as a set of NTSC-standardized RGB triples. Later models of the PaintJet family include support for other schemes as well.

Because of the range of color printer interfaces, a software printer-driver package must be able to handle an assortment of imaging models. This is on top of the many different hardware designs and different control schemes that have been devised for communication with printers. The combined possibilities make for a copious subject that cannot be fully covered here. We will, however, discuss the implementation of printer drivers for several popular printers, which can be taken as models for other drivers.

Communicating with Printers

Printers are normally connected to a system by a parallel port or, less commonly, by a serial port. Under MS-DOS both types of ports are treated as character devices, and are therefore opened in **cooked** or text mode. This mode interprets control characters. For instance, if a tab character (09h) is written to a parallel port, MS-DOS intercepts this and replaces it with some number of blanks. If a control-Z character (1Ah) is written to a port in cooked mode, MS-DOS interprets it to mean end of file, and will send no further output to the device until it is reopened.

This is a problem, obviously, in the printing of a graphical image, which can potentially contain all possible byte values. In this situation, we do not want a byte value that is the same as a control character value to be interpreted as such, but simply sent to the printer as is. To make this happen, the port's I/O must be changed to **raw** or binary mode.

Setting the mode of an open device is accomplished under MS-DOS using the IOCTL function (44h) of interrupt 21h. This service requires the handle of an open file or device. A program using stream I/O can obtain the handle of an open stream using the standard library function `fileno()`. Listing 6.1 shows a suitable implementation of a function to force binary mode on a character device.

Keep in mind that devices are always opened in cooked or text mode. Thus, the statement

```
FILE *fp = fopen( "LPT1", "wb" );
```

opens `LPT1` in text mode, even though the mode string "wb" specifies binary mode. This little-known fact has misled many developers into concluding that binary stream I/O is not possible to a parallel or serial port under MS-DOS.

Listing 6.1   SETBINIO.ASM

```
;-----------------------------------------------------------
;
;   File:     SETBINIO.ASM
;
;   Desc:     Function to force binary mode on a file
;             under MS-DOS
;
;-----------------------------------------------------------

.model large

; argument addressing - 16-bit far calls

arg1   equ   [bp+6]

public _setbinary

.code
```

Listing 6.1 SETBINIO.ASM (continued)

```
;----------------------------------------------------
;  Desc:   Force binary mode on file
;  Use:    void setbinary( int handle );
;  In:     Handle of an open file.
;----------------------------------------------------

_setbinary proc far
     push  bp
     mov   bp, sp
     push  bx

        ; get device info
     mov  bx, arg1
     xor  ax, ax
     xor  dx, dx
     mov  ah, 44h
     int  21h

        ; high bit set if char device
     and  dl, 80h
     jz   setbinary_1

        ; set binary mode
     mov  bx, arg1
     xor  dh, dh
     or   dl, 20h
     mov  ah, 44h
     mov  al, 01h
     int  21h

  setbinary_1:
     pop  bx
     pop  bp
     ret
_setbinary endp

end
```

Escape Sequences

The vast majority of printers are controlled from a program by using command strings known as **escape sequences**. An escape sequence is simply a string of characters; its first character is the so-called **escape character**, a byte with the value 27 (1Bh). The escape character is a signal to the printer that a command follows in the data stream.

The format of the commands themselves varies from printer to printer. In most cases, escape sequences are context dependent; in other words, the printer determines when it has read an entire sequence from the context. For example, on most 24-pin Epson printers, the escape sequence `Esc 3 n` sets the line size to $n/180$ths of an inch. Once the printer receives the escape character and the digit 3, it then interprets the next byte as indicating the line height in 1/180ths of an inch. If you send the string `Esc 3 Z e b r a` to the printer, the characters e b r a print as text on the page. The ASCII value of the character Z is 90, so `Esc 3 Z` sets the line size to 90/180ths or 1/2 inch.

A slightly different approach to escape-sequence syntax is employed by most Hewlett-Packard printers. The escape character has the same meaning, but the end of a sequence is explicitly signaled by the inclusion of a capital letter (more precisely, characters in the range 64 to 94 decimal). This scheme allows parameters to have varying lengths and also makes it possible to combine multiple sequences into a single command. For example, to tell a LaserJet to print five copies of the current page, you send the string `Esc & l 5 X` and to tell it to print 25 copies you send `Esc & l 2 5 X.` Because the X serves to terminate the sequence, the parameter can consist of a variable number of ASCII digits.

There are still other printer control schemes, but those we have illustrated here are typical. We will cover escape sequences in greater detail as we discuss individual printers.

Designing a Printer Driver

At this point we have covered enough information on printers to begin thinking about the design of a printer driver. A good place to start is to consider the tasks involved and then sketch a driver skeleton in pseudocode. Based on a knowledge of how printers work in general, such a skeleton might look like the following:

```
SEND_PRINT_PROLOG( )
For each image:
    SEND_IMAGE_PROLOG( )
    For each image swath:
        SEND_SWATH_PROLOG( )
        SEND_SWATH( )
        SEND_SWATH_EPILOG( )
    End For
    SEND_IMAGE_EPILOG( )
End For
SEND_PRINT_EPILOG( )
```

This general example does not indicate, for instance, what image metrics are needed at each step, or even if a step is necessary. In practice, it may turn out that a given printer does not require a given metric, or that a given step may be only a stub. But because we want to maintain the same overall structure regardless of the printer, and because we want the design to be easily extensible, we should make no assumptions here. All metrics, therefore, should be available at any given step, and all steps should be present.

The only real problem with our driver skeleton is that it is at odds with our preference for dealing with images on a scan-line basis. Scan-line treatment will occur only if a given printer operates with a one-line swath height. Therefore, we will modify the design and then deal with the internal changes as the need arises. The modified driver schematic is now as follows:

```
SEND_PRINT_PROLOG( )
For each image:
    SEND_IMAGE_PROLOG( )
    For each image scan line:
        PROCESS_SCAN_LINE( )
    End For
    SEND_IMAGE_EPILOG( )
End For
SEND_PRINT_EPILOG( )
```

A good overall design approach using C++ implements a generic driver design as an abstract base class from which we derive printer-specific driver classes. The source code for a suitable implementation is presented in Listings 6.2 and 6.3. Note that the `ImageDescriptor` structure is used to pass to the driver any image metrics it might need when performing image-prolog processing. This will vary from printer to printer, and in some cases it is possible that the structure will be unnecessary.

Listing 6.2   PRINTER.HPP

```
//----------------------------------------------------------//
//                                                          //
//    File:     PRINTER.HPP                                 //
//                                                          //
//    Desc:     Base class for printer driver classes       //
//                                                          //
//----------------------------------------------------------//

#ifndef _PRINTER_HPP_
#define _PRINTER_HPP_
```

Listing 6.2   PRINTER.HPP (continued)

```cpp
#include "stdio.h"

#include "color.hpp"

enum PrinterResolutions
{
   rLOW,
   rMEDIUM,
   rHIGH
};

enum PrinterConditions
{
   pOKAY,
   pNOMEMORY,
   pNOPORT,
   pIOERROR
};

enum PrinterFeatures
{
   fLOWRES = 1,
   fMEDRES = 2,
   fHIRES  = 4,
   fPOSN   = 8,
   fCOLOR  = 16
};

//.................Structure to hold image metrics

struct ImageDescriptor
{
   int width;      // width in pixels
   int height;     // height in pixels
   int depth;      // bits per pixel
   int xres;       // horz dots per inch
   int yres;       // vert dots per inch

   ImageDescriptor( )
   {
      width = height = depth = 0;
      xres = yres = 0;
   }
   ImageDescriptor( int w, int h, int d )
   {
      width = w;  height = h;  depth = d;
      xres = yres = 0;
   }
```

Listing 6.2   PRINTER.HPP (continued)

```cpp
    ImageDescriptor( int w, int h, int d, int x, int y )
    {
      width = w;  height = h;  depth = d;
      xres  = x;  yres = y;
    }
   ~ImageDescriptor( )
    {
    }
};

//.................A printer driver base class

class PrinterDriver
{
   protected:
      FILE   * fptr;      // printer stream
      int      feat;      // printer features
      int      res;       // resolution
      int      hdpi;      // horz resolution
      int      vdpi;      // vert resolution
      int      xorg;      // x origin in res units
      int      yorg;      // y origin in res units
      rgb    * pal;       // device palette
      int      nclrs;     // number of palette colors

   public:
      PrinterDriver( char *device );
     ~PrinterDriver( );
      int status( void );
      int features( void ) { return feat; }
      int xres( void )     { return hdpi; }
      int yres( void )     { return vdpi; }
      virtual rgb *devpalette( void ) = 0;
      virtual int  devcolors( void ) = 0;
      virtual void setorg( int xo, int yo );
      virtual void setres( int r );
      virtual int  prtseq( char *seq, int len=0 );
      virtual int  prttext( char *text, int len=0 );
      virtual int  prtline( char *text, int len=0 );
      virtual int  eject( void );
      virtual int  imgprolog( ImageDescriptor& imd ) = 0;
      virtual int  putscanline( unsigned char *pxls,
                                int npxls ) = 0;
      virtual int  imgepilog( void ) = 0;
};

#endif
```

Listing 6.3   PRINTER.CPP

```cpp
//-----------------------------------------------------//
//                                                     //
//   File:     PRINTER.CPP                             //
//                                                     //
//   Desc:     Base class for printer-driver classes   //
//                                                     //
//-----------------------------------------------------//

#include "string.h"

#include "printer.hpp"

extern "C"
{
   void setbinary( int );
}

//.................class PrinterDriver

PrinterDriver::PrinterDriver( char *device )
{
   fptr = fopen( device, "wb" );
   if( fptr ) setbinary( fileno(fptr) );
   hdpi = vdpi = 0;
   xorg = yorg = 0;
   feat = 0;
   pal = 0;
   res = 0;
   nclrs = 0;
}

PrinterDriver::~PrinterDriver( )
{
   if( fptr ) fclose( fptr );
}

int PrinterDriver::status( )
{
   if( fptr == 0 ) return pNOPORT;
   if( ferror(fptr) ) return pIOERROR;
   return pOKAY;
}

void PrinterDriver::setres( int r )
{
   res = r;
}
```

Listing 6.3 PRINTER.CPP (continued)

```cpp
void PrinterDriver::setorg( int xo, int yo )
{
    xorg = xo;
    yorg = yo;
}

int PrinterDriver::prtseq( char *seq, int len )
{
    // write escape character to printer
    fputc( 27, fptr );
    // len=0 implies use string length
    int n = (len < 1) ? strlen(seq) : len;
    fwrite( seq, n, 1, fptr );
    fflush( fptr );
    return status();
}

int PrinterDriver::prttext( char *text, int len )
{
    // len=0 implies use string length
    int n = (len < 1) ? strlen(text) : len;
    fwrite( text, n, 1, fptr );
    fflush( fptr );
    return status();
}

int PrinterDriver::prtline( char *text, int len )
{
    // len=0 implies use string length
    int n = (len < 1) ? strlen(text) : len;
    fwrite( text, n, 1, fptr );
    // send carriage-return line-feed
    fputc( 13, fptr );
    fputc( 10, fptr );
    fflush( fptr );
    return status();
}

int PrinterDriver::eject( void )
{
    // write formfeed char to printer
    fputc( 12, fptr );
    fflush( fptr );
    return status();
}
```

Implementing Printer Drivers

Having discussed issues related to the design of printer drivers, we now turn to their actual implementation. The remainder of this chapter is devoted to implementations for five specific classes of printers that represent a good cross-section of the printer market. The five printers are the HP LaserJet, the HP PaintJet, the Epson LQ Series, the Epson JX80, and a PostScript printer. The HP and Epson software interfaces are widely supported on other printers and the PostScript driver should work on any PostScript device, so these five drivers will actually work with a large portion of the printers in common use. For many other printers, one of these five drivers will work with minor modification. Sometimes the modification simply entails changing the format of escape sequences.

Until now, I have not mentioned that the scope of these printer drivers is limited to the printing of graphical imagery only. Text-related issues, such as font downloading or typeface selection, are not addressed. Keep in mind that these drivers also do not perform any form of image translation or other processing. They, in fact, do little more than encapsulate the process of sending a scan line to a printer while presenting an interface that is reasonably printer independent. This, as it turns out, is all that we require, as we shall see in the next chapter.

HP LaserJet

The Hewlett-Packard LaserJet is one of the most successful of all printer designs, and its success is well deserved. The printer is versatile and rugged, and its print quality is outstanding. One of its more important features is its extensibility through plug-in cartridges and personality modules. These can, for example, turn the LaserJet into a true PostScript printer.

In its native configuration, a program communicates with the LaserJet using PCL, Hewlett-Packard's printer command language. Many other laser printers emulate the LaserJet, so a PCL driver will provide support for quite a few printers. The current release level of PCL is PCL5, introduced with the LaserJet III, but the commands we utilize here are common to all versions of the standard. A print file containing PCL is arguably a graphics file "in the PCL format." However, PCL is not generally treated as a format, so it is not treated as such here.

The task of printing a bitmapped image on a LaserJet breaks down quite nicely into steps that follow our driver design. The specific tasks performed at each step are as follows:

1. PRINT_PROLOG. This corresponds with opening the printer. At this point we would want to reset the printer to initialize it to a known state.

2. IMAGE_PROLOG. Here we specify a graphics resolution, specify the page position at which to print the image on the page, and then signal the start of raster graphics mode. These are all done with escape sequences.

3. SWATH_PROLOG. Here we send to the printer an escape sequence that indicates the number of bytes of graphical data to follow. These are data for a single scan line of the image; they immediately follow the escape sequence in the data stream. This step is repeated for each line in the image.

4. SWATH_EPILOG. The LaserJet does not require any action at this point. Other printers typically require a carriage-return/line-feed pair at this point to reposition the print head for the next swath pass.

5. IMAGE_EPILOG. Here we send an escape sequence to signal the end of raster graphics mode. Additional images can be added to the page by repeating the steps from the image prolog.

6. PRINT_EPILOG. In many cases this is where you would force a page eject. However, this step coincides with closing the printer, so it is possible that a printer state might be restored here.

The driver implementation for the LaserJet is presented in Listings 6.4 and 6.5. Note in Listing 6.5 that, because the LaserJet is a monochrome printer, the printer's device palette consists of two entries only, one for black and one for white.

Listing 6.4   LASERJET.HPP

```
//------------------------------------------------------------//
//                                                            //
//    File:      LASERJET.HPP                                 //
//                                                            //
//    Desc:      Driver class for HP LaserJet and            //
//               compatible printers                          //
//                                                            //
//------------------------------------------------------------//

#ifndef _LASERJET_HPP_
#define _LASERJET_HPP_

#include "printer.hpp"

class LaserJet : public PrinterDriver
{
    public:
        LaserJet( char *device );
```

Listing 6.4   LASERJET.HPP (continued)

```
    ~LaserJet( );
     virtual void setres( int r );
     virtual rgb *devpalette( void );
     virtual int  devcolors( void );
     virtual int  imgprolog( ImageDescriptor& imd );
     virtual int  putscanline( unsigned char *pxls,
                                       int npxls );
     virtual int  imgepilog( void );
};


#endif
```

Listing 6.5   LASERJET.CPP

```
//----------------------------------------------------------//
//                                                          //
//    File:      LASERJET.CPP                               //
//                                                          //
//    Desc:      Driver class for HP LaserJet and           //
//               compatible printers                        //
//                                                          //
//----------------------------------------------------------//

#include "laserjet.hpp"

static rgb printerpal[] =
{
    rgb(   0,   0,   0 ),
    rgb( 255, 255, 255 )
};

static int nprinterpal = 2;

LaserJet::LaserJet( char *device ) : PrinterDriver( device )
{
    // send reset escape sequence
    if( fptr )
       prtseq( "E" );

    // set features
    feat = fLOWRES | fMEDRES | fHIRES | fPOSN;

    // set default parameters
    setres( rMEDIUM );
}
```

Listing 6.5   LASERJET.CPP (continued)

```cpp
LaserJet::~LaserJet( )
{
}

void LaserJet::setres( int r )
{
   switch( r )
   {
      case rLOW :
           res = r;  hdpi = vdpi = 75;    break;
      case rMEDIUM :
           res = r;  hdpi = vdpi = 150;   break;
      case rHIGH :
           res = r;  hdpi = vdpi = 300;   break;
   }
}

int LaserJet::devcolors( void )
{
   return nprinterpal;
}

rgb * LaserJet::devpalette( void )
{
   return printerpal;
}

int LaserJet::imgprolog( ImageDescriptor& imd )
{
   char buf[16];

   // set image position
   sprintf( buf, "*p%dx%dY", xorg, yorg );
   prtseq( buf );

   // set image resolution
   sprintf( buf, "*t%dR", hdpi );
   prtseq( buf );

   // enter raster graphics mode
   prtseq( "*r1A" );

   return status( );
}

int LaserJet::imgepilog( void )
{
   // exit raster graphics mode
```

Listing 6.5   LASERJET.CPP (continued)

```cpp
    prtseq( "*rB" );

    return status( );
}

int LaserJet::putscanline( unsigned char *pxls, int npxls )
{
    // send transfer-raster-data sequence
    int nbytes = (npxls + 7) / 8;
    char buf[16];
    sprintf( buf, "*b%dW", nbytes );
    prtseq( buf );

    // send the raster data
    unsigned char byte = 0;
    unsigned char mask = 0x80;
    for( int i=0; i<npxls; i++ )
    {
        if( pxls[i] == 0 )
            byte |= mask;
        if( (mask >>= 1) == 0 )
        {
            if( fputc( byte, fptr ) < 0 )
                return status( );
            byte = 0;
            mask = 0x80;
        }
    }
    if( mask != 0x80 )
        fputc( byte, fptr );

    return status( );

}
```

HP PaintJet

The PaintJet, another successful Hewlett-Packard design, is an ink-jet color printer. The print quality of ink jets in general is very good, especially compared with the output of the typical color dot-matrix printer. The PaintJet is an especially good quality printer.

There are several different PaintJet models; later models typically provide additional capabilities not found on previous models. The driver implementation provided here is written to the lowest common denominator and should work on all models of the PaintJet. A driver designed specifically for a later model, such as the PaintJet XL, can be simplified considerably by taking advantage of printer capabilities, but, obviously, would not work on earlier models. The PaintJet, like the LaserJet, is a PCL device, and is emulated by a number of printers from other manufacturers.

Listings 6.6 and 6.7 present the PaintJet driver implementation. The two palettes defined in Listing 6.7 probably deserve a bit of explanation. The RGB array named `printerpal` contains NTSC-standard color definitions, which the PaintJet is designed to use. The other array, `devicepal`, contains the same palette converted to the 0 to 255 range that we use throughout this book. It is the form of the palette used for dithering and other operations.

Listing 6.6   PAINTJET.HPP

```
//---------------------------------------------------------//
//                                                         //
//    File:      PAINTJET.HPP                              //
//                                                         //
//    Desc:      Driver class for HP PaintJet and          //
//               compatible printers                       //
//                                                         //
//---------------------------------------------------------//

#ifndef _PAINTJET_HPP_
#define _PAINTJET_HPP_

#include "printer.hpp"

class PaintJet : public PrinterDriver
{
    private:
        int  sendraster( unsigned char *pxls, int npxls,
                         int mask, int passch );

    public:
        PaintJet( char *device );
       ~PaintJet( );
        virtual void setres( int r );
        virtual rgb *devpalette( void );
        virtual int  devcolors( void );
        virtual int  imgprolog( ImageDescriptor& imd );
        virtual int  putscanline( unsigned char *pxls,
                                  int npxls );
        virtual int  imgepilog( void );
};

#endif
```

Listing 6.7   PAINTJET.CPP

```cpp
//------------------------------------------------------------//
//                                                            //
//   File:     PAINTJET.CPP                                   //
//                                                            //
//   Desc:     Driver class for HP PaintJet and              //
//             compatible printers                           //
//                                                            //
//------------------------------------------------------------//

#include "paintjet.hpp"

extern "C"
{
    int iscale( int, int, int );
}

// palette downloaded to printer
// uses NTSC primary color definitions

static rgb printerpal[] =
{
    rgb(  4,  4,  6 ),
    rgb(  4,  4, 85 ),
    rgb(  4, 88,  6 ),
    rgb(  4, 88, 85 ),
    rgb( 90,  4,  6 ),
    rgb( 90,  4, 85 ),
    rgb( 90, 88,  6 ),
    rgb( 90, 88, 85 )
};

// printer's palette scaled to 0..255
// used for actual dithering

static rgb devicepal[] =
{
    rgb(  10,  10,  15 ),
    rgb(  10,  10, 217 ),
    rgb(  10, 224,  15 ),
    rgb(  10, 224, 217 ),
    rgb( 230,  10,  15 ),
    rgb( 230,  10, 217 ),
    rgb( 230, 224,  15 ),
    rgb( 230, 224, 217 )
};
```

Listing 6.7   PAINTJET.CPP (continued)

```cpp
static int nprinterpal = sizeof(printerpal) / sizeof(rgb);

PaintJet::PaintJet( char *device ) : PrinterDriver( device )
{
   // send reset escape sequence
   if( fptr )
      prtseq( "E" );

   // set features
   feat = fHIRES | fLOWRES | fPOSN | fCOLOR;

   // set default parameters
   setres( rMEDIUM );
}

PaintJet::~PaintJet( )
{
}

void PaintJet::setres( int r )
{
   switch( r )
   {
      case rLOW :
            res = r;  hdpi = vdpi = 90;   break;

      case rMEDIUM :
      case rHIGH :
            res = r;  hdpi = vdpi = 180;  break;
   }
}

int PaintJet::devcolors( void )
{
   return nprinterpal;
}

rgb * PaintJet::devpalette( void )
{
   return devicepal;
}

int PaintJet::imgprolog( ImageDescriptor& imd )
{
   char buf[16];

   // specify 3 color planes
   prtseq( "*r3U" );
```

Listing 6.7   PAINTJET.CPP (continued)

```cpp
    // set printer's RGB palette
    for( int i=0; i<nprinterpal; i++ )
    {
        sprintf( buf, "*v%da%db%dc%dI",
                 printerpal[i].red,
                 printerpal[i].grn,
                 printerpal[i].blu,
                 i );
        prtseq( buf );
    }

    // set image position in decipoints
    int x = iscale( xorg, 720, hdpi );
    int y = iscale( yorg, 720, vdpi );
    sprintf( buf, "&a%dh%dV", x, y );
    prtseq( buf );

    // set image resolution
    sprintf( buf, "*t%dR", hdpi );
    prtseq( buf );

    // set image width
    sprintf( buf, "*r%dS", imd.width+xorg );
    prtseq( buf );

    // enter raster graphics mode
    prtseq( "*r1A" );

    return status( );
}

int PaintJet::imgepilog( void )
{
    // exit raster graphics mode
    prtseq( "*rB" );

    return status( );
}

int  PaintJet::sendraster( unsigned char *pxls, int npxls,
                           int mask, int passch )
{
    int nbytes = (npxls + 7) / 8;
    char buf[16];
    sprintf( buf, "*b%d%c", nbytes, passch );
    prtseq( buf );
```

Listing 6.7   PAINTJET.CPP (continued)

```cpp
      unsigned char byte = 0;
      unsigned char bit  = 0x80;
      for( int i=0; i<npxls; i++ )
      {
         if( pxls[i] & mask )
            byte |= bit;
         if( (bit >>= 1) == 0 )
         {
            if( fputc( byte, fptr ) < 0 )
               return status( );
            bit = 0x80;
            byte = 0;
         }
      }
      if( bit != 0x80 )
         fputc( byte, fptr );
      return status( );
}

int PaintJet::putscanline( unsigned char *pxls, int npxls )
{
   if( sendraster( pxls, npxls, 0x01, 'V' ) == pOKAY )
      if( sendraster( pxls, npxls, 0x02, 'V' ) == pOKAY )
         sendraster( pxls, npxls, 0x04, 'W' );

   return status( );
}
```

Epson 24-pin LQ Series

Epson printers are some of the most widely emulated of all printers. In the early days of the IBM PC, Epson printers represented a standard of sorts, in much the same way the Hercules video adapter did. Nowadays, the jungle of available printers has watered down their dominance of the market, but their interface remains important.

The LQ series is a collection of 24-pin printers with varying hardware features, but with much the same software interface from model to model. The graphics driver, presented here in Listings 6.8 and 6.9 should work on all models.

Listing 6.8   EPLQ24.HPP

```
//------------------------------------------------------//
//                                                      //
//    File:    EPLQ24.HPP                               //
//                                                      //
//    Desc:    Driver class for Epson 24-pin LQ and     //
//             compatible printers                      //
//                                                      //
//------------------------------------------------------//

#ifndef _EPLQ24_HPP_
#define _EPLQ24_HPP_

#include "printer.hpp"

class EpsonLQ24 : public PrinterDriver
{
    private :
        int    reschar;      // resolution character
        int    maxdots;      // max dots per line
        int    prtdots;      // printed dots per line
        long   rowmask;      // current row mask
        long  *swath;        // swath buffer
        void   sendswath( void );

    public:
        EpsonLQ24( char *device );
        ~EpsonLQ24( );
        virtual rgb *devpalette( void );
        virtual int  devcolors( void );
        virtual void setres( int r );
        virtual int  imgprolog( ImageDescriptor& imd );
        virtual int  putscanline( unsigned char *pxls,
                                  int npxls );
        virtual int  imgepilog( void );
};

#endif
```

Listing 6.9   EPLQ24.CPP

```
//------------------------------------------------------//
//                                                      //
//    File:    EPLQ24.CPP                               //
//                                                      //
//    Desc:    Driver class for Epson 24-pin LQ and     //
//             compatible printers                      //
//                                                      //
//------------------------------------------------------//
```

Listing 6.9   EPLQ24.CPP (continued)

```cpp
#include "stdlib.h"
#include "stdio.h"
#include "string.h"

#include "eplq24.hpp"

static rgb printerpal[] =
{
   rgb(   0,   0,   0 ),
   rgb( 255, 255, 255 )
};

static int nprinterpal = 2;

EpsonLQ24::EpsonLQ24( char *device ) : PrinterDriver( device )
{
   // send reset escape sequence
   if( fptr )
      prtseq( "@" );

   // set features
   feat = fLOWRES | fMEDRES | fHIRES;

   // other initialization
   swath = 0;
   rowmask = 0;

   // set default parameters
   setres( rMEDIUM );
}

EpsonLQ24::~EpsonLQ24( )
{
}

void EpsonLQ24::setres( int r )
{
   switch( r )
   {
      case rLOW :
            res = r;      reschar = 32;
            hdpi = 60;    vdpi = 180;
            maxdots = 480;
            break;
      case rMEDIUM :
            res = r;      reschar = 38;
            hdpi = 90;    vdpi = 180;
            maxdots = 720;
```

Listing 6.9   EPLQ24.CPP (continued)

```
                    break;
            case rHIGH :
                    res = r;       reschar = 39;
                    hdpi = 180;  vdpi = 180;
                    maxdots = 1440;
                    break;
        }

        // allocate swath buffer
        if( swath ) delete [] swath;
        swath = new long [maxdots];
    }

    int EpsonLQ24::devcolors( void )
    {
        return nprinterpal;
    }

    rgb * EpsonLQ24::devpalette( void )
    {
        return printerpal;
    }

    int EpsonLQ24::imgprolog( ImageDescriptor& imd )
    {
        if( swath == 0 ) return pNOMEMORY;

        // set 24/180 inch line size
        char buf[2];
        buf[0] = '3';
        buf[1] = 24;
        prtseq( buf, 2 );

        // clear swath buffer
        memset( swath, 0, maxdots*sizeof(long) );
        rowmask = 0x800000L;

        // set swath width
        prtdots = (imd.width < maxdots) ?
                    imd.width : maxdots;

        return status( );
    }

    int EpsonLQ24::imgepilog( void )
    {
        if( swath == 0 ) return pNOMEMORY;
```

Listing 6.9   EPLQ24.CPP (continued)

```cpp
        // set 30/180 inch line size
        char buf[2];
        buf[0] = '3';
        buf[1] = 30;
        prtseq( buf, 2 );

        // pending partial swath?
        if( rowmask != 0x800000L )
            sendswath();

        return status( );
    }

    void EpsonLQ24::sendswath( void )
    {
        // send swath prefix
        char buf[4];
        buf[0] = '*';
        buf[1] = reschar;
        buf[2] = prtdots & 0xFF;
        buf[3] = (prtdots>>8) & 0xFF;
        prtseq( buf, 4 );

        // send swath
        for( int i=0; i<prtdots; i++ )
        {
            char *p = (char *) & swath[i];
            if( fputc( p[2], fptr ) < 0 ) return;
            if( fputc( p[1], fptr ) < 0 ) return;
            if( fputc( p[0], fptr ) < 0 ) return;
        }

        // send carriage-return line-feed
        fputc( 13, fptr );
        fputc( 10, fptr );
    }

    int EpsonLQ24::putscanline( unsigned char *pxls, int npxls )
    {
        if( swath == 0 ) return pNOMEMORY;

        int n = (npxls < prtdots) ? npxls : prtdots;
        for( int i=0; i<n; i++ )
            if( pxls[i] == 0 )
                swath[i] |= rowmask;

        if( (rowmask >>= 1) == 0 )
        {
```

Listing 6.9   EPLQ24.CPP (continued)

```
        sendswath( );
        memset( swath, 0, maxdots*sizeof(long) );
        rowmask = 0x800000L;
    }

    return status( );
}
```

Epson JX80

The JX80 was the first important color dot-matrix printer on IBM systems and is emulated by virtually all color dot-matrix printers. Nowadays, an ink-jet printer is generally the best choice for an inexpensive color printer, but there are still enough color dot-matrix units around to warrant their support. The JX80 driver is presented in Listings 6.10 and 6.11.

The device palette provided for the JX80 contains approximations of the nine basic colors producible with its four-color ribbon. The most important aspect of this palette is the order in which the colors appear. They are ordered so that the index into the palette used to select a color also serves as a bit mask to indicate which ribbons are used to produce the color. Here are a few illustrations. Color 0 is white, and is produced by using no ribbon. Color 8 is black, and 8 expressed in binary is 1000. Bit 3 of this value being set to 1 indicates that the black ribbon is used. The color orange is produced by mixing red and yellow. Its index in the palette is 3, or 0011 in binary. Bits 0 and 1 indicate yellow and red respectively.

Listing 6.10   EPJX80.HPP

```
//---------------------------------------------------------//
//                                                         //
//    File:      EPJX80.HPP                                //
//                                                         //
//    Desc:      Driver class for Epson JX-80 and          //
//               compatible printers                       //
//                                                         //
//---------------------------------------------------------//

#ifndef _EPJX80_HPP_
#define _EPJX80_HPP_

#include "printer.hpp"

class EpsonJX80 : public PrinterDriver
{
```

Listing 6.10   EPJX80.HPP (continued)

```cpp
    private:
        int reschar;           // resolution character
        int maxdots;           // max dots per line
        int prtdots;           // printed dots per line
        int rowmask;           // current row mask
        unsigned char *Yel;    // swath pointers
        unsigned char *Red;
        unsigned char *Blu;
        unsigned char *Blk;
        void sendswath( void );

    public:
        EpsonJX80( char *device );
        ~EpsonJX80( );
        virtual rgb *devpalette( void );
        virtual int  devcolors( void );
        virtual void setres( int r );
        virtual int  imgprolog( ImageDescriptor& imd );
        virtual int  putscanline( unsigned char *pxls,
                                  int npxls );
        virtual int  imgepilog( void );
};

#endif
```

Listing 6.11   EPJX80.CPP

```cpp
//----------------------------------------------------------//
//                                                          //
//    File:     EPJX80.CPP                                  //
//                                                          //
//    Desc:     Driver class for Epson JX-80 color dot      //
//              matrix and compatible printers              //
//                                                          //
//----------------------------------------------------------//

#include "stdlib.h"
#include "stdio.h"
#include "string.h"

#include "epjx80.hpp"

// Ribbon color RGBs based upon standardized NTSC RGB
// color definitions.  An index into this palette can
// be used as a mask for determining which ribbon(s)
// are required to produce the color.  The lower 4 bits
// of the index are interpreted as follows:
```

Listing 6.11   EPJX80.CPP (continued)

```
//          3     2     1     0
//        Black  Blue  Red  Yellow

static rgb printerpal[] =
{
   rgb( 255, 255, 255 ),   // white
   rgb( 252, 240,  23 ),   // yellow
   rgb( 145,  12,  26 ),   // red
   rgb( 202, 112,  23 ),   // orange
   rgb(   0,   0,  74 ),   // blue
   rgb(   0,  67,  52 ),   // green
   rgb(  24,   6,  58 ),   // violet
   rgb(  24,  12,  13 ),   // brown
   rgb(   0,   0,   0 )    // black
};

static int nprinterpal =  sizeof(printerpal) / sizeof(rgb);

EpsonJX80::EpsonJX80( char *device ) : PrinterDriver( device )
{
   // send reset escape sequence
   if( fptr )
      prtseq( "@" );

   // set features
   feat = fLOWRES | fMEDRES | fHIRES | fCOLOR;

   // other initialization
   rowmask = 0x80;
   Yel = Red = Blu = Blk = 0;

   // set default parameters
   setres( rMEDIUM );
}

EpsonJX80::~EpsonJX80( )
{
   if( Yel )
      delete [] Yel;
}

int EpsonJX80::devcolors( void )
{
   return nprinterpal;
}

rgb * EpsonJX80::devpalette( void )
{
```

Listing 6.11   EPJX80.CPP (continued)

```cpp
    return printerpal;
}

void EpsonJX80::setres( int r )
{
    switch( r )
    {
        case rLOW :
            res = r;        reschar = 'K';
            hdpi = 60;    vdpi = 72;
            maxdots = 480;
            break;
        case rMEDIUM :
            res = r;        reschar = 'L';
            hdpi = 120;   vdpi = 72;
            maxdots = 960;
            break;
        case rHIGH :
            res = r;        reschar = 'Z';
            hdpi = 240;   vdpi = 72;
            maxdots = 1920;
            break;
    }

    // allocate swath buffers
    if( Yel )
    {
        delete [] Yel;
        Yel = Red = Blu = Blk = 0;
    }
    Yel = new unsigned char [maxdots * 4];
    if( Yel )
    {
        Red = Yel + maxdots;
        Blu = Red + maxdots;
        Blk = Blu + maxdots;
    }
}

void EpsonJX80::sendswath( void )
{
    char buf[4];
    buf[0] = reschar;
    buf[1] = prtdots & 0xFF;
    buf[2] = (prtdots>>8) & 0xFF;

    // yellow pass
    prtseq( "r\x04", 2 );
```

Listing 6.11   EPJX80.CPP (continued)

```cpp
      prtseq( buf, 3 );
      for( int i=0; i<prtdots; i++ )
         if( fputc( Yel[i], fptr ) < 0 )
            return;
      fputc( 13, fptr );

      // red pass
      prtseq( "r\x01", 2 );
      prtseq( buf, 3 );
      for( i=0; i<prtdots; i++ )
         if( fputc( Red[i], fptr ) < 0 )
            return;
      fputc( 13, fptr );

      // blue pass
      prtseq( "r\x02", 2 );
      prtseq( buf, 3 );
      for( i=0; i<prtdots; i++ )
         if( fputc( Blu[i], fptr ) < 0 )
            return;
      fputc( 13, fptr );

      // black pass
      prtseq( "r\x00", 2 );
      prtseq( buf, 3 );
      for( i=0; i<prtdots; i++ )
         if( fputc( Blk[i], fptr ) < 0 )
            return;
      fputc( 13, fptr );

      fputc( 10, fptr );
   }

   int EpsonJX80::imgprolog( ImageDescriptor& imd )
   {
      if( Yel == 0 ) return pNOMEMORY;

      // set graphics line spacing
      prtseq( "A\x08", 2 );

      // clear swath buffer
      memset( Yel, 0, maxdots*4 );
      rowmask = 0x80;

      // set swath width
      prtdots = (imd.width < maxdots) ?
                  imd.width : maxdots;
```

Listing 6.11   EPJX80.CPP (continued)

```cpp
        return status( );
    }

    int EpsonJX80::imgepilog( void )
    {
        if( Yel == 0 ) return pNOMEMORY;

        // partial swath pending?
        if( rowmask != 0x80 )
            sendswath( );

        // set text line spacing
        prtseq( "2" );

        return status( );
    }

    int EpsonJX80::putscanline( unsigned char *pxls, int npxls )
    {
        if( Yel == 0 ) return pNOMEMORY;

        int n = (npxls < prtdots) ? npxls : prtdots;
        for( int i=0; i<n; i++ )
        {
            if( pxls[i] & 1 ) Yel[i] |= rowmask;
            if( pxls[i] & 2 ) Red[i] |= rowmask;
            if( pxls[i] & 4 ) Blu[i] |= rowmask;
            if( pxls[i] & 8 ) Blk[i] |= rowmask;
        }

        if( (rowmask >>= 1) == 0 )
        {
            sendswath( );
            memset( Yel, 0, maxdots*4 );
            rowmask = 0x80;
        }

        return status( );
    }
```

PostScript Printers

Among printers, a PostScript printer is a rare bird—in the sense that PostScript is
a true language. What is sent to a PostScript printer is the source code to a
program rather than a formatted data stream. At the heart of every PostScript
printer is a PostScript language interpreter, which executes the programs sent to

it. Because PostScript is a page description language, the output of a PostScript program is typically a printed page.

The PostScript language is structured around stacks. The syntax will be familiar to anyone who has programmed with the Forth language or who has worked with any of Hewlett-Packard's programmable calculators. In a broad sense, a PostScript program contains two types of constructs: objects and operators. As objects are parsed from the source, they are pushed onto a stack. When an operator is encountered it is executed, which results in zero or more operator parameters being popped from the stack and zero or more operator results being pushed back onto the stack.

Here is a simple example:

```
100 150 add
```

In this example, the PostScript interpreter parses 100, a numeric object, and pushes it onto the stack. It next parses 150, another numeric object, which is also pushed onto the stack. It then parses add, which is an operator and is executed. The add operator pops two numeric objects from the stack, adds them together, and pushes the result back onto the stack. Following the execution of the add operator, the stack in this example contains a single numeric object, 250. Keep in mind that this example omits many details, merely indicating the flavor of the language in a general way.

PostScript programs deal with a device-independent graphics coordinate space. The interpreter is responsible for realizing this virtual space on a physical device, so in most cases a PostScript program is not concerned with the physical device being used. The default coordinate space is right-handed, with the origin of a page in its lower left corner and y coordinates increasing up the page. Note that this scheme is different from most other printers and video adapters, which are left-handed with the origin at the upper left and y coordinates increasing downward. (One of the tasks of our PostScript driver will be to mask this difference.) The default coordinate units are typographic points, of which there are 72 per inch. An 8-by-10-1/2-inch page area is 576 points wide by 756 points high.

Although the PostScript language contains dozens of drawing operators, we are interested in only one here, the *image operator*. This operator renders a gray-scale array over an x–y expanse; in other words, it prints monochrome bitmaps. It does not print an RGB-based color image. That requires use of the *colorimage operator*, which only exists in level 2 or later implementations of the language standard. Although many new PostScript printers contain level-2 interpreters, most existing PostScript printers are based on the level-1 standard and do not support the colorimage operator.

Here is the basic syntax for the PostScript image operator:

```
width height bits/sample matrix procedure image
```

The first five tokens are parameters that are pushed onto the stack prior to the image operator. The parameters are defined as follows:

Parameter	Description
width	Image width in pixels.
height	Image height in pixels.
bits/sample	Bits per pixel, typically 1 or 8.
matrix	A coordinate transform matrix that maps user coordinates to image coordinates. Images are treated as existing in their own coordinate space where each sample spans a unit square. The syntax of a PostScript transform matrix is

$$[a \quad b \quad c \quad d \quad t_x \quad t_y]$$

which represents the mathematical transform matrix

$$\begin{bmatrix} a & b & 0 \\ c & d & 0 \\ t_x & t_y & 1 \end{bmatrix}$$

It is common to map the image array into a unit square in user space with the y-sense reversed to allow for the fact that most bitmapped imagery is stored from the top row down. This corresponds to the following matrix in PostScript syntax:

```
[width 0 0 -height 0 height]
```

procedure	A PostScript procedure to be called to read the image data. The image data, formatted as hexadecimal characters, are commonly placed in the source file following the image operator. If this is done then the following procedure can be used:

```
{ currentfile str readhexstring pop }
```

where str is a string variable defined as follows:

```
/str width string def
```

The use of the image operator is perhaps best understood by illustration. Suppose we want to print on a PostScript printer the El Greco sample image we used earlier. Recall that the image is 354 pixels wide by 446 pixels high. Now suppose we want to size the image to 3 inches wide by 4 inches high and to locate the image 1 inch to the right and 1 inch above the lower left corner of the page. A sample PostScript program to do this is illustrated in Listing 6.12.

Listing 6.12   A Sample PostScript Program

```
%!PS-Adobe-2.0
%%Title: A Sample Program
%%Creator: Marv Luse

% image origin in points
/xorg 72 def
/yorg 72 def

% image size in points
/xsiz 216 def
/ysiz 288 def

% image dimensions
/width 354 def
/height 446 def
/depth 8 def

% a scan line buffer
/scanline width string def

% a procedure to read the image data
/readimg
{
        currentfile scanline readhexstring pop
}
def

% set image origin
xorg yorg translate

% set image size
xsiz ysiz scale

% render the image
width height depth
[ width 0 0 height neg 0 height ]
readimg
```

Listing 6.12   A Sample PostScript Program (continued)

```
image
1A5B1A5B238599FF00FF00FF00...
           :
554040556BFFAAFF00234599CE...

% render the page and eject
showpage
```

Some notes about the sample program in Listing 6.12 are in order.

1. Lines that begin with a percent sign are comments. The percent sign is PostScript's comment delimiter; it functions just like the `//` of C++ or the `;` of assembly language.

2. The first three lines of the program are for reserved comments, and have very specific meanings and uses. In general, any line that begins with `%%` is probably a reserved comment.

3. The very first line, the comment that begins with `%!`, should be included at the start of every PostScript program. Some printers look for it to validate that they are receiving a PostScript program.

4. Variables and procedures are declared before use, as they are in most other languages. A variable definition uses the syntax `/name` *definition* `def`. A procedure can be named using the syntax `/name` *{definition}* `def`.

With this thumbnail sketch of the PostScript language we now turn to the implementation of our PostScript driver. This is presented in Listings 6.13 and 6.14. One note about the implementation: it is wired to print bitmaps of only 1 bit per pixel, which effectively suppresses PostScript's halftone-rendering machinery. The reason for this choice is that it results in much faster printing and also preserves the dithering technique selected by the application. You could let the printer perform the dithering by setting the image depth to 8 and sending the printer the image pixel array converted to gray-scale values. Keep in mind, however, that, if this is done, the resulting print will probably look quite different from the same image printed on non–PostScript printers.

Listing 6.13   PSCRIPT.HPP

```
//----------------------------------------------------------//
//                                                          //
//    File:     PSCRIPT.HPP                                 //
//                                                          //
//    Desc:     Driver class for PostScript Level 1 and     //
//              compatible printers                         //
//                                                          //
//----------------------------------------------------------//

#ifndef _PSCRIPT_HPP_
#define _PSCRIPT_HPP_

#include "printer.hpp"

class PsPrinter : public PrinterDriver
{
   private:
      int vardef( char *name, int value );

   public:
      PsPrinter( char *device );
     ~PsPrinter( );
      virtual void setres( int r );
      virtual rgb *devpalette( void );
      virtual int  devcolors( void );
      virtual int  imgprolog( ImageDescriptor& imd );
      virtual int  putscanline( unsigned char *pxls,
                                int npxls );
      virtual int  imgepilog( void );
      virtual int  eject( void );
};

#endif
```

Listing 6.14   PSCRIPT.CPP

```
//----------------------------------------------------------//
//                                                          //
//    File:     PSCRIPT.CPP                                 //
//                                                          //
//    Desc:     Driver class for PostScript Level 1 and     //
//              compatible printers                         //
//                                                          //
//----------------------------------------------------------//
```

Listing 6.14   PSCRIPT.CPP (continued)

```cpp
#include "pscript.hpp"

extern "C"
{
    int iscale( int, int, int );
}

//..............device palette

static rgb printerpal[] =
{
    rgb(   0,   0,   0 ),
    rgb( 255, 255, 255 )
};

static int nprinterpal = 2;

//................PostScript code

static char *prologbody[] =
{
    "/scanline nbytes string def",
    "gsave",
    "xorg 756 yorg sub ysiz sub translate",
    "xsiz ysiz scale",
    "width height depth",
    "[ width 0 0 height neg 0 height ]",
    "{ currentfile scanline readhexstring pop }",
    "image"
};

static int nprologbody = sizeof(prologbody) / sizeof(char *);

static char *prologhdr[] =
{
    "%..........Begin Image.........."
};

static int nprologhdr = sizeof(prologhdr) / sizeof(char *);

static char *epiloghdr[] =
{
    "grestore",
    "%..........End Image.........."
};

static int nepiloghdr = sizeof(epiloghdr) / sizeof(char *);
```

Listing 6.14   PSCRIPT.CPP (continued)

```cpp
//.................class PsPrinter

PsPrinter::PsPrinter( char *device ) : PrinterDriver( device )
{
   // various initialization
   setres( rMEDIUM );

   // PostScript job header
   prtline( "\x04%!PS-Adobe-2.0" );
   prtline( "%%Title: Graphics File Programming in C++" );
   prtline( "%%Creator: Class PsPrinter" );
}

PsPrinter::~PsPrinter( )
{
   prtline( "\x04" );
}

void PsPrinter::setres( int r )
{
   switch( r )
   {
      case rLOW :
           res = r;  hdpi = vdpi = 75;    break;
      case rMEDIUM :
           res = r;  hdpi = vdpi = 150;   break;
      case rHIGH :
           res = r;  hdpi = vdpi = 300;   break;
   }
}

int PsPrinter::devcolors( void )
{
   return nprinterpal;
}

rgb * PsPrinter::devpalette( void )
{
   return printerpal;
}

int PsPrinter::eject( void )
{
   prtline( "showpage" );

   return status( );
}
```

Listing 6.14   PSCRIPT.CPP (continued)

```
int PsPrinter::vardef( char *name, int value )
{
    char buf[80];
    sprintf( buf, "/%s %d def", name, value );
    prtline( buf );
    return status( );
}

int PsPrinter::imgprolog( ImageDescriptor& imd )
{
    // print prolog header
    for( int i=0; i<nprologhdr; i++ )
        if( prtline( prologhdr[i] ) != pOKAY )
            return status( );

    // print variable definitions
    if( vardef( "width", imd.width )
        != pOKAY ) return status( );
    if( vardef( "height", imd.height )
        != pOKAY ) return status( );
    if( vardef( "depth", 1 )
        != pOKAY ) return status( );
    if( vardef( "nbytes", (imd.width+7)/8 )
        != pOKAY ) return status( );
    if( vardef( "xorg", iscale(xorg,72,hdpi) )
        != pOKAY ) return status( );
    if( vardef( "yorg", iscale(yorg,72,vdpi) )
        != pOKAY ) return status( );
    if( vardef( "xsiz", iscale(imd.width,72,hdpi) )
        != pOKAY ) return status( );
    if( vardef( "ysiz", iscale(imd.height,72,vdpi) )
        != pOKAY ) return status( );

    // print prolog body
    for( i=0; i<nprologbody; i++ )
        if( prtline( prologbody[i] ) != pOKAY )
            return status( );

    return status( );
}

int PsPrinter::imgepilog( void )
{
    // print epilog header
    for( int i=0; i<nepiloghdr; i++ )
        if( prtline( epiloghdr[i] ) != pOKAY )
            return status( );
```

Listing 6.14   PSCRIPT.CPP (continued)

```
        return status( );
    }

    int PsPrinter::putscanline( unsigned char *pxls, int npxls )
    {
        unsigned char byte = 0;
        unsigned char mask = 0x80;
        for( int i=0; i<npxls; i++ )
        {
            if( pxls[i] == 0 )
                byte |= mask;
            if( (mask >>= 1) == 0 )
            {
                byte ^= 255;
                fprintf( fptr, "%02X", byte );
                if( status( ) != pOKAY ) return status( );
                if( (i%320) == 0 ) fprintf( fptr, "\n" );
                byte = 0;
                mask = 0x80;
            }
        }

        if( mask != 0x80 )
        {
            byte ^= 255;
            fprintf( fptr, "%02X", byte );
        }
        fprintf( fptr, "\n" );

        return status( );

    }
```

A Driver Example

Now that we have our printer drivers, let's look at how one is actually used.
Listing 6.15 shows a program that uses the LaserJet driver to print the El Greco
sample image we have used already. Note in this case that, because the printer is
a monochrome printer, a monochrome dither class instance is used. The same
code used for a color printer would use a color dither class instance instead.

Listing 6.15   PDRVTEST.CPP

```cpp
//----------------------------------------------------------//
//                                                          //
//    File:      PDRVTEST.CPP                               //
//                                                          //
//    Desc:      Program to illustrate the use of the       //
//               PrinterDriver class hierarchy              //
//                                                          //
//----------------------------------------------------------//

#include "stdio.h"
#include "conio.h"

#include "dither.hpp"
#include "printer.hpp"
#include "eplq24.hpp"

// test image metrics

#define   PALNAME     "EL-GRECO.PAL"
#define   IMGNAME     "EL-GRECO.IMG"
#define   IMGWIDTH    354
#define   IMGHEIGHT   446
#define   IMGCOLORS   256
#define   IMGBITS     8

rgb imgpalette[IMGCOLORS];

void read_palette( void )
{
   FILE *f = fopen( PALNAME, "rt" );
   for( int i=0; i<IMGCOLORS; i++ )
   {
      int r, g, b;
      fscanf( f, "%d %d %d", &r, &g, &b );
      imgpalette[i] = rgb( r, g, b );
   }
   fclose( f );
}

int main( void )
{
   // read the image's palette
   read_palette();

   // create the printer
   PrinterDriver *prt = new EpsonLQ24( "LPT1" );
```

Listing 6.15 PDRVTEST.CPP (continued)

```cpp
    // create an image descriptor
    ImageDescriptor imd( IMGWIDTH, IMGHEIGHT, IMGBITS );

    // create a dither instance
    Dither *dit = new DiffusionDither( 127, IMGWIDTH );

    // read and print the image...

    unsigned char line[IMGWIDTH];
    FILE *fimg = fopen( IMGNAME, "rb" );

    printf( "printing..." );
    prt->imgprolog( imd );
    for( int i=0; i<IMGHEIGHT; i++ )
    {
        // get scanline
        fread( line, IMGWIDTH, 1, fimg );
        // convert to gray values
        for( int j=0; j<IMGWIDTH; j++ )
            line[j] = imgpalette[line[j]].graylevel();
        // dither the scan line
        dit->dither( line, IMGWIDTH );
        // and print it
        prt->putscanline( line, IMGWIDTH );
    }
    prt->imgprolog( imd );
    printf( "done\n" );
    prt->eject( );

    fclose( fimg );

    return 0;
}
```

This concludes our look at printers. Like the discussion of video display hardware, the discussion of printers has necessarily been basic. However, the principles are widely applicable. Many additional printers can be supported with the code presented here with only minor modifications. In many cases the only changes needed will be to the syntax of individual escape sequences. You can normally find this information in a printer's user manual.

In the next chapter we put the topics of the first six chapters together and discuss the practical implementations of image viewing and printing.

7

Image Display
and Printing

Each of the previous six chapters focused on a different aspect of the overall process of dealing with bitmapped graphics file imagery. In this chapter we will put these pieces together in context, as we discuss the processes of displaying and printing bitmapped images. These two endeavors, after all, represent the ultimate goal of most programs that deal with such images, and are the primary reasons for wanting to read and write graphics formats to begin with.

Most of the complexities that accompany this task result from the vast array of possibilities that must be dealt with in each area in order to obtain a reasonably complete application capability. Thus, if there were but one video display, one printer, one color model, one compression scheme, and one format, this book would, by now, be complete. Fortunately, this is not the case, for, although a world of ones would surely be an easy one, it would be a terribly boring one as well.

If you think about it, the real world of serious commercial applications makes some pretty peculiar demands. It may seem contradictory to print a 24-bit color image on an inexpensive, black and white dot-matrix printer, or to edit such an image in a 16-color video display mode. Yet both of these are standard procedures with most imaging applications. As it turns out, a reasonably versatile and reasonably device-independent imaging design provides these capabilities as a matter of course.

Design Concerns and Constraints

Carpenters have a maxim that say,s "Measure twice, cut once." This precautionary technique makes good sense, in that the net result of a single faulty measurement will be at least two measures and two cuts, possibly with a waste of materials. This philosophy, adapted for the software developer, can be stated in many appropriate ways, including, "Ponder twice, design once, or, Design twice, code once."

Despite our best attempts to follow this philosophy, however, there are still some boards that inevitably get wasted, and there will always be some software designs that eventually get tripped up by an unanticipated glitch. The processes we are dealing with here, mapping many image structures onto many displays or printers, is especially vulnerable to this type of design failure.

It is worthwhile to explore a concrete example of this. Much of the code in this book is structured around a scan-line model of images. We have thus developed classes of objects that read and decode individual scan lines, dither individual scan lines, and print individual scan lines. Suppose we now string several of these objects together to read an image and print it, and suppose we try it out on a Windows BMP file and an Epson dot-matrix printer.

The first time we try this combination we discover that the printed image is upside down! This is because the BMP format stores scan lines from the bottom up, while the printer prints scan lines from the top down. With this particular combination of format and printer there is no way to fashion a workaround—if the file is compressed there is no way it can be decoded backward, and there is no way to force a dot-matrix printer to print up the page from the bottom. It seems our only choices are to redesign the processing model or to resort to an ungainly detour such as decompressing the image to disk and then scanning the disk copy backward with a slew of seeks and reads.

The problem, of course, is that our scan-line primitives are too tightly bound to the objects they represent—`read and decode scan line` is still format dependent and `print scan line` is still printer dependent. When these two operations themselves are tightly bound, as they are in our example, the potential exists for a design mismatch.

The solution is relatively straightforward. What is needed is an object to interface between reading and printing in order to decouple them—a black box, so to speak, that will accept scan lines in any order and give them out in any order. For all intents and purposes, the black box represents an internal image format. As formats are read they are converted to this single internal representation. All output processing derives its input from the same single internal representation. As it turns out, this internal format is automatically realized by employing the image-storage object implemented in Chapter 4.

Without getting sidetracked in a discussion of design methodologies, we'll keep these useful concepts in mind as we tackle the implementations of general-purpose image display and printing. Our specification, if not exactly easy, is quite simply stated: Provide for displaying any supported image type on any supported display, and for printing any supported image type on any supported printer. We start with the implementation of the video display.

The Image-Display Module

A great deal of space has been devoted to the problem of rendering an image on a display when the image's color requirements and the display's color capabilities don't match up. As we have seen, this involves techniques such as color translation and modification and dithering to produce an optimum approximation of the true image.

One pitfall we have yet to talk about is what to do when an image's spatial requirements exceed the display's available space—that is, when the image is bigger than the display aperture. To accommodate this mismatch gracefully, we must employ **panning.** Panning allows a virtual-display aperture to be positioned anywhere on the image, and maps the virtual aperture one for one to the display's physical aperture.

The only real problem in supporting image panning is that screen updates must occur rapidly if we want to avoid frustrating the user. Unfortunately, because many of the operations required to render the image in the first place are already inherently slow, it is not always possible to satisfy this requirement fully.

In the interest of a thorough treatment of our subject, we will go ahead and implement image panning. Keep in mind, however, that you may not always like the result. We will adopt the following operational model:

1. Unshifted cursor key presses pan the virtual aperture one aperture's width or height in the corresponding direction.

2. Shifted cursor key presses pan the aperture one half this amount in the corresponding direction.

3. The Home and End keys reposition the view to the upper left and lower left regions of the image.

4. An Escape or Enter key press terminates the display process.

In addition, a display module should provide some support for controlling the image-rendering process and allowing intensity mapping on the image's palette. As implemented here, they are controlled by two option variables passed to the class constructor. The header file contains valid constant definitions for these options, the use of which should be obvious.

One final decision involves what to do about 24-bit color images. Up to this point, we have more or less constrained our designs by fashioning them around color palettes. Because a 24-bit image is not palette-based, we must abandon this methodology. To handle 24-bit color images, a second version of the `dither()` member function of the `ColorErrorDiffusion` class is provided, called `rgbdither()`. Unlike the `dither()` function, which operates on an array of pixel values, `rgbdither()` operates on an array of RGBs. These are constructed on the fly from each scan line of a 24-bit image.

Using this RGB-based dithering technique, we can reasonably render 24-bit images in both 16- and 256-color display modes. It is also possible to employ a full 256-color device palette in 256-color modes, but this increases computational requirements drastically for only a modest increase in chromatic fidelity. As a general rule, color dithering at display resolutions reaches a practical usefulness limit at about 16 colors. Employing more colors than this, while possible, is not worthwhile.

One potential problem with error diffusion on 24-bit imagery is that cumulative color errors can occasionally exceed the magnitude of a 16-bit signed integer. This shows up as small blotches of pure color in the dithered image. It is a rare occurrence, but if you want to avoid it, the error arrays used by the dithering functions must be changed to use 32-bit integers.

With this brief bit of groundwork we now move to the actual source code, presented in Listings 7.1 and 7.2. Note in the listings that a 24-bit image is assumed if the number of colors in the image's palette is set to zero. A brief demonstration program that uses the `ImageViewer` class to view our El Greco sample image is presented in Listing 7.3.

Listing 7.1   IMGVIEWR.HPP

```
//-----------------------------------------------------------//
//                                                           //
//    File:      IMGVIEWR.HPP                                //
//                                                           //
//    Desc:      Image viewer class                         //
//                                                           //
//-----------------------------------------------------------//

#ifndef _IMGVIEWR_HPP_
#define _IMGVIEWR_HPP_

#include "color.hpp"
#include "colormap.hpp"
#include "intenmap.hpp"
#include "dither.hpp"
```

Listing 7.1   IMGVIEWR.HPP (continued)

```
#include "display.hpp"
#include "imgstore.hpp"

#ifndef _IMAGE_OPTIONS_
#define _IMAGE_OPTIONS_

//................option values

#define   renderNONE      0x0000    // none specified
#define   renderMAP       0x0001    // palette mapping
#define   renderDITHER    0x0002    // dithering
#define   renderGRAY      0x0004    // force gray scale

#define   intensNONE      0x0000    // as-is
#define   intensICNT      0x0001    // increased contrast
#define   intensDCNT      0x0002    // decreased contrast
#define   intensIBRI      0x0004    // increased brightness
#define   intensDBRI      0x0008    // decreased brightness

#endif

//................an image coordinate structure

struct ImCoord
{
   int xo;     // screen origin
   int yo;
   int x1;     // image upper left
   int y1;
   int x2;     // image lower right
   int y2;
};

//................the image viewer class

class ImageViewer
{
   protected :
      // various stuff
      VgaDisplay     *disp;
      ImgStore       *image;
      Dither         *dit;
      // image and display palettes
      rgb            *imgpal;
      int             imgcnt;
      rgb            *devpal;
      int             devcnt;
      int            *clrmap;
```

Listing 7.1   IMGVIEWR.HPP (continued)

```
        // display stuff
        int             scanwid;
        int             scanhgt;
        unsigned char *scanbuf;
        // options and flags
        int             rendopt;
        int             intnopt;
        int             status;
        int             panning;

    private:
        void mv_horz( ImCoord& ic, int dx );
        void mv_vert( ImCoord& ic, int dy );
        void go_home( ImCoord& ic );
        void go_end( ImCoord& ic );
        void alter_palette( rgb *pal, int npal );
        void erase( void );
        void draw( ImCoord& ic );

    public :
        ImageViewer( VgaDisplay *vga, ImgStore *map,
                     rgb *clrs, int nclrs,
                     int ropt, int iopt );
        ~ImageViewer( );
         int view( void );
    };

    #endif
```

Listing 7.2   IMGVIEWR.CPP

```
    //----------------------------------------------------------//
    //                                                          //
    //   File:     IMGVIEWR.CPP                                 //
    //                                                          //
    //   Desc:     Image viewer class                          //
    //                                                          //
    //----------------------------------------------------------//

    #include "stdlib.h"
    #include "string.h"
    #include "conio.h"

    #include "imgviewr.hpp"

    //.................keyboard interface stuff
```

Listing 7.2   IMGVIEWR.CPP (continued)

```cpp
enum ViewerCommands
{
    cmdError,
    cmdEscape,
    cmdEnter,
    cmdPanHalf,
    cmdPanFull,
    cmdHome,
    cmdEnd,
};

static int keys[] =
{
    0x1B, 0x0D,                  // esc, enter
    0x47, 0x4F,                  // home, end
    0x34, 0x4B, 0x36, 0x4D,      // left/right arrow
    0x38, 0x48, 0x32, 0x50,      // up/down arrow
    0x39, 0x49, 0x33, 0x51       // up/down page
};

static int keycmds[] =
{
    cmdEscape,   cmdEnter,
    cmdHome,     cmdEnd,
    cmdPanHalf, cmdPanFull, cmdPanHalf, cmdPanFull,
    cmdPanHalf, cmdPanFull, cmdPanHalf, cmdPanFull,
    cmdPanHalf, cmdPanFull, cmdPanHalf, cmdPanFull
};

static int keydxs[] =
{
     0,  0,
    -1,  1,
    -1, -2,  1,  2,
     0,  0,  0,  0,
     0,  0,  0,  0
};

static int keydys[] =
{
     0,  0,
    -1,  1,
     0,  0,  0,  0,
    -1, -2,  1,  2,
    -1, -2,  1,  2
};
```

Listing 7.2   IMGVIEWR.CPP (continued)

```cpp
static int nkeys = sizeof(keys) / sizeof(int);

static int getkey( int& dx, int& dy )
{
   while( 1 )
   {
      int k = getch();
      if( k == 0 ) k = getch();

      for( int i=0; i<nkeys; i++ )
         if( k == keys[i] )
         {
            dx = keydxs[i];
            dy = keydys[i];
            return keycmds[i];
         }
   }
}

//.................the viewer class

ImageViewer::ImageViewer( VgaDisplay *vga, ImgStore *map,
                          rgb *clrs, int nclrs,
                          int ropt, int iopt )
{
   disp    = vga;
   image   = map;
   dit     = 0;
   imgpal  = 0;
   imgcnt  = 0;
   devpal  = 0;
   devcnt  = 0;
   clrmap  = 0;
   rendopt = ropt;
   intnopt = iopt;
   status  = 0;
   panning = 0;

   // scan line buffer
   scanwid = disp->metric.ncolumns;
   scanhgt = disp->metric.nrows;
   scanbuf = new unsigned char [scanwid];
   if( scanbuf == 0 )
   {
      status = 1;
      return;
   }
```

Listing 7.2   IMGVIEWR.CPP (continued)

```cpp
// allocate and initialize palettes
// if image is palette based
int i;
if( nclrs > 0 )
{
    imgpal = new rgb [nclrs];
    if( imgpal == 0 )
    {
        status = 1;
        return;
    }
    devpal = new rgb [nclrs];
    if( devpal == 0 )
    {
        status = 1;
        return;
    }
    clrmap = new int [nclrs];
    if( clrmap == 0 )
    {
        status = 1;
        return;
    }
    imgcnt = nclrs;
    for( i=0; i<imgcnt; i++ )
    {
        imgpal[i] = clrs[i];
        clrmap[i] = i;
    }

    // apply any requested palette modifications
    alter_palette( imgpal, imgcnt );

    // initialize device palette to image palette
    devcnt = imgcnt;
    for( i=0; i<imgcnt; i++ )
        devpal[i] = imgpal[i];
}

// nclrs == 0 implies a 24-bit color image,
// which has no palette
else
{
    devcnt = ColorDiffusionSize();
    devpal = new rgb [devcnt];
    if( devpal == 0 )
    {
        status = 1;
```

Listing 7.2   IMGVIEWR.CPP (continued)

```
            return;
      }
      imgpal = new rgb [scanwid];
      if( imgpal == 0 )
      {
          status = 1;
          return;
      }
   }

   // if the image must be approximated...
   if( (disp->metric.ncolors < imgcnt) || (imgcnt == 0) )
   {
       if( (ropt & renderDITHER) || (imgcnt == 0) )
       {
           dit = new ColorDiffusionDither( scanwid,
                             imgpal, imgcnt,
                             ColorDiffusionPalette(),
                             ColorDiffusionSize() );
           if( dit == 0 )
           {
               status = 1;
               return;
           }
           devcnt = ColorDiffusionSize();
           for( i=0; i<devcnt; i++ )
               devpal[i] = ColorDiffusionPalette()[i];
       }
       else
       {
           devcnt = disp->metric.ncolors;
           reduce_palette( devpal, imgcnt, devcnt );
           color_map( imgpal, imgcnt, devpal, devcnt,
                     clrmap, 2 );
       }
   }

   // set the device palette
   disp->putpalette( devpal, devcnt );

   // panning necessary?
   if( (image->width() > scanwid) ||
       (image->height() > scanhgt) )
       panning = 1;
}

ImageViewer::~ImageViewer( )
{
```

Listing 7.2   IMGVIEWR.CPP (continued)

```cpp
    if( scanbuf ) delete [] scanbuf;
    if( imgpal )  delete [] imgpal;
    if( devpal )  delete [] devpal;
    if( clrmap )  delete [] clrmap;
    if( dit )     delete    dit;
}

void ImageViewer::alter_palette( rgb *pal, int npal )
{
    // apply any intensity mapping
    if( intnopt & intensICNT )
        contrast_alter( pal, npal, iMORE );
    if( intnopt & intensDCNT )
        contrast_alter( pal, npal, iLESS );
    if( intnopt & intensIBRI )
        brightness_alter( pal, npal, iMORE );
    if( intnopt & intensDBRI )
        brightness_alter( pal, npal, iLESS );

    // force grayscale?
    if( (rendopt & renderGRAY) || (disp->metric.ncolors == 2) )
    {
        for( int i=0; i<npal; i++ )
        {
            int g = pal[i].graylevel();
            pal[i] = rgb( g, g, g );
        }
    }
}

void ImageViewer::go_home( ImCoord& ic )
{
    if( image->width() > scanwid )
    {
        ic.xo = 0;
        ic.x1 = 0;
        ic.x2 = scanwid - 1;
    }
    else
    {
        ic.xo = (scanwid - image->width()) / 2;
        ic.x1 = 0;
        ic.x2 = image->width() - 1;
    }

    if( image->height() > scanhgt )
    {
        ic.yo = 0;
```

Listing 7.2   IMGVIEWR.CPP (continued)

```cpp
            ic.y1 = 0;
            ic.y2 = scanhgt - 1;
      }
      else
      {
            ic.yo = (scanhgt - image->height()) / 2;
            ic.y1 = 0;
            ic.y2 = image->height() - 1;
      }
}

void ImageViewer::go_end( ImCoord& ic )
{
      if( image->width() > scanwid )
      {
            ic.xo = 0;
            ic.x2 = image->width() - 1;
            ic.x1 = ic.x2 - scanwid + 1;
      }
      else
      {
            ic.xo = (scanwid - image->width()) / 2;
            ic.x1 = 0;
            ic.x2 = image->width() - 1;
      }

      if( image->height() > scanhgt )
      {
            ic.yo = 0;
            ic.y2 = image->height() - 1;
            ic.y1 = ic.y2 - scanhgt + 1;
      }
      else
      {
            ic.yo = (scanhgt - image->height()) / 2;
            ic.y1 = 0;
            ic.y2 = image->height() - 1;
      }
}

void ImageViewer::mv_horz( ImCoord& ic, int dx )
{
      int ds = scanwid - ic.xo - 1;
      if( (dx > 0) && (ic.x2 < image->width()-1) )
      {
            ic.x1 += dx;
            if( ic.x1 > ic.x2 )
                  ic.x1 = ic.x2;
```

Listing 7.2   IMGVIEWR.CPP (continued)

```
            ic.x2 = ic.x1 + ds;
            if( ic.x2 >= image->width() )
                ic.x2 = image->width() - 1;
        }
        else if( (dx < 0) && (ic.x1 > 0) )
        {
            ic.x1 += dx;
            if( ic.x1 < 0 )
                ic.x1 = 0;
            ic.x2 = ic.x1 + ds;
            if( ic.x2 >= image->width() )
                ic.x2 = image->width() - 1;
        }
    }

    void ImageViewer::mv_vert( ImCoord& ic, int dy )
    {
        int ds = scanhgt - ic.yo - 1;
        if( (dy > 0) && (ic.y2 < image->height()-1) )
        {
            ic.y1 += dy;
            if( ic.y1 > ic.y2 )
                ic.y1 = ic.y2;
            ic.y2 = ic.y1 + ds;
            if( ic.y2 >= image->height() )
                ic.y2 = image->height() - 1;
        }
        else if( (dy < 0) && (ic.y1 > 0) )
        {
            ic.y1 += dy;
            if( ic.y1 < 0 )
                ic.y1 = 0;
            ic.y2 = ic.y1 + ds;
            if( ic.y2 >= image->height() )
                ic.y2 = image->height() - 1;
        }
    }

    void ImageViewer::erase( void )
    {
        memset( scanbuf, 0, scanwid );
        for( int i=0; i<scanhgt; i++ )
            disp->putscanline( scanbuf, scanwid, 0, i );
    }

    void ImageViewer::draw( ImCoord& ic )
    {
        int            n = ic.x2 - ic.x1 + 1;
```

Listing 7.2   IMGVIEWR.CPP (continued)

```cpp
      int           y = ic.yo;
      unsigned char *p = scanbuf;

      for( int i=ic.y1; i<=ic.y2; i++ )
      {
         if( dit )
         {
            if( imgcnt > 0 )
            {
               image->cpy( scanbuf, i, ic.x1, n );
               dit->dither( scanbuf, n );
            }
            else // 24-bit image
            {
               unsigned char *s;
               s = image->get( i ) + ic.x1*3;
               for( int j=0; j<n; j++ )
                  imgpal[j] = rgb( *s++, *s++, *s++ );
               alter_palette( imgpal, n );
               ColorDiffusionDither *d =
               (ColorDiffusionDither *) dit;
               d->rgbdither( scanbuf, imgpal, n );
            }
         }
         else if( imgcnt > devcnt )
         {
            image->cpy( scanbuf, i, ic.x1, n );
            for( int j=0; j<n; j++ )
               scanbuf[j] = clrmap[scanbuf[j]];
         }
         else
         {
            p = image->get( i ) + ic.x1;
         }
         disp->putscanline( p, n, ic.xo, y++ );
      }
   }

   int ImageViewer::view( void )
   {
      if( status != 0 ) return status;

      ImCoord ic;      // image/screen coords
      int     dx, dy;  // panning deltas

      erase();
      go_home( ic );
      draw( ic );
```

Listing 7.2   IMGVIEWR.CPP (continued)

```cpp
while( status == 0 )
{
    int k = getkey( dx, dy );

    if( (k==cmdEscape) || (k==cmdEnter) )
        status = k;

    else if( panning )
    {
        dx *= scanwid;  dx /= 2;
        dy *= scanhgt;  dy /= 2;

        // home
        if( (dx < 0) && (dy < 0) )
        {
            go_home( ic );
            erase();
            draw( ic );
        }

        // end
        else if( (dx > 0) && (dy > 0) )
        {
            go_end( ic );
            erase();
            draw( ic );
        }

        // pan left/right
        else if( ((dx > 0) && (ic.x2 < image->width()-1)) ||
                 ((dx < 0) && (ic.x1 > 0)) )
        {
            mv_horz( ic, dx );
            erase();
            draw( ic );
        }

        // pan left/right
        else if( ((dy > 0) && (ic.y2 < image->height()-1)) ||
                 ((dy < 0) && (ic.y1 > 0)) )
        {
            mv_vert( ic, dy );
            erase();
            draw( ic );
        }

        // anything else
        else
```

Listing 7.2   IMGVIEWR.CPP (continued)

```
            {
                // printf( "\x07" );
            }
        }
    }

    return status;
}
```

Listing 7.3   VIEWDEMO.CPP

```
//----------------------------------------------------------//
//                                                          //
//    File:     VIEWDEMO.CPP                                //
//                                                          //
//    Desc:     ImageViewer class demonstration program.    //
//                                                          //
//----------------------------------------------------------//

#include "stdio.h"
#include "conio.h"

#include "imgviewr.hpp"

char * palname    = "EL-GRECO.PAL";
char * imgname    = "EL-GRECO.IMG";
int    imgwidth   = 354;
int    imgheight  = 446;
int    imgcolors  = 256;
rgb    imgpalette[256];
CnvImgStore img( 446, 354, 8 );
unsigned char scanline[354];

// read the test image's palette

void read_palette( void )
{
    FILE *f = fopen( palname, "rt" );
    for( int i=0; i<imgcolors; i++ )
    {
        int r, g, b;
        fscanf( f, "%d %d %d", &r, &g, &b );
        imgpalette[i] = rgb( r, g, b );
    }
    fclose( f );
}
```

Listing 7.3   VIEWDEMO.CPP (continued)

```cpp
// read the test image into an ImgStore instance

void read_image( void )
{
    FILE *f = fopen( imgname, "rb" );
    for( int i=0; i<imgheight; i++ )
    {
        fread( scanline, imgwidth, 1, f );
        img.put( scanline, i );
    }
    fclose( f );
}


// perform the demo

int main( int argc, char *argv[] )
{
    // set defaults for display mode, rendering options,
    // and intensity mapping options — see IMGVIEWR.HPP.
    int mode = 0x12;
    int ropt = 0;
    int iopt = 0;

    // override defaults from the command line
    if( argc > 1 ) sscanf( argv[1], "%x", &mode );
    if( argc > 2 ) sscanf( argv[2], "%d", &ropt );
    if( argc > 3 ) sscanf( argv[3], "%d", &iopt );

    // load the image and palette
    printf( "Loading %s...", imgname );
    read_palette();
    read_image();
    printf( "done, press a key\n" );
    getch();

    // instantiate a display and view the image
    VgaDisplay  vga( mode );
    ImageViewer viewer( &vga, &img, imgpalette, imgcolors,
                        ropt, iopt );
    viewer.view();

    return 0;
}
```

The Image-Printing Module

For consistency, the general design of the printing module should be as close as possible to that of the display module. For an operational model it would be desirable to treat the modules as derived classes of the same base class. There is no compelling reason to do this, however, because we can obtain the desired result without using a class hierarchy, so we have not done so.

The constructor requirements for an ImagePrinter class are the same as those of the `ImageViewer class`, except that a printer instance replaces the display instance. We have also added as parameters the image's horizontal and vertical resolutions so that the image can be correctly scaled on the printer to reproduce its true size. Because there is no interaction between the user and the print process, the `print()` method's implementation is simpler than its display counterpart. The panning- and keyboard-handling code is not needed.

There are, however, two significant concerns related to bitmapped imagery printing: aspect ratio correction and image scaling. These two functions are related in the sense that correcting for aspect ratio differences between an image and a printer involves scaling the image. We take some time here to discuss image scaling.

Image Scaling

Arbitrary scaling of a bitmapped image is, in many ways, a messy process, because there is no physical representation of a fractional pixel. If we limit scaling to scaling factors that correspond to integral multiples of an image's original dimensions, the process is simple. However, because aspect-ratio correction can seldom be accommodated in a reasonable manner without using fractional scaling, the simple approach is generally not satisfactory.

The problem is best understood conceptually by considering the scaled version of an image as an entirely new image that must be filled in from the original. Suppose we have a bitmap comprising 100 pixels by 100 pixels. If we want to scale it by 150 percent horizontally and 80 percent vertically, the scaled bitmap will consist of 150 pixels by 80 pixels. Somehow, the pixel values of the scaled bitmap must be derived from the original bitmap.

A simple technique, which yields reasonable results in most cases, maps each scaled pixel position back to the source bitmap and uses the pixel value found at the source location for the value of the corresponding scaled pixel. Given a row–column position of (i,j) in the scaled bitmap, the corresponding source position in the original bitmap is

$$\left(\frac{i \times 100}{80}, \frac{j \times 100}{150} \right)$$

The value of the pixel in the scaled bitmap takes the value of the pixel found at this location in the source bitmap. In this case it makes good sense to perform rounding in the calculations so that the nearest source pixel is used. Our `iscale()` integer scaling function is ideal for this situation. A loop to fill in the scaled bitmap, assuming that scales are expressed as percentages, looks like this:

```
int nrows = iscale( source_hgt, vscale, 100 );
int ncols = iscale( source_wid, hscale, 100 );
            :
for( int i=0; i<nrows; i++ )
{
    isrc = iscale( i, source_hgt, nrows );
    for( int j=0; j<ncols; j++ )
    {
        jsrc = iscale( j, source_wid, ncols );
        scaled_pixel[i][j] = source_pixel[isrc][jsrc];
    }
}
```

This technique effectively treats each source pixel as a small rectangular area of uniform color and each destination pixel as a point location. The location is mapped back to the source image and takes the color of the source area into which it maps.

A more precise approach is to treat both source and destination pixels as point sources, mapping, as before, a destination pixel's position back to the source image. Now, however, the mapped position generally falls within a rectangle, the four vertices of which correspond to four source pixels. A color or gray-scale value for the mapped position is then interpolated from the four known source pixels. This approach is, of course, much more expensive computationally; given the capabilities of the average printer, it is probably not worth the extra effort. It would, however, be useful in other settings, such as creating a precisely scaled version of an existing 24-bit image.

In our `ImagePrinter` class, we implement the simpler scaling technique and use it to scale the printed image to the apparent size of the original. Note that the physical size of a printed image can be effectively manipulated by varying the resolution parameters passed to the class constructor. For example, to double the printed size you would halve the resolution values.

The source code for the class implementation is presented in Listings 7.4 and 7.5, and a brief demonstration program is presented in Listing 7.6.

Listing 7.4   IMGPRNTR.HPP

```
//------------------------------------------------------------//
//                                                            //
//    File:      IMGPRNTR.HPP                                 //
//                                                            //
//    Desc:      Image printer class                         //
//                                                            //
//------------------------------------------------------------//

#ifndef _IMGPRNTR_HPP_
#define _IMGPRNTR_HPP_

#include "color.hpp"
#include "colormap.hpp"
#include "intenmap.hpp"
#include "dither.hpp"
#include "printer.hpp"
#include "imgstore.hpp"

#ifndef _IMAGE_OPTIONS_
#define _IMAGE_OPTIONS_

//.................option values

#define   renderNONE     0x0000    // none specified
#define   renderMAP      0x0001    // palette mapping
#define   renderDITHER   0x0002    // dithering
#define   renderGRAY     0x0004    // force gray scale

#define   intensNONE     0x0000    // as-is
#define   intensICNT     0x0001    // increased contrast
#define   intensDCNT     0x0002    // decreased contrast
#define   intensIBRI     0x0004    // increased brightness
#define   intensDBRI     0x0008    // decreased brightness

#endif

//.................the image printer class

class ImagePrinter
{
   protected :
      // various stuff
      PrinterDriver   *prnt;
      ImgStore        *image;
      Dither          *dit;
      ImageDescriptor *imd;
      // image and display palettes
```

Listing 7.4   IMGPRNTR.HPP (continued)

```
        rgb             *imgpal;
        int             imgcnt;
        // printed image dimensions
        int             scanwid;
        int             scanhgt;
        unsigned char   *scanbuf;
        // options and flags
        int             rendopt;
        int             intnopt;
        int             status;

    private :
        unsigned char * getscan( int row );
        unsigned char * getscan_24( int row );
        unsigned char * getscan_dit( int row );

    public :
        ImagePrinter( PrinterDriver *prt, ImgStore *map,
                      rgb *clrs, int nclrs,
                      int ropt, int iopt,
                      int xres=0, int yres=0 );
        ~ImagePrinter( );
        int print( int eject_pg );
};

#endif
```

Listing 7.5   IMGPRNTR.CPP

```
    //----------------------------------------------------------//
    //                                                          //
    //   File:     IMGPRNTR.CPP                                 //
    //                                                          //
    //   Desc:     Image printer class                         //
    //                                                          //
    //----------------------------------------------------------//

    #include "stdlib.h"
    #include "string.h"
    #include "conio.h"

    extern "C"
    {
       int iscale( int, int, int );
    }

    #include "imgprntr.hpp"
```

Listing 7.5   IMGPRNTR.CPP (continued)

```cpp
//.................the printer class

ImagePrinter::ImagePrinter( PrinterDriver *prt,
                            ImgStore *map,
                            rgb *clrs, int nclrs,
                            int ropt, int iopt,
                            int xres, int yres )
{
   prnt    = prt;
   image   = map;
   dit     = 0;
   imd     = 0;
   imgpal  = 0;
   imgcnt  = 0;
   rendopt = ropt;
   intnopt = iopt;
   status  = 0;

   // image descriptor - reflects printed dimensions
   if( xres == 0 ) xres = prt->xres();
   if( yres == 0 ) yres = prt->yres();
   int w = iscale( map->width(), prt->xres(), xres );
   int h = iscale( map->height(), prt->yres(), yres );
   imd = new ImageDescriptor( w, h, map->depth(),
                                 xres, yres );
   if( imd == 0 )
   {
      status = 1;
      return;
   }

   // printed image and scan line buffer
   scanwid = imd->width;
   scanhgt = imd->height;
   scanbuf = new unsigned char [scanwid];
   if( scanbuf == 0 )
   {
      status = 1;
      return;
   }

   // allocate and initialize palette
   // if image is palette based
   int i;
   if( nclrs > 0 )
   {
      imgpal = new rgb [nclrs];
      if( imgpal == 0 )
```

Listing 7.5   IMGPRNTR.CPP (continued)

```
            {
                status = 1;
                return;
            }
            imgcnt = nclrs;
            for( i=0; i<imgcnt; i++ )
                imgpal[i] = clrs[i];

            // apply any intensity mapping
            if( intnopt & intensICNT )
                contrast_alter( imgpal, imgcnt, iMORE );
            if( intnopt & intensDCNT )
                contrast_alter( imgpal, imgcnt, iLESS );
            if( intnopt & intensIBRI )
                brightness_alter( imgpal, imgcnt, iMORE );
            if( intnopt & intensDBRI )
                brightness_alter( imgpal, imgcnt, iLESS );

            // force grayscale?
            if( (ropt & renderGRAY) || (prnt->devcolors() == 2) )
            {
                for( i=0; i<imgcnt; i++ )
                {
                    int g = imgpal[i].graylevel();
                    imgpal[i] = rgb( g, g, g );
                }
            }
        }

        // nclrs==0, image is 24-bit
        else
        {
            imgpal = new rgb [scanwid];
            if( imgpal == 0 )
            {
                status = 1;
                return;
            }
        }

        // if the image must be approximated...
        if( (prnt->devcolors() < imgcnt) || (imgcnt == 0) )
        {
            dit = new ColorDiffusionDither( scanwid, imgpal, imgcnt,
                                            prnt->devpalette(),
                                            prnt->devcolors() );
            if( dit == 0 )
            {
```

Listing 7.5   IMGPRNTR.CPP (continued)

```
            status = 1;
            return;
        }
    }
}

ImagePrinter::~ImagePrinter( )
{
    if( scanbuf ) delete [] scanbuf;
    if( imgpal )  delete [] imgpal;
    if( dit )     delete    dit;
    if( imd )     delete    imd;
}

unsigned char * ImagePrinter::getscan( int row )
{
    int irow = iscale( image->height(), row, scanhgt );
    unsigned char *p = image->get( irow );
    for( int j=0; j<scanwid; j++ )
    {
        int jcol = iscale( image->width(), j, scanwid );
        scanbuf[j] = p[jcol];
    }
    return scanbuf;
}

unsigned char * ImagePrinter::getscan_dit( int row )
{
    int irow = iscale( image->height(), row, scanhgt );
    unsigned char *p = image->get( irow );
    for( int j=0; j<scanwid; j++ )
    {
        int jcol = iscale( image->width(), j, scanwid );
        scanbuf[j] = p[jcol];
    }
    dit->dither( scanbuf, scanwid );
    return scanbuf;
}

unsigned char * ImagePrinter::getscan_24( int row )
{
    int irow = iscale( image->height(), row, scanhgt );
    unsigned char *p = image->get( irow );
    for( int j=0; j<scanwid; j++ )
    {
        int jcol = iscale( image->width()*3, j, scanwid );
        imgpal[j] = rgb( p[jcol], p[jcol+1], p[jcol+2] );
    }
```

Listing 7.5   IMGPRNTR.CPP (continued)

```cpp
      ColorDiffusionDither *d = (ColorDiffusionDither *) dit;
      d->rgbdither( scanbuf, imgpal, scanwid );
      return scanbuf;
   }

int ImagePrinter::print( int eject_pg )
{
   if( status != 0 ) return status;

   if( prnt->imgprolog( *imd ) != pOKAY )
      return prnt->status();

   for( int i=0; i<scanhgt; i++ )
   {
      if( prnt->status() != pOKAY )
         return prnt->status();

      unsigned char *p;

      if( imgcnt == 0 )
         p = getscan_24( i );
      else if( dit == 0 )
         p = getscan( i );
      else
         p = getscan_dit( i );

      prnt->putscanline( p, scanwid );
   }

   if( prnt->imgepilog( ) != pOKAY )
      return prnt->status();

   if( eject_pg )
      if( prnt->eject( ) != pOKAY )
         return prnt->status();

   return status;
}
```

Listing 7.6   PRNTDEMO.CPP

```cpp
#include "stdio.h"
#include "conio.h"

#include "imgprntr.hpp"

#include "eplq24.hpp"
```

Listing 7.6 PRNTDEMO.CPP (continued)

```cpp
#include "epjx80.hpp"
#include "laserjet.hpp"
#include "paintjet.hpp"

// test image metrics

char * palname    = "EL-GRECO.PAL";
char * imgname    = "EL-GRECO.IMG";
int    imgwidth   = 354;
int    imgheight  = 446;
int    imgcolors  = 256;
rgb    imgpalette[256];
CnvImgStore img( 446, 354, 8 );
unsigned char scanline[354];

// read test image palette

void read_palette( void )
{
   FILE *f = fopen( palname, "rt" );
   for( int i=0; i<imgcolors; i++ )
   {
      int r, g, b;
      fscanf( f, "%d %d %d", &r, &g, &b );
      imgpalette[i] = rgb( r, g, b );
   }
   fclose( f );
}

// read test image bitmap

void read_image( void )
{
   FILE *f = fopen( imgname, "rb" );
   for( int i=0; i<imgheight; i++ )
   {
      fread( scanline, imgwidth, 1, f );
      img.put( scanline, i );
   }
   fclose( f );
}

// perform the demo

int main( int argc, char *argv[] )
{
   // rendering and intensity mapping options
   int ropt = 0;
```

Listing 7.6   PRNTDEMO.CPP (continued)

```cpp
    int iopt = 0;
    if( argc > 1 ) sscanf( argv[1], "%d", &ropt );
    if( argc > 2 ) sscanf( argv[2], "%d", &iopt );

    // load image palette and bitmap
    printf( "Loading %s...", imgname );
    read_palette();
    read_image();
    printf( "done, press a key\n" );
    getch();

    // print the image
    EpsonLQ24 prt( "LPT1" );
    prt.setres( rHIGH );
    ImagePrinter iprt( &prt, &img, imgpalette, imgcolors,
                       ropt, iopt, 100, 100 );
    printf( "Printing..." );
    iprt.print( 1 );
    printf( "done\n" );

    return 0;
}
```

This concludes Chapter 7, and with it the material that constitutes the first part of the book. We now possess all the tools needed to tackle individual graphics file formats and write meaningful programs to use and manipulate them. The remainder of the book presents a wide range of formats that are in current use within the industry, with code to read and write each one. This code, combined with the code from Chapters 1 through 7, forms a reasonably complete graphics file processing system.

Part Two

Simple Bitmapped Formats

8

The Windows Bitmap Format

The Windows Bitmap Format is a general-purpose format for storing **device-independent bitmaps** (called DIBs for short). Files in this format use the extension BMP. The format is referred to as the **BMP format.** It is most often used to store screen- and scanner-generated imagery.

The device-independent nature of the format implies that the physical representation of an image and its palette are fixed, without regard to the requirements of a potential display device. One result of this design constraint is that images for VGA mode 12h are not stored in a multiplanar format, but in a single bit plane consisting of 4-bit pixels. In its current incarnation, the BMP format supports only single-plane bitmaps of 1, 4, 8, or 24 bits per pixel.

One curious (and slightly annoying) aspect of the format is that images are stored by scan line proceeding from the bottom row to the top. Virtually all other formats use the reverse order, or at least support top-to-bottom order as an option. Although there is no compelling reason to prefer one order over another, common practice sets top-down as a de facto standard. We have also seen, in Chapter 7, how bottom-up ordering can complicate the task of printing an image on a dot-matrix printer.

Another quirk of the BMP format is that it supports two separate and completely incompatible sets of data structures for storing image-header and palette information. We will get into the details of this later when we look at the format's structure definitions.

The overall structure of a BMP file breaks down into four separate components: a file header, an image header, an array of palette entries, and the actual bitmap. The palette array is never present with a 24-bit image; it is optional with all other pixel sizes, but is usually present. If you implement a BMP format writer, it is recommended that you include a palette, unless of course you are dealing with a 24-bit image.

As noted, there are two versions of the format's image-header and palette-entry structures. One version predates Windows 3.0 and is compatible with OS/2 1.x. The second version appeared with Windows 3.0 and is not OS/2 compatible. The only way to tell which set of structures is actually present is to read the bitmap header partially and inspect its size field. The Windows 3.0 version of the format is preferred when you are implementing a format writer, but a format reader should ideally handle either version.

The Windows BMP format supports image compression by a simple RLE encoding scheme. Only images with 4-bit and 8-bit pixel sizes can be encoded— the interpretation of encoded image data varies slightly depending on which pixel size is present. In an image with 8 bits per pixel (bpp), a repeating byte represents a single pixel value. By contrast, a repeating byte in an encoded 4-bpp image represents a 2-pixel pair, and the two pixel values are strictly alternated until a specified run length is achieved.

Despite the fact that the format supports compression, it is rare to find an application that actually bothers to encode image data in this format. Even Microsoft's own Windows Paintbrush does not write a compressed BMP file. Although compression support is entirely optional for a format writer, a format reader should be prepared to deal with compressed images.

Scan lines in the BMP format are padded at the end with unused bits so that their length is an integral number of double words—that is, the number of bytes is evenly divisible by 4. To see how to compute scan-line lengths for various pixel sizes, refer to the code for the `BmpDecoder` class presented in Listing 8.2.

Format Structures

For consistency, our implementation of BMP data structures uses the same structure and member names as those found in the Windows SDK, adding a prefix with the letter *x*. The prefix allows the code to be used in a Windows application without conflicting with the BMP structure names defined in `windows.h`. I will discuss dealing with the format under Windows later in the chapter. For the time being, assume a DOS environment.

The BMP structure definitions are presented in Listings 8.1 and 8.2. Because we are using C++, constructors and destructors have been added to each of the structures, where appropriate. Also, don't forget that we are dealing with two format versions simultaneously: the structures `xBITMAPCOREHEADER` and `xRGBTRIPLE` duplicate the functionality of the later `xBITMAPINFOHEADER` and `xRGBQUAD` structures.

Listing 8.1 BMP.HPP

```
//--------------------------------------------------------//
//                                                        //
//    File:     BMP.HPP                                   //
//                                                        //
//    Desc:     Class and structure definitions for the  //
//              Windows BMP format - DOS version          //
//                                                        //
//--------------------------------------------------------//

// Note: This file duplicates structure and member names
//       from windows.h, so it cannot be used in a wn app.

#ifdef WINVER
#error Use WBMP.HPP for Windows - BMP.HPP is for DOS
#endif

#ifndef _BMP_HPP_
#define _BMP_HPP_

#include "color.hpp"
#include "codec.hpp"

//.................File signature

#define BMP_SIGNATURE_WORD 0x4D42

//.................Bitmap compression schemes

enum BiCompressionMethods
{
    xBI_NONE = 0,
    xBI_RGB  = 0,
    xBI_RLE4 = 2,
    xBI_RLE8 = 1
};

//.................xBITMAPFILEHEADER

struct xBITMAPFILEHEADER
{
    unsigned short bfType;        // signature - 'BM'
    unsigned long  bfSize;        // file size in bytes
    unsigned short bfReserved1;   // 0
    unsigned short bfReserved2;   // 0
    unsigned long  bfOffBits;     // offset to bitmap
    xBITMAPFILEHEADER( )
```

Listing 8.1   BMP.HPP (continued)

```cpp
    {
        bfType = BMP_SIGNATURE_WORD;
        bfSize = bfOffBits = 0;
        bfReserved1 = bfReserved2 = 0;
    }
    void list( void );
};

//............xRGBTRIPLE, xBITMAPCOREHEADER, xBITMAPCOREINFO

struct xRGBTRIPLE
{
    unsigned char rgbBlue;     // 0..255
    unsigned char rgbGreen;    // 0..255
    unsigned char rgbRed;      // 0..255
    xRGBTRIPLE( )
    {
        rgbBlue = rgbGreen = rgbRed = 0;
    }
    xRGBTRIPLE( int r, int g, int b )
    {
        rgbBlue  = b;
        rgbGreen = g;
        rgbRed   = r;
    }
    void set( int r, int g, int b )
    {
        rgbBlue  = b;
        rgbGreen = g;
        rgbRed   = r;
    }
    void list( int index );
};

struct xBITMAPCOREHEADER
{
    unsigned long  bcSize;      // size of this struct
    short          bcWidth;     // bitmap width in pixels
    short          bcHeight;    // bitmap height in pixels
    unsigned short bcPlanes;    // num planes - always 1
    unsigned short bcBitCount;  // bits per pixel
    xBITMAPCOREHEADER( )
    {
        bcSize = sizeof(xBITMAPCOREHEADER);
        bcWidth = bcHeight = 0;
        bcPlanes = 1;
        bcBitCount = 0;
    }
```

Listing 8.1 BMP.HPP (continued)

```
    void list( void );
};

struct xBITMAPCOREINFO
{
    xBITMAPCOREHEADER bmciHeader;
    xRGBTRIPLE        bmciColors[1];
};

//...........xRGBQUAD, xBITMAPINFOHEADER, xBITMAPIFO

struct xRGBQUAD
{
    unsigned char rgbBlue;       // 0..255
    unsigned char rgbGreen;      // 0..255
    unsigned char rgbRed;        // 0..255
    unsigned char rgbReserved;   // 0
    xRGBQUAD( )
    {
        rgbBlue = rgbGreen = rgbRed = 0;
        rgbReserved = 0;
    }
    xRGBQUAD( int r, int g, int b )
    {
        rgbBlue  = b;
        rgbGreen = g;
        rgbRed   = r;
        rgbReserved = 0;
    }
    void set( int r, int g, int b )
    {
        rgbBlue  = b;
        rgbGreen = g;
        rgbRed   = r;
    }
    void list( int index );
};

struct xBITMAPINFOHEADER
{
    unsigned long  biSize;        // size of this struct
    long           biWidth;       // bmap width in pixels
    long           biHeight;      // bmap height in pixels
    unsigned short biPlanes;      // num planes - always 1
    unsigned short biBitCount;    // bits per pixel
    unsigned long  biCompression; // compression flag
    unsigned long  biSizeImage;   // image size in bytes
    long           biXPelsPerMeter; // horz resolution
```

Listing 8.1   BMP.HPP (continued)

```cpp
      long            biYPelsPerMeter; // vert resolution
      unsigned long  biClrUsed;        // 0 -> color table size
      unsigned long  biClrImportant;   // important color count
      xBITMAPINFOHEADER( )
      {
         biSize = sizeof(xBITMAPINFOHEADER);
         biWidth = biHeight = 0;
         biPlanes = 1;
         biBitCount = 0;
         biCompression = biSizeImage = 0;
         biXPelsPerMeter = biYPelsPerMeter = 0;
         biClrUsed = biClrImportant = 0;
      }
      void list( void );
};

struct xBITMAPINFO
{
   xBITMAPINFOHEADER  bmiHeader;
   xRGBQUAD           bmiColors[1];
};

//............class BmpDecoder

class BmpDecoder : public Decoder
{
   public:
      int cond;            // condition code

   protected:
      int   rle_method;    // RLE compression method
      int   pxl_size;      // bits per pixel
      FILE *bmp_file;      // input file

   private:
      void read_none( unsigned char *buf, int npxls );
      void read_rle4( unsigned char *buf, int npxls );
      void read_rle8( unsigned char *buf, int npxls );

   public:
      BmpDecoder( FILE *f_in, int rle, int nbits );
      ~BmpDecoder( ) { }
      virtual int decode( unsigned char *buf, int npxls );
      virtual int init( void );
      virtual int term( void );
      virtual int status( void );
};
```

Listing 8.1   BMP.HPP (continued)

```
//.............class BmpEncoder

class BmpEncoder : public Encoder
{
   protected:
       int   pxl_size;      // bits per pixel
       FILE *bmp_file;      // output file

   private:
       void wrt_line( unsigned char *buf, int npxls );

   public:
       BmpEncoder( FILE *f_out, int nbits );
      ~BmpEncoder( ) { }
       virtual int encode( unsigned char *buf, int npxls );
       virtual int init( void );
       virtual int term( void );
       virtual int status( void );
};

   #endif
```

Listing 8.2   BMP.CPP

```
//----------------------------------------------------------//
//                                                          //
//    File:    BMP.CPP                                      //
//                                                          //
//    Desc:    Class and structure definitions for the      //
//             Windows BMP format - DOS version             //
//                                                          //
//----------------------------------------------------------//

#include "stdlib.h"
#include "stdio.h"
#include "string.h"

#include "bmp.hpp"

//................struct xBITMAPFILEHEADER

void xBITMAPFILEHEADER::list( void )
{
   printf( "xBITMAPFILEHEADER::bfType      = '%c%c'\n",
           bfType & 0xFF, (bfType>>8) & 0xFF );
   printf( "xBITMAPFILEHEADER::bfSize      = %lu\n",
           bfSize );
```

Listing 8.2 BMP.CPP (continued)

```
    printf( "xBITMAPFILEHEADER::bfReserved1 = %d\n",
            bfReserved1 );
    printf( "xBITMAPFILEHEADER::bfReserved2 = %d\n",
            bfReserved2 );
    printf( "xBITMAPFILEHEADER::bfOffBits   = %lu\n",
            bfOffBits );
}

//...............struct xRGBTRIPLE

void xRGBTRIPLE::list( int index )
{
    printf( "xRGBTRIPLE[%3d]::  ", index );
    printf( "rgbRed=%3d  rgbGreen=%3d  rgbBlue=%3d\n",
            rgbRed&0xFF, rgbGreen&0xFF, rgbBlue&0xFF );
}

//..............struct xBITMAPCOREHEADER

void xBITMAPCOREHEADER::list( void )
{
    printf( "xBITMAPCOREHEADER::bcSize     = %lu\n",
            bcSize );
    printf( "xBITMAPCOREHEADER::bcWidth    = %d\n",
            bcWidth );
    printf( "xBITMAPCOREHEADER::bcHeight   = %d\n",
            bcHeight );
    printf( "xBITMAPCOREHEADER::bcPlanes   = %u\n",
            bcPlanes );
    printf( "xBITMAPCOREHEADER::bcBitCount = %u\n",
            bcBitCount );
}

//..............struct xRGBQUAD

void xRGBQUAD::list( int index )
{
    printf( "xRGBQUAD[%3d]::  ", index );
    printf( "rgbRed=%3d  rgbGreen=%3d  rgbBlue=%3d",
            rgbRed&0xFF, rgbGreen&0xFF, rgbBlue&0xFF );
    printf( " rgbReserved=%d\n", rgbReserved );
}

//..............struct xBITMAPINFOHEADER

void xBITMAPINFOHEADER::list( void )
```

Listing 8.2 BMP.CPP (continued)

```cpp
{
    printf( "xBITMAPINFOHEADER::biSize          = %lu\n",
            biSize );
    printf( "xBITMAPINFOHEADER::biWidth         = %ld\n",
            biWidth );
    printf( "xBITMAPINFOHEADER::biHeight        = %ld\n",
            biHeight );
    printf( "xBITMAPINFOHEADER::biPlanes        = %d\n",
            biPlanes );
    printf( "xBITMAPINFOHEADER::biBitCount      = %d\n",
            biBitCount );
    printf( "xBITMAPINFOHEADER::biCompression   = %lu\n",
            biCompression );
    printf( "xBITMAPINFOHEADER::biSizeImage     = %lu\n",
            biSizeImage );
    printf( "xBITMAPINFOHEADER::biXPelsPerMeter = %ld\n",
            biXPelsPerMeter );
    printf( "xBITMAPINFOHEADER::biYPelsPerMeter = %ld\n",
            biYPelsPerMeter );
    printf( "xBITMAPINFOHEADER::biClrUsed       = %lu\n",
            biClrUsed );
    printf( "xBITMAPINFOHEADER::biClrImportant  = %lu\n",
            biClrImportant );
}

//.................class BmpDecoder

BmpDecoder::BmpDecoder( FILE *f_in, int rle, int nbits ) :
            Decoder( tRLE )
{
    cond = xOKAY;
    rle_method = rle;
    pxl_size = nbits;
    bmp_file = f_in;
}

int BmpDecoder::status( void )
{
    if( ferror(bmp_file) ) cond = xIOERROR;
    if( feof(bmp_file) ) cond = xOUTOFSYNC;
    return cond;
}

int BmpDecoder::init( void )
{
    return status();
}
```

Listing 8.2 BMP.CPP (continued)

```cpp
int BmpDecoder::term( void )
{
    return status();
}

void BmpDecoder::read_none( unsigned char *buf, int npxls )
{
    int i, j, nbytes;
    switch( pxl_size )
    {
        case 1 :
            nbytes = (npxls + 7) / 8;
            nbytes = (nbytes + 3) / 4;
            nbytes *= 4;
            while( npxls > 0 )
            {
                nbytes--;
                int x = fgetc( bmp_file );
                int m = 0x80;
                while( (npxls > 0) && (m != 0) )
                {
                    *buf++ = (x & m) ? 1 : 0;
                    m >>= 1;
                    npxls--;
                }
            }
            while( nbytes-- > 0 )
                fgetc( bmp_file );
            break;

        case 4 :
            nbytes = (npxls + 1) / 2;
            nbytes = (nbytes + 3) / 4;
            nbytes *= 4;
            while( npxls > 0 )
            {
                nbytes--;
                int x = fgetc( bmp_file );
                int p2 = x & 0x0F;
                int p1 = (x>>4) & 0x0F;
                *buf++ = p1;
                npxls--;
                *buf++ = p2;
                npxls--;
            }
            while( nbytes-- > 0 )
                fgetc( bmp_file );
            break;
```

Listing 8.2 BMP.CPP (continued)

```
          case 8 :
             nbytes = (npxls + 3) / 4;
             nbytes *= 4;
             fread( buf, npxls, 1, bmp_file );
             nbytes -= npxls;
             while( nbytes- > 0 )
                fgetc( bmp_file );
             break;

          case 24 :
             nbytes = (npxls*3 + 3) / 4;
             nbytes *= 4;
             fread( buf, npxls, 3, bmp_file );
             nbytes -= npxls*3;
             while( nbytes- > 0 )
                fgetc( bmp_file );
             // reorder bgr to rgb
             for( i=0, j=0; i<npxls; i++, j+=3 )
             {
                int k = buf[j];
                buf[j] = buf[j+2];
                buf[j+2] = k;
             }
             break;
      }
}

void BmpDecoder::read_rle4( unsigned char *buf, int npxls )
{
   int b1, b2;
   while( cond == xOKAY )
   {
      b1 = fgetc( bmp_file );
      b2 = fgetc( bmp_file );
      if( b1 == 0 )  //.... absolute or escape
      {
         switch( b2 )
         {
            case 0 :  //.... end-of-line
               return;

            case 1 :  //.... end-of-image
               cond = xENDOFIMAGE;
               return;

            case 2 :  //.... delta
               cond = xUNSUPPORTED;
               return;
```

Listing 8.2 BMP.CPP (continued)

```
                default : //.... nonrepeating run
                    while( b2- )
                    {
                        if( npxls > 0 )
                        {
                            *buf++ = fgetc( bmp_file );
                            npxls-;
                        }
                    }
                    break;
            }
        }
        else  //............ encoded
        {
            unsigned char p1 = b2       & 0x0F;
            unsigned char p2 = (b2>>4) & 0x0F;
            unsigned char p;
            if( b1 & 1 ) { p=p1; p1=p2; p2=p; }
            while( b1- )
            {
                if( npxls > 0 )
                {
                    *buf++ = (b1 & 1 ) ? p1 : p2;
                    npxls-;
                }
            }
        }
    }
}

void BmpDecoder::read_rle8( unsigned char *buf, int npxls )
{
    int b1, b2;
    while( cond == xOKAY )
    {
        b1 = fgetc( bmp_file );
        b2 = fgetc( bmp_file );
        if( b1 == 0 )  //.... absolute or escape
        {
            switch( b2 )
            {
                case 0 :  //.... end-of-line
                    return;

                case 1 :  //.... end-of-image
                    cond = xENDOFIMAGE;
                    return;
```

Listing 8.2 BMP.CPP (continued)

```cpp
                case 2 :  //.... delta
                   cond = xUNSUPPORTED;
                   return;

                default : //.... nonrepeating run
                   while( b2— )
                   {
                      if( npxls > 0 )
                      {
                         *buf++ = fgetc( bmp_file );
                         npxls—;
                      }
                   }
                   break;
            }
         }
         else  //............. encoded
         {
            while( b1— )
            {
               if( npxls > 0 )
               {
                  *buf++ = b2;
                  npxls—;
               }
            }
         }
      }
   }
}

int BmpDecoder::decode( unsigned char *buf, int npxls )
{
   switch( rle_method )
   {
      case xBI_NONE :
            read_none( buf, npxls );
            break;

      case xBI_RLE8 :
            read_rle8( buf, npxls );
            break;

      case xBI_RLE4 :
            read_rle4( buf, npxls );
            break;
```

Listing 8.2 BMP.CPP (continued)

```cpp
        default :
            cond = xBADPARAM;
            break;
    }

    return status();
}

//................class BmpEncoder

BmpEncoder::BmpEncoder( FILE *f_out, int nbits ) :
            Encoder( tRLE )
{
    pxl_size = nbits;
    bmp_file = f_out;
}

int BmpEncoder::status( void )
{
    return ferror(bmp_file);
}

int BmpEncoder::init( void )
{
    return status();
}

int BmpEncoder::term( void )
{
    return status();
}

void BmpEncoder::wrt_line( unsigned char *buf, int npxls )
{
    int i, j, nbytes, x, m;
    switch( pxl_size )
    {
        case 1 :
            nbytes = (npxls + 7) / 8;
            nbytes = (nbytes + 3) / 4;
            nbytes *= 4;
            x = 0;
            m = 0x80;
            while( npxls-- > 0 )
            {
                if( *buf++ )
                    x |= m;
                if( (m>>=1) == 0 )
```

Listing 8.2 BMP.CPP (continued)

```cpp
            {
                fputc( x, bmp_file );
                x = 0;
                m = 0x80;
                nbytes--;
            }
        }
        if( m != 0x80 )
        {
            fputc( x, bmp_file );
            nbytes--;
        }
        while( nbytes-- > 0 )
            fputc( 0, bmp_file );
        break;

    case 4 :
        nbytes = (npxls + 1) / 2;
        nbytes = (nbytes + 3) / 4;
        nbytes *= 4;
        x = 0;
        while( npxls > 0 )
        {
            x = (*buf++) << 4;
            if( npxls > 1 )
                x |= *buf++;
            fputc( x, bmp_file );
            npxls -= 2;
            nbytes--;
        }
        while( nbytes-- > 0 )
            fgetc( bmp_file );
        break;

    case 8 :
        nbytes = (npxls + 3) / 4;
        nbytes *= 4;
        fwrite( buf, npxls, 1, bmp_file );
        nbytes -= npxls;
        while( nbytes-- > 0 )
            fputc( 0, bmp_file );
        break;
    case 24 :
        // reorder rgb to bgr
        for( i=0, j=0; i<npxls; i++, j+=3 )
        {
            int k = buf[j];
            buf[j] = buf[j+2];
```

Listing 8.2 BMP.CPP (continued)

```
            buf[j+2] = k;
        }
        nbytes = (npxls*3 + 3) / 4;
        nbytes *= 4;
        fwrite( buf, npxls, 3, bmp_file );
        nbytes -= npxls*3;
        while( nbytes- > 0 )
            fputc( 0, bmp_file );
        break;
    }
}

int BmpEncoder::encode( unsigned char *buf, int npxls )
{
    wrt_line( buf, npxls );
    return status();
}
```

The Bitmap File Header Structure

The `xBITMAPFILEHEADER` structure occurs at the start of every BMP file and is used primarily to validate the format. This is done by checking the `bfType` member for the value 4D42h, which corresponds to the ASCII codes for the letters BM. Note that the low order byte contains B and the high order byte contains M. Because of the way Intel processors store word quantities in memory, they appear in the correct order, B followed by M, within a file.

A second useful member of this structure is `bfOffBits`, which contains the offset from the start of the file to the actual bitmap, expressed in bytes. Using this value is the most reliable method for locating the start of the bitmap. In contrast, the `bfSize` member, which supposedly contains the size of the file in bytes, is not reliable. Some applications interpret this value to mean the size of the file in words, while the Windows SDK documentation indicates units of bytes. Which interpretation is correct is a moot point, because either can be encountered.

One potential problem of reading or writing the file header structure is its sensitivity to the structure-packing assumptions of a compiler. Forcing double-word alignment on structure members, for instance, causes an extra word of padding to be inserted after the `bfType` member. You should always ensure that the `sizeof()` operator indicates a size of 14 bytes for this structure. Note that this problem is more likely to occur with a 32-bit compiler, where `sizeof(int)` is 4.

All reserved structure members, in this as well as other structures, should be zero filled and otherwise ignored. Here is a summary of the `xBITMAPFILEHEADER` structure members:

`bfType`	Signature word with the value 4D42h
`bfSize`	Size of the BMP file in bytes (not reliable)
`bfReserved1`	Reserved value; should be set to zero
`bfReserved2`	Reserved value; should be set to zero
`bfOffBits`	Offset from top of file to the start of the actual bitmap, in bytes

The Bitmap Information Header Structure

The `xBITMAPINFOHEADER` structure serves as the header for the actual bitmap and contains all of the bitmap's important metrics. This structure duplicates the functionality of an earlier version of Windows' `xBITMAPCOREHEADER` and is preferred for new application development.

The meanings of most of the structure's data members are reasonably self-evident. Exceptions are `biClrUsed` and `biClrImportant`—these are intended to indicate the number of palette colors actually used in the bitmap and the number of colors in the palette that are to be considered important. Most applications insert zeroes in these two fields. To get a better feel for their use, see the section that discusses Windows' handling of color, later in this chapter.

`biSize`	Size of the structure in bytes; should be 40
`biWidth`	Width of the bitmap in pixels
`biHeight`	Height of the bitmap in pixels
`biPlanes`	Number of planes in the bitmap; must be 1
`biBitCount`	Number of bits per pixel; can be 1, 4, 8, or 24
`biCompression`	Flag indicating the type of compression used on the image; 1 indicates RLE-8 , 2 indicates RLE-4
`biSizeImage`	Size of the bitmap in bytes; value includes any scan-line padding (keep in mind that scan lines must be padded to an integral number of double words in length)
`biXPelsPerMeter`	Bitmap's horizontal resolution in pixels per meter
`biYPelsPerMeter`	Bitmap's vertical resolution in pixels per meter
`biClrUsed`	Number of colors actually used in the bitmap, or zero
`biClrImportant`	Number of colors in the image palette that are considered important, or zero

The RGB Quad Structure

The xRGBQUAD structure is used to define a single palette entry, or color, as relative intensities of red, green, and blue. Each intensity is expressed as an 8-bit unsigned quantity. In practice, what are nominally RGB triples are manipulated as unsigned long values, which accounts for this structure's two bizarre traits: an 8-bit unused, reserved member, and reverse element ordering (BGR instead of RGB). This structure duplicates the functionality of the earlier xRGBTRIPLE structure and is preferred for new application development.

rgbBlue	Blue primary intensity in the range 0 to 255
rgbGreen	Green primary intensity in the range 0 to 255
rgbRed	Red primary intensity in the range 0 to 255
rgbReserved	Unused byte; value should be zero

The Bitmap Core Header Structure

The xBITMAPCOREHEADER structure represents an earlier version of the xBITMAPINFOHEADER structure. It was used prior to the introduction of Windows 3.0. A BMP format reader should be prepared to recognize this form of the format, but new code to write the format should not use this structure.

bcSize	Size of structure in bytes; should be 12
bcWidth	Width of the bitmap in pixels
bcHeight	Height of the bitmap in pixels
bcPlanes	Number of planes in the bitmap; must be 1
bcBitCount	Number of bits per pixel; can be 1, 4, 8, or 24

The RGB Triple Structure

The xRGBTRIPLE structure is used to define a single palette entry, or color, as relative intensities of red, green, and blue. Each intensity is expressed as an 8-bit unsigned quantity. Note that this structure represents an earlier version of the format.

rgbBlue	Blue primary intensity in the range 0 to 255
rgbGreen	Green primary intensity in the range 0 to 255
rgbRed	Red primary intensity in the range 0 to 255

A BMP Query Program

A good way to get your feet wet with a new format is to write a query program that will print a formatted listing of the format's data structures. Such a program for the BMP format is presented in Listing 8.3. Note that, because `list()` member functions have been implemented for all BMP structures, the program is relatively simple to write. The `list()` functions also come in handy when a program that deals with the format is being debugged.

Listing 8.3 QBMP.CPP

```
//----------------------------------------------------------//
//                                                          //
//    File:     QBMP.CPP                                    //
//                                                          //
//    Desc:     Program to list information in a            //
//              Windows BMP Graphics File                   //
//                                                          //
//----------------------------------------------------------//

#include "stdlib.h"
#include "stdio.h"
#include "string.h"

#include "bmp.hpp"

//................program usage

void explain_pgm( void )
{
   printf( "\n" );
   printf( "Windows BMP File Query Program\n" );
   printf( "\n" );
   printf( "Usage:  QBMP  bmp_file  [-p]\n" );
   printf( "\n" );
   printf( "-p includes palette in listing\n" );
   printf( ".BMP extension is assumed\n" );
   printf( "\n" );
}

//................listing of core-based format

void core_listing( FILE *fbmp, int listpal )
{
   xBITMAPCOREHEADER bmch;
   if( fread(&bmch,sizeof(xBITMAPCOREHEADER),1,fbmp) != 1 )
```

Listing 8.3 QBMP.CPP (continued)

```
      {
         printf( "Error reading xBITMAPCOREHEADER\n" );
         return;
      }
      bmch.list();

      if( listpal )
      {
         // list palette
         printf( "\n" );
         int ncolors = 0;
         switch( bmch.bcBitCount )
         {
            case 1 : ncolors = 2;   break;
            case 4 : ncolors = 16;  break;
            case 8 : ncolors = 256; break;
         }
         for( int i=0; i<ncolors; i++ )
         {
            xRGBTRIPLE rgb;
            fread( &rgb, sizeof(xRGBTRIPLE), 1, fbmp );
            rgb.list( i );
         }
      }
   }

   //.................listing of info-based format

   void info_listing( FILE *fbmp, int listpal )
   {
      xBITMAPINFOHEADER bmih;
      if( fread(&bmih,sizeof(xBITMAPINFOHEADER),1,fbmp) != 1 )
      {
         printf( "Error reading xBITMAPINFOHEADER\n" );
         return;
      }
      bmih.list();

      if( listpal )
      {
         // list palette
         printf( "\n" );
         int ncolors = 0;
         switch( bmih.biBitCount )
```

Listing 8.3 QBMP.CPP (continued)

```cpp
        {
           case 1 : ncolors = 2;   break;
           case 4 : ncolors = 16;  break;
           case 8 : ncolors = 256; break;
        }
        for( int i=0; i<ncolors; i++ )
        {
           xRGBQUAD rgb;
           fread( &rgb, sizeof(xRGBQUAD), 1, fbmp );
           rgb.list( i );
        }
     }
}

//.................main
int main( int argc, char *argv[] )
{
   // check args
   if( (argc < 2) || (*argv[1] == '?') )
   {
      explain_pgm();
      return 0;
   }

   // create file name
   char fn[80];
   strcpy( fn, argv[1] );
   char *p = strchr( fn, '.' );
   if( p == 0 )
      strcat( fn, ".bmp" );
   else if( *(p+1) == 0 )
      *p = 0;

   // open file
   FILE *fbmp = fopen( fn, "rb" );
   if( fbmp == 0 )
   {
      printf( "File '%s' not found\n", fn );
      return 0;
   }

   // read header and check
   xBITMAPFILEHEADER bmfh;
   if( fread(&bmfh,sizeof(xBITMAPFILEHEADER),1,fbmp) != 1 )
   {
      printf( "Error reading file '%s'\n", fn );
      return 0;
   }
```

Listing 8.3 QBMP.CPP (continued)

```cpp
    if( bmfh.bfType != BMP_SIGNATURE_WORD )
    {
        printf( "File '%s' is not a valid BMP file\n", fn );
        return 0;
    }

    printf( "Listing of BMP file '%s'\n", fn );
    printf( "\n" );
    bmfh.list();
    printf( "\n" );

    // determine which format version is used
    // from structure size field value
    long offset = ftell( fbmp );
    long nbytes = 0;
    fread( &nbytes, sizeof(long), 1, fbmp );
    fseek( fbmp, offset, SEEK_SET );

    // list palette ?
    int lpal = 0;
    if( argc > 2 )
      if( (strcmp( argv[2], "-p" ) == 0) ||
          (strcmp( argv[2], "-P" ) == 0) )
        lpal = 1;

    // list bitmap header and palette
    if( nbytes == sizeof(xBITMAPCOREHEADER) )
        core_listing( fbmp, lpal );
    else if( nbytes == sizeof(xBITMAPINFOHEADER) )
        info_listing( fbmp, lpal );
    else
        printf( "Format error or not a BMP file\n" );

    fclose( fbmp );
    return 0;
}
```

A DOS BMP File Viewer

Now that we have a basic understanding of the format's data structures and file layout, we can move on to nontrivial operations on BMP files. We start here with the implementation of a program for MS-DOS to view or print a BMP file. Much of the program consists of code from the first seven chapters, which by now should look reasonably familiar. The program's source code is presented in Listing 8.4.

The task of parsing the BMP file on input is handled by the function `load_bmp()`. This function reads the BMP file whose name has been placed in the variable `fn` by the `process_args()` function. The `load_bmp()` function reads the format header structures, creates an instance of `ImgStore` that is compatible with the image, and loads the file's bitmap into the `ImgStore` instance. Once this has been accomplished, the image is displayed using an instance of `ImageViewer` or printed using an instance of `ImagePrinter`.

Note that all BMP-specific code is localized in the `load_bmp()` function, so the program is easily adaptable to other formats. You will see this basic program reused, with only minor changes, for each of the other formats discussed in the book.

Listing 8.4 VBMP.CPP

```
//------------------------------------------------------------//
//                                                            //
//    File:      VBMP.CPP                                     //
//                                                            //
//    Desc:      Program to view or print a BMP file          //
//                                                            //
//------------------------------------------------------------//

#include "stdlib.h"
#include "stdio.h"
#include "string.h"
#include "conio.h"
#include "ctype.h"

#include "bmp.hpp"
#include "imgviewr.hpp"
#include "imgprntr.hpp"
#include "laserjet.hpp"
#include "paintjet.hpp"
#include "epjx80.hpp"
#include "eplq24.hpp"
#include "pscript.hpp"

//.................Printer types

#define  LJ   0x4C4A
#define  PJ   0x504A
#define  JX   0x4A58
#define  LQ   0x4C51
#define  PS   0x5053

//.................Program globals
```

Listing 8.4 VBMP.CPP (continued)

```cpp
   char      fn[80];        // path to BMP file

   int       gmode;         // video display mode
   int       pmode;         // printer ID
   int       ropt;          // rendering flags
   int       iopt;          // itensity mapping flags

   ImgStore *imgmap;        // image bitmap
   rgb      *imgpal;        // image palette
   int       imgcnt;        // number of palette colors

   //................Exit with a message

   void exit_pgm( char *msg )
   {
      printf( "%s\n", msg );
      exit( 0 );
   }

   //................Program usage

   void explain_pgm( void )
   {
      printf( "\n" );
      printf( ".........Windows BMP File Viewer/Printer..........\n"
   );
      printf( "\n" );
      printf( "Usage:      VBMP  bmp_file  [ switches ]\n" );
      printf( "\n" );
      printf( "Switches: -h      = display program usage\n" );
      printf( "          -vXX    = force video display mode XX\n" );
      printf( "                    (XX = 12, 13, 2E, 62)\n" );
      printf( "          -pXX    = print using printer XX\n" );
      printf( "                    (XX = LJ, PJ, JX, LQ, PS)\n" );
      printf( "          -b[+|-] = increase or decrease
   brightness\n" );
      printf( "          -c[+|-] = increase or decrease contrast\n"
   );
      printf( "          -d      = force dithered rendering\n" );
      printf( "          -g      = force gray scale rendering\n" );
      printf( "          -m      = force palette mapping\n" );
      printf( "\n" );
      printf( "...................................................\n"
   );
      printf( "\n" );
   }

   //................Process pgm argument list
```

Listing 8.4 VBMP.CPP (continued)

```cpp
void process_args( int argc, char *argv[] )
{
    // establish default values
    fn[0] = 0;
    gmode = 0x12;
    pmode = 0;
    ropt  = 0;
    iopt  = 0;

    // process the program's argument list
    for( int i=1; i<argc; i++ )
    {
        if( (*argv[i] == '-') || (*argv[i] == '/') )
        {
            char sw = *(argv[i] + 1);
            switch( toupper(sw) )
            {
                case 'H' :
                    explain_pgm();
                    exit( 0 );
                    break;

                case 'V' :
                    sscanf( argv[i]+2, "%x", &gmode );
                    break;

                case 'P' :
                    pmode = toupper( *(argv[i]+2) );
                    pmode <<= 8;
                    pmode += toupper( *(argv[i]+3) );
                    break;

                case 'B' :
                    if( *(argv[i]+2) == '-' )
                        iopt |= intensDBRI;
                    else
                        iopt |= intensIBRI;
                    break;

                case 'C' :
                    if( *(argv[i]+2) == '-' )
                        iopt |= intensDCNT;
                    else
                        iopt |= intensICNT;
                    break;
```

Listing 8.4 VBMP.CPP (continued)

```cpp
                case 'D' :
                    ropt |= renderDITHER;
                    break;

                case 'G' :
                    ropt |= renderGRAY;
                    break;

                case 'M' :
                    ropt |= renderMAP;
                    break;

                default:
                    printf( "Unknown switch '%s' ignored\n",
                                argv[i] );
                    break;
            }
        }
        else  // presumably a file identifier
        {
            strcpy( fn, argv[i] );
            char *p = strchr( fn, '.' );
            if( p == 0 )
                strcat( fn, ".bmp" );
            else if( *(p+1) == 0 )
                *p = 0;
        }
    }

    // was a file name specified?
    if( fn[0] == 0 )
    {
        explain_pgm();
        exit( 0 );
    }
}


//................Determine palette size

int color_count( int nbits )
{
    int ncolors = 0;
    if( nbits < 24 )
        ncolors = 1 << nbits;
    return ncolors;
}
```

Listing 8.4 VBMP.CPP (continued)

```cpp
//................Create an image storage buffer

ImgStore * istore( int h, int w, int d )
{
    ImgStore *ist = 0;

    // attempt to create in order of preference
    ist = new XmsImgStore( h, w, d );
    if( (ist != 0) && (ist->status != imgstoreOKAY) )
    {
        delete ist;
        ist = new EmsImgStore( h, w, d );
        if( (ist != 0) && (ist->status != imgstoreOKAY) )
        {
            delete ist;
            ist = new CnvImgStore( h, w, d );
            if( (ist != 0) && (ist->status != imgstoreOKAY) )
            {
                delete ist;
                ist = new DskImgStore( h, w, d );
                if( (ist != 0) && (ist->status != imgstoreOKAY) )
                {
                    delete ist;
                    ist = 0;
                }
            }
        }
    }

    return ist;
}

//................Create a printer

PrinterDriver * printer( int which )
{
    PrinterDriver *p;

    switch( which )
    {
        case LJ : p = new LaserJet( "LPT1" );
                  break;
        case PJ : p = new PaintJet( "LPT1" );
                  break;
        case JX : p = new EpsonJX80( "LPT1" );
                  break;
        case LQ : p = new EpsonLQ24( "LPT1" );
                  break;
```

Listing 8.4 VBMP.CPP (continued)

```
            default : p = new PsPrinter( "LPT1" );
                    break;
    }

    return p;
}

//.................Load the BMP file

void load_bmp( void )
{
    // open file
    FILE *fbmp = fopen( fn, "rb" );
    if( fbmp == 0 )
       exit_pgm( "BMP file not found" );

    // read header and check
    xBITMAPFILEHEADER bmfh;
    if( fread(&bmfh,sizeof(xBITMAPFILEHEADER),1,fbmp) != 1 )
       exit_pgm( "Error reading BMP file" );
    if( bmfh.bfType != BMP_SIGNATURE_WORD )
       exit_pgm( "File is not a valid BMP file" );

    // determine which format version is used
    // from structure size field
    long offset = ftell( fbmp );
    long nbytes = 0;
    fread( &nbytes, sizeof(long), 1, fbmp );
    fseek( fbmp, offset, SEEK_SET );

    // read bitmap header and palette
    int width, height, depth, rle;

    // pre Windows 3.0 version
    if( nbytes == sizeof(xBITMAPCOREHEADER) )
    {
       xBITMAPCOREHEADER bmch;
       if( fread(&bmch,sizeof(xBITMAPCOREHEADER),1,fbmp) != 1 )
          exit_pgm( "Error reading xBITMAPCOREHEADER" );
       width  = bmch.bcWidth;
       height = bmch.bcHeight;
       depth  = bmch.bcBitCount;
       rle    = 0;
       imgcnt = color_count( depth );
       if( imgcnt > 0 )
       {
          imgpal = new rgb [imgcnt];
          if( imgpal == 0 )
```

Listing 8.4 VBMP.CPP (continued)

```
                exit_pgm( "Error allocating image palette" );
            xRGBTRIPLE t;
            for( int i=0; i<imgcnt; i++ )
            {
                if( fread(&t,sizeof(xRGBTRIPLE),1,fbmp) != 1 )
                    exit_pgm( "Error reading xRGBTRIPLE" );
                imgpal[i] = rgb(t.rgbRed,t.rgbGreen,t.rgbBlue);
            }
        }
    }

    // Windows 3.0 and later version
    else if( nbytes == sizeof(xBITMAPINFOHEADER) )
    {
        xBITMAPINFOHEADER bmih;
        if( fread(&bmih,sizeof(xBITMAPINFOHEADER),1,fbmp) != 1 )
            exit_pgm( "Error reading xBITMAPINFOHEADER" );
        width  = (int) bmih.biWidth;
        height = (int) bmih.biHeight;
        depth  = bmih.biBitCount;
        rle    = (int) bmih.biCompression;
        imgcnt = color_count( depth );
        if( imgcnt > 0 )
        {
            imgpal = new rgb [imgcnt];
            if( imgpal == 0 )
                exit_pgm( "Error allocating image palette" );
            xRGBQUAD q;
            for( int i=0; i<imgcnt; i++ )
            {
                if( fread(&q,sizeof(xRGBQUAD),1,fbmp) != 1 )
                    exit_pgm( "Error reading xRGBQUAD" );
                imgpal[i] = rgb(q.rgbRed,q.rgbGreen,q.rgbBlue);
            }
        }
    }

    // unknown format
    else
    {
        exit_pgm( "Format error or file is not a BMP file" );
    }

    // set pixel size in bytes
    int pxlsize = 1;
    if( depth == 24 ) pxlsize = 3;
```

Listing 8.4 VBMP.CPP (continued)

```cpp
        // position to start of bitmap
        fseek( fbmp, bmfh.bfOffBits, SEEK_SET );

        // create a scan line buffer
        int rowbytes = (width * pxlsize + 3) / 4;
        rowbytes *= 4;
        unsigned char *scanline = new unsigned char [rowbytes];

        // create an image storage buffer
        imgmap = istore( height, width, depth );

        // and check
        if( (imgmap == 0) || (scanline == 0) )
        {
            if( imgmap )   delete imgmap;
            if( scanline ) delete scanline;
            exit_pgm( "Insufficient memory to load image" );
        }

        // load the image
        printf( "Loading file '%s'...", fn );
        BmpDecoder bmp( fbmp, rle, depth );
        bmp.init( );
        int n = height;
        for( int i=0; i<height; i++ )
        {
            bmp.decode( scanline, width );
            imgmap->put( scanline, —n );
        }
        bmp.term( );
        printf( "done\n" );

        // at this point we're done with the file
        // and the scan line buffer
        fclose( fbmp );
        delete scanline;
    }

    //.................Main

    int main( int argc, char *argv[] )
    {
        process_args( argc, argv );

        load_bmp( );

        // print the image
        if( pmode != 0 )
```

Listing 8.4 VBMP.CPP (continued)

```
    {
        PrinterDriver *prt = printer( pmode );
        if( prt )
        {
            printf( "Printing..." );
            ImagePrinter ip( prt, imgmap, imgpal, imgcnt,
                             ropt, iopt, 100, 100 );
            ip.print( 1 );
            printf( "done\n" );
            delete prt;
        }
        else
            printf( "Printer instantiation failed\n" );
    }

    // display the image
    else
    {
        VgaDisplay vga( gmode );
        ImageViewer iv( &vga, imgmap, imgpal, imgcnt,
                        ropt, iopt );
        iv.view( );
    }

    delete [] imgpal;
    delete imgmap;

    return 0;
}
```

A Windows BMP File Viewer

Microsoft Windows provides many functions that deal with the individual components of the BMP format, but there is no single Windows function to read or write an instance of the format. For that reason, we will take some time to implement a simple BMP file viewer for Windows.

To avoid getting bogged down with too many details of the complex Windows environment, we will forgo many essential program features, such as scroll bars or an adequate file-selector dialog. This will be a truly bare-bones implementation, but it can be used as a template for a more elaborate version.

The program's file-selector dialog contains an edit field and an okay–cancel button pair. The edit field is used to obtain a path specification to a BMP file to be loaded. A second dialog uses two radio button sets to obtain brightness and contrast options that are applied to the file's palette when it is loaded. When a

BMP file is loaded, it is drawn in the client area of the program's window. Although scrolling of the image is not supported, the window's size can be adjusted to display more or less of the full image.

As noted previously, the code in Listings 8.1 and 8.2 uses the same BMP structure and member names that are declared in windows.h, but with the prefix letter x to distinguish them from the actual Windows structures. A version of our structures for Windows, WBMP.HPP and WBMP.CPP, is presented in Listings 8.5 and 8.6 respectively. This version implements a single class, named xBMP, which is designed to take advantage of the available functionality of Windows. For this reason it bears little resemblance to the DOS version presented earlier.

The xBMP class does little more than load BMP file components into memory. However, the class member function xBMP::dib(), creates a device-independent bitmap from the file components and returns a handle to the bitmap. This function requires as a parameter a **device-context handle**. The required HDC value is obtained using the Windows function GetDC(), which takes a window instance handle as a parameter. Details of this process can be seen in Listing 8.7, which presents the source code to WVBMP.CPP. Once the DIB is created, it is drawn in the main window's client area using the draw_bitmap() function. It is drawn whenever the main window procedure receives a WM_PAINT message.

The bitmap is drawn using the BitBlt() function provided by Windows. This process is quite indirect from an application's point of view, because the function's parameter list implies that a region is copied from one device context to another. To this end, **a memory-device context** is temporarily created for the bitmap whose handle was returned by the dib() member function, and this serves as the source context for the copy operation.

A couple of final notes are provided for those unfamiliar with Windows programming. The program's main menu and two dialogs are implemented in a resource script, WVBMP.RC, which is shown later in Listing 8.8. This file and the main source file both reference identifiers that are placed in the file WVBMP.H, shown later in Listing 8.9. WVBMP.H is included in both WVBMP.RC and WVBMP.CPP. To build a Windows executable, the main source file is compiled and linked and then the Windows Resource Compiler is run on the resulting EXE file to bind the menu and dialog resources to it. Assuming that you are using the Borland C++ compiler, the following commands can be run from the DOS prompt:

```
bcc -ml -W WVBMP
rc WVBMP
```

Listing 8.5 WBMP.HPP

```
//---------------------------------------------------------//
//                                                         //
//    File:   WBMP.HPP                                     //
//                                                         //
//    Desc:   Version of BMP.HPP for MS Windows            //
//                                                         //
//---------------------------------------------------------//

#ifndef _WBMP_HPP_
#define _WBMP_HPP_

#include "stdlib.h"
#include "stdio.h"
#include "string.h"

#include "windows.h"

#include "codec.hpp"

#define  BMPSGN   0x4D42
#define  HDRSIZ   (sizeof(BITMAPINFO)+(sizeof(RGBQUAD)*256))

//................class xBMP

class xBMP
{
   public:

      BITMAPFILEHEADER    bmfh;
      BITMAPINFO          *bmi;
      BITMAPINFOHEADER    *bmih;
      RGBQUAD             *rgbq;
   private:

      HGLOBAL      hhdr;
      LPSTR        phdr;
      HGLOBAL      hbits;
      char _huge * pbits;
      int          status;

   public:

      xBMP( char *bmppath );
      ~xBMP( );
      HBITMAP dib( HDC hdc );
      int okay( void ) { return status; }
};

#endif
```

Listing 8.6 WBMP.CPP

```cpp
//----------------------------------------------------------//
//                                                          //
//    File:  WBMP.CPP                                       //
//                                                          //
//    Desc:  Version of BMP.CPP for MS Windows              //
//                                                          //
//----------------------------------------------------------//

#include "wbmp.hpp"

// Note: This version assumes an uncompressed BMP file
//       compatible with Windows 3.0 or later.

//.................class xBMP

xBMP::xBMP( char *bmppath )
{
    // set uninitialized state
    hhdr = hbits = 0;
    phdr = 0;
    pbits = 0;
    status = -1;

    // open file
    HFILE hIN = _lopen( bmppath, READ );
    if( hIN == 0 ) { status = xIOERROR; return; }

    // read header and validate
    if( _lread( hIN, &bmfh, sizeof(BITMAPFILEHEADER) ) !=
        sizeof(BITMAPFILEHEADER) )
    {
        _lclose( hIN ); status = xIOERROR; return;
    }
    if( bmfh.bfType != BMPSGN )
    {
        _lclose( hIN ); status = xBADPARAM; return;
    }

    // load bitmap header and palette
    hhdr = GlobalAlloc( GMEM_MOVEABLE, HDRSIZ );
    if( hhdr == 0 )
    {
        _lclose( hIN ); status = xNOMEMORY; return;
    }
    phdr = GlobalLock( hhdr );
    if( _lread( hIN, phdr, HDRSIZ ) != HDRSIZ )
```

Listing 8.6 WBMP.CPP (continued)

```
      {
          _lclose( hIN ); status = xIOERROR; return;
      }
      bmi  = (BITMAPINFO *) phdr;
      bmih = (BITMAPINFOHEADER *) phdr;
      rgbq = bmi->bmiColors;

      // compute row,bitmap sizes
      long rowbytes = (bmih->biWidth + 3) / 4;
      rowbytes *= 4;
      long nbytes = bmih->biHeight * rowbytes;

      // load bitmap
      hbits = GlobalAlloc( GMEM_MOVEABLE, nbytes );
      if( hbits == 0 )
      {
          _lclose( hIN ); status = xNOMEMORY; return;
      }
      pbits = (char _huge *) GlobalLock( hbits );
      _llseek( hIN, bmfh.bfOffBits, 0 );
      if( _hread( hIN, pbits, nbytes ) != nbytes )
      {
          _lclose( hIN ); status = xIOERROR; return;
      }

      // done!
      _lclose( hIN );
      status = xOKAY;
   }

xBMP::~xBMP( )
{
   if( hhdr )
   {
      GlobalUnlock( hhdr );
      GlobalFree( hhdr );
   }
   if( hbits )
   {
      GlobalUnlock( hbits );
      GlobalFree( hbits );
   }
}
HBITMAP xBMP::dib( HDC hdc )
{
   return CreateDIBitmap( hdc, bmih, CBM_INIT, pbits,
                          bmi, DIB_RGB_COLORS );
}
```

Listing 8.7 WVBMP.CPP

```
//----------------------------------------------------------//
//                                                          //
//   File:  WVBmp.Cpp                                       //
//                                                          //
//   Desc:  A simple Windows BMP file viewer                //
//                                                          //
//----------------------------------------------------------//

#include "intenmap.hpp"
#include "wbmp.hpp"
#include "wvbmp.h"

static HWND main_window_handle;

// contrast and brightness options
static  int  copt = idCNONE;
static  int  bopt = idBNONE;
//................draw a bitmap

void draw_bitmap( HDC hdc, HBITMAP hbm, short xo, short yo )
{
   BITMAP  bm;
   HDC     hdcMem;
   POINT   bmSiz, bmOrg;

   hdcMem = CreateCompatibleDC( hdc );
   SelectObject( hdcMem, hbm );
   SetMapMode( hdcMem, GetMapMode( hdc ) );
   GetObject( hbm, sizeof( BITMAP ), (LPSTR) &bm );

   bmSiz.x = bm.bmWidth;
   bmSiz.y = bm.bmHeight;
   DPtoLP( hdc, &bmSiz, 1 );

   bmOrg.x = 0;
   bmOrg.y = 0;
   DPtoLP( hdc, &bmOrg, 1 );

   BitBlt( hdc, xo, yo, bmSiz.x, bmSiz.y,
           hdcMem, bmOrg.x, bmOrg.y, SRCCOPY );

   DeleteDC( hdcMem );
}

//................load BMP file
static xBMP    *xbmp = 0;
static HBITMAP hbmp = 0;
```

Listing 8.7 WVBMP.CPP (continued)

```cpp
void load_bmp( char *fn, HDC hdc )
{
    if( xbmp ) delete xbmp;
    xbmp = new xBMP( fn );
    if( xbmp->okay() != xOKAY )
    {
        char msg[40];
        sprintf( msg, "Error %d loading file!", xbmp->okay() );
        TextOut( hdc, 10, 10, msg, strlen(msg) );
        MessageBeep( 0 );
        delete xbmp;
        xbmp = 0;
        hbmp = 0;
    }
    else
    {
        if( copt != idCNONE )
        {
            int sgn = (copt == idCMORE) ? 1 : -1;
            for( int i=0; i<256; i++ )
            {
                int r = xbmp->rgbq[i].rgbRed;
                int g = xbmp->rgbq[i].rgbGreen;
                int b = xbmp->rgbq[i].rgbBlue;
                rgb x( r, g, b );
                contrast_alter( &x, 1, sgn );
                xbmp->rgbq[i].rgbRed   = x.red;
                xbmp->rgbq[i].rgbGreen = x.grn;;
                xbmp->rgbq[i].rgbBlue  = x.blu;
            }
        }
        if( bopt != idBNONE )
        {
            int sgn = (bopt == idBMORE) ? 1 : -1;
            for( int i=0; i<256; i++ )
            {
                int r = xbmp->rgbq[i].rgbRed;
                int g = xbmp->rgbq[i].rgbGreen;
                int b = xbmp->rgbq[i].rgbBlue;
                rgb x( r, g, b );
                brightness_alter( &x, 1, sgn );
                xbmp->rgbq[i].rgbRed   = x.red;
                xbmp->rgbq[i].rgbGreen = x.grn;;
                xbmp->rgbq[i].rgbBlue  = x.blu;
            }
        }
        hbmp = xbmp->dib( hdc );
        if( hbmp == 0 )
```

Listing 8.7 WVBMP.CPP (continued)

```cpp
        {
            TextOut( hdc, 10, 10, "DIB creation failed!", 20 );
            MessageBeep( 0 );
        }
        else
            draw_bitmap( hdc, hbmp, 0, 0 );
    }
}

//.................load-file dialog procedure

static  HANDLE    load_file_hand;
static  FARPROC   load_file_proc;
static  char      file_name[81] = "";

BOOL FAR PASCAL load_file( HWND hdlg, UINT message,
                           WPARAM wParam, LPARAM lParam )
{
    switch( message )
    {
        case WM_INITDIALOG :
            SendDlgItemMessage( hdlg, idFNAME,
                                EM_LIMITTEXT, 80, 0L );
            SetDlgItemText( hdlg, idFNAME, file_name );
            return 1;

        case WM_COMMAND :
            switch( wParam )
            {
                case idFNAME :
                    if( HIWORD(lParam) == EN_CHANGE )
                    {
                        HWND h = GetDlgItem( hdlg, IDOK );
                        LONG r = SendMessage( LOWORD(lParam),
                                WM_GETTEXTLENGTH, 0, 0L );

                        EnableWindow( h, (BOOL) r );
                    }
                    return 1;

                case IDOK :
                    GetDlgItemText( hdlg, idFNAME, file_name, 80 );
                case IDCANCEL :
                    EndDialog( hdlg, 0 );
                    if( wParam == IDOK )
                    {
                        HDC hdc = GetDC( main_window_handle );
                        load_bmp( file_name, hdc );
```

Listing 8.7 WVBMP.CPP (continued)

```
                            ReleaseDC( main_window_handle, hdc );
                    }
                    return 1;
            }
            break;
    }

    return 0;
}

//.................load-options dialog procedure

static  HANDLE   get_opt_hand;
static  FARPROC  get_opt_proc;
BOOL FAR PASCAL get_opt( HWND hdlg, UINT message,
                         WPARAM wParam, LPARAM lParam )
{
    switch( message )
    {
        case WM_INITDIALOG :
            CheckRadioButton( hdlg, idCNONE, idCLESS, copt );
            CheckRadioButton( hdlg, idBNONE, idBLESS, bopt );
            return 1;

        case WM_COMMAND :
            switch( wParam )
            {
                case idCNONE :
                case idCMORE :
                case idCLESS :
                    copt = wParam;
                    CheckRadioButton( hdlg, idCNONE,
                                        idCLESS, copt );
                    return 1;

                case idBNONE :
                case idBMORE :
                case idBLESS :
                    bopt = wParam;
                    CheckRadioButton( hdlg, idBNONE,
                                        idBLESS, bopt );
                    return 1;

                case IDOK :
                case IDCANCEL :
                    EndDialog( hdlg, 0 );
```

Listing 8.7 WVBMP.CPP (continued)

```cpp
                        return 1;
            }
            break;
    }

    return 0;
}

//................main window procedure

long FAR PASCAL WndProc( HWND hwnd, UINT message,
                         WPARAM wParam, LPARAM lParam )
{
    HDC          hdc;
    PAINTSTRUCT  ps;

    switch( message )
    {
        case WM_COMMAND :
            switch( wParam )
            {
                case 1 : // Load
                    DialogBox( load_file_hand,
                               "LoadFile",
                               hwnd,
                               load_file_proc );
                    return 0;

                case 2 : // Options
                    DialogBox( get_opt_hand,
                               "GetOptions",
                               hwnd,
                               get_opt_proc );
                    return 0;

                case 3 : // Quit
                    SendMessage( hwnd, WM_CLOSE, 0, 0L );
                    return 0;
            }
            break;

        case WM_CREATE :
            load_file_hand =
                ((LPCREATESTRUCT) lParam)->hInstance;
            load_file_proc =
                MakeProcInstance( (FARPROC) load_file,
                                  load_file_hand );
            get_opt_hand =
```

Listing 8.7 WVBMP.CPP (continued)

```cpp
                     ((LPCREATESTRUCT) lParam)->hInstance;
            get_opt_proc =
                MakeProcInstance( (FARPROC) get_opt,
                                   get_opt_hand );
            return 0;

        case WM_PAINT :
            hdc = BeginPaint( hwnd, &ps );
            if( hbmp )
            {
                hbmp = xbmp->dib( hdc );
                draw_bitmap( hdc, hbmp, 0, 0 );
            }
            EndPaint( hwnd, &ps );
            return 0;

        case WM_DESTROY :
            if( xbmp ) delete xbmp;
            PostQuitMessage( 0 );
            return 0;
    }

    return DefWindowProc( hwnd, message, wParam, lParam );
}

//.................windows main

static char AppName[] = "WVBmp";

int PASCAL WinMain( HANDLE hInstance, HANDLE hPrevInstance,
                    LPSTR lpszCmdParam, int nCmdShow )
{
    WNDCLASS  wc;
    if( ! hPrevInstance )
    {
        wc.style         = CS_HREDRAW | CS_VREDRAW;
        wc.lpfnWndProc   = WndProc;
        wc.cbClsExtra    = 0;
        wc.cbWndExtra    = 0;
        wc.hInstance     = hInstance;
        wc.hIcon         = LoadIcon( NULL, IDI_APPLICATION );
        wc.hCursor       = LoadCursor( NULL, IDC_ARROW );
        wc.hbrBackground = GetStockObject( WHITE_BRUSH );
        wc.lpszMenuName  = AppName;
        wc.lpszClassName = AppName;
        RegisterClass( &wc );
    }
```

Listing 8.7 WVBMP.CPP (continued)

```cpp
        // get screen dimensions
        int sw = GetSystemMetrics( SM_CXSCREEN );
        int sh = GetSystemMetrics( SM_CYSCREEN );

        HWND hwnd;
        hwnd = CreateWindow( AppName,
                             "BMP File Viewer",
                             WS_OVERLAPPEDWINDOW,
                             sw/4,
                             sh/4,
                             sw/2,
                             sh/2,
                             NULL,
                             NULL,
                             hInstance,
                             NULL );

        main_window_handle = hwnd;
        ShowWindow( hwnd, nCmdShow );
        UpdateWindow( hwnd );

        MSG msg;
        while( GetMessage( &msg, NULL, 0, 0 ) )
        {
            TranslateMessage( &msg );
            DispatchMessage( &msg );
        }

        return msg.wParam;
    }
```

Listing 8.8 WVBMP.RC

```
/*-----------------------------------------------------------*/
/*                                                           */
/*     File:    WVBMP.RC                                     */
/*                                                           */
/*     Desc:    Resource script for WVBmp.Exe                */
/*                                                           */
/*-----------------------------------------------------------*/

#include "windows.h"

#include "wvbmp.h"
```

Listing 8.8 WVBMP.RC (continued)

```
/*
 *................WVBmp Main Menu
 */

WVBmp MENU
{
    MENUITEM "&File",     1
    MENUITEM "&Options",  2
    MENUITEM "&Quit",     3
}

/*
 *................WVBmp Load File Dialog
 */

LoadFile   DIALOG  10 10 150 100
           STYLE   WS_POPUP | WS_DLGFRAME
{
    CTEXT   "— Load BMP File —"
            -1,         0,  10,  150,   8

    LTEXT   "Path to file..."
            -1,        15,  30,   60,   8
    EDITTEXT
            idFNAME,   15,  40,  120,  12

    DEFPUSHBUTTON  "Okay"
            IDOK,      30,  70,   40,  14

    PUSHBUTTON  "Cancel"
            IDCANCEL,  80,  70,   40,  14
}

/*
 *................WVBmp Get Options Dialog
 */

GetOptions  DIALOG  10 10 150 100
            STYLE   WS_POPUP | WS_DLGFRAME
{
    CTEXT   "— Load Options —"
            -1,         0,  10,  150,   8

    GROUPBOX  "Contrast"
            -1,        10,  20,   60,  50, WS_GROUP
    RADIOBUTTON  "None"
            idCNONE,   20,  35,   40,   8, WS_GROUP|WS_TABSTOP
    RADIOBUTTON  "More"
```

Listing 8.8 WVBMP.RC (continued)

```
          idCMORE,    20, 45,     40,     8
     RADIOBUTTON  "Less"
          idCLESS,    20, 55,     40,     8


     GROUPBOX  "Brightness"
          -1,          80, 20,     60,    50, WS_GROUP
     RADIOBUTTON  "None"
          idBNONE,     90, 35,     40,     8, WS_GROUP|WS_TABSTOP
     RADIOBUTTON  "More"
          idBMORE,     90, 45,     40,     8
     RADIOBUTTON  "Less"
          idBLESS,     90, 55,     40,     8


     DEFPUSHBUTTON  "Okay"
          IDOK,        55, 80,     40,    14, WS_GROUP
}
```

Listing 8.9 WVBMP.H

```
/*------------------------------------------------------*/
/*                                                      */
/*   File:    WVBMP.H                                   */
/*                                                      */
/*   Desc:    Identifiers used in WVBMP.RC and WVBMP.CPP */
/*                                                      */
/*------------------------------------------------------*/

#define idFNAME    ( WM_USER + 1 )

#define idCNONE    ( WM_USER + 2 )
#define idCMORE    ( WM_USER + 3 )
#define idCLESS    ( WM_USER + 4 )

#define idBNONE    ( WM_USER + 5 )
#define idBMORE    ( WM_USER + 6 )
#define idBLESS    ( WM_USER + 7 )
```

Handling Color under Windows

One problem arises in any multiprocess environment in which a palette-based display can be used by more than one process at any given time–namely, what to do about color conflicts. For instance, say we have a 256-color display and one process is attempting to render a 256-color bitmap. If that process is allowed to set a 256-color palette for the image, it is likely that the displays of other processes will be adversely affected by the resulting color changes.

Windows deals with this problem by reserving hardware palette control for itself and by using a system palette of its own choosing. If an application then requests a color that is not in the current system palette, Windows attempts to approximate that color in one of two ways. If the color is being used to fill an area, Windows approximates the color by means of dithering, and if the color is being used to set a pixel, Windows substitutes the closest matching color in the system palette. Both approaches are, in general, unsatisfactory if visual or chromatic fidelity are important.

The only situation in which an application can expect to reproduce color exactly under Windows is when the video subsystem uses a 24-bit color adapter. Even a 15-bit color display poses problems, because the lower 3 bits of an 8-bit primary intensity value are lost when the 8-bit value is reduced to 5 bits. In this situation, the adapter can produce 32,767 simultaneous colors; however color distinctions even in a 16-color image can be lost because of the adapter's lower primary resolution.

It is ironic that, if accurate color reproduction in 16-color and 256-color images on VGA-compatible video hardware is important, then DOS is the better application environment.

Writing the BMP Format

Writing a format is generally somewhat easier than reading it, because a program is able to control all details of the process and is not responding to the external input that a graphics file represents. Listings 8.1 and 8.2 define a `BmpEncoder` class that can be used to write image data to a BMP file, so all that remains is to develop code to initialize and output the format's header structures.

Listing 8.10 presents two versions of a `WriteBMP` function that has been overloaded for use under C++. This code will output a BMP file from an instance of either the `VgaDisplay` class or the `ImgStore` class.

A sample program that illustrates the use of the `WriteBMP()` function is presented in Listing 8.11. This program displays the El Greco sample image and then creates a BMP file from the video display. Note that the program's output can be tested with the QBMP and VBMP programs.

Listing 8.10 WRTBMP.CPP

```
//----------------------------------------------------------//
//                                                          //
//    File:     WRTBMP.CPP                                  //
//                                                          //
//    Desc:     Code to output a BMP file from a            //
//              VGA Display or a Memory Bitmap              //
//                                                          //
//----------------------------------------------------------//

#include "stdlib.h"
#include "stdio.h"
#include "string.h"

#include "display.hpp"
#include "imgstore.hpp"
#include "bmp.hpp"

//.................Abort macro

#define  ABORT( f, r )  { fclose(f); return r; }

//.................Write VGA screen to BMP file 'fn'

int WriteBMP( VgaDisplay& vga, char *fn,
              int x1, int y1, int x2, int y2 )
{
   FILE *f = fopen( fn, "wb" );
   if( f == 0 )
      ABORT( f, xIOERROR );

   // image metrics
   int nrows    = y2 - y1 + 1;
   int ncols    = x2 - x1 + 1;
   int nbits    = vga.metric.nplanes * vga.metric.nbits;
   int ncolors  = (nbits <= 8) ? 1 << nbits : 0;
   int rowbytes = ((ncols*nbits + 31) / 32) * 4;

   // write an empty file header as a place holder
   xBITMAPFILEHEADER fh;
   if( fwrite( &fh, sizeof(xBITMAPFILEHEADER), 1, f ) != 1 )
      ABORT( f, xIOERROR );

   // initialize and write the image header
   xBITMAPINFOHEADER ih;
   ih.biSize = sizeof(xBITMAPINFOHEADER);
   ih.biWidth = ncols;
   ih.biHeight = nrows;
```

Listing 8.10 WRTBMP.CPP (continued)

```cpp
ih.biPlanes = 1;
ih.biBitCount = nbits;
ih.biSizeImage = nrows * rowbytes;
if( fwrite( &ih, sizeof(xBITMAPINFOHEADER), 1, f ) != 1 )
   ABORT( f, xIOERROR );

// write the display's palette
xRGBQUAD x;
if( ncolors > 2 )
{
   rgb *pal = new rgb[ncolors];
   if( pal == 0 )
      ABORT( f, xNOMEMORY );
   vga.getpalette( pal, ncolors );
   for( int i=0; i<ncolors; i++ )
   {
      x.set( pal[i].red, pal[i].grn, pal[i].blu );
      if( fwrite( &x, sizeof(xRGBQUAD), 1, f ) != 1 )
      {
         delete [] pal;
         ABORT( f, xIOERROR );
      }
   }
   delete [] pal;
}
else if( ncolors > 0 )
{
   x.set( 0, 0, 0 );
   if( fwrite( &x, sizeof(xRGBQUAD), 1, f ) != 1 )
      ABORT( f, xIOERROR );
   x.set( 255, 255, 255 );
   if( fwrite( &x, sizeof(xRGBQUAD), 1, f ) != 1 )
      ABORT( f, xIOERROR );
}

// save offset to start of bitmap
long bmofs = ftell( f );

// output the bitmap
unsigned char *pxls = new unsigned char [ncols];
if( pxls == 0 )
   ABORT( f, xNOMEMORY );
BmpEncoder bmp( f, nbits );
for( int i=y2; i>=y1; i-- )
{
   vga.getscanline( pxls, ncols, x1, i );
   bmp.encode( pxls, ncols );
   if( bmp.status() != xOKAY )
```

Listing 8.10 WRTBMP.CPP (continued)

```
            {
                delete pxls;
                ABORT( f, bmp.status() );
            }
        }

        // save offset to end of file
        long fisiz = ftell( f );

        // update and rewrite file header
        fh.bfSize = fisiz;
        fh.bfOffBits = bmofs;
        fseek( f, 0L, SEEK_SET );
        if( fwrite( &fh, sizeof(xBITMAPFILEHEADER), 1, f ) != 1 )
            ABORT( f, xIOERROR );

        fclose( f );
        return xOKAY;
}

//.................Write an ImgStore to BMP file 'fn'

int WriteBMP( ImgStore& img, rgb *pal, char *fn )
{
    FILE *f = fopen( fn, "wb" );
    if( f == 0 )
        ABORT( f, xIOERROR );

    // image metrics
    int nrows    = img.height();
    int ncols    = img.width();
    int nbits    = img.depth();
    int ncolors  = (nbits <= 8) ? 1 << nbits : 0;
    int rowbytes = ((ncols*nbits + 31) / 32) * 4;
    // write an empty file header as a place holder
    xBITMAPFILEHEADER fh;
    if( fwrite( &fh, sizeof(xBITMAPFILEHEADER), 1, f ) != 1 )
        ABORT( f, xIOERROR );

    // initialize and write the image header
    xBITMAPINFOHEADER ih;
    ih.biSize = sizeof(xBITMAPINFOHEADER);
    ih.biWidth = ncols;
    ih.biHeight = nrows;
    ih.biPlanes = 1;
    ih.biBitCount = nbits;
```

Listing 8.10 WRTBMP.CPP (continued)

```cpp
ih.biSizeImage = nrows * rowbytes;
if( fwrite( &ih, sizeof(xBITMAPINFOHEADER), 1, f ) != 1 )
   ABORT( f, xIOERROR );

// write the palette
xRGBQUAD x;
if( ncolors > 2 )
{
   for( int i=0; i<ncolors; i++ )
   {
      x.set( pal[i].red, pal[i].grn, pal[i].blu );
      if( fwrite( &x, sizeof(xRGBQUAD), 1, f ) != 1 )
      {
         delete [] pal;
         ABORT( f, xIOERROR );
      }
   }
}
else if( ncolors > 0 )
{
   x.set( 0, 0, 0 );
   if( fwrite( &x, sizeof(xRGBQUAD), 1, f ) != 1 )
      ABORT( f, xIOERROR );
   x.set( 255, 255, 255 );
   if( fwrite( &x, sizeof(xRGBQUAD), 1, f ) != 1 )
      ABORT( f, xIOERROR );
}

// save offset to start of bitmap
long bmofs = ftell( f );

// output the bitmap
BmpEncoder bmp( f, nbits );
for( int i=nrows-1; i>=0; i- )
{
   bmp.encode( img.get(i), ncols );
   if( bmp.status() != xOKAY )
      ABORT( f, bmp.status() );
}

// save offset to end of file
long fisiz = ftell( f );
```

Listing 8.10 WRTBMP.CPP (continued)

```
        // update and rewrite file header
        fh.bfSize = fisiz;
        fh.bfOffBits = bmofs;
        fseek( f, 0L, SEEK_SET );
        if( fwrite( &fh, sizeof(xBITMAPFILEHEADER), 1, f ) != 1 )
            ABORT( f, xIOERROR );

        fclose( f );
        return xOKAY;
}
```

Listing 8.11 BMPDEMO.CPP

```
//----------------------------------------------------------//
//                                                          //
//   File:      BMPDEMO.CPP                                 //
//                                                          //
//   Desc:      Example code to write a BMP file           //
//                                                          //
//----------------------------------------------------------//

#include "wrtbmp.cpp"

char *        palname    = "EL-GRECO.PAL";
char *        imgname    = "EL-GRECO.IMG";
int           imgwidth   = 354;
int           imgheight  = 446;
int           imgcolors  = 256;
rgb           imgpalette[256];
unsigned char scanline[354];

// read the test image's palette

void read_palette( VgaDisplay& vga )
{
    FILE *f = fopen( palname, "rt" );
    for( int i=0; i<imgcolors; i++ )
    {
        int r, g, b;
        fscanf( f, "%d %d %d", &r, &g, &b );
        imgpalette[i] = rgb( r, g, b );
    }
    fclose( f );
    vga.putpalette( imgpalette, imgcolors );
}
```

Listing 8.11 BMPDEMO.CPP (continued)

```cpp
// read the test image onto the screen

void read_image( VgaDisplay& vga )
{
    FILE *f = fopen( imgname, "rb" );
    for( int i=0; i<imgheight; i++ )
    {
        fread( scanline, imgwidth, 1, f );
        vga.putscanline( scanline, imgwidth, 0, i );
    }
    fclose( f );
}

// output a BMP file

int main( void )
{
    VgaDisplay vga( 0x2E );

    read_palette( vga );
    read_image( vga );

    WriteBMP( vga, "BMPDEMO.BMP", 0, 0, imgwidth-1, imgheight-1 );

    return 0;
}
```

This concludes our look at the BMP format. As you can see, except for a few quirks, it is a straightforward format to deal with. This makes it an attractive option for a program that must read or write graphics files. An added bonus is the fact that most graphics programs written for MS Windows support the BMP format, which means the format can be used to exchange image data among a wide variety of commercial applications. The growing importance of Windows itself also contributes to this format's usefulness.

9

The Paintbrush
PCX Format

Of all of the common graphics file formats in use on MS-DOS systems, the PCX format is perhaps the most venerable. It is, of course, the native format of PC Paintbrush, one of the earliest paint programs for the IBM personal computer. At one time, if you bought a Microsoft mouse, you received a copy of PC Paintbrush whether you wanted it or not. If you owned four or five Microsoft mice then you owned four or five copies of PC Paintbrush. While the version of Paintbrush bundled with the mouse was not a very compelling application, it was nonetheless frequently pressed into service, so instances of the format were eventually to be found almost everywhere.

The PCX format is widely supported among graphics applications, having been revised over the years to keep up with the pace of emerging graphics display technology. It originally supported only monochrome- and 16-color-palette-based imagery. After IBM released its PS/2 line, the VGA adapter quickly became the new display standard, and the PCX format was revised to support 256-color imagery. The format was recently upgraded again to add support for 24-bit color imagery.

The overall structure of the format is relatively straightforward, consisting of a 128-byte header and an RLE-encoded bitmap. The header contains a palette area that provides room for 16 RGB triples. When 256-color imagery appeared, the format obviously had to be modified. It was decided that the header would remain as written and that 256-color palettes would be appended to the end of the file, following the bitmap.

The RLE encoding scheme used in the PCX format is a bit odd, in that runs and sequences are differentiated by the top two bits of a byte rather than the more usual single high-order bit. It seems likely that the format's creators originally contemplated using more than two encoding constructs, but this is only conjecture. In any case, a format reader must read a data byte and inspect the top two bits. If they are both set, then a run is indicated, and the lower six bits indicate the number of times to repeat the next byte in the data stream. If the top two bits are not set then a repeat count of 1 is assumed and the byte is an actual image data value.

Because repeat counts are expressed in only six bits, the maximum repeat count value is 63. Also, single image bytes that have the top two bits set must be handled specially. These must be encoded using two bytes to indicate a repeating run of 1 byte. Otherwise, the single byte with the top two bits set would be erroneously interpreted as indicating a repeating run.

The PCX format is intended primarily for screen-based imagery, and the overall structure of the encoded bitmap is derived from its display-based representation. The format is thus device dependent. For example, images for VGA mode 12h are encoded as separate bit planes, in keeping with the planar organization of that video mode. This allows an encoded image to be decoded and displayed quite rapidly; it also means that format encoders and decoders must handle individual display modes separately.

Another characteristic of the encoded bitmap is that runs can span both planes and scan lines. That is, a run can extend beyond the end of the current scan line or plane and wrap into the start of the next scan line or plane. Although it might seem that this convention would complicate the logic of an encoder or decoder, this is not actually the case if the logic is developed around this premise to begin with. Note that individual scan lines are padded with unused bits to make their length an integral number of 16-bit words.

PCX file names typically use one of two specific extensions, .PCX or .PCC, both of which indicate the PCX format. The .PCC extension was originally intended to indicate a "cut" image, that is, a rectangular region cut from a complete screen image. The distinction is meaningless from a software perspective, however and few commercial applications bother to observe it.

The PCX File Header

The PCX file header occupies the first 128 bytes of a PCX file. The header can be read using the structure shown in Listing 9.1. Many of the header's fields are of esoteric origin and use and can be ignored when the header is dealt with in a program. In a PCX header, all unused header members should be zero-filled. A brief description of each header structure member follows.

format	Byte value originally intended to indicate a manufacturer. However, the only valid value is 10 (0Ah). About the only practical use for this field is to validate the format—a value other than 10 indicates that the file is probably not a PCX file.
version	Byte value indicating what version of the format is present. Possible values are 0 for version 2.5, 2 for version 2.8 with a palette, 3 for version 2.8 without a palette, or 5 for version 3.0 and later. The value does not affect the interpretation of other header values, except that a value of 3 implies that the header's palette should be ignored.
rleflag	Flag set to 1 to indicate that the bitmap is RLE encoded. Because the bitmap must always be encoded, this field is always 1.
bitpx	Number of bits per pixel in the image. Valid values are 1, 2, 4, or 8. Color images with 24 bits per pixel are normally indicated as 3 planes of 8 bpp each.
x1, y1	Pixel coordinates of the upper left corner of the image. If the image encompasses the full screen, this pair has the value (0,0).
x2, y2	The pixel coordinates of the lower right corner of the image. If the image encompasses the entire screen of a particular video mode, this pair has the value (W-1,H-1) where WxH are the screen dimensions. For example, a full screen image for VGA mode 12h would show the values (639,479) here.
hres, vres	Horizontal and vertical resolutions of the image in dots per inch. Typical values for a VGA display are 75 to 100 dpi.
colors	48-byte buffer containing 16 RGB triples. Each byte indicates a primary intensity value. The triples are ordered as you might expect: r1, g1, b1, r2, g2, b2, and so on. In most cases the full 8 bits of each byte are used, for a range of 0 to 255. However, some specimens of the format may contain actual VGA DAC register values, which use only 6 bits and a range of 0 to 63. Note that this palette buffer is not used for 256-color imagery.
vmode	Byte value that is supposed to indicate the BIOS mode number of the image's native video mode. However, a value is seldom found here, and this field can be ignored in any case.

nplanes	Number of bit planes in the image. This value is typically 1 or 4, but will be 3 for 24-bit imagery. Although 24-bit images are not really multiplanar, they are treated as such for the convenience of the format.
bplin	Number of bytes per scan line per plane. For instance, a VGA-mode 12h image would show a value of 80 here; a 640x480x256-color image would show a value of 640. Note that this value reflects padding of line widths to an even number of bytes.
paltype	Byte value indicating the type of palette present. A value of 1 indicates a color palette; a value of 2 indicates a gray-scale palette.
scrnw, scrnh	Size of the display screen, in pixels, on which the image was created. These fields are optional and can be set to 0.
xtra	54-byte unused area in the header. It should be zero-filled and otherwise ignored.

Listing 9.1 PCX.HPP

```
//----------------------------------------------------------//
//                                                          //
//    File:    PCX.HPP                                       //
//                                                          //
//    Desc:    Class and structure definitions for the      //
//             PC Paintbrush PCX format                      //
//                                                          //
//----------------------------------------------------------//

#ifndef _PCX_HPP_
#define _PCX_HPP_

#include "stdlib.h"
#include "stdio.h"
#include "string.h"

#include "color.hpp"
#include "codec.hpp"
#include "revbyte.hpp"

//.............struct PCXHEADER

struct PCXHEADER
{
    char          format;       // Always 10 for PCX
    char          version;      // Version info
    char          rleflag;      // Set to 1
```

Listing 9.1 PCX.HPP (continued)

```cpp
        char            bitpx;        // Bits per pixel
        unsigned short x1;            // Image bounds in pixels
        unsigned short y1;            //      "
        unsigned short x2;            //      "
        unsigned short y2;            //      "
        unsigned short hres;          // Image resolution in dpi
        unsigned short vres;          //      "
        unsigned char  colors[48];    // Palette
        char            vmode;        // (ignored)
        char            nplanes;      // Plane count (v2.5=0)
        unsigned short bplin;         // Bytes per line
        unsigned short paltype;       // 1 for color, 2 for gray
        unsigned short scrnw;         // Screen size in pixels
        unsigned short scrnh;         //      "
        char            xtra[54];     // Extra space (filler)

        PCXHEADER( );
       ~PCXHEADER( ) { }
        void list( void );
    };

    //............struct PCXPALETTE

    struct PCXPALETTE
    {
        int nopal;
        int ncolors;
        rgb *colors;
        PCXPALETTE( FILE *f, PCXHEADER& h );
        PCXPALETTE( )
        {
            nopal = 0;
            ncolors = 0;
            colors = 0;
        }
        ~PCXPALETTE( )
        {
            if( colors )
                delete colors;
        }
    };

    //............class PcxDecoder

    class PcxDecoder : public Decoder
    {
        protected:
            int   cond;          // condition code
```

Listing 9.1 PCX.HPP (continued)

```
        int    pxl_bits;        // bits per pixel
        int    pxl_planes;      // planes per pixel
        int    row_bytes;       // bytes per plane
        FILE *pcx_file;         // output file

    private:
        int    hdr_byte;        // decode variables
        int    cnt_byte;
        int    dat_byte;
        int    shift_msk;
        int    shift_cnt;
        void   read_124( unsigned char *buf, int npxls );
        void   read_8( unsigned char *buf, int npxls );

    public:
        PcxDecoder( FILE *f_in, PCXHEADER& pcx );
        virtual ~PcxDecoder( ) { }
        virtual int decode( unsigned char *buf, int npxls );
        virtual int init( void );
        virtual int term( void );
        virtual int status( void );
};

//............class PcxEncoder

class PcxEncoder : public Encoder
{
    protected:
        int    cond;            // condition code
        int    pxl_bits;        // bits per pixel
        int    pxl_planes;      // planes per pixel
        int    row_bytes;       // bytes per plane
        FILE *pcx_file;         // output file

    private:
        char *scanbuffer;       // output buffer
        int    scanmask;        // output bit mask
        int    scanbyte;        // output byte pointer
        void   initbuffer( void );
        void   putbits( int bits, int nbits );
        void   putbyte( int byte );
        int    flush( void );
        void   write_124( unsigned char *buf, int npxls );
        void   write_8( unsigned char *buf, int npxls );

    public:
        PcxEncoder( FILE *f_out, PCXHEADER& pcx );
        virtual ~PcxEncoder( )
```

Listing 9.1 PCX.HPP (continued)

```
        {
            if( scanbuffer )
                delete scanbuffer;
        }
        virtual int encode( unsigned char *buf, int npxls );
        virtual int init( void );
        virtual int term( void );
        virtual int status( void );
    };

    #endif
```

Listing 9.2 PCX.CPP

```
//----------------------------------------------------------//
//                                                          //
//    File:     PCX.CPP                                     //
//                                                          //
//    Desc:     Class and structure definitions for the     //
//              PC Paintbrush PCX format                     //
//                                                          //
//----------------------------------------------------------//

#include "pcx.hpp"

#define   RUN_MASK   0xC0      // mask top 2 bits
#define   CNT_MASK   0x3F      // mask bottom 6 bits
#define   MAX_RUN    0x3F      // max repeat count

//.................struct PCXHEADER

PCXHEADER::PCXHEADER( )
{
    format  = 10;
    version = 5;
    rleflag = 1;
    paltype = 1;
    vmode   = 0;
    memset( colors, 0, 48 );
    memset( xtra, 0, 54 );
}

void PCXHEADER::list( void )
{
    printf( "PCXHEADER::format  = %d\n", format );
    printf( "PCXHEADER::version = %d, ", version );
    switch( version )
    {
```

Listing 9.2 PCX.CPP (continued)

```
        case 0  : printf( "version 2.5\n" );
                  break;
        case 2  : printf( "version 2.8 with palette\n" );
                  break;
        case 3  : printf( "version 2.8 without palette\n" );
                  break;
        case 5  : printf( "version 3.0 or later\n" );
                  break;
        default : printf( "unknown version\n" );
    }
    printf( "PCXHEADER::rleflag = %d\n", rleflag );
    printf( "PCXHEADER::paltype = %d, ", paltype );
    switch( paltype )
    {
        case 1  : printf( "color image\n" );
                  break;
        case 2  : printf( "grayscale image\n" );
                  break;
        default : printf( "unknown image type\n" );
    }
    printf( "PCXHEADER::vmode   = %d\n", vmode );
    printf( "PCXHEADER::bitpx   = %d\n", bitpx );
    printf( "PCXHEADER::nplanes = %d\n", nplanes );
    printf( "PCXHEADER::bplin   = %d\n", bplin );
    printf( "PCXHEADER::x1      = %d\n", x1 );
    printf( "PCXHEADER::y1      = %d\n", y1 );
    printf( "PCXHEADER::x2      = %d\n", x2 );
    printf( "PCXHEADER::y2      = %d\n", y2 );
    printf( "PCXHEADER::hres    = %d\n", hres );
    printf( "PCXHEADER::vres    = %d\n", vres );
    printf( "PCXHEADER::scrnw   = %d\n", scrnw );
    printf( "PCXHEADER::scrnh   = %d\n", scrnh );
}

//................struct PCXPALETTE

PCXPALETTE::PCXPALETTE( FILE *f, PCXHEADER& h )
{
    ncolors = nopal = 0;
    colors = 0;
    // 16 colors or less
    if( h.bitpx < 8 )
    {
        ncolors = 1 << (h.bitpx * h.nplanes);
        if( ncolors == 2 )
        {
            colors = new rgb[2];
            colors[0] = rgb( 0, 0, 0 );
```

Listing 9.2 PCX.CPP (continued)

```cpp
          colors[1] = rgb( 255, 255, 255 );
      }
      else
      {
         colors = new rgb[16];
         if( colors )
         {
           int n = 0;
            for( int i=0; i<16; i++ )
               colors[i] = rgb( h.colors[n++],
                                h.colors[n++],
                                h.colors[n++] );
         }
         else
            ncolors = 0;
      }
      nopal = (h.version == 3) ? 1 : 0;
   }
   // 256 colors
   else if( (h.bitpx == 8) && (h.nplanes == 1) )
   {
      fseek( f, -769, SEEK_END );
      nopal = (fgetc( f ) == 12) ? 0 : 1;
      ncolors = 256;
      colors = new rgb[256];
      if( colors )
      {
        for( int i=0; i<256; i++ )
        {
           int r = fgetc( f );
           int g = fgetc( f );
           int b = fgetc( f );
           colors[i] = rgb( r, g, b );
        }
      }
      else
         ncolors = 0;
   }
}

//.................class PcxDecoder

PcxDecoder::PcxDecoder( FILE *f_in, PCXHEADER& pcx )
{
   pxl_bits   = (pcx.bitpx==0)   ? 1 : pcx.bitpx;
   pxl_planes = (pcx.nplanes==0) ? 1 : pcx.nplanes;
   row_bytes  = pcx.bplin;
```

Listing 9.2 PCX.CPP (continued)

```cpp
    pcx_file = f_in;

    shift_cnt = pxl_bits;
    shift_msk = (1 << pxl_bits) - 1;
    cond = xOKAY;
}

int PcxDecoder::status( void )
{
    if( ferror( pcx_file ) ) cond = xIOERROR;
    if( feof( pcx_file ) )   cond = xENDOFFILE;
    return cond;
}

int PcxDecoder::init( void )
{
    cond = xOKAY;
    hdr_byte = cnt_byte = dat_byte = 0;
    // seek to start of bitmap
    fseek( pcx_file, 128, SEEK_SET );
    return status();
}

int PcxDecoder::term( void )
{
    return status();
}

// decodes 1, 2, or 4 bits per pixel
void PcxDecoder::read_124( unsigned char *buf, int npxls )
{
    // initial values
    int bytecnt       = 0;
    int curplane      = 0;
    int pixelsperbyte = 8 / pxl_bits;
    int setpxlshfitcnt = 0;
    int curpxl        = 0;

    // zero the buffer
    memset( buf, 0, npxls );

    while( bytecnt < row_bytes )
    {
        // time to get a data byte?
        if( cnt_byte < 1 )
```

Listing 9.2 PCX.CPP (continued)

```cpp
   {
      // get a byte
      if ( (hdr_byte=fgetc(pcx_file)) < 0 )
         break;

      // decode it
      if ( (hdr_byte & RUN_MASK) == RUN_MASK )
      {
         cnt_byte = hdr_byte & CNT_MASK;
         if ( (dat_byte=fgetc(pcx_file)) < 0 )
            break;
      }
      else
      {
         cnt_byte = 1;
         dat_byte = hdr_byte;
      }

      // reverse the data byte's pixel pattern
      dat_byte = reverse( dat_byte, pxl_bits );
   }

   // fill in pixel buffer
   while( cnt_byte- )
   {
      int p = dat_byte;
      int n = pixelsperbyte;
      while( n- )
      {
         // isolate pixel value
         unsigned char mask = p & shift_msk;
                              p >>= shift_cnt;
         // shift into current plane position
         mask <<= setpxlshfitcnt;
         // OR into pixel buffer
         if( curpxl < npxls )
            buf[curpxl++] |= mask;
      }
      if( ++bytecnt == row_bytes )
      {
         if( ++curplane < pxl_planes )
```

Listing 9.2 PCX.CPP (continued)

```cpp
                    {
                        bytecnt = curpxl = 0;
                        setpxlshfitcnt += shift_cnt;
                    }
                }
            }
        }
    }

    // decodes 8 bits per pixel
    void PcxDecoder::read_8( unsigned char *buf, int npxls )
    {
        // initial values
        int bytecnt  = 0;
        int curplane = 0;
        int curpxl   = 0;
        int pxlindex = 0;

        // zero the buffer
        memset( buf, 0, npxls*pxl_planes );

        while( bytecnt < row_bytes )
        {
            // time to get a data byte?
            if( cnt_byte < 1 )
            {
                // get a byte
                if ( (hdr_byte=fgetc(pcx_file)) < 0 )
                    break;

                // decode it
                if ( (hdr_byte & RUN_MASK) == RUN_MASK )
                {
                    cnt_byte = hdr_byte & CNT_MASK;
                    if ( (dat_byte=fgetc(pcx_file)) < 0 )
                        break;
                }
                else
                {
                    cnt_byte = 1;
                    dat_byte = hdr_byte;
                }
            }

            // fill in pixel buffer
            while( cnt_byte- )
            {
                if( curpxl++ < npxls )
```

Listing 9.2 PCX.CPP (continued)

```
            {
                buf[pxlindex] = dat_byte;
                pxlindex += pxl_planes;
            }
            if( ++bytecnt == row_bytes )
            {
                if( ++curplane < pxl_planes )
                {
                    bytecnt = curpxl = 0;
                    pxlindex = curplane;
                }
            }
        }
    }
}

int PcxDecoder::decode( unsigned char *buf, int npxls )
{
    if( cond == xOKAY )
    {
        if( pxl_bits == 8 )
            read_8( buf, npxls );
        else
            read_124( buf, npxls );
    }
    return status();
}

//.................class PcxEncoder

PcxEncoder::PcxEncoder( FILE *f_out, PCXHEADER& pcx )
{
    pxl_bits   = (pcx.bitpx==0)  ? 1 : pcx.bitpx;
    pxl_planes = (pcx.nplanes==0) ? 1 : pcx.nplanes;
    row_bytes  = pcx.bplin;

    pcx_file = f_out;
    scanbuffer = new char[row_bytes];
    cond = (scanbuffer == 0) ? xNOMEMORY : xOKAY;
}

int PcxEncoder::status( void )
{
    if( ferror( pcx_file ) ) cond = xIOERROR;
    return cond;
}

int PcxEncoder::init( void )
```

Listing 9.2 PCX.CPP (continued)

```cpp
{
   cond = (scanbuffer == 0) ? xNOMEMORY : xOKAY;
   return status();
}

int PcxEncoder::term( void )
{
   return status();
}

void PcxEncoder::initbuffer( void )
{
   memset( scanbuffer, 0, row_bytes );
   scanmask = 0x80;
   scanbyte = 0;
}

void PcxEncoder::putbits( int bits, int nbits )
{
   int mask = 1 << nbits;
   while( (mask >>= 1) != 0 )
   {
      if( bits & mask )
         scanbuffer[scanbyte] |= scanmask;
      if( (scanmask >>= 1) == 0 )
      {
         scanbyte++;
         scanmask = 0x80;
      }
   }
}

void PcxEncoder::putbyte( int byte )
{
   scanbuffer[scanbyte++] = byte;
}

int PcxEncoder::flush( void )
{
   // encode and write scanbuffer
   int n1, n2=0;
   while( n2 < row_bytes )
   {
      n1 = n2;
      n2 = n1 + 1;
      while( (scanbuffer[n2] == scanbuffer[n1]) &&
             (n2 < row_bytes) )
         n2++;
```

Listing 9.2 PCX.CPP (continued)

```cpp
            // n is number of bytes in this run
            int n = n2 - n1;
            while( n > MAX_RUN )
            {
                fputc( 0xFF, pcx_file );
                fputc( scanbuffer[n1], pcx_file );
                n -= MAX_RUN;
            }
            if( (n > 1) || ((scanbuffer[n1]&RUN_MASK) == RUN_MASK) )
                fputc( n|RUN_MASK, pcx_file );
            fputc( scanbuffer[n1], pcx_file );
        }

    return status();
}


// encodes 1, 2, or 4 bits per pixel
void PcxEncoder::write_124( unsigned char *buf, int npxls )
{
    int n = pxl_planes;
    int shft = 0;
    while( n-- )
    {
        initbuffer();
        int m = 0;
        while( m < npxls )
        {
            int p = buf[m++] >> shft;
            putbits( p, pxl_bits );
        }
        if( flush() != xOKAY )
            break;
        shft += pxl_bits;
    }
}


// encodes 8 bits per pixel
void PcxEncoder::write_8( unsigned char *buf, int npxls )
{
    int n = 0;
    while( n < pxl_planes )
    {
        initbuffer();
        int m = 0;
        int i = n;
        while( m++ < npxls )
        {
            putbyte( buf[i] );
```

Listing 9.2 PCX.CPP (continued)

```
         i += pxl_planes;
      }
      if( flush() != xOKAY )
         break;
      n++;
   }
}

int PcxEncoder::encode( unsigned char *buf, int npxls )
{
   if( cond == xOKAY )
   {
      if( pxl_bits == 8 )
         write_8( buf, npxls );
      else
         write_124( buf, npxls );
   }
   return status();

}
```

A PCX Query Program

The PCX format represents one of the simpler formats covered in this book (although not the simplest—that honor goes to the MacPaint format, discussed in Chapter 12), so writing a PCX query program is a straightforward task. The only real difficulty is determining if a palette is present and where it is located. Recall that the header provides room for a 16-color palette, so if the image contains 16 colors or less then the palette is found in the header. The palette for a 256-color image, however, is located at the very end of the file.

The procedure for obtaining a 256-color palette is to use `fseek()` or a similar function to position an open file pointer to 768 bytes before the end of a PCX file and then read the following 768 bytes into a buffer. These 768 bytes represent the 256 RGB triples that constitute the image's palette.

In actual practice the 768-byte palette is prefixed by a single byte with the value 12 (0Ch). This byte authenticates the presence of the palette, and a format writer should always include the prefix byte. Presumably, if you encounter a 256-color PCX file in which byte number 769 from the end of the file does not have the value 12, then the file does not possess a palette. However, this is not a foolproof test. In any case, it is unlikely that you will ever encounter a 256-color file without a palette.

The best strategy for a PCX format reader is always to assume the presence of a palette but also to provide a user-controllable option to ignore the palette. This approach has the advantage that format errors can be compensated for by the program user from inspection of the image. We will use this approach throughout this chapter. The query program will indicate the likelihood that a valid palette is not present, but will still list the palette if requested. The query program source code is presented in Listing 9.3.

Listing 9.3 QPCX.CPP

```
//-----------------------------------------------------------//
//                                                           //
//    File:     QPCX.CPP                                     //
//                                                           //
//    Desc:     PCX File Query Program                       //
//                                                           //
//-----------------------------------------------------------//

#include "stdlib.h"
#include "stdio.h"
#include "string.h"

#include "pcx.hpp"

//.................program usage

void explain_pgm( void )
{
    printf( "\n" );
    printf( "PC Paintbrush PCX File Query Program\n" );
    printf( "\n" );
    printf( "Usage:  QPCX  pcx_file  [-p]\n" );
    printf( "\n" );
    printf( "-p includes palette in listing\n" );
    printf( ".PCX extension is assumed\n" );
    printf( "\n" );
}


//.................main

int main( int argc, char *argv[] )
{
    // check args
    if( (argc < 2) || (*argv[1] == '?') )
    {
        explain_pgm();
        return 0;
    }
```

Listing 9.3 QPCX.CPP (continued)

```cpp
// create file name
char fn[80];
strcpy( fn, argv[1] );
char *p = strchr( fn, '.' );
if( p == 0 )
    strcat( fn, ".pcx" );
else if( *(p+1) == 0 )
    *p = 0;

// list palette too?
int lpal = 0;
if( argc > 2 )
  if( (strcmp( argv[2], "-p" ) == 0) ||
      (strcmp( argv[2], "-P" ) == 0) )
    lpal = 1;

// open the file
FILE *fpcx = fopen( fn, "rb" );
if( fpcx == 0 )
{
    printf( "File '%s' not found\n", fn );
    return 0;
}

// read the header and list
PCXHEADER pcx;
if( fread( &pcx, sizeof(PCXHEADER), 1, fpcx ) != 1 )
{
    printf( "Error reading header of '%s'\n", fn );
    fclose( fpcx );
    return 0;
}
printf( "Listing of PCX file '%s'\n", fn );
printf( "\n" );
pcx.list();
printf( "\n" );
// compute color count
int np = (pcx.nplanes == 0) ? 1 : pcx.nplanes;
int nb = (pcx.bitpx == 0)   ? 1 : pcx.bitpx;
int nbits = np * nb;
long ncolors = 1L << nbits;
printf( "Size of pixel in bits     = %d\n", nbits );
printf( "Number of colors in image = %ld\n", ncolors );
printf( "\n" );
```

Listing 9.3 QPCX.CPP (continued)

```
// list palette if requested
if( lpal )
{
   int pal_unlikely = 0;
   unsigned char *pal;

   if( nbits < 8 )
   {
      pal = new unsigned char [48];
      memcpy( pal, pcx.colors, 48 );
      if( pcx.version == 3 ) pal_unlikely = 1;
   }
   else if( nbits == 8 )
   {
      pal = new unsigned char [768];
      fseek( fpcx, -769, SEEK_END );
      pal_unlikely = (fgetc(fpcx) == 12) ? 0 : 1;
      fread( pal, 768, 1, fpcx );
   }
   else
   {
      pal = 0;
   }

   if( pal == 0 )
      printf( "Image is not palette based\n" );
   else
   {
      if( pal_unlikely )
         printf( "Note - valid palette is unlikely\n\n" );
      printf( "Image palette..........\n" );
      int n = 0;
      for( int i=0; i<ncolors; i++ )
         printf( "RGB(%3d) = (%3d,%3d,%3d)\n",
                  i, pal[n++], pal[n++], pal[n++] );
      delete pal;
   }
}

fclose( fpcx );
return 0;
}
```

A PCX File Viewer

Listings 9.1 and 9.2 include encoder and decoder class definitions for the PCX format. The decoder class, `PcxDecoder`, is used by the PCX file-viewer program that is presented in Listing 9.6. This program bears many similarities to the BMP file viewer that was presented in Chapter 8. Before the viewer program is presented, let's take a closer look at the decoder class.

The PCX Decoder Class

The PCX decoder class was designed to handle any type of PCX image, from monochrome images through 24-bit color images. In fact, it will work on image types that are not included in the format specification, such as a 4-plane, 2-bpp image. This design methodology was adopted on purpose, so that if new image types are covered by the format, then the code should work with them without modification.

The decoder class implementation was developed without concern for performance, and as a result, decoding an image is not especially fast. The performance is, however, acceptable, and the source code is much easier to follow than would have been the case if it had been written for performance. A truly high-speed implementation would require extensive use of assembly language, and each specific image structure would need to be handled separately.

As noted, the PCX format is highly device dependent, and its overall emphasis is on rapidly decoding and displaying an image. For the 16-color display modes of the EGA and VGA adapters, this means writing each color plane separately, so multiplanar images are stored as a multiplexed series of scan lines for each plane.

This structure was exploited to some extent when the format was extended to handle 24-bit color imagery. Rather than a 24-bit image being stored as a single plane of 24-bit pixels, which is perhaps the most natural arrangement, it is stored as three planes of 8-bit pixels. Thus, when a 24-bit image is decoded, each scan line is read as a line of red intensities followed by a line of green intensities followed by a line of blue intensities. This scheme does nothing to expedite the display process, but it does increase the likelihood that a given image will actually compress. Consider, for example, three pixels of the same color where none of the color's primary intensities is the same. Here is an example:

```
223 11 99 223 11 99 223 11 99
```

This sequence of values will not compress at all with the PCX format's RLE compression scheme. However, when presented by plane, the sequence becomes:

```
223 223 223 11 11 11 99 99 99
```

This does compress, from 9 bytes to 6 bytes. Unfortunately, most 24-bit imagery is complex and exhibits little chromatic coherence, so you will seldom find runs of uniform color. Most formats do not attempt to compress 24-bit imagery. The PCX format is a lone exception.

One implementation detail that warrants a note of explanation is the process by which pixels are extracted from individual bytes. Because the PCX format encodes multiplanar images by plane, a given data byte can contain pixel data from several consecutive pixels. For instance, a byte of an image encoded from a VGA mode 12h display will contain 1 bit from each of 8 consecutive pixels. The bits are also arranged such that the leftmost pixel bit occupies the high-order bit position of the byte. Because each line of an image is decoded from left to right, the high-order bit of a byte is used first and the low-order bit is used last.

It is generally easier to extract and use bits from the low-order positions of a multibit quantity. This can be implemented by first reversing the bit order of data bytes. This is done in the PCX decoder using a table lookup. Three tables are actually used, one each for bit fields of 1, 2, and 4 bits in width. Note that the table for 1-bit subfields reverses the bit order of a byte, whereas the table for 4-bit subfields reverses the order of a byte's 2 nibbles. The implementation details are presented in Listings 9.4 and 9.5. The three tables require 768 bytes of space, but a table lookup is much faster than computing the reversed bit order.

Listing 9.4 REVBYTE.HPP

```
//-----------------------------------------------------------//
//                                                           //
//   File:     REVBYTE.HPP                                   //
//                                                           //
//   Desc:     Function to reverse a bit pattern             //
//                                                           //
//-----------------------------------------------------------//

extern unsigned char _reversed_bytes_1[],
                     _reversed_bytes_2[],
                     _reversed_bytes_4[];
```

Listing 9.4 REVBYTE.HPP (continued)

```
inline int reverse( int i, int nbits )
{
    if( nbits == 1 ) return _reversed_bytes_1[i&255];
    if( nbits == 2 ) return _reversed_bytes_2[i&255];
    if( nbits == 4 ) return _reversed_bytes_4[i&255];
    return i;
}
```

Listing 9.5 REVBYTE.CPP

```
//-----------------------------------------------------//
//                                                     //
//    File:      REVBYTE.CPP                           //
//                                                     //
//    Desc:      Table used to reverse a bit pattern   //
//                                                     //
//-----------------------------------------------------//

// Table of bytes where the Ith entry is a
// reversed bit pattern for the value I.
// Valid values for I are 0 <= I <= 255.
// 7 6 5 4 3 2 1 0 -> 0 1 2 3 4 5 6 7
unsigned char _reversed_bytes_1[] =
{
    0x00, 0x80, 0x40, 0xC0, 0x20, 0xA0, 0x60, 0xE0,
    0x10, 0x90, 0x50, 0xD0, 0x30, 0xB0, 0x70, 0xF0,
    0x08, 0x88, 0x48, 0xC8, 0x28, 0xA8, 0x68, 0xE8,
    0x18, 0x98, 0x58, 0xD8, 0x38, 0xB8, 0x78, 0xF8,
    0x04, 0x84, 0x44, 0xC4, 0x24, 0xA4, 0x64, 0xE4,
    0x14, 0x94, 0x54, 0xD4, 0x34, 0xB4, 0x74, 0xF4,
    0x0C, 0x8C, 0x4C, 0xCC, 0x2C, 0xAC, 0x6C, 0xEC,
    0x1C, 0x9C, 0x5C, 0xDC, 0x3C, 0xBC, 0x7C, 0xFC,
    0x02, 0x82, 0x42, 0xC2, 0x22, 0xA2, 0x62, 0xE2,
    0x12, 0x92, 0x52, 0xD2, 0x32, 0xB2, 0x72, 0xF2,
    0x0A, 0x8A, 0x4A, 0xCA, 0x2A, 0xAA, 0x6A, 0xEA,
    0x1A, 0x9A, 0x5A, 0xDA, 0x3A, 0xBA, 0x7A, 0xFA,
    0x06, 0x86, 0x46, 0xC6, 0x26, 0xA6, 0x66, 0xE6,
    0x16, 0x96, 0x56, 0xD6, 0x36, 0xB6, 0x76, 0xF6,
    0x0E, 0x8E, 0x4E, 0xCE, 0x2E, 0xAE, 0x6E, 0xEE,
    0x1E, 0x9E, 0x5E, 0xDE, 0x3E, 0xBE, 0x7E, 0xFE,
    0x01, 0x81, 0x41, 0xC1, 0x21, 0xA1, 0x61, 0xE1,
    0x11, 0x91, 0x51, 0xD1, 0x31, 0xB1, 0x71, 0xF1,
    0x09, 0x89, 0x49, 0xC9, 0x29, 0xA9, 0x69, 0xE9,
    0x19, 0x99, 0x59, 0xD9, 0x39, 0xB9, 0x79, 0xF9,
    0x05, 0x85, 0x45, 0xC5, 0x25, 0xA5, 0x65, 0xE5,
    0x15, 0x95, 0x55, 0xD5, 0x35, 0xB5, 0x75, 0xF5,
    0x0D, 0x8D, 0x4D, 0xCD, 0x2D, 0xAD, 0x6D, 0xED,
    0x1D, 0x9D, 0x5D, 0xDD, 0x3D, 0xBD, 0x7D, 0xFD,
```

Listing 9.5 REVBYTE.CPP (continued)

```
        0x03, 0x83, 0x43, 0xC3, 0x23, 0xA3, 0x63, 0xE3,
        0x13, 0x93, 0x53, 0xD3, 0x33, 0xB3, 0x73, 0xF3,
        0x0B, 0x8B, 0x4B, 0xCB, 0x2B, 0xAB, 0x6B, 0xEB,
        0x1B, 0x9B, 0x5B, 0xDB, 0x3B, 0xBB, 0x7B, 0xFB,
        0x07, 0x87, 0x47, 0xC7, 0x27, 0xA7, 0x67, 0xE7,
        0x17, 0x97, 0x57, 0xD7, 0x37, 0xB7, 0x77, 0xF7,
        0x0F, 0x8F, 0x4F, 0xCF, 0x2F, 0xAF, 0x6F, 0xEF,
        0x1F, 0x9F, 0x5F, 0xDF, 0x3F, 0xBF, 0x7F, 0xFF
    };

// 76 54 32 10 -> 10 32 54 76
unsigned char _reversed_bytes_2[] =
{
        0x00, 0x40, 0x80, 0xC0, 0x10, 0x50, 0x90, 0xD0,
        0x20, 0x60, 0xA0, 0xE0, 0x30, 0x70, 0xB0, 0xF0,
        0x04, 0x44, 0x84, 0xC4, 0x14, 0x54, 0x94, 0xD4,
        0x24, 0x64, 0xA4, 0xE4, 0x34, 0x74, 0xB4, 0xF4,
        0x08, 0x48, 0x88, 0xC8, 0x18, 0x58, 0x98, 0xD8,
        0x28, 0x68, 0xA8, 0xE8, 0x38, 0x78, 0xB8, 0xF8,
        0x0C, 0x4C, 0x8C, 0xCC, 0x1C, 0x5C, 0x9C, 0xDC,
        0x2C, 0x6C, 0xAC, 0xEC, 0x3C, 0x7C, 0xBC, 0xFC,
        0x01, 0x41, 0x81, 0xC1, 0x11, 0x51, 0x91, 0xD1,
        0x21, 0x61, 0xA1, 0xE1, 0x31, 0x71, 0xB1, 0xF1,
        0x05, 0x45, 0x85, 0xC5, 0x15, 0x55, 0x95, 0xD5,
        0x25, 0x65, 0xA5, 0xE5, 0x35, 0x75, 0xB5, 0xF5,
        0x09, 0x49, 0x89, 0xC9, 0x19, 0x59, 0x99, 0xD9,
        0x29, 0x69, 0xA9, 0xE9, 0x39, 0x79, 0xB9, 0xF9,
        0x0D, 0x4D, 0x8D, 0xCD, 0x1D, 0x5D, 0x9D, 0xDD,
        0x2D, 0x6D, 0xAD, 0xED, 0x3D, 0x7D, 0xBD, 0xFD,
        0x02, 0x42, 0x82, 0xC2, 0x12, 0x52, 0x92, 0xD2,
        0x22, 0x62, 0xA2, 0xE2, 0x32, 0x72, 0xB2, 0xF2,
        0x06, 0x46, 0x86, 0xC6, 0x16, 0x56, 0x96, 0xD6,
        0x26, 0x66, 0xA6, 0xE6, 0x36, 0x76, 0xB6, 0xF6,
        0x0A, 0x4A, 0x8A, 0xCA, 0x1A, 0x5A, 0x9A, 0xDA,
        0x2A, 0x6A, 0xAA, 0xEA, 0x3A, 0x7A, 0xBA, 0xFA,
        0x0E, 0x4E, 0x8E, 0xCE, 0x1E, 0x5E, 0x9E, 0xDE,
        0x2E, 0x6E, 0xAE, 0xEE, 0x3E, 0x7E, 0xBE, 0xFE,
        0x03, 0x43, 0x83, 0xC3, 0x13, 0x53, 0x93, 0xD3,
        0x23, 0x63, 0xA3, 0xE3, 0x33, 0x73, 0xB3, 0xF3,
        0x07, 0x47, 0x87, 0xC7, 0x17, 0x57, 0x97, 0xD7,
        0x27, 0x67, 0xA7, 0xE7, 0x37, 0x77, 0xB7, 0xF7,
        0x0B, 0x4B, 0x8B, 0xCB, 0x1B, 0x5B, 0x9B, 0xDB,
        0x2B, 0x6B, 0xAB, 0xEB, 0x3B, 0x7B, 0xBB, 0xFB,
        0x0F, 0x4F, 0x8F, 0xCF, 0x1F, 0x5F, 0x9F, 0xDF,
        0x2F, 0x6F, 0xAF, 0xEF, 0x3F, 0x7F, 0xBF, 0xFF,
    };
```

Listing 9.5 REVBYTE.CPP (continued)

```
// 7654 3210 -> 3210 7654
unsigned char _reversed_bytes_4[] =
{
    0x00, 0x10, 0x20, 0x30, 0x40, 0x50, 0x60, 0x70,
    0x80, 0x90, 0xA0, 0xB0, 0xC0, 0xD0, 0xE0, 0xF0,
    0x01, 0x11, 0x21, 0x31, 0x41, 0x51, 0x61, 0x71,
    0x81, 0x91, 0xA1, 0xB1, 0xC1, 0xD1, 0xE1, 0xF1,
    0x02, 0x12, 0x22, 0x32, 0x42, 0x52, 0x62, 0x72,
    0x82, 0x92, 0xA2, 0xB2, 0xC2, 0xD2, 0xE2, 0xF2,
    0x03, 0x13, 0x23, 0x33, 0x43, 0x53, 0x63, 0x73,
    0x83, 0x93, 0xA3, 0xB3, 0xC3, 0xD3, 0xE3, 0xF3,
    0x04, 0x14, 0x24, 0x34, 0x44, 0x54, 0x64, 0x74,
    0x84, 0x94, 0xA4, 0xB4, 0xC4, 0xD4, 0xE4, 0xF4,
    0x05, 0x15, 0x25, 0x35, 0x45, 0x55, 0x65, 0x75,
    0x85, 0x95, 0xA5, 0xB5, 0xC5, 0xD5, 0xE5, 0xF5,
    0x06, 0x16, 0x26, 0x36, 0x46, 0x56, 0x66, 0x76,
    0x86, 0x96, 0xA6, 0xB6, 0xC6, 0xD6, 0xE6, 0xF6,
    0x07, 0x17, 0x27, 0x37, 0x47, 0x57, 0x67, 0x77,
    0x87, 0x97, 0xA7, 0xB7, 0xC7, 0xD7, 0xE7, 0xF7,
    0x08, 0x18, 0x28, 0x38, 0x48, 0x58, 0x68, 0x78,
    0x88, 0x98, 0xA8, 0xB8, 0xC8, 0xD8, 0xE8, 0xF8,
    0x09, 0x19, 0x29, 0x39, 0x49, 0x59, 0x69, 0x79,
    0x89, 0x99, 0xA9, 0xB9, 0xC9, 0xD9, 0xE9, 0xF9,
    0x0A, 0x1A, 0x2A, 0x3A, 0x4A, 0x5A, 0x6A, 0x7A,
    0x8A, 0x9A, 0xAA, 0xBA, 0xCA, 0xDA, 0xEA, 0xFA,
    0x0B, 0x1B, 0x2B, 0x3B, 0x4B, 0x5B, 0x6B, 0x7B,
    0x8B, 0x9B, 0xAB, 0xBB, 0xCB, 0xDB, 0xEB, 0xFB,
    0x0C, 0x1C, 0x2C, 0x3C, 0x4C, 0x5C, 0x6C, 0x7C,
    0x8C, 0x9C, 0xAC, 0xBC, 0xCC, 0xDC, 0xEC, 0xFC,
    0x0D, 0x1D, 0x2D, 0x3D, 0x4D, 0x5D, 0x6D, 0x7D,
    0x8D, 0x9D, 0xAD, 0xBD, 0xCD, 0xDD, 0xED, 0xFD,
    0x0E, 0x1E, 0x2E, 0x3E, 0x4E, 0x5E, 0x6E, 0x7E,
    0x8E, 0x9E, 0xAE, 0xBE, 0xCE, 0xDE, 0xEE, 0xFE,
    0x0F, 0x1F, 0x2F, 0x3F, 0x4F, 0x5F, 0x6F, 0x7F,
    0x8F, 0x9F, 0xAF, 0xBF, 0xCF, 0xDF, 0xEF, 0xFF,
};
```

The Viewer Program

Listing 9.6 presents the PCX file viewer program, which is based on the same program skeleton used by the other format viewers implemented in this book. The bulk of the PCX-dependent code is localized in the `load_pcx()` function, which decodes a file and produces an `ImgStore` instance and an `RgbPalette` instance. These are passed to an `ImageViewer` instance to perform the actual display of the image, or, optionally, to an `ImagePrinter` instance to print the image. The program can handle the display of any PCX file, including 24-bit color PCX files.

Listing 9.6 VPCX.CPP

```cpp
//------------------------------------------------------------//
//                                                            //
//    File:     VPCX.CPP                                       //
//                                                            //
//    Desc:     Program to view or print a PCX file            //
//                                                            //
//------------------------------------------------------------//

#include "stdlib.h"
#include "stdio.h"
#include "string.h"
#include "conio.h"
#include "ctype.h"

#include "pcx.hpp"
#include "imgviewr.hpp"
#include "imgprntr.hpp"
#include "laserjet.hpp"
#include "paintjet.hpp"
#include "epjx80.hpp"
#include "eplq24.hpp"
#include "pscript.hpp"


//.................Printer types

#define  LJ   0x4C4A
#define  PJ   0x504A
#define  JX   0x4A58
#define  LQ   0x4C51
#define  PS   0x5053


//.................Program globals

char      fn[80];         // path to PCX file

int       gmode;          // video display mode
int       pmode;          // printer ID
int       ropt;           // rendering flags
int       iopt;           // itensity mapping flags
int       nopal;          // if set, ignore file palette
ImgStore  *imgmap;        // image bitmap
PCXPALETTE *pcxpal;       // image palette


//.................Exit with a message
```

Listing 9.6 VPCX.CPP (continued)

```
void exit_pgm( char *msg )
{
   printf( "%s\n", msg );
   exit( 0 );
}

//................Program usage

void explain_pgm( void )
{
   printf( "\n" );
   printf( ".......PC Paintbrush PCX File Viewer/Printer.......\n"
);
   printf( "\n" );
   printf( "Usage:      VPCX  pcx_file  [ switches ]\n" );
   printf( "\n" );
   printf( "Switches:  -h      = display program usage\n" );
   printf( "           -vXX    = force video display mode XX\n" );
   printf( "                     (XX = 12, 13, 2E, 62)\n" );
   printf( "           -pXX    = print using printer XX\n" );
   printf( "                     (XX = LJ, PJ, JX, LQ, PS)\n" );
   printf( "           -b[+|-] = increase or decrease
brightness\n" );
   printf( "           -c[+|-] = increase or decrease contrast\n"
);
   printf( "           -d      = force dithered rendering\n" );
   printf( "           -g      = force gray scale rendering\n" );
   printf( "           -i      = ignore file palette\n" );
   printf( "           -m      = force palette mapping\n" );
   printf( "\n" );
   printf( "................................................\n"
);
   printf( "\n" );
}

//................Process pgm argument list

void process_args( int argc, char *argv[] )
{
   // establish default values
   fn[0] = 0;
   gmode = 0x12;
   pmode = 0;
   ropt  = 0;
   iopt  = 0;
   nopal = 0;
```

Listing 9.6 VPCX.CPP (continued)

```cpp
// process the program's argument list
for( int i=1; i<argc; i++ )
{
    if( (*argv[i] == '-') || (*argv[i] == '/') )
    {
        char sw = *(argv[i] + 1);
        switch( toupper(sw) )
        {
            case 'H' :
                explain_pgm();
                exit( 0 );
                break;

            case 'V' :
                sscanf( argv[i]+2, "%x", &gmode );
                break;

            case 'P' :
                pmode = toupper( *(argv[i]+2) );
                pmode <<= 8;
                pmode += toupper( *(argv[i]+3) );
                break;

            case 'B' :
                if( *(argv[i]+2) == '-' )
                    iopt |= intensDBRI;
                else
                    iopt |= intensIBRI;
                break;

            case 'C' :
                if( *(argv[i]+2) == '-' )
                    iopt |= intensDCNT;
                else
                    iopt |= intensICNT;
                break;

            case 'D' :
                ropt |= renderDITHER;
                break;

            case 'G' :
                ropt |= renderGRAY;
                break;

            case 'I' :
                nopal = 1;
                break;
```

Listing 9.6 VPCX.CPP (continued)

```
                case 'M' :
                    ropt |= renderMAP;
                    break;

                default:
                    printf( "Unknown switch '%s' ignored\n",
                                argv[i] );
                    break;
            }
        }
        else  // presumably a file identifier
        {
            strcpy( fn, argv[i] );
            char *p = strchr( fn, '.' );
            if( p == 0 )
                strcat( fn, ".pcx" );
            else if( *(p+1) == 0 )
                *p = 0;
        }
    }

    // was a file name specified?
    if( fn[0] == 0 )
    {
        explain_pgm();
        exit( 0 );
    }
}

//................Create an image storage buffer

ImgStore * istore( int h, int w, int d )
{
    ImgStore *ist = 0;

    // attempt to create in order of preference
    ist = new XmsImgStore( h, w, d );
    if( (ist != 0) && (ist->status != imgstoreOKAY) )
    {
        delete ist;
        ist = new EmsImgStore( h, w, d );
        if( (ist != 0) && (ist->status != imgstoreOKAY) )
        {
            delete ist;
            ist = new CnvImgStore( h, w, d );
            if( (ist != 0) && (ist->status != imgstoreOKAY) )
            {
                delete ist;
```

Listing 9.6 VPCX.CPP (continued)

```cpp
                    ist = new DskImgStore( h, w, d );
                    if( (ist != 0) && (ist->status != imgstoreOKAY) )
                    {
                        delete ist;
                        ist = 0;
                    }
                }
            }
        }

    return ist;
}

//.................Create a printer

PrinterDriver * printer( int which )
{
    PrinterDriver *p;

    switch( which )
    {
        case LJ : p = new LaserJet( "LPT1" );
                    break;
        case PJ : p = new PaintJet( "LPT1" );
                    break;
        case JX : p = new EpsonJX80( "LPT1" );
                    break;
        case LQ : p = new EpsonLQ24( "LPT1" );
                    break;
        default : p = new PsPrinter( "LPT1" );
                    break;
    }

    return p;
}

//.................Load the PCX file

void load_pcx( void )
{
    // open file
    FILE *fpcx = fopen( fn, "rb" );
    if( fpcx == 0 )
        exit_pgm( "PCX file not found" );
```

Listing 9.6 VPCX.CPP (continued)

```
// read header
PCXHEADER pcxh;
if( fread( &pcxh, sizeof(PCXHEADER), 1, fpcx ) != 1 )
    exit_pgm( "Error reading PCX header" );

// validate file— note that this is not foolproof!
if( pcxh.format != 10 )
    exit_pgm( "File is not a PCX file" );

// obtain palette
pcxpal = new PCXPALETTE( fpcx, pcxh );
if( pcxpal == 0 )
    exit_pgm( "Error allocating PCX palette" );

// create bitmap
int ncols = pcxh.x2 - pcxh.x1 + 1;
int nrows = pcxh.y2 - pcxh.y1 + 1;
int nb = (pcxh.bitpx == 0) ? 1 : pcxh.bitpx;
int np = (pcxh.nplanes == 0) ? 1 : pcxh.nplanes;
int pxbits  = nb * np;
int pxbytes = (pxbits + 7) / 8;
int rwbytes = pxbytes * ncols;

unsigned char *scanln = new unsigned char [rwbytes];
imgmap = istore( nrows, ncols, pxbytes*8 );
if( (imgmap == 0) || (scanln == 0) )
{
    if( imgmap ) delete imgmap;
    if( scanln ) delete scanln;
    exit_pgm( "Insufficient memory to load image" );
}

// load bitmap
printf( "Loading PCX image from '%s'...", fn );
PcxDecoder pcxd( fpcx, pcxh );
pcxd.init();
memset( scanln, 0, rwbytes );
for( int i=0; i<nrows; i++ )
{
    if( pcxd.decode( scanln, ncols ) != xOKAY )
        break;
    imgmap->put( scanln, i );
}
pcxd.term();
printf( "done\n" );

delete scanln;
}
```

Listing 9.6 VPCX.CPP (continued)

```cpp
//.................Main

int main( int argc, char *argv[] )
{
    process_args( argc, argv );

    load_pcx( );

    // print the image
    if( pmode != 0 )
    {
        PrinterDriver *prt = printer( pmode );
        if( prt )
        {
            printf( "Printing..." );
            ImagePrinter ip( prt, imgmap, pcxpal->colors,
                             pcxpal->ncolors,
                             ropt, iopt, 100, 100 );
            ip.print( 1 );
            printf( "done\n" );
            delete prt;
        }
        else
            printf( "Printer instantiation failed\n" );
    }

    // display the image
    else
    {
        VgaDisplay vga( gmode );
        if( nopal )
        {
            // replace file palette with display palette,
            // but only if it makes sense
            int n = vga.metric.ncolors;
            if( n >= pcxpal->ncolors )
            {
                delete [] pcxpal->colors;
                pcxpal->ncolors = n;
                pcxpal->colors = new rgb [n];
                vga.getpalette( pcxpal->colors, pcxpal->ncolors );
            }
        }
        ImageViewer iv( &vga, imgmap, pcxpal->colors,
                        pcxpal->ncolors, ropt, iopt );
        iv.view( );
    }
```

```
    delete pcxpal;
    delete imgmap;

    return 0;
}
```

Writing the PCX Format

The overall simplicity of the PCX format makes writing the format a relatively straightforward process. It also makes the format an attractive choice for use as an application's native bitmapped graphics file format. An additional advantage is the fact that the PCX format is perhaps the most widely supported of all graphics file formats.

All that is necessary to create a PCX file is to initialize and write a PCX header and then encode and write a bitmap. If the image being encoded is 8 bpp then the encoded bitmap is followed with a byte with the value 12 and the 256 RGB triples making up the image's palette. Here are the values that should be placed in the header:

PCXHEADER.format	The value 10.
PCXHEADER.version	The value 5. This is the latest version number and indicates that the image can potentially contain 8-bit or 24-bit color.
PCXHEADER.rleflag	The value 1. Strictly speaking, there is no such thing as an uncompressed PCX file, so a value of 0 is not allowed.
PCXHEADER.paltype	The value 1, which indicates a color image. Gray-scale images are then a special case in which, for all palette entries, red = green = blue.
PCXHEADER.bitpx	For monochrome and 16-color images, the value 1. For 8-bit and 24-bit images, the value 8.
PCXHEADER.nplanes	For monochrome and 8-bit images, the value 1. For 16-color images, the value 4. For 24-bit images, the value 3.
PCXHEADER.x1	The value 0.
PCXHEADER.y1	The value 0.
PCXHEADER.x2	The width of the image in pixels minus 1.

`PCXHEADER.y2`	The height of the image in pixels minus 1.
`PCXHEADER.hres`	For a standard VGA display, a value in the range 75 to 100 can be used. If the image was created by a scanner, use the scanner's horizontal resolution.
`PCXHEADER.vres`	See `PCXHEADER.hres`.
`PCXHEADER.colors`	If the image uses 16 colors or less, fill this buffer with the image palette. Otherwise, fill it with zeroes.
`PCXHEADER.scrnw`	Use the display mode's width in pixels, or set the field to zero.
`PCXHEADER.scrnh`	Use the display mode's height in pixels, or set the field to zero.
`PCXHEADER.vmode`	Virtually everyone sets this field to zero. If you like, you can place the video BIOS display mode number here.
`PCXHEADER.xtra`	Fill with zeroes.

The PcxEncoder Class

The `PcxEncoder` class, presented in Listings 9.1 and 9.2, is used to encode and output the bitmap of a PCX file. The encoding logic is designed to be as simple as possible, so it does not encode runs that span planes or scan lines (the decoder class, however, will properly handle such runs). Note that this design constraint has no effect on the decoding process. The encoder class will handle any image type, including 24-bit color images.

A WritePCX Function

Listing 9.7 shows the implementation of a `WritePCX()` function that will output a PCX file. The function is overloaded to work with either a display instance, class `VgaDisplay`, or an image instance, class `ImgStore`. In the latter case, an array of RGB values is also required. Note that the parameters to either form of the function can be extracted from the `ImageViewer` constructor call in the VPCX program in Listing 9.6.

In Chapter 8, the `WriteBMP()` function was illustrated using a display instance (Listing 8.11). Here, the `WritePCX()` function is illustrated using an image instance. The image and palette are derived from the El Greco test image. The sample program is presented in Listing 9.8.

Listing 9.7 WRTPCX.CPP

```
//-----------------------------------------------------------//
//                                                           //
//    File:     WRTPCX.CPP                                   //
//                                                           //
//    Desc:     Code to output a PCX file from a             //
//              VGA Display or a Memory Bitmap               //
//                                                           //
//-----------------------------------------------------------//


#include "pcx.hpp"
#include "display.hpp"
#include "imgstore.hpp"


//.................Abort macro

#define  ABORT( f, r )  { fclose(f); return r; }


//.................Write VGA screen to PCX file 'fn'

int WritePCX( VgaDisplay& vga, char *fn,
              int x1, int y1, int x2, int y2 )
{
   FILE *f = fopen( fn, "wb" );
   if( f == 0 )
      ABORT( f, xIOERROR );

   // image metrics
   // int nrows   = y2 - y1 + 1;
   int ncols      = x2 - x1 + 1;
   int nbits      = vga.metric.nbits;
   int nplanes    = vga.metric.nplanes;
   int pxlsize    = nbits * nplanes;
   int pxlbytes   = (nbits * nplanes + 7) / 8;
   int ncolors    = (pxlsize <= 8) ? 1 << pxlsize : 0;
   int planebytes = ((ncols * nbits + 15) / 16) * 2;

   // initialize and write the PCX header
   PCXHEADER pcxh;
   pcxh.x1 = x1;
   pcxh.y1 = y1;
   pcxh.x2 = x2;
   pcxh.y2 = y2;
   pcxh.bitpx = nbits;
   pcxh.nplanes = nplanes;
   pcxh.bplin = planebytes;
   pcxh.hres = 100;  // a typical value
   pcxh.vres = 100;
   pcxh.scrnw = vga.metric.ncolumns;
```

Listing 9.7 WRTPCX.CPP (continued)

```cpp
pcxh.scrnh = vga.metric.nrows;
if( (ncolors <= 16) && (ncolors > 0) )
{
   rgb *pal = new rgb [16];
   if( pal == 0 )
      ABORT( f, xNOMEMORY );
   vga.getpalette( pal, ncolors );
   int n = 0;
   for( int i=0; i<ncolors; i++ )
   {
      pcxh.colors[n++] = pal[i].red;
      pcxh.colors[n++] = pal[i].grn;
      pcxh.colors[n++] = pal[i].blu;
   }
   delete [] pal;
}
if( fwrite( &pcxh, sizeof(PCXHEADER), 1, f ) != 1 )
   ABORT( f, xIOERROR );

// encode and write the image
unsigned char *scanln = new unsigned char [ncols*pxlbytes];
if( scanln == 0 )
   ABORT( f, xNOMEMORY );
PcxEncoder pcxe( f, pcxh );
if( pcxe.status() != xOKAY )
   ABORT( f, pcxe.status() );
pcxe.init();
for( int i=y1; i<=y2; i++ )
{
   vga.getscanline( scanln, ncols, x1, i );
   pcxe.encode( scanln, ncols );
}
pcxe.term();
delete scanln;

// if 256-colors, append the palette
if( ncolors == 256 )
{
   fputc( 12, f );
   rgb *pal = new rgb [256];
   if( pal == 0 )
      ABORT( f, xNOMEMORY );
   vga.getpalette( pal, ncolors );
   for( int i=0; i<ncolors; i++ )
   {
      fputc( pal[i].red, f );
      fputc( pal[i].grn, f );
```

Listing 9.7 WRTPCX.CPP (continued)

```cpp
            fputc( pal[i].blu, f );
        }
        delete [] pal;
    }

    fclose( f );
    return xOKAY;
}

//................Write an image to PCX file 'fn'

int WritePCX( ImgStore& img, rgb *pal, char *fn )
{
    FILE *f = fopen( fn, "wb" );
    if( f == 0 )
        ABORT( f, xIOERROR );

    // image metrics
    int nrows   = img.height();
    int ncols   = img.width();
    int nbits   = 1;
    int nplanes = 1;
    switch( img.depth() )
    {
        case 4 :
            nplanes = 4;
            break;
        case 8 :
            nbits = 8;
            break;
        case 24 :
            nbits = 8;
            nplanes = 3;
            break;
    }
    int pxlsize    = nbits * nplanes;
    // int pxlbytes = (nbits * nplanes + 7) / 8;
    int ncolors    = (pxlsize <= 8) ? 1 << pxlsize : 0;
    int planebytes = ((ncols * nbits + 15) / 16) * 2;

    // initialize and write the PCX header
    PCXHEADER pcxh;
    pcxh.x1 = 0;
    pcxh.y1 = 0;
    pcxh.x2 = ncols - 1;
    pcxh.y2 = nrows - 1;
    pcxh.bitpx = nbits;
    pcxh.nplanes = nplanes;
```

Listing 9.7 WRTPCX.CPP (continued)

```cpp
    pcxh.bplin = planebytes;
    pcxh.hres = 100;  // a typical value
    pcxh.vres = 100;
    pcxh.scrnw = 0;
    pcxh.scrnh = 0;
    if( (ncolors <= 16) && (ncolors > 0) )
    {
        int n = 0;
        for( int i=0; i<ncolors; i++ )
        {
            pcxh.colors[n++] = pal[i].red;
            pcxh.colors[n++] = pal[i].grn;
            pcxh.colors[n++] = pal[i].blu;
        }
    }
    if( fwrite( &pcxh, sizeof(PCXHEADER), 1, f ) != 1 )
        ABORT( f, xIOERROR );

    // encode and write the image
    PcxEncoder pcxe( f, pcxh );
    if( pcxe.status() != xOKAY )
        ABORT( f, pcxe.status() );
    pcxe.init();
    for( int i=0; i<nrows; i++ )
    {
        pcxe.encode( img.get(i), ncols );
    }
    pcxe.term();

    // if 256-colors, append the palette
    if( ncolors == 256 )
    {
        fputc( 12, f );
        for( int i=0; i<ncolors; i++ )
        {
            fputc( pal[i].red, f );
            fputc( pal[i].grn, f );
            fputc( pal[i].blu, f );
        }
    }

    fclose( f );
    return xOKAY;
}
```

Listing 9.8 PCXDEMO.CPP

```cpp
//---------------------------------------------------------//
//                                                         //
//    File:      PCXDEMO.CPP                               //
//                                                         //
//    Desc:      Example code to write a PCX file          //
//                                                         //
//---------------------------------------------------------//

#include "wrtpcx.cpp"

char *        palname     = "EL-GRECO.PAL";
char *        imgname     = "EL-GRECO.IMG";
int           imgwidth    = 354;
int           imgheight   = 446;
int           imgcolors   = 256;
rgb           imgpalette[256];
unsigned char scanline[354];
CnvImgStore img( 446, 354, 8 );

// read the test image's palette

void read_palette( void )
{
   FILE *f = fopen( palname, "rt" );
   for( int i=0; i<imgcolors; i++ )
   {
      int r, g, b;
      fscanf( f, "%d %d %d", &r, &g, &b );
      imgpalette[i] = rgb( r, g, b );
   }
   fclose( f );
}

// read the test image into memory

void read_image( void )
{
   FILE *f = fopen( imgname, "rb" );
   for( int i=0; i<imgheight; i++ )
   {
      fread( scanline, imgwidth, 1, f );
      img.put( scanline, i );
   }
   fclose( f );
}

// output a PCX file
```

Listing 9.8 PCXDEMO.CPP (continued)

```
int main( void )
{
    read_palette( );

    read_image( );

    WritePCX( img, imgpalette, "PCXDEMO.PCX" );

    return 0;
}
```

This concludes our look at the PCX format. It is one of the most widely supported of all graphics formats, and is a good choice for an application that is to support only a single format. We will examine two similar but less important formats in the next two chapters, the Microsoft Paint MSP format and the Digital Research GEM IMG format.

10

The Microsoft Paintbrush MSP Format

Although Microsoft bundled PC Paintbrush with its mouse for many years, it also developed its own Microsoft Paintbrush program. Microsoft Paint, as it is also known, is a descendent of PC Paintbrush, but now bears little, if any, relation to the ZSoft product. Microsoft Paint is one of the accessories supplied with Windows and is familiar to anyone who has worked with that environment.

The native format that was originally developed for Microsoft Paint is referred to as the **MSP format.** Files using it generally have the extension .MSP. The MSP format is, for all practical purposes, now defunct. In fact, Microsoft Paint will no longer write the format. It has been replaced by the Windows BMP format, which should be used for new application development. However, there are still a few MSP files to be found, so it is worthwhile to be able to read the format.

Format Variants

The MSP format, like the MacPaint format (discussed in Chapter 12), is for monochrome imagery only. Two versions of the format were developed. The original version 1 of the format did not support any kind of image compression. Version 2 of the format added image compression using an RLE scheme, similar to the algorithm employed in the PCX format. Version 2 also added a table of encoded scan-line lengths, so individual encoded scan lines can be located and extracted without the necessity of parsing the image from its beginning.

Both format variants use the same 32-byte file header structure. The MSP header is discussed in detail in the next section, and a structure definition for the header is presented in Listing 10.1. The two formats can be distinguished by the values of two key fields in the header.

Version 1

Version 1 of the format defines two file components, a header and a bitmap. The bitmap is unencoded and contains 1 bit per pixel. Thus, each byte of the bitmap defines 8 pixels. Scan lines must contain an even number of bytes, so they may be padded with 0 to 15 unused bits. Scan lines are presented from the top of the image down.

Version 1 files are distinguished by key values of 6144h and 4D6Eh.

Version 2

Version 2 adds RLE image compression to the format. The compression scheme encodes repeating byte runs. During decompression, an image byte is read. If the byte is nonzero, it indicates a count. That number of bytes is read from the file, and the bytes are used as is. If the count byte is zero, then an encoded run is indicated. A second byte is read and is used as the repeat count. A third byte is read; this is the data byte that is repeated the indicated number of times. For example, suppose the bitmap starts with these three bytes:

```
00h  80h  FFh
```

The zero byte indicates a repeating run, and the next two bytes define a run of 128 (80h) bytes with the value 255 (FFh).

Version 2 of the format also includes a table of scan-line lengths, which is located between the file header and the encoded bitmap. The table consists of an array of 16-bit unsigned integers, one for each scan line. Each entry contains the length of the encoded data in bytes for the corresponding scan line.

The scan-line length table can include a zero-length line, indicating that no data are present for the corresponding scan line. For this reason, the bitmap should be decoded in conjunction with the reading of the length table. This approach will work whether or not zero lengths are present.

Version 2 files are distinguished by key values of 694Ch and 536Eh.

The MSP File Header

The MSP file header consists of 32 bytes organized as 16-word values. Only four of the header's values are of any importance: the two keys and the width and height of the bitmap.

The two keys are used to determine which version of the format is present. Why two keys were deemed necessary is an oddity that rivals the possible meanings of the key values actually employed. In any case, be sure that they are read and used as 16-bit integers. If they are treated as a sequence of characters, then the byte order is different from the order of 2-byte ints because of the byte ordering conventions of Intel processors.

The bitmap width in pixels is used to compute the scan-line size in bytes. Remember that scan lines must contain an even number of bytes (that is, an integral number of words). The correct computation is:

```
bytes = ((pixels + 15) / 16) * 2
```

This formula depends on both integer rounding and the specified order of evaluation.

A brief explanation of each header structure member is presented in the following list. The header structure itself can be found in Listing 10.1.

key1	Word value used in conjunction with key2 to indicate the format version. Version 1 files use a value of 6144h; version 2 files use a value of 694Ch.
key2	Word value used in conjunction with key1 to indicate the format version. Version 1 files use a value of 4D6Eh; version 2 files use a value of 536Eh.
width	Width of the bitmap in pixels.
height	Height of the bitmap in pixels.
saspx, saspy	These define the aspect ratio of the screen on which the image was created. They can be ignored, but would be useful if you were to scale the bitmap for a different display.
paspx, paspy	These define the aspect ratio of a printer for which the image was presumably created. They can be ignored.
pdx, pdy	Size of the printer's page in pixels. They can be ignored.
acx, acy	Aspect correction factors. These were never used in either version of the format and can be ignored.
cksum	Checksum computed by XORing the first 12 words of the header. Given that there are already two key fields, there is little purpose in using this value.
resv1, resv2, resv3	Three reserved words that should be set to zero.

As you can see from these descriptions, much of the MSP header consists of information with limited or no usefulness. It is likely that the design is influenced by the GDI of early versions of Windows and presumably would make more sense in that context.

Listing 10.1 MSP.HPP

```
//-------------------------------------------------------//
//                                                       //
//   File:     MSP.HPP                                   //
//                                                       //
//   Desc:     Class and structure definitions for the  //
//             Microsoft Paint MSP format                //
//                                                       //
//-------------------------------------------------------//

#ifndef _MSP_HPP_
#define _MSP_HPP_

#include "stdlib.h"
#include "stdio.h"
#include "string.h"

#include "color.hpp"
#include "codec.hpp"

//.............format keys

#define V1KEY1 0x6144
#define V1KEY2 0x4D6E
#define V2KEY1 0x694C
#define V2KEY2 0x536E

//.............struct MSPHEADER

struct MSPHEADER
{
    unsigned short key1;
    unsigned short key2;
    unsigned short width;
    unsigned short height;
    unsigned short saspx;
    unsigned short saspy;
    unsigned short paspx;
    unsigned short paspy;
    unsigned short pdx;
    unsigned short pdy;
    unsigned short acx;
    unsigned short acy;
```

Listing 10.1 MSP.HPP (continued)

```
    unsigned short cksum;
    unsigned short resv1;
    unsigned short resv2;
    unsigned short resv3;

    void list( void );
};

//...........class MspDecoder

class MspDecoder : public Decoder
{
    protected:
        FILE            *msp_file;
        int             version;
        int             lncnt;
        int             curln;
        int             rwbytes;
        unsigned short *lnlen;

    private:
        void read_v1( unsigned char *buf, int npxls );
        void read_v2( unsigned char *buf, int npxls );

    public:
        MspDecoder( FILE *f_in, MSPHEADER& msp );
        virtual ~MspDecoder( ) { }
        virtual int decode( unsigned char *buf, int npxls );
        virtual int init( void );
        virtual int term( void );
        virtual int status( void );
};

    #endif
```

Listing 10.2 MSP.CPP

```
//------------------------------------------------------------//
//                                                            //
//   File:    MSP.CPP                                         //
//                                                            //
//   Desc:    Class and structure definitions for the        //
//            Microsoft Paint MSP format                      //
//                                                            //
//------------------------------------------------------------//

    #include "msp.hpp"
```

Listing 10.2 MSP.CPP (continued)

```cpp
//............struct MSPHEADER

void MSPHEADER::list( void )
{
    printf( "MSPHEADER::key1   = %04Xh\n", key1 );
    printf( "MSPHEADER::key2   = %04Xh\n", key2 );
    printf( "MSPHEADER::width  = %d\n", width );
    printf( "MSPHEADER::height = %d\n", height );
    printf( "MSPHEADER::saspx  = %d\n", saspx  );
    printf( "MSPHEADER::saspy  = %d\n", saspy  );
    printf( "MSPHEADER::paspx  = %d\n", paspx  );
    printf( "MSPHEADER::paspy  = %d\n", paspy  );
    printf( "MSPHEADER::pdx    = %d\n", pdx    );
    printf( "MSPHEADER::pdy    = %d\n", pdy    );
    printf( "MSPHEADER::acx    = %d\n", acx    );
    printf( "MSPHEADER::acy    = %d\n", acy    );
    printf( "MSPHEADER::cksum  = %d\n", cksum  );
    printf( "MSPHEADER::resv1  = %d\n", resv1  );
    printf( "MSPHEADER::resv2  = %d\n", resv2  );
    printf( "MSPHEADER::resv3  = %d\n", resv3  );
}

//............class MspDecoder

MspDecoder::MspDecoder( FILE *f_in, MSPHEADER& msp )
{
    msp_file = f_in;
    rwbytes = ((msp.width + 15) / 16) * 2;
    lncnt = msp.height;
    curln = 0;
    lnlen = 0;
    version = 0;
    if( (msp.key1==V1KEY1) && (msp.key2==V1KEY2) )
       version = 1;
    if( (msp.key1==V2KEY1) && (msp.key2==V2KEY2) )
    {
       version = 2;
       lnlen = new unsigned short [lncnt];
       if( lnlen )
          fread( lnlen, 2, lncnt, msp_file );
    }
    // for either format, at this point the
    // file pointer is positioned at the start
    // of the bitmap.
}
```

Listing 10.2 MSP.CPP (continued)

```cpp
int MspDecoder::status( void )
{
   if( (version == 2) && (lnlen == 0) )
      return xNOMEMORY;
   if( version == 0 )
      return xBADPARAM;
   if( feof(msp_file) )
      return xENDOFIMAGE;
   if( ferror(msp_file) )
      return xIOERROR;
   return xOKAY;
}

int MspDecoder::init( void )
{
   curln = 0;
   return status();
}

int MspDecoder::term( void )
{
   return status();
}

void MspDecoder::read_v1( unsigned char *buf, int npxls )
{
   int bytecnt = 0;
   int n = 0;
   while( (bytecnt < rwbytes) && (status() == xOKAY) )
   {
      bytecnt++;
      int b = fgetc( msp_file );
      int mask = 0x100;
      while( (mask >>= 1) != 0 )
         if( n < npxls )
            buf[n++] = (b & mask) ? 1 : 0;
   }
}

void MspDecoder::read_v2( unsigned char *buf, int npxls )
{
   // missing pixels are assumed to be white!
   memset( buf, 1, npxls );
   // decode the scan line
   int bytecnt = 0;
   int pixelcnt = 0;
   int scancnt = lnlen[curln++];
   while( (bytecnt < scancnt) && (status() == xOKAY) )
```

Listing 10.2 MSP.CPP (continued)

```
    {
        int hdr, cnt, dat;
        hdr = fgetc(msp_file);
        if( hdr == 0 )   // repeating run
        {
            cnt = fgetc(msp_file);
            dat = fgetc(msp_file);
            bytecnt += 3;
        }
        else                    // unencoded sequence
        {
            cnt = hdr;
            bytecnt += cnt + 1;
        }
        while( cnt- )
        {
            if( hdr ) dat = fgetc( msp_file );
            int mask = 0x100;
            while( (mask >>= 1) != 0 )
                if( pixelcnt < npxls )
                    buf[pixelcnt++] = (dat & mask) ? 1 : 0;
        }
    }
}

int MspDecoder::decode( unsigned char *buf, int npxls )
{
    if( status() == xOKAY )
    {
        if( version == 1 )
            read_v1( buf, npxls );
        else if( version == 2 )
            read_v2( buf, npxls );
    }
    return status();
}
```

An MSP Query Program

Given the extreme simplicity of the MSP format, a format query program for it
has little to report. In the interest of completeness, however, such a program is
developed for all formats without exception. The query program is presented in
Listing 10.3. Because MSP files are monochrome, the display palette option of
the program has been omitted. In its place is an option to dump the scan-line
length table of version 2 MSP files.

Listing 10.3 QMSP.CPP

```cpp
//-------------------------------------------------------//
//                                                       //
//   File:     QMSP.CPP                                  //
//                                                       //
//   Desc:     MSP File Query Program                    //
//                                                       //
//-------------------------------------------------------//

#include "stdlib.h"
#include "stdio.h"
#include "string.h"

#include "msp.hpp"

//.................program usage

void explain_pgm( void )
{
   printf( "\n" );
   printf( "MS Paint MSP File Query Program\n" );
   printf( "\n" );
   printf( "Usage:  QMSP  msp_file  [-t]\n" );
   printf( "\n" );
   printf( "-t includes scan table listing"
           " if format is version 2\n" );
   printf( ".MSP extension is assumed\n" );
   printf( "\n" );
}


//.................main

int main( int argc, char *argv[] )
{
   // check args
   if( (argc < 2) || (*argv[1] == '?') )
   {
      explain_pgm();
      return 0;
   }

   // create file name
   char fn[80];
   strcpy( fn, argv[1] );
   char *p = strchr( fn, '.' );
   if( p == 0 )
      strcat( fn, ".msp" );
   else if( *(p+1) == 0 )
      *p = 0;
```

Listing 10.3 QMSP.CPP (continued)

```cpp
                // list scan table too?
                int ltbl = 0;
                if( argc > 2 )
                  if( (strcmp( argv[2], "-t" ) == 0) ||
                      (strcmp( argv[2], "-T" ) == 0) )
                    ltbl = 1;
                // open the file
                FILE *fmsp = fopen( fn, "rb" );
                if( fmsp == 0 )
                {
                   printf( "File '%s' not found\n", fn );
                   return 0;
                }

                // read the header and list
                MSPHEADER msp;
                if( fread( &msp, sizeof(MSPHEADER), 1, fmsp ) != 1 )
                {
                   printf( "Error reading header of '%s'\n", fn );
                   fclose( fmsp );
                   return 0;
                }
                printf( "Listing of MSP file '%s'\n", fn );
                printf( "\n" );
                msp.list();
                printf( "\n" );

                // compute actual checksum for comparison with header
                unsigned short *ix = (unsigned short *) &msp.key1;
                unsigned short cksum = 0;
                for( int i=0; i<12; i++ )
                   cksum ^= *ix++;

                // indicate version and checksum
                int version = 0;
                if( (msp.key1==V1KEY1) && (msp.key2==V1KEY2) )
                {
                   printf( "Format Version = 1\n" );
                   version = 1;
                }
                else if( (msp.key1==V2KEY1) && (msp.key2==V2KEY2) )
                {
                   printf( "Format Version = 2\n" );
                   version = 2;
                }
```

Listing 10.3 QMSP.CPP (continued)

```
        else
           printf( "Format keys are invalid\n" );
        printf( "Computed Header Checksum = %u\n", cksum );
        printf( "\n" );

        // if requested, list scan length table
        if( ltbl )
        {
           if( version == 1 )
              printf( "Version 1 has no scan length table\n" );
           else if ( version == 2 )
           {
              printf( "Listing of encoded scan line lengths:\n" );
              for( i=0; i<msp.height; i++ )
              {
                 unsigned int sclen;
                 fread( &sclen, 2, 1, fmsp );
                 printf( "%3d = %u\n", i, sclen );
              }
           }
        }

        fclose( fmsp );
        return 0;
}
```

Reading MSP Files

As noted previously, the MSP format can be considered defunct, so there is no
compelling reason to implement a format writer for it. However, there are still
MSP files in use, and the current version of MS Paint still reads the format, so a
format reader has been developed.

Listings 10.1 and 10.2 include a MSP decoder class that is similar in design
and operation to the other format decoders presented in this book. Although all
MSP files are monochrome, the decoder still decodes the format as scan lines of
8-bit pixel values. This is, of course, a concession to compatibility. Most of the
details of dealing with the format in a program can be gleaned from inspecting
the source listing to the VMSP program, which is presented in Listing 10.4.

One aspect of monochrome imagery that we discussed in Part One is that it is
sometimes useful to be able to work with the negative of an image. For instance,
many windowing environments use black on a white background as a default

color scheme, which on most printers will print as white on a black background. Printing such an image is therefore best performed with the image's negative. For this reason a switch, –n, added to the VMSP program will invert an image when it is loaded.

Listing 10.4 VMSP.CPP

```cpp
//-------------------------------------------------------//
//                                                       //
//    File:      VMSP.CPP                                 //
//                                                       //
//    Desc:      Program to view or print a MSP file      //
//                                                       //
//-------------------------------------------------------//

#include "stdlib.h"
#include "stdio.h"
#include "string.h"
#include "conio.h"
#include "ctype.h"

#include "msp.hpp"
#include "imgviewr.hpp"
#include "imgprntr.hpp"
#include "laserjet.hpp"
#include "paintjet.hpp"
#include "epjx80.hpp"
#include "eplq24.hpp"
#include "pscript.hpp"

//.................Printer types

#define  LJ   0x4C4A
#define  PJ   0x504A
#define  JX   0x4A58
#define  LQ   0x4C51
#define  PS   0x5053


//.................Program globals

char fn[80];              // path to MSP file

int gmode;                // video display mode
int pmode;                // printer ID
int negate;               // image negative flag

ImgStore *imgmap;         // image bitmap
```

Listing 10.4 VMSP.CPP (continued)

```
rgb monopal[] =          // image palette
{
   rgb( 0, 0, 0 ),
   rgb( 255, 255, 255 )
};

//.................Exit with a message

void exit_pgm( char *msg )
{
   printf( "%s\n", msg );
   exit( 0 );
}

//.................Program usage

void explain_pgm( void )
{
   printf( "\n" );
   printf( ".........MS Paint MSP File Viewer/Printer..........\n"
);
   printf( "\n" );
   printf( "Usage:      VMSP  msp_file  [ switches ]\n" );
   printf( "\n" );
   printf( "Switches: -h      = display program usage\n" );
   printf( "          -vXX    = force video display mode XX\n" );
   printf( "                    (XX = 12, 13, 2E, 62)\n" );
   printf( "          -pXX    = print using printer XX\n" );
   printf( "                    (XX = LJ, PJ, JX, LQ, PS)\n" );
   printf( "          -n      = use negative of image\n" );
   printf( "\n" );
   printf( "...............................................\n"
);
   printf( "\n" );
}

//.................Process pgm argument list

void process_args( int argc, char *argv[] )
{
   // establish default values
   fn[0]  = 0;
   gmode  = 0x12;
   pmode  = 0;
   negate = 0;
```

Listing 10.4 VMSP.CPP (continued)

```
// process the program's argument list
for( int i=1; i<argc; i++ )
{
   if( (*argv[i] == '-') || (*argv[i] == '/') )
   {
      char sw = *(argv[i] + 1);
      switch( toupper(sw) )
      {
         case 'H' :
            explain_pgm();
            exit( 0 );
            break;

         case 'V' :
            sscanf( argv[i]+2, "%x", &gmode );
            break;

         case 'P' :
            pmode = toupper( *(argv[i]+2) );
            pmode <<= 8;
            pmode += toupper( *(argv[i]+3) );
            break;

         case 'N' :
            negate = 1;
            break;

         default:
            printf( "Unknown switch '%s' ignored\n",
                    argv[i] );
            break;
      }
   }
   else  // presumably a file identifier
   {
      strcpy( fn, argv[i] );
      char *p = strchr( fn, '.' );
      if( p == 0 )
         strcat( fn, ".msp" );
      else if( *(p+1) == 0 )
         *p = 0;
   }
}
```

Listing 10.4 VMSP.CPP (continued)

```cpp
      // was a file name specified?
      if( fn[0] == 0 )
      {
         explain_pgm();
         exit( 0 );
      }
   }

   //.................Create an image storage buffer

   ImgStore * istore( int h, int w, int d )
   {
      ImgStore *ist = 0;

      // attempt to create in order of preference
      ist = new XmsImgStore( h, w, d );
      if( (ist != 0) && (ist->status != imgstoreOKAY) )
      {
         delete ist;
         ist = new EmsImgStore( h, w, d );
         if( (ist != 0) && (ist->status != imgstoreOKAY) )
         {
            delete ist;
            ist = new CnvImgStore( h, w, d );
            if( (ist != 0) && (ist->status != imgstoreOKAY) )
            {
               delete ist;
               ist = new DskImgStore( h, w, d );
               if( (ist != 0) && (ist->status != imgstoreOKAY) )
               {
                  delete ist;
                  ist = 0;
               }
            }
         }
      }

      return ist;
   }

   //.................Create a printer

   PrinterDriver * printer( int which )
   {
      PrinterDriver *p;
```

Listing 10.4 VMSP.CPP (continued)

```
    switch( which )
    {
        case LJ : p = new LaserJet( "LPT1" );
                  break;
        case PJ : p = new PaintJet( "LPT1" );
                  break;
        case JX : p = new EpsonJX80( "LPT1" );
                  break;
        case LQ : p = new EpsonLQ24( "LPT1" );
                  break;
        default : p = new PsPrinter( "LPT1" );
                  break;
    }

    return p;
}

//................Load the MSP file

void load_msp( void )
{
    // open file
    FILE *fmsp = fopen( fn, "rb" );
    if( fmsp == 0 )
        exit_pgm( "MSP file not found" );

    // read header
    MSPHEADER msph;
    if( fread( &msph, sizeof(MSPHEADER), 1, fmsp ) != 1 )
        exit_pgm( "Error reading MSP header" );

    // validate file
    int version = 0;
    if( (msph.key1 == V1KEY1) && (msph.key2 == V1KEY2) )
        version = 1;
    if( (msph.key1 == V2KEY1) && (msph.key2 == V2KEY2) )
        version = 2;
    if( version == 0 )
        exit_pgm( "File is not a MSP file" );

    // create bitmap
    int ncols = msph.width;
    int nrows = msph.height;

    unsigned char *scanln = new unsigned char [ncols];
    imgmap = istore( nrows, ncols, 8 );
    if( (imgmap == 0) || (scanln == 0) )
    {
```

Listing 10.4 VMSP.CPP (continued)

```cpp
        if( imgmap ) delete imgmap;
        if( scanln ) delete scanln;
        exit_pgm( "Insufficient memory to load image" );
    }

    // load bitmap
    printf( "Loading MSP image from '%s'...", fn );
    MspDecoder mspd( fmsp, msph );
    mspd.init();
    for( int i=0; i<nrows; i++ )
    {
        if( mspd.decode( scanln, ncols ) != xOKAY )
            break;
        if( negate )
            for( int j=0; j<ncols; j++ )
                scanln[j] = 1 - scanln[j];
        imgmap->put( scanln, i );
    }
    mspd.term();
    printf( "done\n" );

    delete scanln;
}


//.................Main

int main( int argc, char *argv[] )
{
    process_args( argc, argv );

    load_msp( );

    // print the image
    if( pmode != 0 )
    {
        PrinterDriver *prt = printer( pmode );
        if( prt )
        {
            printf( "Printing..." );
            ImagePrinter ip( prt, imgmap, monopal, 2,
                             0, 0, 100, 100 );
            ip.print( 1 );
            printf( "done\n" );
            delete prt;
        }
        else
            printf( "Printer instantiation failed\n" );
    }
```

Listing 10.4 VMSP.CPP (continued)

```
// display the image
else
{
   VgaDisplay vga( gmode );
   ImageViewer iv( &vga, imgmap, monopal, 2, 0, 0 );
   iv.view( );
}

delete imgmap;

return 0;
}
```

This finishes our brief look at the MSP format. To reiterate, this format should not be used as an output option for new graphics application development. Use the BMP format instead.

11

The GEM IMG Format

In the mid 1980s, Digital Research's GEM operating environment was one of the premier GUI environments for DOS. Today, Digital no longer exists, and GEM has pretty much passed on into history.

GEM will most likely be remembered for its role as the original environment of its most famous application, Ventura Publisher. Ventura put GEM on the map, and made the support of GEM's graphics file formats a widespread practice. Two formats in particular are worth mention, the **GEM** format and the GEM **IMG** format. The first is a vector-based format, similar in many respects to Window's metafile format. The second, the IMG format, is the subject of this chapter. It is a bitmapped format, and is comparable to the PCX format or the Windows BMP format.

Format Overview

A GEM IMG file is simply structured and consists of a file header followed by an encoded bitmap. The header is quite brief, consisting of 8-word values (16 bytes total). The bitmap is encoded using an RLE variant that is slightly more involved than the other RLE compression schemes described in this book.

In GEM's heyday, the state of the art in graphics adapters was the EGA. This is reflected in the range of image types covered by the format. Only multiplanar, 1-bit-per-pixel images can be encoded, limiting the format to monochrome and 16-color imagery. There is no such thing as a 256-color IMG file.

The IMG format is not a particularly well-designed format, and despite its simplicity it is somewhat problematic to work with. For one thing, the format's header does not specify the height of the encoded image. Instead, it indicates the number of **scan-line items**—each item consisting of an optional repeat indicator and an encoded scan line. The repeat indicator indicates the number of times to replicate the following scan line; if it is not present, a repeat count of one is implied. One problem with this scheme is that the actual height of an image can be determined only by fully decoding the file's bitmap.

Another problem with this scheme is that there is no way to determine if a scan line repeat count is present except to try to read it. If it is not present, then a program has just read part of an encoded scan line. This tends to complicate the decoding logic unnecessarily.

The IMG Header

An IMG file's header is contained in the file's first 8 words (16 bytes). One interesting (if irritating) aspect of the header is that the byte order of each word is not consistent with the order employed by Intel processors. As a consequence, the two bytes in each of the header's 8 words must be swapped before being used. A suitable structure for reading an IMG header is presented in Listings 11.1 and 11.2, which include the implementation of a `swap()` member function to handle this chore.

A cautious programmer might want to verify that an IMG header's byte order has been reversed before using the header. Probably the most reliable method is to test the value of the header's length field (see `hdrsize` in the following list). This should be 8, but will be 8 times 256, or 2048, if the header's byte order has not been reversed.

A brief description of each header field follows.

version	Format version number; always 1.
hdrsize	Number of 16-bit words in the header; always 8.
nplanes	Number of bit planes in the image. This is 1 for a monochrome image or 4 for a color image.
patbytes	Number of bytes in a repeating pattern. One of the constructs encoded by the IMG format's RLE encoding scheme is repeating patterns of one or more bytes. For example, the byte sequence 10h 20h 10h 20h 10h 20h can be represented as three occurrences of the 2-byte pattern 10h 20h. The pattern length for a given file is constant and is indicated by this field.
pxlwidth	Physical width of a pixel on the image's source device. The value is expressed in microns (a micron is 10^{-6} meters; there are 25,400 microns in an inch). There is seldom any use for this field.
pxlheight	Physical height of a pixel on the image's source device in microns. There is seldom any use for this field.
scanwidth	Width of a scan line in pixels.

scancount   Number of encoded scan line items in the image. A scan-line item consists of an optional repeat count followed by an encoded scan line. Note that this value will indicate the height of the image only if all repeat counts are 1, and the latter can be determined only by decoding the entire image.

The IMG Compression Scheme

The IMG format specifies an RLE variant for compressing images. Each bit plane of each scan line is encoded separately as an integral number of bytes. If the image width in pixels is not a multiple of 8, then each bit plane raster line is padded with unused bits for compression purposes.

Each encoded scan line is preceded by an optional repetition count, which indicates the number of times to repeat the scan line. If the repetition count is not present, a count of 1 is implied. When present, the repetition count is encoded as 4 bytes in the following format:

```
00h 00h FFh COUNT
```

The count is a single byte with a value in the range 2 to 255. Although a count of 1 can be encoded as shown, it is customary to indicate counts of 1 by simply omitting the repeat count sequence altogether.

In practice, a format reader will read 4 bytes and test the first 3 for the special values. If they match, the fourth byte is used for the count. Otherwise, the count is 1 and the 4 bytes must be "unread." The easiest way to do this is to seek back in the file 4 bytes from the current position. This is implemented in Listing 11.2 as the member function `ImgDecoder::readcnt()`. Note that the function returns -1 if end of file occurs while it tries to read the 4 bytes.

Once the repetition count has been determined, an encoded scan line is decoded. Keep in mind that each plane of a multiplane image is encoded separately. The encoded scan line will consist of one or more of three possible encoding constructs. These are referred to as **solid runs**, **pattern runs**, and **bit strings**. They all encode some number of bytes, not pixels.

A solid run consists of a single byte that indicates a state and the number of bytes possessing that state. The high order bit indicates a byte value of 00h if it is clear and a byte value of FFh if it is set. The remaining 7 bits indicate the number of times to repeat the byte value in the data stream. For example, 83h means 3 bytes of FFh, and 0Fh means 15 bytes of 00h.

A pattern run is indicated when a byte with the value 00h is read. The next byte read determines the number of times to repeat the pattern. The length of the pattern is indicated by the `patbytes` member of the header. A single repetition of the pattern follows the count byte in the data stream. It is read and then replicated in the output stream the indicated number of times. Here's an example: suppose the pattern length is 2 and the image contains these 6 bytes:

```
10h 20h 10h 20h 10h 20h
```

This would be encoded as:

```
00h 03h 10h 20h
```

where 00h indicates a pattern run, 03h is the repetition count, and 10h 20h is the pattern.

If a segment of a scan line cannot be encoded as either a solid run or a pattern run, then it is encoded as a `bit string`. This is signaled when a byte with the value 80h is read. The next byte in the encoded stream indicates a byte count, and that number of bytes is read from the file and used as is. For example, the following sequence of image bytes

```
10h 2Ah 34h 17h
```

can be encoded as the following bit string:

```
80h 04h 10h 2Ah 34h 17h
```

The value 80h signals a bit string, and the next byte indicates that the bit string is 4 bytes long. The bit string itself follows these 2 bytes.

As you can see, the compression scheme is slightly more complex than those of the PCX and MSP formats. On average it delivers about the same degree of compression. Note that the actual results obtained are affected by the choice of pattern length. A good value for typical screen imagery is 1 or 2. Note that a value of 1 causes the algorithm to behave very much like the PCX compression scheme and is perhaps the best default choice.

Listing 11.1 IMG.HPP

```cpp
//-----------------------------------------------------------//
//                                                           //
//    File:      IMG.HPP                                      //
//                                                           //
//    Desc:      Class and structure definitions for the     //
//               GEM IMG format                              //
//                                                           //
//-----------------------------------------------------------//

#ifndef _IMG_HPP_
#define _IMG_HPP_

#include "stdlib.h"
#include "stdio.h"
#include "string.h"

#include "color.hpp"
#include "codec.hpp"

//.............struct IMGHEADER

struct IMGHEADER
{
    unsigned int version;      // version number
    unsigned int hdrsize;      // size of header in words
    unsigned int nplanes;      // planes in image
    unsigned int patbytes;     // length of pattern in bytes
    unsigned int pxlwidth;     // pixel size in microns
    unsigned int pxlheight;    // pixel size in microns
    unsigned int scanwidth;    // image width in pixels
    unsigned int scancount;    // encoded scan line count

    void swap( void );
    void list( void );
};

//.............class ImgDecoder

class ImgDecoder : public Decoder
{
    protected:
        int    cond;        // condition code
        int    img_planes;  // image planes
        int    img_width;   // image width
        int    img_height;  // image height
        int    row_bytes;   // bytes per plane per row
        FILE *img_file;     // output file
```

Listing 11.1 IMG.HPP (continued)

```cpp
    private:
        int repeatcnt;  // cur scan line repeat count
        int scancnt;    // scan item count from header

        unsigned char *scanline;  // cur scan line buffer
        int curpxl;               // index into scanline

        unsigned char *pattern;  // pattern buffer
        int patlen;              // size of pattern;

        int  readcnt( void );
        int  imagehgt( void );
        void putbyte( int byte, int plmask );
        void readplane( int plmask );
        void readline( void );
        void skipline( void );

    public:
        ImgDecoder( FILE *f_in, IMGHEADER& img );
        virtual ~ImgDecoder( ) { }
        virtual int decode( unsigned char *buf, int npxls );
        virtual int init( void );
        virtual int term( void );
        virtual int status( void );
        int width( void )  { return img_width; }
        int height( void ) { return img_height; }
        int depth( void )  { return img_planes; }
    };

    #endif
```

Listing 11.2 IMG.CPP

```cpp
//-----------------------------------------------------//
//                                                     //
//   File:    IMG.CPP                                  //
//                                                     //
//   Desc:    Class and structure definitions for the //
//            GEM IMG format                           //
//                                                     //
//-----------------------------------------------------//

#include "img.hpp"

//............struct IMGHEADER
static unsigned int uswap( unsigned int u )
```

Listing 11.2 IMG.CPP (continued)

```cpp
{
    return( ((u >> 8) & 0x00FF) | ((u << 8) & 0xFF00) );
}

// reverse byte order in each word
void IMGHEADER::swap( void )
{
    version   = uswap( version);
    hdrsize   = uswap( hdrsize );
    nplanes   = uswap( nplanes );
    patbytes  = uswap( patbytes );
    pxlwidth  = uswap( pxlwidth );
    pxlheight = uswap( pxlheight );
    scanwidth = uswap( scanwidth );
    scancount = uswap( scancount );
}

// list header values
void IMGHEADER::list( void )
{
    printf( "IMGHEADER::version   = %d\n", version );
    printf( "IMGHEADER::hdrsize   = %d words\n", hdrsize );
    printf( "IMGHEADER::nplanes   = %d\n", nplanes );
    printf( "IMGHEADER::patbytes  = %d\n", patbytes );
    printf( "IMGHEADER::pxlwidth  = %d microns\n", pxlwidth );
    printf( "IMGHEADER::pxlheight = %d microns\n", pxlheight );
    printf( "IMGHEADER::scanwidth = %d\n", scanwidth );
    printf( "IMGHEADER::scancount = %d\n", scancount );
}

//.............class ImgDecoder

ImgDecoder::ImgDecoder( FILE *f_in, IMGHEADER& img )
{
    cond = xOKAY;

    // we use the header length field to determine
    // if header words have the proper byte order
    if( img.hdrsize != 8 )  img.swap();

    img_file   = f_in;
    img_planes = img.nplanes;
    img_width  = img.scanwidth;
    row_bytes  = (img_width + 7) / 8;
    scancnt    = img.scancount;
    patlen     = img.patbytes;
    img_height = imagehgt();
}
```

Listing 11.2 IMG.CPP (continued)

```cpp
int ImgDecoder::init( void )
{
    cond = xOKAY;
    repeatcnt = 0;
    scanline = new unsigned char [img_width];
    if( scanline == 0 ) cond = xNOMEMORY;
    pattern = new unsigned char [patlen];
    if( pattern == 0 ) cond = xNOMEMORY;
    return status();
}

int ImgDecoder::term( void )
{
    if( scanline )
    {
        delete scanline;
        scanline = 0;
    }
    if( pattern )
    {
        delete pattern;
        pattern = 0;
    }
    return status();
}

int ImgDecoder::status( void )
{
    if( cond == xOKAY )
    {
        if( feof(img_file) )   cond = xENDOFIMAGE;
        if( ferror(img_file) ) cond = xIOERROR;
    }
    return cond;
}

int ImgDecoder::readcnt( void )
{
    // if present, count is 4 bytes formatted
    // as follows:  00 00 FF CNT
    unsigned char uc[4];
    if( fread( uc, 1, 4, img_file ) != 4 )
        return -1;
    if( uc[0] == 0 )
        if( uc[1] == 0 )
            if( uc[2] == 255 )
```

Listing 11.2 IMG.CPP (continued)

```
                return uc[3];
    fseek( img_file, -4, SEEK_CUR );
    return 1;
}

void ImgDecoder::putbyte( int byte, int plmask )
{
    int mask = 0x100;
    while( ((mask>>=1) > 0) && (curpxl < img_width) )
    {
        if( (byte & mask) == 0 )  scanline[curpxl] |= plmask;
        curpxl++;
    }
}

void ImgDecoder::readplane( int plmask )
{
    curpxl = 0;
    int nbytes = 0;
    while( nbytes < row_bytes )
    {
        // get construct type
        int type = fgetc( img_file );
        if( type < 0 ) return;

        // process the construct
        int i, j, cnt;
        switch( type )
        {
            case 0x00 :  // a pattern run
                cnt = fgetc( img_file );
                fread( pattern, patlen, 1, img_file );
                for( i=0; i<cnt; i++ )
                {
                    for( j=0; j<patlen; j++ )
                    {
                        putbyte( pattern[j], plmask );
                    }
                    nbytes += patlen;
                }
                break;

            case 0x80 :  // an unencoded run
                cnt = fgetc( img_file );
                for( i=0; i<cnt; i++ )
```

Listing 11.2 IMG.CPP (continued)

```
                        {
                            j = fgetc( img_file );
                            putbyte( j, plmask );
                        }
                        nbytes += cnt;
                        break;

                default :    // a solid run
                        j = (type & 0x80) ? 0xFF : 0x00;
                        cnt = type & 0x7F;
                        for( i=0; i<cnt; i++ )
                            putbyte( j, plmask );
                        nbytes += cnt;
                        break;
                }
            }
        }

        void ImgDecoder::readline( void )
        {
            int i, mask;
            memset( scanline, 0, img_width );
            for( i=0, mask=1; i<img_planes; i++, mask<<=1 )
                readplane( mask );
        }

        void ImgDecoder::skipline( void )
        {
            for( int i=0; i<img_planes; i++ )
            {
                int nbytes = 0;
                while( nbytes < row_bytes )
                {
                    // get construct type
                    int type = fgetc( img_file );
                    if( type < 0 ) return;

                    // process the construct
                    int cnt;
                    switch( type )
                    {
                        case 0x00 :  // a pattern run
                            cnt = fgetc( img_file );
                            fseek( img_file, patlen, SEEK_CUR);
                            nbytes += patlen*cnt;
                            break;
```

Listing 11.2 IMG.CPP (continued)

```cpp
                case 0x80 :  // an unencoded run
                    cnt = fgetc( img_file );
                    fseek( img_file, cnt, SEEK_CUR);
                    nbytes += cnt;
                    break;

                default :    // a solid run
                    cnt = type & 0x7F;
                    nbytes += cnt;
                    break;
            }
        }
    }
}

int ImgDecoder::imagehgt( void )
{
    int cnt = 0;
    fseek( img_file, sizeof(IMGHEADER), SEEK_SET );
    for( int i=0; i<scancnt; i++ )
    {
        cnt += readcnt();
        skipline();
    }
    fseek( img_file, sizeof(IMGHEADER), SEEK_SET );
    return cnt;
}

int ImgDecoder::decode( unsigned char *buf, int npxls )
{
    if( status() == xOKAY )
    {
        if( repeatcnt < 1 )
        {
            repeatcnt = readcnt();
            if( repeatcnt > 0 )
                readline();
        }
        if( repeatcnt > 0 )
            memcpy( buf, scanline, npxls );
        repeatcnt—;
    }
    return status();
}
```

An IMG Query Program

The IMG format's simple header makes for a simple query program. The source code for QIMG.CPP is presented in Listing 11.3.

One potentially useful enhancement for the program would be to decode the image to determine the actual image height. If you recall, the `scancount` member of the header indicates the number of scan-line items, which is the same as the image height only if all vertical replication counts are 1. The IMG decoder class of Listings 11.1 and 11.2 contains such a function, `imagehgt()`.

Listing 11.3 QIMG.CPP

```
//------------------------------------------------------------//
//                                                            //
//    File:      QIMG.CPP                                     //
//                                                            //
//    Desc:      IMG File Query Program                       //
//                                                            //
//------------------------------------------------------------//

#include "stdlib.h"
#include "stdio.h"
#include "string.h"

#include "img.hpp"

//.................program usage

void explain_pgm( void )
{
   printf( "\n" );
   printf( "GEM IMG File Query Program\n" );
   printf( "\n" );
   printf( "Usage:  QIMG  img_file\n" );
   printf( "\n" );
   printf( ".IMG extension is assumed\n" );
   printf( "\n" );
}


//.................main

int main( int argc, char *argv[] )
{
   // check args
   if( (argc < 2) || (*argv[1] == '?') )
```

Listing 11.3 QIMG.CPP (continued)

```cpp
    {
        explain_pgm();
        return 0;
    }

    // create file name
    char fn[80];
    strcpy( fn, argv[1] );
    char *p = strchr( fn, '.' );
    if( p == 0 )
        strcat( fn, ".img" );
    else if( *(p+1) == 0 )
        *p = 0;

    // open the file
    FILE *fimg = fopen( fn, "rb" );
    if( fimg == 0 )
    {
        printf( "File '%s' not found\n", fn );
        return 0;
    }

    // read the header and list
    IMGHEADER img;
    if( fread( &img, sizeof(IMGHEADER), 1, fimg ) != 1 )
    {
        printf( "Error reading header of '%s'\n", fn );
        fclose( fimg );
        return 0;
    }
    printf( "Listing of IMG file '%s'\n", fn );
    printf( "\n" );
    img.swap();
    img.list();

    fclose( fimg );
    return 0;
}
```

An IMG Viewer Program

Listing 11.4 presents a viewer program for IMG files. Most of the IMG-specific code is concerned with creating an instance of the `ImgStore` class, which contains the IMG file's bitmap. This is passed as a parameter to an `ImageViewer` constructor call.

The IMG file is decoded using an instance of the ImgDecoder class of Listings 11.1 and 11.2. Note that this class inverts the image as it is loaded. This is done in the `putbyte()` member function, which sets a pixel bit if the corresponding image data bit is zero. This is in keeping with the black-on-white convention of monochrome IMG files, in which a 1 bit indicates the foreground color, black. However, it is possible that files from other sources will not follow this convention, so the viewer program supports a command line switch, −n (read "dash n"), that inverts the image if it is monochrome.

As you may have noticed by now, the IMG format does not include a palette specification. The viewer program provides two palettes, one for monochrome and one for color, that represent typical default palettes. It is possible, though unlikely, that a 16-color IMG file would be based on a different palette. However, without palette information there is nothing that can be done to accommodate this.

Listing 11.4 VIMG.CPP

```
//------------------------------------------------------------//
//                                                            //
//   File:      VIMG.CPP                                      //
//                                                            //
//   Desc:      Program to view or print a GEM IMG file       //
//                                                            //
//------------------------------------------------------------//

#include "stdlib.h"
#include "stdio.h"
#include "string.h"
#include "conio.h"
#include "ctype.h"

#include "img.hpp"
#include "imgviewr.hpp"
#include "imgprntr.hpp"
#include "laserjet.hpp"
#include "paintjet.hpp"
#include "epjx80.hpp"
#include "eplq24.hpp"
#include "pscript.hpp"

//................Printer types

#define  LJ   0x4C4A
#define  PJ   0x504A
#define  JX   0x4A58
#define  LQ   0x4C51
#define  PS   0x5053
```

Listing 11.4 VIMG.CPP (continued)

```cpp
//.................Program globals

char fn[80];              // path to IMG file

int gmode;                // video display mode
int pmode;                // printer ID
int negate;               // image negative flag

ImgStore *imgmap;         // image bitmap

rgb monopal[] =           // mono palette
{
   rgb( 0, 0, 0 ),
   rgb( 255, 255, 255 )
};

rgb colorpal[] =          // 16-color palette
{
   rgb(   0,   0,   0 ),
   rgb(   0,   0, 170 ),
   rgb(   0, 170,   0 ),
   rgb(   0, 170, 170 ),
   rgb( 170,   0,   0 ),
   rgb( 170,   0, 170 ),
   rgb( 170,  85,   0 ),
   rgb( 170, 170, 170 ),
   rgb(  85,  85,  85 ),
   rgb(  85,  85, 255 ),
   rgb(  85, 255,  85 ),
   rgb(  85, 255, 255 ),
   rgb( 255,  85,  85 ),
   rgb( 255,  85, 255 ),
   rgb( 255, 255,  85 ),
   rgb( 255, 255, 255 )
};

//.................Exit with a message

void exit_pgm( char *msg )
{
   printf( "%s\n", msg );
   exit( 0 );
}

//.................Program usage
```

Listing 11.4 VIMG.CPP (continued)

```cpp
void explain_pgm( void )
{
   printf( "\n" );
   printf( "...........GEM IMG File Viewer/Printer...........\n"
);
   printf( "\n" );
   printf( "Usage:     VIMG  img_file  [ switches ]\n" );
   printf( "\n" );
   printf( "Switches:  -h      = display program usage\n" );
   printf( "           -vXX    = force video display mode XX\n" );
   printf( "                     (XX = 12, 13, 2E, 62)\n" );
   printf( "           -pXX    = print using printer XX\n" );
   printf( "                     (XX = LJ, PJ, JX, LQ, PS)\n" );
   printf( "           -n      = use negative of image\n" );
   printf( "\n" );
   printf( "....................................................\n"
);
   printf( "\n" );
}

//.................Process pgm argument list

void process_args( int argc, char *argv[] )
{
   // establish default values
   fn[0]  = 0;
   gmode  = 0x12;
   pmode  = 0;
   negate = 0;

   // process the program's argument list
   for( int i=1; i<argc; i++ )
   {
      if( (*argv[i] == '-') || (*argv[i] == '/') )
      {
         char sw = *(argv[i] + 1);
         switch( toupper(sw) )
         {
            case 'H' :
               explain_pgm();
               exit( 0 );
               break;

            case 'V' :
               sscanf( argv[i]+2, "%x", &gmode );
               break;
            case 'P' :
               pmode = toupper( *(argv[i]+2) );
```

Listing 11.4 VIMG.CPP (continued)

```cpp
                    pmode <<= 8;
                    pmode += toupper( *(argv[i]+3) );
                    break;

                case 'N' :
                    negate = 1;
                    break;

                default:
                    printf( "Unknown switch '%s' ignored\n",
                            argv[i] );
                    break;
            }
        }
        else   // presumably a file identifier
        {
            strcpy( fn, argv[i] );
            char *p = strchr( fn, '.' );
            if( p == 0 )
                strcat( fn, ".img" );
            else if( *(p+1) == 0 )
                *p = 0;
        }
    }

    // was a file name specified?
    if( fn[0] == 0 )
    {
        explain_pgm();
        exit( 0 );
    }
}

//.................Create an image storage buffer

ImgStore * istore( int h, int w, int d )
{
    ImgStore *ist = 0;

    // attempt to create in order of preference
    ist = new XmsImgStore( h, w, d );
    if( (ist != 0) && (ist->status != imgstoreOKAY) )
    {
        delete ist;
        ist = new EmsImgStore( h, w, d );
        if( (ist != 0) && (ist->status != imgstoreOKAY) )
        {
            delete ist;
```

Listing 11.4 VIMG.CPP (continued)

```
            ist = new CnvImgStore( h, w, d );
            if( (ist != 0) && (ist->status != imgstoreOKAY) )
            {
               delete ist;
               ist = new DskImgStore( h, w, d );
               if( (ist != 0) && (ist->status != imgstoreOKAY) )
               {
                  delete ist;
                  ist = 0;
               }
            }
         }
      }

   return ist;
}

//.................Create a printer

PrinterDriver * printer( int which )
{
   PrinterDriver *p;

   switch( which )
   {
      case LJ : p = new LaserJet( "LPT1" );
                break;
      case PJ : p = new PaintJet( "LPT1" );
                break;
      case JX : p = new EpsonJX80( "LPT1" );
                break;
      case LQ : p = new EpsonLQ24( "LPT1" );
                break;
      default : p = new PsPrinter( "LPT1" );
                break;
   }

   return p;
}

//.................Load the IMG file

int load_img( void )
{
   // open file
   FILE *fimg = fopen( fn, "rb" );
   if( fimg == 0 )
      exit_pgm( "IMG file not found" );
```

Listing 11.4 VIMG.CPP (continued)

```cpp
        // read header
        IMGHEADER imgh;
        if( fread( &imgh, sizeof(IMGHEADER), 1, fimg ) != 1 )
            exit_pgm( "Error reading IMG header" );

        ImgDecoder imgd( fimg, imgh );

        // create bitmap
        int ncols = imgh.scanwidth;
        int nrows = imgd.height();

        unsigned char *scanln = new unsigned char [ncols];
        imgmap = istore( nrows, ncols, 8 );
        if( (imgmap == 0) || (scanln == 0) )
        {
            if( imgmap ) delete imgmap;
            if( scanln ) delete scanln;
            exit_pgm( "Insufficient memory to load image" );
        }

        // load bitmap
        printf( "Loading IMG image from '%s'...", fn );
        imgd.init();
        for( int i=0; i<nrows; i++ )
        {
            if( imgd.decode( scanln, ncols ) != xOKAY )
                break;
            if( negate && (imgh.nplanes==1) )
                for( int j=0; j<ncols; j++ )
                    scanln[j] = 1 - scanln[j];
            imgmap->put( scanln, i );
        }
        imgd.term();
        printf( "done\n" );

        delete scanln;

        // return number of image colors
        return (imgh.nplanes == 1) ? 2 : 16;
}

//.................Main

int main( int argc, char *argv[] )
{
    process_args( argc, argv );
```

Listing 11.4 VIMG.CPP (continued)

```
      int ncolors = load_img( );
      rgb *imgpal = (ncolors == 2) ? monopal : colorpal;

      // print the image
      if( pmode != 0 )
      {
         PrinterDriver *prt = printer( pmode );
         if( prt )
         {
            printf( "Printing..." );
            ImagePrinter ip( prt, imgmap, imgpal, ncolors,
                             0, 0, 100, 100 );
            ip.print( 1 );
            printf( "done\n" );
            delete prt;
         }
         else
            printf( "Printer instantiation failed\n" );
      }

      // display the image
      else
      {
         VgaDisplay vga( gmode );
         ImageViewer iv( &vga, imgmap, imgpal, ncolors, 0, 0 );
         iv.view( );
      }

      delete imgmap;

      return 0;
   }
```

An IMG-to-PCX Conversion Program

One topic we have yet to address is format conversion. That is, converting an existing graphics file to a file of a different format. As it turns out, this is a relatively simple process given the image-processing tools at our disposal. The process is illustrated here for converting IMG files to the PCX format.

Obviously it is possible to write a program that converts a specific format directly to another specific format. However, this is not a good design strategy. (We touched upon this idea in Chapter 7, in connection with image display and printing.) A better approach is to utilize an intermediate, "formatless" image representation. The source format is converted to this form, and the destination format is created from this form. In our case, the `ImgStore` class and `rgb` structure are the components used to implement this format-independent image representation.

To illustrate the point of our design strategy, suppose we have a domain of five formats and we want to develop a utility to convert any of the five to any other of the five. This means that for each format, four conversion modules are required (we obviously don't need to convert a format to itself), for a total of 5 times 4, or 20 modules.

In contrast, if an intermediate representation is used, then only 10 modules are required. Each format requires only two modules, one to convert the format to the intermediate form and one to create an instance of the format from the intermediate form.

Listing 11.5 presents the source code of the IMG2PCX program. It contains nothing that we have not seen before, so it is presented here without comment.

Listing 11.5 IMG2PCX.CPP

```
//---------------------------------------------------------//
//                                                         //
//    File:      VIMG.CPP                                  //
//                                                         //
//    Desc:      Program to view or print a GEM IMG file   //
//                                                         //
//---------------------------------------------------------//

#include "stdlib.h"
#include "stdio.h"
#include "string.h"
#include "conio.h"
#include "ctype.h"

#include "imgstore.hpp"
#include "pcx.hpp"
#include "img.hpp"


//.................Program globals

char img_fn[80];        // path to IMG file
char pcx_fn[80];        // path to PCX file

ImgStore *imgmap;       // image bitmap
int       ncolors;      //    and
rgb      *imgpal;       // palette
```

Listing 11.5 IMG2PCX.CPP (continued)

```cpp
rgb monopal[] =            // mono palette
{
   rgb( 0, 0, 0 ),
   rgb( 255, 255, 255 )
};

rgb colorpal[] =           // 16-color palette
{
   rgb(   0,   0,   0 ),
   rgb(   0,   0, 170 ),
   rgb(   0, 170,   0 ),
   rgb(   0, 170, 170 ),
   rgb( 170,   0,   0 ),
   rgb( 170,   0, 170 ),
   rgb( 170,  85,   0 ),
   rgb( 170, 170, 170 ),
   rgb(  85,  85,  85 ),
   rgb(  85,  85, 255 ),
   rgb(  85, 255,  85 ),
   rgb(  85, 255, 255 ),
   rgb( 255,  85,  85 ),
   rgb( 255,  85, 255 ),
   rgb( 255, 255,  85 ),
   rgb( 255, 255, 255 )
};

//.................Exit with a message

void exit_pgm( char *msg )
{
   printf( "%s\n", msg );
   exit( 0 );
}

//.................Program usage

void explain_pgm( void )
{
   printf( "\n" );
   printf( "............IMG to PCX File Converter..........\n" );
   printf( "\n" );
   printf( "Usage:      IMG2PCX  img_file  [ pcx_file ]\n" );
   printf( "\n" );
   printf( "Default extensions of IMG and PCX are assumed\n" );
   printf( "\n" );
   printf( "...............................................\n" );
   printf( "\n" );
}
```

Listing 11.5 IMG2PCX.CPP (continued)

```
//...............Create an image storage buffer

ImgStore * istore( int h, int w, int d )
{
    ImgStore *ist = 0;

    // attempt to create in order of preference
    ist = new XmsImgStore( h, w, d );
    if( (ist != 0) && (ist->status != imgstoreOKAY) )
    {
        delete ist;
        ist = new EmsImgStore( h, w, d );
        if( (ist != 0) && (ist->status != imgstoreOKAY) )
        {
            delete ist;
            ist = new CnvImgStore( h, w, d );
            if( (ist != 0) && (ist->status != imgstoreOKAY) )
            {
                delete ist;
                ist = new DskImgStore( h, w, d );
                if( (ist != 0) && (ist->status != imgstoreOKAY) )
                {
                    delete ist;
                    ist = 0;
                }
            }
        }
    }

    return ist;
}

//.................Load the IMG file

int load_img( char *fn )
{
    // open file
    FILE *fimg = fopen( fn, "rb" );
    if( fimg == 0 )
        exit_pgm( "IMG file not found" );

    // read header
    IMGHEADER imgh;
    if( fread( &imgh, sizeof(IMGHEADER), 1, fimg ) != 1 )
        exit_pgm( "Error reading IMG header" );

    ImgDecoder imgd( fimg, imgh );
```

Listing 11.5 IMG2PCX.CPP (continued)

```cpp
        // create bitmap
        int ncols = imgh.scanwidth;
        int nrows = imgd.height();

        unsigned char *scanln = new unsigned char [ncols];
        imgmap = istore( nrows, ncols, 8 );
        if( (imgmap == 0) || (scanln == 0) )
        {
            if( imgmap ) delete imgmap;
            if( scanln ) delete scanln;
            exit_pgm( "Insufficient memory to load image" );
        }

        // load bitmap
        imgd.init();
        for( int i=0; i<nrows; i++ )
        {
            if( imgd.decode( scanln, ncols ) != xOKAY )
            {
                delete scanln;
                delete imgmap;
                exit_pgm( "Error reading IMG bitmap" );
            }
            imgmap->put( scanln, i );
        }
        imgd.term();
        delete scanln;

        // return number of image colors
        return (imgh.nplanes == 1) ? 2 : 16;
}

//.................Load the IMG file

void write_pcx( char *fn )
{
    // open file
    FILE *fpcx = fopen( fn, "wb" );

    // create and write the header
    PCXHEADER pcxh;
    pcxh.bitpx = 1;
    pcxh.nplanes = (ncolors == 2) ? 1 : 4;
    pcxh.x1 = 0;
    pcxh.y1 = 0;
    pcxh.x2 = imgmap->width() - 1;
    pcxh.y2 = imgmap->height() - 1;
    pcxh.bplin = ((imgmap->width() + 15) / 16) * 2;
```

Listing 11.5 IMG2PCX.CPP (continued)

```cpp
        int n = 0;
        for( int i=0; i<ncolors; i++ )
        {
            pcxh.colors[n++] = imgpal[i].red;
            pcxh.colors[n++] = imgpal[i].grn;
            pcxh.colors[n++] = imgpal[i].blu;
        }
        if( fwrite( &pcxh, sizeof(PCXHEADER), 1, fpcx ) != 1 )
        {
            delete imgmap;
            exit_pgm( "Error writing PCX header" );
        }

        // encode and write the bitmap
        PcxEncoder pcxe( fpcx, pcxh );
        pcxe.init();
        for( i=0; i<imgmap->height(); i++ )
        {
            if( pcxe.encode( imgmap->get(i), imgmap->width() )
                != xOKAY )
            {
                delete imgmap;
                exit_pgm( "Error writing PCX bitmap" );
            }
        }
        pcxe.term();
}

//.................Main

int main( int argc, char *argv[] )
{
    // we need at least one argument
    if( argc < 2 )
    {
        explain_pgm();
        exit( 0 );
    }

    // create file names
    if( argc < 3 )
    {
        strcpy( img_fn, argv[1] );
        int n = 0;
        char *p = argv[1];
        while( (*p != 0) && (*p != '.') )
```

Listing 11.5 IMG2PCX.CPP (continued)

```
            pcx_fn[n++] = *p++;
        pcx_fn[n] = 0;
    }
    else
    {
        strcpy( img_fn, argv[1] );
        strcpy( pcx_fn, argv[2] );
    }

    // supply default extensions
    if( strchr( img_fn, '.' ) == 0 )
        strcat( img_fn, ".IMG" );
    if( strchr( pcx_fn, '.' ) == 0 )
        strcat( pcx_fn, ".PCX" );

    // load IMG file
    printf( "Loading '%s'...", img_fn );
    ncolors = load_img( img_fn );
    imgpal = (ncolors == 2) ? monopal : colorpal;
    printf( "done\n" );

    // write PCX file
    printf( "Writing '%s'...", pcx_fn );
    write_pcx( pcx_fn );
    printf( "done\n" );

    delete imgmap;
    return 0;
}
```

This concludes our look at the IMG format. Like the MSP format, it should be considered defunct and should not be used for new application development. For that reason, a format writer has been omitted. A good alternative format is PCX, and the IMG2PCX conversion program provided in Listing 11.5 can be used to convert existing IMG files to this format.

12

The MacPaint Format

The MacPaint format originated with the Apple Macintosh application of the same name. It is the only format in this book that is strictly for the Apple environment. The other distinction of the MacPaint format is its bare simplicity—it is also the simplest format presented in this book. Indeed, it is little more than a compressed screen dump from a single application, MacPaint, for a single system, the Macintosh. There are still many MacPaint files to be found on BBS systems around the world, however, and from that standpoint it is useful to be able to read and write the format.

The real legacy of the MacPaint format is probably its compression scheme, which is known as PackBits. Not only was it one of the first RLE compression schemes to achieve widespread use, it also was adopted as a standard for the TIFF format, which is the subject of Chapter 16. Chapter 3 presents a reasonably detailed discussion of the PackBits algorithm, which you can refer to if you need a reminder.

A MacPaint File Overview

A MacPaint file contains a single, fixed-size bitmapped image that is 576 pixels wide by 720 pixels high by 1 bit deep. Because the image dimensions are fixed, there is no need to store these numbers in the file itself. MacPaint files thus lack a header in a traditional sense. What passes for a header is a 512-byte block at the beginning of the file that contains a 4-byte version number, a set of 38 8-bit-by-8-bit fill patterns, and 204 bytes of filler. None of this information is necessary to decode a MacPaint file, so it can pretty much be ignored.

Following the 512-byte header is the actual bitmap, which is PackBits encoded. Each scan line of 576 pixels, or 72 bytes, is encoded separately. Encoded data do not span scan lines. To decode the complete bitmap, a program normally calls a decode-scan-line function 720 times, passing it a 72-byte buffer to fill.

The file system of the Mac is quite different from that of MS-DOS, which fact can impact the physical layout and content of a MacPaint file that has been transferred to an IBM PC. In the Mac file system, for instance, files contain two **forks**, or components; one is the *data fork* and the other is the *resource fork*. Version 1.0 MacPaint files possess only a data fork. Version 2.0 of the format adds some minor resource information that is, again, not needed to decode the file and can be ignored. Most software ignores the resource fork in any case.

When a MacPaint file is transferred to a PC, the contents of the resulting PC file should match the data fork . . . sometimes.

The problem is that, once transferred to the PC, a MacPaint file can lose enough Mac-specific information that it cannot then be transferred back to the Mac as precisely the same file. File names on the Mac, for instance, can be up to 63 characters in length, while MS-DOS file names are limited to 8 characters. Mac files also possess *file-type* and *file-creator* attributes that have no counterpart on the PC.

Some software programs attempt to preserve this information so that the file can be transferred back to the Mac, if necessary. They normally do this by prefixing the file with an external header that includes this information. One unofficial header widely used for this purpose is known as a *MacBinary header*. The code presented in this chapter deals with MacPaint files that possess this header. The MacBinary header is 128 bytes in length. When present, it occurs at the very beginning of the file, before the paint file's own 512-byte header. Thus, if a file possesses the header, then its bitmap begins at byte offset 640 calculated from the beginning of the file; if it lacks the header, then the bitmap starts at byte offset 512.

Listings 12.1 and 12.2 present the structure definitions for both the MacBinary header and the MacPaint header. We are concerned with these only when decoding a file, since we must be able to recognize them and skip them to locate the file's bitmap. The most reliable method of detecting a MacBinary header is to inspect the `filetype` and `fileownr` members for the values `'PNTG'` and `'MPNT'`, respectively. Most software will fill in at least these two members, although often not much else. The program's procedure, then, is to read the first 128 bytes of a file and treat them as a MacBinary header. If the `filetype` and `fileownr` values check out, the program seeks to byte offset 640, if they do not check out, the program seeks to byte offset 512. It can then begin decoding the bitmap.

Listing 12.1 MACPNT.HPP

```
//----------------------------------------------------------//
//                                                          //
//   File:    MACPNT.HPP                                    //
//                                                          //
//   Desc:    Structures for the MacPaint format            //
//                                                          //
//----------------------------------------------------------//

#ifndef _MACPNT_HPP_
#define _MACPNT_HPP_

#include "stdlib.h"
#include "stdio.h"
#include "string.h"

#include "color.hpp"
#include "codec.hpp"
#include "revword.h"


#define MACLNWIDTH 72


//.................MacBinary telecommunications header

struct MACBINHDR
{
    unsigned char    version;
    unsigned char    namelen;
    char             macname[63];
    char             filetype[4];
    char             fileownr[4];
    char             fflags1;
    char             resv1;
    unsigned short   xposn;
    unsigned short   yposn;
    unsigned short   id;
    char             prot;
    char             resv2;
    unsigned long    rforklen;
    unsigned long    dforklen;
    unsigned long    credate;
    unsigned long    moddate;
    char             resv3[2];
    char             fflags2;
    char             resv4[14];
    unsigned long    unpcklen;
    char             resv5[2];
    unsigned char    macbver1;
    unsigned char    macbver2;
```

Listing 12.1 MACPNT.HPP (continued)

```
        unsigned short   crc;
        char             resv6[2];

        MACBINHDR( )
        {
           memset( &version, 0, sizeof(MACBINHDR) );
        }

        MACBINHDR( char *fn )
        {
           memset( &version, 0, sizeof(MACBINHDR) );
           strcpy( macname, fn );
           namelen = strlen( fn );
           filetype[0] = 'P';    // "PNTG"
           filetype[1] = 'N';
           filetype[2] = 'T';
           filetype[3] = 'G';
           fileownr[0] = 'M';    // "MPNT"
           fileownr[1] = 'P';
           fileownr[2] = 'N';
           fileownr[3] = 'T';
        }
       ~MACBINHDR( )
        {
        }
        int  get( FILE *f );
        int  put( FILE *f );
    };

    //.................MacPaint file header

    struct MACPNTHDR
    {
        unsigned long   version;
        unsigned char   patterns[304];
        unsigned char   resv[204];

        MACPNTHDR( )
        {
           memset( &version, 0, sizeof(MACPNTHDR) );
        }
       ~MACPNTHDR( )
        {
        }
        int  get( FILE *f );
        int  put( FILE *f );
    };
```

Listing 12.1 MACPNT.HPP (continued)

```
//.................class MacPntDecoder

class MacPntDecoder : public Decoder
{
   protected:
      FILE           *MacFile;      // input file
      int            MacCond;       // condition code
      int            MacFg;         // fg color
      int            MacBg;         // bg color
      unsigned char MacBuf[72];     // scan line buffer

   private:
      int readln( void );
      void unpack( unsigned char *buf, int npxls );

   public:
      MacPntDecoder( FILE *f_in, int fg=0, int bg=15 )
      {
         MacFile = f_in;
         MacCond = xOKAY;
         MacFg   = fg;
         MacBg   = bg;
      }
      virtual ~MacPntDecoder( )
      {
      }
      virtual int decode( unsigned char *buf, int npxls );
      virtual int init( void );
      virtual int term( void );
      virtual int status( void );
};

//.................class MacPntEncoder

class MacPntEncoder : public Encoder
{
   protected:
      FILE           *MacFile;      // input file
      int            MacCond;       // condition code
      int            MacFg;         // fg color
      int            MacBg;         // bg color
      int            MacLnCnt;      // scan lines written
      unsigned char MacBuf[72];     // scan line buffer

   private:
      int  writeln( void );
      void pack( unsigned char *buf, int npxls );
```

Listing 12.1 MACPNT.HPP (continued)

```cpp
public:
    MacPntEncoder( FILE *f_out, int fg=0, int bg=15 )
    {
        MacFile = f_out;
        MacCond = xOKAY;
    }
    virtual ~MacPntEncoder( )
    {
    }
    virtual int encode( unsigned char *buf, int npxls );
    virtual int init( void );
    virtual int term( void );
    virtual int status( void );
};

#endif
```

Listing 12.2 MACPNT.CPP

```cpp
//----------------------------------------------------------//
//                                                          //
//    File:     MACPNT.CPP                                  //
//                                                          //
//    Desc:     Structures for the MacPaint format          //
//                                                          //
//----------------------------------------------------------//

#include "macpnt.hpp"

//.................struct MACBINHDR

int MACBINHDR::get( FILE *f )
{
    return (fread( &version, sizeof(MACBINHDR), 1, f ) == 1)
        ? 0 : -1;
}

int MACBINHDR::put( FILE *f )
{
    return (fwrite( &version, sizeof(MACBINHDR), 1, f ) == 1)
        ? 0 : -1;
}

//.................struct MACPNTHDR
```

Listing 12.2 MACPNT.CPP (continued)

```cpp
int MACPNTHDR::get( FILE *f )
{
   return (fread( &version, sizeof(MACPNTHDR), 1, f ) == 1)
          ? 0 : -1;
}

int MACPNTHDR::put( FILE *f )
{
   return (fwrite( &version, sizeof(MACPNTHDR), 1, f ) == 1)
          ? 0 : -1;
}

//................class MacPntDecoder

int MacPntDecoder::readln( void )
{
   int n = 0;              // number of bytes decoded

   while( (n < MACLNWIDTH) && ! feof(MacFile) )
   {
      int ix = fgetc( MacFile );   // get index byte
      if( ix < 0 ) return xIOERROR;

      char cx = ix;
      if( cx == -128 ) continue;

      if( cx < 0 )  //............run
      {
         int i = 1 - cx;
         char ch = fgetc( MacFile );
         while( i-- )
            if( n < MACLNWIDTH )
               MacBuf[n++] = ch;
      }
      else  //....................seq
      {
         int i = cx + 1;
         while( i-- )
            if( n < MACLNWIDTH )
               MacBuf[n++] = fgetc( MacFile );
      }
   }
   return feof( MacFile ) ? xENDOFFILE : xOKAY;
}
```

Listing 12.2 MACPNT.CPP (continued)

```cpp
void MacPntDecoder::unpack( unsigned char *buf, int npxls )
{
   int MacMask = 0x80;
   int MacByte = 0;
   for( int i=0; i<npxls; i++ )
   {
      buf[i] = (MacBuf[MacByte] & MacMask) ?
                  MacFg : MacBg;
      if( (MacMask >>= 1) == 0 )
      {
         MacByte++;
         MacMask = 0x80;
      }
   }
}

int MacPntDecoder::init( void )
{
   return status();
}

int MacPntDecoder::term( void )
{
   return status();
}

int MacPntDecoder::status( void )
{
   if( ferror(MacFile) ) return xIOERROR;
   if( feof(MacFile) )   return xENDOFFILE;
   return xOKAY;
}

int MacPntDecoder::decode( unsigned char *buf, int npxls )
{
   if( status() == xOKAY )
   {
      readln();
      unpack( buf, npxls );
   }
   return status();
}

//...............class MacPntEncoder

int MacPntEncoder::writeln( void )
{
   int cnt = 0;  // bytes encoded
```

Listing 12.2 MACPNT.CPP (continued)

```cpp
    while( cnt < MACLNWIDTH )
    {
       int i = cnt;
       int j = i + 1;
       int jmax = i + 126;
       if( jmax >= MACLNWIDTH ) jmax = MACLNWIDTH-1;

       if( i == MACLNWIDTH-1 )  //..........last byte alone
       {
          fputc( 0, MacFile );
          fputc( MacBuf[i], MacFile );
          cnt++;
       }
       else if( MacBuf[i] == MacBuf[j] )  //......run
       {
          while( (j<jmax) && (MacBuf[j]==MacBuf[j+1]) )
             j++;
          fputc( i-j, MacFile );
          fputc( MacBuf[i], MacFile );
          cnt += j-i+1;
       }
       else  //...........................sequence
       {
          while( (j<jmax) && (MacBuf[j]!=MacBuf[j+1]) )
             j++;
          fputc( j-i, MacFile );
          fwrite( MacBuf+i, j-i+1, 1, MacFile );
          cnt += j-i+1;
       }
    }
    return xOKAY;
}

void MacPntEncoder::pack( unsigned char *buf, int npxls )
{
    memset( MacBuf, 0, MACLNWIDTH );
    int MacMask = 0x80;
    int MacByte = 0;
    for( int i=0; i<npxls; i++ )
    {
       if( buf[i] == MacFg )
          MacBuf[MacByte] |= MacMask;
       if( (MacMask >>= 1) == 0 )
       {
          MacMask = 0x80;
          MacByte++;
       }
```

Listing 12.2 MACPNT.CPP (continued)

```
            if( MacByte == MACLNWIDTH )
               break;
      }
   }
}

int MacPntEncoder::init( void )
{
   MacLnCnt = 0;
   return status();
}

int MacPntEncoder::term( void )
{
   while( (MacLnCnt++ < 720) && (status() == xOKAY) )
   {
      fputc( 185, MacFile );
      fputc( 0, MacFile );
   }
   return status();
}

int MacPntEncoder::status( void )
{
   if( ferror(MacFile) ) return xIOERROR;
   if( feof(MacFile) )   return xENDOFFILE;
   return xOKAY;
}

int MacPntEncoder::encode( unsigned char *buf, int npxls )
{
   if( status() == xOKAY )
   {
      pack( buf, npxls );
      writeln();
      MacLnCnt++;
   }
   return status();
}
```

A MacPaint File Viewer

Listing 12.3 presents the source code to a MacPaint file viewer that is implemented along the lines just discussed. As you can see from the listing, decoding
a MacPaint file is a reasonably simple proposition.

There is one caveat that warrants mention. Some MacPaint files possess scan-line lengths that are greater than or equal to 72 bytes. It seems likely that these are the result of incorrectly implemented encoders. One common mistake would be to look for repeating runs by scanning forward in a line until a different byte value is encountered, without checking if the end of the scan line has been reached. Given this logic, if a scan line ends with a repeating run, then the encoded run's length would possibly be too large. This pitfall is easily avoided by breaking out of a decoding loop when 72 bytes have been decoded, whether or not the run or sequence being decoded is complete.

The viewer program adds one feature we have not encountered before: a switch that causes the decoded image to be scaled to half size. This was added because the bitmap height of a MacPaint image, which is 720 lines, is over twice the height of an EGA display and considerably more than a standard VGA's 480-line display. Scaling by half allows the entire image to be viewed, although obviously with reduced detail.

The scaling algorithm is quite simple. The full image is subdivided into 2-pixel-by-2-pixel cells, and the pixel values in each cell are summed to yield a value between 0 and 4. The corresponding pixel in the scaled bitmap derives its value by thresholding the sum, as in

```
pixel_value = (sum > 2) ? 1 : 0
```

Listing 12.3 VMACPNT.CPP

```
//-----------------------------------------------------------//
//                                                           //
//   File:      VMACPNT.CPP                                  //
//                                                           //
//   Desc:      Program to view or print a MacPaint file     //
//                                                           //
//-----------------------------------------------------------//

#include "stdlib.h"
#include "stdio.h"
#include "string.h"
#include "conio.h"
#include "ctype.h"

#include "macpnt.hpp"
#include "imgviewr.hpp"
#include "imgprntr.hpp"
#include "laserjet.hpp"
#include "paintjet.hpp"
#include "epjx80.hpp"
#include "eplq24.hpp"
#include "pscript.hpp"
```

Listing 12.3 VMACPNT.CPP (continued)

```
//.................Printer types

#define  LJ   0x4C4A
#define  PJ   0x504A
#define  JX   0x4A58
#define  LQ   0x4C51
#define  PS   0x5053

//.................Program globals

char fn[80];            // path to MACPNT file

int gmode;              // video display mode
int pmode;              // printer ID
int negate;             // image negative flag
int reduce;             // scale by 1/2 flag

ImgStore *imgmap;       // image bitmap

rgb monopal[] =         // image palette
{
   rgb( 0, 0, 0 ),
   rgb( 255, 255, 255 )
};

//.................Exit with a message

void exit_pgm( char *msg )
{
   printf( "%s\n", msg );
   exit( 0 );
}

//.................Program usage

void explain_pgm( void )
{
   printf( "\n" );
   printf( ".........MacPaint File Viewer/Printer..........\n" );
   printf( "\n" );
   printf( "Usage:     VMACPNT  macpnt_file [ switches ]\n" );
   printf( "\n" );
   printf( "Switches:  -h    = display program usage\n" );
   printf( "           -vXX  = force video display mode XX\n" );
   printf( "                   (XX = 12, 13, 2E, 62)\n" );
   printf( "           -pXX  = print using printer XX\n" );
   printf( "                   (XX = LJ, PJ, JX, LQ, PS)\n" );
   printf( "           -n    = use negative of image\n" );
```

Listing 12.3 VMACPNT.CPP (continued)

```
        printf( "                  -r   = reduce image by half\n" );
        printf( "\n" );
        printf( "...............................................\n" );
        printf( "\n" );
    }

    //................Process pgm argument list

    void process_args( int argc, char *argv[] )
    {
        // establish default values
        fn[0]  = 0;
        gmode  = 0x12;
        pmode  = 0;
        negate = 0;
        reduce = 0;

        // process the program's argument list
        for( int i=1; i<argc; i++ )
        {
            if( (*argv[i] == '-') || (*argv[i] == '/') )
            {
                char sw = *(argv[i] + 1);
                switch( toupper(sw) )
                {
                    case 'H' :
                        explain_pgm();
                        exit( 0 );
                        break;

                    case 'V' :
                        sscanf( argv[i]+2, "%x", &gmode );
                        break;

                    case 'P' :
                        pmode = toupper( *(argv[i]+2) );
                        pmode <<= 8;
                        pmode += toupper( *(argv[i]+3) );
                        break;

                    case 'N' :
                        negate = 1;
                        break;

                    case 'R' :
                        reduce = 1;
                        break;
```

Listing 12.3 VMACPNT.CPP (continued)

```
            default:
                printf( "Unknown switch '%s' ignored\n",
                        argv[i] );
                break;
            }
        }
        else  // presumably a file identifier
        {
            strcpy( fn, argv[i] );
            char *p = strchr( fn, '.' );
            if( p == 0 )
                strcat( fn, ".mac" );
            else if( *(p+1) == 0 )
                *p = 0;
        }
    }

    // was a file name specified?
    if( fn[0] == 0 )
    {
        explain_pgm();
        exit( 0 );
    }
}

//.................Create an image storage buffer

ImgStore * istore( int h, int w, int d )
{
    ImgStore *ist = 0;

    // attempt to create in order of preference
    ist = new XmsImgStore( h, w, d );
    if( (ist != 0) && (ist->status != imgstoreOKAY) )
    {
        delete ist;
        ist = new EmsImgStore( h, w, d );
        if( (ist != 0) && (ist->status != imgstoreOKAY) )
        {
            delete ist;
            ist = new CnvImgStore( h, w, d );
            if( (ist != 0) && (ist->status != imgstoreOKAY) )
            {
                delete ist;
                ist = new DskImgStore( h, w, d );
                if( (ist != 0) && (ist->status != imgstoreOKAY) )
                {
                    delete ist;
```

Listing 12.3 VMACPNT.CPP (continued)

```
                    ist = 0;
                }
            }
        }
    }

    return ist;
}

//.................Create a printer

PrinterDriver * printer( int which )
{
    PrinterDriver *p;

    switch( which )
    {
        case LJ : p = new LaserJet( "LPT1" );
                break;
        case PJ : p = new PaintJet( "LPT1" );
                break;
        case JX : p = new EpsonJX80( "LPT1" );
                break;
        case LQ : p = new EpsonLQ24( "LPT1" );
                break;
        default : p = new PsPrinter( "LPT1" );
                break;
    }

    return p;
}

//.................Load the MACPNT file

void load_macpnt( void )
{
    // open file
    FILE *fmacpnt = fopen( fn, "rb" );
    if( fmacpnt == 0 )
        exit_pgm( "MACPNT file not found" );

    // test first 128 bytes for a MacBinary header
    MACBINHDR bhdr;
    if( bhdr.get( fmacpnt ) != 0 )
        exit_pgm( "Error reading MacBinary header" );
```

Listing 12.3 VMACPNT.CPP (continued)

```
// if found, bitmap is at offset 640, otherwise 512
if( (strncmp( bhdr.filetype, "PNTG", 4 ) == 0) &&
    (strncmp( bhdr.fileownr, "MPNT", 4 ) == 0) )
   fseek( fmacpnt, 640, SEEK_SET );
else
   fseek( fmacpnt, 512, SEEK_SET );

// bitmap metrics
int ncols = 576;
int nrows = 720;
int fg    = 0;
int bg    = 1;
if( negate )
{
   fg = 1;
   bg = 0;
}

unsigned char *scanln  = 0,
              *scanln1 = 0,
              *scanln2 = 0;
if( reduce )
{
   scanln1 = new unsigned char [ncols];
   scanln2 = new unsigned char [ncols];
   scanln = new unsigned char [ncols/2];
   imgmap = istore( nrows/2, ncols/2, 8 );
   if( (imgmap == 0)  || (scanln == 0) ||
       (scanln1 == 0) || (scanln2 == 0) )
   {
      delete imgmap;
      delete scanln;
      delete scanln1;
      delete scanln2;
      exit_pgm( "Insufficient memory to load image" );
   }
   printf( "Loading MACPNT image from '%s'...", fn );
   MacPntDecoder macpdec( fmacpnt, fg, bg );
   macpdec.init();
   for( int i=0; i<nrows/2; i++ )
   {
      if( macpdec.decode( scanln1, ncols ) != xOKAY )
         break;
      if( macpdec.decode( scanln2, ncols ) != xOKAY )
         break;
      for( int j=0; j<ncols/2; j++ )
      {
         int n = scanln1[j*2] + scanln1[j*2+1] +
```

Listing 12.3 VMACPNT.CPP (continued)

```
                            scanln2[j*2] + scanln2[j*2+1];
                scanln[j] = (n >= 2) ? 1 : 0;
            }
            imgmap->put( scanln, i );
        }
        macpdec.term();
        printf( "done\n" );
    }
    else
    {
        scanln = new unsigned char [ncols];
        imgmap = istore( nrows, ncols, 8 );
        if( (imgmap == 0) || (scanln == 0) )
        {
            delete imgmap;
            delete scanln;
            exit_pgm( "Insufficient memory to load image" );
        }
        printf( "Loading MACPNT image from '%s'...", fn );
        MacPntDecoder macpdec( fmacpnt, fg, bg );
        macpdec.init();
        for( int i=0; i<nrows; i++ )
        {
            if( macpdec.decode( scanln, ncols ) != xOKAY )
                break;
            imgmap->put( scanln, i );
        }
        macpdec.term();
        printf( "done\n" );
    }

    delete scanln;
    delete scanln1;
    delete scanln2;
}

//.................Main

int main( int argc, char *argv[] )
{
    process_args( argc, argv );

    load_macpnt( );

    // print the image
    if( pmode != 0 )
    {
        PrinterDriver *prt = printer( pmode );
```

Listing 12.3 VMACPNT.CPP (continued)

```
    if( prt )
    {
        printf( "Printing..." );
        ImagePrinter ip( prt, imgmap, monopal, 2,
                         0, 0, 100, 100 );
        ip.print( 1 );
        printf( "done\n" );
        delete prt;
    }
    else
        printf( "Printer instantiation failed\n" );
}

// display the image
else
{
    VgaDisplay vga( gmode );
    ImageViewer iv( &vga, imgmap, monopal, 2, 0, 0 );
    iv.view( );
}

delete imgmap;

return 0;
}
```

Writing the MacPaint Format

The MacPaint format is not as important as it once was, so there is seldom any need to be able to write the format. For those interested, however, Listing 12.3 includes a MacPaint encoder class that can be used to implement a format writer. If the format writer is to be used to create files on a PC for transport to the Mac, then the file should include both a MacBinary header and a MacPaint header. In other cases, the MacBinary header is optional, but note that many programs expect to find the MacBinary header. It is therefore a de facto component of the format.

This concludes our look at the MacPaint format. It is a venerable format with many examples to be found, but its many limitations make it obsolete by today's standards.

13

The Sun Raster
File Format

Without a doubt, the Sun SPARC is one of the most popular series of engineering workstations ever produced. Its popularity is well deserved, in that it boasts impressive performance and capability at a reasonable (though substantial) price. For many years there was nothing comparable in the MS-DOS arena to SPARC's graphics display. Lately, however, the graphics capabilities of Intel-based PCs have grown and are beginning to approach the level of SPARC's. At the same time, Sun has introduced new, low-end SPARC's that approach the PC in price.

Graphics has always been a strong suit of SPARCs, as with most workstations, as a typical system is equipped with a display capable of 1152x900 or higher resolutions. This is nearly four times the display area of a standard 640x480 VGA display, and is one likely reason that graphics images created on SPARCs are almost never found on MS-DOS systems. There's not much that can be done with an image if only a fraction of it can be seen.

We can look forward to a change in this situation sometime soon. Several developments are expected, one being the imminent availability of Sun's Solaris operating system for Intel-based systems. Another is that 1024x768 and 1280x1024 display capabilities will eventually become commonplace in the DOS/Windows marketplace, allowing such large images to be fully used.

The indigenous graphics file format of the SPARC is known as the **Sun raster file** format. Files in the format commonly use the file extension RF. There is no established tradition for such files on DOS, so I will employ the same naming convention here.

Format Overview

The Sun raster file format is a simple format that supports color-mapped and RGB-based images of 1, 8, or 24 bits per pixel. Bitmaps can be optionally compressed using a simple RLE encoding scheme. There are some additional capabilities of the format that are both rarely used and poorly documented. We will ignore those here except to point them out in passing.

The overall structure of a file consists of a 32-byte header, an optional color map, and the bitmap itself. The header is composed of eight integer fields. Keep in mind that a SPARC possesses a 32-bit processor, so the C type `int` is 32 bits, or a `long` by DOS standards. We will type all such variables here as `long`, but in their native habitat they would be typed as `int`.

When present, a color map consists of either RGB values or raw values. The interpretation of raw values is somewhat ambiguous. For this reason the code in this chapter does not attempt to interpret a raw color map.

One member of a raster file header is an image type field that describes the composition of the file's bitmap. Typically, this is an uncompressed or RLE-encoded array of pixel values. Other image types are also defined, including one described as "experimental." They will be ignored here.

The number of bits in an image scan line is the image's width in pixels times the image's depth in bits per pixel. This value is always rounded up to a multiple of 16 to determine the actual stored length of a scan line. Thus, a scan line will always contain an integral number of words and may be padded at its end with unused bits.

The Raster File Header

As noted, the header of a Sun raster file consists of eight 32-bit integers. One additional and very important characteristic of the header is that the values use Motorola 68000 byte ordering. If the file is read on an Intel-based system, the byte order of each value must be reversed before it can be used. Listings 13.1 and 13.2 show the implementation of the raster file header as the structure `SRFHEADER`. The structure's member functions `get()` and `put()` attend to the byte ordering of the header: Intel-ordering is produced on input, and the correct Motorola ordering is restored for output to disk.

Here is a description of each field of the header:

`iden`	32-bit "magic number" that can be used to validate the file as a Sun raster file. This is the value 0x59A66A95.
`imwidth`	Width of the image in pixels.

`imheight`	Height of the image in pixels.
`imdepth`	Number of bits per pixel.
`imlength`	Size of the stored bitmap in bytes. Older versions of the format, identifiable by an image type of `imOld`, set this field to zero. For that image type, the size can be computed from the width, height, and depth fields. For all other types, the field should contain the true length, which is equivalent to the file size minus the size of the header and the size of the color map.
`imtype`	Image-type identifier. Valid values are shown in Listing 13.1 as the enumeration `SrfImageTypes`. The only types dealt with here are `imOld`, `imStd`, and `imRle`. `imRle` indicates that the bitmap is RLE encoded, the other two types are uncompressed.
`maptype`	Type of color map present. Valid values are shown in Listing 13.1 as the enumeration `SrfMapTypes`. The type `mapNone` implies that no color map is present, in which case the `maplength` field is set to zero. The type `mapRgb` indicates an RGB color map, and `mapRaw` indicates a raw color map.
`maplength`	Size of the color map in bytes. If there is no color map, this value is zero. For an RGB color map, this value is three times the number of colors in the palette.

The Raster File Bitmap

The bitmap of a raster file can be either uncompressed or RLE encoded, and it can consist of pixels of 1, 8, or 24 bits. Pixels of 1 and 8 bits in length indicate a color-mapped image; 24-bit pixels indicate an RGB-based image.

The RLE encoding scheme employed by the Sun raster file format is relatively simple. An encoded bitmap consists of a series of packets of varying lengths. There are three types of packets, 1, 2, and 3 bytes in length. The packets are most easily described by presenting the decoding algorithm in pseudocode:

- Read a byte.
- If the byte is not equal to 0x80 (128), then it represents a single pixel byte. Output a byte of that value and continue.
- If the byte equals 0x80, read a second byte. If the second byte has the value zero, then the first byte represents a pixel byte of value 0x80. Output a byte of that value and continue.
- If the second byte is nonzero, then it is a count field. Read a third byte, which is a pixel byte. Output count+1 bytes of that value and continue.

It is important to note that the algorithm encodes bytes, not pixels. In a 1-bpp bitmap, each encoded byte represents 8 pixels. In an 8-bpp bitmap, each byte is a pixel. In a 24-bpp bitmap, a pixel is composed of 3 bytes. Also, don't forget that the unencoded scan-line length is an even number of bytes, and can thus contain unused bits at its end.

Listing 13.1 SRF.HPP

```
//----------------------------------------------------------//
//                                                          //
//    File:     SRF.HPP                                     //
//                                                          //
//    Desc:     Class and structure definitions for the     //
//              SUN Raster File format                      //
//                                                          //
//----------------------------------------------------------//

#ifndef _SRF_HPP_
#define _SRF_HPP_

#include "stdlib.h"
#include "stdio.h"
#include "string.h"

#include "color.hpp"
#include "codec.hpp"
#include "gffasm.h"

#define  RF_IDEN    0x59A66A95L
#define  RUN_FLAG   0x80

enum SrfImageTypes
{
    imOld  = 0,      // uncompressed
    imStd  = 1,      // same as 0
    imRle  = 2,      // RLE encoded
    imRgb  = 3,      // RGBs
    imTiff = 4,      // TIFF compatible
    imIff  = 5,      // TAAC compatible
    imExp = 0xFFFF   // experimental
};

enum SrfMapTypes
{
    mapNone = 0,     // no color map present
    mapRgb  = 1,     // RGB color map
    mapRaw  = 2      // nonstandard
};
```

Listing 13.1 SRF.HPP (continued)

```cpp
//.................struct SRFHEADER

struct SRFHEADER          // SRF == Sun Raster File
{
    long    iden;         // rf identifier
    long    imwidth;      // width of image in pixels
    long    imheight;     // height of image in pixels
    long    imdepth;      // bits per pixel - 1,8,24
    long    imlength;     // length of image in bytes
    long    imtype;       // image type
    long    maptype;      // colormap type
    long    maplength;    // colormap length in bytes

    SRFHEADER( );
    SRFHEADER( int w, int h, int d );
   ~SRFHEADER( ) { }
    void list( void );
    int  get( FILE *f );
    int  put( FILE *f );
    RgbPalette * pal( FILE *f );
};

//.................class   SrfDecoder

class SrfDecoder : public Decoder
{
    protected:
        FILE *srf_file;      // input file
        int   cond;          // condition code
        int   rwbytes;       // image width in bytes
        int   pxbits;        // bits per pixel - 1,8,24
        int   pxbytes;       // bytes per pixel - 1,3
        int   encoded;       // flag - RLE or uncompressed

    private:
        int   cnt;
        int   dat;
        int   read_byte( void );
        void  read1( unsigned char *buf, int npxls );
        void  read8( unsigned char *buf, int npxls );
        void  read24( unsigned char *buf, int npxls );

    public:
        SrfDecoder( FILE *f_in, SRFHEADER& hdr );
        virtual ~SrfDecoder( ) { }
        virtual int decode( unsigned char *buf, int npxls );
```

Listing 13.1 SRF.HPP (continued)

```
        virtual int init( void );
        virtual int term( void );
        virtual int status( void );
};

//................class  SrfEncoder

class SrfEncoder : public Encoder
{
    protected:
        int   cond;          // condition code
        int   pxbits;        // bits per pixel - 1,8,24
        int   pxbytes;       // bytes per pixel - 1or3
        int   rwbytes;       // image width in bytes
        int   encoded;       // flag - set for RLE output
        FILE *srf_file;      // output file

    private:
        unsigned char *scanln;
        void flush( void );
        void wrt1( unsigned char *buf, int npxls );
        void wrt8( unsigned char *buf, int npxls );
        void wrt24( unsigned char *buf, int npxls );

    public:
        SrfEncoder( FILE *f_out, SRFHEADER& hdr );
        virtual ~SrfEncoder( ) { delete scanln; }
        virtual int encode( unsigned char *buf, int npxls );
        virtual int init( void );
        virtual int term( void );
        virtual int status( void );
};

#endif
```

Listing 13.2 SRF.CPP

```
//----------------------------------------------------//
//                                                    //
//   File:    SRF.CPP                                 //
//                                                    //
//   Desc:    Class and structure definitions for the //
//            SUN Raster File format                  //
//                                                    //
//----------------------------------------------------//

#include "srf.hpp"
```

Listing 13.2 SRF.CPP (continued)

```cpp
//................various identifiers

struct IMGTYPES
{
    int id;
    char *desc;
}
ImTypes[] =
{
    { imOld,  "Old format version" },
    { imStd,  "Standard uncompressed" },
    { imRle,  "RLE encoded" },
    { imRgb,  "RGB pixels" },
    { imTiff, "TIFF compatible" },
    { imIff,  "IFF compatible" },
    { imExp,  "Experimental" },
    { 999,    "Unknown or Invalid" },
};
static nImTypes = 8;

struct MAPTYPES
{
    int id;
    char *desc;
}
MapTypes[] =
{
    { mapNone, "No color map present" },
    { mapRgb,  "RGB color map" },
    { mapRaw,  "Raw color map data" },
    { 999,     "Unknown or Invalid" },
};

static nMapTypes = 4;

//................struct SRFHEADER

SRFHEADER::SRFHEADER( )
{
    iden = RF_IDEN;
    imwidth = imheight = imdepth = 0;
    imlength = imtype = 0;
    maptype = maplength = 0;
}
```

Listing 13.2 SRF.CPP (continued)

```
SRFHEADER::SRFHEADER( int w, int h, int d )
{
    iden = RF_IDEN;
    imwidth = w;
    imheight = h;
    imdepth = d;
    imlength = imtype = 0;
    maptype = maplength = 0;
}

void SRFHEADER::list( )
{
    printf( "SRFHEADER::iden     = %08lXh\n", iden );
    printf( "SRFHEADER::imwidth  = %ld\n", imwidth );
    printf( "SRFHEADER::imheight = %ld\n", imheight );
    printf( "SRFHEADER::imdepth  = %ld\n", imdepth );
    printf( "SRFHEADER::imlength = %ld\n", imlength );
    printf( "SRFHEADER::imtype   = %ld, ", imtype );
    for( int i=0; i<nImTypes; i++ )
    {
        if( (imtype == ImTypes[i].id) ||
            (ImTypes[i].id == 999) )
        {
            printf( "%s\n", ImTypes[i].desc );
            break;
        }
    }
    printf( "SRFHEADER::maptype  = %ld, ", maptype );
    for( i=0; i<nMapTypes; i++ )
    {
        if( (maptype == MapTypes[i].id) ||
            (MapTypes[i].id == 999) )
        {
            printf( "%s\n", MapTypes[i].desc );
            break;
        }
    }
    printf( "SRFHEADER::maplength = %ld\n", maplength );
}

int SRFHEADER::get( FILE *f )
{
    int    nlongs = sizeof(SRFHEADER) / sizeof(long);
    long * item   = &iden;
```

Listing 13.2 SRF.CPP (continued)

```cpp
        // Motorola-to-Intel byte order
        for( int i=0; i<nlongs; i++ )
        {
           fread( item+i, sizeof(long), 1, f );
           item[i] = rev_dword( item[i] );
        }

        return ferror(f) ? -1 : 0;
    }

    int SRFHEADER::put( FILE *f )
    {
        int    nlongs = sizeof(SRFHEADER) / sizeof(long);
        long * item   = &iden;

        // Intel-to-Motorola byte order
        for( int i=0; i<nlongs; i++ )
        {
           long v = rev_dword( item[i] );
           fwrite( &v, sizeof(long), 1, f );
        }

        return ferror(f) ? -1 : 0;
    }

    RgbPalette * SRFHEADER::pal( FILE *f )
    {
        RgbPalette *pal = new RgbPalette;
        if( pal )
        {
           pal->colors = 0;
           pal->ncolors = 0;
           if( maplength == 0 )  // color map not present
           {
              if( imdepth == 1 )
              {
                 pal->colors = new rgb[2];
                 if( pal->colors )
                 {
                    pal->colors[0] = rgb( 255, 255, 255 );
                    pal->colors[1] = rgb(   0,   0,   0 );
                    pal->ncolors = 2;
                 }
              }
              else if( imdepth == 8 )
```

Listing 13.2 SRF.CPP (continued)

```cpp
            {
                pal->colors = new rgb[256];
                if( pal->colors )
                {
                    for( int i=0; i<256; i++ )
                        pal->colors[i] = rgb( i, i, i );
                    pal->ncolors = 256;
                }
            }
        }
        else if( maptype == mapRgb )   // RGB values present
        {
            int nc = int( maplength / 3 );
            pal->colors = new rgb[nc];
            if( pal->colors )
            {
                for( int i=0; i<nc; i++ )
                {
                    pal->colors[i].red = fgetc( f );
                    pal->colors[i].grn = fgetc( f );
                    pal->colors[i].blu = fgetc( f );
                }
                pal->ncolors = nc;
            }
        }
    }
    return pal;
}

//.................class SrfDecoder

SrfDecoder::SrfDecoder( FILE *f_in, SRFHEADER& hdr )
{
    srf_file = f_in;
    cnt = dat = 0;
    pxbits = int( hdr.imdepth );
    pxbytes = (pxbits + 7) / 8;
    rwbytes = int( (hdr.imwidth * hdr.imdepth + 7) / 8 );
    if( rwbytes & 1 ) rwbytes++;
    encoded = (hdr.imtype == imRle) ? 1 : 0;
    if( (hdr.imtype==imOld) || (hdr.imtype==imStd) ||
        (hdr.imtype==imRle) || (hdr.imtype==imRgb) )
      cond = xOKAY;
    else
      cond = xUNSUPPORTED;
}
```

Listing 13.2 SRF.CPP (continued)

```cpp
int SrfDecoder::status( void )
{
    if( ferror( srf_file ) ) cond = xIOERROR;
    if( feof( srf_file ) )    cond = xENDOFFILE;
    return cond;
}

int SrfDecoder::init( void )
{
    cnt = dat = 0;
    return status();
}

int SrfDecoder::term( void )
{
    return status();
}

int SrfDecoder::read_byte( void )
{
    if( cnt == 0 )
    {
        if( encoded )
        {
            dat = fgetc( srf_file );
            if( dat != RUN_FLAG )
                cnt = 1;
            else
            {
                cnt = fgetc( srf_file );
                if( cnt > 0 )
                {
                    cnt++;
                    dat = fgetc( srf_file );
                }
                else
                    cnt = 1;
            }
        }
        else
        {
            dat = fgetc( srf_file );
            cnt = 1;
        }
    }
    cnt--;
    return dat;
}
```

Listing 13.2 SRF.CPP (continued)

```cpp
void SrfDecoder::read1( unsigned char *buf, int npxls )
{
    int n=0;
    for( int i=0; i<rwbytes; i++ )
    {
        int v = read_byte();
        int mask = 0x100;
        while( mask >>= 1 )
            if( n < npxls )
                buf[n++] = v & mask ? 1 : 0;
    }
}

void SrfDecoder::read8( unsigned char *buf, int npxls )
{
    int n=0;
    for( int i=0; i<rwbytes; i++ )
    {
        int v = read_byte();
        if( n < npxls )
            buf[n++] = v;
    }
}

void SrfDecoder::read24( unsigned char *buf, int npxls )
{
    int n  = 0;
    int nb = npxls * 3;
    for( int i=0; i<rwbytes; i++ )
    {
        int v = read_byte();
        if( n < nb )
            buf[n++] = v;
    }
}

int SrfDecoder::decode( unsigned char *buf, int npxls )
{
    if( status() == xOKAY )
    {
        if( pxbits == 24 )
            read24( buf, npxls );
        else if( pxbits == 8 )
            read8( buf, npxls );
```

Listing 13.2 SRF.CPP (continued)

```cpp
        else
            read1( buf, npxls );
    }
    return status();
}


//.................class SrfEncoder

SrfEncoder::SrfEncoder( FILE *f_out, SRFHEADER& hdr )
{
    srf_file = f_out;
    pxbits = int( hdr.imdepth );
    pxbytes = (pxbits + 7) / 8;
    rwbytes = int( (hdr.imwidth * hdr.imdepth + 7) / 8 );
    if( rwbytes & 1 ) rwbytes++;
    encoded = (hdr.imtype == imRle) ? 1 : 0;
    scanln = new unsigned char [rwbytes];
    cond = scanln ? xOKAY : xNOMEMORY;
}

int SrfEncoder::status( void )
{
    if( ferror( srf_file ) ) cond = xIOERROR;
    return cond;
}

int SrfEncoder::init( void )
{
    return status();
}

int SrfEncoder::term( void )
{
    return status();
}

void SrfEncoder::wrt1( unsigned char *buf, int npxls )
{
    memset( scanln, 0, rwbytes );
    unsigned char *p = scanln;
    int mask = 0x80;
    for( int i=0; i<npxls; i++ )
    {
        if( buf[i] ) *p |= mask;
```

Listing 13.2 SRF.CPP (continued)

```cpp
            if( (mask>>=1) == 0 )
            {
                p++;
                mask = 0x80;
            }
        }
    }
}
void SrfEncoder::wrt8( unsigned char *buf, int npxls )
{
    for( int i=0; i<npxls; i++ )
        scanln[i] = buf[i];
}

void SrfEncoder::wrt24( unsigned char *buf, int npxls )
{
    int n = 0;
    for( int i=0; i<npxls; i++ )
    {
        scanln[n] = buf[n];   n++;
        scanln[n] = buf[n];   n++;
        scanln[n] = buf[n];   n++;
    }
}

void SrfEncoder::flush( void )
{
    if( encoded )
    {
        int n1, n2=0;
        while( n2 < rwbytes )
        {
            n1 = n2;
            n2 = n1 + 1;
            while( (n2 < rwbytes) && (scanln[n1] == scanln[n2]) )
                n2++;
            int n = n2 - n1;    // run is n bytes long
            if( n == 1 )
            {
                fputc( scanln[n1], srf_file );
                if( scanln[n1] == RUN_FLAG )
                    fputc( 0, srf_file );
            }
            else
            {
                while( n > 256 )
                {
                    fputc( RUN_FLAG, srf_file );
                    fputc( 255, srf_file );
```

Listing 13.2 SRF.CPP (continued)

```
                         fputc( scanln[n1], srf_file );
                         n -= 256;
                  }
                  fputc( RUN_FLAG, srf_file );
                  fputc( n-1, srf_file );
                  fputc( scanln[n1], srf_file );
            }
         }
      }
      else
         fwrite( scanln, rwbytes, 1, srf_file );
   }

   int SrfEncoder::encode( unsigned char *buf, int npxls )
   {
      if( status() == xOKAY )
      {
         if( pxbits == 24 )
            wrt24( buf, npxls );
         else if( pxbits == 8 )
            wrt8( buf, npxls );
         else
            wrt1( buf, npxls );
         flush();
      }
      return status();
   }
```

An SRF Query Program

Listing 13.3 presents the source code to a Sun raster file query program. With such a simple format and header there are few kinks to be dealt with, and the program itself needs little comment.

Listing 13.3 QSRF.CPP

```
//------------------------------------------------------------//
//                                                            //
//    File:    QSRF.CPP                                       //
//                                                            //
//    Desc:    Sun Raster File Query Program                  //
//                                                            //
//------------------------------------------------------------//

#include "stdlib.h"
#include "stdio.h"
#include "string.h"
```

Listing 13.3 QSRF.CPP (continued)

```cpp
#include "srf.hpp"

//.................program usage

void explain_pgm( void )
{
    printf( "\n" );
    printf( "Sun Raster File Query Program\n" );
    printf( "\n" );
    printf( "Usage:  QSRF  srf_file  [ -p ]\n" );
    printf( "\n" );
    printf( "-p includes palette in listing\n" );
    printf( ".RF extension is assumed\n" );
    printf( "\n" );
}

//.................main

int main( int argc, char *argv[] )
{
    // check args
    if( (argc < 2) || (*argv[1] == '?') )
    {
        explain_pgm();
        return 0;
    }

    // create file name
    char fn[80];
    strcpy( fn, argv[1] );
    char *p = strchr( fn, '.' );
    if( p == 0 )
        strcat( fn, ".rf" );
    else if( *(p+1) == 0 )
        *p = 0;

    // list palette ?
    int lpal = 0;
    if( argc > 2 )
      if( (strcmp( argv[2], "-p" ) == 0) ||
          (strcmp( argv[2], "-P" ) == 0) )
          lpal = 1;

    // open the file
    FILE *fsrf = fopen( fn, "rb" );
    if( fsrf == 0 )
```

Listing 13.3 QSRF.CPP (continued)

```
    {
        printf( "File '%s' not found\n", fn );
        return 0;
    }

    SRFHEADER srfh;
    srfh.get( fsrf );

    printf( "Listing of SRF file '%s'\n", fn );
    printf( "\n" );
    srfh.list();
    printf( "\n" );

    // list palette ?
    if( lpal )
    {
        if( srfh.maplength == 0 )
            printf( "File does not have a color map\n" );
        else if( srfh.maptype == mapRaw )
            printf( "File has an undefined color map\n" );
        else
        {
            RgbPalette *pal = srfh.pal( fsrf );
            if( pal )
            {
                for( int i=0; i<pal->ncolors; i++ )
                    printf( "RGB(%3d) = (%3d,%3d,%3d)\n", i,
                            pal->colors[i].red,
                            pal->colors[i].grn,
                            pal->colors[i].blu );
            }
            else
                printf( "Error reading file's color map\n" );
        }
    }

    return 0;
}
```

An SRF View Program

Listing 13.4 presents a file viewer for the Sun raster file format. About the only aspect of the program that requires comment is the handling of bilevel images. The Sun raster format uses an implied background color of white, so pixels of value 0 are displayed as white and pixels of value 1 are displayed as black. This is the opposite of common practice on DOS systems. The problem can be addressed in one of two ways: inverting pixel values or inverting the image's palette. The latter is the preferred approach, because it doesn't require physical modification of the bitmap, only of the bitmap's interpretation. The `pal()` member function of the SRFHEADER structure accommodates this convention by returning a default monochrome palette where color 0 is defined as white.

Listing 13.4 VSRF.CPP

```
//---------------------------------------------------------//
//                                                         //
//                                                         //
//    File:    VSRF.CPP                                    //
//                                                         //
//    Desc:    Program to view or print an SRF file        //
//                                                         //
//---------------------------------------------------------//

#include "stdlib.h"
#include "stdio.h"
#include "string.h"
#include "conio.h"
#include "ctype.h"

#include "srf.hpp"
#include "imgviewr.hpp"
#include "imgprntr.hpp"
#include "laserjet.hpp"
#include "paintjet.hpp"
#include "epjx80.hpp"
#include "eplq24.hpp"
#include "pscript.hpp"
//.................Printer types

#define  LJ   0x4C4A
#define  PJ   0x504A
#define  JX   0x4A58
#define  LQ   0x4C51
#define  PS   0x5053


//.................Program globals

char      fn[80];          // path to SRF file

int       gmode;           // video display mode
int       pmode;           // printer ID
int       ropt;            // rendering flags
int       iopt;            // intensity mapping flags

ImgStore   *imgmap;        // image bitmap
RgbPalette *imgpal;        // image palette
```

Listing 13.4 VSRF.CPP (continued)

```
rgb        *pal;       //    "
int         ncolors;    //    "

//.................Exit with a message

void exit_pgm( char *msg )
{
   printf( "%s\n", msg );
   exit( 0 );
}

//.................Program usage

void explain_pgm( void )
{
   printf( "\n" );
   printf( "..........Sun Raster File
Viewer/Printer..........\n" );
   printf( "\n" );
   printf( "Usage:      VSRF  srf_file  [ switches ]\n" );
   printf( "\n" );
   printf( "Switches: -h      = display program usage\n" );
   printf( "          -vXX    = force video display mode XX\n" );
   printf( "                  (XX = 12, 13, 2E, 62)\n" );
   printf( "          -pXX    = print using printer XX\n" );
   printf( "                  (XX = LJ, PJ, JX, LQ, PS)\n" );
   printf( "          -b[+|-] = increase or decrease
brightness\n" );
   printf( "          -c[+|-] = increase or decrease contrast\n"
);
   printf( "          -d      = force dithered rendering\n" );
   printf( "          -g      = force gray scale rendering\n" );
   printf( "          -m      = force palette mapping\n" );
   printf( "\n" );
   printf( "..................................................\n"
);
   printf( "\n" );
}

//.................Process pgm argument list
```

Listing 13.4 VSRF.CPP (continued)

```cpp
void process_args( int argc, char *argv[] )
{
   // establish default values
   fn[0] = 0;
   gmode = 0x12;
   pmode = 0;
   ropt  = 0;
   iopt  = 0;

   // process the program's argument list
   for( int i=1; i<argc; i++ )
   {
      if( (*argv[i] == '-') || (*argv[i] == '/') )
      {
         char sw = *(argv[i] + 1);
         switch( toupper(sw) )
         {
            case 'H' :
               explain_pgm();
               exit( 0 );
               break;

            case 'V' :
               sscanf( argv[i]+2, "%x", &gmode );
               break;

            case 'P' :
               pmode = toupper( *(argv[i]+2) );
               pmode <<= 8;
               pmode += toupper( *(argv[i]+3) );
               break;

            case 'B' :
               if( *(argv[i]+2) == '-' )
                  iopt |= intensDBRI;
               else
                  iopt |= intensIBRI;
               break;

            case 'C' :
               if( *(argv[i]+2) == '-' )
                  iopt |= intensDCNT;
               else
                  iopt |= intensICNT;
               break;
```

Listing 13.4 VSRF.CPP (continued)

```cpp
                case 'D' :
                    ropt |= renderDITHER;
                    break;

                case 'G' :
                    ropt |= renderGRAY;
                    break;

                case 'M' :
                    ropt |= renderMAP;
                    break;

                default:
                    printf( "Unknown switch '%s' ignored\n",
                            argv[i] );
                    break;
            }
        }
        else  // presumably a file identifier
        {
            strcpy( fn, argv[i] );
            char *p = strchr( fn, '.' );
            if( p == 0 )
                strcat( fn, ".rf" );
            else if( *(p+1) == 0 )
                *p = 0;
        }
    }

    // was a file name specified?
    if( fn[0] == 0 )
    {
        explain_pgm();
        exit( 0 );
    }
}

//.................Create an image storage buffer
ImgStore * istore( int h, int w, int d )
{
    ImgStore *ist = 0;

    // attempt to create in order of preference
    ist = new XmsImgStore( h, w, d );
    if( (ist != 0) && (ist->status != imgstoreOKAY) )
    {
        delete ist;
        ist = new EmsImgStore( h, w, d );
```

Listing 13.4 VSRF.CPP (continued)

```
          if( (ist != 0) && (ist->status != imgstoreOKAY) )
          {
             delete ist;
             ist = new CnvImgStore( h, w, d );
             if( (ist != 0) && (ist->status != imgstoreOKAY) )
             {
                delete ist;
                ist = new DskImgStore( h, w, d );
                if( (ist != 0) && (ist->status != imgstoreOKAY) )
                {
                   delete ist;
                   ist = 0;
                }
             }
          }
       }

       return ist;
    }

    //.................Create a printer

    PrinterDriver * printer( int which )
    {
       PrinterDriver *p;

       switch( which )
       {
          case LJ : p = new LaserJet( "LPT1" );
                    break;
          case PJ : p = new PaintJet( "LPT1" );
                    break;
          case JX : p = new EpsonJX80( "LPT1" );
                    break;
          case LQ : p = new EpsonLQ24( "LPT1" );
                    break;
          default : p = new PsPrinter( "LPT1" );
                    break;
       }

       return p;
    }

    //.................Load the SRF file
```

Listing 13.4 VSRF.CPP (continued)

```cpp
void load_srf( void )
{
   // open file
   FILE *fsrf = fopen( fn, "rb" );
   if( fsrf == 0 )
      exit_pgm( "Sun Raster File file not found" );

   // read header
   SRFHEADER srf;
   if( srf.get( fsrf ) != 0 )
      exit_pgm( "Error reading Raster File header" );

   // validate file
   if( srf.iden != RF_IDEN )
      exit_pgm( "Specified file not a Sun Raster File" );

   // obtain palette if present
   imgpal = srf.pal( fsrf );
   pal = imgpal ? imgpal->colors : 0;
   ncolors = imgpal ? imgpal->ncolors : 0;

   // create bitmap
   int pxbytes = (srf.imdepth <= 8) ? 1 : 3;
   int rwbytes = pxbytes * int(srf.imwidth);
   int ncols   = int(srf.imwidth);
   int nrows   = int(srf.imheight);
   unsigned char *scanln = new unsigned char [rwbytes];
   imgmap = istore( nrows, ncols, pxbytes*8 );
   if( (imgmap == 0) || (scanln == 0) )
   {
      delete imgmap;
      delete pal;
      delete imgpal;
      delete scanln;
      exit_pgm( "Insufficient memory to load image" );
   }

   // load bitmap
   printf( "Loading SRF image from '%s'...", fn );
   SrfDecoder srfd( fsrf, srf );
   srfd.init();
   memset( scanln, 0, rwbytes );
   for( int i=0; i<nrows; i++ )
   {
      if( srfd.decode( scanln, ncols ) != xOKAY )
         break;
      imgmap->put( scanln, i );
   }
```

Listing 13.4 VSRF.CPP (continued)

```cpp
   srfd.term( );
   printf( "done\n" );

   delete scanln;
}

//.................Main

int main( int argc, char *argv[] )
{
   process_args( argc, argv );

   load_srf( );

   // print the image
   if( pmode != 0 )
   {
      PrinterDriver *prt = printer( pmode );
      if( prt )
      {
         printf( "Printing..." );
         ImagePrinter ip( prt, imgmap, pal, ncolors,
                          ropt, iopt, 100, 100 );
         ip.print( 1 );
         printf( "done\n" );
         delete prt;
      }
      else
         printf( "Printer instantiation failed\n" );
   }

   // display the image
   else
   {
      VgaDisplay vga( gmode );
      ImageViewer iv( &vga, imgmap, pal, ncolors,
                      ropt, iopt );
      iv.view( );
   }

   delete pal;
   delete imgpal;
   delete imgmap;

   return 0;
}
```

Writing the Sun Raster File Format

Listings 13.1 and 13.2 implement an encoder class for writing instances of the Sun raster format. The SrfEncoder class constructor takes an SRFHEADER instance as a parameter and derives all of its encoding parameters from the header. If the header's imtype field is set to imRle then an RLE encoded bitmap is written. In all other cases an uncompressed bitmap is written.

Listing 13.5 presents two functions for outputing a Sun raster file, both named WriteSRF. One version operates from a VgaDisplay instance; the other operates from an ImgStore instance and a palette. Listing 13.6 illustrates the use of the function with the El Greco sample image.

Listing 13.5 WRTSRF.CPP

```cpp
//----------------------------------------------------------//
//                                                          //
//   File:     WRTSRF.CPP                                   //
//                                                          //
//   Desc:     Code to output an SRF file from              //
//             a VGA Display or a Memory Bitmap             //
//                                                          //
//----------------------------------------------------------//

#include "srf.hpp"
#include "display.hpp"
#include "imgstore.hpp"


//.................Write VGA screen to SRF file 'fn'

int WriteSRF( VgaDisplay& vga, char *fn,
              int x1, int y1, int x2, int y2 )
{
   // image metrics
   int nrows   = y2 - y1 + 1;
   int ncols   = x2 - x1 + 1;
   int nbits   = 8;
   int ncolors = vga.metric.ncolors;

   // scan line buffer
   unsigned char *scanln = new unsigned char [ncols];
   rgb *vgapal = new rgb [ncolors];
   if( (scanln == 0) || (vgapal == 0) )
   {
      delete scanln;
      delete [] vgapal;
      return xNOMEMORY;
   }
```

Listing 13.5 WRTSRF.CPP (continued)

```cpp
    // Sun Raster File output file
    FILE *f = fopen( fn, "wb" );

    // initialize and write the SRF header
    SRFHEADER srf( ncols, nrows, nbits );
    srf.imtype = imRle;
    srf.maptype = mapRgb;
    srf.maplength = ncolors * 3;
    srf.put( f );

    // write the color map
    vga.getpalette( vgapal, ncolors );
    for( int i=0; i<ncolors; i++ )
    {
        fputc( vgapal[i].red, f );
        fputc( vgapal[i].grn, f );
        fputc( vgapal[i].blu, f );
    }
    // write the image
    SrfEncoder enc( f, srf );
    enc.init();
    for( i=0; i<nrows; i++ )
    {
        vga.getscanline( scanln, ncols, x1, y1+i );
        enc.encode( scanln, ncols );
    }
    enc.term();

    // update header image size field
    long n = ftell( f );
    n -= sizeof( SRFHEADER ) + srf.maplength;
    srf.imlength = n;
    fseek( f, 0, SEEK_SET );
    srf.put( f );

    int retv = ferror( f );
    fclose( f );
    delete scanln;
    delete [] vgapal;
    return retv ? xIOERROR : xOKAY;
}

//.................Write an image to SRF file 'fn'

int WriteSRF( ImgStore& img, rgb *pal, char *fn )
{
    // image metrics
    int nrows = img.height();
```

Listing 13.5 WRTSRF.CPP (continued)

```cpp
    int ncols = img.width();
    int nbits = 1;
    if( img.depth() == 24 ) nbits = 24;
    else if( img.depth() > 1 ) nbits = 8;
    int ncolors = 2;
    if( img.depth() == 24 ) ncolors = 0;
    else if( img.depth() > 1 ) ncolors = 256;

    // Sun Raster File output file
    FILE *f = fopen( fn, "wb" );

    // initialize and write the SRF header
    SRFHEADER srf( ncols, nrows, nbits );
    srf.imtype = imRle;
    srf.maptype = mapRgb;
    srf.maplength = ncolors * 3;
    srf.put( f );

    // write the color map
    for( int i=0; i<ncolors; i++ )
    {
        fputc( pal[i].red, f );
        fputc( pal[i].grn, f );
        fputc( pal[i].blu, f );
    }

    // write the image
    SrfEncoder enc( f, srf );
    enc.init();
    for( i=0; i<nrows; i++ )
    {
        enc.encode( img.get(i), ncols );
    }
    enc.term();

    // update header image size field
    long n = ftell( f );
    n -= sizeof( SRFHEADER ) + srf.maplength;
    srf.imlength = n;
    fseek( f, 0, SEEK_SET );
    srf.put( f );

    int retv = ferror( f );
    fclose( f );
    return retv ? xIOERROR : xOKAY;
}
```

Listing 13.6 SRFDEMO.CPP

```cpp
//-----------------------------------------------------------//
//                                                           //
//    File:     SRFDEMO.CPP                                  //
//                                                           //
//    Desc:     Example code to write a SRF file            //
//                                                           //
//-----------------------------------------------------------//

#include "wrtsrf.cpp"

char *       palname     = "EL-GRECO.PAL";
char *       imgname     = "EL-GRECO.IMG";
int          imgwidth    = 354;
int          imgheight   = 446;
int          imgcolors   = 256;
rgb          imgpalette[256];
unsigned char scanline[354];
CnvImgStore img( 446, 354, 8 );

// read the test image's palette

void read_palette( void )
{
   FILE *f = fopen( palname, "rt" );
   for( int i=0; i<imgcolors; i++ )
   {
      int r, g, b;
      fscanf( f, "%d %d %d", &r, &g, &b );
      imgpalette[i] = rgb( r, g, b );
   }
   fclose( f );
}

// read the test image into memory

void read_image( void )
{
   FILE *f = fopen( imgname, "rb" );
   for( int i=0; i<imgheight; i++ )
   {
      fread( scanline, imgwidth, 1, f );
      img.put( scanline, i );
   }
   fclose( f );
}

// output a SRF file
```

Listing 13.6 SRFDEMO.CPP (continued)

```
int main( void )
{
    read_palette( );

    read_image( );

    WriteSRF( img, imgpalette, "SRFDEMO.RF" );

    return 0;
}
```

Colorizing Monochrome Sun Raster Files

Given the typical sizes of Sun raster file images, viewing them on a standard VGA display with the program in Listing 13.4 is not a very rewarding process. It is difficult to appreciate an image when only a fraction of it can be seen at one time. One possible remedy is to scale the image down in size for viewing on VGA-sized displays. However, scaling, combined with operations on an image's colors, can produce some interesting results. In particular, the scaling process can be exploited to produce a colorized version of a monochrome image. We'll take a look at this process in this section.

The simplest and most effective procedure to reduce the scale of a monochrome image is to reduce the image's width and height by half—by representing each cell of 2 pixels by 2 pixels in the original image as a single pixel in the scaled image. Summing the pixel values in each 4-pixel cell yields a new quantity, with values in the range 0 to 4. A simple thresholding filter can then be used to convert these values to zeroes or ones to obtain a new monochrome image.

However, information is lost in the thresholding process. Specifically, the summed values derived from the original image represent relative intensities that can be interpreted, for instance, as values from a five-level gray-scale palette. More generally, the five possible values generated by the reduction process can be interpreted as five different colors. The problem with the last possibility is in picking five different colors that make sense.

The gray-scale interpretation, which does make sense within the context of the original image, suggests a general technique for picking five colors that preserves the luminance relationships of the original image. The five gray-scale values can be represented as equidistant points along a straight line segment in the RGB color cube that starts at the origin (0,0,0) and terminates at (1,1,1). The two endpoints, of course, represent black and white, respectively.

A more general procedure is to pick the five colors that result from the equidistant subdivision of an arbitrary straight line segment in RGB color space. The result of this process is a five-color palette that coherently renders the original image without necessarily reproducing the "correct" colors. There is, obviously, no way to obtain the true color components of a color image once it has been converted to a bilevel or gray-scale form. The colorization process described here, however, can be said to do justice to the original.

Listing 13.7 presents the source code to SRF2CLR.CPP, which implements the colorization process just described. It is designed to work only with bilevel images, which implies only images with 1 bit per pixel. The output of the program is a Sun raster file with an 8-bit-per-pixel image that has an area one quarter of the original in size and a five-entry color map. The colorized output can be viewed with VSRF (Listing 13.4) so you can see the results of the process.

Listing 13.7 SRF2CLR.CPP

```
//-----------------------------------------------------------//
//                                                           //
//   File:      SRF2CLR.CPP                                  //
//                                                           //
//   Desc:      Program to colorize Monochrome   SUN         //
//              Raster Files                                 //
//                                                           //
//-----------------------------------------------------------//

#include "stdlib.h"
#include "stdio.h"
#include "string.h"
#include "conio.h"
#include "ctype.h"

#include "color.hpp"
#include "srf.hpp"

//................Program globals

char       ifn[80],          // path to input SRF file
           ofn[80];          // path to output SRF file

rgb        cmin,             // min/max palette colors
           cmax;

//................Exit with a message
```

Listing 13.7 SRF2CLR.CPP (continued)

```
void exit_pgm( char *msg )
{
   printf( "%s\n", msg );
   exit( 0 );
}

//................Program usage

void explain_pgm( void )
{
   printf( "\n" );
   printf( ".............Sun Raster File
Colorizer.............\n" );
   printf( "\n" );
   printf( "Usage:      SRF2CLR  srf_in  srf_out  [ switches ]\n"
);
   printf( "\n" );
   printf( "Switches:  -h         = display program usage\n" );
   printf( "              -minR,G,B  = palette min color\n" );
   printf( "              -maxR,G,B  = palette max color\n" );
   printf( "\n" );
   printf( "Default extension is .RF\n" );
   printf( "Default colorization is 5-level gray scale\n" );
   printf( "\n" );
   printf( "...............................................\n"
);
   printf( "\n" );
}

//................Process pgm argument list

void process_args( int argc, char *argv[] )
{
   // establish default values
   ifn[0] = 0;
   ofn[0] = 0;
   cmin = rgb( 0, 0, 0 );
   cmax = rgb( 255, 255, 255 );

   // process the program's argument list
   for( int i=1; i<argc; i++ )
   {
      if( (*argv[i] == '-') || (*argv[i] == '/') )
      {
         int r, g, b;
         strupr( argv[i] );
         if( strncmp( argv[i], "-MIN", 4 ) == 0 )
         {
```

Listing 13.7 SRF2CLR.CPP (continued)

```
                char *p = argv[i] + 4;
                sscanf( p, "%d,%d,%d", &r, &g, &b );
                cmin = rgb( r, g, b );
            }
            else if( strncmp( argv[i], "-MAX", 4 ) == 0 )
            {
                char *p = argv[i] + 4;
                sscanf( p, "%d,%d,%d", &r, &g, &b );
                cmax = rgb( r, g, b );
            }
            else
                printf( "Unknown switch '%s' ignored\n", argv[i] );
        }
        else  // presumably a file identifier
        {
            if( ifn[0] == 0 )
            {
                strcpy( ifn, argv[i] );
                char *p = strchr( ifn, '.' );
                if( p == 0 )
                    strcat( ifn, ".rf" );
                else if( *(p+1) == 0 )
                    *p = 0;
            }
            else if( ofn[0] == 0 )
            {
                strcpy( ofn, argv[i] );
                char *p = strchr( ofn, '.' );
                if( p == 0 )
                    strcat( ofn, ".rf" );
                else if( *(p+1) == 0 )
                    *p = 0;
            }
        }
    }

    // were file names specified?
    if( (ifn[0] == 0) || (ofn[0] == 0) )
    {
        explain_pgm();
        exit( 0 );
    }
}


//..................Write the color palette
```

Listing 13.7 SRF2CLR.CPP (continued)

```cpp
void wrt_pal( FILE *f )
{
    int dr = cmax.red;  dr -= cmin.red;
    int dg = cmax.grn;  dg -= cmin.grn;
    int db = cmax.blu;  db -= cmin.blu;

    for( int i=0; i<5; i++ )
    {
        int r = cmin.red;
        if( dr != 0 )
        {
            int x = dr;
            x *= i;
            x /= 4;
            r += x;
        }
        int g = cmin.grn;
        if( dg != 0 )
        {
            int x = dg;
            x *= i;
            x /= 4;
            g += x;
        }

        int b = cmin.blu;
        if( db != 0 )
        {
            int x = db;
            x *= i;
            x /= 4;
            b += x;
        }
        fputc( r, f );
        fputc( g, f );
        fputc( b, f );
        printf( "color[%d] = rgb(%d,%d,%d)\n",
                i, r, g, b );
    }
}

//.................Process the files
```

Listing 13.7 SRF2CLR.CPP (continued)

```cpp
void colorize_srf( void )
{
   FILE *fi = fopen( ifn, "rb" );
   if( fi == 0 )
      exit_pgm( "Input file not found" );
   FILE *fo = fopen( ofn, "wb" );

   // get input header and palette
   SRFHEADER ihdr;
   ihdr.get( fi );
   if( ihdr.iden != RF_IDEN )
      exit_pgm( "Input file not a Sun Raster File" );
   if( ihdr.imdepth > 1 )
      exit_pgm( "Input file not a monochrome Sun Raster File" );
   // skip over any color map
   if( ihdr.maplength > 0 )
      fseek( fi, ihdr.maplength, SEEK_CUR );

   // put output header and palette
   SRFHEADER ohdr;
   ohdr.iden = RF_IDEN;
   ohdr.imwidth = ihdr.imwidth / 2;
   ohdr.imheight = ihdr.imheight / 2;
   ohdr.imdepth = 8;
   ohdr.imtype = imRle;
   ohdr.imlength = 0;
   ohdr.maptype = mapRgb;
   ohdr.maplength = 15;
   ohdr.put( fo );
   wrt_pal( fo );

   // Perform the procedure

   unsigned char *iln1, *iln2, *oln;
   iln1 = new unsigned char [ int(ihdr.imwidth) ];
   iln2 = new unsigned char [ int(ihdr.imwidth) ];
   oln  = new unsigned char [ int(ohdr.imwidth) ];
   if( (iln1==0) || (iln2==0) || (oln==0) )
      exit_pgm( "Out of memory allocating buffers" );

   SrfDecoder srfin( fi, ihdr );
   SrfEncoder srfout( fo, ohdr );
```

Listing 13.7 SRF2CLR.CPP (continued)

```cpp
if( (srfin.status() != xOKAY) || (srfout.status() != xOKAY) )
{
   printf( "in.status() = %d\n", srfin.status() );
   printf( "out.status() = %d\n", srfout.status() );
   exit_pgm( "Error instantiating encoder/decoder" );
}

printf( "Converting %s to %s...", ifn, ofn );

srfin.init();
srfout.init();

int icols = int( ihdr.imwidth );
int ocols = int( ohdr.imwidth );
int orows = int( ohdr.imheight );
for( int i=0; i<orows; i++ )
{
   srfin.decode( iln1, icols );
   srfin.decode( iln2, icols );
   for( int j=0; j<ocols; j++ )
   {
      // since 0=white and 1=black
      // we invert the pixel value
      oln[j]  = 4;
      oln[j] -= iln1[j*2];
      oln[j] -= iln1[j*2+1];
      oln[j] -= iln2[j*2];
      oln[j] -= iln2[j*2+1];
   }
   srfout.encode( oln, ocols );
   // let the world know we're alive...
   if( ((i+1) % 80) == 0 ) printf( "." );
}

srfin.term();
srfout.term();

// update header image length field
long n = ftell( fo );
n -= sizeof(SRFHEADER) + 15;
ohdr.imlength = n;
fseek( fo, 0, SEEK_SET );
ohdr.put( fo );

fclose( fi );
fclose( fo );
```

Listing 13.7 SRF2CLR.CPP (continued)

```
    printf( "done\n" );
}
//................Main

int main( int argc, char *argv[] )
{
    process_args( argc, argv );

    colorize_srf( );

    return 0;
}
```

Although it is not done here, the colorization process that was just described can be implemented to operate on 8-bit and 24-bit color images as well. In these cases, however, colorization is not the objective, because the images are already in color. What the process does do is scale color images down in size without restricting the scaled version to the same set of colors as the original. This normally produces a better result at a cost of larger pixel sizes. An 8-bit-per-pixel image modified in this manner can potentially contain four times as many colors as the original and must be stored using 16-bit or 24-bit pixels. A 24-bit image, on the other hand, yields 24-bit output, so there is no size penalty in this case.

In actual use, each pixel in the reduced image is given an RGB value that is the average of the four RGB values in the 2x2 pixel source cell. Averaging pixel RGBs in a color-mapped image can result in colors that are not in the color map, so it makes sense to realize the scaled version as an RGB-based image. A less effective alternative is to maintain the same color map size but modify its values to approximate the scaled image more closely. This can be accomplished using the palette-mapping process that was described in Chapter 1.

This concludes our look at the Sun raster file format. As noted, it is rare to encounter Sun raster files on IBM PCs, but the format's simplicity makes it an otherwise attractive choice. Obviously, the format represents one avenue for exporting graphical data to the Sun environment.

14

The X Window
Bitmap Format

X Window, or X as it known for short, is a network-transparent graphical windowing system that is widely used in Unix environments. Virtually all important GUIs for Unix are designed around X, including OSF's Motif and Sun's Open Look.

X was originally developed in 1984 and 1985 at MIT. These two years saw the release of the first 10 versions of X, which were primarily the work of a small group at MIT and others from Digital Equipment Corporation. During the following two years, 1986 and 1987, interest in X exploded, and many companies made serious commitments to both the implementation and use of X. The result was release 11 of X Window, which is the version in use today.

Although the version number stuck at 11, X continued to evolve and new versions appeared as revisions to version 11. At this writing, the current production release of X is referred to as X11R5. No doubt there will be others.

Surprisingly, X through version 11R5 never defined anything like a general-purpose graphics-image file format. Despite this, X supports images and image manipulations. It would seem that no one ever bothered to save one of these to disk and thereby create a file format.

X also supports graphical objects such as icons, cursors, and bitmaps. Of these, only the bitmap comes close to defining what might be termed a graphics file format. Because many in MS-DOS circles are not familiar with X, I have elected to include the X bitmap format here as a representative example of the genre from the world of Unix.

The X Bitmap Format

Of all the formats discussed in this book, the X bitmap format is conceptually closest to the Encapsulated Postscript (EPS) format, in the sense that both formats define an image using language source code. But where EPS is complex and uses the PostScript language, the XBM format is simple and uses the C programming language. Here is a complete specification of the format:

```
#define name_width width
#define name_height height
#define name_x_hot xhot
#define name_y_hot yhot
static unsigned char name_bits[] = { 0xNN, ... };
```

As you can see, the format is nothing more than a C source code definition for a two-dimensional array of pixels. The italicized terms are replaced by appropriate variable names and values in an actual file. Although the hot-spot definition is optional, the width, height, and bits members are required. The hot spot is a position within the bitmap defined by offsets from the edges of the bit array, and can be used, for example, to implement a cursor image from the bitmap. Some additional notes on the XBM format follow.

1. The width, height, xhot, and yhot values are in pixel units.

2. The bits array defines a 1-bit-per-pixel bitmap as a series of 8-bit hex constants. Each row of the bitmap is rounded to a multiple of 8. The total number of bytes presented is thus:

```
((width + 7) / 8) * height
```

3. The order of bits stored in each byte is the opposite of most other formats. The least significant bit of a byte represents the leftmost pixel of the byte.

4. The name parameter in the specification is, in practice, derived from the name of the bitmap file, stripped of any drive, directory, and extension specification.

Listing 14.1 shows a representative example of an X Window bitmap file. The image is a 16×16 pixel rendition of the X logo, which consists of a stylized letter X. The image itself is depicted in Figure 14.1.

Listing 14.1 XLOGO16

```
#define xlogo16_width   16
#define xlogo16_height 16
static unsigned char xlogo16_bits[] =
{
    0x0f, 0x80, 0x1e, 0x80, 0x3c, 0x40, 0x78, 0x20,
    0x78, 0x10, 0xf0, 0x08, 0xe0, 0x09, 0xc0, 0x05,
    0xc0, 0x02, 0x40, 0x07, 0x20, 0x0f, 0x20, 0x1e,
    0x10, 0x1e, 0x08, 0x3c, 0x04, 0x78, 0x02, 0xf0
};
```

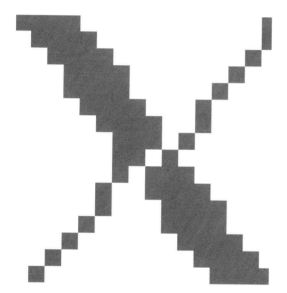

Figure 14.1 The XLOGO16 Image

Reading the X Bitmap Format

Writing an instance of the X bitmap format is a simple exercise, but reading a format instance is slightly more difficult. Reading the format is easiest if the decoder treats the input file as a stream of tokens. To facilitate this process a TKNFILE class has been developed. It treats a file as a collection of tokens and allows reading a file a token at a time. Listings 14.2 and 14.3 present the implementation of the TKNFILE class.

In this instance, the token parser used by the TKNFILE class is specialized, designed around assumptions implied by the XBM format. For example, the characters for both kinds of braces ({ } and [ ]) are treated as white space although the underscore character (_) is not.

Although it might seem that a modification of our format methodology is necessary for the X bitmap format, this is in fact not the case. Because the format lacks a formal file header, one has been devised. This is the XBMHEADER structure in Listing 14.2. We continue to use our standard codec design and implement XbmDecoder and XbmEncoder classes. The only unusual aspect of these classes is that the decoder constructor uses a pointer to a TKNFILE in place of a pointer to FILE.

Listing 14.2 XBM.HPP

```
//-----------------------------------------------------------//
//                                                           //
//    File:    XBM.HPP                                       //
//                                                           //
//    Desc:    Structure and Class definitions for dealing   //
//             with an X Windows bitmap file                 //
//                                                           //
//-----------------------------------------------------------//

#ifndef _XBM_HPP_
#define _XBM_HPP_

#include "stdlib.h"
#include "stdio.h"
#include "string.h"
#include "ctype.h"

#include "codec.hpp"

//.................token handling primitives

int iswhite( int ch );
int tokencnt( char *s );
int token( char *src, char *dst, int which );

//.................class TKNFILE

class TKNFILE
{
    protected:
        FILE    * fin;      // input file
        char    * ln;       // line buffer
        char    * tok;      // extracted token buffer
        int       maxch;    // size of buffers
        int       curtk;    // current token number
        int       cond;     // condition code
```

Listing 14.2 XBM.HPP (continued)

```cpp
   public:
      TKNFILE( char *path );
      ~TKNFILE( );
      int    status( void );
      char * get( void );
};

//................struct XBMNAMES

#define NAMECNT 5

enum XbmNames
{
   xWidth,
   xHeight,
   xXHot,
   xYHot,
   xBits
};

struct XBMNAMES
{
   char *names[NAMECNT];

   XBMNAMES( char *prefix );
  ~XBMNAMES( );
   int which( char *tok );
};

//................struct XBMHEADER

struct XBMHEADER
{
   int    width;
   int    height;
   int    xhot;
   int    yhot;
   char *name;

   XBMHEADER( char *n )
   {
      width = height = 0;
      xhot = yhot = -1;
      name = 0;
      name = new char [strlen(n)+1];
      if( name )
         strcpy( name, n );
   }
```

Listing 14.2 XBM.HPP (continued)

```cpp
    XBMHEADER( int w, int h, char *n )
    {
       width = w;
       height = h;
       xhot = yhot = -1;
       name = new char [strlen(n)+1];
       if( name )
          strcpy( name, n );
    }
   ~XBMHEADER( )
    {
       delete name;
    }
    void list( void );
    int  get( TKNFILE *tf );
    int  put( FILE *f );
};

//................class  XbmEncoder

class XbmDecoder : public Decoder
{
    protected:
       TKNFILE *xbm_file;      // input file
       int      cond;         // condition code

    public:
       XbmDecoder( TKNFILE *f_in );
       virtual ~XbmDecoder( ) { }
       virtual int decode( unsigned char *buf, int npxls );
       virtual int init( void );
       virtual int term( void );
       virtual int status( void );
};

//................class  XbmEncoder

class XbmEncoder : public Encoder
{
    protected:
       FILE *xbm_file;        // output file
       int   cond;            // condition code
       int   cnt;             // bytes written

    public:
       XbmEncoder( FILE *f_out );
       virtual ~XbmEncoder( ) { }
       virtual int encode( unsigned char *buf, int npxls );
```

Listing 14.2 XBM.HPP (continued)

```
        virtual int init( void );
        virtual int term( void );
        virtual int status( void );
    };


    #endif
```

Listing 14.3 XBM.CPP

```
//-----------------------------------------------------------//
//                                                           //
//    File:    XBM.CPP                                       //
//                                                           //
//    Desc:    Structure and Class definitions for dealing   //
//             with an X Window bitmap file                  //
//                                                           //
//-----------------------------------------------------------//

#include "xbm.hpp"

//................token handling primitives

inline int iswhite( int ch )
{
    if( ch == '_' ) return 0;
    if( ch == '#' ) return 0;
    if( isspace(ch) ) return 1;
    if( ispunct(ch) ) return 1;
    if( (ch=='[') || (ch==']') ) return 1;
    if( (ch=='{') || (ch=='}') ) return 1;
    if( (ch=='(') || (ch==')') ) return 1;
    return 0;
}

int tokencnt( char *s )
{
    int n = 0;

    while( *s )
    {
        while( iswhite( *s ) )
        {
            if( *s == 0 ) break;
            s++;
        }
        n++;
        while( ! iswhite( *s ) )
```

Listing 14.3 XBM.CPP (continued)

```cpp
            {
                if( *s == 0 ) break;
                s++;
            }
        }

        return n;
    }

    int token( char *src, char *dst, int which )
    {
        // skip leading tokens
        while( which-- > 0 )
        {
            while( iswhite( *src ) )
            {
                if( *src == 0 ) return 0;
                src++;
            }

            while( ! iswhite( *src ) )
            {
                if( *src == 0 ) return 0;
                src++;
            }
        }

        // extact the desired token
        while( iswhite( *src ) )
        {
            if( *src == 0 ) return 0;
            src++;
        }
        int n = 0;
        while( ! iswhite( *src ) )
        {
            if( *src == 0 ) break;
            *dst++ = *src++;
            n++;
        }
        *dst = 0;
        return n;
    }

    //.................class TKNFILE
```

Listing 14.3 XBM.CPP (continued)

```
TKNFILE::TKNFILE( char *path )
{
    maxch = 133;
    curtk = -1;
    fin = fopen( path, "rt" );
    ln = new char [maxch+1];
    if( ln ) memset( ln, 0, maxch+1 );
    tok = new char [maxch+1];
    if( tok ) memset( tok, 0, maxch+1 );
}

TKNFILE::~TKNFILE( )
{
    if( fin ) fclose( fin );
    delete ln;
    delete tok;
}

int TKNFILE::status( void )
{
    if( ln == 0 )     return xNOMEMORY;
    if( tok == 0 )    return xNOMEMORY;
    if( fin == 0 )    return xIOERROR;
    if( ferror(fin) ) return xIOERROR;
    if( feof(fin) )   return xENDOFFILE;
    return xOKAY;
}

char * TKNFILE::get( void )
{
    curtk++;
    while( token(ln,tok,curtk) == 0 )
    {
        if( fgets(ln,maxch,fin) == 0 )
            return 0;
        curtk = 0;
    }
    return tok;
}

//................struct XBMNAMES
```

Listing 14.3 XBM.CPP (continued)

```cpp
static char *suffix[NAMECNT] =
{
   "_width",
   "_height",
   "_x_hot",
   "_y_hot",
   "_bits"
};

XBMNAMES::XBMNAMES( char *prefix )
{
   int n = strlen(prefix) + 8;
   for( int i=0; i<NAMECNT; i++ )
   {
      names[i] = new char [n];
      if( names[i] )
      {
         strcpy( names[i], prefix );
         strcat( names[i], suffix[i] );
      }
   }
}

XBMNAMES::~XBMNAMES( )
{
   for( int i=0; i<NAMECNT; i++ )
      delete names[i];
}

int XBMNAMES::which( char *tok )
{
   for( int i=0; i<NAMECNT; i++ )
      if( strcmp(names[i],tok) == 0 )
         return i;
   return -1;
}

//.................struct XBMHEADER

void XBMHEADER::list( void )
{
   printf( "XBMHEADER::width  = %d\n", width );
   printf( "XBMHEADER::height = %d\n", height );
   printf( "XBMHEADER::xhot   = %d\n", xhot );
   printf( "XBMHEADER::yhot   = %d\n", yhot );
   printf( "XBMHEADER::name   = %s\n", name );
}
```

Listing 14.3 XBM.CPP (continued)

```cpp
int XBMHEADER::get( TKNFILE *tf )
{
    // set some defaults
    width = height = 0;
    xhot = yhot = -1;

    // now scan tokens from file
    XBMNAMES xn( name );
    int  done = 0;
    while( ! done )
    {
        char *t = tf->get();
        if( t == 0 ) break;
        switch( xn.which( t ) )
        {
            case xWidth:
                width = atoi( tf->get() );
                break;
            case xHeight:
                height = atoi( tf->get() );
                break;
            case xXHot:
                xhot = atoi( tf->get() );
                break;
            case xYHot:
                yhot = atoi( tf->get() );
                break;
            case xBits:
                done = 1;
                break;
        }
    }
    return tf->status();
}

int XBMHEADER::put( FILE *f )
{
    int hdrvals[4];
    XBMNAMES xn( name );

    hdrvals[0] = width;
    hdrvals[1] = height;
    hdrvals[2] = xhot;
    hdrvals[3] = yhot;

    for( int i=0; i<4; i++ )
        fprintf( f, "#define %s %d\n",
                 xn.names[i], hdrvals[i] );
```

Listing 14.3 XBM.CPP (continued)

```cpp
        fprintf( f, "static unsigned char %s[] =\n",
                     xn.names[4] );

        return ferror(f) ? -1 : 0;
}

//................class XbmDecoder

XbmDecoder::XbmDecoder( TKNFILE *f_in )
{
    xbm_file = f_in;
    cond = xbm_file->status();
}

int XbmDecoder::init( void )
{
    return status();
}

int XbmDecoder::term( void )
{
    return status();
}

int XbmDecoder::status( void )
{
    cond = xbm_file->status();
    return cond;
}

int XbmDecoder::decode( unsigned char *buf, int npxls )
{
    if( status() == xOKAY )
    {
        int i, n = 0;
        while( n < npxls )
        {
            sscanf( xbm_file->get(), "%x", &i );
            int mask = 1;
            while( mask < 255 )
            {
                if( n < npxls )
                    buf[n++] = (i & mask) ? 1 : 0;
                mask <<= 1;
            }
        }
    }
    return status();
}
```

Listing 14.3 XBM.CPP (continued)

```cpp
//................class XbmEncoder

XbmEncoder::XbmEncoder( FILE *f_out )
{
    xbm_file = f_out;
}

int XbmEncoder::init( void )
{
    cnt = 0;
    fprintf( xbm_file, "{\n" );
    return status();
}

int XbmEncoder::term( void )
{
    if( cnt > 0 )
        fprintf( xbm_file, "\n" );
    fprintf( xbm_file, "};\n" );
    return status();
}

int XbmEncoder::status( void )
{
    cond = ferror(xbm_file) ? xIOERROR : xOKAY;
    return cond;
}

int XbmEncoder::encode( unsigned char *buf, int npxls )
{
    if( status() == xOKAY )
    {
        int n=0;
        int mask = 1;
        for( int i=0; i<npxls; i++ )
        {
            if( buf[i] ) n |= mask;
            if( (mask <<= 1) > 255 )
            {
                fprintf( xbm_file, " 0x%02x,", n );
                cnt++;
                if( cnt == 12 )
                {
                    fprintf( xbm_file, "\n" );
                    cnt = 0;
                }
                n = 0;
                mask = 1;
```

Listing 14.3 XBM.CPP (continued)

```
            }
        }
        if( mask != 1 )
        {
            fprintf( xbm_file, " 0x%02x,", n );
            cnt++;
            if( cnt == 12 )
            {
                fprintf( xbm_file, "\n" );
                cnt = 0;
            }
        }
    }
    return status();
}
```

An X Bitmap File Viewer

Listing 14.4 presents the source code to VXBM.CPP, a program to view or print X bitmap files. The program is similar in all respects to the other viewers we have developed with two exceptions. First, because X bitmaps are bilevel only, we have added two switches to the program to allow specification of the foreground and background colors for the image. Colors are specified as RGB triples. For example, the following command line will display the xlogo16 file using red on a dark gray background:

```
vxbm xlogo16 -b50,50,50 -f200,0,0
```

Also, a –n switch has been added to allow an override of the variable name prefix that the program expects to find in the file. This is necessary if, for instance, a Unix file with a very long file name is transported to DOS. Suppose, for example, there is an X bitmap file on a Unix system with the name escherknot. It would contain variable names such as escherknot_width, which, of course, use the file's name as the variable prefix. If the file is moved to DOS, its name must be changed to something using eight characters or less, and the file's variable prefix no longer coincides with the file's name. This is handled as follows:

```
vxbm DOSname -nescherknot
```

Listing 14.4 VXBM.CPP

```cpp
//----------------------------------------------------------//
//                                                          //
//    File:     VXBM.CPP                                    //
//                                                          //
//    Desc:     Program to view or print a XBM file         //
//                                                          //
//----------------------------------------------------------//

#include "stdlib.h"
#include "stdio.h"
#include "string.h"
#include "conio.h"
#include "ctype.h"

#include "xbm.hpp"
#include "imgviewr.hpp"
#include "imgprntr.hpp"
#include "laserjet.hpp"
#include "paintjet.hpp"
#include "epjx80.hpp"
#include "eplq24.hpp"
#include "pscript.hpp"


//.................Printer types

#define  LJ   0x4C4A
#define  PJ   0x504A
#define  JX   0x4A58
#define  LQ   0x4C51
#define  PS   0x5053


//.................Program globals

char      fn[80],        // path to XBM file
          name[40];      // XBM var root

int       gmode,         // video display mode
          pmode;         // printer ID

ImgStore  *imgmap;       // image bitmap

rgb pal[] =
{
   rgb( 0, 0, 0 ),
   rgb( 0, 0, 0 ),
   rgb( 255, 255, 255 )
};
```

Listing 14.4 VXBM.CPP (continued)

```
//.................Exit with a message

void exit_pgm( char *msg )
{
   printf( "%s\n", msg );
   exit( 0 );
}

//................Program usage

void explain_pgm( void )
{
   printf( "\n" );
   printf( "...........X Window Bitmap
Viewer/Printer...........\n" );
   printf( "\n" );
   printf( "Usage:      VXBM  xbm_file  [ switches ]\n" );
   printf( "\n" );
   printf( "Switches: -h      = display program usage\n" );
   printf( "             -vXX    = force video display mode XX\n" );
   printf( "                       (XX = 12, 13, 2E, 62)\n" );
   printf( "             -pXX    = print using printer XX\n" );
   printf( "                       (XX = LJ, PJ, JX, LQ, PS)\n" );
   printf( "             -fR,G,B = set foreground color to
(R,G,B)\n" );
   printf( "             -bR,G,B = set foreground color to
(R,G,B)\n" );
   printf( "             -nXXX   = use root name XXX\n" );
   printf( "\n" );
   printf( "................................................\n"
);
   printf( "\n" );
}

//................Process pgm argument list

void process_args( int argc, char *argv[] )
{
   // establish default values
   fn[0]   = 0;
   name[0] = 0;
   gmode   = 0x12;
   pmode   = 0;

   // process the program's argument list
   int   r, g, b;
   char *p;
   for( int i=1; i<argc; i++ )
```

Listing 14.4 VXBM.CPP (continued)

```cpp
{
   if( (*argv[i] == '-') || (*argv[i] == '/') )
   {
      char sw = *(argv[i] + 1);
      switch( toupper(sw) )
      {
         case 'H' :
            explain_pgm();
            exit( 0 );
            break;

         case 'V' :
            sscanf( argv[i]+2, "%x", &gmode );
            break;

         case 'N' :
            strcpy( name, argv[i]+2 );
            break;

         case 'P' :
            pmode = toupper( *(argv[i]+2) );
            pmode <<= 8;
            pmode += toupper( *(argv[i]+3) );
            break;

         case 'B' :
            p = argv[i] + 2;
            sscanf( p, "%d,%d,%d", &r, &g, &b );
            pal[1] = rgb( r, g, b );
            break;

         case 'F' :
            p = argv[i] + 2;
            sscanf( p, "%d,%d,%d", &r, &g, &b );
            pal[2] = rgb( r, g, b );
            break;

         default:
            printf( "Unknown switch '%s' ignored\n",
                     argv[i] );
            break;
      }
   }
   else  // presumably a file identifier
   {
      strcpy( fn, argv[i] );
   }
}
```

Listing 14.4 VXBM.CPP (continued)

```cpp
    // was a file name specified?
    if( fn[0] == 0 )
    {
        explain_pgm();
        exit( 0 );
    }
}

//.................Create an image storage buffer

ImgStore * istore( int h, int w, int d )
{
    ImgStore *ist = 0;

    // attempt to create in order of preference
    ist = new XmsImgStore( h, w, d );
    if( (ist != 0) && (ist->status != imgstoreOKAY) )
    {
        delete ist;
        ist = new EmsImgStore( h, w, d );
        if( (ist != 0) && (ist->status != imgstoreOKAY) )
        {
            delete ist;
            ist = new CnvImgStore( h, w, d );
            if( (ist != 0) && (ist->status != imgstoreOKAY) )
            {
                delete ist;
                ist = new DskImgStore( h, w, d );
                if( (ist != 0) && (ist->status != imgstoreOKAY) )
                {
                    delete ist;
                    ist = 0;
                }
            }
        }
    }

    return ist;
}

//.................Create a printer

PrinterDriver * printer( int which )
{
    PrinterDriver *p;
```

Listing 14.4 VXBM.CPP (continued)

```
    switch( which )
    {
       case LJ : p = new LaserJet( "LPT1" );
                  break;
       case PJ : p = new PaintJet( "LPT1" );
                  break;
       case JX : p = new EpsonJX80( "LPT1" );
                  break;
       case LQ : p = new EpsonLQ24( "LPT1" );
                  break;
       default : p = new PsPrinter( "LPT1" );
                  break;
    }

    return p;
}

//.................Load the XBM file

void load_xbm( void )
{
    // open file
    TKNFILE fxbm( fn );
    if( fxbm.status() != xOKAY )
       exit_pgm( "X Bitmap file not found" );

    // extract bitmap name prefix from file name
    if( name[0] == 0 )
    {
       int n = strlen( fn ) - 1;
       while( n > 0 )
       {
          if( fn[n] == '.' ) fn[n] = 0;
          if( fn[n] == '\\' ) break;
          n--;
       }
       if( fn[n] == '\\' ) n++;
       strcpy( name, fn+n );
    }

    // read header
    XBMHEADER xbm( name );
    if( xbm.get( &fxbm ) != xOKAY )
       exit_pgm( "Error reading X Bitmap header" );

    // create bitmap
    unsigned char *scanln = new unsigned char [xbm.width];
    imgmap = istore( xbm.height, xbm.width, 8 );
```

Listing 14.4 VXBM.CPP (continued)

```cpp
        if( (imgmap == 0) || (scanln == 0) )
        {
            delete imgmap;
            delete scanln;
            exit_pgm( "Insufficient memory to load image" );
        }

        // load bitmap
        printf( "Loading XBM image from '%s'...", fn );
        XbmDecoder xbmd( &fxbm );
        xbmd.init();
        memset( scanln, 0, xbm.width );
        for( int i=0; i<xbm.height; i++ )
        {
            if( xbmd.decode( scanln, xbm.width ) != xOKAY )
                break;
            // convert 0-or-1 to 1-or-2
            for( int j=0; j<xbm.width; j++ )
                scanln[j] += 1;
            imgmap->put( scanln, i );
        }
        xbmd.term();
        printf( "done\n" );

        delete scanln;
    }

    //.................Main

    int main( int argc, char *argv[] )
    {
        process_args( argc, argv );

        load_xbm( );

        // print the image
        if( pmode != 0 )
        {
            PrinterDriver *prt = printer( pmode );
            if( prt )
            {
                printf( "Printing..." );
                ImagePrinter ip( prt, imgmap, pal, 3,
                                 0, 0, 100, 100 );
                ip.print( 1 );
                printf( "done\n" );
                delete prt;
            }
```

Listing 14.4 VXBM.CPP (continued)

```
        else
            printf( "Printer instantiation failed\n" );
    }

    // display the image
    else
    {
        VgaDisplay vga( gmode );
        ImageViewer iv( &vga, imgmap, pal, 3, 0, 0 );
        iv.view( );
    }

    delete imgmap;

    return 0;
}
```

Writing the X Bitmap Format

Listing 14.5 presents functions to output instances of the X bitmap format. The functions work on any image or display, including 24-bit color bitmaps. These are, of course, output as bilevel images, which is done by converting each RGB of a source image to a luminance value and converting the luminance value to a zero or one with a simple threshold. The code is hardwired to use a threshold of 127, which is the best value in most cases. The threshold can, however, be varied to increase or decrease the apparent brightness of the resulting image.

An example of a program that outputs an X bitmap from the El Greco sample image is presented in Listing 14.6.

Listing 14.5 WRTXBM.CPP

```
//----------------------------------------------------------//
//                                                          //
//    File:      WRTXBM.CPP                                 //
//                                                          //
//    Desc:      Code to output an XBM file from            //
//               a VGA Display or a Memory Bitmap           //
//                                                          //
//----------------------------------------------------------//

#include "xbm.hpp"
#include "display.hpp"
#include "imgstore.hpp"

static int threshold = 127;
```

Listing 14.5 WRTXBM.CPP (continued)

```cpp
//................Extract file name from path

void xtrname( char *path, char *name )
{
   int n = strlen( path ) - 1;
   int m = n;
   while( n > 0 )
   {
      if( path[n] == '.' )  m = n;
      if( path[n] == '\\' ) break;
      n--;
   }
   if( path[n] == '\\' ) n++;
   strncpy( name, path+n, m-n+1 );
   name[m-n+1] = 0;
   strlwr( name );
}

//................Write VGA screen to XBM file 'fn'

int WriteXBM( VgaDisplay& vga, char *fn,
              int x1, int y1, int x2, int y2 )
{
   // image metrics
   int nrows   = y2 - y1 + 1;
   int ncols   = x2 - x1 + 1;
   int ncolors = vga.metric.ncolors;

   // scan line buffer and palette
   unsigned char *scanln = new unsigned char [ncols];
   rgb *vgapal = new rgb [ncolors];
   if( (scanln == 0) || (vgapal == 0) )
   {
      delete scanln;
      delete [] vgapal;
      return xNOMEMORY;
   }
   vga.getpalette( vgapal, ncolors );

   // XBM output file
   FILE *f = fopen( fn, "wt" );

   // initialize and write the XBM header
   char name[16];
   xtrname( fn, name );
   XBMHEADER xbm( ncols, nrows, name );
   xbm.put( f );
```

Listing 14.5 WRTXBM.CPP (continued)

```cpp
        // write the image
        XbmEncoder enc( f );
        enc.init();
        for( int i=0; i<nrows; i++ )
        {
            vga.getscanline( scanln, ncols, x1, y1+i );
            // convert to mono
            for( int j=0; j<ncols; j++ )
            {
                int lu = vgapal[ scanln[j] ].graylevel();
                scanln[j] = (lu > threshold) ? 1 : 0;
            }
            enc.encode( scanln, ncols );
        }
        enc.term();

        int retv = ferror( f );
        fclose( f );
        delete scanln;
        delete [] vgapal;
        return retv ? xIOERROR : xOKAY;
    }

    //.................Write an image to XBM file 'fn'

    int WriteXBM( ImgStore& img, rgb *pal, char *fn )
    {
        // image metrics
        int nrows = img.height();
        int ncols = img.width();
        int ncolors = 2;
        if( img.depth() == 24 ) ncolors = 0;
        else if( img.depth() > 1 ) ncolors = 256;

        // scan line buffer
        unsigned char *scanln = new unsigned char [ncols];
        if( scanln == 0 )
            return xNOMEMORY;

        // XBM output file
        FILE *f = fopen( fn, "wt" );

        // initialize and write the XBM header
        char name[16];
        xtrname( fn, name );
        XBMHEADER xbm( ncols, nrows, name );
        xbm.put( f );
```

Listing 14.5 WRTXBM.CPP (continued)

```cpp
    // write the image
    XbmEncoder enc( f );
    enc.init();
    for( int i=0; i<nrows; i++ )
    {
        unsigned char *p = img.get(i);

        // convert to monochrome
        if( ncolors == 0 )
        {
            int n = 0;
            for( int j=0; j<ncols; j++ )
            {
                rgb X( p[n++], p[n++], p[n++] );
                scanln[j] = (X.graylevel() > threshold) ? 1 : 0;
            }
        }
        else
        {
            for( int j=0; j<ncols; j++ )
            {
                int lu = pal[ p[j] ].graylevel();
                scanln[j] = (lu > threshold) ? 1 : 0;
            }
        }

        enc.encode( scanln, ncols );
    }
    enc.term();

    int retv = ferror( f );
    fclose( f );
    return retv ? xIOERROR : xOKAY;
}
```

Listing 14.6 XBMDEMO.CPP

```cpp
//----------------------------------------------------------//
//                                                          //
//   File:    XBMDEMO.CPP                                   //
//                                                          //
//   Desc:    Example code to write a XBM file              //
//                                                          //
//----------------------------------------------------------//

#include "wrtxbm.cpp"
```

Listing 14.6 XBMDEMO.CPP (continued)

```cpp
char *        palname    = "EL-GRECO.PAL";
char *        imgname    = "EL-GRECO.IMG";
int           imgwidth   = 354;
int           imgheight  = 446;
int           imgcolors  = 256;
rgb           imgpalette[256];
unsigned char scanline[354];
CnvImgStore img( 446, 354, 8 );

// read the test image's palette

void read_palette( void )
{
    FILE *f = fopen( palname, "rt" );
    for( int i=0; i<imgcolors; i++ )
    {
        int r, g, b;
        fscanf( f, "%d %d %d", &r, &g, &b );
        imgpalette[i] = rgb( r, g, b );
    }
    fclose( f );
}

// read the test image into memory

void read_image( void )
{
    FILE *f = fopen( imgname, "rb" );
    for( int i=0; i<imgheight; i++ )
    {
        fread( scanline, imgwidth, 1, f );
        img.put( scanline, i );
    }
    fclose( f );
}

// output a XBM file

int main( void )
{
    read_palette( );

    read_image( );

    WriteXBM( img, imgpalette, "LADY" );

    return 0;
}
```

This concludes our look at the X bitmap format. It is a simple format, never intended as a general-purpose graphics-interchange format. Most X applications use EPS or TIFF as their native format. However, X supplies a number of standard tools, including a bitmap editor, that work with the format, and the X run-time library provides functions that also support the format. For the developer dealing directly with X and its bitmap format, the code in this chapter is potentially quite useful.

Part Three

Complex Bitmapped Formats

15

The CompuServe GIF Format

CompuServe's Graphics Interchange Format, GIF for short, is one of the most widely known and widely supported of all bitmapped graphics file formats. Of the formats covered in this book, only the PCX format comes close to GIF in popularity, and it would make an interesting trivia question to ask which is the most prevalent. Much of the format's success derives from CompuServe itself, which is surely the most famous of all on-line BBS systems.

CompuServe has gone to considerable lengths to control the GIF format and its dissemination. GIF is one of a very few formats that have been formally copy-righted. Fortunately, there are no serious strings attached to the format's use—all you need to do to use the format is acknowledge CompuServe's copyright in any printed documentation.

The GIF format is moderately complex as graphics formats go. Much of this complexity is a result of its being designed for optimal handling in telecommunications settings, specifically transmission via modem. When the format first appeared, 300-baud modems were still common and 2400-baud modems were quite expensive. Anything that could be done to shorten transmission times was generally employed. To that end, the GIF format was designed to use LZW compression, to support image interlacing, and to employ a packet-oriented structure, among other things.

The original GIF specification was published in 1987 and is referred to as version 87a of the format. A format revision was published two years later and is known as version 89a. To the best of my knowledge there have been no further revisions. The 89a version contributes various extensions to the previous 87a version without altering any of that format's specifics, so 89a is a true superset of 87a. The full 89a specification is documented in this chapter, but all code to write the format will be restricted to the 87a version. There are a couple reasons for this.

As it turns out, the original 87a format version defines a data protocol for format extensions but does not define any specific extensions. These were all added in the 89a version. Any format decoder that properly implements the 87a specification should be able to read version 89a files and should simply skip any extensions. However, many such decoders look for the 87a format string in a GIF file's header as part of the file verification process and typically will not process an 89a file.

Also, most of the 89a extensions are irrelevant if the format is used simply as a storage medium for a single bitmapped image. The extensions define such things as textual annotation for an image, comments of a noncritical nature, and the manner in which interactions with the user of a GIF viewer are to be handled. These are primarily of interest if the intent is to create a kind of interactive slide show from a GIF file.

A Format Overview

The GIF format supports a number of optional format extensions, so the definition of a typical GIF file is necessarily somewhat vague. However, the 87a version of the format defines what might be termed a **minimal format implementation**. A compliant file will contain at least the following components, in the order listed:

- A file header
- A logical screen descriptor
- A global color map (optional, but usually present)
- One or more image definitions
- A file trailer

An image definition is itself a multicomponent structure, consisting of the following items:

- A logical image descriptor
- A local color table (optional, and usually omitted)
- Compressed image data

Image definitions are repeated as necessary, one following another. They appear in a file following the screen descriptor and global color table but precede the file trailer. The file trailer serves to mark the end of a GIF data stream and therefore implies the end of file as well. The diagrams presented in Figures 15.1 and 15.2 illustrate this layout schematically.

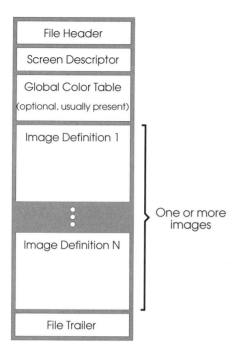

Figure 15.1 Minimal GIF File Structure

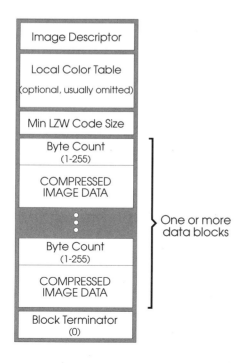

Figure 15.2 GIF Image Definition Structure

The **global color table** (GCT) and **local color table** (LCT) both define image palettes. The GCT possesses file scope and represents a default palette. If an image definition lacks a local color table then the global table is used. When an LCT is present, it applies to the accompanying image only. Most single-image files define a GCT and omit the LCT. GIF palettes are defined as arrays of RGB triples. Primary intensities possess values in the range 0 to 255 and are represented as an 8-bit unsigned quantity.

Version 89a files use the same basic format definition as described for version 87a, but may also include one or more format extensions. I will cover the specifics of each of the defined extensions in some detail a little later, but for now it suffices to note that all format extensions have the same overall structure. This structure is presented schematically in Figure 15.3.

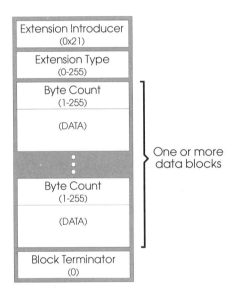

Figure 15.3 GIF Extension Block Structure

Figures 15.2 and 15.3 illustrate the two types of data blocks that can be found in a GIF file, image blocks and extension blocks. Both are formatted as packets varying from 1 to 256 bytes in length and both consist of a 1-byte data-count field followed by 0 to 255 bytes of data. A sequence of data blocks is always terminated by a zero-length packet, which consists of a single byte with the value zero. When writing code to process a sequence of blocks, be sure to structure it so that it terminates only when a zero-length block is encountered.

Image data are compressed using a modified LZW algorithm, which was discussed in detail in Chapter 3. Images can consist of pixels of any size from 1 to 8 bits, but are always encoded as a series of byte values. For example, a monochrome image that is 640 pixels wide will be encoded as scan lines of 640 bytes in size where each byte will possess the value 0 or 1.

Base Format Structures

In this section, we will take a look at the GIF format structures that are common to both the 87a and 89a format versions. This includes all structures illustrated in Figures 15.1 and 15.2, which represent the minimal requirements for a GIF file containing a single bitmapped image. Source code implementations of each structure can be found later in this chapter in Listings 15.1 and 15.2.

The GIF File Header

The GIF file header is quite simple, consisting of only two 3-byte fields. Its purpose is to validate a GIF file and determine the format version used. As a general rule, if you create a file that does not use any of the 89a extensions, then its format string should indicate 87a, even though 89a is the most current format version.

`sig`	3-byte string consisting of the ASCII characters `GIF`. Identifies the file as a GIF file.
`ver`	3-byte string indicating the format version of the file. Valid values are `87a` and `89a`.

The GIF File Trailer

The trailer structure of a GIF file is used to mark the end of a GIF data stream. It should be interpreted to mean end of file. It consists of a single byte with the value 3Bh, which is the ASCII code for a semicolon.

The Logical Screen Descriptor

The logical screen descriptor contains information about the physical display and video mode for which the GIF file's image is intended. It is used primarily to determine if the file contains a global color table, and if so, the number of entries (colors) in the table.

scwidth	Width of the physical display in pixels. For VGA mode 12h, for example, this value is 640. Note that this field does *not* indicate the width of an image.
scheight	Height of the physical display in pixels. For VGA mode 12h, for example, this value is 480. Note that this field does *not* indicate the height of an image.
flags	8-bit quantity containing four subfields. The four field definitions are as follow:

Bit(s)	Description
7	This bit is set to indicate the presence of a global color table.
4–6	A 3-bit subfield indicating the number of bits per pixel required by the video mode, minus 1. Three bits on, for example, is the value 7 and indicates 8 bits per pixel. This field is frequently set incorrectly and should be ignored in practice.
3	This bit is set to indicate that the global color table is sorted in order of color importance. It can be used, for example, in selecting a subset of the available palette for displaying an image in a video mode having fewer available colors than the image requires.
0–2	A 3-bit subfield that indicates the number of entries in the global color table. It is interpreted as a base-two exponent minus 1. For example, 3 bits on is the value 7, representing an exponent of 8, and 2^8 is 256. This value is then multiplied by 3 to determine the size of the GCT in bytes.

bgclr	8-bit quantity indicating the screen background color for all subsequent images; applies only to pixels outside the image area. If this value is nonzero, the screen can be filled with this color before an image is drawn.
pixasp	8-bit quantity that indicates the approximate pixel aspect ratio of images in the file. If this field is nonzero it indicates the approximate ratio of pixel width to pixel height as the quantity (pixasp + 15) / 64. Values of 1 to 255 yield approximate ratios in the range 1:4 to 4:1.

The Logical Image Descriptor

The logical image descriptor contains information describing a local color table and encoded image that immediately follow it in the GIF data stream. Note that the LCT is optional and is frequently omitted.

`id`	Byte value that identifies the structure as a logical screen descriptor; value is 2Ch, the ASCII code for a comma.
`xleft`	Screen pixel position of the left edge of the image.
`ytop`	Screen pixel position of the top edge of the image.
`imwidth`	Width of the image in pixels.
`imheight`	Height of the image in pixels.
`flags`	8-bit value containing five subfields, as follow:

Bit(s)	Description
7	This bit is set to indicate the presence of a local color table.
6	This bit is set to indicate that the image is interlaced. If set, then the scan lines in the image are presented in the following order: every 8 starting with row 1, every 8 starting with row 5, every 4 starting with row 2, and every 2 starting with row 2. In this description, rows are numbered starting with 1.
5	This bit is set to indicate that the image's local color table is sorted in order of color importance. It can be used, for example, in selecting a subset of the available palette for displaying an image in a video mode having available fewer colors than the image requires.
4–3	These bits are reserved and should be set to zero.
2–0	A 3-bit quantity indicating the number of entries in the local color table, if it is present. It is interpreted as a base-two exponent minus 1. For example, 3 bits on is the value 7, representing an exponent of 8, and 2^8 is 256. This value is then multiplied by 3 to determine the size of the GCT in bytes.

Version 89a Extensions

Version 89a of the GIF format adds a number of data extensions to the format definition. While version 87a defines the structure of an extension, it does not, in fact, define any specific extensions. As noted, if the format is being used solely as a storage medium for a bitmapped image, then none of these extensions is required and all can be omitted.

All extensions use the structure illustrated in Figure 15.3. All extensions begin with similar 3-byte prefixes that (1) identify the structure as an extension, (2) identify the type of extension, and (3) indicate the number of data bytes in the first data block of the extension. The size member is in some cases actually the start of a data block that follows the extension. See the comment extension in the next section for an example of this.

Control Extensions

This extension type is used to control the display of images in a multi-image file. It indicates how the image is to be removed (that is, erased), whether or not to wait for a keystroke from the keyboard before continuing, and how long to display the image if there is no wait for user input. When present, a control extension must precede the image definition to which it applies. It only affects the first image definition that follows it.

id	Byte value identifying this as a GIF extension; the value 21h, which is the ASCII code for an exclamation mark.
label	Byte value identifying the type of extension; for a control extension this is the value F9h.
size	Number of bytes remaining in the extension header, but not including any required data blocks that may follow an extension. For a control extension this is the value 4.
flags	8-bit quantity containing four subfields, as follow:

Bit(s)	Description
5–7	A 3-bit reserved field that should be set to zero and ignored.
2–4	A 3-bit value indicating a disposal method, (that is, how the image is to be removed after it is viewed). Four possible values are defined: 0—no method specified; 1—leave the image on the screen; 2—erase the image area to the background color; and

		3—restore the image area to what was showing before it was drawn.
	1	A 1-bit user input flag. If this bit is set, then the program should wait for user input before continuing. The kind of input—key press, mouse press, and so on—is left to the application's discretion.
	0	A 1-bit transparency flag. If set, this flag enables the use of the transparency index (see `trclr`).
delay		16-bit unsigned value that indicates a delay time in thousandths of a second. If this value is nonzero, the accompanying image should be displayed for this amount of time before being removed. If the user input flag is also set, then processing resumes whenever either condition is met.
trclr		8-bit transparency index. If the transparency bit of `flags` is set then image pixels of this value should not be drawn, thus allowing portions of the screen's underimage to show through.

Comment Extensions

Comment extensions are used to add textual information to a GIF file. This can include such things as an author, a title for an image, and so forth. The actual format of comments is not specified. Typically, however, they consist of ASCII text imbedded with carriage-return characters to indicate hard returns.

| id | Byte value identifying this as a GIF extension; the value 21h, which is the ASCII code for an exclamation mark. |
| label | Byte value identifying the type of extension. For a comment extension, this is the value FEh. |

Text Extensions

Text extensions are used to add text to an image itself for annotation or other purposes. A GIF viewer must therefore be able to draw text in graphics mode in order to support this extension type. All such text is assumed to use fixed-pitch character spacing. The actual character string for a text extension immediately follows the extension as a data block of 1 to 255 characters preceded by a 1-byte character count.

`id`	Byte value identifying this as a GIF extension; the value 21h, which is the ASCII code for an exclamation mark.
`label`	Byte value identifying the type of extension. For a text extension, this is the value 01h.
`size`	Number of bytes remaining in the extension header, but not including any required data blocks that may follow. For a text extension, this is always the value 12.
`xleft`	Left edge of the bounding rectangle of the text string expressed in pixels.
`ytop`	Top edge of the bounding rectangle of the text string expressed in pixel coordinates.
`txwidth`	Width of the bounding rectangle of the text string expressed in pixel units.
`txheight`	Height of the bounding rectangle of the text string expressed in pixel units.
`cewidth`	Character cell width in pixel units.
`ceheight`	Character cell height in pixel units.
`fgclr`	Foreground color pixel value for the graphics text.
`bgclr`	Background color pixel value for the graphics text.

Application Extensions

Application extensions provide a mechanism for adding application-specific information to a GIF file. What such information might be or how it is to be interpreted is not specified. Application-specific data are presumed to follow this extension using the standard data-block format and are terminated by a zero-length block terminator.

`id`	Byte value identifying this as a GIF extension; the value 21h, which is the ASCII code for an exclamation mark.
`label`	Byte value identifying the type of extension. For an application extension, this is the value FFh.
`size`	Number of bytes remaining in the extension header, but not including any required data blocks that may follow. For an application extension, this is always the value 11.
`apname`	8-byte printable ASCII string that identifies the application.
`apcode`	3-byte code, possibly binary, that is used by an application to authenticate the extension as belonging to it.

Listing 15.1 GIF.HPP

```
//---------------------------------------------------------//
//                                                         //
//    File:    GIF.HPP                                     //
//                                                         //
//    Desc:    Structure and Class definitions for        //
//             CompuServe's GIF Format, Version 89a        //
//                                                         //
//---------------------------------------------------------//

#ifndef _GIF_HPP_
#define _GIF_HPP_

#include "stdlib.h"
#include "stdio.h"
#include "string.h"
#include "ctype.h"
#include "iostream.h"

#include "codec.hpp"
#include "color.hpp"

//.................struct GIFHEADER

struct GIFHEADER              // GIF File Header
{
   char sig[3];               // "GIF"
   char ver[3];               // "87a" or "89a"
   GIFHEADER( )
   {
      sig[0] = 'G';
      sig[1] = 'I';
      sig[2] = 'F';
      ver[0] = '8';
      ver[1] = '9';
      ver[2] = 'a';
   }
  ~GIFHEADER( )
   {
   }
   void list( void );
   int  get( FILE *f );
   int  put( FILE *f );
   int  isvalid( void );
};

//.................struct GIFSCDESC
```

Listing 15.1 GIF.HPP (continued)

```cpp
#define scdGCT        0x80     // global color table
#define scdGCTCRES    0x70     // color res : nbits-1
#define scdGCTSORT    0x08     // sort flag
#define scdGCTSIZE    0x07     // color cnt as 2^(sss+1)

struct GIFSCDESC               // Screen Descriptor
{
   unsigned short scwidth;     // width in pixels
   unsigned short scheight;    // height in pixels
   unsigned char  flags;       // various flags
   unsigned char  bgclr;       // background color
   unsigned char  pixasp;      // pixel aspect ratio
   GIFSCDESC( )
   {
      scwidth = scheight = 0;
      flags = bgclr = pixasp = 0;
   }
   GIFSCDESC( int w, int h, int d )
   {
      scwidth  = w;
      scheight = h;
      flags = scdGCT | ((d-1)<<4) | (d-1);
      bgclr = pixasp = 0;
   }
   ~GIFSCDESC( )
   {
   }
   void list( void );
   int get( FILE *f );
   int put( FILE *f );
   int isgct( void )
   {
      return (flags & scdGCT) ? 1 : 0;
   }
   int issorted( void )
   {
      return (flags & scdGCTSORT) ? 1 : 0;
   }
   int depth( void )    // bits per pixel
   {
      return ((flags & scdGCTCRES) >> 4) + 1;
   }
   int ncolors( void )  // # entries in GCT
   {
      return 1 << ((flags & scdGCTSIZE) + 1);
   }
};
```

Listing 15.1 GIF.HPP (continued)

```cpp
//................struct GIFIMDESC

#define imdLCT       0x80     // local color table
#define imdINTRLACE  0x40     // interlace flag
#define imdLCTSORT   0x20     // sort flag
#define imdRESV      0x18     // reserved
#define imdLCTSIZE   0x07     // color cnt as 2^(sss+1)

struct GIFIMDESC               // Image Descriptor
{
   unsigned char  id;        // 0x2C
   unsigned short xleft;     // x origin
   unsigned short ytop;      // y origin
   unsigned short imwidth;   // image width
   unsigned short imheight;  // image height
   unsigned char  flags;     // various flags
   GIFIMDESC( )
   {
      id = 0x2C;
      xleft = ytop = 0;
      imwidth = imheight = 0;
      flags = 0;
   }
   GIFIMDESC( int w, int h, int d )
   {
      id = 0x2C;
      xleft = ytop = 0;
      imwidth = w;
      imheight = h;
      flags = 0;
   }
  ~GIFIMDESC( )
   {
   }
   void list( void );
   int  get( FILE *f );
   int  put( FILE *f );
   int islct( void )
   {
      return (flags & imdLCT) ? 1 : 0;
   }
   int issorted( void )
   {
      return (flags & imdLCTSORT) ? 1 : 0;
   }
   int isinterlaced( void )
```

Listing 15.1 GIF.HPP (continued)

```cpp
    {
        return (flags & imdINTRLACE) ? 1 : 0;
    }
    int ncolors( void )  // # entries in LCT
    {
        if( islct() )
            return 1 << ((flags & imdLCTSIZE) + 1);
        return 0;
    }
};

//.................struct GIFCTLEXT

#define ctlRESV      0xE0    // reserved
#define ctlDISPOSE   0x1C    // disposal method
#define ctlINPUT     0x02    // user input flag
#define ctlTRANSPAR  0x01    // transparency flag

struct GIFCTLEXT                 // Control Extension
{
    unsigned char  id;           // 0x21 - extension
    unsigned char  label;        // 0xF9 - extension type
    unsigned char  size;         // always 4
    unsigned char  flags;        // various flags
    unsigned short delay;        // 1/100th seconds
    unsigned char  trclr;        // transparency color
    GIFCTLEXT( )
    {
        id = 0x21;
        label = 0xF9;
        flags = trclr = 0;
        delay = 0;
    }
    ~GIFCTLEXT( )
    {
    }
    void list( void );
    int  get( FILE *f );
    int  put( FILE *f );
};

//.................struct GIFCOMEXT

struct GIFCOMEXT                 // Comment Extension
{
    unsigned char  id;           // 0x21 - extension
    unsigned char  label;        // 0xFE - extension type
    GIFCOMEXT( )
```

Listing 15.1 GIF.HPP (continued)

```cpp
       {
          id = 0x21;
          label = 0xFE;
       }
    ~GIFCOMEXT( )
       {
       }
    void list( void );
    int  get( FILE *f );
    int  put( FILE *f );
};

//................struct GIFTXTEXT

struct GIFTXTEXT                // Text Extension
{
    unsigned char  id;          // 0x21 - extension
    unsigned char  label;       // 0x01 - extension type
    unsigned char  size;        // always 12
    unsigned short xleft;       // x origin
    unsigned short ytop;        // y origin
    unsigned short txwidth;     // text width
    unsigned short txheight;    // text height
    unsigned char  cewidth;     // cell width
    unsigned char  ceheight;    // cell height
    unsigned char  fgclr;       // foreground color
    unsigned char  bgclr;       // background color
    GIFTXTEXT( )
       {
          id = 0x21;
          label = 0x01;
          size = 12;
          xleft = ytop = 0;
          txwidth = txheight = 0;
          cewidth = ceheight = 0;
          fgclr = bgclr = 0;
       }
    ~GIFTXTEXT( )
       {
       }
    void list( void );
    int  get( FILE *f );
    int  put( FILE *f );
};

//................struct GIFAPPEXT
```

Listing 15.1 GIF.HPP (continued)

```cpp
struct GIFAPPEXT                 // Application Extension
{
    unsigned char  id;           // 0x21 - extension
    unsigned char  label;        // 0xFF - extension type
    unsigned char  size;         // always 11
    char           apname[8];    // application name
    char           apcode[3];    // application code
    GIFAPPEXT( )
    {
        id = 0x21;
        label = 0xFF;
        size = 11;
        memset( apname, 0, 8 );
        memset( apcode, 0, 3 );
    }
    ~GIFAPPEXT( )
    {
    }
    void list( void );
    int  get( FILE *f );
    int  put( FILE *f );
};

#endif
```

Listing 15.2 GIF.CPP

```cpp
//-----------------------------------------------------------//
//                                                           //
//   File:   GIF.CPP                                         //
//                                                           //
//   Desc:   Structure and Class definitions for            //
//           CompuServe's GIF Format, Version 89a            //
//                                                           //
//-----------------------------------------------------------//

#include "gif.hpp"

//.................struct GIFHEADER

void GIFHEADER::list( void )
{
    printf( "GIFHEADER::sig = %c%c%c\n",
            sig[0], sig[1], sig[2] );
    printf( "GIFHEADER::ver = %c%c%c\n",
            ver[0], ver[1], ver[2] );
}
```

Listing 15.2 GIF.CPP (continued)

```cpp
int GIFHEADER::get( FILE *f )
{
   return (fread( sig, sizeof(GIFHEADER), 1, f ) == 1) ?
      0 : -1;
}

int GIFHEADER::put( FILE *f )
{
   return (fwrite( sig, sizeof(GIFHEADER), 1, f ) == 1) ?
      0 : -1;
}

int GIFHEADER::isvalid( void )
{
   if( strncmp( sig, "GIF", 3 ) != 0 )
      return 0;
   if( (strncmp( ver, "87a", 3 ) != 0) &&
       (strncmp( ver, "89a", 3 ) != 0) )
      return 0;
   return 1;
}

//................struct GIFSCDESC

void GIFSCDESC::list( void )
{
   printf( "GIFSCDESC::scwidth  = %d\n", scwidth );
   printf( "GIFSCDESC::scheight = %d\n", scheight );
   printf( "GIFSCDESC::flags    = %02Xh\n", flags );
   printf( "           gct?      = %c\n",
         isgct() ? 'Y' : 'N' );
   printf( "           sorted?   = %c\n",
         issorted() ? 'Y' : 'N' );
   printf( "           depth     = %d\n", depth() );
   printf( "           ncolors   = %d\n", ncolors() );
   printf( "GIFSCDESC::pixasp    = %d\n", pixasp );
}

int GIFSCDESC::get( FILE *f )
{
   return (fread( &scwidth, sizeof(GIFSCDESC), 1, f ) == 1) ?
      0 : -1;
}
```

Listing 15.2 GIF.CPP (continued)

```cpp
int GIFSCDESC::put( FILE *f )
{
    return (fwrite( &scwidth, sizeof(GIFSCDESC), 1, f ) == 1) ?
        0 : -1;
}

//................struct GIFIMDESC

void GIFIMDESC::list( void )
{
    printf( "GIFIMDESC::id        = %02Xh\n", id );
    printf( "GIFIMDESC::xleft     = %d\n", xleft );
    printf( "GIFIMDESC::ytop      = %d\n", ytop );
    printf( "GIFIMDESC::imwidth   = %d\n", imwidth );
    printf( "GIFIMDESC::imheight  = %d\n", imheight );
    printf( "GIFIMDESC::flags     = %02Xh\n", flags );
    printf( "          lct?       = %c\n",
            islct() ? 'Y' : 'N' );
    printf( "          sorted?    = %c\n",
            issorted() ? 'Y' : 'N' );
    printf( "          interlaced? = %c\n",
            isinterlaced() ? 'Y' : 'N' );
    printf( "          ncolors    = %d\n", ncolors() );
}

int GIFIMDESC::get( FILE *f )
{
    // assume id has already been read
    return (fread( &xleft, sizeof(GIFIMDESC)-1, 1, f ) == 1)
        ? 0 : -1;
}

int GIFIMDESC::put( FILE *f )
{
    return (fwrite( &id, sizeof(GIFIMDESC), 1, f ) == 1)
        ? 0 : -1;
}

//................struct GIFCTLEXT

void GIFCTLEXT::list( void )
{
    printf( "GIFCTLEXT::id    = %02Xh\n", id );
    printf( "GIFCTLEXT::label = %02Xh\n", label );
    printf( "GIFCTLEXT::size  = %d\n", size );
    printf( "GIFCTLEXT::flags = %02Xh\n", flags );
    printf( "GIFCTLEXT::delay = %d\n", delay );
    printf( "GIFCTLEXT::trclr = %d\n", trclr );
}
```

Listing 15.2 GIF.CPP (continued)

```cpp
int GIFCTLEXT::get( FILE *f )
{
   // assume id-label has already been read
   return (fread( &size, sizeof(GIFCTLEXT)-2, 1, f ) == 1)
          ? 0 : -1;
}

int GIFCTLEXT::put( FILE *f )
{
   return (fwrite( &id, sizeof(GIFCTLEXT), 1, f ) == 1)
          ? 0 : -1;
}

//.................struct GIFCOMEXT

void GIFCOMEXT::list( void )
{
   printf( "GIFCOMEXT::id    = %02Xh\n", id );
   printf( "GIFCOMEXT::label = %02Xh\n", label );
}

int GIFCOMEXT::get( FILE *f )
{
   // assume id-label has already been read
   return 0;
}

int GIFCOMEXT::put( FILE *f )
{
   return (fwrite( &id, sizeof(GIFCOMEXT), 1, f ) == 1)
          ? 0 : -1;
}

//.................struct GIFTXTEXT

void GIFTXTEXT::list( void )
{
   printf( "GIFTXTEXT::id       = %02Xh\n", id );
   printf( "GIFTXTEXT::label    = %02Xh\n", label );
   printf( "GIFTXTEXT::size     = %d\n", size );
   printf( "GIFTXTEXT::xleft    = %d\n", xleft );
   printf( "GIFTXTEXT::ytop     = %d\n", ytop );
   printf( "GIFTXTEXT::txwidth  = %d\n", txwidth );
   printf( "GIFTXTEXT::txheight = %d\n", txheight );
   printf( "GIFTXTEXT::cewidth  = %d\n", cewidth );
   printf( "GIFTXTEXT::ceheight = %d\n", ceheight );
   printf( "GIFTXTEXT::fgclr    = %d\n", fgclr );
   printf( "GIFTXTEXT::bgclr    = %d\n", bgclr );
}
```

Listing 15.2 GIF.CPP (continued)

```cpp
int GIFTXTEXT::get( FILE *f )
{
    // assume id-label has already been read
    return (fread( &size, sizeof(GIFTXTEXT)-2, 1, f ) == 1)
          ? 0 : -1;
}

int GIFTXTEXT::put( FILE *f )
{
    return (fwrite( &id, sizeof(GIFTXTEXT), 1, f ) == 1)
          ? 0 : -1;
}

//................struct GIFAPPEXT

void GIFAPPEXT::list( void )
{
    printf( "GIFAPPEXT::id       = %02Xh\n", id );
    printf( "GIFAPPEXT::label    = %02Xh\n", label );
    printf( "GIFAPPEXT::size     = %d\n", size );
    printf( "GIFAPPEXT::apname   = " );
    for( int i=0; i<sizeof(apname); i++ )
       printf( "%c", apname[i] );
    printf( "\n" );
    printf( "GIFAPPEXT::apcode   = " );
    printf( "%d.%d.%d",
            apcode[0], apcode[1], apcode[2] );
    printf( "\n" );
}

int GIFAPPEXT::get( FILE *f )
{
    // assume id-label has already been read
    return (fread( &size, sizeof(GIFAPPEXT)-2, 1, f ) == 1)
          ? 0 : -1;
}

int GIFAPPEXT::put( FILE *f )
{
    return (fwrite( &id, sizeof(GIFAPPEXT), 1, f ) == 1)
          ? 0 : -1;
}
```

A GIF Query Program

Given the intricate structure of GIF files, a query program for the format is quite a useful accessory. Listing 15.3 presents the source code to a suitable example of such a program. In its particulars it follows the same basic design as the other query programs that have been implemented in this book.

The program takes advantage of the packet-oriented structure of GIF data and extension blocks by skipping over these blocks rather than reading them. This is done by reading the block-size field and then seeking that number of bytes forward in the file to locate the next block or structure.

Listing 15.3 QGIF.CPP

```cpp
//------------------------------------------------------//
//                                                      //
//    File:     QGIF.CPP                                //
//                                                      //
//    Desc:     GIF File Query Program                  //
//                                                      //
//------------------------------------------------------//

#include "stdlib.h"
#include "stdio.h"
#include "string.h"
#include "conio.h"

#include "gif.hpp"

//.................program globals

char fn[80],
     dumpfn[80];

int  listpal,
     dump;

//.................program usage
void explain_pgm( void )
{
   printf( "\n" );
   printf( ".............GIF Query Program.............\n" );
   printf( "\n" );
   printf( "Usage:      QGIF  gif_file  [ switches ]\n" );
   printf( "\n" );
   printf( "Switches:  -dXXX  = dump image to file XXX\n" );
   printf( "           -h     = display program usage\n" );
   printf( "           -p     = display palette (clr tbl)\n" );
   printf( "\n" );
```

Listing 15.3 QGIF.CPP (continued)

```cpp
        printf( ".GIF extension assumed\n" );
        printf( "..............................................\n" );
        printf( "\n" );
    }


//.................process args

void process_args( int argc, char *argv[] )
{
    // establish default values
    fn[0]     = 0;
    dumpfn[0] = 0;
    listpal   = 0;
    dump      = 0;

    // process the program's argument list
    for( int i=1; i<argc; i++ )
    {
        if( (*argv[i] == '-') || (*argv[i] == '/') )
        {
            char sw = *(argv[i] + 1);
            switch( toupper(sw) )
            {
                case 'D' :
                    dump = 1;
                    strcpy( dumpfn, argv[i]+2 );
                    break;

                case 'H' :
                    explain_pgm();
                    exit( 0 );
                    break;

                case 'P' :
                    listpal = 1;
                    break;

                default:
                    printf( "Unknown switch '%s' ignored\n",
                            argv[i] );
                    break;
            }
        }
        else  // presumably a file identifier
        {
            strcpy( fn, argv[i] );
            char *p = strchr( fn, '.' );
            if( p == 0 )
```

Listing 15.3 QGIF.CPP (continued)

```cpp
                    strcat( fn, ".gif" );
                else if( *(p+1) == 0 )
                    *p = 0;
            }
        }

        // was a file name specified?
        if( fn[0] == 0 )
        {
            explain_pgm();
            exit( 0 );
        }
    }

//.................skip data blocks

void skip_blocks( FILE *f )
{
    int nbytes;
    while( (nbytes=fgetc(f)) > 0 )
        fseek( f, nbytes, SEEK_CUR );
}

//.................copy data blocks

void copy_blocks( FILE *fi, FILE *fo )
{
    int nbytes;
    do
    {
        nbytes = fgetc( fi );
        fputc( nbytes, fo );
        for( int i=0; i<nbytes; i++ )
            fputc( fgetc(fi), fo );
    }
    while( nbytes > 0 );
}

//.................list comment blocks

static int nbytes=0;
```

Listing 15.3 QGIF.CPP (continued)

```cpp
int getcomchar( FILE *f )
{
   if( nbytes < 1 )
   {
      nbytes = fgetc( f );
      if( nbytes < 1 )
         return 0;
   }
   nbytes--;
   return fgetc( f );
}
void list_comments( FILE *f )
{
   char word[256];
   int  c, nch=0, nco=0;
   while( (c = getcomchar( f )) > 0 )
   {
      if( c > ' ' )
      {
         word[nch++] = c;
         if( nch == 255 )
         {
            word[nch] = 0;
            printf( "%s\n", word );
            nco = 0;
         }
      }
      else
      {
         if( nch > 0 )
         {
            if( (nco+nch) > 78 )
            {
               printf( "\n" );
               nco = 0;
            }
            word[nch] = 0;
            printf( "%s", word );
            nco += nch;
            nch = 0;
         }
         if( c == ' ' )
         {
            printf( " " );
            nco++;
         }
```

Listing 15.3 QGIF.CPP (continued)

```cpp
            else if( (c == 13) || (c == 10) )
            {
                printf( "\n" );
                nco = 0;
            }
        }
    }
}

//................process image description

void do_image( FILE *f )
{
    GIFIMDESC imd;
    if( imd.get( f ) )
    {
        printf( "Error reading GIF image descriptot\n" );
        exit( 0 );
    }
    imd.list();
    printf( "\n" );
    // process local color table
    if( imd.islct() )
    {
        for( int i=0; i<imd.ncolors(); i++ )
        {
            int r = fgetc( f );
            int g = fgetc( f );
            int b = fgetc( f );
            if( listpal )
                printf( "LCT[%d] = (%d,%d,%d)\n",
                        i, r, g, b );
        }
        if( listpal ) printf( "\n" );
    }

    // read min LZW code size
    int size = fgetc( f );
    printf( "Minimum LZW code size = %d\n", size );
    printf( "\n" );

    if( dump )
    {
        printf( "Dumping image to %s...", dumpfn );
        FILE * fdump = fopen( dumpfn, "wb" );
        fwrite( &imd.imwidth, 2, 1, fdump );
        fwrite( &imd.imheight, 2, 1, fdump );
        fputc( size, fdump );
```

Listing 15.3 QGIF.CPP (continued)

```
            copy_blocks( f, fdump );
            fclose( fdump );
            printf( "done\n" );
            printf( "\n" );
        }
        else
            skip_blocks( f );

    }

    //................process control extension

    void do_ctl_ext( FILE *f )
    {
        GIFCTLEXT ctl;
        if( ctl.get( f ) )
        {
            printf( "Error reading GIF control extension\n" );
            exit( 0 );
        }
        ctl.list();
        printf( "\n" );
        skip_blocks( f );
    }

    //................process comment extension

    void do_com_ext( FILE *f )
    {
        GIFCOMEXT com;
        if( com.get( f ) )
        {
            printf( "Error reading GIF comment extension\n" );
            exit( 0 );
        }
        com.list();
        printf( "\n" );
        list_comments( f );
    }

    //................process text extension

    void do_txt_ext( FILE *f )
    {
        GIFTXTEXT txt;
        if( txt.get( f ) )
        {
            printf( "Error reading GIF text extension\n" );
```

Listing 15.3 QGIF.CPP (continued)

```cpp
        exit( 0 );
    }
    txt.list();
    printf( "\n" );
    skip_blocks( f );
}

//.................process application extension

void do_app_ext( FILE *f )
{
    GIFAPPEXT app;
    if( app.get( f ) )
    {
        printf( "Error reading GIF application extension\n" );
        exit( 0 );
    }
    app.list();
    printf( "\n" );
    skip_blocks( f );
}

//.................process extension

void do_extension( FILE *f )
{
    int label = fgetc( f );
    switch( label )
    {
        case 0xF9 : // control extension
            do_ctl_ext( f );
            break;

        case 0xFE : // comment extension
            do_com_ext( f );
            break;

        case 0x01 : // text extension
            do_txt_ext( f );
            break;

        case 0xFF : // application extension
            do_app_ext( f );
            break;

        default :   // unknown or invalid
            if( label < 0 )
                printf( "Error reading extension\n" );
```

Listing 15.3 QGIF.CPP (continued)

```cpp
            else
                printf( "Unknown or invalid extension %02Xh\n",
                        label );
            exit( 0 );
            break;
    }
}

//.................main

int main( int argc, char *argv[] )
{
    process_args( argc, argv );

    // open the file
    FILE *fgif = fopen( fn, "rb" );
    if( fgif == 0 )
    {
        printf( "File '%s' not found\n", fn );
        return 0;
    }

    // read header and screen descriptor
    GIFHEADER hdr;
    if( hdr.get( fgif ) )
    {
        printf( "Error reading GIF header\n" );
        exit( 0 );
    }
    if( ! hdr.isvalid() )
    {
        printf( "File is not a valid GIF file\n" );
        exit( 0 );
    }
    GIFSCDESC scd;
    if( scd.get( fgif ) )
    {
        printf( "Error reading GIF screen descriptor\n" );
        exit( 0 );
    }

    printf( "Listing of file '%s'\n", fn );
    printf( "\n" );
    hdr.list();
    printf( "\n" );
    scd.list();
    printf( "\n" );
```

Listing 15.3 QGIF.CPP (continued)

```cpp
// process global color table
if( scd.isgct() )
{
    for( int i=0; i<scd.ncolors(); i++ )
    {
        int r = fgetc( fgif );
        int g = fgetc( fgif );
        int b = fgetc( fgif );
        if( listpal )
            printf( "GCT[%d] = (%d,%d,%d)\n",
                    i, r, g, b );
    }
    if( listpal ) printf( "\n" );
}

// process remainder of file
int type;
while( (type=fgetc(fgif)) > 0 )
{
    if( type == 0x2C )      // image descriptor
        do_image( fgif );
    else if( type == 0x21 )  // extension
        do_extension( fgif );
    else if( type == 0x3B )  // trailer
    {
        printf( "..... End of Stream .....\n" );
        break;
    }
    else
    {
        printf( "Unknown type %02Xh\n", type );
        break;
    }
}

return 0;
}
```

Encoding and Decoding GIF Images

In Chapter 3, a detailed discussion was presented of the variant of the LZW compression algorithm that is employed by the GIF format. A compressor and decompressor was implemented for the algorithm. That implementation was designed primarily to make the workings of the algorithm as clear as possible, because the implementation of LZW is fairly complicated.

While a pseudocode description of LZW compression can be stated quite simply, the actual implementation of the algorithm can be quite a bear. In particular, the following three problems must be addressed:

1. The encoder performs many searches of a string table to determine if a given string is already in the table, and the table can become quite large. Some kind of rapid access by means of a hashing algorithm is required for acceptable performance.

2. Because of the way the string table is constructed, the decoder will decode strings backward, from end to beginning. The order of decoded strings must therefore be reversed. This is most easily accomplished using a stack. Pushing a character sequence onto a stack and then popping it off a character at time reverses the byte order of the sequence.

3. Strings are encoded using variable-length bit codes, which requires a great deal of bit shifting and masking. In a conceptual sense, what is required is file I/O one bit at a time, which is tricky to implement if good performance is to be obtained.

To address these problems more effectively, a second implementation of a GIF LZW codec is presented in Lising 15.4 and Listing 15.5. There are still many areas in which the code could be profitably optimized, but this version of the code is more amenable to such changes.

Listing 15.4 GIFCODEC.HPP

```
//----------------------------------------------------------//
//                                                          //
//    File:    GIFCODEC.HPP                                 //
//                                                          //
//    Desc:    Structure and Class definitions for          //
//             a GIF Coder and Decoder                      //
//                                                          //
//----------------------------------------------------------//

#ifndef _GIFCODEC_HPP_
#define _GIFCODEC_HPP_

#include "stdlib.h"
#include "stdio.h"
#include "string.h"
#include "ctype.h"
#include "iostream.h"

#include "codec.hpp"
#include "color.hpp"
```

Listing 15.4 GIFCODEC.HPP (continued)

```cpp
//................class BitString

#define MAXDIGITS ( (sizeof(int) * 8) + 1 )

class BitString
{
   protected :

      char str[MAXDIGITS];
   public :

      BitString( int bits, int width );
     ~BitString( ) { }
      char *rep( void ) { return str; }
};

inline ostream& operator << ( ostream& os, BitString& bs )
{
   return os << bs.rep();
}

//................class iCodeStream

class iCodeStream
{
   protected :

      FILE *        ifile;          // input file
      unsigned char buffer[255];    // data buffer
      int           nbytes;         // bytes in buffer
      int           curbyte;        // index of current byte
      int           nbits;          // current element width
      int           bytecode;       // last byte read
      int           bytemask;       // mask for bytecode
      int           bitcode;        // last bit code read
      int           bitmask;        // mask for bitcode

   private :

      int  getbyte( void );

   public :

      iCodeStream( FILE *f, int size );
      virtual ~iCodeStream( );
      int getcode( void );
      int lastcode( void )
```

Listing 15.4 GIFCODEC.HPP (continued)

```
          {
              return bitcode;
          }
          int width( void )
          {
              return nbits;
          }
          int width( int nb )
          {
            nbits = nb;
            return nbits;
          }
      };


//................class GifDecoder

class GifDecoder : public Decoder, public iCodeStream
{
    protected:
        int   cond;       // condition code
        int   nroots;     // 1 << pixelsize
        int   capacity;   // 1 << 12
        int   rwbytes;    // bytes per scan line

        int   minsize;    // code sizes
        int   cursize;
        int   maxsize;
        int   curcode;    // code values
        int   maxcode;

        int   newc;       // new code
        int   oldc;       // old code
        int   clrc;       // clear code
        int   endc;       // end code
        int   stkp;       // stack pointer

        int *          prefix;
        unsigned char * suffix;
        unsigned char * stack;
        unsigned char * bytes;

    private:
        void clear( void );
        int  push( int s );

    public:
        GifDecoder( FILE* infile, int cobits, int pxcnt );
        ~GifDecoder( );
```

Listing 15.4 GIFCODEC.HPP (continued)

```cpp
            virtual int init( void );
            virtual int term( void );
            virtual int decode( unsigned char *line, int size );
            virtual int status( void );
};

//................class oCodeStream

class oCodeStream
{
   protected :

       FILE *        ofile;          // output file
       unsigned char buffer[255];    // data buffer
       int           nbytes;         // bytes in buffer
       int           nbits;          // current element width
       int           bytecode;       // current output byte
       int           bytemask;       // mask for bytecode

   private :

       int putbyte( int byt );

   public :

       oCodeStream( FILE *f, int size );
       virtual ~oCodeStream( );
       int putcode( int code );
       int flush( void );
       int width( void )
       {
          return nbits;
       }
       int width( int nb )
       {
         nbits = nb;
         return nbits;
       }
};

//................class GifEncoder

class GifEncoder : public Encoder, public oCodeStream
{
   protected :
      int  cond;      // condition code
```

Listing 15.4 GIFCODEC.HPP (continued)

```
        int   started;    // semiphore flag
        int   nroots;     // 1 << pixelsize
        int   capacity;   // prime > (1<<12)

        int   minsize;    // code sizes
        int   cursize;
        int   maxsize;
        int   curcode;    // code values
        int   maxcode;

        int   strc;       // "string"
        int   chrc;       // "character"
        int   clrc;       // clear code
        int   endc;       // end code

        int * codes;
        int * prefix;
        int * suffix;

    private:
        void clear( void );
        int findstr( int pfx, int sfx );

    public:
        GifEncoder( FILE* outfile, int cobits );
        ~GifEncoder( );
        virtual int init( void );
        virtual int term( void );
        virtual int encode( unsigned char *line, int size );
        virtual int status( void );
    };


    #endif
```

Listing 15.5 GIFCODEC.CPP

```
    //----------------------------------------------------------//
    //                                                          //
    //    File:    GIFCODEC.CPP                                 //
    //                                                          //
    //    Desc:    Structure and Class definitions for          //
    //             a Gif Coder and Decoder                      //
    //                                                          //
    //----------------------------------------------------------//


    #include "gifcodec.hpp"

    //.................class BitString
```

Listing 15.5 GIFCODEC.CPP (continued)

```cpp
BitString::BitString( int bits, int width )
{
   int mask = 1 << width;
   for( int n=0; n<width; n++ )
   {
      mask >>= 1;
      str[n] = (bits & mask) ? '1' : '0';
   }
   str[width] = 0;
}

//.................class iCodeStream

iCodeStream::iCodeStream( FILE *f, int size )
{
   ifile = f;
   nbytes = curbyte = 0;
   nbits = size;
   bytecode = 0;
   bytemask = 0x80;
   bitcode = 0;
   bitmask = 0x01;
}

iCodeStream::~iCodeStream( )
{
}

int iCodeStream::getbyte( void )
{
   if( curbyte >= nbytes )
   {
      if( (nbytes = fgetc( ifile )) < 1 )
         return -1;
      if( fread( buffer, nbytes, 1, ifile ) != 1 )
         return -1;
      curbyte = 0;
   }
   return buffer[curbyte++];
}

int iCodeStream::getcode( void )
{
   bitcode = 0;
   bitmask = 1;
   int n = nbits;
   while( n-- > 0 )
```

Listing 15.5 GIFCODEC.CPP (continued)

```cpp
   {
      if( (bytemask<<=1) > 0x80 )
      {
         bytemask = 1;
         if( (bytecode = getbyte( )) < 0 )
            return -1;
      }
      if( bytecode & bytemask )
         bitcode |= bitmask;
      bitmask <<= 1;
   }
   return bitcode;
}

//.................class GifDecoder

GifDecoder::GifDecoder( FILE* infile, int cobits, int pxcnt ) :
            Decoder( ), iCodeStream( infile, cobits+1 )
{
   cond     = xOKAY;
   minsize  = cobits + 1;
   maxsize  = 12;
   nroots   = 1 << cobits;
   capacity = 1 << maxsize;
   rwbytes  = pxcnt;
   prefix   = new int [capacity];
   suffix   = new unsigned char [capacity];
   stack    = new unsigned char [capacity];
   bytes    = new unsigned char [rwbytes];
   if( ! prefix || ! suffix || ! stack || ! bytes )
      cond = xNOMEMORY;
   else
   {
      stkp = 0;
      clear( );
   }
}

GifDecoder::~GifDecoder( )
{
   delete prefix;
   delete suffix;
   delete stack;
   delete bytes;
}
```

Listing 15.5 GIFCODEC.CPP (continued)

```cpp
int GifDecoder::push( int s )
{
   if( stkp < capacity )
   {
      stack[stkp++] = s;
      return xOKAY;
   }
   return xOVERFLOW;
}

void GifDecoder::clear( void )
{
   cursize = minsize;
   width( cursize );
   clrc = nroots;
   endc = clrc + 1;
   curcode = endc + 1;
   maxcode = 1 << cursize;
   for( int i=0; i<curcode; i++ )
   {
      suffix[i] = i;
      prefix[i] = 0;
   }
}

int GifDecoder::init( void )
{
   clear();
   while( (oldc=getcode()) == clrc ) { ; }
   newc = oldc;
   return status();
}
int GifDecoder::term( void )
{
   return status();
}

int GifDecoder::status( void )
{
   if( cond != xOKAY ) return cond;
   if( feof(ifile) ) cond = xENDOFFILE;
   if( ferror(ifile) ) cond = xIOERROR;
   return cond;
}

int GifDecoder::decode( unsigned char *buf, int npxls )
{
    int nb = 0;
```

Listing 15.5 GIFCODEC.CPP (continued)

```cpp
// empty stack into scan line buffer
while( (stkp > 0) && (nb < rwbytes) )
   bytes[nb++] = stack[--stkp];

// loop until a row has been decoded
int code;
while( nb < rwbytes )
{
   //....... get next code
   if( (code=getcode()) < 0 ) break;

   //....... check for a clear code
   if( code == clrc )
   {
      init();
      if( oldc == endc ) break;
      bytes[nb++] = oldc;
      if( nb == rwbytes ) break;
   }

   //....... check for an end code
   else if( code == endc )
   {
      break;
   }

   //....... code is a data code
   else
   {
      if( code == curcode )
      {
         code = oldc;
         cond = push( newc );
      }
      else if( code > curcode )
      {
         cond = xOUTOFSYNC;
         break;
      }
      while( code > endc )
      {
         cond = push( suffix[code] );
         code = prefix[code];
      }
      cond = push( code );
```

Listing 15.5 GIFCODEC.CPP (continued)

```
            // add code to table
            if( curcode < maxcode )
            {
                newc = code;
                suffix[curcode] = newc;
                prefix[curcode] = oldc;
                oldc = lastcode();
                curcode++;
            }

            // current width exhausted?
            if( curcode >= maxcode )
            {
                if( cursize < maxsize )
                {
                    cursize++;
                    width( cursize );
                    maxcode <<= 1;
                }
                else if( (code=getcode()) == clrc )
                {
                    init();
                    if( oldc == endc ) break;
                    bytes[nb++] = oldc;
                    if( nb == rwbytes ) break;
                }
                else
                {
                    cond = xOVERFLOW;
                    break;
                }
            }

            // transfer string from stack to buffer
            while( (stkp > 0) && (nb < rwbytes) )
                bytes[nb++] = stack[--stkp];
        }
    }

    memcpy( buf, bytes, npxls );

    return status();
}

//.................class oCodeStream
```

Listing 15.5 GIFCODEC.CPP (continued)

```cpp
oCodeStream::oCodeStream( FILE *f, int size )
{
    ofile = f;
    nbytes = 0;
    nbits = size;
    bytecode = 0;
    bytemask = 1;
}

oCodeStream::~oCodeStream( )
{
}

int oCodeStream::putbyte( int byt )
{
    buffer[nbytes++] = byt;
    if( nbytes == 255 )
    {
        fputc( nbytes, ofile );
        fwrite( buffer, nbytes, 1, ofile );
        nbytes = 0;
    }
    return ferror(ofile) ? xIOERROR : xOKAY;
}

int oCodeStream::putcode( int code )
{
    int mask = 1;
    int n = nbits;
    while( n-- > 0 )
    {
        if( code & mask )
            bytecode |= bytemask;
        if( (bytemask <<= 1) > 0x80 )
        {
            if( putbyte( bytecode ) != xOKAY )
                return xIOERROR;
            bytecode = 0;
            bytemask = 1;
        }
        mask <<= 1;
    }
    return xOKAY;
}
```

Listing 15.5 GIFCODEC.CPP (continued)

```cpp
int oCodeStream::flush( void )
{
   if( bytemask != 1 )
   {
      putbyte( bytecode );
      bytecode = 0;
      bytemask = 1;
   }
   if( nbytes > 0 )
   {
      fputc( nbytes, ofile );
      fwrite( buffer, nbytes, 1, ofile );
      nbytes = 0;
   }
   return ferror(ofile) ? xIOERROR : xOKAY;
}


//.................class GifEncoder

#define  HASHSIZE  5101
#define  HASHBITS  4
#define  TABLSIZE  4096
#define  EMPTY     -1

GifEncoder::GifEncoder( FILE* outfile, int cobits ) :
            Encoder( ),
            oCodeStream( outfile, cobits+1 )
{
   cond     = xOKAY;
   started  = 0;
   minsize  = cobits + 1;
   maxsize  = 12;
   nroots   = 1 << cobits;
   capacity = HASHSIZE;
   clrc     = nroots;
   endc     = clrc + 1;
   codes    = new int [capacity];
   prefix   = new int [capacity];
   suffix   = new int [capacity];
   if( ! codes || ! prefix || ! suffix )
      cond = xNOMEMORY;
   else
      clear();
}
```

Listing 15.5 GIFCODEC.CPP (continued)

```cpp
GifEncoder::~GifEncoder( )
{
    delete codes;
    delete prefix;
    delete suffix;
}

void GifEncoder::clear( void )
{
    cursize = minsize;
    width( cursize );
    curcode = endc + 1;
    maxcode = 1 << cursize;
    for( int i=0; i<HASHSIZE; i++ )
    {
        codes[i] = EMPTY;
    }
}

int GifEncoder::findstr( int pfx, int sfx )
{
    int i = (sfx << HASHBITS) ^ pfx;
    int di = (i==0) ? 1 : capacity - i;
    while( 1 )
    {
        if( codes[i] == EMPTY )
            break;
        if( (prefix[i] == pfx) && (suffix[i] == sfx) )
            break;
        i -= di;
        if( i < 0 ) i += capacity;
    }
    return i;
}

int GifEncoder::init( void )
{
    started = 0;
    clear();
    putcode( clrc );
    return status();
}
```

Listing 15.5 GIFCODEC.CPP (continued)

```cpp
int GifEncoder::term( void )
{
    putcode( strc );
    putcode( endc );
    flush();
    return status();
}

int GifEncoder::status( void )
{
    if( cond != xOKAY ) return cond;
    if( ferror( ofile ) ) cond = xIOERROR;
    return cond;
}

int GifEncoder::encode( unsigned char *buf, int npxls )
{
    int np = 0;

    // is this the first call?
    if( ! started )
    {
        strc = buf[np++];
        started = 1;
    }

    while( (np < npxls) && (status() == xOKAY) )
    {
        chrc = buf[np++];
        int i = findstr( strc, chrc );
        if( codes[i] != EMPTY )  //...... string found
        {
            strc = codes[i];
        }
        else //........................ string not found
        {
            // add to table
            codes[i]  = curcode;
            prefix[i] = strc;
            suffix[i] = chrc;
            putcode( strc );
            strc = chrc;
            curcode++;
            if( curcode > maxcode )
            {
                cursize++;
                if( cursize > maxsize )
                {
```

Listing 15.5 GIFCODEC.CPP (continued)

```
                    putcode( clrc );
                    clear();
                }
                else
                {
                    width( cursize );
                    maxcode <<= 1;
                    if( cursize == maxsize )
                        maxcode--;
                }
            }
        }
    }

    return status();
}
```

A GIF File Viewer

A program to view or print GIF files is presented in Listing 15.6. As can be seen from the listing, the code is relatively straightforward, despite the complexity of the format. Much of this is a result of the high degree of encapsulation that is obtained from a C++ implementation, particularly the ability to combine both data and code into a single class object.

As written, the program is intended to process only GIF files that contain a single image. It also ignores all format extensions. However, handling multiple images or specific extensions was planned for in the design, and the program can be easily modified for these purposes. Most of the format-specific code is localized in three functions: do_image(), do_extension(), and load-gif().

Listing 15.6 VGIF.CPP

```
//-----------------------------------------------------------//
//                                                           //
//    File:     VGIF.CPP                                     //
//                                                           //
//    Desc:     Program to view or print a GIF file          //
//                                                           //
//-----------------------------------------------------------//

#include "stdlib.h"
#include "stdio.h"
#include "string.h"
```

Listing 15.6 VGIF.CPP (continued)

```cpp
#include "conio.h"
#include "ctype.h"

#include "gif.hpp"
#include "gifcodec.hpp"
#include "imgviewr.hpp"
#include "imgprntr.hpp"
#include "laserjet.hpp"
#include "paintjet.hpp"
#include "epjx80.hpp"
#include "eplq24.hpp"
#include "pscript.hpp"

//.................Printer types

#define  LJ   0x4C4A
#define  PJ   0x504A
#define  JX   0x4A58
#define  LQ   0x4C51
#define  PS   0x5053


//.................Program globals

char      fn[80];         // path to GIF file

int       gmode;          // video display mode
int       pmode;          // printer ID
int       ropt;           // rendering flags
int       iopt;           // itensity mapping flags

ImgStore  *imgmap;        // image bitmap

rgb       *gblpal,        // global palette
          *lclpal;        // local palette

int       ngbl,           // global palette
          nlcl;           // local palette

//.................Exit with a message

void exit_pgm( char *msg )
{
   printf( "%s\n", msg );
   exit( 0 );
}


//.................Program usage
```

Listing 15.6 VGIF.CPP (continued)

```
void explain_pgm( void )
{
    printf( "\n" );
    printf( ".........CompuServe GIF Viewer/Printer.........\n"
);
    printf( "\n" );
    printf( "Usage:      VGIF  gif_file  [ switches ]\n" );
    printf( "\n" );
    printf( "Switches:  -h     = display program usage\n" );
    printf( "           -vXX   = force video display mode XX\n" );
    printf( "                    (XX = 12, 13, 2E, 62)\n" );
    printf( "           -pXX   = print using printer XX\n" );
    printf( "                    (XX = LJ, PJ, JX, LQ, PS)\n" );
    printf( "           -b[+|-] = increase or decrease
brightness\n" );
    printf( "           -c[+|-] = increase or decrease contrast\n"
);
    printf( "           -d     = force dithered rendering\n" );
    printf( "           -g     = force gray scale rendering\n" );
    printf( "           -m     = force palette mapping\n" );
    printf( "\n" );
    printf( "...............................................\n"
);
    printf( "\n" );
}

//................Process pgm argument list

void process_args( int argc, char *argv[] )
{
    // establish default values
    fn[0] = 0;
    gmode = 0x12;
    pmode = 0;
    ropt  = 0;
    iopt  = 0;

    // process the program's argument list
    for( int i=1; i<argc; i++ )
    {
        if( (*argv[i] == '-') || (*argv[i] == '/') )
        {
            char sw = *(argv[i] + 1);
            switch( toupper(sw) )
```

Listing 15.6 VGIF.CPP (continued)

```
            {
              case 'H' :
                  explain_pgm();
                  exit( 0 );
                  break;

              case 'V' :
                  sscanf( argv[i]+2, "%x", &gmode );
                  break;

              case 'P' :
                  pmode = toupper( *(argv[i]+2) );
                  pmode <<= 8;
                  pmode += toupper( *(argv[i]+3) );
                  break;

              case 'B' :
                  if( *(argv[i]+2) == '-' )
                      iopt |= intensDBRI;
                  else
                      iopt |= intensIBRI;
                  break;
              case 'C' :
                  if( *(argv[i]+2) == '-' )
                      iopt |= intensDCNT;
                  else
                      iopt |= intensICNT;
                  break;

              case 'D' :
                  ropt |= renderDITHER;
                  break;

              case 'G' :
                  ropt |= renderGRAY;
                  break;

              case 'M' :
                  ropt |= renderMAP;
                  break;

              default:
                  printf( "Unknown switch '%s' ignored\n",
                          argv[i] );
                  break;
          }
        }
        else  // presumably a file identifier
```

Listing 15.6 VGIF.CPP (continued)

```
      {
         strcpy( fn, argv[i] );
         char *p = strchr( fn, '.' );
         if( p == 0 )
            strcat( fn, ".gif" );
         else if( *(p+1) == 0 )
            *p = 0;
      }
   }

   // was a file name specified?
   if( fn[0] == 0 )
   {
      explain_pgm();
      exit( 0 );
   }
}

//.................Create an image storage buffer

ImgStore * istore( int h, int w, int d )
{
   ImgStore *ist = 0;

   // attempt to create in order of preference
   ist = new XmsImgStore( h, w, d );
   if( (ist != 0) && (ist->status != imgstoreOKAY) )
   {
      delete ist;
      ist = new EmsImgStore( h, w, d );
      if( (ist != 0) && (ist->status != imgstoreOKAY) )
      {
         delete ist;
         ist = new CnvImgStore( h, w, d );
         if( (ist != 0) && (ist->status != imgstoreOKAY) )
         {
            delete ist;
            ist = new DskImgStore( h, w, d );
            if( (ist != 0) && (ist->status != imgstoreOKAY) )
            {
               delete ist;
               ist = 0;
            }
         }
      }
   }
}
```

Listing 15.6 VGIF.CPP (continued)

```cpp
      return ist;
  }

  //.................Create a printer

  PrinterDriver * printer( int which )
  {
     PrinterDriver *p;

     switch( which )
     {
        case LJ : p = new LaserJet( "LPT1" );
                  break;
        case PJ : p = new PaintJet( "LPT1" );
                  break;
        case JX : p = new EpsonJX80( "LPT1" );
                  break;
        case LQ : p = new EpsonLQ24( "LPT1" );
                  break;
        default : p = new PsPrinter( "LPT1" );
                  break;
     }

     return p;
  }

  //.................skip data blocks

  void skip_blocks( FILE *f )
  {
     int nbytes;
     while( (nbytes=fgetc(f)) > 0 )
        fseek( f, nbytes, SEEK_CUR );
  }

  //.................determine interlaced row number

  static int currow   = -8;
  static int curpass  = 0;
  static int delta[]  = { 8, 8, 4, 2 };
  static int origin[] = { 0, 4, 2, 1 };

  int row( int nrows )
  {
     currow += delta[curpass];
     if( currow >= nrows )
```

Listing 15.6 VGIF.CPP (continued)

```cpp
      {
         curpass++;
         currow = origin[curpass];
      }
      return currow;
   }

//..................process image description

void do_image( FILE *f )
{
   GIFIMDESC imd;
   if( imd.get( f ) )
      exit_pgm( "Error reading GIF image descriptor" );

   // process local color table
   lclpal = 0;
   if( imd.islct() )
   {
      nlcl = imd.ncolors();
      lclpal = new rgb [nlcl];
      if( lclpal == 0 )
         exit_pgm( "No memory for local color table" );
      for( int i=0; i<nlcl; i++ )
      {
         int r = fgetc( f );
         int g = fgetc( f );
         int b = fgetc( f );
         lclpal[i] = rgb( r, g, b );
      }
      if( feof(f) || ferror(f) )
         exit_pgm( "Error reading global color table" );
   }

   // create bitmap to be filled
   int ncols = imd.imwidth;
   int nrows = imd.imheight;

   unsigned char *scanln = new unsigned char [ncols];
   imgmap = istore( nrows, ncols, 8 );
   if( (imgmap == 0) || (scanln == 0) )
   {
      delete imgmap;
      exit_pgm( "Insufficient memory to load image" );
   }

   // read min LZW code size
   int size = fgetc( f );
```

Listing 15.6 VGIF.CPP (continued)

```cpp
   // decode image
   printf( "Loading image..." );
   GifDecoder dec( f, size, ncols );
   dec.init();
   for( int i=0; i<nrows; i++ )
   {
      dec.decode( scanln, ncols );
      int n = imd.isinterlaced() ? row( nrows ) : i;
      imgmap->put( scanln, n );
      if( (i % 10) == 9 ) printf( "." );
   }
   dec.term();
   printf( "done\n" );
}

//.................process control extension

void do_ctl_ext( FILE *f )
{
   GIFCTLEXT ctl;
   if( ctl.get( f ) )
      exit_pgm( "Error reading GIF control extension" );
   skip_blocks( f );
}

//.................process comment extension

void do_com_ext( FILE *f )
{
   GIFCOMEXT com;
   if( com.get( f ) )
      exit_pgm( "Error reading GIF comment extension" );
   skip_blocks( f );
}

//.................process text extension

void do_txt_ext( FILE *f )
{
   GIFTXTEXT txt;
   if( txt.get( f ) )
      exit_pgm( "Error reading GIF text extension" );
   skip_blocks( f );
}

//.................process application extension
```

Listing 15.6 VGIF.CPP (continued)

```
void do_app_ext( FILE *f )
{
   GIFAPPEXT app;
   if( app.get( f ) )
      exit_pgm( "Error reading GIF application extension" );
   skip_blocks( f );
}

//.................process extension
void do_extension( FILE *f )
{
   int label = fgetc( f );
   switch( label )
   {
      case 0xF9 : // control extension
           do_ctl_ext( f );
           break;

      case 0xFE : // comment extension
           do_com_ext( f );
           break;

      case 0x01 : // text extension
           do_txt_ext( f );
           break;

      case 0xFF : // application extension
           do_app_ext( f );
           break;

      default :    // unknown or invalid
           if( label < 0 )
              printf( "Error reading extension\n" );
           else
              printf( "Unknown or invalid extension %02Xh\n",
                       label );
           exit( 0 );
           break;
   }
}


//.................Load the GIF file
```

Listing 15.6 VGIF.CPP (continued)

```cpp
void load_gif( void )
{
   // open the file
   FILE *fgif = fopen( fn, "rb" );
   if( fgif == 0 )
      exit_pgm( "GIF file not found" );

   // read header
   GIFHEADER hdr;
   if( hdr.get( fgif ) )
      exit_pgm( "Error reading GIF header" );
   if( ! hdr.isvalid() )
      exit_pgm( "File is not a valid GIF file" );

   // read screen descriptor
   GIFSCDESC scd;
   if( scd.get( fgif ) )
      exit_pgm( "Error reading GIF screen descriptor" );

   // process global color table
   gblpal = 0;
   if( scd.isgct() )
   {
      ngbl = scd.ncolors();
      gblpal = new rgb [ngbl];
      if( gblpal == 0 )
         exit_pgm( "No memory for global color table" );
      for( int i=0; i<ngbl; i++ )
      {
         int r = fgetc( fgif );
         int g = fgetc( fgif );
         int b = fgetc( fgif );
         gblpal[i] = rgb( r, g, b );
      }
      if( feof(fgif) || ferror(fgif) )
         exit_pgm( "Error reading global color table" );
   }

   // scan for image
   int type;
   while( (type=fgetc(fgif)) > 0 )
   {
      if( type == 0x2C )         // image descriptor
      {
         do_image( fgif );
         break;
      }
      else if( type == 0x21 )  // extension
```

Listing 15.6 VGIF.CPP (continued)

```cpp
            do_extension( fgif );
         else if( type == 0x3B )  // trailer
            exit_pgm( "Unexpected GIF trailer" );
         else
            exit_pgm( "Unknown or invalid construct" );
   }
}

//.................Main

int main( int argc, char *argv[] )
{
   process_args( argc, argv );

   load_gif( );

   // determine palette
   int ncolors = nlcl > 0 ? nlcl : ngbl;
   rgb *pal = lclpal ? lclpal : gblpal;

   // print the image
   if( pmode != 0 )
   {
      PrinterDriver *prt = printer( pmode );
      if( prt )
      {
         printf( "Printing..." );
         ImagePrinter ip( prt, imgmap, pal, ncolors,
                          ropt, iopt, 100, 100 );
         ip.print( 1 );
         printf( "done\n" );
         delete prt;
      }
      else
         printf( "Printer instantiation failed\n" );
   }

   // display the image
   else
   {
      VgaDisplay vga( gmode );
      ImageViewer iv( &vga, imgmap, pal, ncolors,
                      ropt, iopt );
      iv.view( );
   }
```

Listing 15.6 VGIF.CPP (continued)

```
    delete imgmap;
    delete gblpal;
    delete lclpal;

    return 0;
}
```

Writing the GIF Format

As with most other formats, writing an instance of the GIF format is somewhat easier than reading an instance. This is particularly true if all that is required is to create a file with a single image and no extensions. Listing 15.7 presents source code for this purpose. Two versions of a `WriteGIF()` function are shown, one that reads its image from the video display and another that gets its input from an in-memory bitmap. The file that is output by these functions is structured like the schematic shown in Figure 15.1 and should be readable by any program that supports version 87a of the GIF format.

An example of the `WriteGIF()` function in actual use is provided in Listing 15.8, which presents the source code to BMPGIF. This program will perform a format translation in both directions, either creating a GIF output file from a BMP input file or creating a BMP output file from a GIF input file. The program can be used as a template for conversions between any two fully implemented formats covered in this book, because a more or less uniform software interface has been enforced for all formats.

The BMPGIF program determines the conversion direction from the supplied filename arguments, and where necessary, attempts to determine the direction. For example, the command line

```
BMPGIF XYZZY.GIF XYZZY.BMP
```

will create a BMP file from the image in the specified GIF file. The argument order is thus "input file—output file." The same conversion is also performed by this command line:

```
BMPGIF XYZZY.GIF
```

because the first argument is assumed to be the input file. Finally, this command line:

```
BMPGIF XYZZY
```

will also work if only one of the two files exists, because the existing file is presumed to be the input file.

It should be noted that the BMPGIF program was constructed from fragments of other programs presented in this book, and as a result, lacks certain niceties of programming style that are generally desirable. However, the code works well enough, and the program is small enough in size that such considerations are not particularly important. The interested reader may nonetheless wish to perform a bit of cosmetic surgery on the code, and do such things as normalize variable and functions names.

Listing 15.7 WRTGIF.CPP

```
//----------------------------------------------------------//
//                                                          //
//    File:      WRTGIF.CPP                                  //
//                                                          //
//    Desc:      Code to output a GIF file from a           //
//               VGA Display or a Memory Bitmap             //
//                                                          //
//----------------------------------------------------------//

#include "gif.hpp"
#include "gifcodec.hpp"
#include "color.hpp"
#include "display.hpp"
#include "imgstore.hpp"

//.................Write VGA screen to GIF file 'fn'

int WriteGIF( VgaDisplay& vga, char *fn,
              int x1, int y1, int x2, int y2 )
{
   // image metrics
   int nrows   = y2 - y1 + 1;
   int ncols   = x2 - x1 + 1;
   int nbits   = vga.metric.nbits * vga.metric.nplanes;
   int size    = (nbits < 8) ? nbits+1 : nbits;
   int ncolors = vga.metric.ncolors;
   rgb *pal    = new rgb [ncolors];
   if( pal == 0 ) return xNOMEMORY;
   vga.getpalette( pal );

   // scan line buffer for encoder
   unsigned char *scanln = new unsigned char [ncols];
   if( scanln == 0 ) return xNOMEMORY;
   // open and write the file
   FILE *f = fopen( fn, "wb" );
```

Listing 15.7 WRTGIF.CPP (continued)

```cpp
    // GIF header - since we don't employ any of the
    // 89a extensions we set the version to 87a
    GIFHEADER hdr;
    hdr.ver[1] = '7';
    if( hdr.put( f ) ) return xIOERROR;

    // GIF screen descriptor
    GIFSCDESC scd( ncols, nrows, nbits );
    if( scd.put( f ) ) return xIOERROR;

    // the Global Color Table
    for( int i=0; i<ncolors; i++ )
    {
       fputc( pal[i].red, f );
       fputc( pal[i].grn, f );
       fputc( pal[i].blu, f );
    }

    // GIF image descriptor
    GIFIMDESC imd( ncols, nrows, nbits );
    if( imd.put( f ) ) return xIOERROR;

    // min LZW code size
    fputc( size, f );

    // output the encoded bitmap
    GifEncoder enc( f, size );
    enc.init();
    for( i=0; i<nrows; i++ )
    {
       vga.getscanline( scanln, ncols, x1, y1+i );
       if( enc.encode( scanln, ncols ) != xOKAY )
       {
          delete scanln;
          fclose( f );
          return enc.status();
       }
    }
    enc.term();

    // output block terminator
    fputc( 0, f );

    // output trailer
    fputc( 0x3B, f );
```

Listing 15.7 WRTGIF.CPP (continued)

```cpp
      // finished
      delete scanln;
      int retv = ferror(f) ? xIOERROR : xOKAY;
      fclose( f );
      return retv;
}

//................Write an image to GIF file 'fn'

int WriteGIF( ImgStore& img, rgb *pal, char *fn )
{
   if( img.depth() == 25 )
      return xUNSUPPORTED;

   // image metrics
   int nrows   = img.height();
   int ncols   = img.width();
   int nbits   = (img.depth() == 1) ? 1 : 8;
   int size    = (nbits < 8) ? nbits+1 : nbits;
   int ncolors = 1 << img.depth();

   // open and write the file
   FILE *f = fopen( fn, "wb" );

   // GIF header - since we don't employ any of the
   // 89a extensions we set the version to 87a
   GIFHEADER hdr;
   hdr.ver[1] = '7';
   if( hdr.put( f ) ) return xIOERROR;

   // GIF screen descriptor
   GIFSCDESC scd( ncols, nrows, nbits );
   if( scd.put( f ) ) return xIOERROR;

   // the Global Color Table
   for( int i=0; i<ncolors; i++ )
   {
      fputc( pal[i].red, f );
      fputc( pal[i].grn, f );
      fputc( pal[i].blu, f );
   }

   // GIF image descriptor
   GIFIMDESC imd( ncols, nrows, nbits );
   if( imd.put( f ) ) return xIOERROR;

   // min LZW code size
   fputc( size, f );
```

Listing 15.7 WRTGIF.CPP (continued)

```
        // output the encoded bitmap
        GifEncoder enc( f, size );
        enc.init();
        for( i=0; i<nrows; i++ )
        {
            unsigned char *p = img.get( i );
            if( enc.encode( p, ncols ) != xOKAY )
            {
                fclose( f );
                return enc.status();
            }
        }
        enc.term();

        // output block terminator
        fputc( 0, f );

        // output trailer
        fputc( 0x3B, f );

        // finished
        int retv = ferror(f) ? xIOERROR : xOKAY;
        fclose( f );
        return retv;
    }
```

Listing 15.8 BMPGIF.CPP

```
    //------------------------------------------------------------//
    //                                                            //
    //   File:      BMPGIF.CPP                                    //
    //                                                            //
    //   Desc:      A program to convert image files in the       //
    //              BMP and GIF formats to the other format       //
    //                                                            //
    //------------------------------------------------------------//

    #include "stdlib.h"
    #include "stdio.h"
    #include "string.h"
    #include "conio.h"
    #include "ctype.h"

    #include "color.hpp"
    #include "imgstore.hpp"
```

Listing 15.8 BMPGIF.CPP (continued)

```
//----------------------------------------------------------//
//                      General Code                        //
//----------------------------------------------------------//


#define UNKNOWN 0
#define BMP2GIF 1
#define GIF2BMP 2


//................Program globals

char       InFn[80],     // path to the input file
           OutFn[80];    // path to the output file

ImgStore   *imgmap;      // image bitmap

rgb        *imgpal,      // image palette
           *gblpal,
           *lclpal;

int        ncolors,      // palette size
           ngbl,
           nlcl,
           cnvdir;       // conversion direction

//................Exit with a message

void exit_pgm( char *msg )
{
   printf( "%s\n", msg );
   exit( 0 );
}


//................Program usage

void explain_pgm( void )
{
   printf( "\n" );
   printf( ".......... BMP <-> GIF File Converter ......\n" );
   printf( "\n" );
   printf( "Usage:  BMPGIF  in_file  out_file\n" );
   printf( "\n" );
   printf( "Args:   in_file  - either a GIF or BMP file\n" );
   printf( "        out_file - name of a file of the\n" );
   printf( "                   opposite format\n" );
   printf( "\n" );
   printf( "...........................................\n" );
   printf( "\n" );
}
```

Listing 15.8 BMPGIF.CPP (continued)

```cpp
//.................Determine if the passed file exists

int file_exists( char *path )
{
   FILE *f;
   if( (f=fopen(path,"rb")) != 0 )
   {
      fclose( f );
      return 1;
   }
   return 0;
}

//.................Process pgm argument list

void process_args( int argc, char *argv[] )
{
   char tmp[133];

   if( argc < 2 )
   {
      explain_pgm();
      exit( 0 );
   }

   cnvdir = UNKNOWN;

   strcpy( InFn, argv[1] );
   strupr( InFn );
   if( strchr(InFn,'.') == 0 )
   {
      strcpy( tmp, InFn );
      strcat( tmp, ".BMP" );
      if( file_exists(tmp) )
      {
         strcat( InFn, ".BMP" );
         cnvdir = BMP2GIF;
      }
      else
      {
         strcpy( tmp, InFn );
         strcat( tmp, ".GIF" );
         if( file_exists(tmp) )
         {
            strcat( InFn, ".GIF" );
            cnvdir = GIF2BMP;
         }
         else
```

Listing 15.8 BMPGIF.CPP (continued)

```
            {
                sprintf( tmp,
                        "Input file %s [BMP|GIF] not found",
                        InFn );
                exit_pgm( tmp );
            }
        }
    }
    else if( file_exists(InFn) )
    {
        if( strstr( InFn, ".BMP" ) != 0 )
            cnvdir = BMP2GIF;
        else if( strstr( InFn, ".GIF" ) != 0 )
            cnvdir = GIF2BMP;
    }

    if( cnvdir == UNKNOWN )
    {
        sprintf( tmp, "Ambiguous or impossible conversion "
                "of '%s' - please be more specific.", InFn );
        exit_pgm( tmp );
    }

    if( argc > 2 )
    {
        strcpy( OutFn, argv[2] );
        strupr( OutFn );
    }
    else
    {
        strcpy( OutFn, InFn );
        char *p = strchr( OutFn, '.' );
        *p = 0;
    }

    if( strchr(OutFn,'.') == 0 )
    {
        if( cnvdir == BMP2GIF )
            strcat( OutFn, ".GIF" );
        else
            strcat( OutFn, ".BMP" );
    }
```

Listing 15.8 BMPGIF.CPP (continued)

```cpp
    if( strcmp( InFn, OutFn ) == 0 )
    {
        sprintf( tmp, "%s == %s - no conversion implied",
                 InFn, OutFn );
        exit_pgm( tmp );
    }

    printf( "Converting %s to %s...", InFn, OutFn );
    if( file_exists(OutFn) )
    {
        printf( "%s exists - overwrite (y|n)? ", OutFn );
        while( 1 )
        {
            int i = getch();
            if( (i=='y') || (i=='Y') )
                break;
            if( (i=='n') || (i=='N') )
                exit( 0 );
        }
    }
    printf( "\n" );
}

//.................Create an image storage buffer

ImgStore * istore( int h, int w, int d )
{
    ImgStore *ist = 0;

    // attempt to create in order of preference
    ist = new XmsImgStore( h, w, d );
    if( (ist != 0) && (ist->status != imgstoreOKAY) )
    {
        delete ist;
        ist = new EmsImgStore( h, w, d );
        if( (ist != 0) && (ist->status != imgstoreOKAY) )
        {
            delete ist;
            ist = new CnvImgStore( h, w, d );
            if( (ist != 0) && (ist->status != imgstoreOKAY) )
            {
                delete ist;
```

Listing 15.8 BMPGIF.CPP (continued)

```cpp
                ist = new DskImgStore( h, w, d );
                if( (ist != 0) && (ist->status != imgstoreOKAY) )
                {
                    delete ist;
                    ist = 0;
                }
            }
        }
    }

    return ist;
}


//----------------------------------------------------------//
//                      BMP-Specific Code                   //
//----------------------------------------------------------//

#include "bmp.hpp"
#include "wrtbmp.cpp"

//.................Load the BMP file

void load_bmp( char *fn )
{
    // open file
    FILE *fbmp = fopen( fn, "rb" );
    if( fbmp == 0 )
        exit_pgm( "BMP file not found" );

    // read header and check
    xBITMAPFILEHEADER bmfh;
    if( fread(&bmfh,sizeof(xBITMAPFILEHEADER),1,fbmp) != 1 )
        exit_pgm( "Error reading BMP file" );
    if( bmfh.bfType != BMP_SIGNATURE_WORD )
        exit_pgm( "File is not a valid BMP file" );
    // determine which format version is used
    // from structure size field
    long offset = ftell( fbmp );
    long nbytes = 0;
    fread( &nbytes, sizeof(long), 1, fbmp );
    fseek( fbmp, offset, SEEK_SET );

    // read bitmap header and palette
    int width, height, depth, rle;

    // pre Windows 3.0 version
    if( nbytes == sizeof(xBITMAPCOREHEADER) )
    {
```

Listing 15.8 BMPGIF.CPP (continued)

```cpp
        xBITMAPCOREHEADER bmch;
        if( fread(&bmch,sizeof(xBITMAPCOREHEADER),1,fbmp) != 1 )
           exit_pgm( "Error reading xBITMAPCOREHEADER" );
        width   = bmch.bcWidth;
        height  = bmch.bcHeight;
        depth   = bmch.bcBitCount;
        rle     = 0;
        ncolors = 1 << depth;
        if( ncolors > 0 )
        {
           imgpal = new rgb [ncolors];
           if( imgpal == 0 )
              exit_pgm( "Error allocating image palette" );
           xRGBTRIPLE t;
           for( int i=0; i<ncolors; i++ )
           {
              if( fread(&t,sizeof(xRGBTRIPLE),1,fbmp) != 1 )
                 exit_pgm( "Error reading xRGBTRIPLE" );
              imgpal[i] = rgb(t.rgbRed,t.rgbGreen,t.rgbBlue);
           }
        }
     }

     // Windows 3.0 and later version
     else if( nbytes == sizeof(xBITMAPINFOHEADER) )
     {
        xBITMAPINFOHEADER bmih;
        if( fread(&bmih,sizeof(xBITMAPINFOHEADER),1,fbmp) != 1 )
           exit_pgm( "Error reading xBITMAPINFOHEADER" );
        width   = (int) bmih.biWidth;
        height  = (int) bmih.biHeight;
        depth   = bmih.biBitCount;
        rle     = (int) bmih.biCompression;
        ncolors = 1 << depth;
        if( ncolors > 0 )
        {
           imgpal = new rgb [ncolors];
           if( imgpal == 0 )
              exit_pgm( "Error allocating image palette" );
           xRGBQUAD q;
           for( int i=0; i<ncolors; i++ )
           {
              if( fread(&q,sizeof(xRGBQUAD),1,fbmp) != 1 )
                 exit_pgm( "Error reading xRGBQUAD" );
              imgpal[i] = rgb(q.rgbRed,q.rgbGreen,q.rgbBlue);
           }
        }
     }
```

Listing 15.8 BMPGIF.CPP (continued)

```
// unknown format
else
{
   exit_pgm( "Format error or input file not a BMP file" );
}

// check pixel size - 24-bit imagery not supported by GIF
if( depth == 24 )
{
   exit_pgm( "Error - BMP file is 24-bit color - "
             "not supported by the GIF format\n" );
}

// position to start of bitmap
fseek( fbmp, bmfh.bfOffBits, SEEK_SET );

// create a scan line buffer
int rowbytes = (width + 3) / 4;
rowbytes *= 4;
unsigned char *scanline = new unsigned char [rowbytes];

// create an image storage buffer
imgmap = istore( height, width, 8 );

// and check
if( (imgmap == 0) || (scanline == 0) )
{
   if( imgmap )   delete imgmap;
   if( scanline ) delete scanline;
   exit_pgm( "Insufficient memory to load BMP image" );
}

// load the image
printf( "Loading BMP file '%s'...", fn );
BmpDecoder bmp( fbmp, rle, depth );
bmp.init( );
int n = height;
for( int i=0; i<height; i++ )
{
   bmp.decode( scanline, width );
   imgmap->put( scanline, --n );
}
bmp.term( );
printf( "done\n" );

fclose( fbmp );
delete scanline;
}
```

Listing 15.8 BMPGIF.CPP (continued)

```cpp
//----------------------------------------------------------//
//                     GIF-Specific Code                    //
//----------------------------------------------------------//

#include "gif.hpp"
#include "gifcodec.hpp"
#include "wrtgif.cpp"

//.................skip data blocks

void skip_blocks( FILE *f )
{
   int nbytes;
   while( (nbytes=fgetc(f)) > 0 )
      fseek( f, nbytes, SEEK_CUR );
}

//.................determine interlaced row number

static int currow   = -8;
static int curpass = 0;
static int delta[]  = { 8, 8, 4, 2 };
static int origin[] = { 0, 4, 2, 1 };

int row( int nrows )
{
   currow += delta[curpass];
   if( currow >= nrows )
   {
      curpass++;
      currow = origin[curpass];
   }
   return currow;
}

//.................process image description

void do_image( char *fn, FILE *f )
{
   GIFIMDESC imd;
   if( imd.get( f ) )
      exit_pgm( "Error reading GIF image descriptor" );

   // process local color table
   lclpal = 0;
   if( imd.islct() )
   {
      nlcl = imd.ncolors();
```

Listing 15.8 BMPGIF.CPP (continued)

```
      lclpal = new rgb [nlcl];
      if( lclpal == 0 )
         exit_pgm( "No memory for local color table" );
      for( int i=0; i<nlcl; i++ )
      {
         int r = fgetc( f );
         int g = fgetc( f );
         int b = fgetc( f );
         lclpal[i] = rgb( r, g, b );
      }
      if( feof(f) || ferror(f) )
         exit_pgm( "Error reading global color table" );
   }

   // create bitmap to be filled
   int ncols = imd.imwidth;
   int nrows = imd.imheight;

   unsigned char *scanln = new unsigned char [ncols];
   imgmap = istore( nrows, ncols, 8 );
   if( (imgmap == 0) || (scanln == 0) )
   {
      delete imgmap;
      exit_pgm( "Insufficient memory to load image" );
   }

   // read min LZW code size
   int size = fgetc( f );

   // decode image
   printf( "Loading GIF file '%s'...", fn );
   GifDecoder dec( f, size, ncols );
   dec.init();
   for( int i=0; i<nrows; i++ )
   {
      dec.decode( scanln, ncols );
      int n = imd.isinterlaced() ? row( nrows ) : i;
      imgmap->put( scanln, n );
   }
   dec.term();
   printf( "done\n" );
}

//.................process control extension
```

Listing 15.8 BMPGIF.CPP (continued)

```cpp
void do_ctl_ext( FILE *f )
{
   GIFCTLEXT ctl;
   if( ctl.get( f ) )
      exit_pgm( "Error reading GIF control extension" );
   skip_blocks( f );
}

//.................process comment extension

void do_com_ext( FILE *f )
{
   GIFCOMEXT com;
   if( com.get( f ) )
      exit_pgm( "Error reading GIF comment extension" );
   skip_blocks( f );
}

//.................process text extension

void do_txt_ext( FILE *f )
{
   GIFTXTEXT txt;
   if( txt.get( f ) )
      exit_pgm( "Error reading GIF text extension" );
   skip_blocks( f );
}

//.................process application extension

void do_app_ext( FILE *f )
{
   GIFAPPEXT app;
   if( app.get( f ) )
      exit_pgm( "Error reading GIF application extension" );
   skip_blocks( f );
}

//.................process extension

void do_extension( FILE *f )
{
   char msg[81];
   int  label = fgetc( f );
   switch( label )
```

Listing 15.8 BMPGIF.CPP (continued)

```
        {
            case 0xF9 : // control extension
                do_ctl_ext( f );
                break;

            case 0xFE : // comment extension
                do_com_ext( f );
                break;

            case 0x01 : // text extension
                do_txt_ext( f );
                break;

            case 0xFF : // application extension
                do_app_ext( f );
                break;

            default :   // unknown or invalid
                if( label < 0 )
                    exit_pgm( "Error reading GIF extension" );
                else
                {
                    sprintf( msg,
                            "Unknown/invalid GIF extension %02Xh\n",
                            label );
                    exit_pgm( msg );
                }
                break;
        }
    }

    //.................Load the GIF file

    void load_gif( char *fn )
    {
        // open the file
        FILE *fgif = fopen( fn, "rb" );
        if( fgif == 0 )
            exit_pgm( "GIF file not found" );

        // read header
        GIFHEADER hdr;
        if( hdr.get( fgif ) )
            exit_pgm( "Error reading GIF header" );
        if( ! hdr.isvalid() )
            exit_pgm( "File is not a valid GIF file" );
```

Listing 15.8 BMPGIF.CPP (continued)

```cpp
      // read screen descriptor
      GIFSCDESC scd;
      if( scd.get( fgif ) )
         exit_pgm( "Error reading GIF screen descriptor" );

      // process global color table
      gblpal = 0;
      if( scd.isgct() )
      {
         ngbl = scd.ncolors();
         gblpal = new rgb [ngbl];
         if( gblpal == 0 )
            exit_pgm( "No memory for global color table" );
         for( int i=0; i<ngbl; i++ )
         {
            int r = fgetc( fgif );
            int g = fgetc( fgif );
            int b = fgetc( fgif );
            gblpal[i] = rgb( r, g, b );
         }
         if( feof(fgif) || ferror(fgif) )
            exit_pgm( "Error reading global color table" );
      }

      printf( "Loading GIF file '%s'...", fn );
      int type;
      while( (type=fgetc(fgif)) > 0 )
      {
         if( type == 0x2C )         // image descriptor
         {
            do_image( fn, fgif );
            break;
         }
         else if( type == 0x21 )  // extension
            do_extension( fgif );
         else if( type == 0x3B )  // trailer
            exit_pgm( "Unexpected GIF trailer" );
         else
            exit_pgm( "Unknown or invalid construct" );
      }
      printf( "done\n" );
   }
```

Listing 15.8 BMPGIF.CPP (continued)

```cpp
//-----------------------------------------------------------//
//                      M A I N                              //
//-----------------------------------------------------------//

int main( int argc, char *argv[] )
{
    process_args( argc, argv );

    if( cnvdir == GIF2BMP )
    {
        load_gif( InFn );
        imgpal  = lclpal ? lclpal : gblpal;
        printf( "Writing BMP file '%s'...", OutFn );
        WriteBMP( *imgmap, imgpal, OutFn );
        printf( "done\n" );
    }
    else
    {
        load_bmp( InFn );
        printf( "Writing GIF file '%s'...", OutFn );
        WriteGIF( *imgmap, imgpal, OutFn );
        printf( "done\n" );
    }

    return 0;
}
```

This concludes our survey of the GIF format. As noted, it is an extremely popular format that is widely supported, and this alone makes it a good choice for use in application development. On the downside, as of this writing, it does not yet support 16-bit or 24-bit color imagery, and the format's many extensions in version 89a represent unnecessary baggage in some situations. (Note, however, that the latter is easily addressed by writing to the 87a specification.) Still, when you survey the incredible number and variety of GIF files that are available on CompuServe and dozens of other BBS systems, it is difficult not to like this format.

16

The Aldus TIFF Format

The TIFF format has done for graphics files what the Swiss army knife did for cutlery. It is an all-purpose, many-in-one format supporting many image types, color models, and compression schemes. It allows specification of a wide range of image metrics. If there is anything wrong with the format, it is that it attempts to do too much. On the other hand, if one were forced to pick a single format to support, TIFF would probably be the best choice.

Fortunately, the TIFF format specification addresses its own wide scope by defining a minimal subset of the format, known as **Baseline TIFF**. This represents the minimum implementation that must be supported by a compliant format reader or writer. All other defined format features are viewed as extensions to the baseline format, and their support is optional.

This chapter will implement the baseline standard as defined by revision 6.0 of the format. Readers interested in the complete specification can obtain documentation on the format from Aldus Corporation. Refer to the bibliography for details.

A TIFF Overview

The operant word in describing the TIFF format is *tag*. It helps to think of a tag in a literal physical sense. A good analogy for it is provided by the wire-and-manila-paper tags one finds attached to articles in hardware stores and repair shops. A tag in this instance is a label that identifies the object to which it is attached.

A TIFF tag is used in pretty much the same sense. As specified in the format, a **tag** is a 16-bit unsigned number that indicates what a given data object is. For instance, suppose that we have an unsigned integer field with the value 32773. By itself, the number connotes nothing. If, however, its tag is 259, then we know that the number indicates compression type, because 259 is the tag identifier for compression type, and a value of 32773 indicates PackBits compression.

In actual use, a tag is one element of a 12-byte structure referred to as an *image file directory entry,* or *IFD entry.* The definition of this structure is given later in Listing 16.1 as the structure IFDENTRY. In addition to the tag, the IFD entry indicates a data type (such as unsigned short), a count indicating the data object's size, and an offset that is used to locate the specified data object within the TIFF file.

IFD entries are elements of a larger structure, the IFD itself. An *image file directory* consists of a count field indicating the number of entries, followed by an array of that number of IFD entries, followed by an offset to the next IFD. A TIFF file must contain at least one IFD but may contain more. If it does contain more, then each IFD and the data it describes are referred to as a TIFF *subfile.* This mechanism allows multiple images to be combined into a single TIFF file. A typical application for this facility is combining the images of each page of a multipage fax into a single file.

A TIFF file begins with a brief 8-byte header that contains three fields. The first field indicates the byte ordering used in the file, which can be either Intel style or Motorola style. (These two byte orderings are also known by the names *little-endian* and *big-endian,* respectively.) The next field is a magic number that can be used to validate the file as a TIFF file. It consists of a 16-bit integer with the value 42. The third field is an offset used to locate the first IFD.

One important concept embraced by the TIFF format is that the various components that make up a file are located using explicit offsets from the beginning of the file. There is no default physical ordering, and you should never make assumptions about physical component order. The only reserved position is for the file's header, which is always in the first 8 bytes of the file. Once that has been read, all subsequent object access is achieved by offsets into the file, starting with the offset to the first IFD. In practice, this can be physically located immediately following the header or at the very end of the file. Again, never assume; use the offsets.

The one ordering convention you *can* assume is that the entries in an IFD are presented in ascending numeric order by tag value. Some tags are optional and have implied default values. If a reader encounters a tag with a higher number before it encounters another lower-numbered tag, then it can assume that the lower-numbered tag is not present. If the missing tag has implied defaults, then they are applied.

Thus far, I have said nothing about a TIFF file's actual image bitmap. It's a safe bet that a TIFF file has one—and that's about the last generalization you can make about bitmaps. Virtually any pixel organization or compression scheme can be used. The specifics of a given file's image (or images) can only be determined by processing the file's tags. Note, too, that images can be presented as a series of strips, or swaths. In those cases, the set of strips needs to be concatenated to obtain a complete image. Also, as you may suspect by now, you cannot assume that the strips will be located physically within a file in any particular order.

With this brief overview, let's turn now to a more detailed inspection of the format. We will begin by looking at the TIFF header, IFD, and IFD entry in more detail. Following that is a discussion of data types and specific tags and how they are interpreted, then a look at several image categories and the tag sets associated with each category.

TIFF Data Structures

This section describes the fixed data structures found in every TIFF file. There are only three, the TIFF header, the IFD, and the IFD Entry. These data structures are used to extract a series of image data from a file that, taken as a whole, define an image and its characteristics.

The TIFF Header

The TIFF header is 8 bytes in length and contains three fields. It always occupies the first 8 bytes of a TIFF file. There is no reliable way to decode a TIFF file without inspecting the header first, so reading the header should always be the first task of a decoder. The TIFF header is defined in Listing 16.1 as the structure `TIFFHEADER`. A description of the header's fields is as follows:

order
: 16-bit integer indicating the byte ordering employed by the file. A value of 0x4949 indicates Intel ordering, a value of 0x4D4D indicates Motorola ordering. Note that these values duplicate the ASCII codes for the letters II and MM respectively. Also note that this field can always be successfully read regardless of the actual byte ordering employed by the file. This is not true for the rest of the header and the file itself. A format reader must therefore account for byte-ordering differences when reading anything other than this field.

iden
: 16-bit magic number that can be used in conjunction with the order field to verify that a file is a valid TIFF file. The value of this field is 42 (decimal) and is byte-order sensitive.

ifdofs
: 32-bit integer indicating the offset, in bytes, from the beginning of the file to the start of the first IFD. Note that all offsets used in a TIFF file are relative to the beginning of the file.

IFD Entries

An IFD entry is a 12-byte structure that is used to define the size and type of individual image data and to indicate where in the TIFF file they are stored. The structure is defined in Listing 16.1 as IFDENTRY. A description of an IFD entry's field is as follows:

tag   16-bit unsigned integer that identifies what a datum is. For example, tag 256 defines image width, tag 282 defines image X resolution, and so on. For a complete list of tags, refer to Appendix B.

type   16-bit unsigned integer that indicates the data type of a datum. Examples include unsigned short, signed char, and null-terminated string. Another way to view this field is as the data unit. Data types defined by revision 6.0 are listed in Listing 16.1 as the enumeration TiffDataTypes.

count   Unsigned long value indicating the number of elements of the specified type that make up the datum. The size of a datum in bytes is therefore

```
count * sizeof(type)
```

Note that scalar data generally have a count of 1. For example, image width is normally defined using a single unsigned short, so its type would be tUShort, and its count would be 1.

valofs   Unsigned long value that indicates the offset from the start of the file to the actual datum value. To read a datum, a decoder seeks to the specified offset and then reads the number of bytes implied by the datum's type and count. *There is one important exception:* If the size of the datum is 4 bytes or less (the size of valofs itself) and the count is one, then valofs contains the actual value, not an offset to locate the value. If the datum size is less than 4 bytes then it is left-justified within the 4 bytes. The creators of the format decided that this convention would be a convenience to format encoders and decoders. In fact, all it does is unnecessarily complicate the format and the logic required to encode or decode the format—typical engineering by committee.

The Image File Directory

The IFD itself is an array of IFD entries that, taken as a whole, represent a complete image definition. A TIFF file always contains at least one IFD. If the file contains multiple images, then it contains one IFD per image. An IFD is said to define a TIFF subfile.

There are three components to an IFD, but we do not use a structure definition to represent them. The three components, described in the order in which they occur in a file are as follow:

count   16-bit unsigned integer field that indicates the number of IFD entries to follow.

array   Sequence of count 12-byte IFD entries.

offset   32-bit offset to the start of the next IFD in the file. If this value is 0, then there are no further IFDs in the file.

The procedure for reading an IFD encompasses the following four steps:

1. Seek to the offset specified for the IFD. If the first IFD is being read then the offset is obtained from the file's header. Otherwise, it is the offset obtained from step 4 from the previous IFD that was read.
2. Read a 16-bit integer and, if necessary, reverse its byte order. This is the number of IFD entries that follow.
3. Read the specified number of IFD entries.
4. Read a 32-bit integer and, if necessary, reverse its byte order. This is the offset to the next IFD in the file. If the offset is zero then there are no further IFDs to be read.

TIFF Data Types

Most of the data types defined by the TIFF format should be familiar to any C or C++ programmer. A few, however, warrant a note of explanation, so we will discuss those here. Table 16.1 lists all the defined data types and provides a description of each. The table is listed by the enumeration constants for TiffDataTypes that can be found in Listing 16.1. Note that the numeric values of each enumeration constant are the actual reserved values specified by the TIFF format for that data type.

One data type familiar to C programmers is the type tAscii, which defines a null-terminated string. The count field of an IFD entry with this type includes the terminating null, if it is present. Thus,

```
count = strlen(value) + 1
```

Both format readers and format writers should not neglect to account for the terminating null. That is, it should always be present.

A second and more unusual data type is represented by the types `tURational` and `tSRational`. A *rational* is a fraction represented as two long integers. The first value is the fraction's numerator, the second is its denominator. Both values are of the same signed type, which can be either signed or unsigned.

Table 16.1 TIFF Data Types

Data Type	Size (Bytes)	Description
tUByte	1	8-bit unsigned integer
tAscii	1	Null-terminated string
tUShort	2	16-bit unsigned integer
tULong	4	32-bit unsigned integer
tURational	8	Two 32-bit unsigned integers forming a fraction
tSByte	1	8-bit signed integer
tByte	1	8-bit undefined (for nonscalar types such as structures)
tSShort	2	16-bit signed integer
tSLong	4	32-bit signed integer
tSRational	8	Two 32-bit signed integers forming a fraction
tFloat	4	Single precision IEEE floating point
tDouble	8	Double precision IEEE floating point

TIFF Tags

The tag member of an IFD entry is used to identify what a given datum represents. All image metrics have an associated tag. Different image types have different sets of tags that are required in order for the image to be properly interpreted. Some tags are optional and have implied default values. Others are required, and it is considered a fatal error if a TIFF file is missing a required tag.

Table 16.2 lists some of the more important tags and what they represent. Keep in mind that this is not a complete list. See Appendix B for a list of all tags defined by revision 6.0 of the format.

The meaning and interpretation of most of the tags in Table 16.2 should be reasonably familiar by now, but a few notes are in order. In particular, the size of a pixel in bits is split into two fields by the TIFF format, bits per sample and samples per pixel. The size of a pixel in bits is the product of these two fields.

The use of the two fields should be apparent from a couple of examples. Gray-scale and palette-based images have a single value associated with each pixel, which is an index into a color map. For these image types, the number of samples per pixel is 1. A 256-color image employs 8 bits per sample while a 16-color image employs 4 bits per sample. Note that samples per pixel does not coincide with number of bit planes. Whether an image is multiplanar or whether it uses multibit pixels is determined from another tag, the planar configuration tag. A 24-bit RGB-based image is specified as having 8 bits per sample and 3 samples per pixel. In this case each sample component corresponds to one of the three primaries, red, green, or blue.

Table 16.2 Important TIFF Tags

Tag	Description
256	Image width in pixels
257	Image height in pixels
258	Bits per sample per primary or component. For a gray-scale image this is the same as the pixel size. For a 24-bit RGB-based image this is 8, because each primary is expressed as an 8-bit quantity.
259	Compression method used on the image. The baseline format definition specifies three possible schemes, uncompressed, PackBits compressed, or CCITT Group 3 one-dimensional modified Huffman encoding.
262	Photometric interpretation. This can indicate white on black or black on white for a bilevel image, or RGB or color-mapped for a color image.
273	Strip offsets. Specifies offsets from the beginning of the file to each strip in an image. This field is used to locate the actual bitmap of an image. If the image is present as a single strip, which is normally the case, only a single offset is specified.
274	Image orientation. This indicates the correspondence between the first encoded image pixel and its relative physical location on the actual image. Depending on this value, the image can be stored vertically mirrored and/or horizontally mirrored. The default is an image oriented with the first pixel at its upper left corner.
277	Samples per pixel. This is normally 1 for bilevel, gray-scale, and color-mapped images, but is 3 for an RGB-based image.

Table 16.2 Important TIFF Tags (continued)

278	Rows per strip. This defines the height, in rows, of each strip of a multistrip image. For a single-strip image, this is some value greater than or equal to the image height, in rows. The default value is the largest unsigned integer expressible in 32 bits, which effectively represents infinity.
282	Image X resolution in pixels-per-resolution unit.
283	Image Y resolution in pixels-per-resolution unit.
282	Planar configuration. This indicates whether pixel components are stored contiguously (**chunky** format) or in separate bit planes (**planar** format).
296	Resolution unit. Possible values are dots (that is, none), inches, or centimeters.
320	Color map. For palette-based images, this tag defines the image's RGB palette. The palette is physically ordered such that all red values come first, followed by all blue values, followed by all green values. Each value is a 16-bit unsigned integer, so black is (0,0,0) and white is (65535,65535,65535).

TIFF Image Types

The baseline TIFF specification supports four image types. These are bilevel, gray-scale, color-mapped, and RGB-based. The type of an image is determined from tag number 262, the photometric interpretation tag.

Versions of the TIFF format prior to revision 6.0 referred to the different image types as TIFF classes. For example, bilevel images were referred to as TIFF class B images. The class terminology is now considered defunct, although it is frequently found in books and references that predate the 6.0 format revision.

Note that TIFF extensions to the baseline specification add additional image types. These include images based on other color models, such as CMYK and YCbCr, and special-purpose image definitions such as transparencies and matted imagery.

In the tables that follow, the data type specification is notated using the `TiffDataTypes` enumeration constants from Listing 16.1.

Bilevel Images

A bilevel image is a 1-bit-per-pixel image that can be interpreted as either black on white (that is, white = 0) or white on black (white = 1). The photometric interpretation tag indicates which interpretation is to be used; the tag's value is the pixel value for white. Table 16.3 indicates the minimum tag requirements for a bilevel image.

Table 16.3 Bilevel Image Tag Requirements

Tag	Name	Data Type	Value(s)
256	Image width	tUShort or tULong	
257	Image height	tUShort or tULong	
259	Compression	tUShort	1, 2, or 32773
262	Photometric interpretation	tUShort	0 or 1
273	Strip offset(s)	tUShort or tULong	
278	Rows per strip	tUShort or tULong	
279	Strip byte count(s)	tUShort or tULong	
282	X resolution	tURational	
283	Y resolution	tURational	
296	Resolution unit	tUShort	1, 2, or 3

Gray-scale Images

As defined by TIFF, a gray-scale image is an image composed of single-valued pixels of 4 or 8 bits in size. This allows for images with either 16 or 256 levels of gray. Note that a color map is not required: a pixel's value indicates gray level directly. Table 16.4 indicates the minimum tag requirements for gray-scale images.

Table 16.4 Gray-scale Image Tag Requirements

Tag	Name	Data Type	Value(s)
256	Image width	tUShort or tULong	
257	Image height	tUShort or tULong	
258	Bits per sample	tUShort	4 or 8
259	Compression	tUShort	1 or 32773
262	Photometric interpretation	tUShort	0 or 1
273	Strip offset(s)	tUShort or tULong	

Table 16.4 Gray-scale Image Tag Requirements (continued)

278	Rows per strip	tUShort or tULong	
279	Strip byte count(s)	tUShort or tULong	
282	X resolution	tURational	
283	Y resolution	tURational	
296	Resolution unit	tUShort	1, 2, or 3

Color-Mapped Images

Color-mapped images are also referred to as palette-based images. This image type requires a palette containing color definitions. Pixel values are interpreted as indexes into the palette. This image type is the natural choice for all 16-color and 256-color VGA display modes. Table 16.5 lists the minimum tag requirements for this image type.

Table 16.5 Color-Mapped Image Tag Requirements

Tag	Name	Data Type	Value(s)
256	Image width	tUShort or tULong	
257	Image height	tUShort or tULong	
258	Bits per sample	tUShort	1, 2, 4 or 8
259	Compression	tUShort	1 or 32773
262	Photometric interpretation	tUShort	3
273	Strip offset(s)	tUShort or tULong	
278	Rows per strip	tUShort or tULong	
279	Strip byte count(s)	tUShort or tULong	
282	X resolution	tURational	
283	Y resolution	tURational	
296	Resolution unit	tUShort	1, 2, or 3
320	Color map	tUShort	

Full-Color RGB Images

The fourth baseline TIFF image type is the full-color RGB image. This type is used for 15-bit and 24-bit color images, among others. In most cases, images of this type specify 8 for bits per sample and 3 for samples per pixel. However, TIFF readers should be prepared to handle values other than these for these two fields. Table 16.6 lists the minimum tag requirements for this image type.

Table 16.6 Full-Color RGB Image Tag Requirements

Tag	Name	Data Type	Value(s)
256	Image width	tUShort or tULong	
257	Image height	tUShort or tULong	
258	Bits per sample	tUShort	8 x 3
259	Compression	tUShort	1 or 32773
262	Photometric interpretation	tUShort	2
273	Strip offset(s)	tUShort or tULong	
277	Samples per pixel	tUShort	3
278	Rows per strip	tUShort or tULong	
279	Strip byte count(s)	tUShort or tULong	
282	X resolution	tURational	
283	Y resolution	tURational	
296	Resolution unit	tUShort	1, 2, or 3

Listing 16.1 TIF.HPP

```
//----------------------------------------------------------//
//                                                          //
//    File:   TIF.HPP                                       //
//                                                          //
//    Desc:   Structure and Class definitions for the       //
//            Tagged Image File Format Revision 6.0          //
//                                                          //
//----------------------------------------------------------//

#ifndef _TIF_HPP_
#define _TIF_HPP_

#include "stdlib.h"
#include "stdio.h"
#include "string.h"
#include "ctype.h"

#include "gffasm.h"
#include "codec.hpp"
#include "color.hpp"

//.................various constants

#define  IntelORDER    0x4949
#define  MotorORDER    0x4D4D
#define  TIFFIDEN      42
```

Listing 16.1 TIF.HPP (continued)

```cpp
// define for system being used
#define  NativeORDER  IntelORDER

enum TiffDataTypes
{
    tNone,              // unspecified
    tUByte,             // 8-bit unsigned
    tAscii,             // Null terminated string
    tUShort,            // 16-bit unsigned
    tULong,             // 32-bit unsigned
    tURational,         // 32-bit unsigned x 2
    tSByte,             // 8-bit signed
    tByte,              // 8-bit undefined
    tSShort,            // 16-bit signed
    tSLong,             // 32-bit signed
    tSRational,         // 32-bit signed x 2
    tFloat,             // 4-byte IEEE
    tDouble             // 8-byte IEEE
};

enum TiffCompressionTypes
{
    cNone,
    cUncompressed,
    cCCITT1d,
    cGroup3Fax,
    cGroup4Fax,
    cLZW,
    cJPEG,
    cPackBits = 32773u
};

enum TiffImageTypes
{
    iBlackOnWhite,
    iWhiteOnBlack,
    iRGB,
    iColorMapped,
    iTransparency,
    iCMYK,
    iYCbCr,
    iCIELab
};

//.................nonmember functions
```

Listing 16.1 TIF.HPP (continued)

```cpp
char *TiffTagName( int tag );
char *TiffDataTypeName( int type );
int   TiffDataTypeSize( int type );
char *TiffCompressionName( int type );
char *TiffPhotometricName( int type );
char *TiffResolutionName( int type );
char *TiffPlanarName( int type );
int   ReverseByteOrder( void );

//................struct TIFFHEADER

struct TIFFHEADER
{
   unsigned short order;    // byte order Intel or Motorola
   unsigned short iden;     // magic number identifier (42)
   unsigned long  ifdofs;   // offset to first IFD
   TIFFHEADER( )
   {
      order = IntelORDER;
      iden  = TIFFIDEN;
      ifdofs = 0;
   }
   TIFFHEADER( unsigned short ord, unsigned long iofs )
   {
      order = ord;
      iden  = TIFFIDEN;
      ifdofs = iofs;
   }
  ~TIFFHEADER( )
   {
   }
   void list( void );
   int  get( FILE *f );
   int  put( FILE *f );
   int  isvalid( void );
};

//................struct IFD

struct IFDENTRY
{
   unsigned short tag;      // tag identifier
   unsigned short type;     // data type
   unsigned long  count;    // number of type values
   unsigned long  valofs;   // offset to value
```

Listing 16.1 TIF.HPP (continued)

```cpp
     IFDENTRY( )
     {
        tag = type = 0;
        count = valofs = 0;
     }
     IFDENTRY( unsigned short t, unsigned short typ,
               unsigned long cnt, unsigned long vofs )
     {
        tag    = t;
        type   = typ;
        count  = cnt;
        valofs = vofs;
     }
    ~IFDENTRY( )
     {
     }

     void list( void );
     int  get( FILE *f );
     int  put( FILE *f );

     // some convenient type conversions
     int cnt( void ) { return int(count); }
     int val( void ) { return int(valofs); }
     unsigned int ucnt( void ) { return (unsigned int) count; }
     unsigned int uval( void ) { return (unsigned int) valofs; }
};

//.................struct TIFFIMAGEDEF

struct TIFFIMAGEDEF
{
     unsigned short imgtype;      // image type              *
     unsigned short cmptype;      // compression type        *
     unsigned short width;        // width in pixels         *
     unsigned short height;       // height in pixels        *
     unsigned short depth;        // depth in bits
     unsigned short bitsamp;      // bits per sample         *
     unsigned short samppix;      // samples per pixel       *
     unsigned short planar;       // planar configuration    *
     unsigned short orient;       // orientation             *
     unsigned short hmirror;      // horz mirrored
     unsigned short vmirror;      // vert mirrored
     unsigned short rotate;       // rotated (landscape)
     unsigned short resunit;      // resolution units        *
     unsigned short xres;         // x resolution            *
     unsigned short yres;         // y resolution            *
     unsigned short nstrips;      // strips in image
```

Listing 16.1 TIF.HPP (continued)

```
    unsigned short striphgt;    // strip hgt in rows       *
    unsigned short ncolors;     // color count in pal
    rgb          *  colors;     // color map               *
    long         *  stripofs;   // array of strip offsets  *

    TIFFIMAGEDEF( );
   ~TIFFIMAGEDEF( );
    void list( void );
    int  get( FILE *f );
};

    #endif
```

Listing 16.2 TIF.CPP

```
//----------------------------------------------------------//
//                                                          //
//    File:   TIF.CPP                                       //
//                                                          //
//    Desc:   Structure and Class definitions for the       //
//            Tagged Image File Format Revision 6.0          //
//                                                          //
//----------------------------------------------------------//

#include "tif.hpp"

//................various constant/name sets

static int reverse_byte_order = 0;

int ReverseByteOrder( void ) { return reverse_byte_order; }
//................various constant/name sets

static struct TAGNAMES
{
   unsigned short tag;
   char           *name;
}
TagNames[] =
{
   { 254,    "NewSubfileType" },
   { 255,    "SubfileType" },
   { 256,    "ImageWidth" },
   { 257,    "ImageHeight" },
   { 258,    "BitsPerSample" },
   { 259,    "Compression" },
   { 262,    "PhotometricInterpretation" },
   { 263,    "Thresholding" },
```

Listing 16.2 TIF.CPP (continued)

```
{ 264,    "CellWidth" },
{ 265,    "CellHeight" },
{ 266,    "FillOrder" },
{ 269,    "DocumentName" },
{ 270,    "ImageDescription" },
{ 271,    "Make" },
{ 272,    "Model" },
{ 273,    "StripOffsets" },
{ 274,    "Orientation" },
{ 277,    "SamplesPerPixel" },
{ 278,    "RowsPerStrip" },
{ 279,    "StripByteCounts" },
{ 280,    "MinSampleValue" },
{ 281,    "MaxSampleValue" },
{ 282,    "XResolution" },
{ 283,    "YResolution" },
{ 284,    "PlanarConfiguration" },
{ 285,    "PageName" },
{ 286,    "XPosition" },
{ 287,    "YPosition" },
{ 288,    "FreeOffsets" },
{ 289,    "FreeByteCounts" },
{ 290,    "GrayResponseUnit" },
{ 291,    "GrayResponseCurve" },
{ 292,    "Group3Options" },
{ 293,    "Group4Options" },
{ 296,    "ResolutionUnit" },
{ 297,    "PageNumber" },
{ 301,    "TransferFunction" },
{ 305,    "Software" },
{ 306,    "DateTime" },
{ 315,    "Artist" },
{ 316,    "HostComputer" },
{ 317,    "Predictor" },
{ 318,    "WhitePoint" },
{ 319,    "PrimaryChromaticities" },
{ 320,    "ColorMap" },
{ 321,    "HalftoneHints" },
{ 322,    "TileWidth" },
{ 323,    "TileHeight" },
{ 324,    "TileOffsets" },
{ 325,    "TileByteCounts" },
{ 332,    "InkSet" },
{ 333,    "InkNames" },
{ 334,    "NumberOfInks" },
{ 336,    "DotRange" },
{ 337,    "TargetPrinter" },
{ 338,    "ExtraSamples" },
```

Listing 16.2 TIF.CPP (continued)

```
        { 339,    "SampleFormat" },
        { 340,    "SMinSampleValue" },
        { 341,    "SMaxSampleValue" },
        { 512,    "JPEGProc" },
        { 513,    "JPEGInterchangeFormat" },
        { 514,    "JPEGInterchangeFormatLngth" },
        { 515,    "JPEGRestartInterval" },
        { 517,    "JPEGLosslessPredictors" },
        { 518,    "JPEGPointTransforms" },
        { 519,    "JPEGQTables" },
        { 520,    "JPEGDCTables" },
        { 521,    "JPEGACTables" },
        { 529,    "YCbCrCoefficients" },
        { 530,    "YCbCrSubSampling" },
        { 531,    "YCbCrPositioning" },
        { 532,    "ReferenceBlackWhite" },
        { 33432u, "Copyright" },
    };
    #define TAGCOUNT ( sizeof(TagNames) / sizeof(TAGNAMES) )
    static struct COMPRESSIONNAMES
    {
        unsigned short type;
        char        *name;
    }
    CompressionNames[] =
    {
        { 1,      "Uncompressed" },
        { 2,      "CCITT1D" },
        { 3,      "Group3Fax" },
        { 4,      "Group4Fax" },
        { 5,      "LZW" },
        { 6,      "JPEG" },
        { 32773u, "PackBits" },
    };
    #define COMPCOUNT ( sizeof(CompressionNames) /\
                        sizeof(COMPRESSIONNAMES) )

    static struct PHOTOMETRICNAMES
    {
        unsigned short type;
        char        *name;
    }
    PhotometricNames[] =
    {
        { 0, "WhiteIsZero" },
        { 1, "BlackIsZero" },
        { 2, "RGB" },
        { 3, "RGB Palette" },
```

Listing 16.2 TIF.CPP (continued)

```cpp
        { 4, "Transparency Mask" },
        { 5, "CMYK" },
        { 6, "YCbCr" },
        { 8, "CIELab" },
};
#define PHOTOCOUNT ( sizeof(PhotometricNames) /\
                          sizeof(PHOTOMETRICNAMES) )

static struct DATATYPENAMES
{
    unsigned short type;
    int            size;
    char           *name;
}
DataTypeNames[] =
{
    {  0,  0,  "Unspecified" },
    {  1,  1,  "8-bit unsigned" },
    {  2,  1,  "ASCIIZ string" },
    {  3,  2,  "16-bit unsigned" },
    {  4,  4,  "32-bit unsigned" },
    {  5,  8,  "32-bit unsigned rational" },
    {  6,  1,  "8-bit signed" },
    {  7,  1,  "8-bit undefined" },
    {  8,  2,  "16-bit signed" },
    {  9,  4,  "32-bit signed" },
    { 10,  8,  "32-bit signed rational" },
    { 11,  4,  "4-byte IEEE floating point" },
    { 12,  8,  "8-byte IEEE floating point" },
};
#define DATACOUNT ( sizeof(DataTypeNames) /\
                         sizeof(DATATYPENAMES) )

static struct RESOLUTIONNAMES
{
    unsigned short type;
    char           *name;
}
ResolutionNames[] =
{
    { 1, "Undefined" },
    { 2, "Inches" },
    { 3, "Centimeters" },
};
#define RESCOUNT ( sizeof(ResolutionNames) /\
                        sizeof(RESOLUTIONNAMES) )
```

Listing 16.2 TIF.CPP (continued)

```cpp
static struct PLANARNAMES
{
   unsigned short type;
   char           *name;
}
PlanarNames[] =
{
   { 1, "Chunky" },
   { 2, "Planar" },
};
#define PLANARCOUNT ( sizeof(PlanarNames) /\
                      sizeof(PLANARNAMES) )

static char *Unknown = "Unknown";

char *TiffTagName( int tag )
{
   for( int i=0; i<TAGCOUNT; i++ )
      if( TagNames[i].tag == tag )
         return TagNames[i].name;
   return Unknown;
}

char *TiffDataTypeName( int type )
{
   for( int i=0; i<DATACOUNT; i++ )
      if( DataTypeNames[i].type == type )
         return DataTypeNames[i].name;
   return Unknown;
}

int TiffDataTypeSize( int type )
{
   for( int i=0; i<DATACOUNT; i++ )
      if( DataTypeNames[i].type == type )
         return DataTypeNames[i].size;
   return 0;
}

char *TiffCompressionName( int type )
{
   for( int i=0; i<COMPCOUNT; i++ )
      if( CompressionNames[i].type == type )
         return CompressionNames[i].name;
   return Unknown;
}
```

Listing 16.2 TIF.CPP (continued)

```cpp
char *TiffPhotometricName( int type )
{
   for( int i=0; i<PHOTOCOUNT; i++ )
      if( PhotometricNames[i].type == type )
         return PhotometricNames[i].name;
   return Unknown;
}

char *TiffResolutionName( int type )
{
   for( int i=0; i<RESCOUNT; i++ )
      if( ResolutionNames[i].type == type )
         return ResolutionNames[i].name;
   return Unknown;
}

char *TiffPlanarName( int type )
{
   for( int i=0; i<PLANARCOUNT; i++ )
      if( PlanarNames[i].type == type )
         return PlanarNames[i].name;
   return Unknown;
}

//.................struct TIFFHEADER

void TIFFHEADER::list( void )
{
   printf( "TIFFHEADER::order  = %04Xh ", order );
   switch( order )
   {
      case IntelORDER :
          printf( "(Intel)\n" );
          break;
      case MotorORDER :
          printf( "(Motorola)\n" );
          break;
      default :
          printf( "(???)\n" );
          break;
   }
   printf( "TIFFHEADER::iden  = %d\n", iden );
   printf( "TIFFHEADER::ifdofs = %ld\n", ifdofs );
}
```

Listing 16.2 TIF.CPP (continued)

```cpp
int TIFFHEADER::get( FILE *f )
{
   if( fread(&order,sizeof(TIFFHEADER),1,f) != 1 )
      return -1;
   reverse_byte_order = (order == NativeORDER) ? 0 : 1;
   if( reverse_byte_order )
   {
      iden  = rev_word( iden );
      ifdofs = rev_dword( ifdofs );
   }
   return 0;
}

int TIFFHEADER::put( FILE *f )
{
   reverse_byte_order = (order == NativeORDER) ? 0 : 1;
   // reverse for writing
   if( reverse_byte_order )
   {
      iden  = rev_word( iden );
      ifdofs = rev_dword( ifdofs );
   }
   int retv = (fwrite(&order,sizeof(TIFFHEADER),1,f) == 1) ?
               0 : -1;
   // restore original order
   if( reverse_byte_order )
   {
      iden  = rev_word( iden );
      ifdofs = rev_dword( ifdofs );
   }
   return retv;
}

int TIFFHEADER::isvalid( void )
{
   if( iden != TIFFIDEN )
      return 0;
   if( (order != IntelORDER) && (order != MotorORDER) )
      return 0;
   return 1;
}

//.................struct IFDENTRY

void IFDENTRY::list( void )
{
   printf( "IFDENTRY::tag    = %u ", tag );
   printf( "(%s)\n", TiffTagName( tag ) );
```

Listing 16.2 TIF.CPP (continued)

```cpp
    printf( "IFDENTRY::type   = %u ", type );
    printf( "(%s)\n", TiffDataTypeName( type ) );
    printf( "IFDENTRY::count  = %lu\n", count );
    int isval = (count * TiffDataTypeSize(type) <= 4) ?
                '*' : ' ';
    printf( "IFDENTRY::valofs = %lu  %c  ", valofs, isval );

    // for a few special tags we interpret the value
    int type = int( valofs );
    switch( tag )
    {
        case 259 : // compression
            printf( "(%s)\n", TiffCompressionName( type ) );
            break;
        case 262 : // image type
            printf( "(%s)\n", TiffPhotometricName( type ) );
            break;
        case 284 : // planar configuration
            printf( "(%s)\n", TiffPlanarName( type ) );
            break;
        case 296 : // resolution units
            printf( "(%s)\n", TiffResolutionName( type ) );
            break;
        default :
            printf( "\n" );
            break;
    }
}

int IFDENTRY::get( FILE *f )
{
    if( fread(&tag,sizeof(IFDENTRY),1,f) != 1 )
        return -1;
    if( reverse_byte_order )
    {
        tag    = rev_word( tag );
        type   = rev_word( type );
        count  = rev_dword( count );
        valofs = rev_dword( valofs );
    }
    return 0;
}

int IFDENTRY::put( FILE *f )
{
    // reverse for writing
    if( reverse_byte_order )
    {
```

Listing 16.2 TIF.CPP (continued)

```
        tag    = rev_word( tag );
        type   = rev_word( type );
        count  = rev_dword( count );
        valofs = rev_dword( valofs );
    }
    int retv = (fwrite(&tag,sizeof(IFDENTRY),1,f) == 1) ?
               0 : -1;
    // restore original order
    if( reverse_byte_order )
    {
        tag    = rev_word( tag );
        type   = rev_word( type );
        count  = rev_dword( count );
        valofs = rev_dword( valofs );
    }
    return retv;
}


//................struct TIFFIMAGEDEF

TIFFIMAGEDEF::TIFFIMAGEDEF( )
{
    imgtype  = 0;      // white is zero
    cmptype  = 1;      // uncompressed
    width    = 0;
    height   = 0;
    depth    = 1;      // bilevel
    bitsamp  = 1;
    samppix  = 1;
    planar   = 1;      // chunky
    orient   = 1;      // upper left org
    hmirror  = 0;
    vmirror  = 0;
    rotate   = 0;
    resunit  = 2;      // inches
    xres     = 100;    // typical screen dpi
    yres     = 100;
    nstrips  = 0;
    striphgt = 0;
    ncolors  = 0;
    colors   = 0;
    stripofs = 0;
}
```

Listing 16.2 TIF.CPP (continued)

```cpp
TIFFIMAGEDEF::~TIFFIMAGEDEF( )
{
    delete colors;
    delete stripofs;
}


// file should be positioned at start of IFD

int TIFFIMAGEDEF::get( FILE *f )
{
    // read IFD entry count
    unsigned short n;
    if( fread( &n, 2, 1, f ) != 1 ) return xIOERROR;
    if( reverse_byte_order ) n = rev_word( n );

    // read each entry
    long curofs, ltmp, ratnl[2];
    unsigned short stmp;
    int j;
    for( int i=0; i<n; i++ )
    {
        IFDENTRY x;
        if( x.get( f ) ) return xIOERROR;
        curofs = ftell( f );

        switch( x.tag )
        {
            case 256 : // ImageWidth
                width = x.uval();
                break;
            case 257 : // ImageHeight
                height = x.uval();
                break;
            case 258 : // BitsPerSample
                bitsamp = x.uval();
                break;
            case 259 : // Compression
                cmptype = x.uval();
                break;
            case 262 : // PhotometricInterpretation
                imgtype = x.uval();
                break;
            case 273 : // StripOffsets
                nstrips = x.ucnt();
                stripofs = new long [nstrips];
                if( stripofs == 0 ) return xNOMEMORY;
                // where are the offsets?
                if( x.count * TiffDataTypeSize(x.type) <= 4L )
```

Listing 16.2 TIF.CPP (continued)

```cpp
                        fseek( f, -4L, SEEK_CUR );
                else
                        fseek( f, x.valofs, SEEK_SET );
                for( j=0; j<nstrips; j++ )
                {
                        if( (x.type == tULong) || (x.type == tSLong) )
                        {
                                fread( &ltmp, 4, 1, f );
                                stripofs[j] = ltmp;
                        }
                        else
                        {
                                fread( &stmp, 2, 1, f );
                                stripofs[j] = stmp;
                        }
                }
                // restore file position
                fseek( f, curofs, SEEK_SET );
                break;
        case 274 : // Orientation
                orient = x.uval();
                break;
        case 277 : // SamplesPerPixel
                samppix = x.uval();
                break;
        case 278 : // RowsPerStrip
                striphgt = x.uval();
                break;
        case 282 : // X Resolution
                fseek( f, x.valofs, SEEK_SET );
                fread( ratnl, 4, 2, f );
                ltmp = ratnl[0] / ratnl[1];
                xres = (unsigned short) ltmp;
                // restore file position
                fseek( f, curofs, SEEK_SET );
                break;
        case 283 : // Y Resolution
                fseek( f, x.valofs, SEEK_SET );
                fread( ratnl, 4, 2, f );
                ltmp = ratnl[0] / ratnl[1];
                yres = (unsigned short) ltmp;
                // restore file position
                fseek( f, curofs, SEEK_SET );
                break;
        case 284 : // PlanarConfiguration
                planar = x.uval();
                break;
```

Listing 16.2 TIF.CPP (continued)

```cpp
        case 296 : // ResolutionUnit
                resunit = x.uval();
                break;
        case 320 : // ColorMap
                ncolors = x.ucnt() / 3;
                colors = new rgb [ncolors];
                if( colors == 0 ) return xNOMEMORY;
                fseek( f, x.valofs, SEEK_SET );
                for( j=0; j<ncolors; j++ )
                {
                    fread( &stmp, 2, 1, f );
                    stmp >>= 8;
                    colors[j].red = (unsigned char) stmp;
                }
                for( j=0; j<ncolors; j++ )
                {
                    fread( &stmp, 2, 1, f );
                    stmp >>= 8;
                    colors[j].grn = (unsigned char) stmp;
                }
                for( j=0; j<ncolors; j++ )
                {
                    fread( &stmp, 2, 1, f );
                    stmp >>= 8;
                    colors[j].blu = (unsigned char) stmp;
                }
                // restore file position
                fseek( f, curofs, SEEK_SET );
                break;
    }
}

// fill in missing values and check...

depth = samppix * bitsamp;

if( striphgt == 0 )
    striphgt = height;

switch( orient )
{
    case 2 :
            hmirror = 1;
            break;
    case 3 :
            hmirror = 1;
            vmirror = 1;
            break;
```

Listing 16.2 TIF.CPP (continued)

```
        case 4 :
            vmirror = 1;
            break;
    }

    if( imgtype > 3 )
        return xUNSUPPORTED;

    if( planar == 2 )
        return xUNSUPPORTED;

    rgb Black( 0, 0, 0 );
    rgb White( 255, 255, 255 );

    if( ncolors == 0 )
        switch( imgtype )
        {
            case 0 : // 0=white
                ncolors = 2;
                colors = new rgb [ncolors];
                if( colors == 0 ) return xNOMEMORY;
                colors[0] = White;
                colors[1] = Black;
                break;
            case 1 : // 0=black
                ncolors = 2;
                colors = new rgb [ncolors];
                if( colors == 0 ) return xNOMEMORY;
                colors[0] = Black;
                colors[1] = White;
                break;
            case 3 : // Color-mapped
                // missing palette
                return xBADPARAM;
        }

    return xOKAY;
}

void TIFFIMAGEDEF::list( void )
{
    printf( "TIFFIMAGEDEF::imgtype  = %u\n", imgtype );
    printf( "TIFFIMAGEDEF::cmptype  = %u\n", cmptype );
    printf( "TIFFIMAGEDEF::width    = %u\n", width   );
    printf( "TIFFIMAGEDEF::height   = %u\n", height  );
    printf( "TIFFIMAGEDEF::depth    = %u\n", depth   );
    printf( "TIFFIMAGEDEF::bitsamp  = %u\n", bitsamp );
    printf( "TIFFIMAGEDEF::samppix  = %u\n", samppix );
```

Listing 16.2 TIF.CPP (continued)

```
    printf( "TIFFIMAGEDEF::planar   = %u\n", planar  );
    printf( "TIFFIMAGEDEF::orient   = %u\n", orient  );
    printf( "TIFFIMAGEDEF::hmirror  = %u\n", hmirror );
    printf( "TIFFIMAGEDEF::vmirror  = %u\n", vmirror );
    printf( "TIFFIMAGEDEF::rotate   = %u\n", rotate  );
    printf( "TIFFIMAGEDEF::resunit  = %u\n", resunit );
    printf( "TIFFIMAGEDEF::xres     = %u\n", xres    );
    printf( "TIFFIMAGEDEF::yres     = %u\n", yres    );
    printf( "TIFFIMAGEDEF::striphgt = %u\n", striphgt);
    printf( "TIFFIMAGEDEF::ncolors  = %u\n", ncolors );
    for( int i=0; i<ncolors; i++ )
        printf( "                colors[%d] = rgb(%d,%d,%d)\n",
            i, colors[i].red, colors[i].grn, colors[i].blu );
    printf( "TIFFIMAGEDEF::nstrips  = %d\n", nstrips );
    for( i=0; i<nstrips; i++ )
        printf( "                stripofs[%d] = %ld\n",
            i, stripofs[i] );
}
```

A TIFF Query Program

Given the relative complexity of the TIFF format, a query program for the format is more of a necessity than a luxury. Listing 16.3 presents the source code to a suitable example of such a program, QTIF.CPP.

A couple of notes about the program are in order. First, it will translate tag and data type values into actual names and display these in parentheses following their values. With so many possible values, this is a necessary feature. Also, if you recall, when an image datum is 4 bytes in size or less, then the offset field of an IFD entry contains the actual value, not an offset to the value. This is indicated in the listing by an asterisk following the value.

One potential snag should be pointed out to programmers who want to use this code on Motorola-based systems. When an IFD entry value offset contains an actual value, it is left-justified within the 4 bytes of the structure's `ofsval` member. If the size of the value is less than 4, then the value must be right-justified before use, or else the address of the value must be cast to a pointer of the desired type. On Intel-based systems this is not necessary; only a cast of the actual value is required.

The program will list all IFD entries for all subfiles found in a TIFF file. An example of the program's output is shown in Figure 16.1. The file being listed is the logo image for MicroGrafx's fine-image editing program, Picture Publisher.

```
Listing of TIF file '\windows\pictpub\logo.tif'
TIFFHEADER::order  = 4949h (Intel)
TIFFHEADER::iden   = 42
TIFFHEADER::ifdofs = 8

IFD at Offset 8 has 11 Entries.....

IFDENTRY::tag    = 255 (SubfileTye)
IFDENTRY::type   = 3 (16-bit unsigned)
IFDENTRY::count  = 1
IFDENTRY::valofs = 1   *

IFDENTRY::tag    = 256 (ImageWidth)
IFDENTRY::type   = 3 (16-bit unsigned)
IFDENTRY::count  = 1
IFDENTRY::valofs = 156   *

IFDENTRY::tag    = 257 (ImageHeight)
IFDENTRY::type   = 3 (16-bit unsigned)
IFDENTRY::count  = 1
IFDENTRY::valofs = 181   *

IFDENTRY::tag    = 258 (BitsPerSample)
IFDENTRY::type   = 3 (16-bit unsigned)
IFDENTRY::count  = 3
IFDENTRY::valofs = 146

IFDENTRY::tag    = 259 (Compression)
IFDENTRY::type   = 3 (16-bit unsigned)
IFDENTRY::count  = 1
IFDENTRY::valofs = 1   *   (Uncompressed)

IFDENTRY::tag    = 262 (PhotometricInterpretation)
IFDENTRY::type   = 3 (16-bit unsigned)
IFDENTRY::count  = 1
IFDENTRY::valofs = 2   *   (RGB)

IFDENTRY::tag    = 273 (StripOffsets)
IFDENTRY::type   = 4 (32-bit unsigned)
IFDENTRY::count  = 1
IFDENTRY::valofs = 168   *

IFDENTRY::tag    = 277 (SamplesPerPixel)
IFDENTRY::type   = 3 (16-bit unsigned)
IFDENTRY::count  = 1
IFDENTRY::valofs = 3   *
```

Figure 16.1 Example of Output from QTIF

```
IFDENTRY::tag    = 282 (XResolution)
IFDENTRY::type   = 5 (32-bit unsigned rational)
IFDENTRY::count  = 1
IFDENTRY::valofs = 152

IFDENTRY::tag    = 283 (YResolution)
IFDENTRY::type   = 5 (32-bit unsigned rational)
IFDENTRY::count  = 1
IFDENTRY::valofs = 160

IFDENTRY::tag    = 284 (PlanarConfiguration)
IFDENTRY::type   = 3 (16-bit unsigned)
IFDENTRY::count  = 1
IFDENTRY::valofs = 1  *
```

Listing 16.3 QTIF.CPP

```cpp
//----------------------------------------------------------//
//                                                          //
//   File:     QTIF.CPP                                     //
//                                                          //
//   Desc:     TIFF File Query Program                      //
//                                                          //
//----------------------------------------------------------//

#include "stdlib.h"
#include "stdio.h"
#include "string.h"
#include "conio.h"

#include "tif.hpp"

//................program globals

char fn[80];
int  list;
int  pglen;

//................program usage

void explain_pgm( void )
{
   printf( "\n" );
   printf( "............TIFF File Query Program..............\n"
);
   printf( "\n" );
   printf( "Usage:     QTIF  tif_file  [ switches ]\n" );
```

Listing 16.3 QTIF.CPP (continued)

```cpp
    printf( "\n" );
    printf( "Switches:  -h       = display program usage\n" );
    printf( "           -d       = list image definition\n" );
    printf( "           -lNN     = page length is NN lines\n" );
    printf( "\n" );
    printf( ".TIF extension assumed\n" );
    printf( "Continuous page length assumed\n" );
    printf( "..................................................\n"
);
    printf( "\n" );
}

//.................process args

void process_args( int argc, char *argv[] )
{
    // establish default values
    fn[0] = 0;
    list  = 0;
    pglen = 0;

    // process the program's argument list
    for( int i=1; i<argc; i++ )
    {
        if( (*argv[i] == '-') || (*argv[i] == '/') )
        {
            char sw = *(argv[i] + 1);
            switch( toupper(sw) )
            {
                case 'H' :
                    explain_pgm();
                    exit( 0 );
                    break;

                case 'L' :
                    sscanf( argv[i]+2, "%d", &pglen );
                    break;

                case 'D' :
                    list = 1;
                    break;
                default:
                    printf( "Unknown switch '%s' ignored\n",
                            argv[i] );
                    break;
            }
        }
        else  // presumably a file identifier
```

Listing 16.3 QTIF.CPP (continued)

```cpp
        {
            strcpy( fn, argv[i] );
            char *p = strchr( fn, '.' );
            if( p == 0 )
                strcat( fn, ".tif" );
            else if( *(p+1) == 0 )
                *p = 0;
        }
    }

    // was a file name specified?
    if( fn[0] == 0 )
    {
        explain_pgm();
        exit( 0 );
    }
}

//.................check for end-of-page

static int nlines = 0;

void more( int n )
{
    if( pglen > 0 )
    {
        nlines += n;
        if( nlines > pglen )
        {
            nlines = 0;
            printf( "(more...)\n" );
            getch();
        }
    }
}

//.................main

int main( int argc, char *argv[] )
{
    process_args( argc, argv );

    // open the file
    FILE *ftif = fopen( fn, "rb" );
    if( ftif == 0 )
    {
        printf( "File '%s' not found\n", fn );
```

Listing 16.3 QTIF.CPP (continued)

```
      return 0;
   }

   // read header and validate
   TIFFHEADER tifh;
   tifh.get( ftif );
   if( ! tifh.isvalid() )
   {
      printf( "Error - file is not a TIFF file\n" );
      exit( 0 );
   }

   printf( "Listing of TIF file '%s'\n", fn );
   printf( "\n" );
   tifh.list();
   more( 5 );

   // list each TIF subfile
   long ifd_offset = tifh.ifdofs;
   while( ifd_offset )
   {
      // seek to start
      fseek( ftif, ifd_offset, SEEK_SET );
      long cur_offset = ifd_offset;

      // get IFD entry count
      unsigned short nentries;
      fread( &nentries, 2, 1, ftif );
      if( ReverseByteOrder() )
         nentries = rev_word( nentries );

      // printf subfile header
      more( 2 );
      printf( "\nIFD at Offset %ld has %d Entries.....\n",
              ifd_offset, nentries );

      // list each IFD entrie
      for( int i=0; i<nentries; i++ )
      {
         more( 5 );
         IFDENTRY ifde;
         ifde.get( ftif );
         printf( "\n" );
         ifde.list();
      }

      // get offset to next subfile
      fread( &ifd_offset, 4, 1, ftif );
```

Listing 16.3 QTIF.CPP (continued)

```
        if( ReverseByteOrder() )
           ifd_offset = rev_dword( ifd_offset );

        // create and list image def?
        if( list )
        {
           more( 999 );
           fseek( ftif, cur_offset, SEEK_SET );
           TIFFIMAGEDEF idef;
           idef.get( ftif );
           printf( "\n" );
           idef.list( );
        }
     }

     return 0;
}
```

Reading and Writing TIFF Files

Given the extent and complexity of the TIFF format, the tasks of reading and writing TIFF files are somewhat more complex than they are for other formats. This of course results in a corresponding increase in program source code volume. To keep the size of source modules manageable, I have elected to split the TIFF source among several source files. Listings 16.1 and 16.2 contain the code for dealing with the various TIFF data structures. Code for encoding and decoding bitmaps is presented separately in Listings 16.4 and 16.5.

As noted, an IFD defines a TIFF subfile. An IFD serves much the same purpose as file and image headers do in other formats. The fact that an IFD can contain an arbitrary collection of data makes it versatile from an architectural point of view but somewhat awkward to work with from a procedural point of view. To address this issue, a fixed structure has been defined that contains all the fields necessary to process a baseline format instance. This is the structure `TIFFIMAGEDEF` in Listings 16.1 and 16.2. Keep in mind that this structure is not a formal part of the format specification, but is a contrivance devised to assist in reading and writing the format.

A codec for the baseline TIFF format is presented in Listings 16.4 and 16.5 as the two classes `TiffEncoder` and `TiffDecoder`. A compliant codec must be capable of handling three compressions schemes, no compression, PackBits compression, and CCITT 1D modified Huffman compression. The latter two were described separately in Chapter 3. Here, slightly modified versions of the code from that chapter are embedded within the TIFF codec classes. This was done to implement both encoder and decoder as a single class.

There is one potentially confusing aspect of the compression schemes defined by the TIFF specification. Fax-based extensions to the baseline format, which were collectively referred to as TIFF class F prior to revision 6.0, add the Group 3 and Group 4 compression schemes specified by the CCITT (the International Telephone and Telegraph Consultative Committee). The modified Huffman compression algorithm of the baseline specification is actually a generalized version of the Group 3 facsimile algorithm, and there is a tendency to confuse the two as a result.

The differences between the two arise from the fact that the baseline format's modified Huffman compression algorithm has had fax-specific requirements removed. For instance, the Group 3 method requires that each scan line be followed by a unique end-of-line (EOL) code, which is used to resynchronize a transmitter-receiver pair in the event of an error burst. The use of EOL codes was dropped in the modified version, because it was never intended for use in facsimile transmission.

If you inspect the constructor code for the `TiffEncoder` and `TiffDecoder` classes, you will note that the setting of an I/O function pointer is based on a specified compression scheme. It is these I/O functions that actually perform encoding and decoding. The remainder of the class implementations are concerned only with packaging a scan line's worth of pixels into a buffer, which is then handed to an I/O function. This arrangement allows the classes to be easily modified to add support for TIFF extensions. You may also note that this arrangement is a bit different from other format codecs developed here.

Listing 16.4 TIFCODEC.HPP

```
//------------------------------------------------------------//
//                                                            //
//   File:     TIFCODEC.HPP                                   //
//                                                            //
//   Desc:     TIFF Encoder and Decoder classes for           //
//             Tagged Image File Format Revision 6.0          //
//                                                            //
//------------------------------------------------------------//

#ifndef _TIFCODEC_HPP_
#define _TIFCODEC_HPP_

#include "tif.hpp"
#include "revbyte.hpp"
```

Listing 16.4 TIFCODEC.HPP (continued)

```
//.................Scan Line I/O Functions

typedef int (*SCANIO)( FILE *, unsigned char *, int );

int ReadG3( FILE *fi, unsigned char *buf, int nbytes );
int ReadPB( FILE *fi, unsigned char *buf, int nbytes );
int ReadNC( FILE *fi, unsigned char *buf, int nbytes );

int WriteG3( FILE *fo, unsigned char *buf, int nbytes );
int WritePB( FILE *fo, unsigned char *buf, int nbytes );
int WriteNC( FILE *fo, unsigned char *buf, int nbytes );

//.................Class TiffDecoder
class TiffDecoder : public Decoder
{
    protected:
        FILE            *ftif;
        SCANIO          read;
        TIFFIMAGEDEF    *idef;
        unsigned char   *ibuf;
        unsigned short  rwbytes;
        int             curline;
        int             curstrip;
        int             cond;

    private:
        void unpack( unsigned char *buf, int npxls );

    public:
        TiffDecoder( FILE *fi, TIFFIMAGEDEF *tid );
        virtual ~TiffDecoder( );
        virtual int init( void );
        virtual int term( void );
        virtual int decode( unsigned char *buf, int npxls );
        virtual int status( void );
};

//.................Class TiffEncoder

class TiffEncoder : public Encoder
{
    protected:
        FILE            *ftif;
        SCANIO          write;
        TIFFIMAGEDEF    *idef;
        unsigned char   *ibuf;
        unsigned short  rwbytes;
        int             cond;
```

Listing 16.4 TIFCODEC.HPP (continued)

```
    private:
        void pack( unsigned char *buf, int npxls );

    public:
        TiffEncoder( FILE *fo, TIFFIMAGEDEF *tid );
        virtual ~TiffEncoder( );
        virtual int init( void );
        virtual int term( void );
        virtual int encode( unsigned char *buf, int npxls );
        virtual int status( void );
};

    #endif
```

Listing 16.5 TIFCODEC.CPP

```
//----------------------------------------------------------//
//                                                          //
//    File:    TIFCODEC.CPP                                 //
//                                                          //
//    Desc:    TIFF Encoder and Decoder classes for         //
//             Tagged Image File Format Revision 6.0         //
//                                                          //
//----------------------------------------------------------//

#include "tifcodec.hpp"

//----------------------------------------------------------//
//         Group 3 Modified Huffman Compression             //
//----------------------------------------------------------//

//................structure to hold code definitions

struct codedef
{
    short bitcode;     // encoded representation
    short codelen;     // length of bitcode in bits
    short runlen;      // run length in pixels
};

// table entry count — note that EOL codes are omitted

#define TBLSIZE 104

// code table for black runs, ordered by code length
static codedef black_bits[] =
{
```

Listing 16.5 TIFCODEC.CPP (continued)

```
{ 0xC000,  2,     2 },    { 0x8000,  2,     3 },
{ 0x4000,  3,     1 },    { 0x6000,  3,     4 },
{ 0x3000,  4,     5 },    { 0x2000,  4,     6 },
{ 0x1800,  5,     7 },    { 0x1400,  6,     8 },
{ 0x1000,  6,     9 },    { 0x0800,  7,    10 },
{ 0x0A00,  7,    11 },    { 0x0E00,  7,    12 },
{ 0x0400,  8,    13 },    { 0x0700,  8,    14 },
{ 0x0C00,  9,    15 },    { 0x0DC0, 10,     0 },
{ 0x05C0, 10,    16 },    { 0x0600, 10,    17 },
{ 0x0200, 10,    18 },    { 0x03C0, 10,    64 },
{ 0x0CE0, 11,    19 },    { 0x0D00, 11,    20 },
{ 0x0D80, 11,    21 },    { 0x06E0, 11,    22 },
{ 0x0500, 11,    23 },    { 0x02E0, 11,    24 },
{ 0x0300, 11,    25 },    { 0x0100, 11,  1792 },
{ 0x0180, 11,  1856 },    { 0x01A0, 11,  1920 },
{ 0x0CA0, 12,    26 },    { 0x0CB0, 12,    27 },
{ 0x0CC0, 12,    28 },    { 0x0CD0, 12,    29 },
{ 0x0680, 12,    30 },    { 0x0690, 12,    31 },
{ 0x06A0, 12,    32 },    { 0x06B0, 12,    33 },
{ 0x0D20, 12,    34 },    { 0x0D30, 12,    35 },
{ 0x0D40, 12,    36 },    { 0x0D50, 12,    37 },
{ 0x0D60, 12,    38 },    { 0x0D70, 12,    39 },
{ 0x06C0, 12,    40 },    { 0x06D0, 12,    41 },
{ 0x0DA0, 12,    42 },    { 0x0DB0, 12,    43 },
{ 0x0540, 12,    44 },    { 0x0550, 12,    45 },
{ 0x0560, 12,    46 },    { 0x0570, 12,    47 },
{ 0x0640, 12,    48 },    { 0x0650, 12,    49 },
{ 0x0520, 12,    50 },    { 0x0530, 12,    51 },
{ 0x0240, 12,    52 },    { 0x0370, 12,    53 },
{ 0x0380, 12,    54 },    { 0x0270, 12,    55 },
{ 0x0280, 12,    56 },    { 0x0580, 12,    57 },
{ 0x0590, 12,    58 },    { 0x02B0, 12,    59 },
{ 0x02C0, 12,    60 },    { 0x05A0, 12,    61 },
{ 0x0660, 12,    62 },    { 0x0670, 12,    63 },
{ 0x0C80, 12,   128 },    { 0x0C90, 12,   192 },
{ 0x05B0, 12,   256 },    { 0x0330, 12,   320 },
{ 0x0340, 12,   384 },    { 0x0350, 12,   448 },
{ 0x0120, 12,  1984 },    { 0x0130, 12,  2048 },
{ 0x0140, 12,  2112 },    { 0x0150, 12,  2176 },
{ 0x0160, 12,  2240 },    { 0x0170, 12,  2304 },
{ 0x01C0, 12,  2368 },    { 0x01D0, 12,  2432 },
{ 0x01E0, 12,  2496 },    { 0x01F0, 12,  2560 },
{ 0x0360, 13,   512 },    { 0x0368, 13,   576 },
{ 0x0250, 13,   640 },    { 0x0258, 13,   704 },
{ 0x0260, 13,   768 },    { 0x0268, 13,   832 },
{ 0x0390, 13,   896 },    { 0x0398, 13,   960 },
{ 0x03A0, 13,  1024 },    { 0x03A8, 13,  1088 },
{ 0x03B0, 13,  1152 },    { 0x03B8, 13,  1216 },
```

Listing 16.5 TIFCODEC.CPP (continued)

```
        { 0x0290, 13, 1280 },    { 0x0298, 13, 1344 },
        { 0x02A0, 13, 1408 },    { 0x02A8, 13, 1472 },
        { 0x02D0, 13, 1536 },    { 0x02D8, 13, 1600 },
        { 0x0320, 13, 1664 },    { 0x0328, 13, 1728 },
    };

    // code table for black runs, ordered by run length

    static codedef black_runs[] =
    {
        { 0x0DC0, 10,    0 },    { 0x4000,  3,    1 },
        { 0xC000,  2,    2 },    { 0x8000,  2,    3 },
        { 0x6000,  3,    4 },    { 0x3000,  4,    5 },
        { 0x2000,  4,    6 },    { 0x1800,  5,    7 },
        { 0x1400,  6,    8 },    { 0x1000,  6,    9 },
        { 0x0800,  7,   10 },    { 0x0A00,  7,   11 },
        { 0x0E00,  7,   12 },    { 0x0400,  8,   13 },
        { 0x0700,  8,   14 },    { 0x0C00,  9,   15 },
        { 0x05C0, 10,   16 },    { 0x0600, 10,   17 },
        { 0x0200, 10,   18 },    { 0x0CE0, 11,   19 },
        { 0x0D00, 11,   20 },    { 0x0D80, 11,   21 },
        { 0x06E0, 11,   22 },    { 0x0500, 11,   23 },
        { 0x02E0, 11,   24 },    { 0x0300, 11,   25 },
        { 0x0CA0, 12,   26 },    { 0x0CB0, 12,   27 },
        { 0x0CC0, 12,   28 },    { 0x0CD0, 12,   29 },
        { 0x0680, 12,   30 },    { 0x0690, 12,   31 },
        { 0x06A0, 12,   32 },    { 0x06B0, 12,   33 },
        { 0x0D20, 12,   34 },    { 0x0D30, 12,   35 },
        { 0x0D40, 12,   36 },    { 0x0D50, 12,   37 },
        { 0x0D60, 12,   38 },    { 0x0D70, 12,   39 },
        { 0x06C0, 12,   40 },    { 0x06D0, 12,   41 },
        { 0x0DA0, 12,   42 },    { 0x0DB0, 12,   43 },
        { 0x0540, 12,   44 },    { 0x0550, 12,   45 },
        { 0x0560, 12,   46 },    { 0x0570, 12,   47 },
        { 0x0640, 12,   48 },    { 0x0650, 12,   49 },
        { 0x0520, 12,   50 },    { 0x0530, 12,   51 },
        { 0x0240, 12,   52 },    { 0x0370, 12,   53 },
        { 0x0380, 12,   54 },    { 0x0270, 12,   55 },
        { 0x0280, 12,   56 },    { 0x0580, 12,   57 },
        { 0x0590, 12,   58 },    { 0x02B0, 12,   59 },
        { 0x02C0, 12,   60 },    { 0x05A0, 12,   61 },
        { 0x0660, 12,   62 },    { 0x0670, 12,   63 },
        { 0x03C0, 10,   64 },    { 0x0C80, 12,  128 },
        { 0x0C90, 12,  192 },    { 0x05B0, 12,  256 },
        { 0x0330, 12,  320 },    { 0x0340, 12,  384 },
        { 0x0350, 12,  448 },    { 0x0360, 13,  512 },
        { 0x0368, 13,  576 },    { 0x0250, 13,  640 },
        { 0x0258, 13,  704 },    { 0x0260, 13,  768 },
```

Listing 16.5 TIFCODEC.CPP (continued)

```
    { 0x0268, 13,   832 },   { 0x0390, 13,   896 },
    { 0x0398, 13,   960 },   { 0x03A0, 13,  1024 },
    { 0x03A8, 13,  1088 },   { 0x03B0, 13,  1152 },
    { 0x03B8, 13,  1216 },   { 0x0290, 13,  1280 },
    { 0x0298, 13,  1344 },   { 0x02A0, 13,  1408 },
    { 0x02A8, 13,  1472 },   { 0x02D0, 13,  1536 },
    { 0x02D8, 13,  1600 },   { 0x0320, 13,  1664 },
    { 0x0328, 13,  1728 },   { 0x0100, 11,  1792 },
    { 0x0180, 11,  1856 },   { 0x01A0, 11,  1920 },
    { 0x0120, 12,  1984 },   { 0x0130, 12,  2048 },
    { 0x0140, 12,  2112 },   { 0x0150, 12,  2176 },
    { 0x0160, 12,  2240 },   { 0x0170, 12,  2304 },
    { 0x01C0, 12,  2368 },   { 0x01D0, 12,  2432 },
    { 0x01E0, 12,  2496 },   { 0x01F0, 12,  2560 },
};

// code table for white runs, ordered by code length

static codedef white_bits[] =
{
    { 0x7000,  4,     2 },   { 0x8000,  4,     3 },
    { 0xB000,  4,     4 },   { 0xC000,  4,     5 },
    { 0xE000,  4,     6 },   { 0xF000,  4,     7 },
    { 0x9800,  5,     8 },   { 0xA000,  5,     9 },
    { 0x3800,  5,    10 },   { 0x4000,  5,    11 },
    { 0xD800,  5,    64 },   { 0x9000,  5,   128 },
    { 0x1C00,  6,     1 },   { 0x2000,  6,    12 },
    { 0x0C00,  6,    13 },   { 0xD000,  6,    14 },
    { 0xD400,  6,    15 },   { 0xA800,  6,    16 },
    { 0xAC00,  6,    17 },   { 0x5C00,  6,   192 },
    { 0x6000,  6,  1664 },   { 0x4E00,  7,    18 },
    { 0x1800,  7,    19 },   { 0x1000,  7,    20 },
    { 0x2E00,  7,    21 },   { 0x0600,  7,    22 },
    { 0x0800,  7,    23 },   { 0x5000,  7,    24 },
    { 0x5600,  7,    25 },   { 0x2600,  7,    26 },
    { 0x4800,  7,    27 },   { 0x3000,  7,    28 },
    { 0x6E00,  7,   256 },   { 0x3500,  8,     0 },
    { 0x0200,  8,    29 },   { 0x0300,  8,    30 },
    { 0x1A00,  8,    31 },   { 0x1B00,  8,    32 },
    { 0x1200,  8,    33 },   { 0x1300,  8,    34 },
    { 0x1400,  8,    35 },   { 0x1500,  8,    36 },
    { 0x1600,  8,    37 },   { 0x1700,  8,    38 },
    { 0x2800,  8,    39 },   { 0x2900,  8,    40 },
    { 0x2A00,  8,    41 },   { 0x2B00,  8,    42 },
    { 0x2C00,  8,    43 },   { 0x2D00,  8,    44 },
    { 0x0400,  8,    45 },   { 0x0500,  8,    46 },
    { 0x0A00,  8,    47 },   { 0x0B00,  8,    48 },
    { 0x5200,  8,    49 },   { 0x5300,  8,    50 },
```

Listing 16.5 TIFCODEC.CPP (continued)

```
        { 0x5400,   8,     51 },    { 0x5500,   8,     52 },
        { 0x2400,   8,     53 },    { 0x2500,   8,     54 },
        { 0x5800,   8,     55 },    { 0x5900,   8,     56 },
        { 0x5A00,   8,     57 },    { 0x5B00,   8,     58 },
        { 0x4A00,   8,     59 },    { 0x4B00,   8,     60 },
        { 0x3200,   8,     61 },    { 0x3300,   8,     62 },
        { 0x3400,   8,     63 },    { 0x3600,   8,    320 },
        { 0x3700,   8,    384 },    { 0x6400,   8,    448 },
        { 0x6500,   8,    512 },    { 0x6800,   8,    576 },
        { 0x6700,   8,    640 },    { 0x6600,   9,    704 },
        { 0x6680,   9,    768 },    { 0x6900,   9,    832 },
        { 0x6980,   9,    896 },    { 0x6A00,   9,    960 },
        { 0x6A80,   9,   1024 },    { 0x6B00,   9,   1088 },
        { 0x6B80,   9,   1152 },    { 0x6C00,   9,   1216 },
        { 0x6C80,   9,   1280 },    { 0x6D00,   9,   1344 },
        { 0x6D80,   9,   1408 },    { 0x4C00,   9,   1472 },
        { 0x4C80,   9,   1536 },    { 0x4D00,   9,   1600 },
        { 0x4D80,   9,   1728 },    { 0x0100,  11,   1792 },
        { 0x0180,  11,   1856 },    { 0x01A0,  11,   1920 },
        { 0x0120,  12,   1984 },    { 0x0130,  12,   2048 },
        { 0x0140,  12,   2112 },    { 0x0150,  12,   2176 },
        { 0x0160,  12,   2240 },    { 0x0170,  12,   2304 },
        { 0x01C0,  12,   2368 },    { 0x01D0,  12,   2432 },
        { 0x01E0,  12,   2496 },    { 0x01F0,  12,   2560 },
    };

    // code table for white runs, ordered by run length

    static codedef white_runs[] =
    {
        { 0x3500,   8,      0 },    { 0x1C00,   6,      1 },
        { 0x7000,   4,      2 },    { 0x8000,   4,      3 },
        { 0xB000,   4,      4 },    { 0xC000,   4,      5 },
        { 0xE000,   4,      6 },    { 0xF000,   4,      7 },
        { 0x9800,   5,      8 },    { 0xA000,   5,      9 },
        { 0x3800,   5,     10 },    { 0x4000,   5,     11 },
        { 0x2000,   6,     12 },    { 0x0C00,   6,     13 },
        { 0xD000,   6,     14 },    { 0xD400,   6,     15 },
        { 0xA800,   6,     16 },    { 0xAC00,   6,     17 },
        { 0x4E00,   7,     18 },    { 0x1800,   7,     19 },
        { 0x1000,   7,     20 },    { 0x2E00,   7,     21 },
        { 0x0600,   7,     22 },    { 0x0800,   7,     23 },
        { 0x5000,   7,     24 },    { 0x5600,   7,     25 },
        { 0x2600,   7,     26 },    { 0x4800,   7,     27 },
        { 0x3000,   7,     28 },    { 0x0200,   8,     29 },
        { 0x0300,   8,     30 },    { 0x1A00,   8,     31 },
        { 0x1B00,   8,     32 },    { 0x1200,   8,     33 },
        { 0x1300,   8,     34 },    { 0x1400,   8,     35 },
```

Listing 16.5 TIFCODEC.CPP (continued)

```
       { 0x1500,  8,   36 },  { 0x1600,  8,   37 },
       { 0x1700,  8,   38 },  { 0x2800,  8,   39 },
       { 0x2900,  8,   40 },  { 0x2A00,  8,   41 },
       { 0x2B00,  8,   42 },  { 0x2C00,  8,   43 },
       { 0x2D00,  8,   44 },  { 0x0400,  8,   45 },
       { 0x0500,  8,   46 },  { 0x0A00,  8,   47 },
       { 0x0B00,  8,   48 },  { 0x5200,  8,   49 },
       { 0x5300,  8,   50 },  { 0x5400,  8,   51 },
       { 0x5500,  8,   52 },  { 0x2400,  8,   53 },
       { 0x2500,  8,   54 },  { 0x5800,  8,   55 },
       { 0x5900,  8,   56 },  { 0x5A00,  8,   57 },
       { 0x5B00,  8,   58 },  { 0x4A00,  8,   59 },
       { 0x4B00,  8,   60 },  { 0x3200,  8,   61 },
       { 0x3300,  8,   62 },  { 0x3400,  8,   63 },
       { 0xD800,  5,   64 },  { 0x9000,  5,  128 },
       { 0x5C00,  6,  192 },  { 0x6E00,  7,  256 },
       { 0x3600,  8,  320 },  { 0x3700,  8,  384 },
       { 0x6400,  8,  448 },  { 0x6500,  8,  512 },
       { 0x6800,  8,  576 },  { 0x6700,  8,  640 },
       { 0x6600,  9,  704 },  { 0x6680,  9,  768 },
       { 0x6900,  9,  832 },  { 0x6980,  9,  896 },
       { 0x6A00,  9,  960 },  { 0x6A80,  9, 1024 },
       { 0x6B00,  9, 1088 },  { 0x6B80,  9, 1152 },
       { 0x6C00,  9, 1216 },  { 0x6C80,  9, 1280 },
       { 0x6D00,  9, 1344 },  { 0x6D80,  9, 1408 },
       { 0x4C00,  9, 1472 },  { 0x4C80,  9, 1536 },
       { 0x4D00,  9, 1600 },  { 0x6000,  6, 1664 },
       { 0x4D80,  9, 1728 },  { 0x0100, 11, 1792 },
       { 0x0180, 11, 1856 },  { 0x01A0, 11, 1920 },
       { 0x0120, 12, 1984 },  { 0x0130, 12, 2048 },
       { 0x0140, 12, 2112 },  { 0x0150, 12, 2176 },
       { 0x0160, 12, 2240 },  { 0x0170, 12, 2304 },
       { 0x01C0, 12, 2368 },  { 0x01D0, 12, 2432 },
       { 0x01E0, 12, 2496 },  { 0x01F0, 12, 2560 },
};

static int   codebyte, codemask;
static FILE* codefile;

int g3rdbit( void )
{
   if( (codemask>>=1) == 0 )
   {
      codebyte = fgetc( codefile );
      codemask = 0x80;
   }
   return (codebyte & codemask) ? 1 : 0;
}
```

Listing 16.5 TIFCODEC.CPP (continued)

```
int g3rdcode( int pxval )
{
   codedef *tbl = pxval ? white_bits : black_bits;
   short code = 0;
   unsigned short mask = 0x8000;
   int len = 0;
   int n = 0;

   while( n < TBLSIZE )
   {
      while( len < tbl[n].codelen )
      {
         if( g3rdbit() ) code |= mask;
         len++;
         mask >>= 1;
      }
      while( (tbl[n].codelen == len) && (n < TBLSIZE) )
      {
         if( tbl[n].bitcode == code )
             return tbl[n].runlen;
         n++;
      }
   }

   // getting here is an error - no matching code found.
   // we signal this by returning a negative run length.
   return -1;
}

int ReadG3( FILE *fi, unsigned char *buf, int nbytes )
{
   // internal initialization
   codefile = fi;
   codebyte = 0;
   codemask = 0;

   // local initialization
   int cnt   = 0;
   int pxval = 1;       // always start with white!
   int mask  = 0x80;
   memset( buf, 0, nbytes );

   while( nbytes > 0 )
   {
      // get next code
      if( (cnt = g3rdcode( pxval )) < 0 )
          return xOUTOFSYNC;
```

Listing 16.5 TIFCODEC.CPP (continued)

```cpp
            // fill in buffer
            int n = cnt;
            while( (n-- > 0) && (nbytes > 0) )
            {
                if( pxval ) *buf |= mask;
                if( (mask >>= 1) == 0 )
                {
                    mask = 0x80;
                    buf++;
                    nbytes--;
                }
            }

            // switch pixel values if terminating code
            if( cnt < 64 )
                pxval = 1 - pxval;
        }
        // if we ended on a makeup code, read what
        // should be a terminating code of runlength 0
        if( cnt > 63 )
        {
            cnt = g3rdcode( pxval );
            if( cnt != 0 ) return xOUTOFSYNC;
        }

        return xOKAY;
    }

    int g3wrtbitcode( int code, int len )
    {
        unsigned short mask = 0x8000;
        while( len-- )
        {
            if( code & mask )
                codebyte |= codemask;
            mask >>= 1;
            if( (codemask >>= 1) == 0 )
            {
                if( fputc( codebyte, codefile ) < 0 )
                    return xIOERROR;
                codebyte = 0;
                codemask = 0x80;
            }
        }
        return xOKAY;
    }
```

Listing 16.5 TIFCODEC.CPP (continued)

```cpp
int g3wrtrun( int pxval, int cnt )
{
    codedef *tbl = pxval ? white_runs : black_runs;
    while( cnt >= 2624 )
    {
        if( g3wrtbitcode( tbl[TBLSIZE-1].bitcode,
                          tbl[TBLSIZE-1].codelen ) != xOKAY )
            return xIOERROR;
        cnt -= 2560;
    }
    if( cnt > 63 )
    {
        int n = cnt >> 6;    // n=pxcnt/64
        int i = n + 63;
        if( g3wrtbitcode( tbl[i].bitcode,
                          tbl[i].codelen ) != xOKAY )
            return xIOERROR;
        n <<= 6;                 // n=n*64
        cnt -= n;
    }
    return g3wrtbitcode( tbl[cnt].bitcode,
                        tbl[cnt].codelen );
}

int WriteG3( FILE *fo, unsigned char *buf, int nbytes )
{
    // internal initialization
    codebyte = 0;
    codemask = 0x80;
    codefile = fo;

    // local initialization
    int mask = 0x80;
    int pxval = 1;    // always start with white!

    // encode the buffer
    while( nbytes > 0 )
    {
        int cnt = 0;
        if( pxval )
        {
            while( *buf & mask )
            {
                cnt++;
                if( (mask >>= 1) == 0 )
                {
                    mask = 0x80;
                    buf++;
```

Listing 16.5 TIFCODEC.CPP (continued)

```
                    if( --nbytes == 0 ) break;
                }
            }
        }
        else
        {
            while( (*buf & mask) == 0 )
            {
                cnt++;
                if( (mask >>= 1) == 0 )
                {
                    mask = 0x80;
                    buf++;
                    if( --nbytes == 0 ) break;
                }
            }
        }
        if( g3wrtrun( pxval, cnt ) != xOKAY ) break;
        pxval = 1 - pxval;
    }

    // flush a partial code byte
    if( codebyte != 0x80 )
        fputc( codebyte, codefile );

    return ferror(codefile) ? xIOERROR : xOKAY;
}

//-----------------------------------------------------------//
//                    PackBits Compression                   //
//-----------------------------------------------------------//

int ReadPB( FILE *fi, unsigned char *buf, int nbytes )
{
    int n = 0;               // number of bytes decoded

    while( (n < nbytes) && ! feof(fi) )
    {
        int ix = fgetc( fi );    // get index byte
        if( ix < 0 ) return xIOERROR;

        char cx = ix;
        if( cx == -128 ) continue;

        if( cx < 0 )  //.............run
        {
            int i = 1 - cx;
            char ch = fgetc( fi );
```

Listing 16.5 TIFCODEC.CPP (continued)

```
            while( i-- )
                if( n < nbytes )
                    buf[n++] = ch;
        }
        else  //....................seq
        {
            int i = cx + 1;
            while( i-- )
                if( n < nbytes )
                    buf[n++] = fgetc( fi );
        }
    }
    return feof(fi) ? xENDOFFILE : xOKAY;
}
int WritePB( FILE *fo, unsigned char *buf, int nbytes )
{
    int cnt = 0;  // bytes encoded

    while( cnt < nbytes )
    {
        int i = cnt;
        int j = i + 1;
        int jmax = i + 126;
        if( jmax >= nbytes ) jmax = nbytes-1;

        if( i == nbytes-1 )  //..............last byte alone
        {
            fputc( 0, fo );
            fputc( buf[i], fo );
            cnt++;
        }
        else if( buf[i] == buf[j] )  //.......run
        {
            while( (j<jmax) && (buf[j]==buf[j+1]) )
                j++;
            fputc( i-j, fo );
            fputc( buf[i], fo );
            cnt += j-i+1;
        }
        else  //............................sequence
        {
            while( (j<jmax) && (buf[j]!=buf[j+1]) )
                j++;
            fputc( j-i, fo );
            fwrite( buf+i, j-i+1, 1, fo );
            cnt += j-i+1;
        }
    }
```

Listing 16.5 TIFCODEC.CPP (continued)

```cpp
    return xOKAY;
}

//-----------------------------------------------------------//
//                      No Compression                       //
//-----------------------------------------------------------//

int ReadNC( FILE *fi, unsigned char *buf, int nbytes )
{
    fread( buf, nbytes, 1, fi );
    return xOKAY;
}

int WriteNC( FILE *fo, unsigned char *buf, int nbytes )
{
    fwrite( buf, nbytes, 1, fo );
    return xOKAY;
}

//-----------------------------------------------------------//
//                      Class TiffDecoder                    //
//-----------------------------------------------------------//
TiffDecoder::TiffDecoder( FILE *fi, TIFFIMAGEDEF *tid )
{
    ftif = fi;
    idef = tid;
    rwbytes = (idef->depth * idef->width + 7) / 8;
    ibuf = new unsigned char [rwbytes];
    cond = ibuf ? xOKAY : xNOMEMORY;
    switch( idef->cmptype )
    {
        case cNone :
        case cUncompressed :
            read = ReadNC;
            break;
        case cCCITT1d :
            read = ReadG3;
            break;
        case cPackBits :
            read = ReadPB;
            break;
        default :
            read = 0;
            cond = xUNSUPPORTED;
            break;
    }
}
```

Listing 16.5 TIFCODEC.CPP (continued)

```cpp
TiffDecoder::~TiffDecoder( )
{
   delete ibuf;
}

int TiffDecoder::status( void )
{
   if( feof(ftif) )    cond = xENDOFFILE;
   if( ferror(ftif) ) cond = xIOERROR;
   return cond;
}

int TiffDecoder::init( void )
{
   curline = curstrip = 0;
   fseek( ftif, idef->stripofs[curstrip], SEEK_SET );
   return status();
}

int TiffDecoder::term( void )
{
   return status();
}

void TiffDecoder::unpack( unsigned char *buf, int npxls )
{
   if( idef->depth >= 8 )
   {
      int nbytes = (idef->depth + 7) / 8;
      nbytes *= npxls;
      for( int i=0; i<nbytes; i++ )
         buf[i] = ibuf[i];
   }
   else
   {
      int mask = (1 << idef->depth) - 1;
      int npix = 8 / idef->depth;
      int ntot = 0;
      int n    = 0;
      while( ntot < npxls )
      {
         int x = reverse( ibuf[n++], idef->depth );
         for( int i=0; i<npix; i++ )
```

Listing 16.5 TIFCODEC.CPP (continued)

```cpp
            {
               if( ntot < npxls )
                  buf[ntot++] = x & mask;
               x >>= idef->depth;
            }
         }
      }
   }

   int TiffDecoder::decode( unsigned char *buf, int npxls )
   {
      if( status() == xOKAY )
      {
         curline++;
         if( curline > idef->striphgt )
         {
            curline = 0;
            curstrip++;
            fseek( ftif, idef->stripofs[curstrip], SEEK_SET );
         }
         cond = (*read)( ftif, ibuf, rwbytes );
         unpack( buf, npxls );
      }
      return status();
   }

   //---------------------------------------------------------//
   //                    Class TiffEncoder                    //
   //---------------------------------------------------------//

   TiffEncoder::TiffEncoder( FILE *fo, TIFFIMAGEDEF *tid )
   {
      ftif = fo;
      idef = tid;
      rwbytes = (idef->depth * idef->width + 7) / 8;
      ibuf = new unsigned char [rwbytes];
      cond = ibuf ? xOKAY : xNOMEMORY;
      switch( idef->cmptype )
      {
         case cNone :
         case cUncompressed :
            write = WriteNC;
            break;
         case cCCITT1d :
            write = WriteG3;
            break;
         case cPackBits :
            write = WritePB;
```

Listing 16.5 TIFCODEC.CPP (continued)

```
                break;
            default :
                write = 0;
                cond = xUNSUPPORTED;
                break;
        }
    }


    TiffEncoder::~TiffEncoder( )
    {
        delete ibuf;
    }

    int TiffEncoder::status( void )
    {
        if( ferror(ftif) ) cond = xIOERROR;
        return cond;
    }

    int TiffEncoder::init( void )
    {
        return status();
    }
    int TiffEncoder::term( void )
    {
        return status();
    }

    void TiffEncoder::pack( unsigned char *buf, int npxls )
    {
        if( idef->depth >= 8 )
        {
            int nbytes = (idef->depth + 7) / 8;
            nbytes *= npxls;
            for( int i=0; i<nbytes; i++ )
                ibuf[i] = buf[i];
        }
        else
        {
            int mask = (1 << idef->depth) - 1;
            int npix = 8 / idef->depth;
            int ntot = 0;
            int n    = 0;
            while( ntot < npxls )
            {
                for( int i=0; i<npix; i++ )
                {
                    ibuf[n] <<= idef->depth;
```

Listing 16.5 TIFCODEC.CPP (continued)

```
                ibuf[n] |= (ntot < npxls) ?
                            buf[ntot++] & mask : 0;
            }
            n++;
        }
    }
}

int TiffEncoder::encode( unsigned char *buf, int npxls )
{
    if( status() == xOKAY )
    {
        pack( buf, npxls );
        cond = (*write)( ftif, ibuf, rwbytes );
    }
    return status();
}
```

Reading or writing an encoded bitmap represents only about half the task of reading or writing a complete TIFF file. A file's header and IFDs must also be dealt with, and in the case of writing a TIFF file, the many offsets found in these structures must be computed and set.

Perhaps the simplest procedure for writing a TIFF file is to have the program output all data items before it writes the corresponding IFD. This allows IFD entry offset fields to be set before the IFD itself is written. Once the IFD has been output then the offset to it can be added to the file's header (if it is the first IFD) or to the previous IFD (if it is the second or subsequent IFD). This arrangement is diagrammed in Figure 16.2. Keep in mind that this is only one of many possible arrangements.

Listing 16.6 presents the source code to functions for writing the TIFF format. These use the same overall design used throughout this book, but note that the implementations are relatively involved. As shown in the listing, the functions will output either a color-mapped or RGB-based TIFF file with a single IFD and image.

The code is easily modified to include bilevel and gray-scale images. One approach for adding a new image type is to implement functions that return a tag array and a tag count, as was done in the listing for color-mapped and RGB-based images. Be sure to include either an enumeration or a set of defined constants for indexing into the tag array, and include these for each image type. If enough specific image types are to be supported, it might be worthwhile to split the code into multiple image-specific output functions to reduce complexity.

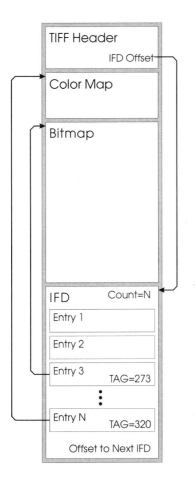

Figure 16.2 One Possible Layout of a TIFF File

Listing 16.7 shows a sample program that uses the `WriteTIF` function. It outputs a TIFF file from the El Greco image used in previous examples.

Listing 16.6 WRTTIF.CPP

```
//----------------------------------------------------------//
//                                                          //
//    File:     WRTTIF.CPP                                  //
//                                                          //
//    Desc:     Code to output a TIFF file from            //
//              a VGA Display or a Memory Bitmap           //
//                                                          //
//----------------------------------------------------------//

#include "tif.hpp"
#include "tifcodec.hpp"
```

Listing 16.6 WRTTIF.CPP (continued)

```cpp
#include "display.hpp"
#include "imgstore.hpp"

//.................Tag set for color-mapped images

enum ColorMappedTagSet
{
   cmWidth,
   cmHeight,
   cmBitSamp,
   cmCompress,
   cmPhotoMet,
   cmStripOfs,
   cmStripHgt,
   cmXres,
   cmYres,
   cmResUnit,
   cmColorMap,
};

static IFDENTRY ColorMappedIFD[] =
{
   IFDENTRY( 256, tUShort,    1, 0L ),   // width
   IFDENTRY( 257, tUShort,    1, 0L ),   // height
   IFDENTRY( 258, tUShort,    1, 0L ),   // bits/samp
   IFDENTRY( 259, tUShort,    1, 0L ),   // compression
   IFDENTRY( 262, tUShort,    1, 0L ),   // photomet intrp
   IFDENTRY( 273, tULong,     1, 0L ),   // strip offsets
   IFDENTRY( 278, tUShort,    1, 0L ),   // rows/strip
   IFDENTRY( 282, tURational, 1, 0L ),   // x res
   IFDENTRY( 283, tURational, 1, 0L ),   // y res
   IFDENTRY( 296, tUShort,    1, 0L ),   // res unit
   IFDENTRY( 320, tUShort,    1, 0L ),   // color map
};

int ColorMappedCnt( void )
{
   return sizeof(ColorMappedIFD) / sizeof(IFDENTRY);
}

IFDENTRY * ColorMappedTags( void )
{
   IFDENTRY *cmt = new IFDENTRY [ ColorMappedCnt() ];
   if( cmt )
      for( int i=0; i<ColorMappedCnt(); i++ )
         cmt[i] = ColorMappedIFD[i];
   return cmt;
}
```

Listing 16.6 WRTTIF.CPP (continued)

```cpp
//................Tag set for RGB images
enum RgbTagSet
{
   rgbWidth,
   rgbHeight,
   rgbBitSamp,
   rgbCompress,
   rgbPhotoMet,
   rgbStripOfs,
   rgbSampPix,
   rgbStripHgt,
   rgbXres,
   rgbYres,
   rgbResUnit,
};

static IFDENTRY RgbIFD[] =
{
   IFDENTRY( 256, tUShort,    1, 0L ),   // width
   IFDENTRY( 257, tUShort,    1, 0L ),   // height
   IFDENTRY( 258, tUShort,    1, 0L ),   // bits/samp
   IFDENTRY( 259, tUShort,    1, 0L ),   // compression
   IFDENTRY( 262, tUShort,    1, 0L ),   // photomet intrp
   IFDENTRY( 273, tULong,     1, 0L ),   // strip offsets
   IFDENTRY( 277, tUShort,    1, 0L ),   // samps/pixel
   IFDENTRY( 278, tUShort,    1, 0L ),   // rows/strip
   IFDENTRY( 282, tURational, 1, 0L ),   // x res
   IFDENTRY( 283, tURational, 1, 0L ),   // y res
   IFDENTRY( 296, tUShort,    1, 0L ),   // res unit
   IFDENTRY( 320, tUShort,    1, 0L ),   // color map
};

int RgbCnt( void )
{
   return sizeof(RgbIFD) / sizeof(IFDENTRY);
}

IFDENTRY * RgbTags( void )
{
   IFDENTRY *rgbt = new IFDENTRY [ RgbCnt() ];
   if( rgbt )
      for( int i=0; i<RgbCnt(); i++ )
         rgbt[i] = RgbIFD[i];
   return rgbt;
}

//................Write VGA screen to TIFF file 'fn'
```

Listing 16.6 WRTTIF.CPP (continued)

```cpp
int WriteTIF( VgaDisplay& vga, char *fn,
              int x1, int y1, int x2, int y2 )
{
   // image metrics
   int nrows   = y2 - y1 + 1;
   int ncols   = x2 - x1 + 1;
   int nbits   = 8;
   int ncolors = vga.metric.ncolors;

   // scan line buffer for encoder
   unsigned char *scanln = new unsigned char [ncols];
   if( scanln == 0 ) return xNOMEMORY;

   // create and initialize a Tiff Image Definition
   TIFFIMAGEDEF idef;
   idef.imgtype = iColorMapped;
   idef.cmptype = cPackBits;
   idef.width = ncols;
   idef.height = nrows;
   idef.depth = nbits;
   idef.bitsamp = nbits;
   idef.nstrips = 1;
   idef.ncolors = ncolors;
   idef.colors = new rgb [ncolors];
   if( idef.colors == 0 ) return xNOMEMORY;
   vga.getpalette( idef.colors, idef.ncolors );

   // create a TIFF header
   TIFFHEADER thdr;

   // create and initialize the tag set
   IFDENTRY *tags = ColorMappedTags();
   if( tags == 0  ) return xNOMEMORY;
   tags[cmWidth].valofs = idef.width;
   tags[cmHeight].valofs = idef.height;
   tags[cmBitSamp].valofs = idef.bitsamp;
   tags[cmCompress].valofs = idef.cmptype;
   tags[cmPhotoMet].valofs = idef.imgtype;
   tags[cmStripHgt].valofs = idef.height;
   tags[cmXres].valofs = idef.xres;
   tags[cmYres].valofs = idef.yres;
   tags[cmResUnit].valofs = idef.resunit;
   tags[cmColorMap].count = idef.ncolors * 3;

   // open and write the file
   FILE *f = fopen( fn, "wb" );
```

Listing 16.6 WRTTIF.CPP (continued)

```cpp
    // output a placeholder for the header
    if( thdr.put( f ) ) return xIOERROR;

    // output the color map
    tags[cmColorMap].valofs = ftell( f );
    unsigned short pri;
    for( int i=0; i<idef.ncolors; i++ )
    {
        pri = idef.colors[i].red;
        pri <<= 8;
        fwrite( &pri, 2, 1, f );
    }
    for( i=0; i<idef.ncolors; i++ )
    {
        pri = idef.colors[i].grn;
        pri <<= 8;
        fwrite( &pri, 2, 1, f );
    }
    for( i=0; i<idef.ncolors; i++ )
    {
        pri = idef.colors[i].blu;
        pri <<= 8;
        fwrite( &pri, 2, 1, f );
    }

    // output the X/Y resolutions
    tags[cmXres].valofs = ftell( f );
    long ltmp = idef.xres;
    fwrite( &ltmp, 4, 1, f );
    ltmp = 1L;
    fwrite( &ltmp, 4, 1, f );
    tags[cmYres].valofs = ftell( f );
    ltmp = idef.yres;
    fwrite( &ltmp, 4, 1, f );
    ltmp = 1L;
    fwrite( &ltmp, 4, 1, f );

    // output the encoded bitmap
    tags[cmStripOfs].valofs = ftell( f );
    TiffEncoder enc( f, &idef );
    enc.init();
    for( i=0; i<nrows; i++ )
    {
        vga.getscanline( scanln, ncols, x1, y1+i );
        if( enc.encode( scanln, ncols ) != xOKAY )
        {
            delete scanln;
            fclose( f );
```

Listing 16.6 WRTTIF.CPP (continued)

```
            return enc.status();
        }
    }
    enc.term();

    // output the IFD
    thdr.ifdofs = ftell( f );
    short ntags = ColorMappedCnt();
    fwrite( &ntags, 2, 1, f );
    for( i=0; i<ntags; i++ )
        tags[i].put( f );
    ltmp = 0L;
    fwrite( &ltmp, 4, 1, f );

    // rewrite the updated header
    fseek( f, 0L, SEEK_SET );
    thdr.put( f );

    // finished!
    delete scanln;
    int retv = ferror(f) ? xIOERROR : xOKAY;
    fclose( f );
    return retv;
}

//.................Write an image to TIFF file 'fn'
int WriteTIF( ImgStore& img, rgb *pal, char *fn )
{
    // image metrics
    int nrows   = img.height();
    int ncols   = img.width();
    int nbits   = (img.depth() == 24) ? 24 : 8;
    int ncolors = 2;
    if( img.depth() == 24 ) ncolors = 0;
    else if( img.depth() > 1 ) ncolors = 256;

    // create and initialize a Tiff Image Definition
    TIFFIMAGEDEF idef;
    idef.imgtype = (nbits==24) ? iRGB : iColorMapped;
    idef.cmptype = (nbits==24) ? cUncompressed : cPackBits;
    idef.width = ncols;
    idef.height = nrows;
    idef.depth = nbits;
    idef.bitsamp = 8;
    idef.samppix = nbits / 8;
    idef.nstrips = 1;
    idef.ncolors = ncolors;
    if( ncolors > 0 )
```

Listing 16.6 WRTTIF.CPP (continued)

```cpp
    {
        idef.colors = new rgb [ncolors];
        if( idef.colors == 0 ) return xNOMEMORY;
        for( int i=0; i<ncolors; i++ )
            idef.colors[i] = pal[i];
    }
    // create a TIFF header
    TIFFHEADER thdr;

    // create and initialize the tag set
    IFDENTRY *tags;
    if( idef.ncolors > 0 )
    {
        tags = ColorMappedTags();
        if( tags == 0 ) return xNOMEMORY;
        tags[cmWidth].valofs = idef.width;
        tags[cmHeight].valofs = idef.height;
        tags[cmBitSamp].valofs = idef.bitsamp;
        tags[cmCompress].valofs = idef.cmptype;
        tags[cmPhotoMet].valofs = idef.imgtype;
        tags[cmStripHgt].valofs = idef.height;
        tags[cmXres].valofs = idef.xres;
        tags[cmYres].valofs = idef.yres;
        tags[cmResUnit].valofs = idef.resunit;
        tags[cmColorMap].count = idef.ncolors * 3;
    }
    else
    {
        tags = RgbTags();
        if( tags == 0 ) return xNOMEMORY;
        tags[rgbWidth].valofs = idef.width;
        tags[rgbHeight].valofs = idef.height;
        tags[rgbBitSamp].valofs = idef.bitsamp;
        tags[rgbCompress].valofs = idef.cmptype;
        tags[rgbPhotoMet].valofs = idef.imgtype;
        tags[rgbSampPix].valofs = idef.samppix;
        tags[rgbStripHgt].valofs = idef.height;
        tags[rgbXres].valofs = idef.xres;
        tags[rgbYres].valofs = idef.yres;
        tags[rgbResUnit].valofs = idef.resunit;
    }

    // open and write the file
    FILE *f = fopen( fn, "wb" );

    // output a placeholder for the header
    if( thdr.put( f ) ) return xIOERROR;
```

Listing 16.6 WRTTIF.CPP (continued)

```cpp
// output the color map if present
if( idef.ncolors > 0 )
{
   tags[cmColorMap].valofs = ftell( f );
   unsigned short pri;
   for( int i=0; i<idef.ncolors; i++ )
   {
      pri = idef.colors[i].red;
      pri <<= 8;
      fwrite( &pri, 2, 1, f );
   }
   for( i=0; i<idef.ncolors; i++ )
   {
      pri = idef.colors[i].grn;
      pri <<= 8;
      fwrite( &pri, 2, 1, f );
   }
   for( i=0; i<idef.ncolors; i++ )
   {
      pri = idef.colors[i].blu;
      pri <<= 8;
      fwrite( &pri, 2, 1, f );
   }
}

// output the X/Y resolutions
int ir = (idef.ncolors > 0) ? cmXres : rgbXres;
tags[ir].valofs = ftell( f );
long ltmp = idef.xres;
fwrite( &ltmp, 4, 1, f );
ltmp = 1L;
fwrite( &ltmp, 4, 1, f );
ir = (idef.ncolors > 0) ? cmYres : rgbYres;
tags[ir].valofs = ftell( f );
ltmp = idef.yres;
fwrite( &ltmp, 4, 1, f );
ltmp = 1L;
fwrite( &ltmp, 4, 1, f );

// output the encoded bitmap
ir = (idef.ncolors > 0) ? cmStripOfs : rgbStripOfs;
tags[ir].valofs = ftell( f );
TiffEncoder enc( f, &idef );
enc.init();
for( int i=0; i<nrows; i++ )
{
   unsigned char *p = img.get( i );
   if( enc.encode( p, ncols ) != xOKAY )
```

Listing 16.6 WRTTIF.CPP (continued)

```
        {
            fclose( f );
            return enc.status();
        }
    }
    enc.term();

    // output the IFD
    thdr.ifdofs = ftell( f );
    short ntags = (ncolors > 0) ?
                  ColorMappedCnt() : RgbCnt();
    fwrite( &ntags, 2, 1, f );
    for( i=0; i<ntags; i++ )
        tags[i].put( f );
    ltmp = 0L;
    fwrite( &ltmp, 4, 1, f );

    // rewrite the updated header
    fseek( f, 0L, SEEK_SET );
    thdr.put( f );

    // finished!
    int retv = ferror(f) ? xIOERROR : xOKAY;
    fclose( f );
    return retv;
}
```

Listing 16.7 TIFDEMO.CPP

```
//----------------------------------------------------------//
//                                                          //
//   File:     TIFDEMO.CPP                                  //
//                                                          //
//   Desc:     Example code to write a TIFF file            //
//                                                          //
//----------------------------------------------------------//

#include "wrttif.cpp"

char *        palname     = "EL-GRECO.PAL";
char *        imgname     = "EL-GRECO.IMG";
int           imgwidth    = 354;
int           imgheight   = 446;
int           imgcolors   = 256;
rgb           imgpalette[256];
unsigned char scanline[354];
CnvImgStore img( 446, 354, 8 );
// read the test image's palette
```

Listing 16.7 TIFDEMO.CPP (continued)

```cpp
void read_palette( void )
{
    FILE *f = fopen( palname, "rt" );
    for( int i=0; i<imgcolors; i++ )
    {
        int r, g, b;
        fscanf( f, "%d %d %d", &r, &g, &b );
        imgpalette[i] = rgb( r, g, b );
    }
    fclose( f );
}

// read the test image into memory

void read_image( void )
{
    FILE *f = fopen( imgname, "rb" );
    for( int i=0; i<imgheight; i++ )
    {
        fread( scanline, imgwidth, 1, f );
        img.put( scanline, i );
    }
    fclose( f );
}

// output a TIF file
int main( void )
{
    read_palette( );

    read_image( );

    WriteTIF( img, imgpalette, "TIFDEMO.TIF" );

    return 0;
}
```

This concludes our look at the TIFF format. It is definitely the most ambitious of all of the formats covered in the book, and it is also definitely the one to pick if only one format is to be supported. Virtually all important graphics applications for DOS, Windows, OS/2, and Unix support the TIFF format, but note that extensions to the baseline format specification tend to be niche-oriented and not widely supported. You should consider this when planning what portion of the full specification is to be implemented.

17

The WordPerfect
WPG Format

WordPerfect is a popular word processing application, justly famous for its many capabilities. It is one of those products that seem to elicit only strong opinions—people either swear at it or swear by it. Personally, I wouldn't use anything else, and, in fact, the manuscript for this book was produced with WordPerfect 5.1.

The product supports an indigenous graphics format known as the WordPerfect Graphics Format. Files that employ the format normally use the extension WPG. Despite WordPerfect's fame, the WPG format has not achieved the widespread acceptance of simpler bitmapped formats such as PCX. This is probably a result of the format's relative complexity and peoples' perception that it is primarily a vector-based format.

Although the WPG format is a general-purpose vector-based format, it supports bitmapped graphics images as well. A convention of the format is that a WPG file can contain either vector graphics or bitmapped graphics, but not both. For this reason the format can be considered to possess two variants—the discussion is confined here to the bitmapped variant. It is important to note, however, that the bitmap-versus-vector distinction does not affect the interpretation of a WPG file's data structures, but rather indicates what subset of those structures will be found in a given file.

Format Overview

The overall structure of a WPG file consists of a brief file header followed by some number of tag-object pairs. The official WPG documentation from WordPerfect Corporation uses the terminology *record type* and *record* instead of *tag* and *object*. I use the latter terms here because they are more descriptive and they also help relate the WPG format to other formats, such as TIFF.

A tag is a structure consisting of two fields, an object identifier and an object size. The identifier member is always a byte value, but the size member can be either a byte, word, or double-word integral value. While this complicates the process of reading and deciphering a tag, once the process has been understood and appropriately encapsulated in code, it can then be pretty much ignored.

Each tag identifies the object that follows it. There are essentially three object types: (1) graphical objects such as lines, polygons, and bitmaps; (2) attribute specifiers, which indicate such things as line color and fill pattern; and (3) control constructs, which indicate generally what is happening. Two control constructs found in every WPG file are "begin WPG data" and "end WPG data." These can be used by an application, for example, to determine when a picture definition is complete. The size member of a tag specifies, in bytes, the length of the object that follows it.

The use of type/size tags makes the process of scanning a WPG file relatively straightforward. As each tag is encountered, its identifier member is used to determine what the object is and thus whether or not it needs to be processed. The size member can then be used to allocate a suitable buffer, for instance, or to control how far ahead to seek to find the next tag. When an "end WPG data" tag is encountered, an application knows that the scan is complete.

The tag sequence for a bitmapped WPG file generally goes as follows:

15—begin WPG data
14—define color map
11—define bitmap
16—end WPG data

The numbers indicate the tag identifier values associated with the specified object. A color map defines a block of RGB values in the current palette. The WPG format specifies a default palette, so strictly speaking, the inclusion of a color map is optional. However, most format specimens contain a color map.

The WPG bitmap object is composed of a brief bitmap header followed by the bitmap data. The bitmap is encoded using an RLE compression scheme. Bitmaps of 1, 4, and 8 bits per pixel are supported, and a 4-bpp bitmap is structured as a single plane with 2 pixels packed into each byte.

The WPG File Header

Listings 17.1 and 17.2 (presented shortly) provide the structure definitions for the various object types defined by the WPG format. A WPG file's header is defined by the structure `WPGHEADER`. This structure is always the first item of a WPG file. A description of each member follows.

`fileid`	4-byte identifier consisting of the values FFh, W, P, C. This validates the file as being a WordPerfect file, but the `filetype` member must also be checked to validate a WPG file.
`dataofs`	32-bit integer that indicates the offset from the beginning of the file to the beginning of the file's data. For a WPG file this is typically 16, which is the size of a `WPGHEADER`.
`prodtype`	Product type identifier, normally the value 1.
`filetype`	File type identifier. A value of 22 indicates a WPG file.
`majver`	Major version number.
`minver`	Minor version number.
`enckey`	Encryption key, normally zero, indicating no encryption.
`resv`	Reserved word with the value zero.

The Begin WPG Data Object

The "begin WPG data" object is always the first data object of a WPG file. Its tag type value is 15 and the tag size is 6. This object is defined in Listing 17.1 as the structure `WPGBEGIN`. Its member descriptions are as follow:

`version`	Byte version number, should have the value 1.
`flags`	Byte flags value, should have the value 0.
`imwidth`	Integer value indicating the width of the file's image space in wpu (wordperfect units). A wpu is 1/1200 of an inch.
`imheight`	Integer value indicating the height of the file's image space in wpu.

When a WPG file contains only a bitmap and a color map, the width and height members of this structure can be ignored. The bitmap's dimensions are instead obtained from the bitmap's header.

The WPG Bitmap Header

A bitmap object has a tag type of 11 and the tag size varies depending on the size of the bitmap. The tag size is the sum of the size of the bitmap header and the size of the encoded bitmap. This object is defined in Listing 17.1 as the structure WPGBMHEADER. Its member descriptions are as follow:

bmwidth	Width of the bitmap in pixels.
bmheight	Height of the bitmap in pixels.
bmdepth	Number of bits per pixel. Possible values are 1, 2, 4, or 8.
bmxres	Horizontal resolution of the bitmap in pixels per inch. A typical value for a VGA-based image is 75.
bmyres	Vertical resolution of the bitmap in pixels per inch. A typical value for a VGA-based image is 75.

Listing 17.1 WPG.HPP

```
//------------------------------------------------------------//
//                                                            //
//    File:     WPG.HPP                                       //
//                                                            //
//    Desc:     Class and structure definitions for the       //
//              WordPerfect Graphics File Format              //
//                                                            //
//------------------------------------------------------------//

#ifndef _WPG_HPP_
#define _WPG_HPP_

#include "stdlib.h"
#include "stdio.h"
#include "string.h"

#include "color.hpp"
#include "codec.hpp"

//............record types and characteristics

enum WpgRecordTypes
{
    wpgFirst,
    wpgFillAttr,
    wpgLineAttr,
    wpgMarkerAttr,
    wpgPolyMarker,
    wpgLine,
    wpgPolyLine,
```

Listing 17.1 WPG.HPP (continued)

```
            wpgRectangle,
            wpgPolygon,
            wpgEllipse,
            wpgCurve,
            wpgBitmap,
            wpgText,
            wpgTextAttr,
            wpgColorMap,
            wpgBegin,
            wpgEnd,
            wpgPostScript,
            wpgOutputAttr,
            wpgLast,
        };

        //............misc nonmember functions

        RgbPalette * WpgPalette( void );
        RgbPalette * WpgPalette( FILE *f );

        //............struct WPGHEADER

        struct WPGHEADER
        {
            char  fileid[4];    // the bytes 0xFF, W, P, C
            long  dataofs;      // offset to start of data
            char  prodtype;     // product type = 1
            char  filetype;     // file type = 22
            char  majver;       // major version number
            char  minver;       // minor version number
            int   enckey;       // encryption key
            int   resv;         // reserved

            WPGHEADER( ) { }
            WPGHEADER( int ftype );
           ~WPGHEADER( ) { }
            int   get( FILE *f );
            int   put( FILE *f );
            int   validate( void );
            void  list( void );
        };

        //............struct WPGTAG

        struct WPGTAG
        {
            char rectype;       // record type identifier
            long reclength;     // length of record following
```

Listing 17.1 WPG.HPP (continued)

```
    WPGTAG( ) { rectype=0; reclength=0; }
    WPGTAG( char rt, long rl ) { rectype=rt; reclength=rl; }
   ~WPGTAG( ) { }
    int get( FILE *f );
    int put( FILE *f, int lenbytes );
    void list( void );
};

//............struct WPGBEGIN

struct WPGBEGIN
{
    char   version;      // WPG version number
    char   flags;        // various flags
    int    imwidth;      // image space width in wpu
    int    imheight;     // image space height in wpu

    WPGBEGIN( )
    {
        version = 1;
        flags = 0;
        imwidth = imheight = 0;
    }
    WPGBEGIN( int w, int h )
    {
        version = 1;
        flags = 0;
        imwidth = w;
        imheight = h;
    }
   ~WPGBEGIN( )
    {
    }
    int get( FILE *f );
    int put( FILE *f );
};

//............struct WPGBMHEADER

struct WPGBMHEADER
{
    int bmwidth;     // width in pixels
    int bmheight;    // height in pixels
    int bmdepth;     // pixel size in bits
    int bmxres;      // x res as pixels/inch
    int bmyres;      // y res as pixels/inch
```

Listing 17.1 WPG.HPP (continued)

```cpp
    WPGBMHEADER( )
    {
       bmwidth = bmheight = bmdepth = bmxres = bmyres = 0;
    }
    WPGBMHEADER( int w, int h, int d )
    {
       bmwidth  = w;
       bmheight = h;
       bmdepth  = d;
       bmxres = bmyres = 75;
    }
  ~WPGBMHEADER( )
    {
    }
    int get( FILE *f );
    int put( FILE *f );
    void list( void );
};


//.............class WpgDecoder

class WpgDecoder : public Decoder
{
   protected:
      FILE *wpg_file;           // output file
      int   cond;               // condition code
      int   pxbits;             // bits per pixel - 1,2,4,8
      int   width;              // image width in pixels
      int   height;             // image height in pixels

   private:
      int count;                // repeats of current scan line
      int pxmask;               // masks 1 pixel's width
      unsigned char *pxls;      // pixel buffer
      int readline( void );
      int putpixel( int pxbyte, int curpx );

   public:
      WpgDecoder( FILE *f_in, int nbits, int w, int h );
      virtual ~WpgDecoder( );
      virtual int decode( unsigned char *buf, int npxls );
      virtual int init( void );
      virtual int term( void );
      virtual int status( void );
};


//.............class WpgEncoder
```

Listing 17.1 WPG.HPP (continued)

```cpp
class WpgEncoder : public Encoder
{
    protected:
        int    cond;             // condition code
        int    pxl_bits;         // bits per pixel
        int    row_bytes;        // bytes per row
        FILE *wpg_file;          // output file

    private:
        char *scanbuffer;        // output buffer
        int    scanmask;         // output bit mask
        int    scanbyte;         // output byte pointer
        void   initbuffer( void );
        void   putbits( int bits, int nbits );
        void   putbyte( int byte );
        int    flush( void );
        void   write_124( unsigned char *buf, int npxls );
        void   write_8( unsigned char *buf, int npxls );

    public:
        WpgEncoder( FILE *f_out, WPGBMHEADER& wpg );
        virtual ~WpgEncoder( )
        {
            if( scanbuffer )
                delete scanbuffer;
        }
        virtual int encode( unsigned char *buf, int npxls );
        virtual int init( void );
        virtual int term( void );
        virtual int status( void );
};

#endif
```

Listing 17.2 WPG.CPP

```cpp
//----------------------------------------------------------//
//                                                          //
//   File:    WPG.CPP                                       //
//                                                          //
//   Desc:    Class and structure definitions for the       //
//            WordPerfect Graphics File Format               //
//                                                          //
//----------------------------------------------------------//

#include "wpg.hpp"
```

Listing 17.2 WPG.CPP (continued)

```cpp
#define  RUN_MASK   0x80     // mask top bit
#define  CNT_MASK   0x7F     // mask bottom 7 bits
#define  MAX_RUN    0x7F     // max repeat count

static char *WpgRecordNames[] =
{
    "Undefined",            // 0
    "Fill Attribute",       // 1
    "Line Attribute",       // 2
    "Marker Attribute",     // 3
    "Poly Marker",          // 4
    "Line",                 // 5
    "Poly Line",            // 6
    "Rectangle",            // 7
    "Polygon",              // 8
    "Ellipse",              // 9
    "Curve",                // 10
    "Bitmap",               // 11
    "Text",                 // 12
    "Text Attribute",       // 13
    "Color Map",            // 14
    "Begin WPG",            // 15
    "End WPG",              // 16
    "PostScript Data",      // 17
    "Output Attribute",     // 18
};

//............default WPG palette

static rgb default_colors[] =
{
    rgb(   0,   0,   0 ),
    rgb(   0,   0, 170 ),
    rgb(   0, 170,   0 ),
    rgb(   0, 170, 170 ),
    rgb( 170,   0,   0 ),
    rgb( 170,   0, 170 ),
    rgb( 170,  85,   0 ),
    rgb( 170, 170, 170 ),
    rgb(  85,  85,  85 ),
    rgb(  85,  85, 255 ),
    rgb(  85, 255,  85 ),
    rgb(  85, 255, 255 ),
    rgb( 255,  85,  85 ),
    rgb( 255,  85, 255 ),
    rgb( 255, 255,  85 ),
    rgb( 255, 255, 255 )
};
```

Listing 17.2 WPG.CPP (continued)

```cpp
static RgbPalette palette;

// return the current palette

RgbPalette * WpgPalette( void )
{
    // if palette is undefined, supply a default
    if( palette.ncolors == 0 )
    {
        palette.ncolors = 16;
        palette.colors = new rgb[16];
        if( palette.colors )
        {
            for( int i=0; i<16; i++ )
            palette.colors[i] = default_colors[i];
        }
        else
            palette.ncolors = 0;
    }

    return &palette;
}

// read a color map from WPG file

RgbPalette * WpgPalette( FILE *f )
{
    // read start index, color count
    int c1, cc;
    fread( &c1, 2, 1, f );
    fread( &cc, 2, 1, f );
    if( (c1 < 0) || (cc < 0) )
        return &palette;

    // total colors
    int nc = cc + c1;

    // need to allocate or reallocate?
    if( palette.ncolors == 0 )
    {
        palette.colors = new rgb[nc];
        palette.ncolors = palette.colors ? nc : 0;
    }
    else if( palette.ncolors < nc )
    {
        rgb *newcolors = new rgb[nc];
        if( newcolors == 0 )
            return &palette;
```

Listing 17.2 WPG.CPP (continued)

```cpp
            for( int i=0; i<palette.ncolors; i++ )
               newcolors[i] = palette.colors[i];
            delete palette.colors;
            palette.colors = newcolors;
            palette.ncolors = nc;
         }

      // read the colors
      while( cc-- )
      {
         palette.colors[c1].red = fgetc( f );
         palette.colors[c1].grn = fgetc( f );
         palette.colors[c1].blu = fgetc( f );
         c1++;
      }

      return &palette;
   }

//...........struct WPGHEADER

WPGHEADER::WPGHEADER( int ftype )
{
   fileid[0] = -1;
   fileid[1] = 'W';
   fileid[2] = 'P';
   fileid[3] = 'C';
   dataofs = 16;
   prodtype = 1;
   filetype = ftype;
   majver = 1;
   minver = 0;
   enckey = 0;
   resv = 0;
}

int WPGHEADER::get( FILE *f )
{
   return ( fread(fileid,sizeof(WPGHEADER),1,f) == 1 ) ?
          0 : -1;
}

int WPGHEADER::put( FILE *f )
{
   return ( fwrite(fileid,sizeof(WPGHEADER),1,f) == 1 ) ?
          0 : -1;
}
```

Listing 17.2 WPG.CPP (continued)

```cpp
int WPGHEADER::validate( void )
{
    if( fileid[0] != -1 )  return -1;
    if( fileid[1] != 'W' ) return 'W';
    if( fileid[2] != 'P' ) return 'P';
    if( fileid[3] != 'C' ) return 'C';
    if( filetype != 22 )   return 22;
    return 0;
}

void WPGHEADER::list( void )
{
    printf( "WPGHEADER::fileid   = %d %c %c %c\n",
              fileid[0], fileid[1], fileid[2], fileid[3] );
    printf( "WPGHEADER::dataofs  = %ld\n", dataofs );
    printf( "WPGHEADER::prodtype = %d\n", prodtype );
    printf( "WPGHEADER::filetype = %d\n", filetype );
    printf( "WPGHEADER::majver   = %d\n", majver );
    printf( "WPGHEADER::minver   = %d\n", minver );
    printf( "WPGHEADER::enckey   = %d\n", enckey );
    printf( "WPGHEADER::resv     = %d\n", resv );
}

//.............struct WPGTAG

int WPGTAG::get( FILE *f )
{
    reclength = 0;
    if( (rectype = fgetc( f )) < 0 ) return -1;
    int i;
    if( (i = fgetc(f)) < 0 ) return -1;
    if( i < 255 ) { reclength = i; return 0; }
    if( fread(&i,1,2,f) != 2 ) return -1;
    if( i > 0 ) { reclength = i; return 0; }
    i &= 0x7FFF;
    reclength = i;
    reclength <<= 16;
    if( fread(&i,1,2,f) != 2 ) return -1;
    reclength |= ((long) i ) & 0x0000FFFFL;
    return 0;
}

int WPGTAG::put( FILE *f, int lenbytes )
{
    char  ch;
    short hi, lo;
```

Listing 17.2 WPG.CPP (continued)

```
fputc( rectype, f );
switch( lenbytes )
{
   case 0 :  // determine appropriate size
        if( reclength < 255 )
        {
           ch = (char) reclength;
           fputc( ch, f );
        }
        else if( reclength < 32767L )
        {
           fputc( 255, f );
           lo = (short) reclength;
           fwrite( &lo, 2, 1, f );
        }
        else
        {
           fputc( 255, f );
           lo = (short) reclength;
           hi = (short) ((long) reclength >> 16);
           hi |= 0x8000;
           fwrite( &hi, 2, 1, f );
           fwrite( &lo, 2, 1, f );
        }
        break;

   case 1 :  // byte
        ch = (char) reclength;
        fputc( ch, f );
        break;

   case 2 :  // word
        fputc( 255, f );
        lo = (short) reclength;
        fwrite( &lo, 2, 1, f );
        break;

   case 4 :  // double word
        fputc( 255, f );
        lo = (short) reclength;
        hi = (short) ((long) reclength >> 16);
        hi |= 0x8000;
        fwrite( &hi, 2, 1, f );
        fwrite( &lo, 2, 1, f );
        break;
```

Listing 17.2 WPG.CPP (continued)

```cpp
        default : // error
                return lenbytes;
    }
    return ferror( f );
}

void WPGTAG::list( void )
{
    printf( "Type = %d", rectype );
    if( (rectype > wpgFirst) && (rectype < wpgLast) )
        printf( ", \"%s\", ", WpgRecordNames[rectype] );
    else
        printf( ", \"(Unknown, Unused, or Undefined)\", " );
    printf( "Length = %ld\n", reclength );
}

//.............struct WPGBEGIN

int WPGBEGIN::get( FILE *f )
{
    return ( fread(&version,sizeof(WPGBEGIN),1,f) == 1 ) ?
            0 : -1;
}

int WPGBEGIN::put( FILE *f )
{
    return ( fwrite(&version,sizeof(WPGBEGIN),1,f) == 1 ) ?
            0 : -1;
}

//.............struct WPGBMHEADER

int WPGBMHEADER::get( FILE *f )
{
    return ( fread(&bmwidth,sizeof(WPGBMHEADER),1,f) == 1 ) ?
            0 : -1;
}

int WPGBMHEADER::put( FILE *f )
{
    return ( fwrite(&bmwidth,sizeof(WPGBMHEADER),1,f) == 1 ) ?
            0 : -1;
}

void WPGBMHEADER::list( void )
{
    printf( "WPGBMHEADER::bmwidth  = %d\n", bmwidth );
    printf( "WPGBMHEADER::bmheight = %d\n", bmheight );
```

Listing 17.2 WPG.CPP (continued)

```cpp
    printf( "WPGBMHEADER::bmdepth  = %d\n", bmdepth );
    printf( "WPGBMHEADER::bmxres   = %d px/in\n", bmxres );
    printf( "WPGBMHEADER::bmyres   = %d px/in\n", bmyres );
}

//.............class WpgDecoder

WpgDecoder::WpgDecoder( FILE *f_in, int nbits, int w, int h )
{
    wpg_file = f_in;
    pxbits   = nbits;
    pxmask   = (1 << pxbits) - 1;
    if( pxbits < 8 )
        pxmask <<= 8 - pxbits;
    width    = w;
    height   = h;
    count    = 0;
    pxls     = new unsigned char [width];
    cond     = pxls ? xOKAY : xNOMEMORY;
}

WpgDecoder::~WpgDecoder( )
{
    if( pxls ) delete pxls;
}

int WpgDecoder::status( void )
{
    if( ferror( wpg_file ) ) cond = xIOERROR;
    if( feof( wpg_file ) )   cond = xENDOFFILE;
    return cond;
}

int WpgDecoder::init( void )
{
    count = 0;
    cond  = pxls ? xOKAY : xNOMEMORY;
    return status();
}

int WpgDecoder::term( void )
{
    return status();
}
```

Listing 17.2 WPG.CPP (continued)

```cpp
int WpgDecoder::putpixel( int pxbyte, int curpx )
{
   int mask = pxmask;
   int n = 8 - pxbits;
   while( mask )
   {
      pxls[curpx++] = (pxbyte & mask) >> n;
      mask >>= pxbits;
      n -= pxbits;
   }
   return curpx;
}

int WpgDecoder::readline( void )
{
   int nlines = 1;
   int n = 0;
   while( n < width )
   {
     int x = fgetc( wpg_file );
     if( x < 0 ) break;
     int highbit = (x & 0x80) ? 1 : 0;
     int cnt = x & 0x7F;
     if( highbit )
     {
        if( cnt > 0 )
        {
           int dat = fgetc( wpg_file );
           while( cnt-- > 0 )
              n = putpixel( dat, n );
        }
        else
        {
           cnt = fgetc( wpg_file );
           while( cnt-- > 0 )
              n = putpixel( 0xFF, n );
        }
     }
     else
     {
        if( cnt > 0 )
        {
           while( cnt-- > 0 )
           {
              int dat = fgetc( wpg_file );
              n = putpixel( dat, n );
           }
        }
```

Listing 17.2 WPG.CPP (continued)

```
            else
            {
               nlines = fgetc( wpg_file );
               break;
            }
         }
      }
      return nlines;
   }

int WpgDecoder::decode( unsigned char *buf, int npxls )
{
   if( status() == xOKAY )
   {
      if( count == 0 )
         count = readline();
      memcpy( buf, pxls, npxls );
      count--;
   }
   return status();
}

//.................class WpgEncoder

WpgEncoder::WpgEncoder( FILE *f_out, WPGBMHEADER& wpg )
{
   pxl_bits = wpg.bmdepth;
   row_bytes = (wpg.bmwidth*wpg.bmdepth + 7) / 8;
   wpg_file = f_out;
   scanbuffer = new char[row_bytes];
   cond = (scanbuffer == 0) ? xNOMEMORY : xOKAY;
}

int WpgEncoder::status( void )
{
   if( ferror( wpg_file ) ) cond = xIOERROR;
   return cond;
}

int WpgEncoder::init( void )
{
   cond = (scanbuffer == 0) ? xNOMEMORY : xOKAY;
   return status();
}
```

Listing 17.2 WPG.CPP (continued)

```cpp
int WpgEncoder::term( void )
{
   return status();
}

void WpgEncoder::initbuffer( void )
{
   memset( scanbuffer, 0, row_bytes );
   scanmask = 0x80;
   scanbyte = 0;
}

void WpgEncoder::putbits( int bits, int nbits )
{
   int mask = 1 << nbits;
   while( (mask >>= 1) != 0 )
   {
      if( bits & mask )
         scanbuffer[scanbyte] |= scanmask;
      if( (scanmask >>= 1) == 0 )
      {
         scanbyte++;
         scanmask = 0x80;
      }
   }
}

void WpgEncoder::putbyte( int byte )
{
   scanbuffer[scanbyte++] = byte;
}

int WpgEncoder::flush( void )
{
   // encode and write scanbuffer
   int n1, n2=-1, n, nt=0;

   while( nt < row_bytes )
   {
      n1 = n2 + 1;
      n2 = n1 + 1;
```

Listing 17.2 WPG.CPP (continued)

```cpp
                // single byte left
                if( n1 == row_bytes - 1 )
                {
                   fputc( 1, wpg_file );
                   fputc( scanbuffer[n1], wpg_file );
                   nt++;
                }

                // repeating run of 2 or more bytes
                else if( scanbuffer[n1] == scanbuffer[n2] )
                {
                   while( (scanbuffer[n1] == scanbuffer[n2]) &&
                          (n2 < row_bytes) )
                      n2++;
                   if( n2 == row_bytes )
                      n2--;
                   n = n2 - n1 + 1;
                   nt += n;
                   while( n > MAX_RUN )
                   {
                      fputc( MAX_RUN|RUN_MASK, wpg_file );
                      fputc( scanbuffer[n1], wpg_file );
                      n -= MAX_RUN;
                   }
                   fputc( n|RUN_MASK, wpg_file );
                   fputc( scanbuffer[n1], wpg_file );
                }

                // nonrepeating run of 2 or more bytes
                else
                {
                   while( (scanbuffer[n2] != scanbuffer[n2-1]) &&
                          (n2 < row_bytes) )
                      n2++;
                   if( n2 == row_bytes )
                      n2--;
                   n = n2 - n1 + 1;
                   nt += n;
                   while( n > MAX_RUN )
                   {
                      fputc( MAX_RUN, wpg_file );
                      fwrite( scanbuffer+n1, MAX_RUN, 1, wpg_file );
                      n -= MAX_RUN;
                      n1 += MAX_RUN;
                   }
```

Listing 17.2 WPG.CPP (continued)

```
            fputc( n, wpg_file );
            fwrite( scanbuffer+n1, n, 1, wpg_file );
        }
    }

    return status();
}

// encodes 1, 2, or 4 bits per pixel
void WpgEncoder::write_124( unsigned char *buf, int npxls )
{
    initbuffer();
    int n = 0;
    while( n < npxls )
        putbits( buf[n++], pxl_bits );
    flush();
}

// encodes 8 bits per pixel
void WpgEncoder::write_8( unsigned char *buf, int npxls )
{
    initbuffer();
    int n = 0;
    while( n < npxls )
        putbyte( buf[n++] );
    flush();
}

int WpgEncoder::encode( unsigned char *buf, int npxls )
{
    if( cond == xOKAY )
    {
        if( pxl_bits == 8 )
            write_8( buf, npxls );
        else
            write_124( buf, npxls );
    }
    return status();
}
```

Reading Object Lengths

The size member of a WPG tag itself varies in size depending on the magnitude of the number it must represent. Possible sizes are 1 byte, 1 word (16 bits), or 1 double word (32 bits). The procedure for reading a tag size field is illustrated by the WPGTAG::get() member function in Listing 17.2. However, the code may be a bit difficult to follow, so the process is described here.

When a tag is read, 2 bytes are read first. The first byte is, of course, the tag ID byte, and the second byte is the size byte. If size is between 0 and 254 inclusive, then you are done. If, however, size is 255 (that is, FFh), two more bytes are read. These are, respectively, the low-order byte and the high-order byte of a 16-bit signed integer. If the integer just read has a value greater than zero, then you are done. If, however, it is less than zero, the high-order bit is cleared and the two bytes are interpreted as the high-order word of a 32-bit integer. The low-order word is obtained by reading two more bytes from the file. Note that this algorithm results in reading 1, 3, or 5 bytes for the size field. The initial byte serves as a flag for 2-byte and 4-byte values and is not part of the actual value.

If you are scratching your head at this point, don't worry—this process is much more complex than it needs to be. It was no doubt developed with the aim of keeping the size of a WPG file as small as possible. By the way, the WPGTAG::get() member function returns a negative value to indicate that an error occurred while a tag was being read.

The WPG Compression Scheme

WPG bitmaps are compressed using an RLE compression algorithm. Each compression construct is preceded by a byte value that identifies the construct. This byte contains two values. The byte's high-order bit is a flag and its lower 7 bits constitute a count field. The two in combination provide for four possible constructs depending on whether the high bit is set and whether the count is nonzero. The possible interpretations are as follow:

High Bit	Count	Interpretation
0	0	The next byte read indicates the number of times to repeat the last scan line that was decoded.
0	1..127	The number of bytes specified by count are read from the file and used as is; that is, they are uncompressed.
1	0	The next byte read indicates the number of times to repeat the byte FFh in the bitmap.
1	1..127	The next byte read is repeated the number of times indicated by count.

This scheme means that a decoder must save the last scan line read in case the next compression construct indicates that the scan line is to be repeated. This convention also implies that each scan line is encoded separately. Finally, note that scan lines are padded with unused bits, if necessary, to form an integral number of bytes.

A WPG Query Program

Listing 17.3 presents a WPG query program that is similar in most respects to the other query programs that have been developed in this book. One WPG-specific option of this program is the ability to scan a file and list the tags it contains. This allows one to ascertain a file's contents at a glance. Assuming a bitmapped WPG file, the output of a scan will look something like the following:

```
Listing of WPG file 'sample.wpg'
WPGHEADER::fileid   = -1 W P C
WPGHEADER::dataofs  = 16
WPGHEADER::prodtype = 1
WPGHEADER::filetype = 22
WPGHEADER::majver   = 1
WPGHEADER::minver   = 0
WPGHEADER::enckey   = 0
WPGHEADER::resv     = 0

Type = 15, "Begin WPG", Length = 6
Type = 14, "Color Map", Length = 772
Type = 11, "Eitmap", Length = 5613
Type = 16, "End WPG", Length = 0
```

Listing 17.3 QWPG.CPP

```cpp
//-----------------------------------------------------------//
//                                                           //
//    File:    QWPG.CPP                                       //
//                                                           //
//    Desc:    WPG File Query Program                        //
//                                                           //
//-----------------------------------------------------------//

#include "stdlib.h"
#include "stdio.h"
#include "string.h"

#include "wpg.hpp"

//.................program usage

void explain_pgm( void )
{
    printf( "\n" );
    printf( "WordPerfect WPG Graphics File Query Program\n" );
    printf( "\n" );
    printf( "Usage:  QWPG  wpg_file  [ -p | -s ]\n" );
    printf( "\n" );
    printf( "-p includes palette in listing\n" );
```

Listing 17.3 QWPG.CPP (continued)

```cpp
    printf( "-s scans and lists all opcodes\n" );
    printf( ".WPG extension is assumed\n" );
    printf( "\n" );
}

//.................main

int main( int argc, char *argv[] )
{
    // check args
    if( (argc < 2) || (*argv[1] == '?') )
    {
        explain_pgm();
        return 0;
    }

    // create file name
    char fn[80];
    strcpy( fn, argv[1] );
    char *p = strchr( fn, '.' );
    if( p == 0 )
        strcat( fn, ".wpg" );
    else if( *(p+1) == 0 )
        *p = 0;

    // list palette ?
    int lpal = 0;
    if( argc > 2 )
        if( (strcmp( argv[2], "-p" ) == 0) ||
            (strcmp( argv[2], "-P" ) == 0) )
            lpal = 1;

    // scan for opcodes ?
    int scan = 0;
    if( argc > 2 )
        if( (strcmp( argv[2], "-s" ) == 0) ||
            (strcmp( argv[2], "-S" ) == 0) )
            scan = 1;

    // open the file
    FILE *fwpg = fopen( fn, "rb" );
    if( fwpg == 0 )
    {
        printf( "File '%s' not found\n", fn );
        return 0;
    }
```

Listing 17.3 QWPG.CPP (continued)

```cpp
WPGHEADER wpgh;
wpgh.get( fwpg );
if( wpgh.validate() != 0 )
{
   printf( "File '%s' is not a valid WPG file\n", fn );
   return 0;
}

printf( "Listing of WPG file '%s'\n", fn );
printf( "\n" );
wpgh.list();
printf( "\n" );

WPGTAG tag;
RgbPalette * pal = WpgPalette();
while( ! tag.get( fwpg ) )
{
   if( scan )
   {
      tag.list();
      fseek( fwpg, tag.reclength, SEEK_CUR );
   }
   else
   {
      WPGBMHEADER bmh;
      switch( tag.rectype )
      {
         case wpgBitmap :
             bmh.get( fwpg );
             bmh.list();
             fseek( fwpg,
                     tag.reclength-sizeof(WPGBMHEADER),
                     SEEK_CUR );
             break;

         case wpgColorMap :
             pal = WpgPalette( fwpg );
             break;

         default :
             fseek( fwpg, tag.reclength, SEEK_CUR );
             break;
      }
   }
}
```

Listing 17.3 QWPG.CPP (continued)

```
// list palette ?
if( lpal )
{
   printf( "\n" );
   for( int i=0; i<pal->ncolors; i++ )
      printf( "pal->colors[%d] = rgb(%d,%d,%d)\n",
                i, pal->colors[i].red,
                   pal->colors[i].grn,
                   pal->colors[i].blu );
}

return 0;
}
```

A WPG View Program

Listing 17.4 presents the source code for a WPG view program. Note that the program is intended for use only with bitmapped WPG files. If it is run with a WPG file that lacks a bitmap, it is terminated with an appropriate error message. Also note that any drawing primitives other than bitmaps and palette specifications are ignored. Other than these two caveats, the program is similar to its many cousins found throughout this book.

Listing 17.4 VWPG.CPP

```
//----------------------------------------------------------//
//                                                          //
//    File:      VWPG.CPP                                   //
//                                                          //
//    Desc:      Program to view or print a WPG file        //
//                                                          //
//----------------------------------------------------------//

#include "stdlib.h"
#include "stdio.h"
#include "string.h"
#include "conio.h"
#include "ctype.h"

#include "wpg.hpp"
#include "imgviewr.hpp"
#include "imgprntr.hpp"
#include "laserjet.hpp"
#include "paintjet.hpp"
```

Listing 17.4 VWPG.CPP (continued)

```
#include "epjx80.hpp"
#include "eplq24.hpp"
#include "pscript.hpp"


//.................Printer types


#define   LJ   0x4C4A
#define   PJ   0x504A
#define   JX   0x4A58
#define   LQ   0x4C51
#define   PS   0x5053


//.................Program globals


char        fn[80];        // path to PCX file

int         gmode;         // video display mode
int         pmode;         // printer ID
int         ropt;          // rendering flags
int         iopt;          // itensity mapping flags

ImgStore     *imgmap;      // image bitmap
RgbPalette   *imgpal;      // image palette

//.................Exit with a message

void exit_pgm( char *msg )
{
   printf( "%s\n", msg );
   exit( 0 );
}

//.................Program usage

void explain_pgm( void )
{
   printf( "\n" );
   printf( ".......WordPerfect WPG File Viewer/Printer.......\n"
);
   printf( "\n" );
   printf( "Usage:       VWPG  wpg_file  [ switches ]\n" );
   printf( "\n" );
   printf( "Switches:  -h      = display program usage\n" );
   printf( "           -vXX    = force video display mode XX\n" );
   printf( "                     (XX = 12, 13, 2E, 62)\n" );
   printf( "           -pXX    = print using printer XX\n" );
```

Listing 17.4 VWPG.CPP (continued)

```
   printf( "                            (XX = LJ, PJ, JX, LQ, PS)\n" );
   printf( "              -b[+|-] = increase or decrease
brightness\n" );
   printf( "              -c[+|-] = increase or decrease contrast\n"
);
   printf( "              -d      = force dithered rendering\n" );
   printf( "              -g      = force gray scale rendering\n" );
   printf( "              -m      = force palette mapping\n" );
   printf( "\n" );
   printf( "..................................................\n"
);
   printf( "\n" );
}

//.................Process pgm argument list

void process_args( int argc, char *argv[] )
{
   // establish default values
   fn[0] = 0;
   gmode = 0x12;
   pmode = 0;
   ropt  = 0;
   iopt  = 0;

   // process the program's argument list
   for( int i=1; i<argc; i++ )
   {
      if( (*argv[i] == '-') || (*argv[i] == '/') )
      {
         char sw = *(argv[i] + 1);
         switch( toupper(sw) )
         {
            case 'H' :
               explain_pgm();
               exit( 0 );
               break;

            case 'V' :
               sscanf( argv[i]+2, "%x", &gmode );
               break;

            case 'P' :
               pmode = toupper( *(argv[i]+2) );
               pmode <<= 8;
               pmode += toupper( *(argv[i]+3) );
               break;
```

Listing 17.4 VWPG.CPP (continued)

```cpp
            case 'B' :
                if( *(argv[i]+2) == '-' )
                    iopt |= intensDBRI;
                else
                    iopt |= intensIBRI;
                break;

            case 'C' :
                if( *(argv[i]+2) == '-' )
                    iopt |= intensDCNT;
                else
                    iopt |= intensICNT;
                break;

            case 'D' :
                ropt |= renderDITHER;
                break;

            case 'G' :
                ropt |= renderGRAY;
                break;

            case 'M' :
                ropt |= renderMAP;
                break;

            default:
                printf( "Unknown switch '%s' ignored\n",
                        argv[i] );
                break;
        }
    }
    else  // presumably a file identifier
    {
        strcpy( fn, argv[i] );
        char *p = strchr( fn, '.' );
        if( p == 0 )
            strcat( fn, ".wpg" );
        else if( *(p+1) == 0 )
            *p = 0;
    }
}
```

Listing 17.4 VWPG.CPP (continued)

```cpp
        // was a file name specified?
        if( fn[0] == 0 )
        {
           explain_pgm();
           exit( 0 );
        }
     }

     //..................Create an image storage buffer

     ImgStore * istore( int h, int w, int d )
     {
        ImgStore *ist = 0;

        // attempt to create in order of preference
        ist = new XmsImgStore( h, w, d );
        if( (ist != 0) && (ist->status != imgstoreOKAY) )
        {
           delete ist;
           ist = new EmsImgStore( h, w, d );
           if( (ist != 0) && (ist->status != imgstoreOKAY) )
           {
              delete ist;
              ist = new CnvImgStore( h, w, d );
              if( (ist != 0) && (ist->status != imgstoreOKAY) )
              {
                 delete ist;
                 ist = new DskImgStore( h, w, d );
                 if( (ist != 0) && (ist->status != imgstoreOKAY) )
                 {
                    delete ist;
                    ist = 0;
                 }
              }
           }
        }

        return ist;
     }

     //.................Create a printer

     PrinterDriver * printer( int which )
     {
        PrinterDriver *p;
```

Listing 17.4 VWPG.CPP (continued)

```
    switch( which )
    {
        case LJ : p = new LaserJet( "LPT1" );
                  break;
        case PJ : p = new PaintJet( "LPT1" );
                  break;
        case JX : p = new EpsonJX80( "LPT1" );
                  break;
        case LQ : p = new EpsonLQ24( "LPT1" );
                  break;
        default : p = new PsPrinter( "LPT1" );
                  break;
    }

    return p;
}

//.................Load a bitmap

ImgStore * read_bm( FILE * f, WPGBMHEADER * h )
{
    unsigned char *scanln = new unsigned char [h->bmwidth];
    ImgStore *imap = istore( h->bmheight, h->bmwidth, 8 );
    if( (imap == 0) || (scanln == 0) )
    {
        if( imap ) delete imap;
        if( scanln ) delete scanln;
        exit_pgm( "Insufficient memory to load image" );
    }

    WpgDecoder d( f, h->bmdepth, h->bmwidth, h->bmheight );
    d.init();
    for( int i=0; i<h->bmheight; i++ )
    {
        d.decode( scanln, h->bmwidth );
        imap->put( scanln, i );
    }
    d.term();

    delete scanln;
    return imap;
}

//.................Load the WPG file
```

Listing 17.4 VWPG.CPP (continued)

```cpp
void load_wpg( void )
{
   // open file
   FILE *fwpg = fopen( fn, "rb" );
   if( fwpg == 0 )
      exit_pgm( "WPG file not found" );

   // read header
   WPGHEADER wpgh;
   if( fread( &wpgh, sizeof(WPGHEADER), 1, fwpg ) != 1 )
      exit_pgm( "Error reading WPG header" );

   // validate file
   if( wpgh.validate() != 0 )
      exit_pgm( "File is not a WPG file" );

   // scan file for palette and bitmap
   imgmap = 0;
   imgpal = WpgPalette();
   WPGTAG tag;
   while( ! tag.get( fwpg ) )
   {
      WPGBMHEADER bmh;
      switch( tag.rectype )
      {
         case wpgBitmap :
              bmh.get( fwpg );
              imgmap = read_bm( fwpg, &bmh );
              break;

         case wpgColorMap :
              imgpal = WpgPalette( fwpg );
              break;

         default :
              fseek( fwpg, tag.reclength, SEEK_CUR );
              break;
      }
   }
   fclose( fwpg );
   if( imgmap == 0 )
      exit_pgm( "WPG file lacks a bitmap" );
}

//.................Main
```

Listing 17.4 VWPG.CPP (continued)

```cpp
int main( int argc, char *argv[] )
{
   process_args( argc, argv );

   load_wpg( );

   // print the image
   if( pmode != 0 )
   {
      PrinterDriver *prt = printer( pmode );
      if( prt )
      {
         printf( "Printing..." );
         ImagePrinter ip( prt, imgmap, imgpal->colors,
                          imgpal->ncolors,
                          ropt, iopt, 100, 100 );
         ip.print( 1 );
         printf( "done\n" );
         delete prt;
      }
      else
         printf( "Printer instantiation failed\n" );
   }

   // display the image
   else
   {
      VgaDisplay vga( gmode );
      ImageViewer iv( &vga, imgmap, imgpal->colors,
                      imgpal->ncolors, ropt, iopt );
      iv.view( );
   }

   delete imgmap;

   return 0;
}
```

Writing the WPG Format

Listings 17.1 and 17.2 include, among other things, the definition for a
WpgEncoder class that can be used in writing instances of the format. Of course,
with a format like WPG, encoding a bitmap represents only about half the task
of writing the format. A format writer must also output the file header, the tags
for each object, and any data structures associated with each object.

The only tricky part of the whole process is writing the bitmap's tag, because the size of the encoded bitmap will not be known beforehand. Obviously, the tag can be output as a placeholder. Once the bitmap has been written and its size determined then the tag can be updated with the proper value. The real problem is determining what size will be needed to represent the bitmap length, which may require a byte, word, or double-word value. The solution is always to write the bitmap length as a double word regardless of its actual size requirement.

A similar problem would occur in writing a color map, except that the size of the color map should always be known ahead of time. But note, for instance, that a 16-color palette requires only a single byte to specify its length (size < 255) while a 256-color palette requires a word value (size > 254).

The `WpgEncoder` class from Listing 17.2 is designed to utilize only two of the four possible compression constructs. It does not encode runs of FFh separately nor does it use the repeat-scan-line construct. What is left is repeating runs and nonrepeating runs, which makes the compression process similar to that of other formats, particularly the PCX format. This design simplification makes implementation of the encoder much easier, and in most cases, does not greatly affect compression efficiency.

Listing 17.5 shows the implementation of two versions of a `WriteWPG` function, one that takes its input from a display and one that operates with an `ImgStore` instance. The WPGDEMO program in Listing 17.6 illustrates the use of `WriteWPG` with the El Greco test image.

Listing 17.5 WRTWPG.CPP

```
//----------------------------------------------------------//
//                                                          //
//    File:     WRTWPG.CPP                                   //
//                                                          //
//    Desc:     Code to output a WPG file from              //
//              a VGA Display or a Memory Bitmap            //
//                                                          //
//----------------------------------------------------------//

#include "wpg.hpp"
#include "display.hpp"
#include "imgstore.hpp"
#include "iscale.h"

//.................Write VGA screen to WPG file 'fn'
```

Listing 17.5 WRTWPG.CPP (continued)

```cpp
int WriteWPG( VgaDisplay& vga, char *fn,
              int x1, int y1, int x2, int y2 )
{
    // various image metrics
    int ncols = x2 - x1 + 1;
    int nrows = y2 - y1 + 1;
    int nbits = vga.metric.nplanes * vga.metric.nbits;
    int nclrs = vga.metric.ncolors;
    rgb *pal = new rgb[nclrs];
    unsigned char *pxl = new unsigned char [ncols];
    if( (pal == 0) || (pxl == 0) )
    {
        delete pal;
        delete pxl;
        return xNOMEMORY;
    }
    vga.getpalette( pal, nclrs );

    // file header
    WPGHEADER wpg( 22 );

    // bitmap header
    WPGBMHEADER hdr( ncols, nrows, nbits );

    // begin WPG data
    int wpuW = iscale( ncols, 1200, hdr.bmxres );
    int wpuH = iscale( nrows, 1200, hdr.bmyres );
    WPGBEGIN bgn( wpuW, wpuH );

    // the four object tags
    WPGTAG bgntag( wpgBegin, 6 );
    WPGTAG clrtag( wpgColorMap, nclrs*3+4 );
    WPGTAG maptag( wpgBitmap, 999999L );
    WPGTAG endtag( wpgEnd, 0 );

    // Write the WPG file
    FILE *f = fopen( fn, "wb" );

    // file header
    wpg.put( f );

    // begin WPG data
    bgntag.put( f,0 );
    bgn.put( f );

    // define·color map
    clrtag.put( f, 0 );
    int ibgn = 0;
```

Listing 17.5 WRTWPG.CPP (continued)

```cpp
        fwrite( &ibgn, 2, 1, f );
        fwrite( &nclrs, 2, 1, f );
        for( int i=0; i<nclrs; i++ )
        {
            fputc( pal[i].red, f );
            fputc( pal[i].grn, f );
            fputc( pal[i].blu, f );
        }

        // bitmap header and data
        long maptagofs = ftell( f );
        maptag.put( f, 4 );

        long mapofs1 = ftell( f );
        hdr.put( f );
        WpgEncoder enc( f, hdr );
        enc.init();
        for( i=0; i<nrows; i++ )
        {
            vga.getscanline( pxl, ncols, x1, y1+i );
            enc.encode( pxl, ncols );
        }
        enc.term();
        long mapofs2 = ftell( f );

        // end WPG data
        endtag.put( f, 0 );

        // update bitmap tag length field
        fseek( f, maptagofs, SEEK_SET );
        maptag.reclength = mapofs2 - mapofs1;
        maptag.put( f, 4 );

        int retv = ferror( f );
        fclose( f );
        return retv;
    }

    //.................Write an image to WPG file 'fn'

    int WriteWPG( ImgStore& img, rgb *pal, char *fn )
    {
        // various image metrics
        int ncols = img.width();
        int nrows = img.height();
        int nclrs = 1 << img.depth();
        int nbits = img.depth();
```

Listing 17.5 WRTWPG.CPP (continued)

```cpp
// file header
WPGHEADER wpg( 22 );

// bitmap header
WPGBMHEADER hdr( ncols, nrows, nbits );

// begin WPG data
int wpuW = iscale( ncols, 1200, hdr.bmxres );
int wpuH = iscale( nrows, 1200, hdr.bmyres );
WPGBEGIN bgn( wpuW, wpuH );

// the four object tags
WPGTAG bgntag( wpgBegin, 6 );
WPGTAG clrtag( wpgColorMap, nclrs*3+4 );
WPGTAG maptag( wpgBitmap, 0 );
WPGTAG endtag( wpgEnd, 0 );

// Write the WPG file
FILE *f = fopen( fn, "wb" );

// file header
wpg.put( f );

// begin WPG data
bgntag.put( f, 0 );
bgn.put( f );

// define color map
clrtag.put( f, 0 );
int ibgn = 0;
fwrite( &ibgn, 2, 1, f );
fwrite( &nclrs, 2, 1, f );
for( int i=0; i<nclrs; i++ )
{
   fputc( pal[i].red, f );
   fputc( pal[i].grn, f );
   fputc( pal[i].blu, f );
}

// bitmap header and data
long maptagofs = ftell( f );
maptag.put( f, 4 );

long mapofs1 = ftell( f );
hdr.put( f );
WpgEncoder enc( f, hdr );
enc.init();
for( i=0; i<nrows; i++ )
```

Listing 17.5 WRTWPG.CPP (continued)

```
    {
        enc.encode( img.get(i), ncols );
    }
    enc.term();
    long mapofs2 = ftell( f );

    // end WPG data
    endtag.put( f, 0 );

    // update bitmap tag length field
    fseek( f, maptagofs, SEEK_SET );
    maptag.reclength = mapofs2 - mapofs1;
    maptag.put( f, 4 );

    int retv = ferror( f );
    fclose( f );
    return retv;
}
```

Listing 17.6 WPGDEMO.CPP

```
//-----------------------------------------------------------//
//                                                           //
//   File:     WPGDEMO.CPP                                   //
//                                                           //
//   Desc:     Example code to write a WPG file             //
//                                                           //
//-----------------------------------------------------------//

#include "wrtwpg.cpp"

char *        palname      = "EL-GRECO.PAL";
char *        imgname      = "EL-GRECO.IMG";
int           imgwidth     = 354;
int           imgheight    = 446;
int           imgcolors    = 256;
rgb           imgpalette[256];
unsigned char scanline[354];
CnvImgStore img( 446, 354, 8 );

// read the test image's palette

void read_palette( void )
{
    FILE *f = fopen( palname, "rt" );
    for( int i=0; i<imgcolors; i++ )
    {
        int r, g, b;
```

Listing 17.6 WPGDEMO.CPP (continued)

```
        fscanf( f, "%d %d %d", &r, &g, &b );
        imgpalette[i] = rgb( r, g, b );
    }
    fclose( f );
}

// read the test image into memory

void read_image( void )
{
    FILE *f = fopen( imgname, "rb" );
    for( int i=0; i<imgheight; i++ )
    {
        fread( scanline, imgwidth, 1, f );
        img.put( scanline, i );
    }
    fclose( f );
}

// output a WPG file

int main( void )
{
    read_palette( );

    read_image( );

    WriteWPG( img, imgpalette, "WPGDEMO.WPG" );

    return 0;
}
```

This concludes our look at the WordPerfect WPG format. It would probably be a much more important format if it were the only image format supported by WordPerfect. However, WordPerfect also reads PCX and IMG files, among others, so there is no compelling reason to prefer the WPG format to those simpler formats.

18

The Encapsulated PostScript Format

In many ways, the Encapsulated PostScript Format, EPS, for short, is the most complex format covered in this book. For all practical purposes an EPS file is an arbitrary PostScript file that is structured according to certain conventions. It is these conventions that make up the actual format specification. An EPS decoder, therefore, must possess the full capability range of a PostScript interpreter—in fact, it *is* a PostScript interpreter.

Writing a PostScript interpreter is beyond the scope of this book, so we won't be discussing an EPS decoder. However, writing a specific instance of an EPS file is a reasonably simple task, so this chapter will develop an encoder. As it turns out, much of the implementation for an EPS encoder has already been done in the PostScript printer driver developed in Chapter 6.

You will find some books and articles in the literature that implement so-called EPS file viewers. These are not, however, true PostScript interpreters. The EPS format allows for the inclusion of a small bitmap that represents a thumbnail sketch of the file's true image. This is relatively easy to locate and process, and provides a quick-and-dirty view of what you will get if the file is actually processed. Finding and displaying this thumbnail image, however, is not the same as actually interpreting the PostScript code.

Format Overview

As noted, an Encapsulated PostScript file is an ordinary PostScript program that conforms to certain structuring conventions. Like an ordinary PostScript program, an EPS file can contain any combination of text, graphics, and bitmapped images. One restriction is that an EPS file describes a single page only.

EPS was designed primarily to allow for the transport of PostScript code between applications and as a means of encapsulating and subsequently reusing portions of a page description. An example is a graphic that depicts a company's logo. The logo graphic would be used in a variety of documents. If placed in a single EPS file, it could be imported as needed into such documents.

PostScript is a true programming language, with its own grammar and syntax, but the language definition specifies nothing about the overall structuring of PostScript programs. This issue was addressed by the implementation of a separate Document Structuring Convention, referred to as DSC, which provides guidelines on how PostScript programs should be structured. Note that these are guidelines, not requirements, so one speaks of a given program as being conforming or nonconforming.

Strictly speaking, an EPS file must conform to the DSC specification; most applications do not attempt to read a nonconforming file. Thus, the EPS format requires an understanding of DSC in addition to PostScript itself.

The Document Structuring Convention

DSC specifies a suggested structure for a PostScript program, but it cannot itself affect the language definition. In order to implement structural markers, DSC specifies a number of *reserved comment* definitions. As described in Chapter 6, a PostScript comment begins with a percent sign, and the PostScript interpreter ignores the remainder of any line when a percent sign is encountered. This is essentially the same as the double-slash (//) comment delimiter of C++.

DSC comments are required to begin with two percent signs, starting in column one of a line, and must be followed immediately by a reserved key word. Because these are only comments as far as the PostScript interpreter is concerned, they have no effect on the interpretation of a program. Here are some examples of DSC reserved comments:

```
%%Title: Gone with the Wind
%%Creator: Margaret Mitchell
%%BoundingBox: 0 0 100 100
```

DSC further specifies a set of comment key words and the information that is to be included with the key word. In the preceding comments, for example, `BoundingBox:` is a reserved key word and must be followed by four numbers that indicate the bounding box of the EPS file's graphics. This allows an application to display a properly sized box for positioning an EPS graphic on a page. The numbers, by the way, use coordinate units of typographic points and indicate the lower left and upper right corners of the graphic respectively. Also note that the terminating colon that follows some key words is considered to be part of the key word, indicating that one or more options or parameters follow the key word.

Because many DSC comments are structural markers, you can get a good idea of the structure of a PostScript program by looking at these comments and their order. In most cases, the interpretation of a comment is clear from the key word. Figure 18.1 lists these structural key words in their proper order and indicates how a DSC-conforming PostScript program is structured. Keep in mind that not every program contains all these key words.

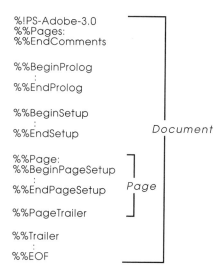

Figure 18.1 DSC Document Structure

EPS Program Structure

Having briefly covered the DSC convention, we can now look at the EPS format itself. EPS is a DSC-conforming PostScript program that requires, at a minimum, the following two DSC comments:

```
%!PS-Adobe-3.0 EPSF-3.0
%%BoundingBox: llx lly urx ury
```

If we were to take the PostScript output of our ImagePrinter class (see Chapter 7) and replace all comments at the top of the file with these two comments (with appropriate values for the `BoundingBox` comment), then we would have a bona fide EPS file conforming with version 3.0 of the format.

That's the good news. The bad news is that you cannot depend on applications that support EPS to be able to read the file. Few developers and companies can afford to license a full-blown PostScript interpreter, and fewer still are able to develop their own. Consequently, their EPS support is very narrow in scope, and will not properly read many valid examples of the format. In my view, this renders the EPS format almost useless from a practical standpoint. However, if your requirements are to export PostScript to a specific application, such as Adobe Illustrator, this objection may not be relevant.

Most applications that export EPS include more than the two minimally required comments. Here is a good model for a typical EPS file:

```
%!PS-Adobe-3.0 EPSF-3.0
%%Creator: An-Application-Name
%%Title: A-File-Name
%%BoundingBox: llx lly urx ury
%%EndComments
%%BeginProlog
    :
  (procedure and variable definitions)
    :
%%EndProlog
    :
  (program code)
    :
%%Trailer
```

EPS Thumbnails

As noted, the EPS format also allows for the inclusion of a small preview or thumbnail sketch of the full EPS graphic. There are actually three preview variants that are supported under MS-DOS: an included TIFF image, an included Windows Metafile, or a device-independent bitmap specification in the DSC comments. On the Macintosh, a PICT preview substitutes for the WMF and TIFF options, and if present, is placed in the resource fork of the EPS file.

The device-independent preview specification is the best choice, as it is not system dependent and is the easiest to implement. It is the only preview option that we will discuss here.

When present, the preview information occurs in a set of DSC comments that must immediately follow the `%%EndComments` statement. The structure of the preview is as follows:

```
%%BeginPreview: width height depth nlines
%
% (hex data)
%
%%EndPreview
```

The hex data in this structure is formatted the same as it would be for the PostScript `image` operator. `Width`, `height`, and `depth` indicate the size of the image. These, too, are the same as the corresponding arguments to the `image` operator. The `nlines` parameter indicates the number of following lines that contain hex data. Note that these lines begin with a percent sign and are thus comments.

Writing the EPS Format

As noted in the previous section, an EPS encoder is very much like a PostScript printer driver. An encoder can be developed from such a driver with only minimal effort. Listings 18.1 and 18.2 present the source code for structure and class definitions that implement an EPS writer. These bear many similarities to the PostScript driver that was presented in Chapter 6. Indeed, the only real differences are in the comments that are output.

Listing 18.3 shows the implementation of two `WriteEPS()` functions that utilize the classes from Listings 18.1 and 18.2. These create an EPS file conforming to Level 1 PostScript that contains a black and white dithered version of the image or screen display that is passed as a parameter. Listing 18.4 shows a sample program that creates an EPS file from the El Greco image. Note that the EPS file includes a `showpage` operator, so it can be printed on any PostScript printer simply by copying the file to the printer. Under MS-DOS, for example, you could print the EPS file as follows:

```
copy EPSDEMO.EPS LPT1:
```

This, of course, assumes that you have a PostScript printer attached to LPT1.

Level 2 of PostScript adds a `colorimage` operator, which allows printing of color bitmaps on PostScript color printers. This operator is similar in most respects to the monochrome `image` operator, except that it takes three procedure parameters instead of one. Each procedure is responsible for reading the data for one of the color primaries, so there is a red proc, a green proc, and a blue proc. The hex data read by these are structured as if they were three interlaced monochrome images, one for each primary.

Unfortunately, color PostScript printers are still very expensive and relatively rare. Unless you know that your output is intended for a color printer it is better to stick with Level 1 monochrome EPS files. For those interested, a color bitmap PostScript program looks like the following:

```
/redstr rowbytes def
/grnstr rowbytes def
/blustr rowbytes def
width height depth
[width 0 0 height neg 0 height]
{currentfile redstr readhexstring pop}
{currentfile grnstr readhexstring pop}
{currentfile blustr readhexstring pop}
true 3
colorimage
R0R1R2R3........RN
G0G1G2G3........GN
B0B1B2B3........BN
     :
etc.
```

Listing 18.1 EPS.HPP

```
//----------------------------------------------------------//
//                                                          //
//   File:      EPS.HPP                                     //
//                                                          //
//   Desc:      Class and structure definitions for the     //
//              Encapsulated PostScript format               //
//                                                          //
//----------------------------------------------------------//

#ifndef _EPS_HPP_
#define _EPS_HPP_

#include "stdlib.h"
#include "stdio.h"
#include "string.h"

#include "color.hpp"
#include "codec.hpp"
#include "dither.hpp"

//.................struct EPSPROLOG
```

Listing 18.1 EPS.HPP (continued)

```cpp
struct EPSPROLOG
{
   char *title;
   char *creator;
   int  llx;
   int  lly;
   int  urx;
   int  ury;

   EPSPROLOG( )
   {
      title = creator = 0;
      llx = lly = urx = ury = 0;
   }
   EPSPROLOG( char *t, char *c, int x1, int y1,
               int x2, int y2 )
   {
      title = t;
      creator = c;
      llx = x1;
      lly = y1;
      urx = x2;
      ury = y2;
   }
  ~EPSPROLOG( )
   {
   }
   int put( FILE *f );
};

//................struct EPSEPILOG

struct EPSEPILOG
{
   int x;    // dummy variable

   EPSEPILOG( )
   {
      x = 0;
   }
  ~EPSEPILOG( )
   {
   }
   int put( FILE *f );
};
```

Listing 18.1 EPS.HPP (continued)

```
//...............struct IMGPROLOG

struct IMGPROLOG
{
   int width;
   int height;
   int depth;
   int xorg;
   int yorg;

   IMGPROLOG( )
   {
      width = height = depth = 0;
      xorg = yorg = 0;
   }
   IMGPROLOG( int w, int h, int d, int xo, int yo )
   {
      width  = w;
      height = h;
      depth  = d;
      xorg   = xo;
      yorg   = yo;
   }
   ~IMGPROLOG( )
   {
   }
   int put( FILE *f );
};

//...............struct IMGEPILOG

struct IMGEPILOG
{
   int x;    // dummy variable

   IMGEPILOG( )
   {
      x = 0;
   }
   ~IMGEPILOG( )
   {
   }
   int put( FILE *f );
};
```

Listing 18.1 EPS.HPP (continued)

```
//.................class  EpsEncoder

class EpsEncoder : public Encoder
{
   protected:
      int             cond;          // condition code
      int             width;         // image width
      FILE            *eps_file;     // output file
      int             nout;          // bytes written
      rgb             *impal;        // image palette
      unsigned char   *scanln;       // scanline buffer
      DiffusionDither *dit;          // dither

   private:
      void writeln( void );

   public:
      EpsEncoder( FILE *f_out, int w, rgb *pal );
      virtual ~EpsEncoder( );
      virtual int encode( unsigned char *buf, int npxls );
      virtual int init( void );
      virtual int term( void );
      virtual int status( void );
};

#endif
```

Listing 18.2 EPS.CPP

```
//----------------------------------------------------------//
//                                                          //
//   File:     EPS.CPP                                      //
//                                                          //
//   Desc:     Class and structure definitions for the      //
//             Encapsulated PostScript format               //
//                                                          //
//----------------------------------------------------------//

#include "eps.hpp"

static char *p0 = "%!";
static char *p1 = "%";
static char *p2 = "%%";


//.................EPS Prolog/Epilog

int EPSPROLOG::put( FILE *f )
{
```

Listing 18.2 EPS.CPP (continued)

```cpp
    fprintf( f, "%sPS-Adobe-3.0 EPSF-3.0\n", p0 );
    if( title && *title )
        fprintf( f, "%sTitle: %s\n", p2, title );
    if( creator && *creator )
        fprintf( f, "%sCreator: %s\n", p2, creator );
    fprintf( f, "%sBoundingBox: %d %d %d %d\n",
             p2, llx, lly, urx, ury );
    fprintf( f, "%sEndComments\n", p2 );
    return ferror(f);
}

int EPSEPILOG::put( FILE *f )
{
    fprintf( f, "showpage\n" );
    fprintf( f, "%sTrailer\n", p2 );
    return ferror(f);
}


//.................Image Prolog/Epilog

int IMGPROLOG::put( FILE *f )
{
    fprintf( f, "%sBeginProlog\n", p2 );
    fprintf( f, "/width %d def\n", width );
    fprintf( f, "/height %d def\n", height );
    fprintf( f, "/depth %d def\n", depth );
    fprintf( f, "/xorg %d def\n", xorg );
    fprintf( f, "/yorg %d def\n", yorg );
    int rwbytes = (width + 7) / 8;
    fprintf( f, "/rwbytes %d def\n", rwbytes );
    fprintf( f, "/scanline rwbytes string def\n" );
    fprintf( f, "%sEndProlog\n", p2 );
    fprintf( f, "%s begin image.....\n", p1 );
    fprintf( f, "gsave\n" );
    fprintf( f, "xorg 756 yorg sub height sub translate\n" );
    fprintf( f, "width height scale\n" );
    fprintf( f, "width height depth\n" );
    fprintf( f, "[width 0 0 height neg 0 height]\n" );
    fprintf( f, "{currentfile scanline readhexstring pop}\n" );
    fprintf( f, "image\n" );
    return ferror(f);
}

int IMGEPILOG::put( FILE *f )
{
```

Listing 18.2 EPS.CPP (continued)

```cpp
      fprintf( f, "grestore\n" );
      fprintf( f, "%s .....end image\n", p1 );
      return ferror(f);
   }

   //.................class EpsEncoder

   EpsEncoder::EpsEncoder( FILE *f_out, int w, rgb *pal )
   {
      cond = xOKAY;
      eps_file = f_out;
      impal = pal;
      width = w;
      scanln = new unsigned char [width];
      if( scanln )
      {
         memset( scanln, 0, width );
         dit = new DiffusionDither( 127, width );
         if( ! dit )
             cond = xNOMEMORY;
      }
      else
         cond = xNOMEMORY;
   }

   EpsEncoder::~EpsEncoder( )
   {
      delete scanln;
      delete dit;
   }

   int EpsEncoder::init( void )
   {
      nout = 0;
      return status();
   }

   int EpsEncoder::term( void )
   {
      if( nout != 0 ) fprintf( eps_file, "\n" );
      return status();
   }

   int EpsEncoder::status( void )
   {
      if( cond == xOKAY )
         if( ferror( eps_file ) )
             cond = xIOERROR;
```

Listing 18.2 EPS.CPP (continued)

```cpp
        return cond;
    }

    void EpsEncoder::writeln( void )
    {
        int mask = 0x80;
        int byte = 0;

        for( int i=0; i<width; i++ )
        {
            if( scanln[i] )
                byte |= mask;
            if( (mask >>= 1) == 0 )
            {
                fprintf( eps_file, "%02X", byte );
                if( status() != xOKAY ) return;
                mask = 0x80;
                byte = 0;
                nout += 2;
                if( nout == 72 )
                {
                    fprintf( eps_file, "\n" );
                    nout = 0;
                }
            }
        }

        if( mask != 0x80 )
        {
            fprintf( eps_file, "%02X", byte );
            nout += 2;
            if( nout == 72 )
            {
                fprintf( eps_file, "\n" );
                nout = 0;
            }
        }
    }

    int EpsEncoder::encode( unsigned char *buf, int npxls )
    {
        if( status() == xOKAY )
        {
            // convert pixel indexes to gray levels
            for( int i=0; i<npxls; i++ )
            {
                int j = buf[i];
```

Listing 18.2 EPS.CPP (continued)

```
            scanln[i] = impal[j].graylevel();
        }

        // dither the gray values
        dit->dither( scanln, npxls );

        // output the PS source
        writeln();
    }
    return status();
}
```

Listing 18.3 WRTEPS.CPP

```
//-----------------------------------------------------------//
//                                                           //
//   File:     WRTEPS.CPP                                    //
//                                                           //
//   Desc:     Code to output an EPS file from               //
//             a VGA Display or a Memory Bitmap              //
//                                                           //
//-----------------------------------------------------------//

#include "eps.hpp"
#include "display.hpp"
#include "imgstore.hpp"

//.................Write VGA screen to EPS file 'fn'

int WriteEPS( VgaDisplay& vga, char *fn,
              int x1, int y1, int x2, int y2 )
{
    // image metrics
    int nrows   = y2 - y1 + 1;
    int ncols   = x2 - x1 + 1;
    int ncolors = vga.metric.ncolors;

    // scan line buffer
    unsigned char *scanln = new unsigned char [ncols];
    rgb *vgapal = new rgb [ncolors];
    if( (scanln == 0) || (vgapal == 0) )
    {
        delete scanln;
        delete [] vgapal;
        return xNOMEMORY;
    }
```

Listing 18.3 WRTEPS.CPP (continued)

```cpp
    // EPS output file
    FILE *f = fopen( fn, "wb" );
    // Prolog code
    EPSPROLOG epsP( fn, "WrtEps.Cpp", 0, 0, ncols, nrows );
    epsP.put( f );
    IMGPROLOG imgP( ncols, nrows, 1, 0, 0 );
    imgP.put( f );

    // write the image
    EpsEncoder enc( f, ncols, vgapal );
    enc.init();
    for( int i=0; i<nrows; i++ )
    {
        vga.getscanline( scanln, ncols, x1, y1+i );
        enc.encode( scanln, ncols );
    }
    enc.term();

    // Epilog code
    IMGEPILOG imgE;
    imgE.put( f );
    EPSEPILOG epsE;
    epsE.put( f );

    int retv = ferror( f );
    fclose( f );
    delete scanln;
    delete [] vgapal;
    return retv ? xIOERROR : xOKAY;
}
//.................Write an image to EPS file 'fn'

int WriteEPS( ImgStore& img, rgb *pal, char *fn )
{
    // image metrics - 24 bit not supported
    int ncols  = img.width();
    int nrows  = img.height();

    // scan line buffer
    unsigned char *scanln = new unsigned char [ncols];
    if( scanln == 0 )
    {
        delete scanln;
        return xNOMEMORY;
    }

    // EPS output file
    FILE *f = fopen( fn, "wb" );
```

Listing 18.3 WRTEPS.CPP (continued)

```
            // Prolog code
            EPSPROLOG epsP( fn, "WrtEps.Cpp", 0, 0, ncols, nrows );
            epsP.put( f );
            IMGPROLOG imgP( ncols, nrows, 1, 0, 0 );
            imgP.put( f );

            // write the image
            EpsEncoder enc( f, ncols, pal );
            enc.init();
            for( int i=0; i<nrows; i++ )
            {
               img.cpy( scanln, i );
               enc.encode( scanln, ncols );
               if( (i & 7) == 0 ) printf( "." );
            }
            enc.term();

            // Epilog code
            IMGEPILOG imgE;
            imgE.put( f );
            EPSEPILOG epsE;
            epsE.put( f );

            int retv = ferror( f );
            fclose( f );
            delete scanln;
            return retv ? xIOERROR : xOKAY;
         }
```

Listing 18.4 EPSDEMO.CPP

```
      //-----------------------------------------------------------//
      //                                                           //
      //    File:     EPSDEMO.CPP                                  //
      //                                                           //
      //    Desc:     Example code to write an EPS file           //
      //                                                           //
      //-----------------------------------------------------------//

      #include "wrteps.cpp"

      char *        palname     = "EL-GRECO.PAL";
      char *        imgname     = "EL-GRECO.IMG";
      int           imgwidth    = 354;
      int           imgheight   = 446;
      int           imgcolors   = 256;
      rgb           imgpalette[256];
```

Listing 18.4 EPSDEMO.CPP (continued)

```cpp
unsigned char scanline[354];
CnvImgStore img( 446, 354, 8 );

// read the test image's palette

void read_palette( void )
{
   FILE *f = fopen( palname, "rt" );
   for( int i=0; i<imgcolors; i++ )
   {
      int r, g, b;
      fscanf( f, "%d %d %d", &r, &g, &b );
      imgpalette[i] = rgb( r, g, b );
   }
   fclose( f );
}

// read the test image into memory

void read_image( void )
{
   FILE *f = fopen( imgname, "rb" );
   for( int i=0; i<imgheight; i++ )
   {
      fread( scanline, imgwidth, 1, f );
      img.put( scanline, i );
   }
   fclose( f );
}


// output a PCX file

int main( void )
{
   read_palette( );

   read_image( );

   WriteEPS( img, imgpalette, "EPSDEMO.EPS" );

   return 0;
}
```

This concludes our look at the Encapsulated PostScript format. As a format for bitmapped graphics it is not especially robust—it is much more useful for vector graphics. However, in many desktop-publishing situations it is the format of choice, and for this reason is a good format to keep in your bag of tricks.

19

The TARGA TGA Format

One of the earliest video subsystems for the PC that was capable of displaying true color imagery was the TARGA board from AT&T's Truevision product family. When it was first introduced, this sophisticated board effectively converted a lowly PC into a graphics-imaging workstation. The price of the board was also quite "sophisticated," so the boards have never become commonplace. Nowadays, much of the board's color capabilities can be found on off-the-shelf, low-cost SVGA adapters. Although the TARGA board's specialized niche is small, the TARGA format has become quite important and is likely to be around for some time to come.

The full range of image types and compression schemes that are handled by the TARGA format make it both extensive in scope and difficult to handle in its entirety. Images can contain pixel sizes of 8, 15, 16, 24, or 32 bits; they can be RGB-based, color-mapped, or gray-scaled; and they can be uncompressed, run-length encoded, or Huffman compressed. An additional complexity for a TARGA decoder is the fact that TARGA images can be stored either vertically or horizontally mirrored; that is, with the scan-line order reversed, the pixel-order within a line reversed, or both.

Despite the TARGA format's support for both RLE and Huffman compression, it is rare to encounter a compressed TARGA file. As noted in the chapter on compression, images with large numbers of simultaneous colors exhibit proportionally less redundancy than simpler images and are therefore difficult to compress by traditional means. Most such images exhibit negative compression with a typical RLE algorithm.

The TARGA format is unique in one respect: in its support for image *transparency* and *overlays*. An **overlay** is an image with transparent regions, and is intended to be placed on top of another image. Where the overlay is transparent the underimage shows through, and where the overlay is opaque it obscures the underimage.

Transparency is an option only with 16-bit and 32-bit images. A 16-bit image pixel is composed of a 15-bit RGB value and a 1-bit transparency flag; a 32-bit image pixel is composed of a 24-bit RGB value and an 8-bit transparency value. While a 1-bit flag indicates only two states, fully transparent or fully opaque, an 8-bit value provides a range of transparency, in effect allowing one image to be blended with another. In actual use, the 8-bit value is interpreted as a 1-bit flag and a 7-bit blending value.

The code in this chapter ignores the overlay capability of the format and treats images utilizing this feature as if they were fully opaque.

Format Overview

Despite its scope, the TARGA format itself is relatively straightforward. It consists of a file header, a palette if the image is color mapped, and the image itself. The header can be optionally extended by up to 255 bytes to include descriptive information.

One peculiarity of RGB-based TARGA images is that RGB triples are stored physically backward; that is, in the order blue-green-red. Depending on an image's color resolution and its transparency options, an RGB-based pixel occupies 2 to 4 bytes. Two-byte pixels contain a 15-bit RGB triple, and 3- and 4-byte pixels contain a 24-bit RGB triple. In all cases, a pixel can be read into a 32-bit-long integer, and the individual primary intensities can be extracted with a suitable mask and some bit shifts.

In contrast, color-mapped images always consist of 8-bit pixel values that index into the image's palette. This, of course, implies a maximum palette size of 256 colors. Also, note that 8-bit pixels are used regardless of the actual number of colors in the palette, including images with 2 to 16 colors.

The TARGA File Header

Listings 19.1 and 19.2 present the definition of the TARGA file header as the structure `TGAHEADER`. The structure's data members are as follow:

idlen
Unsigned byte value indicating the length of any additional descriptive information appended to the header. A value of zero indicates that there is no additional information. When a TARGA file is processed, the number of bytes specified here must be skipped to locate the start of a palette or image bitmap.

cmtype
Byte value that indicates the presence of a color map (palette); 0 indicates no palette is present, 1 indicates that a palette is present. Other values are undefined.

imtype	Byte value indicating the type of image data contained by the file. See the structure initialization list for `tgatypes` in Listing 19.2 for possible values. The code in this chapter handles only types 1, 2, 3, 9, 10, and 11.
cmorg	First palette index for the file's palette, if present. If an entire palette is present, this field has the value zero.
cmcnt	Number of entries in the file's palette, if present. If a complete 256-color palette is present, this field has the value 256.
cmsiz	Number of bits per palette entry. This value is somewhat device dependent. If each primary intensity is expressed in the range 0 to 255, this value is 8 * 3 = 24. Do not confuse this member with the `imdepth` member described later in this list.
imxorg	Horizontal pixel coordinate of the image's lower left corner. This field can be ignored in most cases, including the display of individual TARGA images.
imyorg	Vertical pixel coordinate of the image's lower left corner. This field can be ignored in most cases. See `imxorg`.
imwidth	Width of the image in pixels.
imheight	Height of the image in pixels.
imdepth	Number of bits per pixel. Possible values are 8, 15, 16, 24, or 32. The values 16 and 32 indicate an image with overlay information.
imdesc	Byte value containing several bit fields that indicate various image properties. These are as follows:

Bits	Meaning
0–3	The number of attribute bits (that is, overlay bits) associated with each pixel value. Possible values are 0, 1, and 8.
4	A bit that is set to indicate that the image is horizontally mirrored.
5	A bit that is set to indicate that the image is vertically mirrored. Because the TARGA format assumes a lower left origin, the image must be reversed for the code in this book if the bit is clear.
6-7	A data-storage interleaving flag. This field should always be zero. However, a value of 01, for example, indicates a two-way interleave such as that employed by the CGA adapter.

Note that if the `idlen` member is nonzero, then that number of bytes immediately follows the header structure just described. This is intended for descriptive information such as an image title or a vendor's copyright notice.

TARGA File Palettes

If the `cmtype` member of the TARGA header is set to 1, the file contains a color map (palette) that immediately follows the header and any descriptive text appended to the header. This palette consists of an array of RGB triples, each entry occupying an integral number of bytes. The `cmsiz` header member indicates the number of bits per entry, which is used to compute the number of bytes per entry as follows:

```
nbytes = (hdr.cmsiz + 7) / 8;
```

The simplest method of reading and extracting individual primary values is to read the number of bytes per entry into a long integer, as follows:

```
long cmval;
    :
fread( &cmval, nbytes, 1, infile );
```

Then each primary value can be extracted from the long integer as follows:

```
int nbits = (nbytes == 2) ? 5 : 8;
int mask = (1 << nbits) - 1;
    :
int blue = cmval & mask;
cmval >>= nbits;
int green = cmval & mask;
cmval >>= nbits;
int red = cmval & mask;
```

Two things are worth noting here. First, the RGB components are extracted in reverse order; that is, blue, followed by green, followed by red. Also, the procedure described here depends on the byte ordering employed on Intel processors. This scheme will not work on some processors, notably the Motorola 68000 series.

TARGA File Bitmaps

Most TARGA files possess image types of 1, 2, or 3, meaning that the file's bitmap is uncompressed. In this case the procedure for reading a bitmap is to determine the pixel size in bytes, multiply it by the image width, and read that number of bytes for each scan line. The pixel size is computed in the same manner as an entry in the color map, but note that there is one additional possible size, 8 bits.

If the image is color mapped, then the pixel size is 8 bits, and a pixel is treated as a conventional palette index. In all other cases a pixel is an actual RGB color definition, and the individual primary intensities must be extracted, and possibly normalized. For the image-handling code in this book, each RGB intensity is scaled to the range 0 to 255 and is placed in consecutive bytes of a scan-line array. The scan line contains `imwidth` * 3 bytes in this instance.

Image types 9, 10, and 11 indicate a run-length encoded bitmap, and the algorithm employed encodes pixels, not bytes. Each scan line in an encoded bitmap consists of one or more packets, each packet consisting of a header byte followed by some number of pixel values.

If the high-order bit of a header byte is clear, then the low-order 7 bits are a count value in the range 0 to 127. The count is incremented by 1 to yield a value in the range 1 to 128, and that number of unencoded pixel values is read from the bitmap.

If the high-order bit of a header byte is set, then the low-order 7 bits are also a count, but this count indicates the number of times to repeat the next pixel value read from the bitmap. As with nonrepeating packets, the count is incremented by 1 before use. If each header byte is read as an integer value, the decoding logic looks something like the following:

```
int hdr, cnt;
    :
hdr = fgetc( input_file );
if( hdr > 127 ) // high bit set
{
    cnt = hdr - 127;
    // read a pixel, repeat cnt times
}
else // high bit clear
{
    cnt = hdr + 1;
    // read cnt pixels
}
```

In the statement `cnt=hdr-127`, note that we are combining two operations: subtracting 128 to clear the high bit and incrementing by 1 before use. Because we are decoding pixels, the number of bytes read for each packet is the number of pixels read times the size of a pixel in bytes.

Listing 19.1 TGA.HPP

```
//--------------------------------------------------------//
//                                                        //
//   File:     TGA.HPP                                    //
//                                                        //
//   Desc:     Class and structure definitions for the    //
//             TARGA Format                               //
//                                                        //
//--------------------------------------------------------//

#ifndef _TGA_HPP_
#define _TGA_HPP_

#include "stdlib.h"
#include "stdio.h"
#include "string.h"

#include "color.hpp"
#include "codec.hpp"

struct TGAHEADER
{
    unsigned char   idlen;       // ID field length
    unsigned char   cmtype;      // color map type
    unsigned char   imtype;      // image type
    unsigned short  cmorg;       // index of first cm entry
    unsigned short  cmcnt;       // number of cm entries
    unsigned char   cmsiz;       // bits per cm entry
    unsigned short  imxorg;      // image x origin
    unsigned short  imyorg;      // image y origin
    unsigned short  imwidth;     // image width in pixels
    unsigned short  imheight;    // image height in pixels
    unsigned char   imdepth;     // bits per pixel
    unsigned char   imdesc;      // image descriptor

    TGAHEADER( );
    TGAHEADER( int w, int h, int d );
   ~TGAHEADER( ) { }
    void list( void );
    int  get( FILE * f );
    int  put( FILE * f );
    rgb *pal( FILE *f );
    int  isvertmirror( void )
    {
        return (imdesc & 0x20) ? 0 : 1;
    }
    int  ishorzmirror( void )
```

Listing 19.1 TGA.HPP (continued)

```cpp
    {
        return (imdesc & 0x10) ? 1 : 0;
    }
};

//.............class TgaDecoder

class TgaDecoder : public Decoder
{
    protected:
        FILE *tga_file;         // input file
        int   cond;             // condition code
        int   width;            // image width in pixels
        int   height;           // image height in pixels
        int   pxbits;           // bits per pixel - 8,16,24,32
        int   pxbytes;          // bytes per pixel - 1,2,3,4
        int   mapped;           // color mapped flag
        int   encoded;          // rle flag
        int   mirrored;         // horz mirror flag

    private:
        void readmapped( unsigned char *buf, int npxls );
        void readrlemapped( unsigned char *buf, int npxls );
        void readrgb( unsigned char *buf, int npxls );
        void readrlergb( unsigned char *buf, int npxls );
        void reverse1( unsigned char *buf, int npxls );
        void reverse3( unsigned char *buf, int npxls );

    public:
        TgaDecoder( FILE *f_in, TGAHEADER& hdr );
        virtual ~TgaDecoder( );
        virtual int decode( unsigned char *buf, int npxls );
        virtual int init( void );
        virtual int term( void );
        virtual int status( void );
};

//.............class TgaEncoder

class TgaEncoder : public Encoder
{
    protected:
        int   cond;             // condition code
        int   pxl_bytes;        // bytes per pixel - 1 or 3
        FILE *tga_file;         // output file

    private:
        unsigned char *scanln;
```

Listing 19.1 TGA.HPP (continued)

```cpp
    public:
        TgaEncoder( FILE *f_out, TGAHEADER& tga );
        virtual ~TgaEncoder( ) { delete scanln; }
        virtual int encode( unsigned char *buf, int npxls );
        virtual int init( void );
        virtual int term( void );
        virtual int status( void );
    };


    #endif
```

Listing 19.2 TGA.CPP

```cpp
    //----------------------------------------------------------//
    //                                                          //
    //    File:     TGA.CPP                                     //
    //                                                          //
    //    Desc:     Class and structure definitions for the     //
    //              TARGA Format                                //
    //                                                          //
    //----------------------------------------------------------//


    #include "tga.hpp"


    //.............struct TGATYPES


    struct TGATYPES
    {
        int    id;
        char *desc;
    }
    tgatypes[] =
    {
        {   0, "No Image Data" },
        {   1, "Uncompressed, Color Mapped" },
        {   2, "Uncompressed, RGB" },
        {   3, "Uncompressed, Gray Scale" },
        {   9, "Run-Length Encoded, Color Mapped" },
        {  10, "Run-Length Encoded, RGB" },
        {  11, "Run-Length Encoded, Gray Scale" },
        {  32, "Huffman Encoded, Color Mapped" },
        {  33, "Huffman Encoded, 4-Pass, Color Mapped" },
        { 999, "Unknown or Invalid" }
    };
    static ntypes = 10;
```

Listing 19.2 TGA.CPP (continued)

```cpp
//.............struct TGAHEADER

TGAHEADER::TGAHEADER( )
{
    idlen = cmtype = imtype = 0;
    cmorg = cmcnt = cmsiz = 0;
    imxorg = imyorg = 0;
    imwidth = imheight = 0;
    imdepth = imdesc = 0;
}

TGAHEADER::TGAHEADER( int w, int h, int d )
{
    idlen = 0;
    cmtype = (d == 8) ? 1 : 0;
    imtype = (d == 8) ? 1 : 2;
    cmorg = cmcnt = cmsiz = 0;
    imxorg = imyorg = 0;
    imwidth = w;
    imheight = h;
    imdepth = d;
    imdesc = 0x20;
}

void TGAHEADER::list( void )
{
    printf( "TGAHEADER::idlen    = %d\n", idlen );
    printf( "TGAHEADER::cmtype   = %d\n", cmtype );
    printf( "TGAHEADER::imtype   = %d - ", imtype );
    for( int i=0; i<ntypes; i++ )
    {
        if( (imtype == tgatypes[i].id) ||
            (tgatypes[i].id == 999) )
        {
            printf( "%s\n", tgatypes[i].desc );
            break;
        }
    }
    printf( "TGAHEADER::cmorg    = %d\n", cmorg );
    printf( "TGAHEADER::cmcnt    = %d\n", cmcnt );
    printf( "TGAHEADER::cmsiz    = %d\n", cmsiz );
    printf( "TGAHEADER::imxorg   = %d\n", imxorg );
    printf( "TGAHEADER::imyorg   = %d\n", imyorg );
    printf( "TGAHEADER::imwidth  = %d\n", imwidth );
    printf( "TGAHEADER::imheight = %d\n", imheight );
    printf( "TGAHEADER::imdepth  = %d\n", imdepth );
    printf( "TGAHEADER::imdesc   = %02Xh\n", imdesc );
}
```

Listing 19.2 TGA.CPP (continued)

```cpp
int TGAHEADER::get( FILE *f )
{
   return( fread( &idlen, sizeof(TGAHEADER), 1, f ) == 1 ?
           0 : -1 );
}

int TGAHEADER::put( FILE *f )
{
   return( fwrite( &idlen, sizeof(TGAHEADER), 1, f ) == 1 ?
           0 : -1 );
}

rgb * TGAHEADER::pal( FILE *f )
{
   if( cmcnt == 0 ) return 0;
   rgb *pal = new rgb [cmcnt];
   if( pal )
   {
      long v;
      int  nbytes, nbits, mask;

      if( cmsiz == 32 )
      {
         nbytes = 4;
         nbits = 8;
      }
      else if( cmsiz == 24 )
      {
         nbytes = 3;
         nbits = 8;
      }
      else
      {
         nbytes = 2;
         nbits = 5;
      }
      mask = (1 << nbits) - 1;

      for( int i=0; i<cmcnt; i++ )
      {
         fread( &v, nbytes, 1, f );
         pal[i].blu = v & mask;
         v >>= nbits;
         pal[i].grn = v & mask;
```

Listing 19.2 TGA.CPP (continued)

```cpp
            v >>= nbits;
            pal[i].red = v & mask;
        }
    }
    return pal;
}

//............class TgaDecoder

TgaDecoder::TgaDecoder( FILE *f_in, TGAHEADER& hdr )
{
    tga_file = f_in;
    width    = hdr.imwidth;
    height   = hdr.imheight;
    pxbits   = hdr.imdepth;
    pxbytes  = (hdr.imdepth + 7) / 8;
    mapped   = hdr.cmtype;
    cond     = xOKAY;
    encoded  = 0;
    mirrored = hdr.ishorzmirror();
    if( (hdr.imtype==9)  ||
        (hdr.imtype==10) ||
        (hdr.imtype==11) )
      encoded = 1;
    else if( (hdr.imtype!=1) &&
             (hdr.imtype!=2) &&
             (hdr.imtype!=3) )
      cond = xUNSUPPORTED;
}

TgaDecoder::~TgaDecoder( )
{
}

int TgaDecoder::status( void )
{
    if( ferror( tga_file ) ) cond = xIOERROR;
    if( feof( tga_file ) )    cond = xENDOFFILE;
    return cond;
}

int TgaDecoder::init( void )
{
    return status();
}
```

Listing 19.2 TGA.CPP (continued)

```cpp
int TgaDecoder::term( void )
{
   return status();
}

void TgaDecoder::reverse1( unsigned char *buf, int npxls )
{
   int i1 = 0;
   int i2 = npxls-1;
   while( i1 < i2 )
   {
      int i = buf[i1];  buf[i1] = buf[i2];  buf[i2] = i;
      i1++;
      i2--;
   }
}

void TgaDecoder::reverse3( unsigned char *buf, int npxls )
{
   int i1 = 0;
   int i2 = npxls-3;
   while( i1 < i2 )
   {
      int i = buf[i1];    buf[i1] = buf[i2];    buf[i2] = i;
      i = buf[i1+1];  buf[i1+1] = buf[i2+1];  buf[i2+1] = i;
      i = buf[i1+2];  buf[i1+2] = buf[i2+2];  buf[i2+2] = i;
      i1 += 3;
      i2 -= 3;
   }
}

void TgaDecoder::readmapped( unsigned char *buf, int npxls )
{
   fread( buf, npxls, 1, tga_file );
   if( mirrored )
      reverse1( buf, npxls );
}

void TgaDecoder::readrlemapped( unsigned char *buf, int npxls )
{
   int n = 0;
   int cnt;
   while( n < npxls )
   {
      if( (cnt = fgetc( tga_file )) < 0 )
         break;
      if( cnt > 127 )
```

Listing 19.2 TGA.CPP (continued)

```
            {
                cnt -= 126;
                int pxv = fgetc( tga_file );
                while( cnt- > 0 )
                    buf[n++] = pxv;
            }
            else
            {
                cnt++;
                fread( buf+n, cnt, 1, tga_file );
                n += cnt;
            }
        }
        if( mirrored )
            reverse1( buf, npxls );
    }

    void TgaDecoder::readrgb( unsigned char *buf, int npxls )
    {
        int nbits = (pxbytes == 2) ? 5 : 8;
        int nshft = (pxbytes == 2) ? 3 : 0;
        int mask = (1 << nbits) - 1;
        int n = 0;
        for( int i=0; i<npxls; i++ )
        {
            long pxv;
            if( fread( &pxv, pxbytes, 1, tga_file ) != 1 )
                break;
            buf[n+2] = (pxv & mask) << nshft;
            pxv >>= nbits;
            buf[n+1] = (pxv & mask) << nshft;
            pxv >>= nbits;
            buf[n] = (pxv & mask) << nshft;
            n += 3;
        }
        if( mirrored )
            reverse3( buf, npxls );
    }

    void TgaDecoder::readrlergb( unsigned char *buf, int npxls )
    {
        int nbits = (pxbytes == 2) ? 5 : 8;
        int nshft = (pxbytes == 2) ? 3 : 0;
        int mask = (1 << nbits) - 1;
        int n = 0;
        int cnt;
        long pxv;
        while( n < npxls * 3 )
```

Listing 19.2 TGA.CPP (continued)

```
    {
       if( (cnt = fgetc( tga_file )) < 0 )
          break;
       if( cnt > 127 )
       {
          cnt -= 127;
          fread( &pxv, pxbytes, 1, tga_file );
          int b = (int) ((pxv & mask) << nshft);
          pxv >>= nbits;
          int g = (int) ((pxv & mask) << nshft);
          pxv >>= nbits;
          int r = (int) ((pxv & mask) << nshft);
          while( cnt-- > 0 )
          {
             buf[n++] = r;
             buf[n++] = g;
             buf[n++] = b;
          }
       }
       else
       {
          while( cnt-- > 0 )
          {
             fread( &pxv, pxbytes, 1, tga_file );
             int b = (int) ((pxv & mask) << nshft);
             pxv >>= nbits;
             int g = (int) ((pxv & mask) << nshft);
             pxv >>= nbits;
             int r = (int) ((pxv & mask) << nshft);
             buf[n++] = r;
             buf[n++] = g;
             buf[n++] = b;
          }
       }
    }
    if( mirrored )
       reverse3( buf, npxls );
}

int TgaDecoder::decode( unsigned char *buf, int npxls )
{
    if( status() == xOKAY )
    {
       if( mapped )  // pixels are indexes
       {
          if( encoded )
             readrlemapped( buf, npxls );
          else
```

Listing 19.2 TGA.CPP (continued)

```cpp
                    readmapped( buf, npxls );
            }
            else            // pixels are colors
            {
               if( encoded )
                  readrlergb( buf, npxls );
               else
                  readrgb( buf, npxls );
            }
        }
        return status();
    }

    //............class TgaEncoder

    TgaEncoder::TgaEncoder( FILE *f_out, TGAHEADER& hdr )
    {
        tga_file = f_out;
        cond = xOKAY;
        pxl_bytes = (hdr.cmtype == 0) ? 3 : 1;
        scanln = 0;
        if( pxl_bytes == 3 )
        {
            int n = pxl_bytes * hdr.imwidth;
            scanln = new unsigned char [n];
            cond = (scanln == 0) ? xNOMEMORY : xOKAY;
        }
    }

    int TgaEncoder::status( void )
    {
        if( ferror( tga_file ) ) cond = xIOERROR;
        return cond;
    }

    int TgaEncoder::init( void )
    {
        return status();
    }

    int TgaEncoder::term( void )
    {
        return status();
    }
```

Listing 19.2 TGA.CPP (continued)

```
int TgaEncoder::encode( unsigned char *buf, int npxls )
{
   if( pxl_bytes == 1 )
      fwrite( buf, npxls, 1, tga_file );
   else
   {
      int n = 0;
      for( int i=0; i<npxls; i++ )
      {
         scanln[n] = buf[n+2];
         scanln[n+1] = buf[n+1];
         scanln[n+2] = buf[n];
         n += 3;
      }
      fwrite( scanln, n, 1, tga_file );
   }
   return status();
}
```

A TARGA File Query Program

Listing 19.3 presents the source code to QTGA.CPP, a query program for the
TARGA format. This program is useful for checking the image-type member of a
file's header. Remember, our TARGA decoder handles only uncompressed and
RLE-encoded files.

Listing 19.3 QTGA.CPP

```
//-----------------------------------------------------//
//                                                     //
//   File:     QTGA.CPP                                //
//                                                     //
//   Desc:     TARGA File Query Program                //
//                                                     //
//-----------------------------------------------------//

#include "stdlib.h"
#include "stdio.h"
#include "string.h"

#include "tga.hpp"

//.................program usage
```

Listing 19.3 QTGA.CPP (continued)

```cpp
void explain_pgm( void )
{
   printf( "\n" );
   printf( "TARGA Graphics File Query Program\n" );
   printf( "\n" );
   printf( "Usage:  QTGA  tga_file  [ -p ]\n" );
   printf( "\n" );
   printf( "-p includes palette in listing\n" );
   printf( ".TGA extension is assumed\n" );
   printf( "\n" );
}

//................main

int main( int argc, char *argv[] )
{
   // check args
   if( (argc < 2) || (*argv[1] == '?') )
   {
      explain_pgm();
      return 0;
   }

   // create file name
   char fn[80];
   strcpy( fn, argv[1] );
   char *p = strchr( fn, '.' );
   if( p == 0 )
      strcat( fn, ".tga" );
   else if( *(p+1) == 0 )
      *p = 0;

   // list palette ?
   int lpal = 0;
   if( argc > 2 )
      if( (strcmp( argv[2], "-p" ) == 0) ||
          (strcmp( argv[2], "-P" ) == 0) )
         lpal = 1;

   // open the file
   FILE *ftga = fopen( fn, "rb" );
   if( ftga == 0 )
   {
      printf( "File '%s' not found\n", fn );
      return 0;
   }
```

Listing 19.3 QTGA.CPP (continued)

```
    TGAHEADER tgah;
    tgah.get( ftga );

    printf( "Listing of TGA file '%s'\n", fn );
    printf( "\n" );
    tgah.list();
    printf( "\n" );

    // is there an ID string?
    if( tgah.idlen > 0 )
    {
        while( tgah.idlen-- > 0 )
            printf( "%c", fgetc(ftga) );
        printf( "\n" );
        printf( "\n" );
    }

    // list palette ?
    if( lpal )
    {
        if( tgah.cmtype == 0 )
        {
            printf( "TGA file is not color mapped\n" );
        }
        else
        {
        }
    }

    return 0;
}
```

A TARGA File Viewer

Listing 19.4 presents VTGA.CPP, a TARGA file viewer. Most TARGA files possess 15-bit or 24-bit color. This viewer employs color dithering to display such images in standard 16-color and 256-color VGA modes. The result of this, of course, is slow display times. One method for speeding up the display time, at some sacrifice of image fidelity, is to reduce the size of the device palette used in the error-diffusion-rendering process. This is the palette returned by the function `ColorDiffusionPalette()`, which can be found in DITHER.CPP (Listing 2.2). As coded there, the palette contains 16 entries. It can be reduced in size to 8, but any size smaller than that is not recommended.

Listing 19.4 VTGA.CPP

```
//----------------------------------------------------------//
//                                                          //
//    File:      VTGA.CPP                                   //
//                                                          //
//    Desc:      Program to view or print a TGA file        //
//                                                          //
//----------------------------------------------------------//

#include "stdlib.h"
#include "stdio.h"
#include "string.h"
#include "conio.h"
#include "ctype.h"

#include "tga.hpp"
#include "imgviewr.hpp"
#include "imgprntr.hpp"
#include "laserjet.hpp"
#include "paintjet.hpp"
#include "epjx80.hpp"
#include "eplq24.hpp"
#include "pscript.hpp"

//.................Printer types

#define  LJ   0x4C4A
#define  PJ   0x504A
#define  JX   0x4A58
#define  LQ   0x4C51
#define  PS   0x5053

//.................Program globals

char      fn[80];        // path to TGA file

int       gmode;         // video display mode
int       pmode;         // printer ID
int       ropt;          // rendering flags
int       iopt;          // itensity mapping flags

ImgStore   *imgmap;       // image bitmap
rgb        *imgpal;       // image palette
int         ncolors;      // palette size

//.................Exit with a message
```

Listing 19.4 VTGA.CPP (continued)

```
void exit_pgm( char *msg )
{
    printf( "%s\n", msg );
    exit( 0 );
}

//.................Program usage

void explain_pgm( void )
{
    printf( "\n" );
    printf( "..........TARGA TGA File Viewer/Printer..........\n"
);
    printf( "\n" );
    printf( "Usage:      VTGA  tga_file  [ switches ]\n" );
    printf( "\n" );
    printf( "Switches: -h      = display program usage\n" );
    printf( "          -vXX    = force video display mode XX\n" );
    printf( "                    (XX = 12, 13, 2E, 62)\n" );
    printf( "          -pXX    = print using printer XX\n" );
    printf( "                    (XX = LJ, PJ, JX, LQ, PS)\n" );
    printf( "          -b[+|-] = increase or decrease
brightness\n" );
    printf( "          -c[+|-] = increase or decrease contrast\n"
);
    printf( "          -d      = force dithered rendering\n" );
    printf( "          -g      = force gray scale rendering\n" );
    printf( "          -m      = force palette mapping\n" );
    printf( "\n" );
    printf( "...............................................\n"
);
    printf( "\n" );
}

//.................Process pgm argument list

void process_args( int argc, char *argv[] )
{
    // establish default values
    fn[0] = 0;
    gmode = 0x12;
    pmode = 0;
    ropt  = 0;
    iopt  = 0;
```

Listing 19.4 VTGA.CPP (continued)

```
// process the program's argument list
for( int i=1; i<argc; i++ )
{
   if( (*argv[i] == '-') || (*argv[i] == '/') )
   {
      char sw = *(argv[i] + 1);
      switch( toupper(sw) )
      {
         case 'H' :
            explain_pgm();
            exit( 0 );
            break;

         case 'V' :
            sscanf( argv[i]+2, "%x", &gmode );
            break;

         case 'P' :
            pmode = toupper( *(argv[i]+2) );
            pmode <<= 8;
            pmode += toupper( *(argv[i]+3) );
            break;

         case 'B' :
            if( *(argv[i]+2) == '-' )
               iopt |= intensDBRI;
            else
               iopt |= intensIBRI;
            break;

         case 'C' :
            if( *(argv[i]+2) == '-' )
               iopt |= intensDCNT;
            else
               iopt |= intensICNT;
            break;

         case 'D' :
            ropt |= renderDITHER;
            break;

         case 'G' :
            ropt |= renderGRAY;
            break;

         case 'M' :
            ropt |= renderMAP;
            break;
```

Listing 19.4 VTGA.CPP (continued)

```
                default:
                    printf( "Unknown switch '%s' ignored\n",
                            argv[i] );
                    break;
            }
        }
        else  // presumably a file identifier
        {
            strcpy( fn, argv[i] );
            char *p = strchr( fn, '.' );
            if( p == 0 )
                strcat( fn, ".tga" );
            else if( *(p+1) == 0 )
                *p = 0;
        }
    }

    // was a file name specified?
    if( fn[0] == 0 )
    {
        explain_pgm();
        exit( 0 );
    }
}


//.................Create an image storage buffer

ImgStore * istore( int h, int w, int d )
{
    ImgStore *ist = 0;

    // attempt to create in order of preference
    ist = new XmsImgStore( h, w, d );
    if( (ist != 0) && (ist->status != imgstoreOKAY) )
    {
        delete ist;
        ist = new EmsImgStore( h, w, d );
        if( (ist != 0) && (ist->status != imgstoreOKAY) )
        {
            delete ist;
            ist = new CnvImgStore( h, w, d );
            if( (ist != 0) && (ist->status != imgstoreOKAY) )
            {
                delete ist;
                ist = new DskImgStore( h, w, d );
                if( (ist != 0) && (ist->status != imgstoreOKAY) )
                {
                    delete ist;
```

Listing 19.4 VTGA.CPP (continued)

```cpp
                    ist = 0;
                }
            }
        }
    }

    return ist;
}

//.................Create a printer

PrinterDriver * printer( int which )
{
    PrinterDriver *p;

    switch( which )
    {
        case LJ : p = new LaserJet( "LPT1" );
                  break;
        case PJ : p = new PaintJet( "LPT1" );
                  break;
        case JX : p = new EpsonJX80( "LPT1" );
                  break;
        case LQ : p = new EpsonLQ24( "LPT1" );
                  break;
        default : p = new PsPrinter( "LPT1" );
                  break;
    }

    return p;
}

//.................Load the TGA file

void load_tga( void )
{
    // open file
    FILE *ftga = fopen( fn, "rb" );
    if( ftga == 0 )
        exit_pgm( "TGA file not found" );

    // read header
    TGAHEADER tga;
    if( tga.get( ftga ) != 0 )
        exit_pgm( "Error reading TGA header" );
```

Listing 19.4 VTGA.CPP (continued)

```cpp
        // skip id string if present
        while( tga.idlen-- > 0 )
            fgetc( ftga );

        // obtain palette if present
        imgpal = tga.pal( ftga );
        ncolors = tga.cmorg + tga.cmcnt;

        // create bitmap
        int pxbytes = (tga.imdepth <= 8) ? 1 : 3;
        int rwbytes = pxbytes * tga.imwidth;
        int ncols   = tga.imwidth;
        int nrows   = tga.imheight;
        unsigned char *scanln = new unsigned char [rwbytes];
        imgmap = istore( nrows, ncols, pxbytes*8 );
        if( (imgmap == 0) || (scanln == 0) )
        {
            delete imgmap;
            delete scanln;
            exit_pgm( "Insufficient memory to load image" );
        }

        // load bitmap
        printf( "Loading TGA image from '%s'...", fn );
        TgaDecoder tgad( ftga, tga );
        tgad.init();
        memset( scanln, 0, rwbytes );
        for( int i=0; i<nrows; i++ )
        {
            if( tgad.decode( scanln, ncols ) != xOKAY )
                break;
            int row = tga.isvertmirror() ? nrows-1-i : i;
            imgmap->put( scanln, row );
        }
        tgad.term();
        printf( "done\n" );

        delete scanln;
}

//.................Main

int main( int argc, char *argv[] )
{
    process_args( argc, argv );

    load_tga( );
```

Listing 19.4 VTGA.CPP (continued)

```
// print the image
if( pmode != 0 )
{
   PrinterDriver *prt = printer( pmode );
   if( prt )
   {
      printf( "Printing..." );
      ImagePrinter ip( prt, imgmap, imgpal, ncolors,
                       ropt, iopt, 100, 100 );
      ip.print( 1 );
      printf( "done\n" );
      delete prt;
   }
   else
      printf( "Printer instantiation failed\n" );
}

// display the image
else
{
   VgaDisplay vga( gmode );
   ImageViewer iv( &vga, imgmap, imgpal, ncolors,
                   ropt, iopt );
   iv.view( );
}

delete imgpal;
delete imgmap;

return 0;
}
```

Writing the TARGA Format

Writing the TARGA format is a straightforward proposition as long as the encoder ignores image compression. This is the approach taken with the `TgaEncoder` class in Listings 19.1 and 19.2 and may be considered common practice for this format.

Listing 19.5 presents two versions of a `WriteTGA()` function, which is equivalent to the write functions of the other formats presented in this book. Listing 19.6 show a brief demo program for creating a sample TARGA file using the El Greco test image. Note that in this case the sample TARGA file is color mapped.

Listing 19.5 WRTTGA.CPP

```cpp
//--------------------------------------------------------//
//                                                        //
//   File:     WRTTGA.CPP                                 //
//                                                        //
//   Desc:     Code to output a TGA file from             //
//             a VGA Display or a Memory Bitmap           //
//                                                        //
//--------------------------------------------------------//

#include "tga.hpp"
#include "display.hpp"
#include "imgstore.hpp"

//.................Write VGA screen to TGA file 'fn'

int WriteTGA( VgaDisplay& vga, char *fn,
              int x1, int y1, int x2, int y2 )
{
   // image metrics
   int nrows   = y2 - y1 + 1;
   int ncols   = x2 - x1 + 1;
   int nbits   = 8;
   int ncolors = vga.metric.ncolors;

   // scan line buffer
   unsigned char *scanln = new unsigned char [ncols];
   rgb *vgapal = new rgb [ncolors];
   if( (scanln == 0) || (vgapal == 0) )
   {
      delete scanln;
      delete [] vgapal;
      return xNOMEMORY;
   }

   // TARGA output file
   FILE *f = fopen( fn, "wb" );

   // initialize and write the TGA header
   TGAHEADER tga( ncols, nrows, nbits );
   tga.cmcnt = vga.metric.ncolors;
   tga.cmsiz = 24;
   tga.put( f );

   // write the color map
   vga.getpalette( vgapal, ncolors );
   for( int i=0; i<ncolors; i++ )
   {
      fputc( vgapal[i].blu, f );
```

Listing 19.5 WRTTGA.CPP (continued)

```cpp
        fputc( vgapal[i].grn, f );
        fputc( vgapal[i].red, f );
    }

    // write the image
    TgaEncoder enc( f, tga );
    enc.init();
    for( i=0; i<nrows; i++ )
    {
        vga.getscanline( scanln, ncols, x1, y1+i );
        enc.encode( scanln, ncols );
    }
    enc.term();

    int retv = ferror( f );
    fclose( f );
    delete scanln;
    delete [] vgapal;
    return retv ? xIOERROR : xOKAY;
}

//.................Write an image to TGA file 'fn'

int WriteTGA( ImgStore& img, rgb *pal, char *fn )
{
    // image metrics
    int nrows   = img.height();
    int ncols   = img.width();
    int nbits   = (img.depth() == 24) ? 24 : 8;
    int ncolors = (img.depth() <= 8) ? (1 << img.depth()) : 0;

    // TARGA output file
    FILE *f = fopen( fn, "wb" );

    // initialize and write the TGA header
    TGAHEADER tga( ncols, nrows, nbits );
    tga.cmcnt =  ncolors;
    tga.cmsiz = (ncolors > 0) ? 24 : 0;
    tga.put( f );

    // write the color map
    for( int i=0; i<ncolors; i++ )
    {
        fputc( pal[i].blu, f );
        fputc( pal[i].grn, f );
        fputc( pal[i].red, f );
    }
```

Listing 19.5 WRTTGA.CPP (continued)

```cpp
      // write the image
      TgaEncoder enc( f, tga );
      enc.init();
      for( i=0; i<nrows; i++ )
      {
         enc.encode( img.get(i), ncols );
         printf( "." );
      }
      enc.term();

      int retv = ferror( f );
      fclose( f );
      return retv ? xIOERROR : xOKAY;
   }
```

Listing 19.6 TGADEMO.CPP

```cpp
//-------------------------------------------------------------//
//                                                             //
//   File:      TGADEMO.CPP                                    //
//                                                             //
//   Desc:      Example code to write a TGA file              //
//                                                             //
//-------------------------------------------------------------//

#include "wrttga.cpp"

char *        palname     = "EL-GRECO.PAL";
char *        imgname     = "EL-GRECO.IMG";
int           imgwidth    = 354;
int           imgheight   = 446;
int           imgcolors   = 256;
rgb           imgpalette[256];
unsigned char scanline[354];
CnvImgStore img( 446, 354, 8 );

// read the test image's palette

void read_palette( void )
{
   FILE *f = fopen( palname, "rt" );
   for( int i=0; i<imgcolors; i++ )
   {
      int r, g, b;
      fscanf( f, "%d %d %d", &r, &g, &b );
      imgpalette[i] = rgb( r, g, b );
```

Listing 19.6 TGADEMO.CPP (continued)

```cpp
      }
      fclose( f );
   }

// read the test image into memory

void read_image( void )
{
   FILE *f = fopen( imgname, "rb" );
   for( int i=0; i<imgheight; i++ )
   {
      fread( scanline, imgwidth, 1, f );
      img.put( scanline, i );
   }
   fclose( f );
}

// output a TGA file

int main( void )
{
   read_palette( );

   read_image( );

   WriteTGA( img, imgpalette, "TGADEMO.TGA" );

   return 0;
}
```

This concludes our look at the TARGA format. Because it can be considered one of the principal true-color image formats, it is a good choice for applications that must deal with such images. Its relative simplicity compared with TIFF- and JPEG-based formats, which are other options for true color, is also quite attractive. Yet another advantage is its support of many image types, including overlay capability. TARGA is one of the more thoughtfully designed formats covered in this book.

Appendix A

CCITT Group 3 Compression Codes

The TIFF format supports CCITT Group 3 facsimile compression as one of its possible compression schemes. This scheme uses Huffman compression with a predefined set of bit codes. These can be found in the listings accompanying Chapters 3 and 16 as arrays of 16-bit unsigned integers with the code occupying the high order bits of an integer. It is difficult to look at a hex representation of a code, however, and pick out the actual bit pattern and its length, so we reproduce the codes here for convenience.

Table A.1   Terminating White Codes

Code	Length	Run Length	Code	Length	Run Length
00110101	8	0	0100100	7	27
000111	6	1	0011000	7	28
0111	4	2	00000010	8	29
1000	4	3	00000011	8	30
1011	4	4	00011010	8	31
1100	4	5	00011011	8	32
1110	4	6	00010010	8	33
1111	4	7	00010011	8	34
10011	5	8	00010100	8	35
10100	5	9	00010101	8	36
00111	5	10	00010110	8	37
01000	5	11	00010111	8	38
001000	6	12	00101000	8	39
000011	6	13	00101001	8	40
110100	6	14	00101010	8	41
110101	6	15	00101011	8	42
101010	6	16	00101100	8	43
101011	6	17	00101101	8	44
0100111	7	18	00000100	8	45
0001100	7	19	00000101	8	46
0001000	7	20	00001010	8	47
0010111	7	21	00001011	8	48
0000011	7	22	01010010	8	49
0000100	7	23	01010011	8	50
0101000	7	24	01010100	8	51
0101011	7	25	01010101	8	52
0010011	7	26	00100100	8	53

Table A.1   Terminating White Codes (continued)

Code	Length	Run Length	Code	Length	Run Length
00100101	8	54	01001010	8	59
01011000	8	55	01001011	8	60
01011001	8	56	00110010	8	61
01011010	8	57	00110011	8	62
01011011	8	58	00110100	8	63

Table A.2   Make Up White Codes

Code	Length	Run Length	Code	Length	Run Length
11011	5	64	011010100	9	960
10010	5	128	011010101	9	1024
010111	6	192	011010110	9	1088
0110111	7	256	011010111	9	1152
00110110	8	320	011011000	9	1216
00110111	8	384	011011001	9	1280
01100100	8	448	011011010	9	1344
01100101	8	512	011011011	9	1408
01101000	8	576	010011000	9	1472
01100111	8	640	010011001	9	1536
011001100	9	704	010011010	9	1600
011001101	9	768	011000	6	1664
011010010	9	832	010011011	9	1728
011010011	9	896			

Table A.3   Terminating Black Codes

Code	Length	Run Length	Code	Length	Run Length
0000110111	10	0	0000011000	10	17
010	3	1	0000001000	10	18
11	2	2	00001100111	11	19
10	2	3	00001101000	11	20
011	3	4	00001101100	11	21
0011	4	5	00000110111	11	22
0010	4	6	00000101000	11	23
00011	5	7	00000010111	11	24
000101	6	8	00000011000	11	25
000100	6	9	000011001010	12	26
0000100	7	10	000011001011	12	27
0000101	7	11	000011001100	12	28
0000111	7	12	000011001101	12	29
00000100	8	13	000001101000	12	30
00000111	8	14	000001101001	12	31
000011000	9	15	000001101010	12	32
0000010111	10	16	000001101011	12	33

Table A.3 Terminating Black Codes (continued)

Code	Length	Run Length	Code	Length	Run Length
000011010010	12	34	000001100101	12	49
000011010011	12	35	000001010010	12	50
000011010100	12	36	000001010011	12	51
000011010101	12	37	000000100100	12	52
000011010110	12	38	000000110111	12	53
000011010111	12	39	000000111000	12	54
000001101100	12	40	000000100111	12	55
000001101101	12	41	000000101000	12	56
000011011010	12	42	000001011000	12	57
000011011011	12	43	000001011001	12	58
000001010100	12	44	000000101011	12	59
000001010101	12	45	000000101100	12	60
000001010110	12	46	000001011010	12	61
000001010111	12	47	000001100110	12	62
000001100100	12	48	000001100111	12	63

Table A.4 Make Up Black Codes

Code	Length	Run Length	Code	Length	Run Length
0000001111	10	64	0000001110011	13	960
000011001000	12	128	0000001110100	13	1024
000011001001	12	192	0000001110101	13	1088
000001011011	12	256	0000001110110	13	1152
000000110011	12	320	0000001110111	13	1216
000000110100	12	384	0000001010010	13	1280
000000110101	12	448	0000001010011	13	1344
0000001101100	13	512	0000001010100	13	1408
0000001101101	13	576	0000001010101	13	1472
0000001001010	13	640	0000001011010	13	1536
0000001001011	13	704	0000001011011	13	1600
0000001001100	13	768	0000001100100	13	1664
0000001001101	13	832	0000001100101	13	1728
0000001110010	13	896			

Table A.5 Extended Make Up Codes (Black and White)

Code	Length	Run Length	Code	Length	Run Length
00000001000	11	1792	000000010110	12	2240
00000001100	11	1856	000000010111	12	2304
00000001101	11	1920	000000011100	12	2368
000000010010	12	1984	000000011101	12	2432
000000010011	12	2048	000000011110	12	2496
000000010100	12	2112	000000011111	12	2560
000000010101	12	2176			

Appendix B

TIFF Tag Identifiers

This appendix lists all tag identifiers defined by revision 6.0 of the TIFF format specification. Refer to Chapter 16 for additional details.

Table B.1 TIFF Tag Identifiers

Tag Name	Dec	(Hex)	Data Type	Count
NewSubfileType	254	(FE)	LONG	1
SubfileType	255	(FF)	SHORT	1
ImageWidth	256	(100)	SHORT/LONG	1
ImageLength	257	(101)	SHORT/LONG	1
BitsPerSample	258	(102)	SHORT	SamplesPerPixel
Compression	259	(103)	SHORT	1
PhotometricInterpretation	262	(106)	SHORT	1
Thresholding	263	(107)	SHORT	1
CellWidth	264	(108)	SHORT	1
CellLength	265	(109)	SHORT	1
FillOrder	266	(10A)	SHORT	1
DocumentName	269	(10D)	ASCII	nchars
ImageDescription	270	(10E)	ASCII	nchars
Make	271	(10F)	ASCII	nchars
Model	272	(110)	ASCII	nchars
StripOffsets	273	(111)	SHORT/LONG	nvalues
Orientation	274	(112)	SHORT	1
SamplesPerPixel	277	(115)	SHORT	1
RowsPerStrip	278	(116)	SHORT/LONG	1
StripByteCounts	279	(117)	LONG/SHORT	nvalues
MinSampleValue	280	(118)	SHORT	SamplesPerPixel
MaxSampleValue	281	(119)	SHORT	SamplesPerPixel
XResolution	282	(11A)	RATIONAL	1
YResolution	283	(11B)	RATIONAL	1
PlanarConfiguration	284	(11C)	SHORT	1
PageName	285	(11D)	ASCII	nchars

Table B.1   TIFF Tag Identifiers (continued)

Tag Name	Dec	(Hex)	Data Type	Count
XPosition	286	(11E)	RATIONAL	nvalues
YPosition	287	(11F)	RATIONAL	nvalues
FreeOffsets	288	(120)	LONG	nvalues
FreeByteCounts	289	(121)	LONG	nvalues
GrayResponseUnit	290	(122)	SHORT	1
GrayResponseCurve	291	(123)	SHORT	2**BitsPerSample
Group3Options	292	(124)	LONG	1
Group4Options	293	(125)	LONG	1
ResolutionUnit	296	(128)	SHORT	1
PageNumber	297	(129)	SHORT	2
ColorResponseCurves	301	(12D)	SHORT	3* (2**BitsPerSample)
Software	305	(131)	ASCII	nchars
DateTime	306	(132)	ASCII	20
Artist	315	(13B)	ASCII	nchars
HostComputer	316	(13C)	ASCII	nchars
Predictor	317	(13D)	SHORT	1
WhitePoint	318	(13E)	RATIONAL	2
PrimaryChromaticities	319	(13F)	RATIONAL	6
ColorMap	320	(140)	SHORT	3* (2**BitsPerSample)
HalftoneHints	321	(141)	SHORT	2
TileWidth	322	(142)	SHORT/LONG	1
TileLength	323	(143)	SHORT/LONG	1
TileOffsets	324	(144)	LONG	TilesPerImage
TileByteCounts	325	(145)	SHORT/LONG	TilesPerImage
InkSet	332	(14C)	SHORT	1
InkNames	333	(14D)	ASCII	nchars
NumberOfInks	334	(14E)	SHORT	1
DotRange	336	(150)	BYTE/SHORT	2 * NumberOfInks
TargetPrinter	337	(151)	ASCII	nchars
ExtraSamples	338	(152)	BYTE	nvalues
SampleFormat	339	(153)	SHORT	1
SMinSampleValue	340	(154)	any	SamplesPerPixel
SMaxSampleValue	341	(155)	any	SamplesPerPixel
JPEGProc	512	(200)	SHORT	1
JPEGInterchangeFormat	513	(201)	LONG	1
JPEGInterchangeFormatLngth	514	(202)	LONG	1

Table B.1   TIFF Tag Identifiers (continued)

Tag Name	Dec	(Hex)	Data Type	Count
JPEGRestartInterval	515	(203)	SHORT	1
JPEGLosslessPredictors	517	(205)	SHORT	SamplesPerPixel
JPEGPointTransforms	518	(206)	SHORT	SamplesPerPixel
JPEGQTables	519	(207)	LONG	SamplesPerPixel
JPEGDCTables	520	(208)	LONG	SamplesPerPixel
JPEGACTables	521	(209)	LONG	SamplesPerPixel
YCbCrCoefficients	529	(211)	RATIONAL	3
YCbCrSubSampling	530	(212)	SHORT	2
YCbCrPositioning	531	(213)	SHORT	1
ReferenceBlackWhite	532	(214)	LONG	2 * SamplesPerPixel
Copyright	33432	(8298)	ASCII	nchars

Appendix C

Source Listing Index ▬▬▬▬▬▬▬▬▬▬▬

This appendix presents a tabulation of all source files contained in the body of the book together with a brief description of each file.

Appendix D

Bibliography

Adobe Systems. *PostScript Language Reference Manual*, Reading, MA: Addison-Wesley, 1990.

Aldus Corporation. *Tag Image File Format Revision 6.0*, 1992.

Anson, Louisa. "Graphics Compression Technology," *SunWorld*, October 1991.

Apple Computer, Inc. *Inside Macintosh*, Reading, MA: Addison-Wesley, 1988.

Asente, Paul. *X Window System Toolkit*, Bedford, MA: Digital Press, 1990.

Autumn Hill Software, Inc. *Baby Driver Printer Interface Library Programmer's Guide*, 1991.

Binstock, Andrew, Babcock, David P., and Luse, Marv, *HP LaserJet Programming*, Reading, MA: Addison-Wesley, 1991.

CompuServe, Inc. *Graphics Interchange Format Version 87a*, 1987.

CompuServe, Inc. *Graphics Interchange Format Version 89a*, 1989.

Digital Research, Inc. *GEM Programmer's Toolkit*, 1988.

Duncan, Ray (Ed.). *The MS-DOS Encyclopedia*, Redmond, WA: Microsoft Press, 1988.

Foley, James. *Computer Graphics Principles and Practice*, Reading, MA: Addison-Wesley, 1990.

Hewlett-Packard. *LaserJet Series II Printer Technical Reference Manual*, 1987.

Hewlett-Packard. *HP PaintJet Color Graphics Printer User's Guide*, 1987.

Luse, Marv. "Printing PCX Files," *The C Gazette*, Winter, 1990–1991.

McGee, Pat. "Format for Byte Encoded Rasterfiles," *Sun-Spots Digest*, 6:84.

Microsoft Corporation. *Extended Memory Specification Version 3.0*, 1991.

Microsoft Corporation. *Microsoft Paint Format Technical Note*, 1988.

Microsoft Corporation. *Microsoft Windows Programmer's Reference*, Redmond, WA: Microsoft Press, 1990.

Nelson, Mark. "LZW Data Compression," *Dr. Dobb's Journal*, October 1989.

Pavlidis, Theodosios. *Algorithms for Graphics and Image Processing*, Rockville, MD: Computer Science Press, 1982.

Phoenix Technologies Ltd. *System BIOS for IBM PC/XT/AT Computer and Compatibles*, Reading, MA: Addison-Wesley, 1989.

Roth, Stephen. *Real World PostScript*, Reading, MA: Addison-Wesley, 1988.

Scheifler, Robert. *X Window System*, Bedford, MA: Digital Press, 1990.

Storer, James. *Data Compression Methods and Theory*, Rockville, MD: Computer Science Press, 1988.

Truevision, Inc. *Targa File Format Specification Version 2.0*, 1991.

Ulichney, Robert. *Digital Halftoning*, Cambridge, MA: MIT Press, 1987.

Welsh, Terry. "A Technique for High-Performance Data Compression," *Computer*, June 1984.

Wilton, Richard. *Programmer's Guide to PC and PS/2 Video Systems*, Redmond, WA: Microsoft Press, 1987

WordPerfect Corporation. *WordPerfect Developer's Toolkit*, 1988.

ZSoft Corporation. *Technical Reference*, 1991.

Index

Addison-Wesley warrants the enclosed disk to be free of defects in materials and faulty workmanship under normal use for a period of ninety days after purchase. If a defect is discovered in the disk during this warranty period, a replacement disk can be obtained at no charge by sending the defective disk, postage prepaid, with proof of purchase to:

Addison-Wesley Publishing Company
Editorial Department
Trade Computer Books Division
One Jacob Way
Reading, MA 01867

After the 90-day period, a replacement will be sent upon receipt of the defective disk and a check or money order for $10.00, payable to Addison-Wesley Publishing Company.

Addison-Wesley makes no warranty or representation, either express or implied, with respect to this software, its quality, performance, merchantability, or fitness for a particular purpose. In no event will Addison-Wesley, its distributors, or dealers be liable for direct, indirect, special, incidental, or consequential damages arising out of the use or inability to use the software. The exclusion of implied warranties is not permitted in some states. Therefore, the above exclusion may not apply to you. This warranty provides you with specific legal rights. There may be other rights that you may have that vary from state to state.

Attention 3 1/2″ Disk Drive Users:

The *Bitmapped Graphics Programming in C++* disk is available in 3 1/2″ high density format. Please return the order form below to Addison-Wesley, along with your check for $10.00 made payable to Addison-Wesley, or your credit card information. Send to:

Addison-Wesley Publishing Company
Order Department
One Jacob Way
Reading, MA 01867-9984

To order by phone with credit card call (800) 822-6339.

Please send me the 3 1/2″ high density disk to accompany *Bitmapped Graphics Programming in C++* by Marv Luse (ISBN 0-201-62655-1).

☐ I am enclosing a check for $10.00.

☐ I'd like to pay by credit card.

Name: _____ Phone: _____

Address: _____

City: _____ State: _____ Zip: _____

Circle type of credit card: Visa   MasterCard   American Express

Name of cardholder: _____

Credit card number: _____ Expiration Date: _____